ENGAGING JAPANESE PHILOSOPHY: A SHORT HISTORY

Engaging Japanese Philosophy

A SHORT HISTORY

Thomas P. KASULIS

University of Hawai'i Press

HONOLULU

23 22 21 20 19 18   6 5 4 3 2 1

Library of Congress Cataloging-in-Publication Data

Names: Kasulis, Thomas P., author.
Title: Engaging Japanese philosophy : a short history / Thomas P. Kasulis. Description:
Honolulu : University of Hawai'i Press, [2018] | Series: Nanzan Library of
    Asian religion and culture | Includes bibliographical references and index.
Identifiers: LCCN 2017036842 | ISBN 9780824869793 (cloth alk. paper)
| ISBN 9780824874070 (pbk alk. paper)
Subjects: LCSH: Philosophy, Japanese—History.
Classification: LCC B5241 .K293 2018 | DDC 181/.12—dc23
LC record available at https://lccn.loc.gov/2017036842

The design and typesetting for this book were prepared by
the Nanzan Institute for Religion and Culture.

University of Hawai'i Press books are printed on acid-free
paper and meet the guidelines for permanence and
durability of the Council on Library Resources.

To my teachers,
some of whom came to me disguised as students

Contents

REFERENCE MATERIAL

Preface

The first of its kind in English, this book treats comprehensively the Japanese philosophical tradition from ancient times through the turn of the twenty-first century. I designed it to serve multiple audiences. For example, some may want to explore Japanese philosophy as an alternative or complement to western philosophy while others may be generally interested in Japanese culture, thought, and history. Readers with different priorities bring different backgrounds as well. One group may be familiar with western philosophy and its terminology but have little if any previous exposure to Japan, while others may be able to read Japanese philosophical texts in the original languages. Still others may have practical knowledge of some Japanese art, but wonder about its place within the larger tradition of the country's ideas and values.

Writing a book suitable for such a range of readers is daunting. Yet, for over four decades I have taught Japanese philosophy to both undergraduates and graduates and directed workshops for college teachers, many with equally diverse backgrounds. I have delivered professional papers to academic groups from a variety of disciplines, and lectured to audiences at Japanese art exhibits and to American business and military leaders, and even to Japanese managers working in a global context. In engaging such different audiences, I learned that *what* I said varied less than *how* I said it. Examples, vocabulary, and kinds of details might change to suit the audience, but the general points remained constant. With experimentation, I also found analogies, metaphors, and examples from everyday life that often crossed boundaries separating different audiences. Of course, that does not mean every explanation will work equally well for everybody.

As our world widens in complexity, our knowledge narrows through specialization. Outside what we know well, we often don't know much, at least in any depth. While we may be world-renowned experts in one field, in others we are lucky to have a college sophomore level of understanding. For example, when lecturing on Japan to a college or university audience, I may give a simplified explanation of some historical event or western philosophical distinction. By reading the expressions of my audience, I see a philosopher react to the historical description with a nod of assent suggesting "Oh really. That explains something I've wondered about." Meanwhile the historian harrumphs while

1

thinking, "Well, yes. But that is hardly the *whole* story." Conversely, my brief explanation of some Aristotelian distinction evokes the opposite reaction in the historian and the philosopher. In approaching this book, therefore, readers will, I hope, remember what is familiar to them may not be so for others and vice versa. I ask their indulgence if not for my sake, at least in consideration for their fellow readers.

If I say something that strikes you as overgeneralized, just skim through it. That passage was not written for a person of your background. When you come across unfamiliar territory, however, the sophomore in you will be glad I write as I do. Only when I am expressly interpreting or explaining the central ideas of Japanese philosophy itself will I stand by my statements as being not only accurate, but up to the standards of my fellow specialists in the field.

The terms in the title, *Engaging Japanese Philosophy: A Short History,* suggest the rationale behind this book. I'll let them guide most of what follows in this Preface. *The full orientation for the reader, however, is in Chapter 1.* That chapter is an essential preliminary even for those interested in reading only specific chapters later in the text.

Engaging Japanese Philosophy: A Short History

Let us analyze the title by starting with the word *history,* which in this context means specifically a *history of philosophy.* In the world of scholarship, history and philosophy intersect to form three fields. For understanding the purpose of this book, it is helpful to bear in mind how those fields are distinct.

History: Intellectual histories, histories of ideas, and histories of philosophy

An intellectual history, a history of ideas, and a history of philosophy may overlap in some cases but they fundamentally differ in method and purpose. An intellectual history is a task for a historian and as a subject is taught in history departments. It traces the institutions and organizations, the political and social contexts for ideas and values in specific times and places. Such intellectual histories enrich our appreciation of how class, gender, race, power relations, and authority influence the development and acceptance of ideas. They are strongest in tracking ideological movements and trends, but weakest in analyzing the distinctiveness of individual thinkers and the details of their arguments.

Intellectual histories may run the risk of reducing the individuality of philosophers to their being no more than examples of an intellectual, political, or social movement. Yet, as individual thinkers, philosophers not only reflect but also reflect upon the events and trends of their time, formulating qualifications, critiques, modifications, and counterpositions. That individuality of the particular thinker can elicit distinctively philosophical reflection in readers from different times and places, a type of reflection not typically generated by reading an intellectual history.

A history of ideas, by contrast, may be written by either a historian or a philosopher (and is often taught by faculty from multiple disciplines). In that genre the ideas formulated by individuals and the interplay of those ideas across contexts and periods take center stage. On the grandest scale, a history of ideas can try to explain the great concepts or theories that changed a society or even the world. The critical evaluation of the ideas or arguments themselves are typically subordinated to their impact on society. Sometimes a philosopher may write a history of ideas and might trace one idea through a long stretch of history, including its rise, transformations, and decline (such as A. O. Lovejoy's masterwork, *The Chain of Being*). True to its name, a history of ideas emphasizes ideas over those who had the ideas and their reasoning in arriving at those ideas.

Although intellectual histories and histories of ideas often better fit historians' interests, histories of philosophy are written by philosophers and are commonly taught as courses in philosophy departments. (Unfortunately, such departments still too often focus only on the philosophies of Western Europe, Canada, and the United States.) Unlike intellectual histories, histories of philosophy tend to reduce the historical and social context of thought to thumbnail sketches. They focus instead on a historical series of individual thinkers such as Aristotle, Thomas Aquinas, Descartes, Locke, Kant, Hegel, Nietzsche, Russell, Husserl, Wittgenstein, and Heidegger. Alternatively, they might concentrate on a series of philosophical clusters instead of individuals such as the pre-Socratics, Scholastics, British empiricists, continental rationalists, German idealists, existentialists, and logical positivists.

In either case, the historian of philosophy, as a philosopher, takes pains to expose the contours of the various thinkers' positions, assumptions, and arguments, whether explicit or implicit. The historian of philosophy may even evaluate how well theses are argued or articulated. A hope is often that by attending to arguments and theories from the past, the quality of present-day philosophy might improve. Such analysis is not commonly done nor expected to be done in works by historians.

At the risk of caricature, I can summarize the differences as follows. Intellectual histories focus on the social, political, institutional, and economic conditions that have influenced philosophical ideas through history. The history of ideas focuses on the ideas themselves, their interaction, and their impact on historical events. The history of philosophy isolates and assesses the individual philosophers' arguments and the thinking by which they came to their conclusions. That focus includes, when relevant, the impact of one thinker on another and the author's evaluation of the philosophical theories presented.

A Short (?) History

As a physical tome, this book is hardly short. I included *short* in the title for two reasons. First, from a long list of candidates (our *Japanese Philosophy: A Sourcebook* [JPS] has chapters on over a hundred Japanese philosophers, for example), I selected only seven for special treatment: Kūkai, Shinran, Dōgen, Ogyū Sorai, Motoori Norinaga, Nishida Kitarō, and Watsuji Tetsurō (Chapters 3, 5, 6, 9, 10, 12, and 13). Two criteria informed my choices.

Since one audience for this book is readers with philosophical interests, by having seven chapters devoted to single philosophers, those chapters can be richer in philosophical detail, allowing the arguments and positions of the respective philosophers to be clearer. Moreover, I consider the seven to be paradigmatic of the Japanese tradition, enough so that if readers can understand them, they will have the background to read and understand a rich array of other Japanese philosophers. Lastly, those seven philosophers collectively represent a range of historical periods and traditions.

Specifically, three of the seven are Buddhist: one esoteric—Shingon's Kūkai (774–835)—and two exoteric—Pure Land Buddhism's Shinran (1173–1263) and Zen Buddhism's Dōgen (1200–1253). In historical chronology, Kūkai represents the classical while Shinran and Dōgen the medieval. The Edo or Tokugawa period is represented by the classical Confucianism of Ogyū Sorai (1666–1728) and the Shintō Native Studies tradition of Motoori Norinaga (1730–1801). For the forms of academic philosophy in the modern period, I have focused on Nishida Kitarō (1870–1945), the founder of the globally influential Kyoto School, and Watsuji Tetsurō (1889–1960), the leading philosopher from that era not directly advancing that school and its problematics.

The second sense of *short* concerns the six chapters (2, 4, 7, 8, 11, and 14) dealing with the historical contexts in which the thinkers lived rather than the detailed analysis of individual philosophers. Therein I depict events with the broadest of strokes in an effort to expedite the narrative. My goal is mainly to set the mood and spirit of the historical periods in which Japanese philosophers developed their systems. Furthermore, the historical chapters allow me to acknowledge, however briefly, the contributions of nearly a hundred Japanese and a dozen Chinese philosophers beyond the key seven. In that respect, by their inclusion in the historical chapters, some intellectual history and history of ideas enters my narrative.

I previously claimed that most histories of philosophy focus on individuals and schools of thought with only thumbnail sketches of historical, political, and social conditions. I deviate from that principle somewhat because my earlier comment was referring to *western* histories of *western* philosophy written for *western* readers. Thus, the authors of those intellectual histories could assume their readers had at least a general knowledge of ancient Greece, medieval Christendom, the Reformation, the Russian Revolution, the rise of psychoanalysis, and so forth. A significant number of those for whom I wrote this book, however, might not have a comparable familiarity with equally significant events in Japanese history. So I expanded a bit my historical discussions for their benefit. I have included some photographs that may also help communicate some of the spirit of the times being discussed.

Those expert in Japanese history will not find much new information in the six historical chapters. At least, I would think not. Since my primary contribution is philosophical not historical, I have included historical information that can be found in a variety of standard sources. In the Bibliography, before the general listing of references, I have a short list of "General reference works in western languages." I take those works to contain widely accepted historical facts among experts in the field and to be reliable resources for English readers. If I mention an event found in at least two of the sources, I omit a citation in my notes on the grounds that the event is apparently well-known and documented. That process allowed me to cut back on an already long list of citations and supplementary notes. If there is something innovative in my historical accounts, it is the way I use them to frame the Japanese philosophical tradition. After all, I am not a general historian of Japan, but a historian of Japanese philosophy.

Japanese Philosophy

Some readers may be troubled by my not defining Japanese philosophy at the outset of this book. Without a preliminary definition, how could I know what to include in a book on "Japanese philosophy?" Fortunately, in assembling the entries for JPS, James Heisig, John Maraldo, and I did our preliminary work by intensive consultations with several dozens of scholars from Europe, North America, and Asia. We asked for their recommendations about which figures to include in our *Sourcebook* without our stipulating any particular definition of philosophy. In discussing with them their nominations and justifications, we noticed some recurring points of analysis, argument, terminology, and thematic orientations.

From that consultation I have distilled in my own terms some characteristics commonly displayed by Japanese philosophers. I emphatically reject, however, the idea that Japanese philosophies share some common essence that can be captured in a simple definition. To those who think such a definition is a prerequisite, I invite them to produce such a concise definition that would sufficiently embrace all of the history of western philosophy. What is the single clear and distinct characteristic shared by such a motley assemblage of western thinkers as Heraclitus, Aristotle, Plotinus, Augustine, Spinoza, Hume, Kant, Hegel, Kierkegaard, Bentham, Nietzsche, Ayer, Wittgenstein, Whitehead, Heidegger, Merleau-Ponty, Quine, and Derrida? I doubt any essentialist, all-inclusive definition befitting such a list could be concocted in good faith by anyone. I see no reason to concoct one for Japanese philosophy either.

Instead, when speaking of commonalities within Japanese philosophy, we should look for a list of characteristics lending them what Ludwig Wittgenstein called in his *Philosophical Investigations* (§67) a *family resemblance*. Not all members of any family share some single defining characteristic (shape of nose, type of hair, height, shape of face, general physiology, etc.) that distinguishes them from members of other families. Yet, we still often see a so-called family resemblance. How is that possible?

Basically because, Wittgenstein explained, of a long list of possible physical characteristics, members of the same family share a larger number of them than do members of other families. So, to identify a family member (or a philosophical tradition), you should not seek a single essential, defining quality. Instead, you should compile a list of characteristics that perhaps no single member of the (philosophical) family meets completely, but as a group the (philosophical) family members share a large number (a much larger number than people from other philosophical families).

Of course, before you can start cataloguing family resemblances, you have to meet the family. Hence, I reserve my most important general statements about the nature of Japanese philosophy for my Conclusion after we have completed our survey of Japanese philosophers. In Chapter 1 I will, however, give some general orientations about what to look for. But you will find no preliminary definitions there.

In the aforementioned process of interviews, analysis, and generalization involved in editing JPS, one *exclusionary* criterion did emerge, however. In Japan today most faculty members of academic philosophy programs show only a distant resemblance to the Japanese philosophy family. (I will address the reason for this postwar development in Chapter 14 and in the Conclusion.) In fact, those academic philosophers clearly and self-avowedly belong to a different family, that of western philosophy, preferring its methods, terminology, and problematics. Despite their important philosophical contributions, their work would fit more comfortably in a history of western philosophy than a history of Japanese philosophy.

When I come to discussing modern Japanese philosophy in this book, the difference between the two families of philosophers in Japan will be clearer. By my criteria, modern Japanese philosophy explicitly draws on western philosophy, but it does not *derive* from western philosophy in the way the work of many professional philosophers in Japan does today. Japanese philosophy is not simply philosophy done in Japan any more than "German philosophy" is only pursued in Germany by Germans. Nor does every philosopher in Germany do only German philosophy.

In my Conclusion I will say more about the contribution Japanese philosophy can make to philosophy both inside and outside Japan. Only as I came to the end of this project did I notice how well some aspects of Japanese philosophy resonate with the spirit of the forefathers of western philosophy: Socrates, Plato, and Aristotle. That led me to an unexpected conclusion. Some have argued that *by definition* "philosophy" is the tradition started by those ancient Greeks and therefore cannot include Asian traditions with different origins. Yet, by the conclusion of this book, I will have presented evidence suggesting that many values and themes central to Japanese philosophy are shared by ancient Greek philosophers. Indeed, Japanese philosophy in some ways may be more true to the spirit of ancient Greek philosophy than are some projects undertaken in today's philosophy departments, in either the West or Japan. So, in the final analysis, who really is most in the tradition of ancient Greek philosophers?

Engaging Philosophy

An aspect of Japanese philosophy that accords with the tradition of the ancient Greeks (and many western philosophers after them, especially before the Enlightenment) is an emphasis on engagement over detachment as the source of insight. As I argued in my 1998 Gilbert Ryle Lectures, *Intimacy or Integrity: Philosophy and Cultural Difference,* engaged (intimacy-oriented) knowing and detached (integrity-oriented) knowing each have their own coherence, benefits, and limitations. Yet, for logical reasons, the two do not easily mesh.

Since the Enlightenment of the seventeenth century, western philosophy has increasingly turned to detached knowing as its preferred paradigm. As I show in this book, though, Japanese philosophy has generally stressed engaged knowing throughout most of its history. (*Intimacy or Integrity* shows that neither Japan, nor even Asia, is unique in that emphasis incidentally.) This presents both an opportunity and a conundrum.

The opportunity is that in studying Japanese philosophy, many western readers can glimpse a way of relating to the world that differs from how they have likely been enculturated, especially in academic settings. The conundrum is that one cannot fully understand engagement by reading about it in a detached manner. If engagement is a special form of knowing, one must engage it to know it. In Chapter 1 I try to prepare the reader for engaging rather than simply learning about Japanese philosophy. The chapter also introduces some special vocabulary and methods used in the subsequent chapters.

Finally, in this book I often write in a style somewhat more conversational than is typical of much academic writing. The problem with the normal academic style is that it privileges detachment to the detriment of engagement. It creates a linguistic world in which "one" does things and what "we" know refers not to you and me, but to a disembodied consciousness from a transcendent standpoint. Chapter 1 will argue, however, that objectivity can also arise from a community of expert knowers who undergo a common praxis of engagement.

So, if you find my writing style colloquial at times, don't assume that in itself proves a lack objectivity or rigor. After all, we *engage* in philosophical conversations. We learn through engagement at least as much as through detachment. In this work I will try to initiate a conversation between you, me, and several major Japanese philosophers. How we can do that and its implications for understanding are, again, explored in Chapter 1.

CONVENTIONS

Citations and Notes

Marginal page references. I was well into working on this book when the opportunity arose to be one of the three coeditors of *Japanese Philosophy: A Sourcebook* (JPS). Since I envisioned the two books as complementary, I deferred work on this one until we completed our editing of JPS. I realized that if JPS were already available when this volume appeared, readers could easily pursue issues from this book that they could not do otherwise (unless they could read Japanese). JPS not only has some material unavailable in English elsewhere but about a hundred specialists contributed its translations. To support the synergy between the two volumes, I give cross-references to JPS via small page numbers listed in the margins. This has the benefit, I hope, of being both convenient and unobtrusive. Context determines whether the JPS pages refer to the location of a quoted passage or to further readings in JPS related to the particular discussion.

Japanese and English sentences as well as the meaning of individual words do not map neatly into a one-to-one correspondence. A translation can highlight one nuance only at the expense of another. When I have wanted to stress some connotation in the original that is not sharply delineated in the passage as translated in JPS, I either used another translation (the source of which appears in a supplementary note) or I translated it myself (citing the original source). In those cases I also include the JPS page number for the same passage so the reader can not only compare the translation appearing here with another good translation, but can also see the larger context of the passage quoted.

Furthermore, in quoting a translated passage, I have occasionally changed the translation of a term here or there to make it consistent with my text and other translated passages in this book. That is not meant as a criticism of the original translation, but merely a convenience imposed so as not to confuse readers with multiple translations of the same term when not absolutely necessary.

Another merit of listing the JPS citations is that JPS gives in its bibliography not only the source of the original text in Japanese or Chinese, but also a list of other English translations available at the time of publication. So those able to read Japanese or Chinese may consult the original, and those who cannot are directed to other western language translations.

When I taught my first course in Japanese philosophy some forty years ago, I could fill only about a shelf or two in my office with good English translations of works in Japanese philosophy. A joy of my career has been to see the rapid growth of the field and superlative contributions by scholars from around the world. It is now possible, especially with the publication of JPS and this book as primers, to undertake a focused study of Japanese philosophy totally in European languages (as one can study Kierkegaard in depth without necessarily knowing any Danish, for example).

To encourage readers along those lines, I have tried when possible to cite works written in English, even taking precedence over those only available in Japanese. A trove of resources in Japanese philosophy already exists in European languages and the bounty increases monthly. Those resources are referenced in the supplementary notes and in the bibliography of cited sources. Hoping this book may serve as a gateway to further readings in Japanese philosophy for English readers, when there is a good English translation of a particular passage that is not included in JPS, I have tried to use and cite it as well.

Supplementary notes. Supplementary notes are of two kinds. The first gives a minimal amount of information such as the source of a passage, a supporting quotation, a small qualification, or a citation for where further information may be found. They are numbered and printed in the ordinary way. I assume most readers would consult those supplementary notes mainly when researching or checking some issue of particular personal interest.

The other type of supplementary note—usually much more extended than the others—elaborates, augments, or qualifies the topic under discussion. Such notes may be too technical or specialized for most readers, but might still be of importance to scholars or general readers with a particular interest. To alert the reader that there is such a substantive note on a certain point, particularly one of possible philosophical significance, the number in the text for the supplementary note is followed by a small star, so the note marker looks like this: ˣˣ*.

Footnotes. Footnotes also serve two purposes. First, and most commonly, they cross-reference relevant passages in this book itself. That is, the footnote *See pages xxx–yyy* refers to the page numbers in *Engaging Japanese Philosophy.* I realize that this book might be used for reference as well as a text to be read through. In the former case, the footnoted cross-references may be more helpful than using the index as they indicate my judgment about which pages in the book most directly relate to the subject at hand. In reading the book straight through, on the other hand, the footnotes serve as reminders of where the issue or philosopher had been discussed previously in case the readers wish to refresh their memory.

The second, less common, use for a footnote is to briefly explain a common term or convention at its first occurrence. Although such an item might be known to many readers, it might be a stumbling block for others. Rather than interrupting the flow by having the reader stop to refer to a dictionary or reference book, the footnote is an inconspicuous aid to those who need it. As an example, see the definition of *bodhisattva* in Chapter 1.

Incidentally, JPS includes an extensive glossary of key Japanese philosophical terms, giving not only the definitions and the sinograph in each instance, but also a concordance to every occurrence of the term in the sourcebook. Hence, the reader can easily acquire a sense of a technical term's use through fifteen centuries of Japanese philosophy in its various manifestations.

Sinographs

I have omitted sinographs (Sino-Japanese characters) in the main text so as not to disrupt the flow of the English. Exceptions occur when the sinograph itself is the topic (such as 会 and 学 in Chapter 1) or when different words with identical pronunciation are under discussion. The sinographs for names and Japanese terms, as well as the dates for people, appear by the the appropriate entries in the Index. So that information is readily available there for those who want it. When pronunciations other than Japanese appear, (C.) indicates Chinese, (K.) Korean, (S.) Sanskrit, and (P.) Pali.

Romanization

To render East Asian names and terms into the English roman alphabet, Pinyin is used for Chinese and the Modified Hepburn system for Japanese (a pronunciation guide for Japanese is included in *Pointers for Studying Japan,* pages 681-3). When texts in English are quoted, I have changed any Chinese romanization from Wade-Giles to Pinyin and from alternate romanizations of Japanese into Hepburn. The following place names, by English convention, drop the macron marking the long-vowel sound: Tōkyō, Kyōto, and Ōsaka. Terms listed in major dictionaries as English words (such as "shogun") also drop any macrons occurring in the Japanese (*shōgun*) as well as the italics.

Notes on the Japanese Language

Sometimes issues about characteristics of the Japanese language arise in philosophical discussions. To appreciate more fully what is at stake in those debates, readers unfamiliar with the language may benefit from an orientation to the semantic, syntactic, and orthographic aspects of Japanese. *Pointers for Studying Japan* includes a brief section (pages 685–96) on the Japanese language for that purpose.

Names of People

Following the native convention, Japanese, Chinese, and Korean names are given with the family name first, followed by the personal name (with the exception of those scholars who have worked primarily in the West and who prefer the western name order in their writings). Since Japanese often refer to classical personalities by their personal name, artistic name, or ordination name (for example, Motoori Norinaga is referred to as Norinaga), an unknowing reader might look up the name in an index under *N* instead of the family name beginning with *M*. For major figures mentioned frequently in different parts of the book, an index entry will refer the reader to the name in its proper form (Norinaga. See Motoori Norinaga). For more details about Japanese names, see *Pointers for Studying Japan*, pages 683-5.

Map

To aid readers unfamiliar with Japan's geography, a simple map on page 697 lists several of the main sites mentioned in the book.

Dates

Events do not have dates, calendars do. Calendars are devised by scholars who do not always agree on how to date historical eras. In the case of the Tokugawa or Edo period, for example, scholars may use for its beginning date 1600, 1601, or 1603. For the sake of consistency and simplicity, I followed the dating system of the *Kodansha Encyclopedia of Japan*.

Moreover, readers familiar with the accepted chronologies will notice that my historical chapters do not always follow the strict fracture points demarcating the standard eras and that, furthermore, I discuss some events or people in two different chapters. That should not be puzzling since the historical or philosophical significance of one event may be to culminate a preceding series; another to presage what is to follow. Some do both and may occur, therefore, in two different chapters in my account.

Scholars sometimes disagree about dates of events or people. In such cases I have tried to determine the more commonly accepted dates in the Japanese and English sources. For discrepancies in the birth and death years for premodern people, I have followed the *Kodansha Encyclopedia of Japan*, but only if confirmed by a major Japanese dictionary of names (*jinmei jiten*) or specialized encyclopedic work.

ACKNOWLEDGEMENTS

I wish to thank the Entsuba Katsuzō Family Foundation and the Japan National Supreme Court for permission to reproduce the photograph of Lady Justice in Chapter 1 and Professor Takada Yasunari of Tokyo University for assisting in securing those permissions. Thanks also to the U.S. Geological Survey for the public domain photograph of Tokyo after the Great Kantō Earthquake and to the National Archives for the photo of the aftermath of Operation Meeting House, both in Chapter 14. All other photographs are mine.

As I read through this book's final draft, I sometimes smiled at a sentence I remember first writing decades ago as my involvement with Japanese philosophy moved from study notes, to teaching notes, to publications, to public lectures and workshops. This book has deep roots in time, not only in Japanese history but in my own biography. It may not be surprising, therefore, that my list of indebtedness is extensive, indeed too extensive to list here. Still, special mention is absolutely necessary in some cases.

Parts of this project have been generously funded with the aid of the Robert Roche Fellowship Foundation of the Nanzan Institute for Religion and Culture, the Japan Foundation, the National Endowment for the Humanities, and the Joint Committee of the American Council of Learned Societies and the Social Science Research Council. The Ohio State University research programs have been crucial to my work: Grants-in-aid, Faculty Professional Leaves (sabbaticals), and its University Distinguished Scholar Research Grant.

Throughout this project, the Nanzan Institute for Religion and Culture in Nagoya has been a fount of moral support, resources, collaboration, and funding. My interaction with NIRC over the decades has benefitted from the leadership of five directors: James Heisig, Paul Swanson, Watanabe Manabu, Okuyama Michiaki, and Kim Seung Chul, not to mention the founding director who was already emeritus when I first arrived, the late Jan Van Bragt.

In recent years, the University of Tokyo Center for Philosophy (UTCP) has stimulated my work with collaborations, critiques, and friendship. It is hard for me to think of Japanese philosophy without thinking of Kobayashi Yasuo, Takada Yasunari, and Nakajima Takahiro. Their enthusiasm has convinced me that my work can be of value to Japanese as well as westerners.

I also thank the University of Hawai'i Press, its external readers, editors, and proofreaders who transformed an unwieldy manuscript into published form. The project began under the general editorship of Patricia Crosby and ended with Stephanie Chun after Pat retired. Remaining errors are mine alone.

Especially important were those who supported me in this project on a continuing basis. James Heisig of the Nanzan Institute has been a colleague and friend through so much of my work on Japan. Without him, this book would never have been completed. At times he was a Zen Master, figuratively beating me with a stick to persevere. At other times, especially when I had medical difficulties, his support nursed both me and the project along at a slower but still constant rate. His patience, insight, and enthusiasm kept me going.

My family has always been there when I needed them. My three sons, their wives, and our seven grandchildren—Maya, Anna, Ewan, Gabriella, Alexandra, James, and Eva—have brought pride and joy to daily life and buoyed my spirits in times both good and bad. Most of all, I am indebted to my wife, Ellen, who has stoically watched me battle with this project for decades, wondering whether I would finish the book before the book finished me. That I won was as much her accomplishment as mine.

In the years I have been working on this book, three of my doctoral students have died and I want to mention them here. Shim Jae-ryong (Seoul National University) was my first doctoral dissertation advisee at the University of Hawai'i and we first worked together when he was my research assistant collecting Japanese articles on Dōgen. Nikki Bado (Iowa State University), whose doctoral studies at Ohio State I co-advised, was through the years a stimulating conversation partner and personal inspiration. She was the first to convince me that my work on Kūkai had relevance far beyond Japanese religion and philosophy. Lastly, Justin Isom (Ohio State University) was just beginning his doctoral studies when he died rather suddenly of cancer. Justin had great philosophical acuity and a wonderful sense of humor that made him a joy in any graduate seminar. He inspired all of us as he proved time and again that philosophical vision does not require eyesight.

Lastly, this book is dedicated to my teachers, many of whom kindly mentored me without ever being my teacher in a classroom. Their insights and interest in my questions made me the philosopher I am. Zen Master Dōgen said that when he sat in meditation, he sat with all the buddha-ancestors of the past. When I think philosophically, I am engaged with all the teachers and mentors of my past, both in Japan and in the U.S. Almost all of them, including Robert J. J. Wargo who introduced me to Japanese philosophy at the University of Hawai'i in 1973, have passed. Yet, they continue to live through the ideas in my mind and through the words on these pages. The common sinograph in the Japanese words for teacher (sensei 先生) and student (gakusei 学生) is life (生).

1. Engagement

I begin with a question seldom asked in the opening pages of a book although it is relevant to reading any text, especially one such as this. The question: What do you the reader bring to your reading of this book? While that may seem an odd query, it is a typically Japanese concern. Hasegawa Kai (1954–), a present-day poet and scholar of haiku speaks from the mainstream of classical Japanese poetics when he says:

> …A haiku is not completed by the poet. The poet creates half of the haiku, while the remaining half must wait for the appearance of a superior reader. Haiku is literature created jointly by the poet and the reader.[1]

In his discussion of Nō (Noh) drama, Zeami (1363–1443) as well noted the indispensable role of the audience:

> Even if the actor is an unsurpassed master of a level suited to the play, unless the play is performed for a discerning audience in a grand venue, it will not always be such a great success.[2]

When characterizing the verbal exchange between teacher and disciple, Zen Master Dōgen (1200–1253) wrote that the "lines [of discourse] leap out of themselves; student and master practice together." Of the premise behind Zen praxis, he added:†

162

> Intimate action does not know self vs. other, as if I alone can know my intimate self and do not understand any other person's intimate self.… Everything exists through intimacy; each half exists through intimacy.

161

Japanese philosophy, I submit, is equally demanding on its readers. Its significance resides not in the words on a page, but in the engaged reading of those words by what Hasegawa called "a superior reader," Zeami the "discerning audience," and Dōgen the true "student." In using such terminology, those Japanese theorists were not speaking of the audience's cache of factual knowledge, professional training, or even basic intelligence. They were instead referring to

---

† Throughout this book, numbers listed in the margins refer to the relevant page numbers from *Japanese Philosophy: A Sourcebook* (JPS).

a way of interrelating, interacting, and participating with an expressive act such as a text. The primary and most appreciated mode of knowing in the Japanese intellectual tradition, including philosophy, is what I call *engaged knowing* as contrasted with *detached knowing*.

To begin to explore the difference between the two and what is at stake for the project of this book, I start with an instance of cultural misrecognition. This was a case where I believed I understood something but did not. The cause was my being initially oblivious to cultural assumptions I had brought to my interpretation of what I saw.

A CASE OF MISTAKEN IDENTITY

A few years ago I was being led down the towering cathedral-like main corridor of the Japanese Supreme Court Building in Tokyo on the way to the Law Library. I spied ahead a statue of the Greco-Roman goddess of justice, Themis or Justitia. Its presence in a court building was no surprise because such statues of Lady Justice—adorned with toga, crown, sword, and balance scale—

are found these days throughout the world, including in many Japanese judicial sites. As I approached, I could make out that this Lady Justice was not blindfolded, a notable feature but not extraordinary. Images of Lady Justice in the post-Roman times did not commonly begin to include the blindfold as an option until around the sixteenth century.

When I drew up close enough to see the face in more detail, however, my jaw dropped. The ears of the Goddess were elongated, the eyes just barely slit open, and most strikingly, in the forehead centered between the eyebrows was the protuberance colloquially known as the third eye, the center of compassionate wisdom. This Themis was a buddha! Or at least a hybrid between a Greek goddess and a buddha.

To my eye, not expert in Buddhist iconography, the statue reminded me a bit of Kannon, the Bodhisattva[†] of Compassion. Kannon hears the cry of human distress (with the elongated ears), sees the need for com-

---

† The technical meaning of the term *bodhisattva* varies across centuries, cultures, and Buddhist subtraditions. In Japan a bodhisattva is generally understood to be a celestial embodiment of buddha, a heavenly being who can intercede in the human world to help others reach enlightenment. For further discussion of buddhas and bodhisattvas, see pages 80–3.

passionate intervention (with the third eye), and brings with her the instruments needed to alleviate that suffering. Kannon is commonly portrayed as having multiple heads and arms, the heads to see in all directions and the arms ready with the implements for addressing the pain: a flaming jewel to grant wishes, a pilgrim's staff with six rings to open the doors to alternate realms of existence, a wheel of the true teachings to replace ignorance, a trident to vanquish the three causes of delusion, and so forth (see images below). If my association between the two images is valid, the Lady Justice in the Japanese Supreme Court Building embodies compassionate wisdom coming to the aid of suffering human beings with the implements of legal fairness (the balance scales) and authority (the sword).

So yet again I had learned my lesson (for the nth time in my scholarly career). Whatever the cross-cultural similarities visible at a distance, a closer look at a specific cultural artifact—whether a sculpture, a gesture, or a philosophical text—often reveals cardinal differences. In this case I had seen statues of Justice in many other places throughout the world and assumed I was encountering just another example, this one happened to be by Entsuba Katsuzō (1905–2003). Only as I drew near did the statue suddenly shift to its appropriate Japanese context.

Once I fixed my attention on its Buddhist characteristics, the statue started to appear as a buddha in the form of Justice instead of Justice with a few Buddhist stylized flourishes. The balance scales were transformed from being simply a metaphor for weighing evidence objectively (in which case a blindfold would have been appropriate) into an instrument of cosmic compassion. As I engaged Entsuba's statue more intently, trying to view it within its cultural frames, further levels of interpretation opened up. His sculpture is not just an innovative artistic expression; it also represents a radically different vision of justice itself, a difference with a direct bearing on the distinction between detached knowing and engaged knowing I will develop in this introductory chapter.

The traditional western icon portrays judicial integrity. Applying legal principles, Justice decides cases with detachment. She balances the rights and arguments of both litigants, blind to the individuals involved and any special interests they might represent. The western image highlights rule of law over personal fiat. That symbology, incidentally, helps explain the reappearance of the blindfold during the western Renaissance and Enlightenment, the era when rational objectivity was increasingly identified with being a "disinterested party" and "detached observer."

Entsuba's Japanese image, by contrast, is a compassionate Justice who engages each case with penetrating discernment rather than blindly applying principles. Her objectivity arises not from standing back but from intently focusing on the situation before her. (Notice that her right foot is stepping down from her pedestal to get closer to the particulars.) Each situation is unique, needing not only careful observation (the two ordinary eyes slit open in undistracted reflection), but also insight into the human predicament (the third eye). The Greco-Roman toga and balance scale reflect the modern Japanese legal system's debt to the western legal heritage. Yet, they only embellish a more ancient Japanese vision of justice: Buddhist compassion informed by wisdom, that is, the ability to empathize and engage with the litigants involved. In the final analysis, Japan's Justice has the objective of not simply balancing the opposing rights of those who come before her court, but more especially, of establishing social harmony (*wa*).

TWO KINDS OF KNOWING, TWO KINDS OF READING

This returns us to you the reader. In my encounter with the statue of Justice, my cultural assumptions, reinforced by years of enculturation in the western tradition, misdirected my initial evaluation of the sculpture's meaning. I would have liked to think that after more than four decades studying Japanese thought and values, I would not be so susceptible to such cultural misrecognition. Yet, I was.

As I argued in my book, *Intimacy or Integrity: Philosophy and Cultural Difference,* the process of enculturation allows us to be selective in the face of the bombardment of sensations we absorb at any moment. Culture guides us in what to make foreground and what to leave in the background, on what to focus and what to relegate to the periphery. In short: culture tells us what counts. Enculturation is effective to the extent its workings become so second-nature as to be invisible. Like the syntax of our native language, cultural proclivities are more often the medium of thought than an object for reflection.

Yet, it is critical you have at least a modest sense of what enculturated philosophical preferences you bring to your reading. That does not mean I assume every reader of this book is a philosopher. Still, everyone has some deeply held and viscerally felt assumptions about how to understand our world and flourish within it. Those assumptions can influence which philosophical ideas immediately make sense to us and which others leave us flustered and flabbergasted. As my students sometimes say when I begin to introduce an idea from another culture, "How could anyone actually believe *that*?"

For those of you who are philosophers, by contrast, such assumptions will likely be more obvious to you since, as philosophers, we are often asked what we believe and why. That does not mean, however, that we necessarily better understand the true *source* of all our beliefs. I will illustrate with an anecdote.

In the late 1970s when I was teaching in the philosophy department at the University of Hawai'i, we hosted a lecture by a prominent U.S. logician and philosopher of language. It was the heyday of what was known as *possible worlds* analysis. Our lecturer spoke to us on the logic of indexicals (demonstrative pronouns like *this* and *that*) and at one point said, "I think we can all agree that we share an intuition that in no possible world would one use indexicals in the following way...."

When he finished his description, I looked over at my colleague, Roger Ames, in alarm. We wondered if we should immediately leave the lecture to make an emergency phone call to China. The description our speaker just gave was, in fact, how some indexicals may function in the Chinese language. [3] Should we not alert 1.2 billion people that they were populating an "impossible world" before disaster struck?

Humor aside, the anecdote shows that even a sophisticated philosophical thinker can confuse a culturally instilled assumption for a logical necessity. The lecturer's "intuition" about what was possible was formed in a particular cultural milieu, what the modern philosopher Watsuji Tetsurō called the cultural "climate."[†] If he had come of age intellectually in a different climate, even

---

† See pages 487–92. Unless stated otherwise, pages in footnotes refer to pages in this book.

a different academic environment, our lecturer in Hawai'i would likely have had some different intuitions. So, if you have cultural propensities that might obstruct your ability to understand Japanese philosophy, it is best to bring them to light at the outset. Then at least you can be aware of them and how they might skew your understanding of a tradition quite different from what is second nature to you.

I hasten to add that I am not expecting you to *agree* with every Japanese philosopher. I do not do so myself. However, before you can decide on whether you agree or disagree on some point, it is incumbent on you to first understand the point. As your guide through the history of Japanese philosophy, I urge you to have handy a list of your philosophical allergies and vaccinations. If at some point you start experiencing strange symptoms when you read what follows, you might want to check that list to help understand why and take appropriate remedial action.

Identifying Your Cultural Orientation

A most important presupposition for you to examine is how you tend to conceive of knowledge. For diagnostic purposes, I invite you to consider the following questions. I urge you take a moment to consider them, not just to decide your answer but, to the extent you can, to determine why you favor that answer.

Who better knows clay: (A) a geologist or (B) a potter?
Who better knows words: (A) a philologist or (B) a poet?
Who better knows light: (A) a physicist or (B) a photographer?
Who better knows breath: (A) a pulmonologist or (B) a meditator?
Who better knows families: (A) a sociologist or (B) a family counselor?

From the little I have said thus far, it is probably clear the (A) alternatives represent detached knowing and the (B) engaged knowing.

For engaged knowers. Suppose you are a person who tends to favor (B) as the answer in the list of questions. Since most (but not all) Japanese philosophers usually foreground engaged knowing, you may surmise you will likely experience little philosophical discomfort in reading this book. You anticipate meeting kindred spirits, fellow wayfarers on the path you are already taking.

Don't get too comfortable, however. In this book, you will be walking that path with *philosophers,* those gadflies who bring critical reflection and rational analysis to every twist and turn along the way. Precisely because you share a basic orientation with them, you may be all the more startled by their demand for philosophical rigor. You may even have chosen the path of engaged knowing because it seemed an escape from a society you find too rational, too self-reflective, or too scientific.

Yet, the philosophers of engaged knowing you will encounter in this book are not at all adverse to philosophical analysis and argument. Indeed, what makes them *philosophers* of engaged knowing is not that they avoid analysis or argumentation, but instead what they analyze and how they argue in favor of their position. As a result, in engaging their ideas, you may have to think through the consequences of a philosophical orientation you had previously taken for granted. It can be challenging, but also immensely rewarding to survey fourteen centuries of ideas from people who share some of your personal orientation about what reality is, what we can know, and how we should respond to problems of thought and value.

For detached knowers. How about those of you who favor the alternative of detached knowing, the (A) option? Detached knowing became prominent in the West during the modern period of philosophy beginning in the seventeenth century. Since then, it has become increasingly dominant in the western halls of academic learning, and so the majority of you readers may ascribe to it, or at least, think you should. You may want to hedge your philosophical allegiance a bit by quickly adding that you gladly accept engaged knowing as a species of practical understanding, technical know-how, or physical skill. Perhaps no one admires a Chihuly glass bowl or Ansel Adams photograph more than you.

Yet, the bottom line is that if you are periodically having a minor problem with shallow breathing, your first stop is a physician, not a yoga teacher. Such an inclination is revealing. In times of illness, you are likely to assign your body to someone else's care who will do something to it so you can get on with your life.

Notice the detached attitude: your body is a mechanized apparatus you inhabit and is, in some sense, separate from you. When you go to a physician, you metaphorically disconnect from your ordinary sense of the body as the physical expression of your self-agency. You hand your body over to the expert with her detached, scientific or medical expertise about how to treat the disorder with as much assuredness as when you bring your ailing car to the auto mechanic. Indeed, the physician's inclination is to treat the illness roughly the same regardless of who the patient might be. (Note the blindfolds paradigm again.) And why not? You assume your mind and your body, your personality and your physical anatomy—maybe even *you* and your body—can, for the most part, be disconnected from each other.

If you are usually inclined toward detached knowing, your initial purpose in reading this book might be to acquire more information about the history of Japanese philosophy, thereby increasing your knowledge about that intriguing and globally influential culture. Furthermore, if you have a personal fascination with, say, Japanese woodblock prints or samurai values, you may hope to gain a better grasp of the historical and cultural contexts in which those phenomena arose. Because I require of my readers no detailed previous knowledge about Japanese history and culture, I have tried to supply the basic background necessary for understanding the historical, social, political, and economic context in which Japanese philosophers' thought took shape. Accordingly, some of your interest in factual information will likely be addressed, especially in Chapters 2, 4, 7, 8, 11, and 14, which are mostly *about* Japanese philosophy. As the preposition *about* suggests, they will give you an intellectual survey of Japanese philosophy, allowing you to circumambulate its artifacts as you might tour through an exhibit in a museum.

Yet, I urge you to recognize your predisposition about how to read this book and to open yourself to reading it in another way as well. If you approach it in a strictly detached manner, no matter how much information you might accumulate, it will still be as if you were viewing Japanese philosophy as I first viewed Japanese Lady Justice from afar; your interpretation will be formed only around familiar categories. You will see only what you re-cognize. I urge you instead to move in closer and to risk finding what you did not expect, to cognize differently from your original impulse. Perhaps again an anecdote may clarify.

In the 1980s during the Japanese economic boom, I sometimes met U.S. business executives on the plane to Japan. Once they saw I had picked up a Japanese newspaper, they were quick to start a conversation. Finding themselves in awkward negotiations with their Japanese corporate equivalents, they bombarded me with questions about Japanese management styles, business dynamics, and cultural values. As we talked, I was often amazed at their detailed grasp of Japanese history (premodern as well as modern) and command of information gleaned from books about Japanese business, politics, and law. Clearly, they had been excellent students, voraciously digesting books and attending seminars to help them understand Japan.

Yet, they confided, as soon as they entered a meeting room with a group of Japanese executives, "it always becomes immediately evident that I have no idea of what is going on." The problem was that they had confused learning *about* the Japanese with *engaging* the Japanese.

I propose that the principle applies to studying Japanese philosophy as well. Learning about Japanese philosophy should not be confused with engaging Japanese philosophy: its thinkers, its intellectual contexts, and its ideas. Otherwise, we may end up knowing a lot about Japanese philosophy but having "no idea of what is going on."

I have made a sharp distinction between readers who bring to the text a preference for either engaged knowing or detached knowing. That said, I should add that only rarely have I encountered someone who commits to one kind of knowing to the complete exclusion of the other. Most people move back and forth between the two depending on context. So my suggestion is merely that you recognize the difference between the two kinds of knowing and be aware of which you are privileging at any given time.

Even so, scientism, the theory that scientific neutrality presents us with the only truly reliable means of knowing, has so permeated modern society, including its academic institutions, that there is pressure to trust only detached knowing. As we will see in Chapters 11–14, twentieth-century Japanese philosophers felt that same pressure and some have pursued strategies for granting scientific thinking its rightful place in Japanese society while preserving the value of engaged knowing. Perhaps therein will lie some advice for all of us.

An Engaged Reading of Japanese Philosophy

If engaged knowing is, as I claim, dominant in Japanese philosophy, we should make some effort to *engage* our subject matter, rather than stand back and accumulate information about it. What would be involved in such an understanding? Here two Japanese sinographs[†] may help. The first is 会, which in classical Japanese can mean either "to meet" or "to know (or realize)." If we are to *know* Japanese philosophers and not merely know about them, we have to *meet* them. For this book, I have picked seven Japanese philosophers for you to meet. (In the Preface to this book I explained how I selected them.) To help your meetings go smoothly, I have tried to make them flesh-and-blood people, each of whom lived in particular times, were influenced by specific people, and who were driven by one or two key philosophical problems. In other words, I have made them protagonists in a narrative.

Like a Japanese go-between (*nakōdo*) for arranged marriages, I have tried to tell you about your prospective partner's background and personality, often gleaning information either from autobiographical comments or traditional biographies. My doing so will undoubtedly raise red flags in the minds of some scholarly readers. The hermeneutics of suspicion rightly warns us that both first-hand accounts and biographies of great masters written by doting disciples are notoriously unreliable. Autobiographies often color memories to suit the self-image one would like others to accept, while hagiographies often do not serve the agenda of conveying historical truth but rather serve as devotional or

---

† A sinograph is a character used in written Chinese and also in writing unrelated languages within the Chinese cultural sphere, most notably Japanese and classical Korean. See "Pointers for Studying Japan," (pages 685–95) for a brief discussion of the Japanese language. It includes descriptions of the writing system, basic syntax, and a guide giving foreign speakers a rough approximation of how to pronounce Japanese words and names.

authority-conferring narratives that enhance the virtues or miraculous powers of a tradition's founder. Yet, in response I would argue that such narratives can also serve a different purpose, communicating not necessarily historical, positivistic truth, but instead heuristic truth. Most importantly, such narratives often play a constructive role in helping us engage people we do not know. An everyday example will illustrate my point.

Suppose that I am hosting a picnic and would like you to meet another guest, Jim. I might introduce him to you as "the man who taught me all I know about barbecue." Most likely, literally speaking, that is not completely true, yet it introduces Jim so that you know much more about him than if I said, "Jim was born in Chicago, lives in Akron, and owns a townhouse." The former introduction has one fact (and a suspect one at that), the latter three unvarnished pieces of objective data. Yet, the former gets to the truth of the man in question much more effectively because (1) it suggests something of Jim's personality, likes and dislikes; (2) it establishes a point of contact among you, him, and me, a possible start-up for a conversation (I may have heard you saying you liked the barbecue I cooked and so of all the things I might have said about Jim, I picked that to highlight as the most engaging). If the point I conveyed about Jim was heuristically effective, by the end of the day you will know Jim better than if I had merely supplied a long list of empirical, verifiable, facts about him. As we will see in Chapter 4, *The Tale of Genji* explained a thousand years ago that even fiction has its own quality of truth.†

1118–19

Now that we have seen how knowing overlaps with meeting to such an extent that they can be expressed with the same sinograph, let us turn to a second sinograph, 学, which can mean either "to study" or "to imitate." Once I have introduced you to one of the seven selected philosophers, the next step in engaged knowing is to think along with him as he philosophizes. We speak of "following a thinker's line of thought" as if we were walking along with the philosopher, engaged in discussion. In such a way of studying, the two meanings of the sinograph merge. An example from the classroom may help clarify.

In teaching philosophy—western as well as Asian—a test of my students' insight into a philosopher is whether, based on what they have studied so far, they can predict what the philosopher would likely say about some point we have not yet studied. That test helps distinguish whether they really know the philosophy or only know about it. You don't fully understand a philosopher if all you can do is detail what that philosopher said; rather, you need to acquire the ability to think along with that philosopher to see where a line of thought leads (even if, in the end, you disagree with the conclusions).

† See pages 141–4.

When you understand a person well and that person makes an initial state-ment on some topic, you already have a good sense of what will follow in the ensuing next several sentences. You know the gait of that person's progression in thinking. To bridge the gap between today's English readers and the Japanese philosophers I introduce, to help today's western reader be sensitive to the gait of Japanese thinkers, I will at times resort to analogies with philosophical top-ics relevant to us today, or to posing short thought experiments, or even, in a couple of cases, simple exercises involving the body as well as the mind. Such techniques prove especially helpful when we study/emulate thinkers from pre-modern times, those who are most distant from our world.

An approach of that kind requires a tolerant attitude toward anachronisms and analogies. It would be absurd to claim that our debates between scientific reason and religious faith in today's US culture are identical with the tensions between *hakarai* and *shinjin* in Shinran's Japan of the thirteenth century. Yet, if we think through what is at stake in our contemporary controversy and its lines of argument, we can bring that experience to Shinran's philosophical project, thereby making the unfamiliar seem a little less so and therefore more open to our engagement.[4*]

Earlier I related my experience of misreading the meaning of the Statue of Justice. The bad news in that anecdote was that, my exposure to Japanese culture notwithstanding, how easily I fell into misrecognition because of my cultural assumptions. The good news was that once I was attuned to the sculp-ture's Japanese context and realized that it was portraying Justice as a form of engagement rather than detachment, my training in Japanese culture facilitated my discovering multiple layers of meaning. My second, more appropriate, inter-pretation of the sculpture emerged from my recognizing the Buddhist signs of compassionate wisdom, a major expression of engaged knowing in the Japanese philosophical tradition.

How can you as a reader apply that lesson to engaging Japanese philosophy? There are indeed signs of engaged knowing in Japanese philosophy as clear as Justice's elongated ears or third eye if, that is, we are attuned to recognizing them. In the rest of this chapter, I will briefly point out what to watch for as you read the chapters that follow, signals that we are dealing with a case of engaged rather than detached knowing.

There are two kinds of markers. The first are thematic, that is, the recurring motifs and concerns that Japanese philosophers, when they are stressing the engaged model of thinking, tend either to assume or to make an explicit focus for reflection. The opening of this chapter already presented one such thematic motif, namely, the idea that the audience, not just the writer, performer, or philosopher, is an intrinsic part of the event of meaning. The second set of markers relates to forms of analysis and argumentation. Not surprisingly, they are sometimes unlike the forms typical of philosophies dominated by the paradigm of detached thinking. Let us begin with the thematic motifs.

THEMATIC MOTIFS OF ENGAGEMENT

Stress on Internal Relations

If I say "a and b are related," the paradigm of external relations—which is associated with detachment—assumes that a and b can exist independently (each with its own integrity), but since they are related, some third factor R must bridge or connect the two. That is, a and b are detached unless something external connects them. It follows as well that if the relation is terminated, a and b become again detached without any loss to either of them.

By contrast, the paradigm of internal relations—which is associated with engagement—assumes that if I say "a and b are related," I mean that a and b are intrinsically interlinked or overlapping, and that the R is the shared part of a and b. It also follows that since the relation is intrinsic to both a and b, if that relation were terminated, a and b would be less than what they were while in relation. This subtle difference profoundly influences how philosophy in each orientation proceeds.[5]

To illustrate the two kinds of relationality, consider what is different in regarding a marriage as a legal relation as contrasted with marriage as a loving relation. Legally, marriage is an external connection, a contract R connecting two otherwise separate individuals, a and b. If the marriage ends, the rights of the individuals are preserved, both detached persons return to being the discrete individuals they were previously, namely, a and b. In the case of a marriage viewed as a loving relation, by contrast, love is the bond R that a and b share internally and if that bond is dissolved, a becomes less than fully a and b less than fully b. As Emily Dickinson wrote in a poem after the death of a loved one, she became a "crescent" of her former self.

In western and Japanese philosophies alike, we find thinkers and texts that use both paradigms of relationality, but there is what we can call the "default setting" in each tradition. A philosophical tradition's default setting is, like the default settings in a computer program, not something absolute or unchangeable. It is simply what is assumed unless one makes special efforts to override

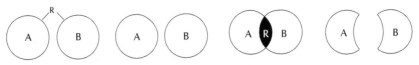

EXTERNAL RELATION   LOST EXTERNAL RELATION   INTERNAL RELATION   LOST INTERNAL RELATION

the defaults. Defaults are normally very helpful; they let us get on with the task at hand with a minimum of preliminary preparation.

We have all probably had the experience of using a computer not our own to run a program we know well. If we encounter different default settings on the unfamiliar computer, we are puzzled and perhaps even annoyed. In the same way, if we bring to our reading of a philosophical text detached knowing's default assumption that relations are regularly external, while the text we are reading is assuming the internal relations of engagement for its default, we may easily miss the point of what is being said. We may well be puzzled, even annoyed.

Because western philosophies in the past four centuries have increasingly made external relations their default assumption, whereas most Japanese philosophies throughout history have tended to make internal relations the default, we can experience frustrating difficulties in our attempt to think through Japanese philosophical positions. Thus, it is useful to keep in mind internal relations when interpreting Japanese philosophical statements.

For example, if a political theory maintains the emperor is the relation between the Japanese people and the state, unless otherwise specified, we should assume that the statement does not mean the emperor *creates* a connection linking the two, but rather, the emperor is an *overlap* between the people and the state. That is, the statement likely implies the Japanese people would not be fully the Japanese people without the emperor, nor would the state be fully the Japanese state without the emperor. As we will see later in this book, the relation of the emperor to the Japanese people has been understood to be more familial than contractual.

Or consider how the two models would construe the relation between knower and known. In detached knowing, the subject (the knower) and the object (the known) exist independently, and are connected only through the introduction of a third term, the relational connector called *knowledge*. Reality preexists our knowing it. We preexist the knowledge. Knowledge then appropriately connects what we think to what is.

Various theories will arise to explain what makes that detached knowledge "true." For example, some philosophers claim that knowledge occurs when the representations or concepts in the mind of the knower correspond with the state of affairs in the known. That is the gist of the so-called correspondence theory of knowledge, a theory with a history in the West traceable back at least to Aristotle.

Now consider what happens when we make internal, rather than external, relations the default model for knowledge. Then knowledge represents not what connects the independently existing knower and known, but instead, knowledge is found in the overlap, the interdependence between knower and known.

The more expansive the knowledge, the greater the overlap and the more insep-arable knower and known become. The knowledge lies, then, not in reference or correspondence, but rather in conference or mutual interpenetration. It is a model of knowledge that stresses not observation and analysis, but instead engagement and praxis. The difference between knowledge as external or inter-nal relation helps pinpoint the previously mentioned distinction between how the geologist and the potter know clay or between how the philologist and the poet know words.

Philosophical themes. The difference between detachment and engagement distinguishes not only kinds of knowing but also affects how philosophy con-structs itself thematically. The following two diagrams show how some themes

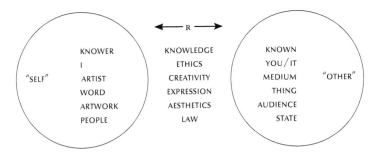

Philosophical Themes Built on External Relations

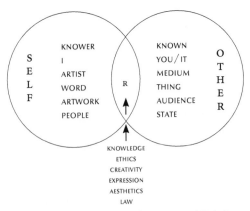

Philosophical Themes Built on Internal Relations

of philosophy may assume a different configuration depending on whether external or internal relations are taken to be the default.

For example, as the second diagram indicates, from the standpoint of engagement, ethics does not study the rules, duties, virtues, or the calculus of outcomes that bridge the divide between the discrete I and discrete Other (whether other person or other thing). Engaged ethics instead discovers the common ground shared by the I and other, using that as a standpoint for its analysis of value. Similarly, the philosophy of language does not study how linguistic expression spans the gap between mental words/concepts and things in the world, but instead studies the internal resonance between words and things that generates human expression.

Further, as noted already, within engagement, art is incomplete without its audience; the artist (the potter, for example) and the medium (the clay) create the pottery together; a constitution does not create a bond between individuals and the state, but instead arises from the preexisting, intrinsic overlap of individual and group. (We will examine a good example of this in the Shōtoku Constitution discussed in Chapter 2.) And so forth.

Bodymind

A second recurring motif in Japanese philosophy is the notion that body and mind form a single complex such that the two cannot be sharply separated. Earlier, I used the case of consulting a pulmonologist to illustrate how the separation between body and mind can arise from assuming detachment as the paradigm for knowing. Not surprisingly, for engagement, as the compound term bodymind suggests, the relation between the body and mind is internal, not external.

Therefore, the philosophical question becomes not what third thing connects the mind and body (the R as the bridge between them), but rather, the analysis of how the body and mind intrinsically overlap and function as a unit to various degrees. The bodymind as a unit does not perform so well in a novice typist, but does very well when the novice becomes an expert touch typist, for example.

Consequently, engaged knowing is inherently a somatic as well as intellectual event. It involves not merely thinking, but also bodymind praxis. If knowledge engages rather than maps reality, it must involve the whole person. This emphasis on the internal relation called bodymind has crucial corollaries in Japanese philosophy.

Knowing can be affective as well as intellectual. If the mind and body are not discrete, independently existing entities, how can we completely isolate the intellectual from the affective or thinking from feeling? Favoring the metaphors of detachment, we often speak of thinking as in the mind and feeling as in the gut or in the heart. What if we shift the paradigm, though, and consider bodymind to be a single complex?

In Japanese, the ordinary verb *omou* can refer to either thinking or feeling, or perhaps better stated, it names what arises from where the two are not easily split. There are other verbs that more specifically mean just thinking or just feeling, but it is revealing that the Japanese have preserved and widely use a word that blurs the line between the two. Likewise, Japanese aesthetics places great weight on the word *kokoro*, which as we will see in the discussion of poetics in Chapters 4 and 10, has an extraordinary range of nuances, but for convenience I sometimes translate it as the "mindful heart." *Kokoro* is the source of meanings that arise from both the sensitivity of feelings and the precision of thinking.

Even in English when we speak of an expert who has a hunch, does that hunch derive from a logical deduction based on previously gathered information? Or is a hunch a cultivated feeling derived from previous experience that allows one to engage the present situation holistically in a unified moment of thought-and-feeling? When a close friend says to another, "I knew you were going to say that," in what was that knowing based? Probably many years of shared experiences: both exchanging ideas and sharing feelings, both thinking through things and doing things together. When we start our philosophical reflections based in those kinds of experiences, to separate bodymind into a discrete body and discrete mind is not, as our lecturer in Hawai'i might say, *intuitive*.

I am not saying most Japanese philosophers fail to distinguish thinking from feeling or mind from body. They certainly can and do make the distinction as they find it relevant, but it is not typically their starting point. Their default is to begin with the overlapping and interconnectedness of the two.

Consider this analogy. As I look up from my computer, I see my grandson's red ball is over there in the corner of the room. Yes, I can think about the redness of the ball independently from its spherical shape, but that is not my starting point. If, for some reason only interesting to us philosophers, I think of the red of the ball and the shape of the ball as two separate data and ruminate on how the two came together in one entity or in one phenomenon, I am no longer engaging the ball, but engaging in a sequence of abstractions taking me ever further from everyday reality. Indeed, such an analysis leaves out entirely what is to me almost always the ball's most significant characteristic, namely, it is my *grandson's* ball; the overlap between *ball* and *grandson* is to me more crucial than the relation between *red* and *sphere*. That is not to say some truth cannot be extracted from ruminations about color and shape, but the point is that those philosophical reflections are derivative and abstract.

Japanese philosophers prefer to start with the primary and concrete. For the most part, they have discovered enough conundrums on that level to keep themselves philosophically engaged with only occasional excursions into the more ethereal realms of shapeless colors and colorless shapes, or of worlds without grandchildren.

Learning as the praxis of modeling oneself after a master. If engaged knowing assumes an inherent interdependence of knower and known, that has implications for how knowledge can be taught, what is often called in Japanese philosophy the issue of *transmission*. The standpoint of engagement will be more readily understood if we clarify, again, what distinguishes it from the standpoint of detachment.

In the detachment paradigm, knowledge can be the external relation R that connects the thoughts in my mind with the things out there in reality. Knowledge can also be the external relation between teacher and student. Once knowledge is imagined to be a discrete thing, even a thing that bridges two other things (mind and reality; teacher and student), it becomes a parcel of information or facts. The model of teaching then becomes the delivery of that parcel to the student.

In the default Japanese position, however, one does not isolate knowledge as something existing independently of the knower and known or teacher and student; knowledge resides in the intrinsic *overlap* within the pairs. So, the teacher does not delineate or outline knowledge for the sake of the student, packaging it into a self-contained "lesson plan." In the traditional Japanese context, we have seen how the sinographs suggest intrinsic connections among knowing, meeting, and imitating, such that the transmission of the truth is a process whereby the student assimilates the insight of the master. This pedagogical model assumes that in some respect the teacher and student undertake a praxis together and the student learns by emulating the way the master engages reality. Hence, from a Japanese standpoint, a philosophical text is not like a cookbook or a manual for operating a piece of machinery in which a parcel of information is wrapped up and delivered to the reader. Instead, it is an invitation to join the writer and to learn not simply from what the writer says, but also how she or he arrives there. This brings us to the final thematic motif I will discuss.

The emphasis on how instead of what. A philosophical tradition that places more value on engagement than detachment forces us to recast certain philosophical questions and, consequently, the form of their answers as well. The central epistemological question, for example, becomes not "what is knowledge?" but "how does knowing occur?"

Thus, when thinking about judgment, the modern Japanese philosopher, Nishida Kitarō, focused not so much on the propositional statements of judgment, but in the act of judging itself, an analysis of how different kinds of judgments come about. Similarly, the ethical question for many Japanese philosophers is not "what is moral?" or "what criteria determine what is good?" but instead "how does one negotiate a moral dilemma?" or "how does a concern for good and evil arise?" Likewise, in Japanese poetics the question is not usually "what are the characteristics of a good poem?" but more often "how does a good poem come into being?" or "how do certain practices lead to the sensitivity and clarity required of a good poet?"

The preference for *how* over *what* accounts for Japanese philosophy's celebrated emphasis on the "Way" (*michi* or *dō*): the Way of tea, the Way of the buddhas, the Way of the warrior, the Way of the Confucian scholar, the Way of calligraphy, and so on. We miss the point if we think those are just names for various practices.[6*] Rather, they are ways of engaging the world and each other. Thus, they have not only practical, moral, or aesthetic dimensions, but often epistemic, metaphysical, and even political dimensions as well.

FORMS OF ANALYSIS AND ARGUMENT

When we compare philosophical traditions stressing external relations, detached knowing, and the separation between the mind and body with those stressing internal relations, engaged knowing, and bodymind, it is not surprising we find differences in methods of analysis and rational persuasion. Three of those differences are especially important for engaging Japanese philosophy.

The Relation of Whole and Part as Holographic

A common problem in any philosophical analysis is understanding the relation between parts and whole. Most (but not all) modern western philosophers begin with the assumption that "the parts constitute the whole" or,

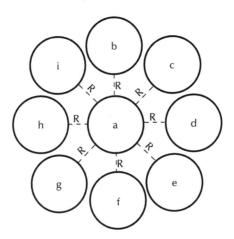

Reality As External Relations

more precisely because they also likely assume external relations, the "whole consists of its parts and the relations connecting those parts to each other."

Atomistic analysis, one of the most common forms of philosophical reasoning in the West (and often in classical India), makes that assumption and has the following regimen. To understand something, break it down into its smallest constituents, analyze the nature of those constituents, and then explain how the discrete parts are linked by external relationships with each other. Thus, in the physical sciences, a substance can be broken down into its atomic components, each analyzed in terms of its composition and the additional chemical bonds linking them. This yields the common, simplified model of the atom as schematically represented on the previous page. Many modern western philosophies use the same model for understanding and analyzing reality as a whole.

The holographic model of part and whole is strikingly different, however, and leads to an alternative mode of analysis. In the holographic model the whole (holo-) is inscribed (-graph) in each of its parts. So, it is not only the case that the parts are in the whole, but also that the pattern of the whole is in each of its parts. Moreover, the parts themselves are internally related. The result is that in the holographic mode of analysis, the part, once identified, is not then reconnected to make the whole by the addition of external relations, but instead, the part is more closely studied so that the pattern of the whole is discovered within it.

Consider a hair left in my hairbrush this morning. That hair is certainly only a part of my whole body, yet if that hair were discovered at a crime scene and became part of a forensic analysis, the technician would not try to determine my identity by finding other parts of me and attaching them together. Instead, the technician would focus even more closely on the hair itself to capture the DNA that yields the holistic information about my physical constitution.

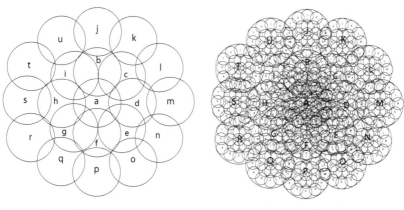

Internally Related Whole   Holographic Whole

That is, the forensic laboratory recaptures the whole by looking into a single part of the whole. That is an example of a holographic analysis that finds the whole written in each of its parts. Schematically, it would look like the diagrams on the preceding page. On the left is an internally related whole; on the right that same whole viewed as inscribed in each of its parts. If we take part E, for example, in the left diagram and look closely at it through the holographic analysis, we find inscribed within it (as shown by the diagram on the right) the entire pattern of the whole, parts A–U.

The holographic analysis of finding the whole-in-every-of-its-parts is not extensively used in most modern western philosophical theories. Yet, as the DNA example shows, it is part of the *modus operandi* in some scientific analyses, not only in genetics but also in fractal analysis and recursive set theories. Oddly enough, some of its strongest western proponents in recent centuries were the Romantics as when William Blake in "Auguries of Innocence" famously wrote:

> To see a world in a grain of sand,
> And a heaven in a wild flower,
> Hold infinity in the palm of your hand,
> And eternity in an hour.

The link between the Romantics and some modern-day scientists may be a surprise to both groups, but their common commitment to holographic thinking puts them on the same page, or perhaps better stated, they are turning their pages in unison although reading the same book in different languages.

In the Japanese intellectual and religious tradition, by contrast, the holographic mode of analysis is far more mainstream throughout its tradition from ancient animism up to today. That is so much the case that western commentators who are unaware of the privileged role of the holographic in Japanese culture are susceptible to misconstruing aspects of Japanese culture.[7]*

Take the example of the well-known Japanese proclivity for so-called minimalism. It is not a matter of simply leaving out what is functionally unnecessary. Rather, by reducing the painting to a single blossom on a branch, the poem to just seventeen syllables, or the Ryōan-ji rock garden to fifteen rocks, the audience is forced to engage the particular, but for the purpose of experiencing the whole of reality in that particular. Nothing is left out, at least not if you engage it properly. The Japanese are minimalists or particularists in the sense that the technicians in a DNA laboratory are.

Let us turn now from analysis to argumentation.

Argument by Refutation, Allocation, Hybridization, and Relegation

Japan is renowned for its ability to assimilate foreign ideas and methods, often being called "imitative," or "syncretistic," or "hybrid." Such general terms are too crude for the kinds of careful philosophical analysis we will engage in this book. So it is useful to examine three common rhetorical or argumentative techniques Japanese thinkers have commonly used when assimilating foreign ideas and theories.

First, however, it is helpful to think about how argument can be used to exclude rather than assimilate the new. I will call the primary form of exclusionary rhetoric "argument by refutation." It typifies the dominant mode of logical argument in the West (and generally in India as well, for that matter).

Refutation. First of all, refutation commonly does more than simply exclude or refute a position. It often does so to argue for an opposing position, a form of logical demonstration known as *reductio ad absurdum.* The purpose of refutation is to annihilate or nullify the opposing position by showing it to be faulty in either premises or logic.[8] As an argumentative form, refutation implicitly accepts Aristotle's Laws of Excluded Middle and Noncontradiction. Through refutation, therefore, I can establish my position simply by proving the opposing position false. Let us look more closely at how this is done.

In a *reductio* argument, specifically, I affirm the truth of my initial thesis by initially assuming its opposite and then refuting the latter by demonstrating it entails a contradiction. Formally speaking, I begin by taking my original thesis p and formulating its contradictory, *not-p.* By the Law of Noncontradiction, p and *not-p* cannot both be true in the same way at the same time and by the Law of Excluded Middle, there is no third possibility. It follows that either one of the theses p or *not-p* must be true. Hence, if I disprove *not-p*, p is affirmed.

As a technique, refutation is not limited to the rarefied forms of proof we find in symbolic logic or geometry, though. It also lies at the heart of our everyday arguments with colleagues, friends, family, and strangers. As long as we are disagreeing in a rational, cool-headed way, when you and I argue about the truth of a position, the protocol is basically as follows.

If I believe your view is wrong, we break it down into its propositional premises, some (even most) of which I accept as true. Then we can isolate the precise pivotal point (or points) of disagreement wherein we find that I hold position p and you position *not-p.* With that logical binary, applying Aristotle's two laws, only one of us can be right but in practice it is usually easier to prove something false rather than true (to be shown false, it need only be proven false in some one respect; to be proven true, however, it needs to be demonstratively true in all respects). So once the argument gets fully underway, most of our time is spent in your trying to refute my position *p* and my trying to refute your position *not-p*.

This process of argumentation is so inculcated in the western tradition as to be second-nature. Indeed, it seems to most westerners to define the very essence of argumentation in our adversarial exchanges in the courtroom, in the techniques of rebuttal in debate, and in the structuring of philosophical or political disputes. The rules of refutation are so entrenched that is easy to overlook assimilative forms of argument.

Yet, for the most part, the refutation form of argument and analysis is not the most dominant one in Japan where assimilation tends to trump exclusion. This brings us to the three common forms of argument that best serve assimilation, namely, allocation, hybridization, and relegation.

In an argument by *allocation*, we look not to refute the other position but to find out how in *certain contexts*, for *some purposes*, it can be accepted alongside what we already accept. It generates locutions such as "Oh, if you are talking about an umpire's judgment in a ballgame and not a judgment in a court of law, I can agree with you about how judgments are made." By my allocating your position to baseball and mine to law, each position is given its own appropriate domain or application so that my position and your position can logically coexist. *Hybridization,* by contrast, tries to fuse the two positions into something new, a hybrid of the two. "Let's see, if we take those aspects of your position and blend it with these from mine, we'll have a new theory that improves on both." Finally *relegation* accepts the other position but argues it is only part of the larger truth that my position already represents. "I couldn't agree with you more, but that is only part of the whole story. Let me explain."

Admittedly, it is not true that Japanese philosophers never use refutation and western philosophers never use allocation, hybridization, or relegation. I am speaking in generalities and generalities not only have exceptions, they *must* have exceptions (otherwise, they would be universalizations not generalities). Yet, my experience has been that the defaults for how to argue and why to argue are set differently in Japanese philosophy from how the defaults are set in western philosophy.

Of course, you can always override defaults, but in general, unless explicitly qualified, the western mode of rational persuasion favors refutation. Japanese thinkers, by contrast, tilt in favor of the three assimilative forms of rational persuasion. Given that premise, I will discuss the latter three in a bit more detail.

Allocation. As I have already said, allocation embraces the new by giving it a specified domain or role alongside the already accepted theories, thereby allowing the old and new to coexist without fundamentally changing either. For example, as we will see later in this book,[†] in the nineteenth century a popular slogan for Japan's modernization was that it should represent "Japanese spirit and western ingenuity" (*wakon yōsai*), itself an echo of a motto from a millennium earlier when the imported ideas were coming from a different direction: "Japanese spirit and Chinese ingenuity" (*wakon kansai*). In both cases by allocating a special role to the newly introduced ideas, the old and new could stand side-by-side in a complementary manner. The second way of integrating old and new—hybridization—is different in that it dissolves rather than preserves the integrity of each position.

Hybridization. Hybridization cross-pollinates ideas from different traditions to create a new theory or way of thinking. A thinker who was particularly clear about the difference between allocation and hybridization was Ninomiya Sontoku (1787–1856). He claimed to have developed a philosophical "medicine" for the health of the Japanese nation and its people, a "round pill" consisting of one-half the "essence" of Shintō, one-quarter the essence of Confucianism, and one-quarter the essence of Buddhism. When asked the function of each (as if they had been *allocated* discrete roles), Sontoku laughed and said,

> When I mentioned that the pill was round, I meant that it well combines and harmonizes the ingredients so that one does not know what the pill actually contains. If it were not like this, when you placed it in your mouth, it would sting your tongue, and when it entered your stomach, it would upset it. When making such a pill as this, it is essential that the ingredients are combined and harmonized so that no one notices them.

451

Sontoku recognized that hybridization, unlike allocation, often disguises its mixed genealogical parentage. For example, a loganberry is a species in itself, although a botanist knows it came into existence as a hybrid between a blackberry and a raspberry. The Japanese Way of the Warrior (*bushidō*) had its own ideology but a genealogical study of its heritage clearly shows it cross-bred elements of Confucian virtue theory, Buddhist discipline, and Shintō purity and sincerity. Modern Japanese philosophy presents us with many hybrids born of the cross-pollination of western ideas with traditional Japanese ideas, resulting in a new theory, no longer simply Asian or simply western. Watsuji Tetsurō's ethics is a good example insofar as it is a hybrid of Confucian collectivism, existential individualism (following Heidegger and Kierkegaard), and a Buddhist dialectic of emptiness, creating in the end a new and creative theory in its own right.

† See page 450.

Despite their difference in whether they preserve or dissolve the discrete character of the original theories, allocation and hybridization do share one trait: the traditional, already accepted ideas and the newly introduced ones are kept on roughly equal footing; neither is fully subordinated by the other. That is not the case with the third common Japanese option for assimilation, namely, relegation.

Relegation. Relegation rejects the segregation of ideas found in allocation, but does not go as far as hybridization in creating something completely new. In relegation the preferred theory accepts intact a new or opposing theory but only by consigning it to a subordinate position within an enlarged version of itself. Relegation preserves the other, but only by demonstrating it was already assumed in the original (preferred) system of thought. That is, it sets a clear hierarchy. By being inclusive and expansive, relegation can effectively produce holistic or systematic theories that absorb rather than exclude opposing ideas. Its hierarchical technique does not reject the competing view. Indeed it affirms the competing view as *completely* true but not the *whole* truth.

Relegation has been a popular technique throughout Japanese intellectual history. We find it, on one hand, as early as the ninth century in Kūkai's theoretical systemization of the ten mindsets (*jūjūshinron*) used to characterize all philosophies known in Japan at the time, showing each to be included in, but subordinate to, the mindset of Shingon Buddhism. In terms of praxis, on the other hand, Japanese esoteric Buddhism accepted the indigenous Shintō *kami*, but only by relegating them to being no more than the surface manifestations of the more foundational pantheon of buddhas (a relegating hermeneutic called *honji suijaku*).† Like Shingon, both the Kegon and Tendai traditions imported from China the stratagem of relegating the teachings of other schools into the lower tiers of their own inclusive system.

On the modern end of the Japanese spectrum, we find relegation used by such philosophers as Nishida Kitarō when he attempted to find a "place" within his system for all the major modern philosophical perspectives such as western empiricism and idealism. In his "logic of *basho* (place),"‡ Nishida consigned all the other philosophies to their respective loci, each subordinate to the most inclusive locus defined by what he called absolute nothing. That is, Nishida used the Buddhist notion of nothingness to absorb western philosophies, accepting their truth, but showing them to be partial when compared with his own theory.

Because refutation functions as the default form of argument for so many people today, it is instructive to consider some advantages in using relegation

---

† See pages 145–6; and 156.
‡ See pages 464–8.

as an argumentative mode. First, there is a logical point behind it. Suppose you and I have philosophic positions that are in fundamental disagreement. If my view of reality is comprehensive, I should be able to account for not only how my position is correct, but also how it is possible for someone to hold your (not fully correct) view. Your view, even if it is false in some respect, is nevertheless a *real* point of view and my theory of reality must be able to account for it. Whereas an argument by refutation often sets out to show an opposing view is ignorant or wrongheaded, an argument by relegation tries instead to show how, given the way reality is, such a partial or inadequate view is even possible. Notice, by the way, the shift from refutation's proving *what* is wrong (your position) to relegation's explaining *how* it is right, but only partially so.

Second, in line with the East Asian cultural stress on saving face, an argument by relegation has the appearance of being irenic or conciliatory rather than agonistic or adversarial. When we disagree in the relegation form of argument, I do not say you are wrong. To the contrary, I agree that your position is correct although limited and I assert that my position includes yours in some way. Of course, the conciliatory tone is more rhetorical than substantive because if we share the model of argument by relegation, we will indeed be competing over which position can relegate which.

To those acquainted with Hegel's philosophy, there is something familiar in building an ever more inclusive system that relegates—dare we say "sublates" (*aufheben* in German)—all other philosophical systems. It seemed that way to many Japanese philosophers as well, especially in the late nineteenth and early twentieth centuries when Hegelianism first reached Japan. That led to a fascination with Hegelian terminology, including the concept of "dialectics" (J. *benshōhō*). Yet, as the term developed within Japanese philosophy, dialectics came to mean something quite different from Hegel's notion due to another aspect of analysis fundamental to Japanese philosophy, one unlike Hegel's. We turn to that now as our last topic in this chapter.

Philosophy's Ground as the "In Medias Res"

The Hegelian dialectic is a progressive movement from one position to its antithesis, continuing on to ever more inclusive positions. Hegel's theory was a new twist on a deeply embedded western premise that truth, progress, or creativity comes about through the confrontation of opposites, what the pre-Socratic philosopher Heraclitus called "Strife." Hegel's term "dialectic," after all, traces back to the so-called Socratic method of philosophy as striving to reach the truth by arguing through opposing positions.

The western judicial system is based on the adversarial confrontation of prosecution and defense (remember Justice's balance scales?). Negotiation, whether in business or politics, generally aims for a compromise between two or more clearly defined opposing positions rather than for building a consensus from the ground up. The Abrahamic religions, following their Near Eastern Zoroastrian and Manichean brethren, saw creation as an eternal struggle between the cosmic forces of good and evil, namely, God and Satan or angels and demons. Even the mind and body were seen as a conflict between soul and temptations of the flesh, the sacred and the profane. Notice that those aspects of western thought and value all generally privilege external relations and argument by refutation. Yet almost all those cultural proclivities and presuppositions were foreign to early Japanese culture.

It is commonly claimed that Japanese culture is not dualistic. That is not true. Dualities of we and them, inner and outer, *yin* and *yang*, obligation and taboo, even subjective and objective are all part of the Japanese vocabulary of everyday life and the subject of philosophical reflection. There is a sense, however, that the Japanese philosophers tend to see the dualism as derivative rather than primary.

Think of a magnetic field with a positive and negative pole. To understand magnetism, should we start with the analysis of the positive and negative poles and see how their interaction "creates" the magnetic field or should we start with the field itself and study how the poles function within it? To most Japanese philosophers (but not all, of course) the latter approach makes more sense. Start with what is concretely experienced and see how the opposing poles can be abstracted out of that if, and only if, that process of abstraction has some practical value. That is what I mean by starting "in the midst of things," *in medias res*, and working outward from there.

As modern Japanese philosophers assimilated the idea of dialectic, therefore, they often used the idea in ways unlike Hegel. Rather than embrace Hegel's vision of a future goal or *telos* towards which history was evolving, they turned the question on its head to ask where the dialectic had come from. If Hegel recapitulated a long-standing western tradition of bringing opposites into a final unity, Japanese philosophers were more often drawn to the logical place, the ontological or experiential ground of unity out of which reality split into discrete, mutually exclusive polarities. The question is not how the positive and negative poles got together to make magnetism, but how the poles came to be abstracted out of the originally experienced single magnetic field.

When inquiring into how a unified process was abstracted into opposing polarities, Japanese philosophers do not necessarily seek a halcyon past without strife and opposition (although, admittedly, some of their political theories do try to do that). Rather, they are more often concerned with recovering and expressing the experience of the here-and-now within which the originally unified aspect of an active reality can be recognized. The preference for doing philosophy *in medias res* resides in the gaps left by abstract concepts about reality.

Therefore, Japanese philosophy often proceeds by starting with the overlap of internal relations and then analyzes how the opposing positions can be seen as abstractions in one direction or the other of that overlapping. How can we describe this *in medias res,* this being in the midst of the confluence of various events? Quite often, Japanese philosophers think of this field—what precedes the abstraction into opposites—as inexpressible in itself, but serving as the ground out of which meaningful expression arises.

To suggest that elusive quality, Japanese philosophers resort to terms like "emptiness" or "nothingness" or vacuous expressions like "as-ness" or "thusness." In Buddhism, that ground can be expressed as a root enlightenment that must be initialized in praxis so it can assume meaning. The field that serves as the home ground for the beginning of philosophizing is not far from the "blooming, buzzing confusion" out of which, William James believed, all thought and reflection emerges.

JUMPING IN

I hope by now you have an idea of what I mean by "engaging Japanese philosophy" as both a description of the tradition and a challenge about how to read that tradition. I end with two points before our journey through the history of Japanese philosophy begins.

First, I want to reiterate that everything in this chapter is not a universal statement about Japanese philosophy but a generality. A universal statement would be true in all instances, but in Japanese philosophy, as in any philosophical tradition, we find a variety of positions and intellectual temperaments. As a result, no statement about Japanese philosophy is true of all Japanese philosophers. If I were making universal claims, asserting that there is some essence shared by all Japanese philosophers or, even more bizarrely, by all Japanese, you could refute me simply by offering one counter-example. I certainly know of many myself. So, I am not making any universal claims or trying to delineate some mysterious Japanese essence. (As we will see later in this book, that search for a unique Japanese essence has been the agenda of a certain ilk of Japanese scholarship starting in the eighteenth century with Native Studies and continuing even today among many who spout *nihonjinron,* "theories of Japaneseness.")

Why then in this opening chapter have I engaged in so much generalization? Although this is not the place to go into the evidence, human beings typically learn new ideas by beginning with the general. Indeed, without the process of generalizing from recurrent patterns found in many experiences, we could never have learned a concept as simple as *cat,* for example. As we encounter ever more evidence, generalizations improve with modification and qualification. Yet, the generalization is the starting point.

As for refuting a generalization, there is only one logically valid way of doing so, namely, by positing a *better* generalization, one that accounts for more of the evidence. If someone can come up with better generalizations than the ones I offer in this chapter, I would welcome that effort and would like to see the evidence so that the study of Japanese philosophy can be improved.

Second, I doubt there is any major theory or idea in Japanese philosophy that is totally foreign or unintelligible to western philosophical thinking. (Again, I do not argue for Japanese uniqueness.) Take the idea of engaged knowing. The dramatic character of Plato's dialogues, Aristotle's theory of *phronēsis* (practical wisdom), and the central role of praxis in religious philosophies are all classical western sources highlighting engaged knowing. In the modern West, too, we find Gadamerian hermeneutics, William James's pragmatism, and Merleau-Ponty's phenomenology of embodiment as points of comparison.

A particularly striking statement along these lines was by the French philosopher, Henri Bergson, who wrote in the opening pages of his *Introduction to Metaphysics* in 1903:

> Philosophers, in spite of their apparent divergencies, agree in distinguishing two profoundly different ways of knowing a thing. The first implies that we move round the object; the second that we enter into it.... [9]

If you prefer a more East Asian invitation, consider this Zen kōan from China:

> The student asked Master Xuansha how to enter Zen.
> The master replied, "Do you hear the rushing of the mountain stream?"
> "Yes."
> "Enter there."

This book aspires to help you not just stand by as a detached observer of Japanese philosophy, not just hear about it from a distance, but to enter into it. Walk down that corridor to get up close to the statue of Justice and see what you discover and discover how you see.

The Ancient and Classical Periods

2. Blueprints for Japan

Shōtoku's *Constitution* and Shōmu's Nara (604–794)

> Take harmony to be of the highest value....
> Shōtoku's *Seventeen-Article Constitution*　　　36

Every narrative needs to begin somewhere, but we should not confuse how we open a history of Japanese philosophy with the beginning of Japanese philosophy itself. Philosophy is no physical invention like a light bulb: at one time, there were no light bulbs and, after that, there were. Philosophy is more a disposition, a reasoned thinking through matters, or a rational discourse that unfolds in spurts. It may come as an inspiring vision, a moment of analytic reflection, a need to convince by rational persuasion, or an impulse to figure out "what it all means."

To pin down the origin of philosophy in any culture is as quixotic as designating the precise moment when the darkness of night turns into the light of day. To become Japan's first philosopher was no one's conscious intent and the very word the Japanese have used to translate the western term "philosophy" (*tetsugaku*) is itself only a little over a century old. Still, the story of Japanese philosophy must originate somewhere with someone and I have chosen to begin this history with the writings attributed to Prince Shōtoku from the early seventh century. In making that choice I was inspired by Aristotle's selecting Thales as the point of departure for his history of Hellenic philosophy in his *Metaphysics* I.3.

Ever since he crowned Thales of Miletus the first philosopher, most histories of western philosophy have followed Aristotle's lead. A novice might assume that since western philosophy began with Thales, one should commence philosophical studies by reading Thales's complete works. It wouldn't take long. Most scholars today assume that Thales himself wrote little and whatever he did write is lost. Secondary accounts, which seem to be all that Aristotle had available as well, inform us that Thales asserted "all things are water" and "everything is full of gods." Such was the birth (out of holy water, perhaps?) of western philosophy, at least as Aristotle tells it.

45

Most revealing is not the selection of Thales, but the criterion applied for making that choice. Aristotle singled out Thales as the earliest Hellenic thinker to seek not merely an explanation for everything, but an explanation based in the natural rather than the supernatural or mythological. That is, Thales based his theories not in tales about Olympian gods and goddesses but in reason and observation, an approach that Aristotle believed epitomized the philosophical legacy he and his contemporaries had inherited.

The lesson we take from Aristotle's narrative is that a historical account of a culture's philosophy discusses origins not to identify a pristine moment when philosophy first appeared, but to explain the nature of philosophy itself by selecting an ancient figure or text as emblematic of what would follow. To compose a good story of origins, you start from the present and work backward until you find the apt starting point. In the Japanese case that takes us back to Shōtoku, the main figure in the first half of this chapter.

THE ICONIC PLACE OF PRINCE SHŌTOKU (574–622)

The *Seventeen-Article Constitution*, purportedly issued by Shōtoku in 604, is not much more philosophically sophisticated than Thales's pronouncements. Yet, it represents the first document to undertake what has been a major endeavor in Japanese philosophy ever since, namely, the attempt to harmonize ideas from different traditions.

The Japanese often consider Shōtoku the founder of the Japanese state. Of the four denominations of Japanese paper currency in the 1960s, two used Shōtoku's portrait for their central image. For most of the twentieth century, three huge portraits of Shōtoku served as the backdrop for the high bench in the Japanese Supreme Court. One portrays Shōtoku as a babe in his mother's arms, one as a princely general astride his horse, and one as sitting on his throne receiving from a scribe a copy of the *Constitution*. Understood as respectively signifying Shōtoku's loving compassion, courage, and justice, the paintings depict the three virtues for an ideal judge. The Japanese word translated "Constitution" in the title of Shōtoku's document is *kenpō* and Japan did not have another *kenpō* until the Meiji Constitution of 1889. Clearly, Shōtoku serves as an icon of law and the state, but just as notable is his religious import.

Shōtoku supposedly wrote the first three major Japanese commentaries on Buddhist texts and his *Constitution* declared Buddhism a state religion. Furthermore, since antiquity, popular folklore has considered him an incarnation of the aforementioned Kannon, the Bodhisattva of Compassion.† The folk narratives and practices surrounding Shōtoku are so thickly layered that it is

† See pages 16–17.

difficult to reach the core historical reality. In any case, for the past thirteen or fourteen centuries Shōtoku has served as a political and religious centerpiece in Japan's narrative about its national roots. Moreover, the writings attributed to him have inspired much Japanese philosophy to follow.

I will begin by explaining philosophical resources Shōtoku had at his disposal as he articulated his vision for a unified and harmonious Japan. As will soon be obvious, the number and complexity of ideas available to him were staggering. We can only imagine how it must have been for him and his contemporaries to make sense of it all. Still, Shōtoku at least laid the intellectual foundation for the Nara culture that will be our concern in the second half of this chapter, the culture that spawned Kūkai's career in the early ninth century as Japan's first systematic philosopher. Only with Kūkai and his contemporaries do we find true philosophical system-building in Japan. Yet, that intellectual creativity might never have flourished were it not for Shōtoku's promulgating a vision for Japan's intellectual, political, and moral development.

Shōtoku's Political Context

Shōtoku Taishi ("prince of saintly virtue") is the posthumous title for Prince Umayado or Kamitsumiya, the nephew regent of Empress Suiko (554–628).[1] To appreciate Shōtoku's political context, a brief overview of Japan's social evolution up to that point is in order. The archeological evidence from the Jōmon era (ca. 10,000–300 BCE), the Japanese stone age, indicates the people were then mostly hunter-gatherers living on game, nuts, fish, and shellfish. They buried their dead in simple graves alongside their campsites. Archeologists surmise the Jōmon—the name stems from the "straw rope pattern" of their pottery—were for most of the era small nomadic groups taking shelter in caves or thatched-covered pits.

On one hand, with its regular seasonal rains, fertile plains, and proximity to bountiful marine food, Japan's geography favors human sustenance. On the other hand, unpredictable natural catastrophes are common: earthquakes, tsunami, volcanoes, mudslides, and typhoons. In such a predominantly benevolent but erratically threatening environment, the Jōmon people likely understood the natural world to be influenced by capricious *kami,* spiritual presences inspiring awe and demanding appeasement. The extant Jōmon pottery figurines (*dogū*) of strange animals and humanoid, usually female, shapes likely functioned as talismans for warding off angry *kami* or ensuring fertility.

To put this in historical perspective, by the end of the Japanese Jōmon period the writings of Confucius and Laozi were shaping classical Chinese civilization and the *Upanishads, Bhagavad Gītā,* and Buddhist teachings were doing the same for India. In both countries those textual developments were the culmination of a literary tradition already a millennium old. Meanwhile, the Japanese Jōmon people were still eking out an existence in caves and pits. Japan was indeed a latecomer to the family of Asian civilizations.

The Japanese social structure continued to evolve into the ensuing iron and bronze ages, the still prehistoric Yayoi period[2] (300 BCE to 300 CE). It signaled notable changes, mainly via the increasing influence of Japan's nearest continental neighbor, the Korean peninsula. With the expansion of wet rice culture, more of the hunter-gatherers began to move down from the steep foothills into the plains, settling as fishers and farmers. In sedentary communities sustained by agricultural and fishing collectives, social classes began to solidify.

Besides the information gathered from archeological digs, we know a bit more about Yayoi culture from early Chinese visitors.[3] Ritual apparently revolved around taboo violations and purification while the social order was hierarchical with regional sovereigns, or at least what Chinese visitors understood to be sovereigns. For example, third-century Chinese accounts describe a female shaman-queen named Himiko (or Pimiko).[4] Guided by trance-induced visions, she lived in a protected compound apart from the rest of the settlement while a male priest interpreted her visions to the community and attended to the daily affairs of governance.[5]* Himiko's model of combined political and spiritual rulership continues today insofar as the Japanese emperor is both Shintō high priest and titular head of state.[6]

Yayoi social trends and the further influence of the continent intensified in the ensuing Kofun ("ancient mounds" or "ancient tombs") period (300–710 CE), which includes the time of Shōtoku (the subperiod of Asuka 593–710). Politically, regional kinship groups or clans (*uji*) gained prominence throughout Japan, each with its own shaman priests ministering to the clan's guardian deity. Unlike the egalitarian, spartan burial sites of the Jōmon, the deceased Kofun leaders commanded keyhole-shaped burial mounds ranging up to 586 meters long, significantly larger than, say, the Great Pyramids of Egypt. Often large, simple pottery figures of people, animals, and houses accompanied them to the grave, suggesting belief in an afterlife.

The smattering of such burial mounds throughout the islands of Kyūshū, Honshū, and Shikoku indicates a common culture was taking form across the discrete clan territories. The stronger kinship groups gradually absorbed weaker ones and in the end, the clan of the Yamato plain dominated. Its tribal *kami* was the Sun Goddess, Amaterasu. As the Yamato established itself as the imperial family for the entire archipelago, she emerged as a celestial *kami* of nationwide significance.[7]

This returns us to the early seventh century, the time of Shōtoku and his *Constitution*. Only then are there early signs of an emergent centralized Japanese government under imperial rule, a process that would continue to evolve into the early eighth century. In interpreting the *Constitution*, it is instructive to know how the Empress Suiko and her nephew, Prince Regent Shōtoku, came to power.

During the sixth century, intrigue and violence rather than the rule of law determined imperial succession. The Soga clan, led by Soga no Umako (?–626), had defeated and almost annihilated its major competitor, the Mononobe, after which Umako installed his nephew Sushun as emperor. Finding Sushun too independent, Umako had him assassinated two years later and then enthroned his niece Suiko,[8] making Shōtoku the prince regent and heir apparent.

Shōtoku's *Constitution*, along with his twelve-cap system for ranking courtiers (headgear signified the levels of aristocratic hierarchy), were efforts to bring stability to the newly emergent central government. Increasing threats of invasion from the continent and an understandable fear that other kinship groups within Japan might attempt a *coup d'état* at any moment lent all the more urgency to his unification project.

In formulating his ideas for the *Constitution*, Shōtoku could draw on three traditions: Confucianism, the indigenous *kami*-worship heritage I will call proto-Shintō, and Buddhism. Here the comparison with Thales clearly breaks down. Since Japan became literate much later than its East Asian neighbors, Shōtoku had available to him all at once more than a millennium of philosophical thought. Unlike Thales, Shōtoku did not have to conceive *ex nihilo* new ideas or new ways of thinking but instead could direct his talents to puzzle through how best to coordinate, make coherent, and enhance an array of ideas and values already at hand. Because the three traditions he engaged have continued to shape Japanese philosophy up to the present, I will summarize a few enduring ideas from each that can be traced back to Shōtoku's era. My discussion is intended to serve readers with little previous knowledge of these traditions and to emphasize those ideas most relevant to the major philosophical thinkers we will encounter in subsequent chapters of this book.

SHŌTOKU'S THREE INTELLECTUAL RESOURCES

Confucianism

The impact of Confucianism on early seventh-century Japan starts with the introduction of literacy. The Japanese had no form of writing, no orthography, until they adopted Chinese characters, the sinographs. Because Chinese and Japanese are such different languages,[9] the imported orthography was so cumbersome for rendering Japanese that Shōtoku and his contemporaries simply wrote in Chinese. Even after the early ninth century when a hybrid orthography evolved for writing Japanese with some efficiency, for many centuries most Japanese philosophers continued to write in Chinese.[10]

Confucianism[11] entered Japan with the introduction of writing in the early fifth century. As in China, the ancient Japanese students acquired literacy by reading and copying classical Chinese texts, a canon including poetry, histories, and the ancient "Confucian" classics.[12] Although Japanese Confucianism was not religious in the sense that Shintō and Buddhism were,[13] its social, political, and moral ideals did nurture the maturation of Japanese culture. While relations between China and ancient Japan were not always friendly,[14] the Japanese, like most other East Asians, historically respected Chinese cultural accomplishments. To unify its own state, therefore, it is not surprising the early Japanese would draw on successful Chinese models for their own institutions.

Confucianism introduced two particularly important teachings into ancient Japan: the five relationships and five virtues. Stressing the social character of human existence, Confucianism maintains that self-understanding arises from analyzing the web of human relations: your identity is inseparable from your interconnections with other people. Tradition distilled those relations down to five elemental binaries: lord-subject, parent-child, elder-younger, husband-wife, and friend-friend. If those foundational dyadic relations function harmoniously, society as their composite will also be harmonious.

At least the first four relations are hierarchical: the person of lower status trusts and complies with the one of higher status, whereas the person of higher status cares for the lower. That universal reciprocity is the bedrock for building a Confucian society and philosophy's role within it is to analyze how to perform those duties, responsibilities, and interdependencies.

When social concord rules, people's behavior accords with the meanings of the names defining their relations with others: to be a good father is to act like what the term *father* implies; to be a good son is to act like a *son*. That correspondence between relational roles and behavior is the Confucian principle of "using terms properly" or the "rectification of (in the sense of trueing up) names" (*seimei*). That is, what the relation *is*, its descriptive name, prescribes how one *ought* to act. In effect, to be a bad father, for instance, is not to be truly a father at all. This Confucian inseparability of *is* and *ought* has played a central role in Japanese moral and ethical thinking throughout its history.[15]

The Confucian tradition also brought to Japan the "five constant excellences" or "virtues" (*toku*)[16] to explain how to accord names with social roles: being "authentically human" or "benevolent" (*jin*), being "apropos" or "righteous" (*gi*), being "ritually proper" (*rei*), being "wise" or "realizing" (*chi*), and being "sincere," "trustworthy," or "faithful" (*shin*).[17] The Confucian tradition analyzed the virtues in detail, debating which to be most central or logically prior.

As we will see in later chapters, a millennium after Shōtoku, the Japanese Edo-period philosophers developed their own variations of Confucian philosophy, but in ancient Japan there was little creative Confucian thought or critical reflection. Confucianism's main contribution was limited to supplying a new terminology and general template for political and social behavior. In that, it was highly successful.

To sum up: Confucian thought influenced ancient Japan in three areas. First, it emphasized the socially relational person rather than the atomistic individual. Next, Confucian or classical Chinese principles lent the Japanese a rationale for the social hierarchy conducive to a monarchy-centered, bureaucratic government. Lastly, the Confucian tradition endowed the ancient Japanese with a system of virtues defining interpersonal relations and setting the performance standards for state officials. The Japanese inculcated those principles in their young men by imitating China's educational program for training aristocrats and government officials to meet the ideal of the Confucian scholar-official.[18]

Let us turn now to the ideas and values in *kami*-worship that likely influenced Shōtoku's thinking at the time of the *Constitution*.

Proto-Shintō

In discussing the prehistory and early history of Japan, I referred both to aspects of the native spirituality and to the relation among the clans, sovereigns, and *kami*. In this book, I will use the term *proto-Shintō* rather than simply *Shintō* to refer to that indigenous spirituality.[19*] The word *Shintō* is a sinicized (Chinese-influenced) Japanese reading[20] of the phrase *kami no michi*, the "Way of the *kami*," a name coined to distinguish the indigenous tradition from the continental imports, namely, "*butsudō*" (the Way of the buddhas) and *judō* ("the Way of Confucian literati").[21*]

By using the term *proto-Shintō*, I am stressing the point that Japan's indigenous spirituality did not originally see itself as a discrete tradition with its own history and nomenclature. Not being self-reflective, it also did not explicitly define for itself any core ideas or orthopraxis that would prevent intermixing with other traditions such as shamanism, Daoism, or folk religious practices introduced from the continent.

As a result, the ancient native spirituality was not what we today think of as Shintō, a religious and philosophical system with advocates that have tried at times to divorce it from Buddhism, Confucianism, and Daoism[22] by articulating, modifying, and codifying aspects of that ancient spiritual orientation. Such self-conscious reflection began in the medieval period at major shrines such as Ise and Yoshida, but did not reach its full philosophical expression until the eighteenth century with the Native Studies philosophy of Motoori Norinaga (1730–1810), whom we will engage at length in Chapter 10.

Both proto-Shintō and Shintō focus on *kami*. As used so far in this book, the term *kami* has primarily designated personal deities such as the tutelary gods of kinship groups or the celestial deities like the Sun Goddess, Amaterasu. The term's semantic range is much broader, however. To the proto-Shintō Japanese, as implied in my account even of the Jōmon period, awe-inspiring presences called *kami* pervaded the world in various forms besides those of celestial deities. Such *kami* could include natural objects (striking mountains, rocks, waterfalls, or trees), human beings (the emperor and some extraordinary warriors, shamans, and artisans), ghosts, spirits, and eventually also wondrous artifacts (swords, tea bowls, and so on).

Tama is the most common term for a *kami*'s power to inspire awe.[23] As in other animistic traditions, the Japanese *kami* are not necessarily benevolent. They can also be mischievous, deceptive, or destructive, although not falling into the hard-and-fast distinction between good and evil typical of religions originating in the Middle East. In the Japanese spiritual ontology, we find no angels and demons in eternal conflict—even a benevolent buddha might take a demonic form if the situation calls for it. And a fox could be a shape-shifter harmful or helpful to humans (but always a little wily in doing so). Consequently, without attaching moral categories, the term *kami* can as readily apply to a destructive tsunami as to the life-sustaining sun. What has *tama* is *kami* and people must simply engage them for what and how they are.

In brief: the word *kami* refers to any wondrous, awe-inspiring presence in whatever form, regardless of whether it is beneficial or harmful to humans. We live in an animated world, pulsing with wondrous energy and agency. *Nihonshoki* (*Chronicle of Japan*), an eighth-century record of myths and history, tells us that rocks, plants, and various other natural objects could once move about and speak, but they were so noisy, querulous, and violent that the celestial *kami* had to deprive them of those powers.[24] Such intervention is a theme in many Japanese myths: the coordination with spirited elements to make the world better for human habitation. The further implication is often that the emperors, as direct descendants of the Sun *kami*, should guide the human world in that harmonizing.

In other words, the spiritual force that orders the natural world is akin to the force that, through the emperors, brings political and social harmony to the human world. As I will discuss later in this chapter, such an assumption probably lent its own hue to the *Seventeen-Article Constitution*'s recurrent call for respecting the emperor. A century after the *Constitution*, the *Kojiki* (*Record of Ancient Events*) and *Nihonshoki* accounts of creation, purportedly tracing from ancient oral traditions, directly linked the imperial and aristocratic families to the *kami* from the time of creation. The detailed lineage and hierarchy of the various *kami* in the myths may also have reflected the hierarchy of the kinship groups associated with those specific *kami,* not only lending spiritual authority to the imperial family, but also through relegation, conferring some lesser levels of spiritual authority to other kinship groups as well.

It is easy to understand animism in a way that misrepresents Japan's proto-Shintō world view about the links among the sacred, the natural, and the human. Scholarly treatments of so-called primitive or archaic religions often define animism as a belief that spirits *inhabit* such natural items as trees, rivers, mountains, animals, and rocks. If we accept that definition, then the Japanese myths commonly portray something additional.

The ancient Japanese believed natural objects themselves, as they are, consist of spirit or more precisely spirit-matter, either fragments of *kami* or the progeny of *kami*. In the creation myths, the *kami* generate the world as much by serendipity and parthenogenesis as by design. According to *Kojiki,* for example, the effluent from the eyes of the *kami* Izanagi when he bathed in a river became physical objects—the material sun and moon—that were themselves inseparable from the Sun *kami* Amaterasu and the Moon *kami* Tsukuyomi. Such descriptions present the physical and spiritual as an indissoluble whole. In that proto-Shintō vision of internal relatedness, natural things share in the inherent character of the *kami,* and the *kami* share in the inherent character of natural things.

The ancient Japanese, therefore, did not sharply distinguish matter and spirit as western thinking has so frequently done since Plato. In the proto-Shintō world view, when the rocks and plants lost their power of speech and movement, they did not lose their spiritual qualities. Nature and humanity, matter and spirit, or the divine and human are so intimately related that to isolate them into independently existing entities would destroy part of their fundamental character. They would become a crescent of their former, fully developed selves.

Such internal relations are experienced affectively as much as intellectually; they are a matter of sensing or feeling an already existing overlap rather than making rational connections that bridge discrete entities. We can find that affective overlap between the natural and human in many Japanese-language poems from the eighth-century anthology of verse called *Man'yōshū* (*The Collection of Ten Thousand Leaves*), for example. A few representative lines from "Elegy on the Death of a Wife" (*Man'yōshū*: 794–9) by Yamanoue no Okura (660–*ca* 733) illustrates the point. After relating how the man's wife had died while accompanying him on a journey to Tsukushi, the widower expresses his grief:

Not knowing	言はむ術	*Iwamusube*
What to do or say,	せむ術知らに	*Semusubeshirani*
I uncomprehendingly cry out (for response)	石木をも	*Iwakiomo*
From stones and trees.	問ひ放け知らず	*Tohisakeshirazu*

From our modern perspective, we might wonder why the speaker in the poem sought soothing words from trees and stones. Crying out (*tohisake*) to them for comfort, sympathy, or understanding, he receives no response. A gap separates the bereaved and the natural, a gap where the speaker in the poem feels there should be an intimate connection within an inter-responsive field (*kokoro*[25]) shared by the widower and the world.

1220–4

Insofar as the widower seeks a spiritual response, the grieving husband's cry may at first seem to resemble a Christian widower's looking up at the sky and asking: "God, why did this happen?" Yet, the Christian looks to a heavenly deity, an external "other" who is transcendent to this world, while the ancient Japanese seeks spiritual engagement within the natural world. Furthermore, the westerner asks why, whereas the Japanese seeks consolation, not explanation. The Japanese is not associating the sacred with teleology, rational analysis, or supramundane intention, but instead seeks resonance with it. This interpretation is reinforced by Okura's envoy (*hanka*) appended to the end of the poem:

On Mount Ōno	大野山	*Ōnoyama*
The mist rises;	霧立ち渡る	*Kiritachiwataru*
With the wind	我が嘆く	*Waganageku*
From my sighs of grief,	おきその風に	*okisonokaze ni*
The mist rises.	霧立ちわたる	*kiritachiwataru*[26]

As that concluding stanza depicts, the widower's wail interfuses with the natural force driving the mist upward: "With the wind from my sighs of grief, the mist rises."[27] Thus, the last line implies that in the poet's experience at least, the natural world is at last responding magically and empathically to his grief. Again, it is not a response to prayer directed to a transcendent divine being, nor a natural sign of divine covenant like the rainbow shown Noah (Gen 9:12–13).

Instead, the poet discovers for himself the natural harmony between the physical and affective, the material and spiritual, the natural and the human. Although verbally silenced in the primordial past, the natural world can still resonate with the man's sighs of grief. In the poem, the mutual movement of air and the affect's capacity to connect the psychological and material have restored the empathy between the man and nature.[28]*

Three features emerge from this discussion of the indigenous Japanese or proto-Shintō world view. To begin, the assumption was that spiritual forces are everywhere and people can contact them directly either through rituals, shamanistic trances (as with Empress Himiko), or through emotive sensitivity (as suggested by the poem).

Next, as noted in my account of how the centralized Japanese state took form, there was a hierarchy of elite and ordinary people within each clan and each clan had its own *kami*. With the rise of the Yamato as the dominant—eventually imperial—clan, its central *kami*, Amaterasu (the Sun Goddess), would achieve national preeminence. By that means, proto-Shintō added a religious factor to the Japanese view of rulership. In fact, it seems *kami* is the primary term and all other agencies of power—human, natural, and political—derive from it.

Lastly, because the ancient Japanese understood sacred power to permeate both the natural and the human, both the material and the spiritual, harmony stemmed from recognizing, celebrating, and preserving the existing internal connections. One discovers and nurtures, rather than creates, harmony. Social and political harmony derives from sensitivity and intuition without the need for a Lockean or Hobbesian social contract to supply a rational principle behind the formation of the state. According to Shintō, to form a society, we need originally only recognize the internal relations already there.

As I will show in Chapter 10, in the eighteenth century Motoori Norinaga based his ideal of the state in the aesthetic of *kokoro*, while in Chapter 13, we will see how the twentieth-century philosopher, Watsuji Tetsurō, reformulated this idea of inherent relationship into a modern theory explicitly critical of the western social contract model. But for now, let us stay in Shōtoku's world to examine his third philosophical asset: Buddhist thought.

Buddhism

Like Confucianism, Buddhism enjoyed from the time of its founder more than a millennium of literary, cultural, and intellectual development before finding its way to Japan. Understandably, it took the Japanese some time to assimilate the newly introduced tradition before they could engage in advancing their own Buddhist philosophies. Yet, once Buddhism did take root in Japan, it dominated the Japanese intellectual scene for the next thousand years, a trajectory of success that can be considered to have begun with Prince Shōtoku.

As already explained, the Soga family of Empress Suiko and Shōtoku had acquired the throne through a military victory over the Mononobe, a bone of contention between the two families being the role Buddhism should play in Japan's future. Buddhism had formally entered Japan in the sixth century and by the late seventh, the Soga hoped to make it a state religion. Meanwhile, the Mononobe, as overseers of court rituals related to *kami*-worship, determinedly opposed that plan, predicting repercussions from the jealous native *kami* should Buddhism be granted undue sponsorship from the court. Thus, the Soga victory ensured Buddhism unquestioned imperial support.

Many welcomed Buddhism not only for its literary works, which accompanied the Confucian classics as sourcebooks for learning Chinese, but even more so for its arts, rituals, and purported wonder-working or thaumaturgy.[29]* In stark contrast with the austere proto-Shintō tradition, Buddhism offered sculpture, painting, impressive architectural styles, and ritual elegance involving new forms of music and dance—all of which became part of court spectacle.

As a result, the court aristocrats sponsored the flow of monks and artisans into Japan from Korea and China and financially backed an increasing number of Japanese emissaries sent to the continent for cultural enrichment. Another factor in Buddhism's favor was that when Japan began its formal relations with China in the Sui Dynasty (581–618), the Chinese court supported Buddhism. For example, the first emperor of the Sui Dynasty, the Emperor Wen (r. 581–604), was fervently Buddhist and Sui imperial rule was informed by the Buddhist ideology of statecraft.[30] Thus, for the Japanese of the period, Buddhism as well as Confucianism embodied Chinese high culture.

Since spirits, ghosts, deities, taboos, totems, and sacred rituals for worldly benefit were part of the fabric of everyday life, the ancient Japanese relished Buddhism's reputed power to win battles, protect the state, cure disease, appease angry spirits, and generate prosperity. Understanding Buddhist celestial beings to have powers analogous to those of the *kami* from the indigenous tradition, the Japanese tapped both as sources of spiritual potency. The official records note Shōtoku supported public festivals for the *kami,* issuing an edict in 607 encouraging *kami*-worship.[31]

Still, Shōtoku targeted his patronage on Buddhism. In what is now southern Osaka, for example, he constructed the Temple of the Four Celestial Kings (Shitennō-ji) in gratitude for the Soga victory over the anti-Buddhist Mononobe. The complex included a hospital and a school, signs that Shōtoku understood Buddhism to have a social as well as spiritual mission. Since our interest is in the Buddhist ideas and values affecting the unfolding of Japanese philosophy, however, I will begin with the core Buddhist analysis of human existence, depicting in very broad strokes some of the central ideas that would be familiar to Japanese court Buddhists even as far back as Shōtoku's early seventh century. This will present us with a Buddhist world view in its most generic form, lacking the doctrinal subtleties we will find a century later in the schools of Nara-period Buddhism and, indeed, even parts of the Buddhist commentaries attributed to Shōtoku. This account will also serve to familiarize us with some technical terms and introduce us to Buddhist praxis, both of which are critical for understanding the later development of Japanese philosophy.

The human situation according to Buddhism. Buddhism teaches that ordinary human existence is marked by unsatisfactoriness, impermanence, and insubstantiality. The unsatisfactoriness derives from our ego's continually thwarted attempt to find ongoing happiness and pleasure while avoiding the pain of illness, aging, and death.

The second mark, that of impermanence, refers to the source for that frustration: the objects of our desire and repulsion continue to come and go. A moment of pleasure or a brief respite from pain further fuels the desire for that state to endure, but it cannot. Because every pleasure or pain, every material thing, every desire, and every thought is fleeting, it is futile to fixate on any object as something to be forever preserved or permanently annihilated.

The last characteristic—the insubstantiality of all things—accounts for that impermanence: what we think of as stable things are really processes. Desperately seeking constancy, we delude ourselves into believing that behind or beneath any change is an unchanging essence or substance that undergoes the change. We have no direct evidence to support such a belief, but we nonetheless fabricate the fiction to avoid facing reality as it is, replacing it with how we wish it were.

Buddhism insists that however much we may wish for constancy, nothing permanent exists—not God, not Brahman, not the soul. Instead, each "thing" is really an event interdependent with other events. (Here we find one basis for the general tendency in Japanese thought to give primacy to *how* rather than *what*.) According to Buddhism, the most harmful delusion is taking ourselves to be substances: "I have experiences" (instead of I am experiences); "things happen to me" (instead of I am a happening); "I am getting old" (instead of aging is how I am). That delusional, reified, substantialized self is the "ego" (*ga*; S. *ātman*) and the general Buddhist word for insubstantiality is the negation of it (*muga*; S. *anātman*).

The mismatch between desire and reality feeds the unsatisfactoriness haunting our existence. To be enlightened, therefore, is to face reality and to engage it fully without deluding ourselves into thinking of it otherwise. Only then will the unsatisfactoriness of ordinary life cease.

To understand that Buddhist view of impermanence and insubstantiality more clearly, consider a phenomenon in which we have less vested interest than in the reality of I or of God—a river for instance. To the Buddhist way of thinking, the Mississippi River is not the *thing* that flows from Minnesota to the Gulf of Mexico, but is rather that watery *flow* coursing its way from Minnesota to the Gulf. That flow is a process, itself dependent on other processes (rainfall, temperature, gravity, erosion, human engineering projects, and so forth).

Analogously, we do not navigate our way down the river of life; we are the sheer flowing of that river. Buddhism claims that recognizing this truth, not merely intellectually, but also emotionally and practically, is enlightenment. To be enlightened is to engage the world on its own terms: to see, hear, taste, touch, feel, and know what is there without any delusional longing for it to be otherwise.

Karma. Admittedly, viewing reality as interdependent processes with neither substance nor ego might lead us to question the reality of free human agency, lapsing into a fatalistic submission to the conditions of destiny or fate (*unmei*). Fatalists may point to the Buddhist idea of karma (*gō*) to justify their pessimism, but that would be a mistake. The root meaning of the Sanskrit word *karman* is not fate but *action,* particularly volitional action.

The Buddhist interpretation is this: every time I decide to act (an act can be a thought, word, or deed), there is a dual effect. The first is the obvious one that likely factored into my decision to act in the first place—getting what I desired, for example. Suppose I see my favorite dessert on the menu and I decide to suspend my diet to delight in its pleasures, gleefully ordering a double portion, knowing that such an act might affect my long-range project of losing weight. That first effect from an action is a matter of simple physical causality: eating the dessert increases my caloric intake causing a gain in weight.

The second karmic effect of my eating the dessert is more subtle. By excusing my adherence to the strict diet "just this once," I have planted a psycho-physical propensity to do it again. My physical cravings will get only stronger by my having surrendered to them and, now that I have blazed the trail of rationalization, my thinking processes have a clear pathway to follow in allowing my next detour off the road to good health. In Buddhist terms, I will be "karmically conditioned" to deviate from my diet again.

The English idiom is "we are what we eat" but a Buddhist might add that "we are also *how* we eat," shifting the emphasis from the substantialized *what* to the process-based *how.* By the first effect, that of physical causality, I endangered my diet by indulging in a fattening dessert. Yet, that is a *what,* something I can correct tomorrow by cutting back from my usual caloric daily intake to compensate. Far more pernicious, the Buddhist says, is *how* I indulged, using rationalization to set a propensity for how I will later deviate again from the regimen. For understanding and transforming how we are, Buddhist analysis zeroes in on those psycho-physical propensities, mental tendencies, or habit formations (*gyō;* S. *saṃskāras*). Since propensities are part of a larger analysis defining personal identity, let us turn to that.

According to traditional Buddhist teachings, psycho-physical propensities are one of five key processes (*un,* literally "heapings"; S. *skandhas*) composing the experiential flow constituting a person. The full set is as follows. (1) First are the physical processes constituting the structure of my *body* (e.g., my sense organs). (2) Those physical processes yield the *sensations* (both internal and external) of, say, the raw data of seeing a red blotch of a particular size and shape, smelling a sweet aroma, and feeling a certain firmness. (3) Based on previous experience, I then can have the *perception* of those sensations as constituting what I conceive of, or recognize as, an "apple." Those first three heapings represent a rather mechanistic aspect of experience. (4) Next comes the volitional process of *psycho-physical propensities* that introduce conscious attitudes and behavioral responses toward what I perceive or conceive. For example, I may respond to the apples as something I desire and covet, leading me to steal some from a neighbor's tree. At this level, volitional action (karma) comes into play and sets the patterns or dispositions for future behaviors. Such karmic actions lead to repercussions in future attitudes and behaviors to such an extent that the habits established become second-nature to the way I subsequently live, even to the extent that I may not recognize why I act as I do. (5) *Consciousness* allows, through reflexive awareness, access to this whole set of processes making possible both delusional and enlightened thought and action.

If our concern is human agency, it is instructive to see how the fivefold list allows for personal uniqueness and individuality. What distinguishes you from me is not that we each have our own discrete, underlying essence, ego, "I," or soul—where many western philosophies locate agency. Buddhism instead finds your personal distinctiveness in the details of your five processes (the sum of interdependent processes in your experiential flow) as being distinct from my five processes. Again, let us turn to an analogy.

Both the Mississippi River and the Colorado River are alike in being the downward flowing of water along a subtly ever-changing river bank affected by the processes of rain, erosion, pollution, human engineering, and so forth. Yet, the details of those processes lend each river enough uniqueness—how much rainfall, which erosive processes on what kind of rock, which polluting compounds, which engineering projects, etc.—that there is no confusing the Mississippi for the Colorado. This allows us to say, for example, that the Colorado not the Mississippi carved out the Grand Canyon. We can accurately identify the causal agency even though there is no discrete *thing* acting as that agent, but only a set of interlinked processes. The Buddhist theory gives us agency without a substantial thing's being the agent.

The theory of the psycho-physical propensities undergirds the Buddhist analysis of karma. The propensities establish the continuity of self-identity over time, a continuity that (like the rivers) guarantees at once both the lack of independent substantiality as well as the uniqueness of each individual. Even more strikingly, karma is understood to drive personal continuity across lifetimes. Yet, in terms of the fivefold processes, what is there to continue from one rebirth to the next? Certainly, not the dead body or its attendant sensations and perceptions. Nor can it be a disembodied consciousness either, because if it were, we would all be conscious of our previous lives. That leaves the special role for the propensities. The propensities are like a vector, a directional arrow of forces or tendencies that guide the continuity from one lifetime to the next.

Consider cutting an outlet from a mountain lake to form an irrigation stream for the village below. As the water flows downhill, a rock obstructs its way. If today our newly made stream flows left around that rock, it is likely to do so tomorrow as well since it would have already cut its own channel. In our actions in this life, we are cutting the channels we will "naturally" follow in this life and the next. The life flow may stop with our death, but as it begins again in the next life, the pre-cut channels give it an initial direction. As a result, we often consider even infants to have their own personalities. Those innate personalities, the Buddhist theory of karma maintains, are the propensities of a person's previous life being carried over into this one.

Since the aforementioned artifacts in the Japanese pre-Buddhist Kofun tombs suggest belief in an afterlife within some other dimension or realm, the introduction of Buddhism seems to have been the catalyst for the Japanese belief in reincarnation, transmigration, or rebirth. With Buddhism came the idea that when we die, we will be reborn back into this world or some other worldly realm, there to live, die, and be born again.

Thus Buddhism depicts a maelstrom of birth-death-rebirth through billions upon billions of lifetimes without any obvious gain in cumulative insight accrued from previous lives. That prospect so depressed the ancient Indian Buddhists that an original meaning of enlightenment was the "extinguishing" (nehan; S. nirvāṇa) of that vicious cycle. That is, unless one eliminates the propensity to be attached to life, even death cannot end that recurring pattern. The craving for ongoing existence, the addiction to continuing life through endless rebirths however tainted they may be with unsatisfactoriness, the delusory belief that perhaps in the next life (after billions and billions of tries already?) we will find true unending happiness—that psycho-physical propensity fuels the sequence of birth-death-rebirth.

That Buddhist theory of karma must have jolted the world view of the ancient Japanese: their views of self, of the consequences of choice, and of the continuity of life and death. Yet, karma has a puzzling Janus-headed character. On one hand, it looks to the past to see why I am as I am. That is, the karmic effects of previous volitional acts so permeate my existence that their influence on my present actions becomes second-nature and unnoticed. Such karmic results from past actions may either help or hinder my engaging reality. For example, as I write these sentences in my native language, I can focus my attention on what to say rather than on the intricacies of English grammar. English is second-nature to me, built on a lifetime of using the language. In such an instance, the unconscious propensities involved in writing my native language can be fruitful—I can write about Buddhist thought more effectively because I do not have to simultaneously reflect on the grammar of each sentence. English syntax and vocabulary are part of *how* I exist in the world.

Not all propensities are so benign though. Consider those toward racism, sexism, elitism, egoism, or homophobia, for example. Those too can be so inculcated that they also seem natural. Yet, such psycho-physical tendencies obstruct my ability to see the uniqueness of individuals, to recognize the subtle processes of oppression in which I unself-consciously participate, and to engage sympathetically and responsively to the needs of others.

This brings us to the second face of Janus-headed karma, the one that looks not to the past but rather the future. The decisions I now make influence the propensities that condition what happens hereafter. So, I must be resolute in identifying my propensities, in sorting out the positive from the negative, and in augmenting the former while disengaging the latter.

However, in the two faces of karma lies the riddle: how can I be free enough of my past propensities to see them clearly, evaluate them objectively, and act on them? Put in our present-day terms, how can *I* reprogram who *I* am? Consciousness, we recall, was one of the five constituent processes making me how I am. How can I become conscious of patterns so engrained that they function without my being aware of them? If I could be aware of them, however, I might sort out which propensities are helpful for engaging reality and which are not.

When we today think about identifying counter-productive habits of the heart and mind and about how to treat them, we venture into the domain of counseling and psychotherapy. In the case of premodern Japan, that domain was left to Buddhist praxis.

The need for Buddhist praxis.† On one hand, the Buddhist message is simple. We already know all we need to know. Who can honestly deny the reality of impermanence? Or that the root of unhappiness lies within our own unrealistic desires? On the other hand, we have deeply engrained patterns of interaction with the world that inhibit our ability to grasp reality's true nature. Our desire for this, our avoidance of that, our thirst for substantiality, and our resistance to dissolving our ordinary sense of ego collectively project distortions on the way reality is, what the Buddhists call reality's as-ness (*nyoze, shinnyo,* or *inmo;* S. *tathatā*).‡

---

† Despite a common trend to equate the words "practice" and "praxis," in this book, I make a slight distinction, namely, "praxis" refers to the *system* of interrelated practices in a given tradition. Thus, Zen praxis, for example, designates a coordinated array of interrelated practices such as meditation, chanting, and kōan training. Similarly, Christian praxis is an interlinked set of practices including prayer, reading the Bible, and attending church services, for example.

‡ This term is commonly translated "suchness" or "thusness" instead of "as-ness." Its central idea is that—however it is translated—it names a how not a what, that is, it designates the way a process unfolds, not a cause behind it.

The propensities behind those distorting projections must be unmasked so they can be addressed and we may embrace reality as it actually is. Self-reflection, especially that informed by meditation, yields insight into our experiential flow. The better we understand the dynamics of our negative propensities, the better our chances of breaking the bad habits they support.

Consider the emotions. Emotions can either distort reality, blinding us to its real nature or, alternatively, emotions can sensitize us to what is happening so we can respond with insight and compassion. Buddhist praxis has historically developed two strategies for dealing with the emotions.

The first strategy (and the one most favored in the earliest Buddhist teachings from India) aims to quiet all emotions into a state of equanimity. Then we can allow affective responses to arise only as they befit the situation. The other strategy is not to quell the emotions but to delve into them as they arise, unmasking their hidden propensities so they can be appropriately corrected. The former disconnects the emotions to neutralize them; the latter engages the emotions to transform them. The former filters *out* affect (eliminating emotion) through praxis and the other filters affect *through* praxis (purifying emotion). In most cases, the Japanese Buddhist tradition has favored the latter approach.

Those two Buddhist strategies for dealing with the emotions led to a divergence in how to address impermanence. The early Buddhist tradition understood impermanence as a reality to which one had to be resigned with stoic detachment, disengaging the emotional response to inevitable change. In Japanese culture, by contrast, impermanence is to be engaged as an aspect of how things are, not merely coolly witnessed without involvement. That engagement will trigger a variety of affective responses, the Buddhist goal being to discover the ego's desire for constancy and to root out all propensities associated with it. What remains would then not be neutralized observation, but instead, an affective engagement with flux without any self-centered wish for permanence.

As we will see in Chapter 4, the Heian-period aesthetic valorized an engagement with impermanence as what they called in Japanese *aware*,† an expression of aesthetic sensitivity not found in Indian Buddhism. In the Buddhism known to Shōtoku, of course, such subtleties about emotions and impermanence were likely still a bit hazy, but within two or three centuries, their clarification would affect the heart of Japanese Buddhist theory and praxis.

The overview of the human situation I have just described has been the working assumption in most Japanese Buddhist philosophy up to the present. The high-water mark for the analysis of Buddhist teachings in Shōtoku's time

† See pages 140–1.

was the three commentaries attributed to him.[32] So let us briefly look at those as suggestive of how Buddhism might have been understood by its intellectual Japanese followers at that point in history.

Shōtoku's Buddhist commentaries. Shōtoku's commentaries address three Buddhist sutras, namely, the *Lotus,* the *Shōman* (S. Śrīmālā), and the *Yuima* (S. *Vimalakīrti*). The Buddhist canon classically contains three genres of texts: discourses by the Buddha, analytic commentaries, and ecclesiastical rules with accompanying historical case studies and precedents.[33] Often more didactic or symbolic than analytic or logical, many discourses or sutras (*kyō*) only intermittently offer sustained philosophical arguments. The third canonical genre (*ritsu*) defines the rule for the Buddhist community and its historical development. Community can be defined either narrowly as including only the institutions for monks and nuns or, sometimes more broadly, as including rules for the laity as well. Still, the most sustained philosophical analysis is generally reserved for the second grouping, the commentaries (*ron* or *gisho*). Shōtoku's Buddhist writings fit that category.

The first question is how the three sutras fit together and what themes they represent. The choice of those three particular scriptures reflects the state of Korean-Japanese Buddhist development at the time. Once grouped as a triad with the added authority of Shōtoku's commentaries, however, they came to hold a special place in the Japanese Buddhist canon.[34]

The *Lotus Sutra*—arguably the most influential sacred text in the history of Japanese Buddhism—emphasizes the universal availability of enlightenment, the need to adapt teachings to the audience, and the theory of the cosmic (or "eternal") Shakyamuni (Śākyamuni) Buddha that is the source of all other buddhas, including the historical Shakyamuni who founded the religion twenty-five centuries ago. The *Lotus Sutra* also purports to be the highest formulation of the Buddha's teaching, claiming a unique standpoint allowing it to fathom how all other Buddhists paths, when properly understood, converge into one. Simply put, the *Lotus Sutra* stresses inclusiveness, relegating all other positions to subordinate status under its all-embracing umbrella.

The *Shōman Sutra,* by contrast, narrates an account of an enlightened Buddhist queen Śrīmālā (J. Shōman) who espouses the pure ground of the mind found in everyone. In addition, it highlights the monarch's responsibility to rule in a way conducive to Buddhist praxis. The third text, the *Yuima Sutra,* tells of an enlightened layman (Vimalakīrti) who gives a sermon to celestial beings and the Buddha's most advanced disciples, stating that emptiness is the ground of both wisdom and compassion.

Even in those brief summaries of the three sutras, two common threads appear. First, they stress the availability of enlightenment to everyone, including women and laity. Moreover, they all accentuate compassion as a sign of the most profound wisdom. (Shōtoku, we recall, came to be associated with the Bodhisattva of Compassion.†) More philosophically salient than the sutras, however, is Shōtoku's commentaries on them.

Three themes run through the commentaries. To begin with, Shōtoku repeatedly suggests that the sutras emphasize that enlightenment is directly accessible. In his commentary on the *Yuima*, he uses a *reductio* argument to prove the ground of enlightenment must always be present; it can be tapped right here and now, regardless of one's social status or karmic situation.[35] Specifically, referring to karmic causality, Shōtoku argues that what makes enlightenment possible cannot derive from events in a past life, a future life, or even cumulatively from actions in this life. What is past does not still exist and what is future does not yet exist so they cannot be *causes* of enlightenment in the present—for there to be a causal connection, the cause must at some point exist simultaneously with its effect. As for the present, it is fleeting: it does not linger long enough for us to eliminate all the negative propensities blocking the path to enlightenment. Hence, Shōtoku concludes, enlightenment must be grounded in something universal and readily available to anyone regardless of their karmically conditioned circumstances.[36]

Since that ground of enlightenment is found even in non-Buddhists, Shōtoku says "Even heretics are your teachers."[37] Applying the same principle of equality to social justice, he asserted that "The buddhas are those who should be most respected. Beggars are those who should be most loved."[38] Such spiritually egalitarian sensitivities befit his including a hospital and school within the precincts of the aforementioned Temple of the Four Celestial Kings.

This leads directly to his second theme: rejecting otherworldly spirituality in favor of social activism. According to Shōtoku, deeds—not passive meditation or contemplation—are the litmus test of enlightenment. "Do not approach a person who always sits in religious meditation."[39] In stressing good works, Shōtoku claimed in the opening of his commentary on the *Shōman Sutra* that the queen was called "Shōman" ("Glorious Garland") not because of her jewels, but because of her true adornments, her compassionate deeds.[40]

A final theme in Shōtoku's commentaries concerns the origin of the virtues resulting in good works. Following his reading of the *Yuima Sutra*, Shōtoku insists repeatedly that virtues arise from the mind: "The forthright mind is the beginning of all deeds."[41] This statement deviates from the classical Confucian teaching that the virtues arise from modeling one's social behavior on that of the ancient sages. Admittedly, the classical Chinese Confucian, Mencius, did

† See page 73.

argue for the intrinsic goodness of human nature, but Shōtoku's Buddhist commentary differed slightly by stressing the ground of that goodness as "mind," imparting a psychological, rather than ontological, nuance.

The forthright mind of which Shōtoku speaks is revealed through meditation's dissolving the ego, granting immediate access to the virtuous and pure mental ground.[42] Over time, this emphasis on mind as intrinsically good would evolve so that Japanese readily accepted the imported assumption that enlightenment is inherent; it need only be realized, manifested, or initialized rather than achieved.

To sum up: Shōtoku's Buddhist commentaries add egalitarianism, social activism, and a psychological theory of the virtues to the mix of ideas and values already outlined in relation to Confucianism and proto-Shintō. Now let us finally turn to the *Constitution* itself to see how Shōtoku put the three traditions in service to his vision for the Japanese state.

SHŌTOKU'S SEVENTEEN-ARTICLE CONSTITUTION

If you were to expect from its English name that Shōtoku's *Seventeen-Article Constitution* would be a set of laws outlining government organization and some principles for penal or civil legal procedures, you would be in for a surprise. The work focuses instead on the appropriate attitudes and conduct among officials, accompanied by a few general statements about how to establish amity within a society. The opening line sets the tone: "Take harmony to be of the highest value and take cooperation to be what is most honored." In other words, the *Constitution* is less about what the government institutions are and more about how leaders should act within them.

I mentioned in Chapter 1 that Japanese thinkers have often been their most creative in assimilating foreign ideas through the logical and rhetorical devices I labeled allocation, hybridization, and relegation.† Shōtoku favored the first and second, as will be clear when we examine three themes in his *Constitution* particularly relevant to Japan's later philosophical reflection: his assigning different roles to Confucianism and Buddhism, his analysis of human nature (his philosophical anthropology), and his justification for monarchical rule by the imperial family.

35–9

---

† See pages 35–9.

The Respective Domains of Confucianism and Buddhism

Shōtoku believed that both Confucianism and Buddhism were essential to his vision for the ideal Japanese state, but each philosophy was allocated its own relevant sphere. From the ideas already covered in this chapter, it is not surprising that an astute student of Chinese thought like Shōtoku would find Confucianism's value in its analysis of social and political relations, whereas Buddhism's strength lies in its analysis of the inner self and the delineation of praxis for managing human drives and motives. As a result, when the *Constitution* discusses *human relations*, Confucian values dominate, but when it discusses the *mastery of psychological forces*, Buddhist values come to the fore. Let us see how this works out in the text itself.

As one might expect of a document inspired by Confucianism, Shōtoku's *Constitution* proclaims:

> The lord is the sky and the ministers are the earth. When the sky covers and shelters all and the ministers provide their support, the cycle of the four seasons turns smoothly and all of the life forces in nature flourish.[43] (Article 3)

That is immediately followed by an exhortation to develop the cardinal Confucian virtue of ritual propriety (*rei*; C. *li*) as the means to political order and concord:

> The conduct of all of the various high ministers and officials must be rooted in the observance of ritual propriety. As for the root of bringing proper order to the people, its very core lies in the observance of ritual propriety.... Thus, when the various ministers comport themselves according to ritual propriety, rank and status are properly observed. And when the people comport themselves with ritual propriety, the nation is properly ordered of its own accord. (Article 4)

Such passages have led some scholars to regard the *Constitution* as an essentially Confucian document. And yet, if that were true, how could we explain the article immediately preceding those purportedly Confucian statements?

> Revere in earnest the three treasures: the Buddha, the dharma [the true teachings of Buddhism], and the clergy, for these are the final refuge for all sentient beings and are the most sacred and honored objects in the faith of all nations. What persons in what age would fail to cherish this dharma? There are few persons who are truly wicked. Most can be instructed and brought into the fold. Without repairing to these three treasures, wherein can the crooked be made straight? (Article 2)

Thus, Article 2 proclaims Buddhism to be essentially a state religion, going so far as to imply it should be so for all nations. Furthermore, it assigns to

Buddhism, not Confucianism, the role of instructing and transforming the people who have gone astray. In subsequent articles Shōtoku bids his audience to control anger (Article 10), to eliminate envy and jealousy (Article 14), and to be free of private interests and resentment toward others (Article 15). Those negative characteristics are basically like the psycho-physical propensities that Buddhism analyzes and the *Constitution's* advice is to address them through "sustained reflection" (*kokunen*) (Article 7), presumably a praxis of self-awareness that leads to governing the emotions.

In sum, the *Constitution* is clearly both Confucian and Buddhist, but it is important to see how the two relate. For the most part, the *Constitution* sees Buddhism and Confucianism as being able to function side-by-side with little adaptation and minimal interaction—a classic case of allocation as a method for accepting the new and foreign. Shōtoku seems disinterested in formulating a new theory of his own, but instead is intent on preserving the insights of both philosophies by allowing them to coexist as long as each serves its own province. It seems Shōtoku's design for Japan is to be a Confucian society inhabited by practicing Buddhists. Why that model would be so attractive derives from his understanding of human nature. Therein we find allocation is not the only principle of assimilation at work in the *Constitution*.

The Constitution's View of Human Nature

We have seen Shōtoku alternately arguing for hierarchical social and governmental relations while insisting on parity when it comes to sagacity or spiritual potential. How do the two fit together? The difference is between knowing how one should conduct oneself and having the self-understanding and control to be able to do so. Decades ago I heard a western Buddhist teacher be asked about the difference between Jesus and the Buddha. The answer went something like this:

> Jesus was a wise and compassionate man who unfortunately died when he was only thirty-three years old. So, he left us with great teachings such as "love thy enemies," but the problem is that he did not live long enough to tell us how to transform ourselves so that we may become capable of doing that. What if we already hate our enemies? Then what? The Buddha, on the other hand, lived to be eighty so he had plenty of time to develop teachings and techniques to help us undergo the needed personal transformation.

Shōtoku seems to have had a somewhat similar view when it came to the difference between Confucianism and Buddhism. To see how this is so, look again at the opening of the *Constitution*, this time considering the first article in full but paying special attention to the phrases I italicize:

Take harmony to be of the highest value and take cooperation to be what is most honored. All persons are *partisan*, and *few indeed are sufficiently broadminded. It is for this reason that some offend against lord and father*, and some transgress wantonly against neighboring villagers. But *when those above are harmonious and those below live congenially with each other*, and when mutual accord prevails in resolving the affairs of the day, then all matters without exception will be properly and effectively dispatched. (Article 1)

In my discussion of the five Confucian relations, we saw the lord-subject and father-child relations to be two pillars upholding a Confucian society. The problem is, according to the *Constitution*, that we are all innately flawed, caught up in partisanship and lacking broad-mindedness (the result of our propensities driven by self-interest and ego). If we could only transform our character we could live up to the ideals Confucianism teaches, letting harmony reign over both those above and those below.

How do we make that transformation? If we continue our rereading of the *Constitution*, we come next to the aforementioned Article 2 and its claim that by revering Buddhism we can straighten the crooked. No one, it says, is irremediably wicked; Buddhism has the techniques to turn our lives around from the inside. Then the following Articles 3 and 4 (containing the aforementioned "Confucian" passages) tell us how wonderful a society we could then achieve, just as Confucius had envisioned.

We saw allocation at work when we ask how we should behave (Confucianism answers that) versus how we should transform our natural propensities (Buddhism has that one covered). But if we ask what it means to be a human being, Shōtoku's analysis seems to drift into hybridization instead of allocation. Rather than saying we are part Buddhist and part Confucian, Shōtoku hints at a unified theory of human nature which maintains we are intrinsically liable to delusions that inhibit the concord we seek in our primary relationships.

The *Constitution*'s model of human flourishing seems to be a *hybrid* of idealized Confucian role-defined behavior (which is hierarchical in establishing reciprocity between those above and those below) and Buddhism's call for the personal surveillance of our innermost motives and propensities (a project in which we are all equals). The result is no longer simply Confucian since Shōtoku does not claim that virtue is achieved by studying and emulating the ancient sage kings of Chinese lore. Nor is it any longer simply Buddhist since the *Constitution* is less interested in personal liberation than in the fulfillment of the social roles needed in a harmonious society. As in many other hybrids, the parentage disappears into the new species created by the cross-breeding.[44] Only a genealogy of ideas such as the one we have just undertaken can trace the process of hybridization found in Shōtoku's *Constitution*.

Shōtoku's perspective on human nature and its flourishing has specific implications for how a ruler should govern. The *Constitution* reminds us that we come across a truly worthy person only once in five centuries and a sage at best once in a millennium (Article 14). Not able to rely on the availability of sagely rulers, we must make do with whom and what we have. "We all have our share of wisdom and foolishness...." (Article 10). Article 17 advises the ruler to consult with others on important matters of state; key decisions should result from "shared deliberation." To recognize one's own humanity is to recognize one's own limitations. As virtue and wisdom can be found in anyone, the emperor as an individual is no better than anyone else ("We are all just ordinary people"— Article 9). Since insight might come from any of us, Shōtoku asserts that open discussion and consensus should define government decision-making. When we proceed in that way, mutual trust will reign and "If the various ministers trust each other, what cannot be accomplished?" (Article 10).

That almost seems like Shōtoku is arguing for an oligarchy rather than a strict monarchy, but surface appearances are misleading in this case. Consider again the unqualified language of Article 3:

> ... Thus the lord dictates and the minister receives; those above take action and those below obey. Therefore on receiving imperial commands attend to them scrupulously; to do otherwise would be disastrous. (Article 3)

Shōtoku could not have been more clear about the unique and unassailable status of the emperor. Although the emperor is not superior to us as a human being, the emperor's *role* is hierarchically superior to ours. That status is the linchpin in his vision of political order, but wherein lies its legitimacy? Chinese Confucianism derives it from the "mandate of heaven" (*tenmei*; C. *tianming*), that is, the emperor's authority lies outside the emperor as an individual and if the emperor loses the mandate of heaven, also lost is the basis of imperial authority.

Indeed, the Chinese Confucian Mencius argued in the third century BCE that we can apply the principle of the rectification of names (the trueing up of terms) to an emperor who does not meet the criteria defining imperial behavior. Not living up to the meaning of the term *emperor*, that person loses the mandate of heaven and becomes *de facto* an imposter whom the people should overthrow (*Book of Mencius*, 1B.8).

Shōtoku's *Constitution* makes no mention of the mandate of heaven as the basis of imperial authority, nor is it granted any sustained attention in the ensuing history of Japanese political philosophy. The reason is that in Japan, the throne's legitimacy resides elsewhere. This brings us to the final theme in the *Constitution* I want to highlight—the justification for imperial rule. Here we will find that the third leg of the ideological tripod buttressing Japanese political theory—proto-Shintō—plays a key, though disguised, role.

Justifying Monarchical Rule

Shōtoku's *Constitution* not only asserts the final and absolute authority of the monarch, but lest there be any confusion, specifies in Articles 12 and 16 explicit limits on the provincial governors' powers concerning taxation and conscripted labor, summing up the point in Article 12 by baldly stating, "The nation cannot have two lords and the people do not serve two masters." Yet, if this Confucian-like deference to authority is not based in the traditional Chinese mandate of heaven, what warrants imperial rule?

Not only is the term "mandate of heaven" missing from the *Constitution*, but even the term for heaven or sky occurs but once, in the previously cited passage from Article 3: "The lord is the sky and the ministers are the earth." In my discussion of proto-Shintō I mentioned the *kami* Amaterasu, the "heaven-illuminating one" is the progenitrix of the imperial family. Could that be a source of imperial authority that Shōtoku assumes but does not mention?

That the term *kami* does not appear anywhere in the text weighs against that interpretation. Yet, in Shōtoku's time, there certainly was a proto-Shintō view of heaven and it used the same sinograph as the Chinese heaven, 天 *tian*, pronounced in Japanese either *ten* in its Chinese-derived reading or *ama* (as in *Amaterasu*) in its native Japanese reading. Thus, when the *Constitution* says the ruler is 天, should we read it as the Chinese or the Japanese heaven, or as some hybrid of the two? Certainly, if Shōtoku had wanted to put forward the authority of the throne as deriving from the *kami,* he could have been much more explicit. Yet, maybe he was, but in different texts.

The eighth-century *Nihonshoki* lists two histories of imperial lineage written by the Soga clan during the reign of Suiko-Shōtoku: *Chronicle of the Emperors* (*Tennōki*) and *Chronicle of the Country* (*Kokki*). Since they were both destroyed by fire in 645 when the Soga were overthrown, we do not know their content. It is plausible they described the imperial ancestral line as descended from the *kami* (not necessarily specifically Amaterasu). Additionally, narratives from the early sixth-century work called *Compendium of Ancient Times* (*Kyūji*) supposedly found their way into *Kojiki* and *Nihonshoki,* but unfortunately, we have no extant copy of that text either. In any case, if myths about the link between the imperial family and the heavenly deities were already widely accepted in Shōtoku's time, that might explain why the *Seventeen-Article Constitution* made no direct mention of such an ideology justifying imperial rule.

Does Buddhism play any role in establishing the validity of imperial rule for Shōtoku? In only one small respect—the *Shōman Sutra* and Shōtoku's commentary both praise Queen Shōman as a propagator of Buddhism (much like Empress Suiko?). The authoritarian Article 3 of the *Constitution* does directly follow Article 2's making Buddhism a state religion. So, it might be surmised that as long as the throne is propagating Buddhism, the authority of the throne is justified.

To sum up: the wording and organization of the *Constitution* suggest the authority of the central government is supported in one way or another by all three traditions: certainly Confucianism and Buddhism, and possibly also proto-Shintō. Admittedly, this involves reading a lot into the text, but even if such a hybridized defense for imperial authority is not found in the *Constitution* itself, it certainly does foreshadow what did become the tripodal foundation of imperial rule in the immediately ensuing centuries. In any particular historical period, one or another of the three legs—Confucianism, Buddhism, or Shintō—may dominate over the others, but the three are usually there in some form or another.

SHŌTOKU'S CONTRIBUTION TO JAPANESE *PHILOSOPHY*

In his famous poem "The Road Not Taken," Robert Frost relates traveling in a yellow wood and coming upon a fork in the road. Although the two paths before him seem about the same, he realizes that once he chooses one route, it is highly unlikely ("knowing how way leads on to way") that he would ever circle back to try the other. He chooses the "one less traveled by," musing that when he reflects on the incident in the distant future, he would know that however arbitrary the original choice might seem now, in the end it will have "made all the difference."

In its early formation a culture's philosophical tradition comes to such forks in the road. On purely logical grounds the choice of path might seem arbitrary, but if we look back at it from later history we can see how that choice has shaped the ensuing tradition, at least in a rudimentary way. It can define philosophy's purposes, methods, and themes, presenting it with a list of questions whose answers would inspire the next generation's questions in an ongoing series through time. As I mentioned at the outset, Aristotle picked Thales as his first philosopher for that very reason.

When I read Shōtoku from the standpoint of later Japanese history, I see him also as one who chose a certain path that set the course for Japanese philosophy. In Shōtoku's first tentative steps in his own yellow wood, we find him opting for a path different from the one taken by the ancient Greeks such as Socrates and Plato, for example. Shōtoku, of course, knew nothing of the western philosophical tradition, but he did face an initial decision that set Japanese philosophy in a somewhat different direction from that of the West.

Shōtoku and the early Greek thinkers most markedly diverged over their techniques in doing philosophy. In dealing with oppositional theories or ideas, ancient Greece favored dialectic and refutation whereas ancient Japan favored modes of assimilation. From the times of Socrates and the Sophists, a popular western assumption has been that philosophical progress derives from adversarial competition and the confrontation between opposing views. Ideally, the dialectic proceeds on its course by following only reason, purging the discussion of any distractions and distortions contributed by the emotions, imagination, or naïve dependence on sense appearance. Philosophical argument and analysis, believed its Greeks founders, succeeds best when reason can refute all false views so that the truth alone remains.

How different was Shōtoku's approach. He proceeded with the assumption that people are unlikely ever to be *completely* wrong in their views. The highborn can learn from the commoner, the religiously committed from the heretic. The goal is not to refute the opposing view but rather to search within it for a germ of truth that can be profitably assimilated into your own theory. Moreover, unlike Plato's belief that only some people are innately capable of the wisdom deriving from discursive thinking and intuitive insight, Shōtoku maintained that everyone is capable. His Buddhist sensitivities led him to see both the universal capacity for wisdom or compassion in everyone as well as our common challenge to overcome our own negative karmic propensities.

Grounded in the practical world, Shōtoku was suspicious of those who spent too much time in otherworldly contemplation (even of those who might contemplate Plato's Forms presumably?), focusing instead on how we can mutually serve each other and the society as a whole. We think most effectively, he said, when we compensate for each other's weaknesses by working together in building consensus rather than against each other in adversarial opposition. Shōtoku might grant that a purely rational argument might be possible, but he questioned whether *any human being making an argument* could be totally free of the poisonous influence of self-aggrandizement. Shōtoku said he found in his world no sages, so we have to make do with each other. It is very unlikely, then, that he would suggest we wait for one of Plato's philosopher-kings to guide us.

I hope by now it is clear why Prince Shōtoku (or at least the legendary Shōtoku) would become such a Japanese cultural icon. His egalitarian view of human nature recognizes human fallibility, but also sees us all as capable of enlightened engagement with the world and its social needs. He believes that learning is for the good of our fellow human beings, assuming that social harmony is inextricably bound to harmony within each person. For him, there can be no Confucian behavior without the inner self-awareness and self-governance offered by Buddhist introspection and, through it all, we Japanese should maintain our reverence for the *kami*.

Regardless of who the real man was or might have been like, it is understandable that the celebrated Shōtoku would be considered an incarnation of the Bodhisattva of Compassion (Kannon) and that his three portraits would have hung from the walls of the old Japanese Supreme Court Building. Unsurprisingly, his spirit would also inspire later Japanese philosophers in various ways. The most striking example is from the life of Shinran, the founder of Shin Buddhism. In his darkest moment, he retreated to a temple in Kyoto built by Shōtoku that housed a sculpture of Kannon. That retreat precipitated his turning to Pure Land Buddhism, becoming a disciple of Hōnen. In gratitude Shinran even composed a series of hymns in praise of Shōtoku.

As I have said before, sophisticated Japanese philosophizing did not begin until the ninth century with Kūkai, whom we will engage in our next chapter. Before turning to him, however, we should consider some eighth-century developments. The intellectual imports of the sixth and seventh centuries brought to Japan provocative world views and insights into human nature, but the analytic tools were still rather blunt. The eighth century would bring further imports— an increasing number of sophisticated Buddhist philosophical commentaries of the sort attributed to Shōtoku, a steady flow of scholar monks from Korea and China, and new forms of art, music, and architecture. In the Nara period, the nascent Japanese nation would continue to absorb and assimilate. Yet, with its exposure to new ideas and practices, the establishment of elite educational centers, the stabilization of the state, and the aspiration to emulate China as a great civilization, Japan would acquire a new assertiveness and confidence. That attitude describes the next great architect of ancient Japanese culture after Shōtoku, namely, the Emperor Shōmu of the mid-Nara period.

PHILOSOPHICAL FOUNDATIONS FROM THE NARA PERIOD (710–794)

After Shōtoku died in 622, followed by his aunt, the Empress Suiko, in 628, it became clear that if Japan aspired to be a harmonious country, it had a long way to go. The Soga family continued to work behind the scenes to maintain its grip on power, but it fell in a coup engineered by the imperial Prince Naka no Ōe (614–669) with the assistance of Nakatomi no Kamatari in 645. To honor his longtime ally, when Naka no Ōe became Emperor Tenji (or Tenchi),[45] he bestowed upon the Nakatomi family a new name—Fujiwara. Legend has it that the name commemorated their having plotted the 645 *coup d'état* while in a grove of wisteria (*fujiwara*). Whatever the truth of that charming story, that newly christened Fujiwara family eventually came to dominate the Japanese political and cultural scene for the next half millennium.

Such intricacies of political history are not our concern here, but they suggest a tonal shift from Shōtoku's chord of harmony. Not surprisingly, the downfall of the Soga attenuated somewhat Buddhism's imperial influence. The throne and the aristocratic power brokers continued to support Buddhism, often lavishly, but probably as much to accrue its charismatic and political capital as to express personal piety. For the most part, furthermore, in the seventh century, the temple-building was for the welfare of the families that built them rather than for the welfare of the nation as a whole. That would change somewhat in the next century. Government regulation, a leitmotif of the latter half of the eighth century, was the instrument for bringing about that broadening of Buddhism's role in relation to the state.

The first flourish of legalism followed almost immediately upon the success of the 645 coup, namely, the Taika Reforms, an attempt to shore up the finances of imperial rule by increasing its centralized control of land, taxation, and peasant labor conscripted for public works. Although it is questionable how effectively the still weak central government could have enforced the Reforms, the change in tone was clear and further legal initiatives soon ensued, most notably, a more effective series of penal laws (*ritsu*) and administrative regulations (*ryō*). Taking the Chinese model of centralized government for their template, the *Ritsuryō* laws gave further legitimacy to the imperial system as the unifying force in the nation.

With escalating financial and legal authority, the last piece to fall into place was public image. The Japanese empire had to *look* like an East Asian empire and that involved building a new grand capital city in Nara. Before Nara became the capital in 710, whenever a sovereign died, the Japanese had built a new palace somewhere else in the Yamato plain. Presumably, that practice reflected the native attitude that death is a defilement—a violated taboo, however involuntary—requiring ritual purification and change of venue for the government.

By repeatedly constructing new imperial residences, however, the center of the court did not stay in place long enough to accumulate the appropriate accoutrements of power and prestige: a large, geometrical and geomantic city fitted with monumental architecture oozing opulence and elegance. An impressive new permanent capital like Nara would enhance Japan's image both at home and abroad as a new center of civilization in East Asia.

With the Nara court's intricate network of bureaucratic offices, a newly established system of laws, and an urban plan resembling Chinese models, it might have seemed that Chinese (and ultimately Confucian) strains would drown out the previous harmony of traditions envisioned by Shōtoku. There were contrapuntal movements, however, beginning with new texts for the new empire.

Kojiki and Nihonshoki: Marshalling the Past to Serve the State

Although at this point in history the ancient Japanese continued to write in the foreign language of Chinese, still intact was a rich Japanese oral tradition of myth, song, prayers, and history. Consequently, the Nara court included not only masters of Chinese Confucian and Buddhist texts, but also a group of oral storytellers (*kataribe*), what we might think of as masters of orature. In brief: literature was in Chinese; orature in Japanese. If that situation were to continue much longer, however, the literati might overwhelm the tonalities of proto-Shintō and all resonances of an earlier Japanese identity. In response, the Japanese wanted to transcribe the orature—the ancient creation myths, imperial genealogies, proto-Shintō incantations, and native poetry— thereby preserving the native element in an otherwise increasingly sinicized Japan. The result was *Kojiki* (Record of Ancient Matters) completed in 712.

For compiling the narrative, the text itself informs us that the charge went to a specialist of orature, Hieda no Are, to gather and unify the oral narratives preserved in the Japanese language. Ō no Yasumaro then assumed the task of devising how to transform the oral account into writing since there was at the time still no standard way to write Japanese. Although some passages in *Kojiki* are in classical Chinese and Japanese poems are usually rendered phonetically by using sinographs to represent sounds rather than words, for much of the text Yasumaro used an arcane and highly idiosyncratic writing system, a form of literary Japanese now considered by historical linguists to be an early form of "altered (or deviant) Chinese writing" (*hentai kanbun*).[46*]

Kojiki's blend of creation myths with the genealogies of the prehistorical sovereigns explained unequivocally that the imperial family is directly descended from the Sun *kami*, Amaterasu, thereby reinforcing the idea that the relation between the emperor and celestial *kami* was a blood relation. That reiteration of the ancient creation myths established a familial model for the Japanese state: the *kami* as the progenitors, the emperor as the parent, and the people as the children. The corollary was that the sovereigns should play a sacerdotal role as the rulers of Japan, serving as mediators between heaven and earth.

The project of establishing imperial legitimacy by transcribing the Japanese oral traditions dovetailed with the need for a new official Chinese-style court chronicle to secure a historical record of imperial lineage and authority. Earlier official accounts, written in Chinese of course, were either lost or corrupted.[47] Individual clans did have their own records, but they had to be collated and edited into a single critical edition. The final product was *Nihonshoki* (*Written Chronicle of Japan*), completed in 720 and written in a style mimicking the dynastic histories of China with the expected allusions and rhetorical flourishes. The editor of *Kojiki*, Ō no Yasumaro, also supposedly assisted in compiling *Nihonshoki* (or, as it was sometimes called, *Nihongi*).

Kojiki and *Nihonshoki* were twin publications similar in purpose insofar as they traced the story of Japan's imperial rule from creation to around the time of publication. It is easy to think of the two as complementary: for example, *Kojiki* is most detailed in the prehistoric period through the reign of Suiko, whereas *Nihonshoki* is most detailed about events from the fifth century onward. Yet, we should not be blind to their differences, especially those incongruities important to the later development of Japanese thought.

First, we already noted *Kojiki* rendered orature into literature. *Nihonshoki*, on the other hand, was a work of literature based on previous literature—not only incomplete writings extant at the time in Japan, but also some from China and Korea. Where there were important variants in the narratives, the compilers often simply included alternative accounts. In compiling *Kojiki*, by contrast, Hieda no Are's charge had been to weave the various oral narratives into a single story, blending variations into a consistent account. In short, *Kojiki* tried to give a definitive rendition culled from orature, whereas *Nihonshoki* tried to be a balanced, historiographically sophisticated account based in the extant literature.

Second, since *Nihonshoki* copied the style of Chinese dynastic histories, some Chinese creation myths found their way into the text. *Kojiki*, by contrast, used its hybrid Chinese-Japanese language to present what purported to be a fully native narrative.

Third, in comparison with *Kojiki*, *Nihonshoki* often favored naturalistic over miraculous descriptions. Let us consider just one revealing case, the origin of Amaterasu, the Sun *kami* and progenitrix of the imperial family. According to *Kojiki*, Izanagi had gone to the underworld (the Land of Yomi) to find Izanami, his wife who had died giving childbirth to the Fire God. To his horror, he found the underworld a place of filth and decay, escaping it as fast as he could and sealing the entrance behind him. At the first opportunity, Izanagi ritually bathed to remove the impurities of death and as he did so, Amaterasu sprang forth from the effluent of his left eye.

The *Nihonshoki* narrative, on the other hand, explains that Izanagi and Izanami "produced" Amaterasu in the ordinary way, that is, by sexual intercourse. Her birth was motivated by their desire to bear a daughter who could take over the responsibilities of overseeing the human world. With its characteristic concern for historiographical thoroughness, *Nihonshoki* even notes two alternative names for Amaterasu.[48] Obviously, those are two very different narratives. One might say that *Kojiki* represents the end of the age of myth and *Nihonshoki* the emergence of historical method. Yet, why did the court want to have two texts compiled at the same time, even to the extent of purportedly having a common editor, Yasumaro? This suggests something more than a transition from myth to history, but rather an instance of the insider-outsider distinction so common in Japanese culture.

On one hand, *Nihonshoki*, like the Chinese-style government bureaucracy, the new civil and penal legal system, and the new capital of Nara, was part of Japan's face shown to the outside world. *Nihonshoki* hoped to prove that Japan was "civilized," as modern as any other culture in the Chinese-dominant world of East Asia. Its compilers were interested in preserving the integrity of the historical facts, keeping the text consistent with the style of classic Chinese chronicles, and maintaining an objective distance in evaluating alternative accounts. *Kojiki*, on the other hand, was a hint at what is innermost, a narrative by and for Japanese that identified and preserved the roots of ancient Japanese culture, celebrating its native mentality and history. As we will see in Chapter 10, the Native Studies philosopher, Motoori Norinaga analyzed the difference between the texts along those lines some ten centuries later, a reading that came to have striking nationalistic implications in events leading even up to World War II.

The Poetry Collections: Man'yōshū and Kaifūsō

A similar analysis applies to the two poetic collections appearing around the same time. Completed sometime after 759, *Man'yōshū* (*Collection of Ten Thousand Leaves*) is an assemblage of Japanese verse written in Japanese. Compared with *Kojiki*, *Man'yōshū* represents an improved, but still awkward and inefficient, technique of using sinographs alone to render Japanese.[49]* *Man'yōshū* appeared just eight years after an official compilation of Chinese-language court poetry called *Kaifūsō* (*Fond Recollections of Poetry*).

I previously analyzed a *Man'yō* poem and its intimate overlapping of human feelings, nature, and language.[†] Over time the Japanese came to regard *Man'yōshū* poems as representing pure, unfiltered sentiments in a direct, not necessarily strictly defined, stylistic form. The poems of *Kaifūsō*, in contrast, were exquisitely refined in their allusions and rhetoric, that is, they mimicked the most elegant classic poetic forms from contemporaneous China. So, again, we find one text for outsiders trying to meet Chinese-derived standards and a kindred text aimed for Japanese to celebrate and preserve native poetic expressions.

This situation is not, strictly speaking, a tension of Chinese vs. Japanese— both faces are genuinely Japanese—but one is more the profile presented to the outside world and the other the profile for the local, personal, inner world. As we will see, this outside/inside differentiation will occasionally recur in the development of Japanese culture and its various philosophies.

† See pages 53–5.

To review: the Nara period's twin mythicohistorical chronicles and its twin collections of poetry shared a common purpose. As Japan looked increasingly to China as a prototype for its civilizational aspirations, it also wanted to preserve its native or indigenous elements (or at least what were purported to be native and indigenous elements). In the face of the potent Chinese cultural impact, *Kojiki* and *Man'yōshū* could, at least in theory, manage to demarcate, codify, and preserve at least a slice of Japan's non-Chinese cultural legacy. By that means, early patterns of animistic naturalism and human sentimentality could maintain a place within the tapestry of Japanese cultural accomplishment.

Through the device of producing paired mythicohistorical and poetic texts, Japan maintained a continuing juxtaposition, though perhaps not full intermixing, of proto-Shintō and Chinese-based tonalities in the culture. As we saw with Shōtoku's mix of inward Buddhist psychology and outward Confucian social forms, by these two pairs of Nara literary texts, the Chinese and the native continued to coexist as two layers within Japanese society. Each was allocated to its own stratum within a single, newly emergent Japanese cultural civilization. When we look to Buddhism in this period, we find further evidence of that stratification.

Buddhist Ideas in the Nara Period

Earlier in this chapter I explained some basic Buddhist doctrines as they would have been known to any educated layperson like Shōtoku with access to Korean Buddhist scholarship in the early seventh century. The Shōtoku commentaries set a standard for later Buddhist critical reflection, but in the ensuing two centuries the scholarly efforts in Japan increased markedly in quantity as Japan moved to having a permanent capital with sites for various Buddhist study centers, each specializing in a specific set of texts.

In fact, the proliferation in Buddhist thought and practice likely led to some confusion in the Japanese Buddhist world: how could that variety be categorized and evaluated? What were the *philosophical* reasons for choosing one set of doctrines or one system of praxis over the others? Which Buddhist traditions were compatible and which not? As we will see in our next chapter, Kūkai brought some order to this chaos and, in so doing, set a trajectory for the future development of Japanese Buddhist philosophy.[50]

To appreciate the extent of Kūkai's encyclopedic knowledge of the tradition and his use of it in developing Japan's first homegrown philosophical system, however, we need to understand the range of ideas on which he was able to draw. As I will now show, he had much to work from.

The rise of Buddhist study centers. I already mentioned the court's attempt to regulate the growth of Buddhism. This was evident in severely limiting the number of official Buddhist ordinations (to just ten annually at the end of the seventh century, for example). Only the officially ordained could enjoy privileges such as exemption from taxes and from the corvée labor force conscripted for public works.

Administratively, if the Ritsuryō legal system was mainly for governing the secular realm, special government oversight was needed for the religious orders. In response, the court established an office for the regulation of Buddhist institutions and clergy. The Office of Clerics (sōgō) was headed by imperially appointed monks and in the Nara period the Office put in place a ranking system for monks appointed by the court as well as an extensive set of ordinances for monks and nuns (the sōniryō). One such ordinance, likely introduced to prevent charismatic monks from gaining too much influence over the ordinary people, prohibited clergy from preaching to commoners, restricting Buddhist activities to the monastic compounds.[51]

Those attempts to rein in Buddhism notwithstanding, the aristocrats lavishly endowed Buddhist institutions with temple buildings, gifts of land, support for elegant rituals, libraries, and study centers for scholarly research on a greater range of Buddhist texts. Out of those study centers or research groups (shū 衆) came more nuanced and scholarly commentaries on various Buddhist texts and philosophies.

Later in this chapter I will say more about those study centers and research groups. First, though, I will explain briefly some central themes to come collectively from their analyses. In so doing, I will most emphasize those having a broad impact beyond any one school of thought and of enduring importance in Japanese Buddhist thinking throughout its subsequent history. That is, I will here stress those ideas that were not only important in the Nara period, but which will be referenced by the philosophers discussed in later chapters of this book. Japanese philosophers are seldom scholars of Buddhism and so the range of ideas important to their own thinking is more restricted than might be the range for a buddhologist, for example. On the other hand, philosophers are interested not only in the ideas as originally stated but also in what they logically entail in a philosophical view of reality.

One major contrast drawn was that between the Mahayana (S. mahāyāna) and the so-called Hinayana (S. hīnayāna) branches of Buddhism, both of which had a presence in Japan during the seventh century. The distinction between Hinayana (shōjō, "Small Vehicle") and Mahayana (daijō, "great vehicle") Buddhism was a construct of the Mahayanists. Because the term Hinayana might be considered pejorative, scholars have tried using alternative terms to replace it.[52*] Yet, because the focus in this book is Japan, where almost all the philosophers I discuss used the term equivalent to Hinayana, I have decided to stay with that terminology to maintain consistency with the translation of their texts.

The Mahayana branch flourished in Buddhism's northern transmission from India and Nepal into Tibet, China, Vietnam, Korea, and Japan, whereas the Hinayana spread southward to settle permanently in Sri Lanka and Southeast Asia. Hinayana did reach Tibet and China but it was not dominant there, serving mainly as a philosophical resource for commentarial treatises (as it was for some sects of Japanese Buddhism as well).

Although both branches of Buddhism also had found their way to Japan, from the late seventh century forward, virtually all Japanese Buddhist philosophers, like Shōtoku before them, wrote from the Mahayanist perspective. In developing their own arguments, Japanese philosophical thinkers sometimes referred to the distinction between Mahayana and Hinayana as a foil against which to explicate their own Mahayana position (much as Mahayana polemicists had sometimes done earlier in China and India).[53] In the following discussion of some key Mahayana Buddhist concepts, therefore, I will also point out how they were often thought to differ from the ideas Japanese philosophers often associated (rightly or wrongly) with Hinayana concepts. In many contexts, *Hinayana* was used less as a historically descriptive term and more as a subset of ideas and values from which the Japanese Mahayanist Buddhists wanted to distance themselves.

The meaning of "buddha." The Hinayanists were generally assumed to believe the Buddha was an ordinary person called Shakyamuni—a popular title for Siddhartha Gautama—who lived some 2,500 years ago in what is today Nepal and north India.[54] Through many rebirths and lifetimes of dedicated practice, he was able at last to find the way to extinguish the thirst for permanence, and with that, the unsatisfactoriness marking ordinary existence. At that point, he became "the awakened one," that is, the *Buddha*. In order to alleviate the suffering of others, Shakyamuni preached how to meditate on the inner dynamics of mind and body so as to live a life without ego-centered desire. Free of attachments, even free of the clinging to life, the Buddha was not reborn, but "extinguished" (the literal meaning of *nirvāṇa*).

By that account, by heeding Shakyamuni's guidelines, we can ourselves achieve nirvana.[55] Thus, the Hinayana schools emphasize precepts, lifestyle restrictions, and forms of contemplation. By strictly adhering to such a praxis, people can undergo a series of rebirths that bring them ever closer to enlightenment. After eons of diligence, they can finally achieve enlightenment as Shakyamuni did: they can extinguish the desires that fuel their anguish and thereby be released from the cycle of birth-death-rebirth.

In distinguishing themselves from that view, the Mahayana Buddhists, elaborating on the doctrines of the insubstantiality and interdependence of the self as a process, tended to see enlightenment as a universal rather than individual accomplishment. Thus, one's personal enlightenment, at least theoretically, involves the enlightenment of all other sentient beings as well. Therein we find the basis for Mahayana's distinctive *bodhisattva vow.*

Traditionally construed, the bodhisattvas (beings on the path to awakening) defer their own final extinction for the sake of helping others in this world, transferring her or his own karmic merit to others in service to the collective enlightenment of everyone. The transferred merit of bodhisattvas working on our behalf constitutes a spiritual momentum in the cosmos helping us achieve enlightenment in our own lives. That notion of a cosmic spiritual power relates to the Mahayana theory of the Buddha's threefold embodiment,[56] a second difference from Hinayana Buddhism.

The Buddha's embodiments. The Mahayana threefold embodiment theory maintains there are three expressions of buddha, three forms or bodies of concrete enlightened existence: (1) buddha can be embodied as a flesh-and-blood person teaching in this world; (2) buddha can be embodied as a heavenly being (like the aforementioned Kannon) who is transferring merit to help others achieve enlightenment; (3) buddha can be embodied as the universal principle whose spiritual presence permeates everything.[57] Thus, Shakyamuni represents for Mahayanists the first way of being buddha, "the historical Buddha."

Representative of the second embodiment in Mahayana Buddhism, the "celestial buddhas" include such marvelous buddhas and bodhisattvas as Amida, Miroku (Maitreya), Yakushi, Jizō, and the aforementioned Kannon. Most Mahayana Buddhist art in Japan and indeed throughout Asia focuses on the celestial buddhas. The celestial buddhas are intangible, accessible to ordinary people only insofar as they engage in devout contemplative praxis. Nonetheless, they have individual personalities and work for our spiritual welfare, sometimes temporarily assuming a physical form in this world to intercede on our behalf (as in the aforementioned folk belief of Kannon's taking the form of Shōtoku). Whether they are technically buddhas or bodhisattvas (the distinction often blurs in Japan), those buddhas fulfill the bodhisattva vow by working toward enlightening others. Devotional visualization and invocation of such celestial buddhas define much Mahayana ritual.

The third way of being a buddha in Mahayana Buddhism is that of "the cosmic buddha." The least apparent manifestation, it can also at times be considered the most immanent and pervasive. The ambiguity is in the original term itself: *hosshin* (S. *dharmakāya*). Some Mahayanists see the cosmic embodiment as the transcendent reality (*dharma*) underlying all phenomena. Others understand the cosmic embodiment to be the sum of all phenomena (*dharmas*). As we will see in Chapter 3, the latter is closer to the esoteric view promulgated by such philosophers as Kūkai. In itself, the cosmic buddha is usually impersonal and formless, the ontological ground of which the other two embodiments are expressions.[58]

The cosmic buddha is not necessarily a transcendent being and certainly not the creator of the cosmos, however. The cosmic buddha is more a quality of the cosmos, or even the sum of all cosmic functions. While the cosmic buddha can sometimes be understood as personal rather than a transcendent principle, it is nonetheless not a divine person behind the functions of the cosmos.

The cosmic buddha can, therefore, be understood as ubiquitous. The term *cosmic buddha* thus means that the cosmos itself is a way of being buddha, that is, the cosmic buddha is the cosmos-as-buddha and buddha-as-cosmos. As we shall see in later chapters, some Japanese Buddhists did give the cosmic buddha a personal name and occasionally depicted it as having a specific personal form, usually that of either Dainichi or Amida, but in doing so, they were personalizing reality rather than saying there was a person beyond reality.

The last comment brings us to a major variation of this triple embodiment theory, the theory of the so-called eternal buddha revealed, for example, in chapter eleven of the *Lotus Sutra*. As I noted earlier, the *Lotus Sutra* is undeniably one of the single most influential sutras in Japan and, as we have seen, the subject of one of Shōtoku's commentaries. In its eleventh chapter, Shakyamuni (the historical buddha) makes the startling claim that all buddhas are his emanations. In chapter sixteen, we find the equally remarkable assertion that he became an enlightened buddha many eons ago, going back in time indefinitely. Since then, he has periodically taken a physical form in this world in order to teach.

That is, according to the *Lotus Sutra*, the Shakyamuni we know as the historical buddha is only an earthly manifestation of Shakyamuni as the eternal buddha. A particular buddha, not an impersonal cosmic embodiment, is in this case the universal source for all other buddhas. This idiosyncratic theory of Shakyamuni as eternal is not, incidentally, restricted to the *Lotus Sutra*, but is also found in other major popular texts such as the *Nirvana Sutra* and the *Kegon Sutra*.

For understanding either the Mahayanist triple-embodiment or the eternal buddha theories, it is critical to keep in mind that the Buddhist teaching of insubstantiality still holds. On the popular level, many Buddhists may think of the cosmic or eternal buddha as a discrete, divine individual—perhaps resembling an eternal God of some sort. That is decidedly not the understanding of most Japanese Buddhist philosophers, however. Philosophically, as we have seen, a "person" in Buddhism is the name for a specific set of interdependent processes or functions, not an independent agent who performs actions or has functions.

In saying the cosmos itself is a buddha, then, the claim is that the cosmic buddha is a name for a combination of ubiquitous interdependent processes with no independent ego-identity as agent behind them. Since these processes are eternally undergoing cycles of interdependent genesis and destruction, one can appropriately speak of an eternal buddha, but that buddha is no more than a name for a specific cluster of interrelated events without beginning or end. It is emphatically *not* the name for a being who exists independently of the cosmos or who created the world.

Even when the cosmic buddha is depicted as an individual being such as Dainichi, that is technically still only a name for interdependent cosmic processes. As processes rather than substances, it can be seen as much as a *how* the cosmos is as *what* it is. The actual cosmic buddha *per se* has no form, or perhaps more precisely, its form is the whole of reality itself. Granted, that is the *philosophical* understanding and on the level of popular practice, devotees may view that image of Dainichi much as they would a celestial buddha.

Enlightenment. A third Mahayana doctrine separating it from Hinayana is its emphasis on the affective or emotive dimension of enlightenment. In emphasizing the bodhisattva vow, Mahayana Buddhists stress that the bodhisattva's engagement with human suffering is not just cognitive, but also affective. The more intimately one understands suffering, the more compassion one feels; the more one feels compassion, the more one understands suffering.

Because engaged knowing implies an overlap between the knower and the known, to know intimately the suffering of another can sometimes mean feeling that suffering. Thus in the aforementioned *Yuima* (S. *Vimalakīrti) Sutra*, when Vimalakīrti becomes sick, he says it is because beings are sick. Parents are pained when their child is in pain. This sensitivity is akin to what we might feel when we see someone get injured (perhaps if only in a movie we are watching); we often wince and may even say "ouch!" To know the other's pain may, therefore, imply feeling that pain in some way, even if we know the pain is illusory (as in the movie). To engage the suffering in the world is to both know and experience it. In their definition of enlightenment, Mahayana Buddhists typically express this as the inseparability, or even identity, of wisdom and compassion.

The Hinayana traditions, by contrast, are assumed to emphasize enlightenment as detachment and equanimity, asserting we should overcome all such affective engagement on the path to complete enlightenment. For traditional Hinayanists, an enlightened person does indeed respond to the suffering of others, but only by helping them understand the nature and causes of unsatisfactoriness and by teaching the method to extinguish such suffering. I would put the distinction between the two traditions in the following way. When encountering another person's suffering, the Hinayanist diagnoses the interdependent *system* of psychological and physical causes and addresses those. By contrast, when Mahayanists know the person's pain through compassion, they address the problem in a more *interpersonal* manner.

A further aspect of enlightenment said to distinguish the Mahayanists from the Hinayanists is that the former emphasize the universality and immediate availability of enlightenment. For Mahayana Buddhism, enlightenment is available to anyone regardless of social status, gender, ordination, or education. Furthermore, in principle at least, enlightenment is attainable by anyone right here and now in this lifetime without entailing eons of praxis through innumerable rebirths as often implied in Hinayanist texts. In Japan, nearly all Buddhist philosophers, going back to Shōtoku, have accepted some version of the Mahayana perspective on enlightenment's immediate availability to anyone. That orientation influences how to distinguish delusion from enlightenment.

Hinayanist rhetoric commonly favors the language of transition from one state to another: enlightenment is the liberation from this world of delusion and rebirth. Mahayana rhetoric favors instead the language of inseparability: the world of enlightenment is exactly the same as the world of delusion and rebirth. For the Mahayanists the state of existence remains the same, but the *mode of engagement* changes when one moves from delusion to enlightenment. In short: for Mahayana the difference between delusion and enlightenment is a matter of *how* the world is experienced.

Emptiness. A fourth distinctively Mahayanist emphasis concerns the meaning of *emptiness*, a traditional term with broad application in many Japanese philosophies, both traditional Buddhist and modern academic. As we have seen from the general doctrine of the three marks of human existence, both branches of Buddhism recognize the impermanence and insubstantiality of all things,

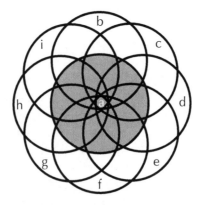

Identity without Substance

including the self. That suggests that each thing is "empty" in itself and is only defined by the flux of interrelated processes designating it. To refer back to an earlier example, the Mississippi River is not the thing that undergoes change, but is instead the name for an interrelated set of functions. The figure on the preceding page illustrates the point.

In the diagram, *a* represents the thing (or the self) in question. The *a* has its own identity insofar as we can define its limits (the shaded area). Yet, there is no part of *a* that is not overlapping with, interdependent with, something else. Therefore, if we were to ask what *a* might be in itself without any other things (*b-i*), the answer is "nothing;" it is empty; it has no substantial or independent identity. The emptiness of all things is a theme in Japanese Buddhism tracing back to Shōtoku's commentaries.[59]

Starting in India, Mahayana Buddhists expanded the notion of emptiness to apply not only to things, but also to concepts and words. They argued that words cannot be simple labels we attach to reality, one word for one thing. Words are interdependent with other words, serving as part of a linguistic network just as things are part of an ontological network. Pressing the issue further, the Mādhyamaka (or the Japanese Sanron) philosophy of Mahayana Buddhism developed a sophisticated analysis showing that the interdependent web among concepts or words is different in kind from the interdependent web among things or processes.[60] For that reason, even if individual words or concepts could correspond precisely to individual things, the relations among words or concepts cannot correlate with the relations among things. Although language is pragmatically useful as *ad hoc* approximations, there is always going to be a gap, an emptiness, separating it from reality.

A consequence of the Madhyamaka standpoint is that philosophy can never be more than contextually pragmatic, because its concepts cannot precisely characterize reality as it is in itself. At most, philosophy can address certain problems on an *ad hoc* basis as they arise in a specific situation. Not surprisingly, metaphysics, if we mean by that a systematic philosophy about reality that transcends perspective and pragmatic concerns, is rarely practiced in Japanese philosophy, especially when contrasted with its prominence in the western tradition.

In China, the Mahayana Buddhists added yet another twist to this idea of emptiness. Drawing on the Daoist notion of nonbeing, the Buddhist idea of emptiness acquired the nuance of serving as the "source," "locus," or "field" in which beings are articulated. Being is configured against the field of nonbeing. In the diagram above we could say that *a*, although void in itself, is the filled-to-capacity locus for various interdependent processes. It can be designated or named only insofar as it is such a fulfilled locus and as that locus it is part of the interdependence defining *b-i*.

According to that line of thought, the East Asian Buddhist notion of empti-ness, or *nothingness* as it was sometimes also called, came to refer to the engaged openness associated with creativity, whether natural or human. That is, creation requires an empty site for its ground. Personal creativity arises from an empty-ing of ego to make room, as it were, for creative interdependence to emerge.[61]

I would sum up this East Asian Buddhist view of emptiness as follows:

1. emptiness means that things are intersections of interdependent pro-cesses lacking individual substantiality;
2. emptiness means there is an unavoidable gap between how words or concepts can describe reality and the way reality actually is;
3. emptiness means that all phenomena are processes filling an empty locus that serves as the source or site of being and meaning, the ground behind all figures.

Heuristic expressions. As explained already, Mahayana Buddhist philosophers maintain that enlightenment is universally available. To transform this potential universality into actual enlightenment for everyone, the exposition of Buddhist doctrine has to be suited to its various audiences, different people requiring dif-ferent styles of instruction. This is the celebrated idea of *heuristic expression* or *skill-in-means* (*hōben*; S. *upāya*).[62] Because its implications influence so much later Japanese thinking, let us examine it more closely.

In a heuristic expression, we do not separate the truth of an expression from its impact on its audience. A heuristic is not a direct expression of *what* truth is, but is instead an expression about *how to act or think* that will allow the readers or listeners to discover the truth for themselves. As directed more toward praxis than reality, the heuristic's model of truth resembles assimilation more than correspondence. In the correspondence theory, which is not based in heuristics, truth is an external relation that occurs when what is in my mind (or in what I assert in the words I say) corresponds with the way things are.

For example, if I know about John or know of John, there are various things I believe about him. If those things jibe with the way John is, the beliefs are true. For the assimilation theory, by contrast, truth occurs when the knower and the known form an internal relation; they overlap. If John is my son or an intimate friend, my knowledge is not *about* him or *of* him as much as it is *with* him. John and I share ourselves so that our lives are, at least in part, lives in common. When I know John in that sense, I know how he feels because "I feel for him" and I know what he is thinking because "I can see things through his eyes." To teach heuristically, to help others assimilate the truth for themselves, we need both empathy (or compassion) and knowledge (or wisdom).

Suppose I have a similar relation with Mary as I have with John. For the sake of argument, let us assume, on one hand, that John has personal problems engaging daily life because he is agonizingly hesitant and self-conscious, a modern-day Hamlet. Let us further assume, on the other hand, that Mary also struggles with daily life, but for the opposite reason: she is too aggressive and impetuous. In that case, it is perfectly appropriate—it is heuristically efficacious—for me to say to John, "He who hesitates is lost. Thinking too much can get us into trouble; it is best to just go for it." But when talking to Mary, I might say instead, "Haste makes waste. We've got to be aware of what we are doing; we should think twice before acting." In both cases, the value of my advice is shaped to the listener's ability to get the point. Yet, if we consider the endpoint of the advice—helping the two people get on better in life—the different statements can have similar heuristic force.

For the correspondence theory, the truth of a statement is independent of the audience to whom the statement is made, but when we look at the situation from the standpoint of heuristic expression, note what would occur if I reversed my advice to John and Mary. In that case, my advice and claims about how things are ("he who hesitates is lost" and "haste makes waste") would be taken differently and have a different result. For all intents and purposes, my statements would not be the same as before, conveying in effect a different intention and having a different effect.

To appreciate the significance of heuristic expression, then, we need to expand our notion of truth to include how a statement is assimilated, to consider its impact on the audience as well as what is in the mind of the speaker. This is not a simple relativism. The key to heuristics is that in both John's and Mary's cases, I am helping them get *to the same goal*—an effective way to go through life, to engage reality as it is. Although there is no difference in the goal or purpose of the heuristic expression, because John and Mary are different people with different personalities and proclivities, I say something different to each.

With that understanding, we can now see two reasons why buddhas as enlightened beings may use heuristics in their teachings. First, most of us are not enlightened buddhas. By definition, buddhas engage things as they are without delusional modifications, whereas we unenlightened people develop a view of the world permeated with delusions. As we know from ordinary contexts, when people are truly delusional, even if we explain to them their delusion, they will not be able to assimilate what we are saying without filtering it through the delusion. Paranoid patients, for example, will interpret our insistence that no one is trying to harm them as a plot to get them to lower their guard. If we had no delusions—if we were all already buddhas—the other buddhas would not need to adjust their message to us. So, the first reason for the buddhas' not expressing the truth directly is because to do so would not help us. There is no point in a buddha's expressing the truth to us if we cannot *get it.*

The second reason is that it is impossible to perfectly explain the truth anyway. By the principle of emptiness discussed earlier, words and concepts are never fully adequate to describing reality as it is. So, the absolute truth—the truth not relative to audience—can only be shown or pointed out; it cannot be straightforwardly said. A buddha cannot tell us the truth, but a buddha can heuristically lead us to it so we can experience it ourselves. Whenever the goal is showing rather than describing, the standpoint of the listener is especially critical. We must know where the other person is so that our directions—right, left, up, down—will effectively get them to see what we are directing them toward. Analogously, buddhas must assume the position of their audiences so they can show them how things are.

Based on such an analysis, many Buddhist traditions maintain a theory of "two truths." One is said to be absolute and can be engaged only from the standpoint of enlightenment: buddha-to-buddha communication, so to speak. Such truth is beyond, or more than, words and concepts. It is *enacted* or *performed*, not explained. As with other forms of expert knowledge, it is not publicly expressible or provable. Only another expert, in this case another buddha, can engage it.

The second kind of truth is said not to be absolute but relative or provisional; it is adapted to the audience and functions as heuristic expression (*hōben*). If one gets the point and is transformed, the provisional truth is no longer necessary. To borrow a metaphor from the early Buddhist tradition, it is like a raft that gets one across the river. Once reaching the destination, we no longer need it.

Having investigated some of the more general themes, let us return to the Nara study groups or research institutes that enhanced the Japanese understanding of such ideas.

The Six Nara Schools of Buddhism. Through continuing contact with the continent, the Buddhist temples of the late seventh and eighth centuries amassed large libraries of Buddhist works, thereby spawning research institutes and study groups to copy, classify, and analyze the ever-growing treasury of texts. Although those centers were within temple complexes, for the most part they were sites of philosophical or scholarly analysis rather than places for religious praxis. In fact, in the Nara period, if one wanted to enter a period of intense discipline, the ideal site would more likely be a mountain retreat rather than a temple in the capital.

Each study group tended to highlight a single text or a cluster of closely allied texts. The groups were not particularly sectarian in the religious sense and individual monks were free to move from one group to another without restriction, motivated more by intellectual curiosity than religious conversion. Indeed, a single temple complex might house more than one such study center, much as today's universities might house any number of discrete research institutes. The study centers were in some respects the Buddhist equivalent of the academy (*daigaku*) in which aristocrats would train for positions in the court bureaucracy by attaining a mastery of the Chinese, especially Confucian, classics.

This is not to say that there was no competition among the Buddhist groups. In fact, by studying the points of disagreement among the texts, some distilled from philosophical debates dating back to Indian Buddhism, the scholar monks continued to grow more sophisticated in analysis and argumentation, skills that would later serve Japan well in its own creative philosophizing. Since patrons underwrote their operating costs, the rival groups strove for prestige and political recognition.

By the mid-eighth century, six groups (*shū*,[63] "schools" or "sects") stood out, partly because each had its own major center in the Great Temple to the East (Tōdai-ji), the focal point of Nara imperial Buddhism (which I will address later in this chapter). Because of that visibility, they became known as the "Six Nara (Buddhist) Schools." Again, those institutions generally lacked the sectarianism of later Japanese Buddhism and should not be labeled "sects," although in later years Hossō especially did come to function as a discrete sect or religious order, often contesting with the religious groups originating in the Heian and Kamakura periods. As we will later see, Japanese sectarianism in later history frequently precipitated skirmishes, assassinations, arson, and open warfare, but that extreme sectarianism was not typical of Nara Buddhism.

The Six Nara Schools were the Ritsu, Kusha, Jōjitsu, Sanron, Hossō, and Kegon.[64] None exist today in Japan as prominent forms of Buddhism in their own right, but they do endure as philosophical resources for Japanese Buddhist philosophy. That is especially true of the three Mahayana schools, namely, Sanron, Hossō, and Kegon as well as the quasi-Mahayana Kusha school. Among the six, we find groups concentrating on Buddhist texts from each of the previously mentioned three groupings: discourses (or sutras), philosophical commentaries, and ecclesiastical rule. The Ritsu was the least philosophical of the six schools, focusing on moral laws, monastic regulations, and their legal precedents, collectively called the *ritsu* (S. *Vinaya*). As part of its oversight of Buddhism, the Nara court authorized only the Ritsu school to perform Buddhist ordinations regardless of the study center to which the ordinands belonged.[65]

The Kusha school focused on Vasubandhu's analytic commentary found in the *Abhidharma-kośa* (J. *Kusha*), sharing many philosophical concerns with the Jōjitsu (the "fulfilled actuality") school. The philosophers of both schools analyzed events (physical or mental) by first breaking them down into their atomistic components, what are called in this context *dharmas* (*hō*). Those atoms are not, however, material things like those in western theories of atomism from Democritus up to today. First of all, the dharmas can be mental as well as physical, often both. Secondly, they are insubstantial. How to understand that insubstantiality is where complications arose and the two schools, like many other schools derived from early Indian Buddhism, engaged in arguments about causality, the reality of past-present-future, the role of the mental in generating the dharmas, and so forth. If I had to distinguish these two Nara schools, I would say the Kusha insists that although the atoms are insubstantial, they are nonetheless real. The Jōjitsu school, on the other hand, maintains that their very insubstantiality makes them unreal.

For explaining the Kusha view, consider again my earlier analogy of the Mississippi River where I argued the Buddhist view is that the river is not *what* flows from Minnesota to the Gulf of Mexico, but *how* the flow—gravity's downward pull on water, erosive patterns, amount of rainfall, human engineering, and even the influx of polluting chemicals—occurs from northern Minnesota to the Gulf. The point is that the river is a process not a thing and, even more importantly, its identity as a process is nothing more than an overlapping network of other processes. The Kusha analysis, of course, analyzes reality into much smaller units than rainfall or erosive patterns, but the point is the same: the processes are insubstantial and ever-changing, but nonetheless real. On the second part of that point, the Jōjitsu school disagrees.

From the Jōjitsu standpoint, when the Kusha maintain that something can be insubstantial and yet real, they are surreptitiously reintroducing the idea of an enduring essence. For the Jōjitsu, what does not endure unchanged through time is not a real thing. It does not exist because there is no *it* and what does not exist cannot be real. That is why, they say, the Buddha spoke of their "emptiness" (*kū*; S. *śunyata*).

Despite appearances, this disagreement is more than a semantic debate over the meaning of "really exist." The difference between the schools can be explained in light of my previous depiction of insubstantial identity. Consider the "*a*" in the diagram on page 84 above. For the Kusha school, all the lettered components in the diagram are ever-changing, real processes. In that case process *a* is the overlap of processes *b-i*. Since the process really exists, *a* really exists. But that is exactly the point, replies the Jōjitsu proponent. Since (as the theory of insubstantiality maintains and the Kusha school agrees) there is no *a* without *b-i*, that means *a* is not real, not even a real process. It is no more than a *name* we have superimposed on reality. (On this point, Jōjitsu resembles some western nominalist schools.) Indeed, the same can be said for *b-i* as well. It is merely a convenient and, admittedly pragmatically useful, product of conceptualizing, but that process is not itself enough to grant ontological *reality* to something.

A simplified way of putting the issue: for Kusha the *a* is real because it is perceived; for Jōjitsu, because perception (unlike simple sensation) involves conceptualization, it superimposes meaning on what is in fact empty of meaning. So *a* is unreal. In a sense, Jōjitsu represents a logical and epistemological approach, Kusha one more experiential or psychological.[66] In that distinction, we find a parallel in the difference between the Mahayana schools of Sanron and Hossō.

The Mahayanist Sanron ("three treatise") School, born out of the aforementioned Indian Madhyamaka tradition, emphasized emptiness and the logical analysis of conceptual arguments. By the end of the eighth century, Sanron relegated Jōjitsu teachings to being a subdivision of its own system, leading to Jōjitsu's losing its status as an independent group in the Great Temple to the East complex. Based in the theories of emptiness, of language's limited capacity to characterize reality in its as-ness, and of the two truths, Sanron granted that epistemological and metaphysical analyses had some practical or pedagogical value, but in the long run subordinated that to an absolute, direct, nonconceptual form of insight (S. *prajñā*: J. *e, chie,* or *hannya*).

If we want to know reality exactly as it is, the Sanron School maintains, that knowing would have to be an experience without conceptualization because concepts fail to perfectly capture the way things are. For many Japanese Buddhists in later centuries, the attempt to achieve such an insight became a primary goal of praxis and the philosophers among them often explored how to how to integrate nonconceptual insight into their philosophical epistemologies.

An even stronger emphasis on consciousness was typical of the Mahayanist Hossō ("phenomenal aspect") school, whose roots are in the Indian Yogācāra tradition. Hossō argued that reality is not simply a given, but inevitably also a mental construct. Hossō hoped to explain the functions of consciousness, the mechanisms for how delusory experiences arise, and to give practical meditative techniques for disengaging those mechanisms. A distinctive theory was its delineation of eight kinds of consciousness.

The first six correspond to the five senses ordinarily recognized in the West with the addition of inner awareness (such as of my hunger or anger, for example). The seventh consciousness superimposes the idea of ego onto the activities of the other six, not only stamping each experience as "mine," but developing the delusional idea that the "I" exists separately from the experiential flow. Lastly, the eighth, the "storehouse" consciousness, is a deep stream of conscious flow that lacks intrinsic characteristics, but stores seeds deposited by the other consciousnesses until they germinate. The germinated seeds form the phenomenal world, both true and deluded. Karmic cause and effect, the habituated patterns of delusions reinforcing other delusions, the possibility of enlightenment—all these are explained by Hossō as phenomena developed through the complex mechanism of the eightfold consciousness.

Both Hossō and Kusha emphasized the reality of mental constructions and opposed the radical emptiness of the Jōjitsu and Sanron. As a result, on the institutional level, the Kusha study center officially became a subsidiary of Hossō in 793. That is not to say the Kusha analyses lost their significance. Vasubandhu's text continued to be part of the curricula for the training of scholar monks in multiple traditions throughout the ensuing centuries.

In subsequent Japanese Buddhist philosophy, the category of "mind" has remained central, often with resonances derived from the Hossō (and Kusha) analyses. Furthermore, after the eighth century, through further contacts with continental developments, the Hossō school supplemented its Yogācāra doctrines with expertise in Buddhist logic and debate, playing an important role in medieval Japanese Buddhism's evolution. The main temple with Hossō associations in Nara was Kōfuku-ji (Temple for Extending Good Fortune). Under Fujiwara sponsorship, its prestige rose with the ascendancy of its patrons. That is a major reason why, of the Six Nara Schools, Hossō maintained its institutional prominence the longest, making the successful transition from study center to full-fledged religious sect.

Japanese Kegon ("Garland") derives from Chinese Huayan Buddhism, a philosophical school focused on the *Kegon* (S. *Avataṃsaka*: C. Huayan) *Sutra*. The primary vision of Kegon is that the totality of reality is so intertwined that each thing ultimately depends on the existence of *every other thing*. That theory expands on a central Buddhist doctrine, so-called conditioned co-production[†] (S. *pratītya-samutpāda*; J. *innen*). The original teaching of the Buddha was simply that no thing comes to exist or ceases to exist in and of itself without being dependent on some other thing or things. Kegon went further, claiming that each thing is interdependent with *everything* else.

Kegon's central metaphor is the image of Indra's net in which each individual phenomenon is compared to a multi-faceted jewel at a nodal point in the web of reality. Each facet reflects another jewel in the net so that in any one thing or one phenomenon, every other thing or phenomenon is reflected. The result is a holographic relation between whole and part. Every part of the whole reflects the pattern for the whole, much like the DNA in every cell of my body contains the blueprint for all the cells of my body. As noted in Chapter 1, this model of the whole (holo-) inscribed (-graph) in each of its parts has been profoundly influential on East Asian philosophy and Japanese philosophy specifically.[‡]

---

† The term is also commonly translated as "conditioned genesis" or "dependent origination."

‡ See pages 32–4.

A second central Kegon teaching was first propounded by the founder of the tradition in China, Dushun (557–640). In his theory of the phenomenal realms (J. *hokkai*; S. *dharmadhātu*), the most profound level of reality is expressed as *jijimuge hokkai*, "the phenomenal world [viewed as] the unimpeded interpenetration of all things." Expanding on the point behind the imagery of Indra's net, Dushun's formulation of *jijimuge* is part of his more extensive fourfold general theory about how pattern or principle (J. *ri*; C. *li*) relates to events or things (*ji*).

The Kegon position is that how we experience phenomenal worlds is how we understand reality. In other words, the idea of *hokkai* approximates what we call in English a *world view*. The tradition analogizes this to how we can view the ocean. At first sight, on a superficial level, we see waves, each with a discrete shape and movement. That is the view of reality as sequential individual events (*ji hokkai*). Going deeper, we recognize the waves are a patterning within the ocean water, the constantly undulating ocean base itself. Such is the world view of the patterned ground (*ri hokkai*). We then go on to ascertain the ocean water and the waves are in internal relation, intermeshed and inseparable. That is the world view of the interpenetration of the patterning ground and the individual events (*rijimuge hokkai*). Finally, on the most profound level, there is no separate, transcendent ground, but just the complete interpenetration of all events from within themselves, the inseparability of waves and water. That extrapolates to the full internal relationship among all things, the "interpenetration of all events" (*jijimuge hokkai*).

Notice that in the fourth phenomenal world, the phenomena are interrelated by their own intrinsic nature rather than linked by external principles. Hence, it is a shift from an externally related world view to an internally related one. Although the notion may have been latent in prehistoric animism, the theoretical differentiation between internal and external relations in Japanese philosophy, including the explicit preference for the former, may trace to this Kegon theory.

Kegon's third philosophical impact on later thinking was its detailed system of classifying all Buddhist teachings and sutras into a single system. Although I noted that the *Lotus Sutra* engages in some relegation by claiming all Ways are included in its One Way, the Kegon system—as one would expect of a highly sophisticated commentarial tradition based on a sutra rather than a sutra alone—is far more systematic and formal in its use of relegation. Kegon's hierarchical relegation of opposing teachings presented Japan with a paradigm that would inspire later thinkers such as Kūkai.

It is not accidental that Kegon highlights both the holographic relation and the relegation of all other teachings. If you believe every part of the whole contains the pattern for the whole, even in an opposing theory you can discover

School	Branch	Textual Focus	General Orientation
Ritsu ("[Religious] Regulations")	Hinayana	*Ritsu* (S. *Vinaya*)	Analysis of monastic and moral regulations; liturgical protocols, including ordination rites; legal precedents
Kusha ("[Abhidharma] kośa")	Hinayana	*Abidatsuma kusharon* (S. *Abhidharmakośa*)	Categorization of the psycho-material processes constituting reality that are without underlying substance but nonetheless real [strictly philosophical; few dedicated religious adherents]
Jōjitsu ("Culmination of Reality")	Hinayana	*Jōjitsuron* (*Satyasiddhi śastra*) by Harivarman	Analysis of the processes constituting reality as "empty" conceptual constructs useful for provisional purposes
Sanron ("Three Commentaries")	Mahayana	Three commentaries from Indian Madhyamaka tradition	Emphasis on "emptiness" as reality; two truths: absolute and conventional; Formally absorbed Jōjitsu study group into its system in the late 8th century
Hossō ("Phenomenal Aspects")	Mahayana	Grouping of sutras and commentaries from Indian Yogācāra tradition	Investigation of reality as forms of consciousness and the mental constructs they establish; Made use of Kusha ideas and, later, traditions of Buddhist logic and debate
Kegon ("Garland Wreath")	Mahayana	*Kegon* (S. *Avataṃsaka*; C. *Huayan) Sutra*	Totalistic system using holographic relation of whole-in-every-part; levels of phenomenal realms culminating in interpenetration of all things; inclusive system that tries to relegate all other Buddhist theories into itself

Nara Buddhist Schools

its holographic relation to your more holistic theory. Then you can make that formerly opposing theory into a subordinate part of your own theory.

Although Kegon philosophy began its career in Japan during the Nara period with the enthusiastic support of the Emperor Shōmu, it never prospered as an independent sect in later centuries. Yet, even today its model of the holographic relation between whole and part, its theorization of world views, and its skill at relegation continue to inspire the highest theoretical levels of Japanese philosophizing.

For understanding the historical development of Japanese Buddhist thought, the detailed teachings of the Six Nara Schools are less important than the kinds of questions they raised and their forms of analysis. Beginning with the methodological techniques first witnessed in the Shōtoku commentaries, Buddhism brought to ancient Japan a new vision accompanied by doctrines, texts, rituals, and artworks. Furthermore, by the Nara period it had become increasingly clear that Buddhism was as much about questions as answers, even questions about previous answers.

The Nara scholar monks had become more acutely aware of the broad horizons of Buddhist philosophy and the wider variety of competing teachings within the tradition. Different Buddhist groups answered the same questions differently. If there is no "I," what is human agency? If everything is impermanent, in what sense are things real? In our comprehension of reality, what is the role of language and of mental constructs? What does it mean to "know?" How is such knowing related to praxis? And so on. The Nara schools brought to the attention of Japan's intellectuals that there were contentious issues among the Buddhist teachings imported from abroad. That realization revealed the need for further independent philosophizing in Japan, a need that was addressed by the end of the eighth century, the beginning of the Heian period.

Meanwhile, proto-Shintō had little formal doctrinal development. As for Japanese Confucianism, it seems the debates within Chinese Confucianism were either muted or unknown in Japan during this period. This lends further credence to the theory that the ancient Japanese used Confucianism mainly as a template for how to organize society and the government bureaucracy, a complete vision of the ideal society without the need for further analysis, debate, and argumentation.

Given that situation, it is not surprising that in the ensuing several centuries, Japan's most creative philosophical thinkers would gravitate toward Buddhist rather than Confucian or (proto-)Shinto thought. The Buddhist schools of philosophy in Nara started that trend. Since their theories will occasionally recur throughout this book, the table on the facing page may be helpful.

EMPEROR SHŌMU (701–756)
AND HIS SUN BUDDHA

The main buddha in the *Kegon Sutra* is the Great Sun Buddha, Dainichi (S. Mahāvairocana), a buddha who played a major role in Japanese culture for the next several centuries. The sutra treats Dainichi as the cosmic embodiment, the cosmos-as-buddha or buddha-as-cosmos. Dainichi's most stunning early appearance in Japanese history is Emperor Shōmu's extraordinary artifact, the Great Buddha image in the Great Temple to the East (Tōdai-ji) in Nara.

The sculpture is of a seated Birushana (a Japanized phonetic rendering of "Vairocana") seated on a lotus shaped pedestal. The original image was destroyed in a fire and today's building and statue date from the seventeenth-century. The present version is significantly smaller than the original, and likely much less elaborate, but it still stands almost twenty meters high and is said to be the largest seated bronze figure in the world. It is enclosed within the largest wooden building in the world, which is itself only about two-thirds the size of the original edifice. Emperor Shōmu's vision was obviously of a grand scale.

Today if we visit Tōdai-ji, we cannot avoid the throngs of visitors, including busloads of school children in their uniforms, the boys shouting, pushing each other, and making wisecracks. Families visit the temple as part of a holiday outing and tourists consider it an obligatory stop on any visit to Nara. The general tone is one of gaiety rather than piety. We might feel sorry for the ancient emperor Shōmu to see the lack of reverence being shown to his great religious edifice but, to the contrary, I suspect that if he could have seen this behavior some thirteen centuries into the future, he might actually have been pleased.

Tōdai-ji: The Great Temple to the East in Nara

Shōmu made the official opening of the temple into an international coming-out party for the new Empire of Japan, sending invitations throughout the known world. The temple treasury house has kept intact congratulatory gifts received from as far away as Persia. A Buddhist monk from India, Bodhisena (704–760), officiated at its opening ceremony.[67] Institutionally, Shōmu made Tōdai-ji the hub of a nationwide network of temples, with both monasteries and nunneries in every province. Just as the Great Sun Buddha radiated its protecting and illuminating light throughout the universe, Nara's central monastic temple radiated its power throughout the land.

To associate his own potency with that radiance, Shōmu formally vowed allegiance to Buddhism and characterized himself as participating in the activity of Birushana. To show his loyalty to the Buddhist Way even further, as the temple complex was nearing completion, Shōmu retired from the throne and took tonsure as a Buddhist cleric.

That said, Shōmu did not miss the opportunity to involve the *kami* progenitrix of his family in his elaborate symbol system. Before building the Great Temple to the East, he had sent an emissary to secure the blessing of Amaterasu, the Sun Goddess. The *kami* of the sun and the buddha of the sun were, therefore, intimately linked through the imperial personage of Shōmu. Through such actions, Shōmu brought Buddhism—with a dash of proto-Shintō—back to the political forefront in what had seemed to be an increasingly Sinicized, and basically Confucian-related, process of national development, especially within the legal system and court bureaucracy.

It is instructive to compare Shōmu's ideal of Buddhist sovereignty with Shōtoku's. Shōtoku had used the *Shōman Sūtra* to portray the ideal sovereign as one who establishes a social and political milieu conducive to the blossoming of Buddhist spirituality. According to that interpretation, Queen Śrīmālā (J. Shōman) was an exemplary Buddhist ruler because of how she governed.

For Shōmu, however, his own identification with Dainichi symbolically implied he was a holographic part of the cosmic whole. As such, Japan as a whole would be reflected within him. That made Shōmu's authority intrinsic and ontological rather than dependent on performance or intention. As such, it aligned his Buddhist ideology of legitimacy with proto-Shintō's, rather than the performance-based Confucian ideology based in the mandate of heaven. Again,

Nara's Great Temple to the East (Tōdai-ji)

however powerful the Confucian models of courtier behavior in the Nara court might have been, the legitimization of the imperial rule remained more embedded in Shintō and Buddhist ideas.

Shōmu's fervent support for Buddhist temples and sculptures manifested itself in the extraordinary flourishing of art in what is known as the Tenpyō era (729–749). Yet, those expenditures not only depleted imperial coffers, but also intensified political volatility. The Fujiwara family, spawned in the wisteria-draped plot to overthrow the emperor a century earlier, was on the rise. In clear violation of Ritsuryō law, Shōmu's wife, Kōmyō, had been given the title of "nonreigning empress" (kōgō) despite her lack of imperial blood. She was, however, a Fujiwara, the first in a long line of Fujiwara kōgō that gave the Fujiwara access to the imperial family, its bloodline, and its power.

Along with her cousin Fujiwara no Nakamaro (706–764), Kōmyō insinuated her way into court affairs starting in the latter years of Shōmu's rule (he abdicated the throne in 749) and continuing through the reign of Shōmu's daughter, Empress Kōken.[68] In 764 Nakamaro attempted a coup to snatch direct power for himself, triggered primarily it seems, by the actions of the retired Empress Kōken. The coup was a disaster. Not only was Nakamaro killed, but his whole family, a branch of the Fujiwara, was executed. Empress Kōken then promptly deposed Emperor Junnin and put herself back on the throne, this time under the title of Empress Shōtoku.

The question remains why Nakamaro would have attempted such a rebellion. It seemed he had been a successful puppeteer behind the major political maneuvers within the court already and had little to gain, but a lot to lose. A common theory is that a primary motivation was Kōken's special relationship with a Buddhist monk known as Dōkyō. A discussion of this shadowy figure will lend us one final insight into the status of Buddhism during the Nara period.

THE DŌKYŌ AFFAIR

Dōkyō (?–772) was a Rasputin to the Nara court. I mentioned earlier that Buddhist scholarship was in the capital and the most intense Buddhist praxis in the mountains. Even the heads of Nara study centers would go into the mountains for spiritual retreats. Dōkyō was a Buddhist monk from the Hossō school who practiced for years in the Yoshino mountains near Nara, an isolated area full of wizards, folk religious practitioners, criminals on the lam, and monks practicing rituals or training in thaumaturgy. Through that praxis, he became, it seems, a thaumaturgist par excellence.

Dōkyō came to Empress Kōken's notice when she fell seriously ill and he was summoned to her bed chamber. After his private time with her, during which he worked his magic, Kōken miraculously recovered. Dōkyō's reputation in the court for his bedazzling powers and his personal closeness to the former empress only intensified as years passed, perhaps to the point he threatened Nakamaro's clutch on political power, thereby triggering the unsuccessful coup. If so, Nakamaro's fears about Dōkyō were well-founded.

Once Kōken seized back the throne under the new name of Shōtoku, Dōkyō was given power as head of both the secular bureaucracy and of the Buddhist institutional hierarchy, appointing his Buddhist cronies to important government posts. In 769 a plan was afoot to have Dōkyō named the imperial successor to Empress Shōtoku, but court aristocrats foiled the plot and Dōkyō was banished.

The Dōkyō affair shines light on events both political and religious. First of all, it shows how Buddhism had insinuated itself into the court, so much so that there was a plan to make an emperor of a Buddhist monk, one of common rather than royal blood at that. Further, the story shows that thaumaturgical power—to heal, to affect the weather, to bring prosperity, to protect the state—was still a mainly Buddhist province. Lastly, the Dōkyō affair illustrates that Buddhist practice, centered in the mountains, could sway court politics, but not necessarily through the institutions of the Six Nara Schools. The mountains hosted unregulated, sometimes fantastic, religious praxis in contrast with the city's more disciplined and refined scholarly Buddhist study centers. The mountains were home to the animistic forces of nature, the playground of ghosts and goblins, the pulsating womb of life forces; the capital was sophisticated, cultured, literate, and urbane. The mountains, like the rural areas, had roots in proto-Shintō; the city, in the Confucian literati tradition. Buddhism planted its feet in both the mountains and the city, giving it a strategic advantage in the competition for intellectual and cultural hegemony.

Which leg of the tripod—proto-Shintō, Confucianism, or Buddhism—would dominate had been up to this point more a reflection of court intrigue and personal idiosyncrasy than any considered ideological consensus. No one had yet given a good *philosophical* reason to prefer one tradition over the other. At the turn of the ninth century, particularly with the impact of Kūkai and Saichō, that would change.

The Dōkyō affair also suggests one reason why the Emperor Kanmu (737–806; r. 781–806) decided to abandon Nara to establish a new capital elsewhere: to create a little distance from Nara politics and perhaps the Buddhist influence as well. Further, he might have felt his position more secure if he could move the capital closer to his own home base of power.[69] After an aborted trial in relocating the capital to nearby Nagaoka, he moved it permanently (that is, until 1868) to Heian-kyō in present-day Kyoto. The Six Nara Schools continued to be headquartered in Nara rather than Kyoto, but their influence persisted in the new court. The more significant impact of Buddhism on the Heian court, however, would be centered in the persons of Saichō and Kūkai along with the new traditions of Buddhism they introduced, namely, Tendai and Shingon.

Saichō and Kūkai escorted Japanese Buddhism into a new phase. Both were excellent scholars and acute thinkers, evidence that the Nara study centers had successfully established the intellectual conditions for creative Japanese philosophizing. That said, Saichō and Kūkai also abandoned the capital for solitary praxis in the mountains. And when Saichō established his Tendai school and Kūkai his Shingon, they both centered their institutions in mountain settings, forming monastic centers of *combined* study and praxis. Furthermore, both Saichō and Kūkai journeyed to China to hone their mastery of Buddhist philosophy and praxis. In fact, although unknown to each other at the time, they departed for China in the same fleet of ships.

Of the two, however, Kūkai was to become the more influential philosopher. In fact, he is generally recognized as not only the first systematic philosopher of Japan, but also one of the greatest Japanese thinkers of all time. He will be our interest in the next chapter and so we now need to prepare ourselves to shift our approach.

Up to this point, we have studied *about* Japanese philosophy, as meager and disjointed as it might have been. We have stood back as onlookers watching the events unfold as if on a screen. As explained in the last chapter, however, that is not the primary mode of knowing emphasized by Japanese thinkers throughout history. For them, knowledge involves engagement, not objectifying detachment. To understand Kūkai in a Japanese way, we should not be bystanders or onlookers, but participants. We must enter the narrative of Japanese philosophy and play our own role within it. We must think through Kūkai's philosophy with him, not think about it.

The first step in that project is to meet Kūkai on his home ground, to engage the thinker and not just the thought. To do that we leave the capital area to go to where it is dark, a spiritual retreat in a cave on the island of Shikoku.

3. Kūkai 空海 (774–835)

The Man Who Wanted to Understand Everything

Wherever the six elements reach,
that is my body;
wherever the ten worlds exist,
that is my mind.
Kūkai

Late into the night, a young man meditates in a waterfront cave, sitting with his back to the sea, its waves pummeling the shoreline in crashes that reverberate off the walls, enveloping him in sound. Incense perfumes the musty air. The cave is in the savage wilds of Shikoku, the island itself far distant from Japan's refined centers of learning and culture.

He has closed his eyes and crossed his legs in the lotus position, visualizing a figure of the bodhisattva Kokūzō, whose chest is aglow with the image of a full moon against which written mantra syllables flash by. No novice, the man sits as solidly and immovably as the stone womb in which he gestates. His parched lips are moving, the cave resonating with the low rumble of the mantra conjoined with the echoes of the sea. His fingers flick a Buddhist rosary, counting the mantric recitations with a goal of one million repetitions, ten thousand a day for a hundred days.

As he finishes this set, he pauses a few moments before starting again. He stands to stretch his legs, turning to look out the cave's vista on the sea, the light from the not-yet-risen sun brightening the cloudless, azure sky. The waves continue to roll in. Adjusting to the light, the man's eyes flutter as he scans the horizon in front of him, an indistinct line separating the empty sky (*kū*) above and the roiling sea (*kai*) below. When this man would later take an ordination name, it would be "Kūkai." He is also known by his imperially bestowed posthumous title: Kōbō Daishi ("the great teacher who disseminated the Buddhist teachings").

My interest in this event is not just to introduce you to Kūkai's intensity, resolve, and focus, but also to have you reflect on his purpose for undertaking such a strenuous exercise. He is not doing it to gain the supernormal powers of Dōkyō whose thaumaturgy and charisma a few decades earlier had nearly secured him the throne. Nor is he doing it to achieve a favorable rebirth after he dies. He is not even doing it to reach enlightenment. No, this practice called *Kokūzō gumonjihō* has one specific purpose: to grant him the power to be able to memorize and understand every line of every Buddhist sacred text.

Kūkai has a fervent wish: he wants to understand everything and he will go to any lengths to achieve that goal. As much as we can admire his diligence, we might question his methods. Surely, to expand his knowledge, there had to be better options: enrolling in the national imperial academy (*daigaku*) or in the research institutes of the Nara Buddhist temples, for example. Actually Kūkai had tried that. He came to this cave after dropping out of the Confucian academy and leaving behind the Buddhist study centers in the capital. To appreciate his philosophical motives, let's retrace the steps that brought him to the cave.

KŪKAI'S SPIRITUAL QUEST

In the opening lines of his stylized biography, Shiba Ryōtarō (1923–1996) discusses Kūkai's birthplace in Shikoku across the Inland Sea from the main island of Honshū.

> The province of Sanuki in which Kūkai was born borders on the five inner provinces around the capital, separated from them by the waters of Chinu. The plains are broad, the mountains exceptionally low. Conical hills dot the landscape as though sprinkled here and there across the fields. Probably because the plains are so broad, the sky—shining with the light off the sea—is opened up in its terrible expanse. Formed in the shoals, the clouds shift through their varied forms. Is this not the sort of natural environment that would nurture visions in a man?[70]

As a member of the Saeki clan (a branch of the Ōtomo),[71] Kūkai had enjoyed the privileged education of an aristocrat. His maternal uncle, Atō no Ōtari, was a prominent Confucian scholar, a tutor to the imperial family in fact. Seeing promise in the lad, he had brought him as a fifteen-year old to the capital (then Nagaoka) for training in Chinese literature and culture. The special tutoring paid off when, at eighteen, Kūkai gained admission to the national academy where upper-class young men studied Chinese histories, poetry, and the Confucian classics as preparation for civil service exams leading to government service.[72]

Yet, early on Kūkai grew disenchanted with the courtly life where he studied the Confucian ideals of the harmonious society in the library, while witnessing in the corridors and wisteria groves the intrigue of realpolitik.[73] Kūkai wanted to make sense of the world, but a career in the court bureaucracy didn't seem a way to do that.

According to his first philosophical work, *Aims of the Three Teachings* (*Sangōshiiki*) written in 797[74] when he was twenty-four, Kūkai also had philosophical reasons for his turn toward Buddhism away from Confucianism and Daoism. A piece of didactic fiction in dialogue form, *Aims* recounts a tale of three teachers who try to reform a self-indulgent young man.

To the question "Why be moral?", the Confucian teacher in the dialogue promises that if the young man were to follow the ideals of duty, filial piety, and loyalty, he would find peace, respect, and harmony both within himself and in his social world. The Daoist in the narrative promotes instead the alchemical arts and introspection as the path to personal purity and longevity. The Buddhist character then chastises his two colleagues for advocating such temporal benefits, really offering not much more than an upgrade to the kinds of pleasure already sought by the young man. He argues instead that the true religious goal should be to forsake desire itself. Only by recognizing the impermanence of all worldly gains can a person achieve the one worthwhile aim, the transcendent bliss of nirvana, the ground of universal wisdom and compassion.

That early work, although immature in its escapist understanding of Buddhism, shows that even as a young man, Kūkai was trying to differentiate, assess, and rank doctrinal traditions, a tendency that would persist into his later philosophy. As I explained in Chapter 2, by the end of the eighth century, Japan was awash with imported teachings and would welcome someone with Kūkai's talents at classifying and analyzing.

Aims may have had another purpose as well. It might have been an apologia, justifying to his family his decision to leave the imperial academy, turning his back on the career path laid out for him by his uncle. Still, we might wonder, if Kūkai were so enthralled with Buddhism, why would he have left the Nara Buddhist study centers to retreat into the wilds? What could he learn in the mountains, forests, and caves that he could not learn in a library or school?

With his rural upbringing, it is perhaps not surprising that throughout his life Kūkai preferred the mountains to the cities.[75] Moreover, since even the abbots of Nara temples periodically retreated to the mountains for spiritual renewal, Kūkai's praxis could be understood as only a more strenuous and prolonged version of what others did but intermittently. Yet, the available practices were even more a jumble than were the doctrines of the day, being little more than a grab bag of psycho-physical exercises garnered from various sources: religious Daoism, indigenous *kami*-worship, shamanism, animism, and varieties of Buddhism.

Such disarray likely irritated Kūkai's penchant for order but he persisted. As his practice in the Shikoku cave shows, he felt there must be a path to insight beyond the desiccated perusal of texts in a library, a path that would engage him totally in mind, body, and spirit. At this point in his career, Kūkai could not yet articulate that difference between detached study and engaged knowing, but later he would, calling it the "difference between exoteric and esoteric." Let's now return to Kūkai's cave to resume our biographical narrative to see how that distinction became so central to his philosophy and eventually to the later course of Japanese philosophy at large.

After successfully completing his hundred-day practice, Kūkai continued his spiritual quest in the mountain regions. He came across a Buddhist text that struck him as something different, the *Dainichi Sutra* (*Dainichikyō*, the "sutra of the Great Sun [Buddha])." Dainichi was the Buddha whose image presided over Shōmu's Great Temple to the East, but this text drew on an esoteric, rather than Kegon's exoteric, interpretation of the cosmic buddha. The sutra not only contained Sanskrit incantations (mantras) that Kūkai could not read, but it also shed light on why they were effective as part of spiritual praxis.

Imagine that: a text that could philosophically explain and justify a system of praxis—a *metapraxis*. Perhaps hidden within this obscure text was also the nucleus of a metaphysics disclosing the nature of reality and how to understand it. Might there not be in this text, Kūkai wondered, the key to a comprehensive understanding for the multifarious disciplines he had undertaken: the chanting of mantras, the visualization of buddhas, and performance of ritual hand gestures (mudras)? Might there be a way to link such practices to the ideas taught in Nara's Buddhist study centers?

If so, this *Dainichi Sutra* might help him intertwine the disconnected strands of his life, the tensions mirrored in Japanese culture at large: the Chinese versus the native, the scholastic versus the ascetic, the intellectual versus the affective, the city versus the mountains, and the intellectual versus the physical. If he could pull all this together, then maybe he could finally understand everything.

Yet, no matter how hard he tried, he could not penetrate the sutra's inner meanings and no one in Japan was qualified to assist. He had but one option, to go to the Chinese capital of Chang'an, arguably (along with Baghdad) the most cosmopolitan center of culture and learning in the entire world at the time. It was also where the Chinese translation of the *Dainichi Sutra* from Sanskrit had originated. Kūkai later wrote about this time in his life:

> Since my awakening to the Buddha Dharma [the Truth of Buddhism], I, Kūkai, was striving to return to the home of originally enlightened mind. However, I was still in the midst of a labyrinth and had lost my way back. Standing at a loss at the crossroads, there was many a time when I cried.

3. KŪKAI | 105

With the kind guidance of the Buddhas, I then discovered this secret gate of Dharma. However, as soon as I opened the [*Dainichi Sutra*] scroll to read its lines, my mind was darkened again. It was at this time that I vowed to travel to China to study it.[76]

Hastily securing a formal Buddhist ordination (and the name Kūkai), he received government sponsorship to go to China as a student monk in 804. His stipend was for ten years.

Kūkai: The Shingon Master

Once in China Kūkai studied Sanskrit intensively for a short time and then moved on to Huiguo (746–805), Master of Zhenyan (J. *Shingon*) Buddhism, the tradition associated with the *Dainichi Sutra*. The name of the school literally means "truth word" and was a common Chinese rendering of the Sanskrit "*mantra*" or ritual incantation. Shingon (henceforth, I will use the Japanese pronunciation of the school) is an East Asian form of Buddhism classified as *esoteric* (J. *mikkyō*), a term misunderstood often enough that I will briefly explain it generally before turning to Kūkai's specific interpretation.

First of all, *esoteric* suggests something secret and open only to initiates, a characteristic making esoteric traditions subject to abuse. For example, in the name of confidentiality, elite cabals may form to withhold knowledge from being distributed to outsiders and ordinary people. That is not, however, esotericism's fundamental meaning and certainly not what Kūkai meant by the term.

Using terminology familiar to readers of this book, the crux of the matter is that esotericism promotes engaged knowing of the sort that cannot be understood via explanations in readings or lectures, but must be experienced for oneself under the guidance of a master. The master teaches by showing and doing rather than by saying and listening, conducting rituals that employ the entire bodymind, not just the intellect, rituals that the student replicates for oneself. Thus, esotericism does not study reality in a detached way but is known through a performative engagement with it. An offshoot of Mahayana Buddhism, esoteric Buddhism is associated with the so-called Diamond/Thunderbolt tradition (S. Vajrayāna) or Mantra tradition (S. Mantrayāna) prominent in India and Tibet as well as parts of East Asia.[77]*

Staying with that working definition for now, let us return to Huiguo and his encounter with Kūkai in China to observe that ritualistic transfer of understanding from master to apprentice. Then I will be able to unpack Kūkai's specific interpretation of esotericism and its philosophical significance.

A disciple of those who had translated texts like the *Dainichi Sutra*, Huiguo immediately recognized Kūkai's potential and, the story goes, had been waiting for him to arrive so that Shingon Buddhism could be transmitted beyond China to the East. In the initiation ritual, Huiguo had Kūkai stand on a balcony in a temple building and throw a flower backward over his head onto the Diamond Mandala painted on the floor, the significance being that the flower would land on the square that depicted the stage of practice at which Kūkai should begin his praxis. The flower landed in the middle on the image of Dainichi, signifying the final stage of transformation wherein the initiate merges with Dainichi himself, that is, with the self-expressive cosmos.

Thus began Kūkai's rigorous training in the Shingon's formal doctrines and in the ritual use of mantras (incantations), mandalas (visualized geometric maps), and mudras (hand gestures). Huiguo died in 805, but not before he had trained Kūkai well enough to make him one of his six major successors, along with one from Java, one from Korea, and three from China.[78] The oldest biography of Huiguo, written in the year after his death, quotes his saying of Kūkai:

> Whether in Chinese or Sanskrit, he has absorbed all my instructions in his mind. It was just like pouring water from one vase into another.[79]

It seems that in his ascetic praxis in the mountains and caves of Japan Kūkai had unwittingly shaped himself into a vessel ideally suited for the transmission of Shingon esotericism.

Kūkai returned to Japan in 806, having spent only a small portion of his allotted ten years in China, but still managing to spend his entire stipend by buying texts, images, and ritual implements to carry back to Japan. He likely felt justified in such expenditures because he was returning as an authorized master of esoteric Buddhism, a form of Buddhism he was keen to introduce to his home country. Upon returning to Japan, he was stunned, therefore, to receive a cool response from the court, by then having relocated to the new capital in Kyoto.

The court officials seemed to think Japan already had a master of esoteric Buddhism, namely, Saichō (767–822), the senior Tendai Buddhist monk who had left for China in the same fleet as Kūkai. When Saichō had returned to Japan before Kūkai, he had brought some esoteric teachings and practices he had fortuitously learned in China when not studying Tiantai (J. Tendai) Buddhism. Accordingly, to Kūkai's consternation, esotericism had arrived in Japan before he did.

Eventually, with the succession of a new emperor, Kūkai won over the court with his charisma and talents. His thaumaturgical powers, his vast knowledge of Chinese poetry, and his extraordinary artistic skills, especially in calligraphy (an art particularly favored by the reigning emperor), made him a confidant of the throne and a regular at the court. Meanwhile, Kūkai also forged friendships and alliances with key figures in Nara Buddhist circles, avoiding much of the competitive backbiting common among their intellectuals.

To be sure, as the founder of a new Japanese sect, Kūkai did have his own philosophical critics, but he usually maintained amicable relations even with them. A case in point is Tokuitsu (781?–842?), an astute scholar-monk from the Hossō school who had also aggressively criticized Saichō. The exchange between the Saichō and Tokuitsu was often hostile and *ad hominem*, but the interactions between Kūkai and Tokuitsu were more cordial.

For example, in 815 in response to Kūkai's deferential request for help in copying and disseminating esoteric texts, Tokuitsu replied with a courteous but pointed critique of Shingon teachings, asking for clarification on eleven questions.[80] Kūkai's response, although partial, was again tactful. Ryūichi Abe surmises that the Tokuitsu exchange might have precipitated Kūkai's flurry of philosophical writings in the immediately ensuing years, writings central to his intellectual development.[81] Before turning to those philosophical writings, though, let us finish the account of Kūkai's life.

Despite, or perhaps because of, his increasing political interactions in the capital, Kūkai longed for the mountains. With imperial authorization and financial backing he began construction in 819 of an impressive monastic complex located on Mt Kōya, some eighty kilometers from Nara and one hundred twenty from Kyoto. Around 832 Kūkai retired there permanently until he passed on in 835. As Kūkai's resting site, Mt Kōya retains its mystique even today.

The temple complex is only two or three hours by train and cable car from the metropolitan Kyoto-Osaka area, but to visit Kōya is to enter another realm. Because the mountaintop lacks hotels, the crowds of overnight guests must arrange lodging in the subtemples, many with treasured artworks and artifacts. There in the early morning they can witness the sensuality of the Shingon rituals that has so entranced the Japanese through the centuries: gold-plated altar utensils shimmer in darkened rooms; bells, drums, and gongs reverberate; incantations and chants rhythmically rumble on; the *mudras* punctuate the sacred space; pungent wafts of incense filter through the air; fierce sculptures glower at the pilgrims; geometrically intricate mandalas embellish walls or ceilings. To witness Shingon ritual is to encounter the primordial, the mystical, and the magical. A walk to Okunoin, Kūkai's mausoleum, heightens that impression as the juncture of historical and religious realities.

The long, broad path takes us through an extensive cemetery, a necropolis of moss-covered stone tablets among towering Japanese cedars over ten stories tall. Following the walkway, admiring the imposing yet graceful Buddhist statues amid the tombstones, no student of history can help but be impressed by the names on the gravesites, including many of Japan's most distinguished families or individuals from ancient times up to the present. Throughout history, it seems, the famous have fancied burial in Kūkai's cemetery. Walking deeper into the forest, we gradually become aware that the mist nestled among the rocks, trees, and gravestones is fragrant with incense billowing from the temple building up ahead.

On entering, we again find a dark interior to which our eyes must adjust for the glittering ritual objects to become visible, but immediately we can see the translucent white veil covering a large opening at the back of the hall. If we go around behind the building, we see that the window opens to a separate, simple hut with a thatched roof overgrown with moss. In that humble building is Kūkai.

Previously I said Kūkai had "passed on" in 835. Believers say he has not died in the ordinary sense of the word but rather sits in unwavering meditation, awaiting reentrance into the world at the end of this cycle of time when Miroku, the buddha of the future (and perhaps incarnate as Kūkai himself), will come to usher everyone into the state of collective enlightenment.[82] People say Kūkai's fingernails and hair are still growing and the emperor sends him a new robe annually.

Behind this modern phenomenon are centuries of folktales about his wonder-working, including his curing plagues, ending droughts, carving wooden buddha images that would not burn, and inscribing mantras deep into rocks using only his fingernails. Collectively, these make Kūkai seem a mythical figure, a Japanese Merlin. Still, Kūkai the wonder-worker is only half his story. The other half is the part that concerns us: Kūkai the philosopher. As we will now see, Kūkai was as much a Thomas Aquinas as a Merlin.

THE TWO KINDS OF KNOWING

Think back to Kūkai's motivation in the cave: the wish to understand every Buddhist text. The preliminary question was the nature of such understanding and how it might be attained. To understand everything is not the same as knowing everything, as simply amassing all the facts about reality. If that had been Kūkai's goal, he would have been better served by studying in either the imperial academy or the Buddhist study centers.

Kūkai's intention was instead to know reality somewhat like how we *know a person*. Not to be confused with knowing *about* a person (which derives from reading and hearing about that individual), truly knowing a person involves some shared intimacy. To know another is to be inside that person's world, to interact or overlap with the person in such a way that the other person becomes part of your own life. Rather than objectifying the other, you share something with the other.

Even in knowing an object, there can be a difference between a detached and engaged form of knowing. For example, skilled craftspeople do not just know about their tools and their media; they know them intimately by working with them, modeling their technique after the exemplary masters of the craft. By that process, woodcarvers come to perceive the uniqueness of each piece of wood and each chisel. They work *with* the wood based on an engaged, embodied knowing that allows the wood, the chisels, the artist's hands, and the artist's mind to be a harmonious whole, a single act of engagement.

Similarly, when Kūkai left the academies on his quest to understand, he wanted to engage the world intimately, not as a detached observer. He wanted to know all of reality the way a potter, not a geologist, knows clay. By the time he returned from China, Kūkai had experienced firsthand the difference between the two kinds of knowing and was ready to explain it as the contrast between *exoteric* and *esoteric*.

Before we look more closely at Kūkai's own words, this is an opportune point for a reminder of this book's objectives. Its purpose is only secondarily to help you learn about Japanese philosophy; its primary goal is to enable you to know Japanese philosophy by engaging it in some way. If I am right in claiming that engaged rather than detached knowing is the main paradigm of most Japanese philosophy throughout history, we should not be satisfied with knowing about it in a detached way. That would be like learning to be a potter by reading about pottery or getting to know someone by reading a biography in a *Who's Who*. The challenge is to understand engaged knowing by actually engaging it in some way.

That insight struck home for Kūkai when he read the *Dainichi Sutra*. Before coming across that text, Kūkai had probably believed, as did most of his contemporaries, that we learn about Buddhism through scholarly study and we engage it through praxis. That helps explain the geographical separation of the two at the time: scholastic study in the city, ascetic praxis in the mountains. In reading the *Dainichi Sutra,* though, Kūkai realized that the text could only be fully appreciated by engaging it with a master from the tradition. He had to go to China and become Huiguo's disciple. Likewise, to appreciate Kūkai's philosophy of engagement, you cannot simply read about it with detachment; you must be willing to follow his lead.

A major challenge will be penetrating Kūkai's technical terminology. His vocabulary is foreign not only to most western readers, even western philosophers; it is equally alien to most Japanese readers, even Buddhists. Kūkai's writings are redolent with allusions to a staggering array of buddhas, images, incantations, doctrines, and liturgical practices. To comprehend all those references would take years of study and practice at Mt Kōya. Fortunately for us, to engage Kūkai as a philosopher, those references are not what is most critical. To use a phrasing that will, I hope, be more meaningful by the end of this chapter, we are less interested in what Kūkai's words *refer to* than in what they *confer with*.

Accordingly, I will try to use as few technical terms as possible and, at least to the extent feasible, I will translate those terms into ordinary English words, although with explicit qualifications or additional nuances. If Kūkai's words do not, to some extent, mesh with the words in which we English speakers think, the hope of engagement will fail before we begin.

To address this situation, in our engaging Kūkai and this book's other six major philosophers, especially the premodern ones, I will try a binocular interpretation, merging two slightly different perspectives in the hopes of perceiving depth. On one hand, in order to be fair to the authenticity of the philosopher's thought, I will present the ideas in their original context as much as possible. On the other, for us to appreciate the more general philosophical issues at stake, I will reframe the ideas slightly as we go along, putting them in terms a little more familiar to our own contemporary context.

If, in doing this to analyze Kūkai for example, I use an idea from a time and place foreign to Kūkai, that will be only one lens through which we are looking at his philosophizing. What is anachronistic to one lens is not necessarily so for the other. What is culturally foreign to one is not necessarily so for the other. By harmonizing the two, I will try to help us perceive a dimension that neither alone could fully access. After all, if as a reader you bring (as I explained in the opening of Chapter 1) "your half of the intimacy" to this analysis, you become part of the text and what is anachronistic for Kūkai's contemporaries is not so to you and your contemporaries. With those caveats, let us now turn to Kūkai's words and how he distinguished two kinds of knowing.

In his essay "Treatise on Distinguishing the Two Teachings: Exoteric and Esoteric" (*Benkenmitsu nikyōron*) written in about 814 or 815 when he was in his early forties, Kūkai explained in detail the essence of esotericism as he understood it. The opening sentences make the key points:

> Whereas the Buddha has three bodies, there are two kinds of teachings. Those delivered by the celestial (ō) and historical (ke) embodiments are "exoteric teachings" (kengyō). Being publicly expressed and abridged, those words are suited to the audience's circumstances. The speeches of the cosmic embodiment (hosshin), on the other hand, are "esoteric teachings" (mikkyō). Obscure and interior, those words are the authentic exposition.[83]

In that passage, Kūkai makes three points of contrast between esoteric and exoteric teachings: the source of the teaching, the audience for the teaching, and the form of expression. We need to address all three.

The Source of Esoteric Teaching

The difference between the exoteric and esoteric correlates with the buddha embodiment doing the teaching. Exoteric doctrines—what we can generally consider the fruits of detached knowing—are the teachings of a historical buddha such as Śākyamuni or, less commonly, of a celestial buddha such as Amida or Kannon. For esoteric teachings, however, the cosmic embodiment itself teaches. Kūkai often expresses this latter point with the pithy formula *hosshin seppō*: "the buddha-as-cosmos expounds the truth."[84] Although the verbal expression may vary, the basic notion behind this phrase is central to many Japanese philosophers we will study. In fact, the prominent Japanese scholar of Buddhism, Tamaki Kōshirō, considered it the fundamental idea in the development of Japanese Buddhism.[85] So, with its first occurrence in this book, I will try to be as clear as possible about what this idea entails.

In general Mahayana Buddhist teachings, the cosmic embodiment, as explained in Chapter 2, is the principle at the base of all that exists or, alternatively, is the cosmos itself. One literal meaning of the technical term *hosshin* (S. *dharmakāya*) is "reality embodiment," that is, the buddha as all reality. Most Mahayana Buddhists understand this embodiment to be formless, intangible, impersonal, and nameless, that is, an abstract principle or theoretical ground for the omnipresent spiritual force. That force links the enlightenment of all beings to the personal buddhas of the other two kinds of embodiment, historical and celestial.

However, like Kegon Buddhism whose tradition inspired the image of the Great Buddha in Nara's Great Temple to the East, Shingon maintains the cosmic embodiment does have a name and is, in some sense, a person, both schools referring to it as the specific buddha, the "Great Sun" Buddha, Dainichi. By giving the cosmic embodiment a personal name, both Kegon and Shingon make it out to be more than a theoretically necessary premise for their metaphysics; it becomes instead the source and goal of Buddhist practice. That is, to attain enlightenment is to have an *interpersonal encounter* with reality as a buddha: to know reality is somehow analogous to knowing a person. One engages or works with reality; one does not observe it, analyze it, or manipulate it. One does not *refer to* it, but rather, *confers with* it.

As an exoteric rather than esoteric school, Kegon Buddhists do not emphasize the second part of the *hosshin seppō* formula, however. For them, Dainichi may be the personal name of the cosmic embodiment, but it is still abstract enough that they do not ordinarily think of it as being able to "teach" or "expound the truth (*seppō*)." According to Shingon esotericism, by contrast, Dainichi teaches. Thus, we have the startling claim that the cosmic embodiment—whether by that we mean the cosmos itself or the principle behind the cosmos—can expound the truth. If you find this bizarre, it may be consoling to know that many of Kūkai's Japanese contemporaries felt the same. Can it really be the case that the cosmos itself is actually telling us something? This very point, it turns out, was the gist of the ninth of Tokuitsu's previously mentioned eleven questions for Kūkai. Before looking at Kūkai's response to that skepticism, however, let us deal with the other two points of differentiation between exoteric and esoteric: audience and form of expression.

The Audience of Esoteric Teaching

When Kūkai wrote that the esoteric teaching is not "suited to the audience's circumstances," he was referring to the popular idea of *hōben*, that is, "heuristic expression" or "skill-in-means" as I discussed it in Chapter 2.† As I explained there, the theory is that, for the sake of universal enlightenment, Buddhist teachings are heuristically adjusted to fit the capacity and needs of the audience. As *hōben*, expressions are not so much true or false, but effective or ineffective, that is, if they do not lead the audience to experience the truth for themselves, they are not *hōben*. If we do speak of expedient teachings as true, it is in a pragmatic not referential sense, meaning that the truth of an expression depends on what it *does* for the listener, not on the reality it designates.

Kūkai points out that the theory of heuristic expression applies only to the exoteric, not the esoteric. If the cosmos-as-Dainichi is expounding the teachings, there can be no audience outside the cosmos to which Dainichi would have to adjust his or her‡ message. This means that Dainichi is expounding the truth not for any external audience, but rather, for his own sake (*jijūyū*). Rather than being a teaching tailored to a specific audience, it is more akin to speech acts we say aloud to ourselves when no one else is present, "*That's* it," or "Ah, there it is," or "Oh, oh." This view of expression-without-audience segues into the third distinguishing mark of esotericism: its form of expression.

Esotericism's Form of Expression

Kūkai said that esoteric teachings are "obscure and interior" rather than "publicly expressed and abridged." The difference is obvious even in ordinary teaching contexts. Suppose a novice asks you about something in which you have expertise, a complex computer program, for example. Do you explain it in the detail in which you think about it yourself? Of course not. You tell the person just what he or she needs to know, omitting complexities or alternatives beyond their needs or level of understanding. Your message is abridged and

---

† See pages 86–8.

‡ Technically, the gender of Dainichi is indeterminate as Chinese and Japanese do not typically use gendered personal pronouns. Artistic representations of Dainichi, however, are male and so, henceforth, I will use the male personal pronouns. More importantly, since Kūkai insists Dainichi is a person, we should avoid referring to the cosmos-as-buddha as "it."

expressed for the public so that almost anyone could understand: you look for the heuristic expression that will be pedagogically most effective for the particular context and audience.

In thinking about the computer program intimately to yourself, however, there is no need for expediency, adaptation, or abridgement. The complexity in your inner thoughts would be to the novice obscure or secret, but it is obscure not because you are intentionally concealing it from outsiders or being secretive, but because what is most intimate to you would not ordinarily be intelligible to outsiders. Therefore, Dainichi's expounding the truth is, as we have already noted, akin to our own internal expressions to ourselves. But that is only half the story with relation to audience.

As part of the cosmos, *we* are also part of Dainichi. To the extent we can differentiate ourselves from the cosmos at large, there is an interpersonal dimension to Dainichi's expounding the truth. Yet, this cannot be an interpersonal encounter like public communication because that too sharply contrasts speaker and listener. So, consider instead the communication between two intimate friends or a longtime married couple. Because they are intimate, in communicating with each other, they read each other's intimations. They do not explain everything, but complete understanding occurs with just a few words and or perhaps a subtle gesture. They may not even be explicitly communicating anything to anyone else, but if one of the pair is thinking about something and is worried, the other intimate will "read the signs." To an outsider, such communication would be "obscure," but it is not necessarily because the people are being secretive or obfuscating.

I chose to use the phrase *reading the signs*, incidentally, because it suits well Kūkai's own articulation about how the practitioner engages Dainichi's expressions, what Kūkai calls *monji* (words, signs, symbols, or even sinographs). I will come back to this point shortly, but for now, just register the everyday sense of *reading the signs* as I just used it. In the context where you will encounter the term later, it might be tempting to overly mystify the term, but Kūkai's point is that we are always reading the signs. Yet, that act usually occurs so offhandedly that when we reflect on its process, it suddenly seems so complex and profound that we might think it a mysterious function beyond our ken.

Kūkai's analysis of expression coalesces around his theory of the so-called three intimacies of body, speech, and mind.

> Accompanied by his retinue of celestial buddhas, the cosmic embodiment in himself and for himself preaches—for their own enjoyment of the truth—entrance into the "three intimacies" (*sanmitsu*). This is the esoteric teaching. This entrance to the three intimacies is the so-called realm of the Buddha's innermost wisdom.[86]

Let us examine more closely what Kūkai means by these three (*san*) intimacies (*mitsu*). The basic meanings of the Japanese sinograph *mitsu* are "secret,"[87] "intimate," or "detailed." So, the term itself suggests a link between praxis and reality: through the praxis of the three intimacies, we achieve a profound, intimate, detailed engagement with the processes of reality. *Mitsu* is commonly translated "mysteries," but for the reason just discussed in relation to *read the signs*, the English word *mystery* does not here mean enigma. The three *mitsu* are enigmatic only when approached externally, discursively, or publicly—that is, with detachment—rather than intimately with engagement. As Kūkai said in initially making his distinction, outside the praxis of the intimacies, the truth is hidden or "obscure and interior."

For example, not being a banjo player, I understand theoretically how an expert musician makes the sounds by strumming and plucking the strings, but that does not mean I can pick up a banjo and play. In fact, the actual music-making is to me hidden: it is a mystery to me how one can move one's fingers so precisely and rapidly, not to mention improvise, as one plays with others. Yet, to a fellow banjo player, there is nothing hidden or obscure here.

Likewise, to those within the intimate circle of Shingon praxis, the *mitsu* are not "mysterious" either. If one thinks of the English word "mysteries" in its religious sense—as in mystery cults, the Christian Holy Mysteries (the sacraments), and so forth—the translation may be acceptable, but what makes it so is its direct link with praxis, a link that explains why Kūkai specifies *three* intimacies or mysteries.

60-1

THE THREE INTIMACIES

The three intimacies are the bodily, the verbal, and the mental. From the general Indian understanding out of which Buddhist thought arose, the three forms of volitional action or karma are, as mentioned in Chapter 2,† deed, word, and thought, that is, the actions of body, speech, and mind. In defining actions that are virtuous or sinful, the medieval western Christian theologians used the same three categories: "thought, word, and deed." There is an important difference from Buddhism, however, and it is essential to understanding how Kūkai could think of the cosmos as a person.

In the western model, the person is what performs the thoughts, words, and deeds, whereas for Buddhism, the person *is* the thoughts, words, and deeds. Because it denies substantiality, Buddhism understands the person to be a set of intrinsically interlinked processes and activities. As I explained previously,‡

---

† See pages 58–61.

‡ See pages 57 and 59 for my analysis of a river as an example of nonsubstantiality.

because of the interdependence within the processes themselves, the Buddhist theory of the person requires no soul, ego, or "I" to account for their connectedness.

Therefore, when Kūkai's esotericism teaches the cosmos is a person named Dainichi, it is saying the cosmos is a set of interdependent actions or processes, not an independently existing agent who does things. That is basically the general Buddhist claim about any person.

My experience has been that a danger of cultural misrecognition among westerners is to think of Kūkai's Dainichi as a variant of a monotheistic God. So I will say again, Dainichi is not the creator of the universe, nor a personal deity who takes action in this world from a transcendent location behind it. Nor does Dainichi communicate with humans through revelation or inerrant texts. Dainichi *is* the universe. If you need some western idea to start from, it would be better to think of Dainichi as the whole of reality, rather than as God.

Moreover, in the Shingon Buddhists' interpersonal relation with the universe, the processes that define the practitioner are a subset of Dainichi's processes, that is, each of us is a subset of the universe's function. It follows then that my knowing reality is part of reality's self-knowing. For me to know is to enter "the so-called realm of the buddha's innermost wisdom." When Kūkai had been ignorant of all this before his trip to China, he thought the cosmos was a secret hidden from him. He wanted to know everything about it. Once he came to understand everything, however, he discovered what was most intimately available to him all along. He had at last found the *way* to understanding everything: to understand everything is to partake in everything's knowing itself.

Since Dainichi is the behavior of the entire cosmos, we can think of reality as Dainichi's self-expressive style. Reality is not *what* the universe is; instead, it is *how* the universe is. In that context, we human beings—like everything else— are no more than letters or syllables or words (*monji*) in Dainichi's expression of the truth to himself. If that is so, then everything in the universe is an intimation of Dainichi's preaching the truth. To grasp this truth, though, you must be able, as I previously said, to "read the signs."

The question then becomes how you can become intimate with Dainichi's preaching so you can read the universe as Dainichi's intimations. Kūkai's answer is as follows. Metaphysically speaking, there is only one reality: Dainichi as intimately interlinked activity. Because Dainichi and you are both persons, however, you engage in the same three forms of action, namely, the three intimacies of body, speech, and mind expressed as deed, word, and thought. So, as a human being, you can fathom the universe as an intimation of Dainichi's personal style by deliberately harmonizing your own bodily, verbal, and mental styles with Dainichi's. The way to understand everything is not to analyze it, but to engage it harmoniously, to be in tune with it.

It follows, then, that in Kūkai's system, ritual is a form of knowing. As the theory of three intimacies implies, ritual is a three-part harmony among verbal, mental, and bodily action. Let us now examine more closely each of the three intimacies, bearing in mind that in the end they fuse into a single expressive act or performance.

62-4

The Intimacy of Speech

Let us begin with verbal intimacy, Dainichi's language of intimation. In some ways, this is the most straightforward of the three intimacies for us to grasp, but it is probably still not easy, at least at first. Dainichi's verbal intimations are the entire cosmos: the universe of stars, planets, sunsets, snowflakes, birdcalls, telephone poles, stop signs, worms, and cow manure. To understand how Kūkai could read such things as signs of Dainichi's expounding the truth, I suggest we look to his essay "On the Significance of 'Sound[88*]-Word-Reality'" (*Shōjijissōgi*), the gist of which I will now characterize.

Three levels of reality. To follow Kūkai's analysis, it is helpful to think of Dainichi's verbal activity as operating on three levels: the cosmic, the macrocosmic, and the microcosmic. Let us start with the cosmic. As we have seen, Kūkai believes the entire universe is just the Buddha as interlinked processes. This cosmic person, we could say, practices the rituals of Shingon Buddhism. That may seem ludicrous—like saying God is a Methodist or a Lutheran—but to take Kūkai's point in that way would be reversing cause and effect. Dainichi is a Shingon practitioner of rituals because Shingon practice was designed to harmonize with Dainichi's activity, to mirror or emulate how the cosmos functions. So Dainichi's activity, conversely, must be the same as the Shingon Buddhist's praxis.

The Shingon practice of verbal intimacy is to intone a sacred syllable or phrase: a mantra. Therefore, Dainichi's verbal intimation is a sound. What sound? We can hear the sound of a birdcall, but what is the sound of a sunset or a telephone pole? The answer lies in the function of mantras, or as they are called in Japanese, *shingon*—"truth words."

Of all the mantras, Shingon ritual singles out six as so-called seed mantras, namely, *A, Va, Ra, Ha, Kha* and *Hūṃ*.[89] When reciting those mantras with the correct posture and mental attitude, one becomes attuned to the basic "resonances" or "echoes" (*kyō*) constituting the cosmos. These voiced seed mantras are not themselves the basic constituents of reality, but by intoning them within the proper ritualistic context, one becomes sensitive to the "truth words" inaudible to ordinary hearing. That is the cornerstone of Kūkai's metaphysics: reality as resonance.

Metaphysics. We modern people, whether western or Japanese, may find that claim exotic and outlandish: the cosmos is a giant buddha's mumbling mantras, filling the void with resonances that coalesce into the world we experience all around us. Yet, metaphysical theories are never, we should remember, empirically verifiable. If they were, they would be theories of physics, not metaphysics. Even the notion that empirical evidence should play the central role in understanding reality is itself a metaphysical assumption: it presupposes that reality is completely knowable through disengaged, publicly shared, sense experience—the basic input / output system of detached knowledge.

We cannot empirically prove why empirical methods work, however, without falling into circularity: the evidence in the proof would itself have to be empirically derived to have validity. It would be like saying, "we know we can trust empiricism because it matches so well the way things appear to us." That begs the question: the issue is how we know the way things appear to our senses is the way things are, or more precisely, the *complete* picture of the way they are. Empiricism itself cannot answer that question without making a leap of faith that the world is as it appears. In sum: a metaphysics is always a set of *assumptions* about reality that explains why certain ways of understanding the world are effective.

That said, what if two cultures differ in their models of what it means to understand the world? Would that not imply a different metaphysics? For example, empiricism believes an understanding occurs when you detach yourself from the world to observe it, collect data through your external senses, and cull recurrent patterns, often mathematical, out of that array of data. Those patterns are considered the laws of reality and if you understand them, you can manage and statistically predict the impact of your actions. The better you articulate those patterns and control the results of your actions, the better you understand everything. A metaphysics supporting such an empiricist view might envision, for example, a universe of discrete things (elements, substances, atoms) along with forces (energy, God, entropy). Those forces bring the things into and out of relations with one another to form complexes that you can empirically perceive and logically analyze.

Now contrast that with a strikingly different model of what it means to understand everything. Shift your paradigm of knowing from that of the geologist to that of the potter. In that case, to understand the world is to engage it, to be interdependent and inter-responsive with it, to be part of the universe's self-unfolding or self-expression. The better you can feel at home in the world or the more you feel part of it instead of separate from it, the better you can understand everything. A metaphysics supporting such a view of understanding might characterize reality as a single, vital system of interrelated processes and resonances, each responding with the others like the notes in a chord instead of bricks in a wall.

Rather than taking vision for its primary metaphor of knowing, that model of engaged understanding might well stress hearing instead.[90] When you look with your eyes, you take a single standpoint at a time, a focused perspective in which you are separate from the thing seen; you put yourself in external relation with what you see. Even if you look at it with other people, each person stands alone vis-à-vis the object: you cannot merge your vision with my vision in the way you can merge the visual data from your left eye with your right.

Sound, by contrast, can engulf you from all directions; you can hear what is all around you simultaneously, even though you cannot see all around you simultaneously. Even when you make the conscious effort to listen intently, you still feel the sound comes to you, meeting you halfway. Although you may say you hear from someone, you cannot say you see from someone, suggesting that in listening, the sound seems half "out there" and half "in your head."[91] Consequently, you can experience sound communally in a way you cannot a visual object.

Imagine a jazz nightclub, the patrons' heads bobbing, toes tapping, and fingers snapping in unison. Their bodily gestures indicate they are listening to the same music. Contrast that with an art gallery: the patrons' body movements are more individualized than communal, postures telling us little about the object being viewed. If someone were wearing headphones, you could probably guess correctly from their body movements whether they are listening to a march or a waltz, but if you observe a person in an art gallery, you probably cannot determine from their body movements if the painting they are viewing is an abstract or impressionist. To sum up: the rhythms in the jazz club are objective and transpersonal in a way that the visual experience of the art gallery's visitors is not. That helps explain why Kūkai finds hearing rather than seeing to be an apt root metaphor for engagement.

As a manifestation of his enlightenment, Dainichi intones the sacred syllables or, more precisely, Dainichi is the intoning of the syllables. His "truth words" are a spontaneous expression of his situation rather than reference to a situation. It is analogous to our spontaneously voicing "Brr!" as we open the door into the bitter cold of a wintry day or "ouch!" if we stub a toe. A word like "Brr!" is a responsive expression of feeling the cold, not a word referring to the cold.[92] In a sense I will soon explain more fully, we can say "Brr!" *confers with*, rather than *refers to*, the cold. Voicing the syllables of the seed mantras, Dainichi emits resonances that are the microcosmic nature of the cosmos.

Those basic resonances, like notes in a musical chord, coalesce into the elements making up the universe as we know it, what I will call the *macrocosmos*. Kūkai accepts the East Asian tradition that recognizes six elements forming our macrocosmic world: earth, water, fire, wind, space, and consciousness. Each accords with the resonance from one of the six seed mantras being uttered by Dainichi (and the Shingon practitioner in ritual).⁹³*

The main point is that the *cosmic* behavior of Dainichi is manifest as a subperceptible, *microcosmic* resonance which in turn forms the six elemental resonances. The elements combine to form the *macrocosmic* reality perceptible to our ordinary sense organs, the world of everyday experience. Living in this macrophysical world, perceiving it with our senses, we are normally unaware of the deeper levels of reality: the cosmic and the microcosmic. In its schematic logic, we may note, this model resembles using a periodic table of elements to explain the physical constitution of reality. Most of the time, we live our daily lives paying no attention to the microphysical level of atoms or, alternatively, the cosmic level of planetary gravity and the expansion of galaxies.

For Kūkai, though, in the esoteric experience of reality, there is no sharp separation of levels. Like every other item in the universe, the sense organs can be broken down into the six elements which are themselves composed of the six resonances. Yet, just as the naked eye cannot perceive the subatomic level known to us through physics, we cannot perceive the subaudible world of Dainichi's resonance. If we are to understand reality on that level, we need to engage it directly. We need to harmonize with it, not study it. That is the purpose behind the mantra practice.

By practicing the forms under a master, one can learn how the world functions and how to act accordingly. We cannot exoterically explain adequately what we engage and understand esoterically. When the mantras are practiced within the correct context, the resonance shatters our entrapment in the macrophysical view of reality as suddenly and dynamically as the resonance of the opera singer's voice shatters the crystal goblet. As soon as the Shingon Buddhist breaks through the macrocosmic to the microcosmic, yet another dimension opens: the *cosmic*.

When known intimately through Shingon practice, the microcosmic does not appear as the probabilistic world of field effects and quanta. Rather, it has its own patterns; the universe is a personal act. We can know that cosmic act because we, too, are persons with bodily, verbal, and mental behavior. We can grasp the style of the universe because it is Dainichi's style and Dainichi's style can inspire our own style. The world is an intimation of what is most intimate in our intimate teacher, the cosmos-as-buddha—Dainichi. To know the universe as an event is to harmonize with it, not to objectify it as something outside us.

Hence, to know the universe is to join its tonal resonances. For that reason I said earlier that for Kūkai, language does not so much *refer to* reality as it *confers with* it. In fact, for the enlightened Shingon Buddhist, every act is an intimation of Dainichi's act. Here we find the holographic relation between whole and part. Our behavior may only be part of the behavior of the cosmos. Yet, if we delve into it through Shingon praxis, our behavior reflects the patterns of the cosmos. As Kūkai famously expressed it: "Wherever the six great elements reach, that is my body."

Explanation for thaumaturgy. I have mentioned Kūkai's associations with thaumaturgy, the miraculous wonder-working power to cure plagues, end droughts, and perform superhuman feats. Regardless of whether we accept the accounts literally, we can at least understand how Kūkai's metaphysical system could explain such events through his theory of "spiritual empowerment" (*kaji*), Kūkai's term for Dainichi's resonance in the individual.[94]* The two sinographs in the word literally mean "add" (*ka*) and "hold" (*ji*). The implication is that Dainichi's actions fill the cosmos with resonant power, while the practicing Shingon Buddhist preserves that resonance by harmonizing with it in one's own actions.

In everyday Japanese speech today, *kaji* usually means magical power, but Shingon interprets the term metaphysically in terms of Dainichi's presence as the world. For Shingon, *kaji* amounts to *nyūga ganyū*, "(the Buddha's or reality's) entering me and my entering (the Buddha or reality)." Spiritual empowerment is always occurring, although we may typically be unaware of it. During periods of religiously charged experience as well as at times of thaumaturgical display, however, we become acutely conscious of its activity. At such times the cosmos is spiritually vibrant with Dainichi's vibration.

From the standpoint of engagement, to be a buddha is not a change in what you are, but in how you know. When achieving enlightenment, you realize what you have been all along, an aspect of Dainichi's function, a small subset of the resonances composing the universe. Among your elemental resonances is consciousness and, therefore, you can realize how your small part of the whole contains the pattern of the whole within it.

An analogy with music may again help. When you merge with Dainichi through empowerment, it is not so much that your individuality disappears, but rather that your thoughts, words, and deeds harmonize into the chorus of cosmic sound. When we hear a choir of carolers singing "Jingle Bells," for example, we often cannot help but nod our heads to the rhythm, humming along, or even joining in. We have not really lost our free will, but as the music resonates within us, it beckons us to join. Even when we self-consciously hold back, the music still fills us, resounding through us. Later that night, we may catch ourselves singing the song in our minds. A song can stick in our heads, our minds drifting off to sing it silently now and again throughout the day. It is, in the final analysis, unnatural to not be part of the music. The more distracted we are, the more caught up in our individual turmoils and problems, the more we may try to shut out the music. But it is still there. So also is the resonance of Dainichi's activity.

Participation in Dainichi's resonance, like joining the music, has a creative aspect as well. For example, should you sing the melody or the harmony? The selection of the song may not be your choice, but how you engage it can subtly affect the way the song sounds. Analogously, the wonder-worker does not miraculously change or suspend the laws of nature—that would be like changing the song being sung. No one has that power; it is always Dainichi's song. Yet, like the individual in the choir, the wonder-worker can subtly influence the overall sound, particularly to the extent the wonder-worker is acting in accord with the natural.

When a piano string is out-of-tune and the piano tuner strikes it at the same time as the appropriate tuning fork, the two notes emit a third, unpleasant sonic pulse. When the string is then properly tuned to the pitch of the tuning fork, the notes from the piano and from the tuning fork merge into one. As the sonic pulse from the out-of-tune piano is a disruption of harmony, so also are phenomena like disease or drought. A strong singer standing next to an off-key singer in a choir can bring the weak singer back on pitch just by the power of his or her voice. Analogously, the wonder-worker can bring the resonance of the universe into better harmony. Attuned[95] to the right pitch of Dainichi's resonance, the pulsating disharmony disappears into the harmonious whole.

For Kūkai, the true wonder-worker performs miracles simply by better expressing Dainichi's style as one's own. So, the wonder-worker does not act as an individual agent; Dainichi's enlightened function (*yū*) resounds powerfully through the individual, drawing other beings into the harmony. On the macrophysical level, this can seem miraculous.[96] That which enters the self and that which the self enters is, again, a cluster of functions: Dainichi as the thought, word, and deed of the universe. So, the theory of spiritual empowerment necessarily applies to the bodily and mental intimacies as well as the verbal. As the "mantra school," Shingon theory focuses most on the verbal intimacy, but it applies essentially the same model to bodily form and mental intention as well.

In Shingon Buddhism, one does not practice the mantra by itself, but accompanied by the appropriate sacred hand gestures (S. *mudrā*; J. *in*) and meditative visualizations, especially of mandalas. The sacred gestures and mandalic visualization mirror Dainichi's bodily and mental intimacy, as the mantras mirror Dainichi's verbal intimacy. The mantra is the sound of Dainichi's empowerment, the ritual hand gesture his pose and movement, the visualization his outlook. As Dainichi's act is one, the three practices are one. Because the functional relation between self and Dainichi in the other two intimacies—mind and body—parallels our discussion of the verbal intimacy, I can treat them briefly here, adding only a few points specific to each of these other two dimensions.

The Intimacy of Mind

Dainichi's actions do not merely fill the universe with resonance; they also lend it structure and pattern, what is understood to be Dainichi's mental function. To understand that pattern intimately, the Shingon practitioner must engage it through praxis. As the mantra is to the verbal intimacy, the mandala is to the mental. The Sanskrit term *mandala* (J. *mandara*) simply means "circle," an appropriate name given the basic shape of the mandalas themselves: sets of circles, either concentric or juxtaposed within squared off areas. In ancient Indian religious life, the mandalas were initially drawn as a site for the deities to assemble during rituals. Shingon scholars often interpret the etymology of the word *mandala* to mean "possessing (*la*) the essence (*manda*)." The essence of what? Of the universe as the activity of Dainichi. So, a mandala is a sacred site, what I refer to as a *holographic entry point* in Shingon praxis, that is, a point at which the practitioner recognizes oneself to be part of Dainichi (the whole) and at the same time a holographic reflection of the configuration of that whole.[†] In Shingon tradition, the circles generally contain either images of buddhas or sacred letters.

In a sense, in focusing on a mandala, my mind is focusing on its own mental configurations that are, in turn, the configuration of everything. It is somewhat analogous to my looking at a periodic table of chemicals. In doing so, I am looking at the mental construct of the elements comprising reality, but yet, insofar as I myself am also comprised of those elements, it is something like the compounded elements looking at their own configuration. This theme of truth as reality looking at itself recurs, as we will see, intermittently throughout the history of Japanese philosophy.

Although innumerable mandalas might be used in Shingon praxis, Shingon is a so-called dual mandala (*ryōbu mandara*) form of esotericism in that it places its primary philosophical emphasis on the Womb and the Diamond mandalas. From the philosophical standpoint, we can regard the Womb Mandala (*taizō mandara*), the mandala associated with the *Dainichi Sutra*, as a depiction of the previously mentioned principle of "the cosmic embodiment expounds the truth," *hosshin seppō*. The term *taizō* (S. *garbha*) literally means "womb," "embryo," or "matrix." By visualizing the mandala, therefore, you enter the innermost, most intimate structure of the universe, the source of everything. In effect, the mandala pictorially expresses the procreative or, more precisely, emanative function of the cosmic embodiment's activities. Specifically, in each nested box are various pantheons of celestial buddhas emanating outward from

---

† For further explanation of the holographic relation in which the whole is in each of its parts, see pages 32–4.

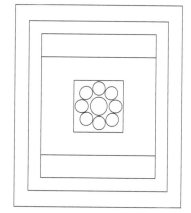

The Womb Mandala and Its Schematic

the central square in which Dainichi is surrounded by his most intimate retinue of celestial buddhas. Each depicted buddha (and the paintings may show
dozens of them) has his or her own specific symbolic markers: posture, garb,
sacred hand gesture, and color.

The meaning and use of the mandalas in Shingon praxis are intricate and
the paintings themselves are mere prompts for the real mandala envisioned in
meditation over years of esoteric practice under the tutelage of a master. This is
understandable when we consider the purpose of mandala praxis is to pattern
one's own mind as Dainichi's mind patterns the universe. Through mandala
praxis, the focus is not so much the specific content of the cosmos, but rather
the patterns of interrelation within that content. Again, reality is not a *what*; it
is a *how*. Obviously, the relations within the mandala practice, as in reality, are
internal and holographic, just as we found with the mantra practice of attuning
one's speech with the cosmic resonances.

Because the Womb Mandala depicts the *hosshin seppō* theory as the underlying metaphysics in Kūkai's teaching, it is associated with the undifferentiated
ground or principle from which patterns (*ri*) emerge.[†] The configuration of
reality emanates concentrically outward from the center of the mandala where
Dainichi resides.

As mentioned earlier, however, Shingon Buddhism is a dual mandala tradition and we now turn to the other member of the pair, the Diamond Mandala
(*kongō mandara*). Whereas the Womb Mandala represents the metaphysical
principle, the Diamond Mandala depicts the attainment of wisdom (*chi*), which

---

† For an explanation of *ri* as "principle" or "pattern" in the Kegon Buddhist system, see
pages 92–3.

 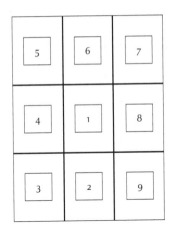

The Diamond Mandala and Its Schematic

is to say, the configuration of Shingon praxis as represented in the *Diamond Peak Sutra*. Like the Womb Mandala, the Diamond Mandala has multiple clusters of celestial buddhas and bodhisattvas, but unlike the Womb Mandala's concentric organization, the nine squares of the Diamond Mandala are typically interpreted as a spiral symbolizing the flow of spiritual empowerment in practice.

Each aspect of Shingon practice has, as it were, its place in the map of reality depicted by the mandala. Dainichi is again at the center and the Buddha's empowerment moves clockwise around the mandala, starting at the middle (frame 1), proceeding downward (frame 2), and spiraling until reaching the lower right corner (frame 9). Conversely, from the practitioner's standpoint, the approach to Dainichi is counterclockwise, moving from frame 9 sequentially down to frame 1 at the center. In Kūkai's initiation ritual with Huiguo that I described earlier, Kūkai's blind toss of the flower landed in the middle of the Diamond Mandala, signifying he had already progressed to the final stage of praxis before even formally beginning his Shingon training.

If we can associate the Womb Mandala with the "cosmic buddha expounds the truth," *hosshin seppō*, we can think of the Diamond Mandala as related to the principle of *sokushin jōbutsu*, "this very body attains buddha." That is, it depicts the progress toward enlightenment and its immediate accessibility. This brings us to the third intimacy, the intimacy of body.

The Intimacy of Body

Like *hosshin seppō*, the principle of *sokushin jōbutsu* derives from China, but Kūkai gave it his own twist, especially in his later years. As *hosshin seppō* explains empowerment from Dainichi's standpoint, *sokushin jōbutsu* articulates the individual practitioner's perspective. We could say that *hosshin seppō* characterizes Shingon metaphysics, the structure of embodiment behind events (*physis*), whereas *sokushin jōbutsu* characterizes Shingon metapraxis, the structure of embodiment behind practice (*praxis*). Shingon commentaries on Kūkai have found it convenient to explain his interpretation of the phrase "*sokushin jōbutsu*" in terms of three Japanese ways to read (and therefore interpret) the Chinese-based phrase.

First, it means *sunawachi mi nareru butsu*, "this body in itself is the fulfilled Buddha." This is sometimes called the interpretation in terms of essence (*tai*) or inherence of principle (*rigu*). The point is that self and Buddha are ontologically inseparable.

The second Japanese reading of *sokushin jōbutsu* is *mi ni sokushite butsu to naru*, "I become the Buddha through my own body." This is the interpretation in terms of aspect (*sō*) or empowerment (*kaji*). Although essentially one with Dainichi, I must participate in his empowerment to unify the outward aspects of self and Buddha. In other words, although metaphysically speaking, I am always part of Dainichi's activity, I can only experientially recognize this unity through embodied praxis: detached knowing alone will not suffice.

Finally, *sokushin jōbutsu* means *sumiyaka ni mi butsu to naru*, "the body immediately becomes the Buddha." This interpretation is from the standpoint of function (*yū*) or manifestation (*kendoku*). My own actions, insofar as they merge through practice with Dainichi's actions, are right here and now able to manifest enlightenment. Through my own ritualized style, I manifest Dainichi's style.

Although the three readings of *sokushin jōbutsu* are technically not Kūkai's own exegesis, they do capture well the gist of his teaching and Kūkai himself used the tripartite labels *tai*, *sō*, and *yū* in some of his explanations. More to the point, Kūkai emphasized the idea of "attaining enlightenment in this very body" to affirm three major points.

First, contrary to the teachings of some exoteric Buddhist schools, especially the Hinayana schools, that maintain enlightenment is available to us only after millions of lifetimes spent in assiduous practice, Kūkai wished to affirm that enlightenment is available to any of us in this very body, that is, this present lifetime. Japanese Buddhist commentaries had emphasized that idea as far back as Prince Shōtoku.[†] In this regard, Shingon belongs to the Buddhist traditions that emphasize enlightenment as sudden and complete, rather than gradual and cumulative.[97]

† See pages 63–4.

Next, enlightenment is attainable to us in this embodiment because Dainichi is embodied right now as this world, including our very own bodies. In this special sense, our own bodies are buddha embodiments.

Lastly, Shingon praxis is a means to identifying with the buddha.[98] To know the buddha, one has to engage the buddha with one's whole self, including the body. Returning to Henri Bergson's two kinds of knowing discussed in Chapter 1, one knows the buddhas-as-cosmos not by "moving around it" but by "entering it."[†]

The bodily intimacy is expressed most directly through the physical hand gestures used in ritual, the aforementioned *mudras* (J. *in*). The gestures bring both a tactile dimension and sense of physical location to the praxis. If we think of the mantras resonating with the elements constituting reality and the mandalas as mirroring the structures of reality, the mudras participate in the patterns of change. Of course, the body and the mind are ultimately inseparable as bodymind, the subject to which we now turn.

BODYMIND: THE PROPRIOCEPTIVE COSMOS

Although we have found Kūkai uniformly using the term *shin* for body, we have already come across three terms related to the mental: consciousness (*shiki*) used in connection with the six great elements, the mental (*i*) used in reference to the three intimacies, and mind (*shin*) used in connection with either the intimacies or the mental-and-affective faculty that forms experience. How do these three notions of the mental interrelate? And how do they overlap with the body?[99]

Let us return to a quote previously cited, this time including the next sentence: "Wherever the six great elements reach, that is my body. Wherever the ten worlds exist, that is my mind (*shin*[‡])."[100] Since one of the six elements is consciousness (*shiki*), that brief statement gives us a clue about the connections among body (*shin*), consciousness (*shiki*), and mind (*shin*). Identified through empowerment with Dainichi's body, the person's body permeates the elements constituting the universe including the element of consciousness, but the person's mind structures that universe into the ten, which is to say all, worlds.

So the body (*shin*) is essentially the bodily intimacy (*shinmitsu*), the embodiment of Dainichi's style as one's own. Through Shingon practice, one can identify with the cosmos itself, but that cosmos is not just a grand unintelligent machine since one of its elements is consciousness (*shiki*). Conscious-

† See page 42.

‡ Although the two words can be pronounced the same, we must take care to distinguish the *shin* that means "mind" (心) and the *shin* that means "body" (身).

ness does not necessarily include thought or intention, however.[101] In other words, although the bodily intimacy is associated with consciousness, it is not necessarily associated with thought and intention. What could it then mean to regard consciousness as a constitutive element of reality? To pose the question in terms akin to the mind-body problem in western philosophy: how does this consciousness relate to body?

Any explanation I (or Kūkai) could offer here would be limited in two ways. First, it would necessarily be an exoteric explanation adapted to you, the reader of this book, whereas the real answer should involve your own engaged knowing achieved in ritual. You should know the answer through yourself, not via someone else's explanation. Second, you cannot fathom the consciousness element of the body with just your discriminating mind of thought and intention. (To try to explain the mind-body relation with just your mind begs, rather than answers, the question.)

What to do? If you want to engage Kūkai's understanding of bodymind—the body as containing the consciousness element—you must engage your own bodymind. Hence, I propose a little bodymind experiment for you to try.

A Bodymind Experiment

Open your right hand, holding it up in front of you so you can see your palm. With the fingers spread, look at each fingertip. Now, using the left index finger, touch the fingertips of each of the right fingers.

Please put down the book and try this now. Only after finishing, return to reading.

In looking at your fingers, you were using what neurologists call your exteroceptors ("outwardly directed receivers") to gather perceptual information about external stimuli.

Now do the same experiment with your eyes closed.

Again, put down the book and after performing the exercise, return to reading.

Remarkably, it wasn't at all difficult to do, was it? Yet, without the aid of the exteroceptors, how does your left hand know where the right fingers are? To do the exercise, you depended on your proprioceptors ("towards-oneself-directed receivers") to give you information about the location of your hands and fingers. Those neural sensors are deep within your flesh and continuously process information about such phenomena as muscle tension to inform you about, among other things, the location and movement of your limbs.† Without

---

† These are not the interoceptors ("inwardly directed receptors") that inform you about

continuously processing all the complex information from the proprioceptors, you would not be able to do everyday activities such as touching your fingers or walking.

You might think that using only your external senses and mind, you would be able to touch your fingers without having recourse to the proprioceptors, but that is not the case. Neurology teaches us that even when your eyes were open in the first run of the exercise, the information from the proprioceptors was essential. If your proprioceptors were malfunctioning, you could not touch your fingers even if you could see them clearly. Conversely, even if your exteroceptors were malfunctioning (as in blindness, for example), you could still perform the touching experiment successfully (as you did with your eyes closed).

Two points illustrate Kūkai's theory of the body's consciousness element. First, when using the proprioceptors to blindly touch the fingers of one hand with a finger from the other, your bodymind is using its consciousness (*shiki*). That consciousness is the bodymind of self-awareness, a self-awareness that does not objectify the self. It contrasts with your intellectual self-consciousness that is your mind (as *shin*). That mind is aware of yourself as an object, self-consciously watching your left finger touch your right fingertips.

When Kūkai says, therefore, that enlightenment is to "know your own mind,"[102] he probably means something more like understanding what you learned from our experiment rather than understanding your disembodied sequence of thoughts. Furthermore, since consciousness (*shiki*) is one of the basic six elements of the cosmos, the entire universe, not just you, is proprioceptive. The universe knows where and how it is without thinking about it.

Second, when you first touched your fingers with your eyes opened, that was only possible because of the function of the proprioceptors. Yet, although the proprioceptors were informing you of where your fingers were, you were totally unaware of that neural function. The relation of the esoteric to the exoteric is like that for Kūkai. The esoteric dimension is always in the background of all activity, although we ordinarily do not realize it. Thus, as I will explain in the next section of this chapter, Kūkai goes so far as to say the esoteric even functions behind the scenes in the development of exoteric philosophies.

However "obscure" as it initially may seem, the esoteric dimension opens up as soon as we ask of any experience, "How was it possible for me to do what I just did?" A previously hidden dimension in your experience revealed itself when you did something as simple as ask how it was possible to touch your fingers. The esoteric is not exotic; it is intimate.

---

inner functions such as how your lunch is making its way through your alimentary canal.

If (the proprioceptive) consciousness (*shiki*), as one of the six elements, is on the border between the micro- and macrocosmic, mind (*shin*) is more decidedly on the macrocosmic side, the level of ordinary perception in everyday life. Mind is the reflective function, involving both affect as well as thought, that interprets the macrophysical as a world, a world in which that mind lives, its *Lebenswelt* (life-world) as it is called in German philosophy. Each of us lives in the world as structured and interpreted by our own minds. There are multiple lived-in worlds, each depending on the assumptions and value orientations we give them. Of course, these are not literally worlds, but more *mindsets*, the frameworks in which our minds dwell, what Shingon calls the *jūshin* (literally, "mental abodes"). A mindset is a fixed web of beliefs and values from within which we experience and interpret the world.

64-74

This brings us to Kūkai's influential "theory of the ten mindsets" (*jūjūshinron*). Here we will witness what I believe is the first appearance of an innovative argument by relegation† performed in the history of Japanese philosophy. And what a virtuoso performance it will be.

THE TEN MINDSETS

Kūkai developed his theory in two closely related treatises: *Theory of the Ten Mindsets* (*Jūjūshinron*) and *The Precious Key to the Obscure Treasury* (*Hizō hōyaku*) the latter being somewhat of an abridged version of the former.[103] Kūkai apparently wrote the first in response to an imperial request that each officially recognized Japanese Buddhist school write a compendium of its doctrine. In meeting this request, Kūkai wrote not just a summary of Shingon teaching, but also a summary of all other schools from the Shingon perspective. Since Shingon is for Kūkai the answer to understanding everything, even the views of other schools must fit into Shingon's system. Partly because the work was so long, Kūkai wrote the much shorter *Precious Key*, a document that the court authorities would accept and might even actually read. Before examining details of the ten mindsets themselves, I will mention a few salient points about the general form of the two treatises.

First, they are not impartial studies: Kūkai criticizes and ranks, not merely describes, the mindset representative of each school. In taking that stance, Kūkai was acting as a philosopher instead of a scholar of Buddhism. In fact, he evaluates the crucial doctrines of each in light of quotations from Shingon texts, not the texts of the exoteric schools themselves. To cite proof texts, incidentally, is a common rhetorical device in much premodern Buddhist philosophizing and

---

† For my explanation of argument by relegation as contrasted with argument by refutation, see pages 35–6 and pages 38–9.

we will encounter it frequently in this book. Yet, it is not quite the same as citing proof texts in, say, western theological treatises. In its canonical development Buddhism was extraordinarily inclusive, developing a corpus of many hundreds of texts representing wildly different philosophical positions. So, regardless of one's own position, it was usually possible to find a quotation someplace in the canon supporting it. Seen in that context, the citation was more a sign of one's mastery of the canon than an appeal to an inerrant authority.

Second, Kūkai's system is unlike the doctrinal classification systems of contemporaneous China and Saichō's Japanese Tendai school insofar as Kūkai did not classify the teachings themselves. Instead he explained the mindsets generating and abiding in the various world views those teachings characterize. Kūkai was not as interested in *what* doctrinal schemes were found in other schools (which is a product only of the mind) as he was in *how* people have interpreted the world and lived in it (through their mind, body, and speech). He focused less on the ideas than on the fully human context defining the mindset generating those ideas.

We find another clue to Kūkai's intent in the formal title of the longer treatise: although commonly called simply *Jūjūshinron* (*Theory of the Ten Mindsets*), its full title is *Himitsu mandara jūjūshinron*, that is, *The Secret Mandala Jūjūshinron*. In Kūkai's rhetoric the term *the secret mandala* frequently refers to the Shingon view in general, so the title forthrightly admits it is a view of other schools from within the Shingon perspective, which is to say it is self-admittedly an argument by relegation. The term *mandala* may also have special implications in this case, however.

Like the Diamond Mandala, the ten mindsets can be construed as points of spiritual development leading to intimacy with Dainichi. They are numbered in a hierarchical order from the point of the completely irreligious to the highest point, that of esoteric Buddhism. For this reason, some translators render "the ten mindsets" as "the ten stages of mind." Unfortunately, the term "stages" suggests a fixed sequence, but that is clearly not Kūkai's main intent, as I will now explain.

Similar to the chambers of buddhas depicted in the Womb Mandala, the mindsets represent emanations from Dainichi. As all things are manifestations, however distant, of Dainichi's act, all teachings must manifest the reality as described in the Shingon system. As the embodiment of reality, Dainichi must be the basis not only of the true teachings in Shingon, but also of all teachings, even those apparently opposed to Shingon. If the *hosshin seppō* principle holds true, Dainichi's exposition must be present even in the incorrect ideas of others.

(Note how this is a twist on Shōtoku's advice to "learn even from heretics.")†
Kūkai's systematic project required him to explain how even those who do not
know or accept Shingon Buddhism are still unwittingly enacting Dainichi's
style, are still empowered with Dainichi's *kaji*. (Just as people who know nothing of their own proprioceptive system still depend on it all the time.)

Hence, Kūkai's goal was to recognize the reality of all positions, identify the
germ of esoteric insight within each, and to *relegate* them to various subordinate regions in Shingon's comprehensive system. As with all Shingon mandalas,
ontology spins off centrifugally from the core of being: the activity of Dainichi
Buddha. At the same time, all things are axiologically pulled centripetally
into the heart of spirituality: the activity of Dainichi Buddha. So, Dainichi's
empowerment is pulling people up through the ten mindsets just as it pulls
practitioners into the middle of the mandala.[104]

There is yet a further sense in which the system of ten mindsets is like a mandala. As I already explained, we can read the Diamond Mandala as a map showing the progress of spiritual praxis (from box nine to box one in my diagram).
Yet, because "the body immediately becomes the Buddha" (the third gloss of
the phrase *sokushin jōbutsu*), one can jump, as it were, from any of the eight
surrounding boxes directly into the center of mandala, merging with Dainichi.
Similarly, one can enter Shingon (mindset ten) directly and immediately from
any other mindset. To shift from the exoteric to the esoteric requires a radical shift in perspective, however. It is a contrast between making progress and
abruptly skipping all intermediate steps to suddenly "get it."[105]*

Yet, at the same time, Kūkai's system also allows that even if we stay within
the exoteric model of understanding, we can still progress in sequence from
one mindset up to the next in the system, at each point gradually expanding
our comprehension of reality. In that progression, to go from the most inclusive exotericism of mindset nine to the all-inclusive esotericism of mindset ten
would be only one further step—however profound and life-changing. In that
way Dainichi's empowerment leads even exoteric Buddhists to progress in the
direction of the esoteric.

How does one accept Dainichi's empowerment? In his preface to *Jūjūshinron*
Kūkai quoted the *Dainichi Sutra*, asserting that enlightenment is, as I noted
above, to "know your own mind (*shin*) as it actually is."[106] As already noted, *shin*
is the intellectual and affective activity that develops concepts, emotions, and
values—in short, world views. So Dainichi's empowerment facilitates spiritual
progress through the person's questioning the basis of his or her own world view.

† See page 64.

This will be clearer if I summarize Kūkai's list of the ten mindsets.†

I. *The Ram-like Mind of Common People*[107] A materialistic, egocentric, hedonistic mindset with no sense of ideals or the ability to regulate desires. Capable of affection but unable to transform it into egoless love. (the nonspiritual mindset driven by animal appetites)

II. *The Abstinent Mind of the Foolish Child.* A socially responsible mindset, following virtues and moral authority robotically like a child. (the mindset of Confucians or overly scrupulous Buddhists attached to rules of asceticism)

III. *The Fearless Mind of the Young Child.* A mindset renouncing the secular world in hopes of transcendent serenity and immortality. Like a newborn suckling, oblivious to the outside world, finding peace only within oneself. (the religious Daoist or any other mindset seeking immortality)

IV. *The Mind of Aggregates-only and No-I.* A mindset appreciative of Buddhist impermanence and the self as an insubstantial aggregate of interrelated processes. In its escapism, cannot recognize the working of the cosmic buddha as this very world. (the Hinayana Buddhist mindset)

V. *The Mind that Has Eradicated the Causes and Seeds of Karma.* Without hearing the doctrines of any teacher, a mindset achieving insight by discovering for itself that the roots of suffering are self-generated delusions. Lacking teacher and community, remains incapable of showing compassion toward others. (the mindset of the masterless, hermit buddhas)

VI. *The Mind of the Mahayana Concerned for Others.* A mindset recognizing experience as mental constructs. Freed of ego, displays a bodhisattva's compassion expressed toward all. Yet, still caught in dualistic distinctions such as that between self and other. (the Hossō Buddhist mindset)

VII. *The Mind Awakened to the Non-Birth of the Mind.* Via the insights of logic and argument, a mindset knowing the emptiness of both mind and object. In emphasizing emptiness, misses the internal relation between language and world. (the Sanron Buddhist mindset)

VIII. *The Unconditioned Mind of the One Path.* Accepting the emptiness of all concepts but affirming their heuristic value, a mindset that sees all approaches as having the same ultimate goal, thereby seeking the oneness of mind as containing all things. Fails to see the delusory nature and limits of a detached standpoint as a basis for knowledge. (the Tendai Buddhist mindset)

---

† To review the basic perspectives of the Six Nara Schools mentioned in this list, see the table on page 94 and the explanations on the pages preceding it.

IX. *The Mind Utterly without Any Nature of Its Own.* A mindset recognizing the complete interpenetration of all things without need for any transcendent principle or a separation between mind and reality. Enlightenment as completely immanent. The most advanced of the exoteric mindsets, but lacking a praxis to move from detached to engaged knowing. (the Kegon mindset)

X. *The Mind of Secret Adornment.* Subordinating all exoteric teachings to the immediacy and comprehensiveness of esoteric practice, a mindset that engages, rather than merely detachedly understands, the interpenetration of all things. (the Shingon Buddhist mindset)

Kūkai's psychological insight was that our experience seems to confirm for each of us our particular mindset because we structure our experiences *through* the mindset. Think of the optimists who see their glasses as half-full and the pessimists who see them as half-empty: the same event, whatever it might be, reinforces each group's dispositional attitude. For Kūkai, that explains the strong grip ignorance can have on us. In its own terms, each delusional mindset seems consistent; it repeatedly confirms itself.

Therefore, as explained in Chapter 2's discussion of psycho-physical propensities,† it is often futile to argue against a wrong view by showing inconsistency or counter-evidence because the delusional mindset itself will skew the evidence or inconsistency to fit its own viewpoint. Assuming that mindsets have confined our own ability to understand the way things truly are, how then can we break through our own self-delusions? How can the mind come to "know itself as it actually is?"

Search for ground. This brings us to a line of analysis popular in Japanese philosophy: what I will call the *search for ground.* Basically, this method assumes that even to understand an idea, not to mention evaluate it, we have to know whence it came, the experiential standpoint and circumstances from which it arose. In Kūkai's case, we know the limits of our own mindset only when we try to fathom how that mindset came about.

For example, if my mindset is that animal drives compel human choice, I should be able to explain the basis for that claim. What animal drive compels me to believe in the dominance of animal impulses? If there were only self-centered animal drives, why would I be able to consider other possibilities (altruism, for example) even if only to reject them? While entrenched in the egocentric standpoint of the first mindset, I will insist I "put myself first" and "watch out for number one." Yet, how could I get the idea of a "myself" without

† See pages 58–62.

a sense of "other," or put myself as "number one" without assuming there are others who are "number two," "number three," and so forth?

Such a train of thought could then lead me to realize that even my idea of self is defined out of a web of social relations. That is, I have to depend on the reality of my relations with others in order to even imagine putting myself first. By looking for the ground of the first mindset, I find it opens into the second mindset: I move out of the mindset of animal urges into Confucianism's humanistic mindset of social relations.

We might wonder if this is an infinite process, each mindset opening up into another as it tries to fathom its own ground. If that were so, the mind could never "know itself as it really is." But what, then, grounds and justifies Kūkai's system of mindsets?

The general issue of a philosophical system's inability to justify itself is a problem not only for Kūkai but for modern western philosophy as well. Immanuel Kant explained the irresolvable antinomies at the basis of any metaphysical system. Bertrand Russell's theory of types tried to find a way out of the logical inconsistencies in set theory once we consider the notion of a set which includes all sets, even itself. Kurt Gödel demonstrated that, despite all attempts to the contrary, no arithmetic system can ground itself. Positivists have grappled with the conundrum of how to verify their own principle of empirical verification.

Common to those modern western projects is the attempt to discover a ground or basis for a theory that would avoid both the Scylla of infinite regress and the Charybdis of circularity. The first peril arises from seeking to justify one theory through another theory, which itself requires a further justification in yet another theory, and so on *ad infinitum*; the second from assuming a theory as part of a proof for the very theory it is trying to validate.

Kūkai's strategy was not to ground his theory in theory at all, neither its own theory nor another one. Instead, he grounds his theory in a theory-praxis nexus where the metaphysics of *hosshin seppō* meets the metapraxis of *sokushin jōbutsu*, where the two mandalas merge. That was why I urged you to undertake the little proprioceptive bodymind experiment so that you could get the point of Kūkai's theory through the actions of your bodymind instead of just as a theory in your mind. The "proof" must not be detached from the praxis.

Degrees of internal relatedness. Kūkai stresses internal relations in his ranking of the ten mindsets. His ranks from one through nine reflect to what degree each of those mindsets recognizes the interpenetration of things over atomistic discreteness: the higher the ranking for the exoteric mindset, the more it is steeped in internal rather than external relations. Let us briefly examine how this plays out in his system.

The Confucians (mindset two), unlike the lowest level of people who see only the animal and egocentric side of human nature, recognize the internal relations among people and their accompanying moral ideals, but do not see the internal relation between the social and natural, which the Daoists (mindset three) do. Yet, the Daoists do not understand that internal relations mean that reality cannot be static, that is, that there can be no immortality (the goal of alchemical Daoism).

Proceeding further along the same lines of analysis, Kūkai argues that the Hinayana Buddhists (mindsets four and five) do understand that interdependence entails rejection of the changeless. Yet, they do not realize that their enlightenment is in an internal relation with the enlightenment of others, the reality which all Mahayanist exoteric Buddhists (mindsets six through nine) do recognize in upholding the principle that enlightenment is universal.[108] The universalistic perspective of the Mahayana Buddhists is a step toward realizing the totality of the microcosmic and its link with the cosmic, but they are not equal in how profoundly they realize that link.

In Kūkai's scheme, all four Mahayana mindsets emphasize their own particular form of nonduality, with the degree of interpenetration among things increasing as one moves up the hierarchy. Specifically, Hossō (mindset six) stresses the internal relation between compassion and wisdom, Sanron (mindset seven) the internal relation between delusion and nirvana, Tendai (mindset eight) the interpenetration of all spiritual paths into the single path to enlightenment, and Kegon (mindset nine) the interpenetration of thing with thing.

What then distinguishes Shingon's esoteric mindset from Kegon's exoteric mindset? That was the issue that incited Kūkai to leave his cave to go to China. Kūkai's interpretation was that Kegon (and, to a slightly lesser extent, Tendai) attained the highest level of understanding available through detached knowing. Strictly through the analysis of the macrocosmic, those mindsets have grasped complete interpenetration as the fundamental nature of reality. By logic and analysis, their exoteric philosophies reached the pinnacle of metaphysical understanding.

Yet, how can that exoteric understanding, spawned as it is from the disembodied intellect, solidify its own foundation? It cannot, at least it cannot if it simply resorts to further theorizing. A full-bodied exoteric theory of the perfect interpenetration of all things such as what we find in Kegon encounters its own logical limit. If people try to fathom the basis of their eighth or ninth mindset, explaining what makes their own mindset possible, they cannot do so from within the mindset. That is, *they* cannot explain their basis for knowing metaphysical interpenetration, because they are *in* it and yet their detached form of knowing requires the knower to be distinct from the known. That leaves them with an ineluctable dilemma. Specifically, the most comprehensive theory of interpenetration, precisely because it is comprehensive, cannot find its justification in either another theory or in itself.

Detached knowledge cannot ground itself in its own detached knowledge. That is why Kūkai believed exotericism could never philosophically suffice as the source of a mindset. To justify a metaphysics of complete interpenetration, Kūkai insisted, one has to confirm it in a way such that the knower and known interpenetrate each other, a model of understanding based in engagement, a form of knowing that involves the whole bodymind. According to Kūkai, only esotericism can supply that. The shift from the exoteric to the esoteric vision of knowledge goes from pure theory to theory-as-praxis. In conclusion: the only mindset that can confirm itself is one based in a model of engaged bodymind rather than detached intellection.

KŪKAI'S CONTRIBUTION TO JAPANESE PHILOSOPHY

Advocating engaged over detached knowing, assimilating opposing views through relegation, philosophizing with bodymind rather than disembodied intellect, searching for ground as an evaluative technique, stressing the holographic relation of whole-in-every-part, distinguishing self-awareness from conceptual reflection, envisioning reality as self-expressive, and engaging in a proprioceptive cosmos—all those aspects of Kūkai's philosophy would shape the trajectory of Japanese philosophy up to today. He may not have invented all those methods and theories on his own, but he did systematize them, supply them with his own arguments, and make them part of the Japanese philosophical tradition. Not limited to the temples, shrines, and academies of philosophy, Kūkai's ideas resonate with the rhythms of everyday Japanese life as well.

Consider this. Before Kūkai, Japan was a world where the mountain mist could respond to a widower's grief, where people believed nature could teach us lessons with a cicada's chirp or a whispering pine or the babbling of a mountain brook, where the somatic was as primary as the intellectual, where ritualized behavior was a primary way to engage the world, and where extraordinary people could do what seemed miraculous. After Kūkai, Japan was a world where the mountain mist could respond to a widower's grief, where people believed nature could teach us lessons with a cicada's chirp or a whispering pine or the babbling of a mountain brook, where the somatic was as primary as the intellectual, where ritualized behavior was a primary way to engage the world, and where extraordinary people could do what seemed miraculous.

In short: thanks to Kūkai, the archaic remained intact in Japan, but it was henceforth draped in a mantle embroidered with a millennium of Buddhism's most grand philosophical insights. Through his thought, words, and deeds,

Kūkai interlaced the urban study centers with the mountains of praxis, Chinese learning with Japanese sensitivities, and animistic spirituality with a system of metaphysics and metapraxis.

In 1929 Alfred North Whitehead wrote in *Process and Reality*, "The safest general characterization of the European philosophical tradition is that it consists of a series of footnotes to Plato."[109] Because of the continuing reverberations of Kūkai's ideas, it is tempting to say the same for him in the Japanese tradition. Yet, it would not be true. Kūkai does not appear in many footnotes. Indeed, except for a small contingent of Buddhist scholars and a handful or two of philosophers, few Japanese even know the details of his theories or works. Yet, everyone knows his name; no one denies his brilliance even if they have no idea what he said. Perhaps Kūkai's greatest marvel was his gradual disappearance from center stage of Japanese intellectual culture. Where did he go?

He disappeared into esotericism (*mikkyō*), a bodymind theory of engaged knowing that would dominate Buddhism, as later chapters will show, for many centuries to come. Moreover, Whitehead's metaphor of the footnote, a discrete citation detached from the main text, is no home for Kūkai and his mantras.

Instead I think of Kūkai's philosophical performance as a riff, one of those classic riffs that every jazz or rock musician knows, but the origin of which is lost to history. The riff is not blindly repeated, but in the highest tribute of appreciation, it is constantly recast, renewed with a new twist or new context. Kūkai's riff is no static reference at the bottom of the page in small print, but the invitation to ever new expressions of creativity. Thus, I venture to suggest that the safest general characterization of the Japanese philosophical tradition is that it consists of a series of riffs on Kūkai.[110*] In the next chapter, we will begin to see how that played out.

4. Shining Prince, Shining Buddha

Heian to Kamakura (794–1333)

Back in the capital
we gazed at the moon, calling
our feelings deep (*aware*)—
mere shallow diversions
that here don't count at all.
SAIGYŌ (1118–1190)[111]

From the ninth through the twelfth centuries, an elite Japanese culture bloomed in the Heian court. To glimpse this cloistered aristocratic society, we can visit Kyoto's Heian Shrine. Because of fires, the buildings are recent. Even the originals dated only from 1895, when the government enshrined there the spirits of the first and last emperors to reside in Kyoto during its tenure as the capital from 794 to 1868. Reproducing a bit of the original Heian court complex, the buildings are smaller than the ninth-century prototypes. Still, they successfully convey the mood of the imperial palace grounds during the Heian period (794–1185).

Passing through the front gate, we find ourselves in the Tang Chinese cultural sphere: vermillion buildings with sloping tiled roofs surrounding a wide expanse of graveled courtyard. (See photo, page 139.) As explained in Chapter 2, in the seventh and eighth century, aristocrats rapidly and enthusiastically assimilated Chinese culture. Moving the capital from Nara-Nagaoka to Heian in what is now Kyoto, the Japanese court could have a fresh start, but the early city planners decided to build again a city modeled on the Chinese capital of Chang'an, much as they had started to do in Nara. The architecture around us at the Heian Shrine proves they did just that.

As we enter the little gate leading to the Heian Shrine gardens, nestled behind the buildings and invisible from the courtyard, the cultural context shifts again. The south garden is our particular interest since it most closely resembles the Heian-period style, punctuated with seasonal colorings from cherry trees, azaleas, irises, and maples. Even some fauna (turtles, fish, and birds) in the garden are species mentioned in court poems of the classical age. The grand expanse of

Chinese-style Heian Palace Courtyard (Heian Shrine)

the Chinese-style palatial courtyard is now just a memory as we lose ourselves in the intimate spaces—mossy banks by a meandering stream, resting spots beneath trellised wisteria, narrow winding gravel pathways—that lent themselves to picnics, moon-viewing parties, romantic trysts, and political intrigue. (See photo, page 140.)

Here we have a portrayal, however limited and concocted, of the setting for Murasaki Shikibu's *The Tale of Genji* and Sei Shōnagon's *Pillow Book*. To go from the Chinese courtyard to the Japanese garden is to follow the Heian aesthetic as it went from something borrowed to something new. No longer simply reflecting Chinese civilization, Heian Japan increasingly refracted the continental influence through its own prism, projecting its own spectrum of Japanese sensitivities.

THE AESTHETIC OF THE HEIAN COURT

The Heian court society was elite, a fraction of one percent of Japan's population. When Heian poets wrote about the emotions of a poor farmer, it was not firsthand information, but pure fantasy. The Heian courtiers spent their days and nights among themselves: composing poems in Chinese or Japanese, admiring or snickering at the color scheme in a woman's seven-layered kimono, writing semi-public diaries and scandal sheets, or trying to guess the author of

Japanese Style Strolling Garden (Heian Shrine)

an unsigned poem from its literary and calligraphic style. Marriages anchored political alliances that lent access to the higher aristocratic echelons even, as the Fujiwara family was particularly adept at proving, to the imperial bloodline itself. The goals were power and wealth; the cultural capital that could secure those goals was courtly elegance or refinement (*miyabi*). The more elegant the person, the more desirable.[112]

An expression of that courtly elegance was an enhanced sensitivity called *aware*, later commonly expressed more fully as *mono no aware*. Deriving from a common exclamation meaning "ah!," it signals coming across something striking. Mixed with attentiveness to the ephemeral, *aware* transformed the traditional Buddhist resignation toward impermanence into an aesthetic of poignancy. The cherry blossoms, for example, are all the more stunning because they bloom for such a short time. The Heian period lacked a developed philosophy of *aware*, but even the use of such a term suggests engagement rather than detached observation.

1257-8

Aware is neither simply in the object nor fully in the human subject, but rather in their convergence as an internal relation. Years of aesthetic cultivation and praxis nurture a sense of *aware*, an acquired sensitivity that transcends mere personal opinion or preference to become an objective insight that can be verified only by another expert with the appropriate training and discipline. Even in our modern technological society, we still recognize such expert knowledge when, for example, we require scientific studies to be peer reviewed by other experts. Or, to cite an example from a different field, only those who spend their careers in gymnastics have the expert knowledge to judge the style of a performance. In like manner, the Heian court was a community of experts in the aesthetics of *miyabi* and *aware*.

To sum up: *aware* is a form of engagement both affective and cognitive, both personal and objective, both somatic in its repetitive praxis and intellectual in its literary expression. In Kūkai's terminology, it arises from the esoteric rather than exoteric. Although *aware* is intensely personal, it is cultivated in community and is subject to peer review. Within *aware* is a sensitivity that enables a person to both know reality and to express it creatively—a recurrent motif in subsequent Japanese philosophy.

Lady Murasaki on Fiction

The emphasis on courtly refinement accompanied the ascent of women's writing as a notable cultural product of Heian Japan. Murasaki Shikibu's *The Tale of Genji* and Sei Shōnagon's *The Pillow Book* (both written around the beginning of the eleventh century) are the most famous of these writings and have come to be classics of not only Japanese but also world literature. Because women generally wrote in Japanese, using only the Japanese syllabary without the Chinese-derived sinographs, they were free of many cultural strictures often imposed on male writers who, except for some poetry and an occasional prose piece, wrote in classical Chinese.[113]

Because words like *aware* did not derive from the Chinese aesthetic vocabulary, such terminology was a step toward Japanizing the aesthetic experience, freeing Japanese notions from Chinese norms. In fact, in the texts written in Japanese by women, we find snippets of philosophical reflection on the difference between Chinese and Japanese values. A famous example is the discussion of fiction within a work of fiction: a conversation, really more a monologue, in Lady Murasaki's *The Tale of Genji*, chapter 25 "Fireflies."[114]

In that chapter, Prince Genji (The Shining Prince) hears that the ladies in his household are whiling away the dreary rainy season by reading and copying romantic novels. Genji catches Tamakazura in the act and chides her for reading fiction, which is, from his male view of literature, just a bunch of lies.

1118–19

"There is hardly a word of truth in all this, as you know perfectly well...." From a narrowly construed Confucian perspective, narratives should engender virtuous behavior by recounting exemplary deeds, but Tamakazura's readings were more titillating than edifying.

Then Prince Genji, thinking aloud, concedes the engaging aspect of the medium:

> ... and yes, we know they are fictions, but even so we are moved and half drawn for no real reason to the pretty, suffering heroine.

It might seem the prince is praising fiction precisely for what Plato distrusted in poetry, namely, its ability to stir the emotions, but that is not Genji's point. For him, fiction's value resides in its particularity and concreteness.

> I have been very rude to speak so ill to you of tales! They record what has gone on ever since the Age of the Gods. The *Chronicles of Japan* and so on give only a part of the story. It is tales that contain the truly rewarding particulars.

Since the topic is fiction, Genji is obviously not referring to the particulars of historical fact. Instead, he is alluding to the details of human feelings and interpersonal relations that fiction can depict so sharply because it is exempt from the need to conform to actual events. We often learn about people by observing how they behave under extraordinary conditions. Yet, to witness such events firsthand in the real world is fortuitous; we must be at the right place at the exact right moment. In contrast, because fiction writers can create the extraordinary circumstances for us at will, their tales open us to new insights about the human situation we could not otherwise access.

> Not that tales accurately describe any particular person; rather, the telling begins when all those things the teller longs to have pass on to future generations—whatever there is about the way people live their lives...—overflow the writer's heart.

Though similar in some ways, the Heian aesthetic of *aware* deviates from Kūkai's esotericism in an important respect. Although both share an appreciation of elegantly ritualized forms, mystery, and the preference for direct engagement over detached observation, the dynamic between the particular and the universal is not the same in the two. For esotericism, because every particular is in holographic relation to the whole, its universal significance derives from its being an inscription of Dainichi's (or reality's) self-expression. That is, the universal meaning comes via the metaphysical connection in the particular.

In *The Tale of Genji*'s aesthetic of *aware*, though, the singularity of the event remains particular while *aware* itself is the generalizing force. To put the contrast starkly: for *aware*, human sensitivity rather than Dainichi, gives the particular its universal import. Through esotericism, we discover the cosmos; through *aware* we discover our humanity. This contrast foreshadows a shift in focus that will be a major theme in Kamakura-period Buddhist philosophy, namely, the transition from the cosmic to the personal.

The quote from *The Tale of Genji* also suggests that fiction arises from the writer's sensitivity to human feeling. In other words, the writing is emotive. A contrast with classical Greek aesthetics is again illuminating. Like Plato, Aristotle thought fiction (mainly drama) could stir up the emotions, but unlike Plato, he found value in that provocation if it leads to an emotional catharsis in the members of the audience. It purges them of their overpowering emotions and thereby calms them for rational contemplation.

By contrast, Murasaki has Prince Genji defend the value of a tale for its capacity to generate empathy with the fictional character. Through fiction, the readers come to better understand and even appreciate their own emotions, an agenda unlike either Confucian didacticism or Aristotelian catharsis. In engaged knowing, you understand another person's emotion not by observing it as an outsider, but by entering into it so you can feel it for yourself. Reading fiction develops such an empathic understanding.

Prince Genji concludes his musings by noting a link between fiction and the Buddhist use of heuristic expressions (*hōben*). As we have seen, a heuristic expression adapts teachings to the members of its audience in order to lead them to a point from which they can achieve insight on their own. Analogously, Genji suggests, fictional tales can teach us about ourselves in ways not otherwise available. Even if fiction is not the deepest truth, it is no empty fabrication; it speaks a truth beyond factual reportage. As if to leave no doubt that Genji represents her own view, Murasaki has the narrator comment at the end, "He mounted a very fine defense of tales."

Murasaki's fictional conversation may not be a tight philosophical argument, but it does circumscribe a specific understanding of language. For Murasaki language is more than just reference and edification. Although fiction depicts states of affairs that never actually occurred, it nonetheless portrays accurately the affairs of the heart. By describing real feelings and human interactions, fictional accounts evoke a corresponding response in their readers. Therefore, *The Tale of Genji* suggests that if Chinese-style didactic literature is for instilling moral virtues, romantic fiction instills sensitivity, the most admired quality of the Heian aesthete. We do in the end find a form of truth in fictional narratives, the truth of genuineness or authenticity referred to as *makoto*.

Such truth is evident only to those sensitized to it, however. Engaging the genuine arouses the impulse to write, the hope being that what engages the author will also engage the reader. Expression makes sensitivity communal, overcoming the separation between writer and reader. In that view of language, the relations among author, language, and audience are clearly internal, perhaps again reminiscent in some respects of Kūkai's theory.

Yet, that view of language omits Kūkai's emphasis on the sound of words and their resonant power. Further, Murasaki's theory of poetics involves conferring with the aesthetic community while responding to the impermanence of things; Kūkai's Shingon theory involves instead conferring with the self-expression of the cosmos itself. Murasaki's language is part of a social, not explicitly religious, praxis. Still, there is much in common between the two theories and both contrast with what I will discuss next.

Sei Shōnagon and the Zuihitsu Style

Murasaki's contemporary, Sei Shōnagon, took a different approach to writing in her *Pillow Book*. Like Murasaki, Sei was free of the strict rules associated with Chinese language and literature as taught to male courtiers, but her response was to just write, developing a literary genre called *zuihitsu*, literally, "following the brush [as it writes along]." Whereas Murasaki emphasized an intimate immersion in events, even fictional ones, Sei stood back from them for the sake of detached observation and comment. The *Pillow Book* amounted to being an eleventh-century Japanese version of a blog in which Sei shared with others whatever struck her fancy that day.[115]

Compared to Murasaki, Sei preserved more of her integrity as a discrete subject, commenting on objects around her instead of losing herself within them. Sei wrote what moved her and, given her personality (which was quite unlike Murasaki's), she was moved most by what brought her a smile or even a smirk. This could be something curiously charming (*okashi*) like pussy willows or, perhaps better yet, the delicious foibles, shenanigans, and *faux pas* of her court contemporaries.

Between Murasaki and Sei we have two parameters defining a space within which styles of Japanese writing flourished over the centuries. With Murasaki we find the touching, the poignant, the acculturated, and the elegant. With Sei we find mixed with her cultivated background the amusing, the cavalier, the spontaneous, and the mundane.[116]

Although the Heian court culture was only a sheltered sliver of Japanese society at the time, subsequent Japanese generations have so esteemed its aesthetic that many of its terms and sensitivities eventually found their way into the popular idiom. Today, when Japanese wear an elegant kimono, read a classical Japanese poem, or engage in the arts of gardening or calligraphy, we feel resonances with that aesthetic legacy. Consider the following anecdote.

I was taking a Japanese tour of a medieval detached imperial palace and the docent pointed to the wall of the room, saying that the artists had tried to achieve a "*miyabi* effect." There was a hush in the crowd and one elderly woman whispered, nodding with recognition and reverence, "Ah, *miyabi*." The general tone was that we had identified something ancient, valuable, and quintessentially Japanese.

Of course, such continuity of tradition does not happen by chance. Tradition is born not in the past but in the present. A culture retrospectively decides what it wants to preserve and how to construe its significance, even if in doing so, the result is more a romanticized reconstruction than a strict retrieval of bygone times. As we will see in Chapter 10, led by Motoori Norinaga, the Native Studies movement in the eighteenth century defined what the Japanese even now think is "traditional" about the Heian aesthetic.

Since the denizens of the Heian court represented only a minuscule portion of the country's population, for a fuller picture of the mood of the times and its spiritual timbre, we must leave the cloistered Heian court and explore the streets, the countryside, and the mountain monasteries.

POPULAR BUDDHISM: AMIDISM

Outside the court walls and beyond the great monastic centers, the ordinary people practiced devotional religion directed toward various buddhas and *kami*. The Nara court had originally resisted the spread of Buddhism among the general populace, but the attempted restrictions eventually proved futile.[117] Kūkai, for example, believed Shingon Buddhism should be widely disseminated. So he advocated using art to illustrate the teachings for the illiterate and at his Temple to the East (Tō-ji) in Kyoto he founded a public school open to all children, regardless of class or gender. The result was that in the Heian period, Buddhist practices and elementary teachings were widespread among the general populace. Buddhism promised people not only spiritual rewards such as rebirth in a heavenly domain presided over by a buddha or bodhisattva, but also material benefits such as bountiful harvests, good health, and easy childbirth.

Buddhist practices did not supplant *kami*-worship because most people thought of buddhas and *kami* as interchangeable deities. Hence, they did not have to choose between being loyal to the Way of the buddhas or the Way of the *kami*. Eventually, esoteric Buddhist metapraxis justified what was already a part of everyday Japanese religious life, devising a theory that maintained that the universal buddha "ground" (*honji*) had local "surface traces" (*suijaku*) in the form of *kami*. According to this *honji suijaku* doctrine, proto-Shintō syncretic practices devoted to the *kami* were, upon deeper understanding, really expressing reverence for buddhas. The theory, therefore, relegated *kami*-

worship to being a subset of esoteric Buddhist praxis, allowing the two to exist harmoniously.

Amida Buddha and the Pure Land

235-41

Of the celestial buddhas and bodhisattvas, Miroku (the Buddha of the future) and Kannon (the bodhisattva of compassion) were especially popular, but Amida (the Buddha of Immeasurable Light and Immeasurable Life) became increasingly prominent in this era. An influential Amidist was the tenth-century itinerant monk, Kūya or Kōya (903–972). Kūya, who in later life took ordination as a Tendai monk, began as a disaffected aristocrat who vowed to follow Buddhism and to live among the common people. He became renowned for his traveling from village to village, doing good deeds and distributing alms, while continuously chanting the *nenbutsu*.

For Kūya and his lay contemporaries, *nenbutsu* meant the recitation of the formula *namu amida butsu* ("I take refuge in Amida Buddha") but, as we will see, other kinds of *nenbutsu* practice would soon gain popularity in the monastic centers. Because Amidism and its associated Pure Land forms of Buddhism will be a theme running throughout this and the next chapter, I will make a few preliminary comments here.

First, what is a pure land? Often considered the same as a buddha realm (*bukkokudo*), in Mahayana Buddhism a pure land (*jōdo*) most broadly means the field of a particular buddha's or bodhisattva's spiritual power and activity. More narrowly, it can refer to the specific realm created by such a buddha when taking the bodhisattva vow to assist others, assuming the distinctive character of that buddha and her or his vow. Although people often understand these pure lands to be actual physical heavens separate from this world, they do not have to be so. The same locale can appear or not appear as a pure land, depending on the observer's state of mind.

For example, for the cosmic embodiment (such as Shingon's Dainichi), the whole cosmos is the pure land. For the historical buddha, Shakyamuni, our human world is a pure land. Meanwhile, celestial buddhas may have their pure lands anywhere in the many universes. Amida's celestial pure land, the Pure Land of Perfect Bliss, is located to the west and is therefore sometimes called the Western Paradise. In East Asia, devotion to Amida Buddha has become so prominent that when people speak of "the pure land" without qualification, they usually mean Amida's Pure Land.

The Pure Land tradition originated in India, developing further in China and Korea (as well as Tibet[118]) before reaching Japan. That span of historical eras and cultures complicates generalities about the Pure Land tradition in all its manifestations. So here I will note just a few key ideas important to Japanese philosophy, beginning with the background narrative of Amida that frames the tradition. For the origin of their tradition, Japanese Pure Land Buddhists recognize three foundational sacred texts called in English, *The Larger Sutra of Immeasurable Life, The Amida Sutra,* and *The Sutra of Contemplation on [the Buddha of] Immeasurable Life* (or simply *The Contemplation Sutra*).[119] The first is most important for its account of Amida's Vow, the gist of its narrative being as follows.

The historical Buddha, Shakyamuni, was with his disciples at Vulture Peak when he was asked about the cause for the unusual glow in his face. The Buddha recounted the story of the bodhisattva Hōzō (S. Dharmākara) who had spiritually developed over countless lifetimes to the point of achieving nirvana. Feeling compassion for his fellow human beings, especially for those spiritually unable to reach enlightenment on their own, he paused to survey the variety of already existing pure lands to determine which characteristics would most assist those who could not help themselves.

As a result, Hōzō vowed to establish a pure land where conditions for Buddhist practice would be so ideal that even those who could not previously succeed in the Buddhist path would now be able to do so. After dying in this world, people could be reborn in his Pure Land, where the spiritual environment would allow them to quickly develop spiritually so as reach the brink of attaining enlightenment. Then they could be reborn again in this world to complete their enlightenment and help others as bodhisattvas. Hōzō Bodhisattva promised that if he could not keep his vow to establish such a pure land, he would not allow himself to become a buddha. Shakyamuni was so pleased that day because he saw that Hōzō had fulfilled his Vow and had become the Buddha, Amida.[120]

Hōzō's vow was actually forty-eight separate vows, detailing the characteristics of his Pure Land and the Way to rebirth in it. For Shinran, the philosopher whom we will engage in our next chapter, the eighteenth vow was the most important. It states (in as convoluted Chinese syntax as the English translation suggests):

> Suppose I [the bodhisattva Hōzō] were to attain Buddhahood [as Amida Buddha]. Suppose sentient beings anywhere had a sincere mind entrusting themselves to me, aspiring to be born in my land, saying my Name even ten times, and then suppose they were (still) not born in my land. If that were to be the case, then may I not attain the supreme enlightenment [and become Amida Buddha]. Excluded are those who have committed the five grave offenses[121] or who have slandered the buddha's true teachings.

One consequence of the peculiar wording is that when the Pure Land Buddhist "takes refuge in Amida Buddha," that implicitly means the person trusts that the vows have been fulfilled, because if they had not, there would not be an Amida Buddha but only a Hōzō Bodhisattva.

The other vows most often cited by Japanese commentators, all with similar wording, can be summarized as follows:

> 11th: guarantees enlightenment will be attained in the Pure Land.
>
> 12th: guarantees Amida will be a buddha of immeasurable light.
>
> 13th: guarantees Amida will be a buddha of immeasurable life.
>
> 17th: guarantees all buddhas will praise the name of Amida.
>
> 19th: guarantees Amida will appear at the deathbed of the devout Buddhist who has lived a meritorious life and sincerely wishes rebirth in the Pure Land.
>
> 20th: guarantees rebirth in the Pure Land to everyone who hears Amida's name, sincerely wishes to be reborn there, and turns all the merits of their good deeds over to that wish.
>
> 22nd: guarantees that those born in the Pure Land may out of compassion return to this world to help others.

Besides their intricate language, the vows' sheer variety opens them to multiple interpretations, but let us not lose sight of the main point: they reflect the characteristics of the Pure Land that Hōzō specifically selected as being most relevant in helping those people who could not achieve enlightenment strictly through their own efforts. So the vows respond to a spiritual crisis and presume an assessment of the human situation. In short: they derive from a philosophical anthropology, a theory of what is means to be human.

Are all forty-eight vows equally important? What exactly do the vows require of us so that we can be born in Amida's Pure Land? We know the power of the vows to create a pure land, but do the vows have power to transform us as well? Why do we need Amida's help to engage reality as it is? How could there have been so many people in history who reached enlightenment without the help of Amida's Pure Land? Such questions became the stuff of Pure Land philosophizing in both China and, later, Japan.[122]

Mappō: The Degenerate Age

I will treat the further unfolding of Pure Land religion and philosophy at appropriate places in the rest of this book including Chapter 5's engagement with the Pure Land philosopher, Shinran. Still, there is one further point that had a great impact on not only Japanese Pure Land thought, but also Japanese Buddhism in general. Indeed its earliest mention in Japan traces back to Shōtoku's commentaries. I am referring to the notion of mappō, what I will usually call simply the Degenerate Age.[123] Mappō literally means "the Dharma of the final (era)," the term dharma in this case meaning the truth as expressed by the historical buddha, Shakyamuni.

According to a venerable Buddhist teaching, after the death of Shakyamuni, the ensuing centuries would bring a gradual decline in people's ability to achieve enlightenment. The Buddhist truths—its doctrines and praxis—remain always true, of course, and human nature does not change, but external circumstances certainly do. Insights get watered down, values co-opted, institutions corrupted, and good intentions sidetracked. The Japanese thinkers treated in this book generally assumed three phases in this process.

The first period after Shakyamuni's death is when conditions were correct or ideal for understanding, praxis, and spiritual achievement. In Japanese, that is known as *shōbō*, "the dharma of the correctness (era)." In the second phase the conditions look right, but are not: religious institutions continue, but people in them only go through the motions of studying doctrine and performing the praxis. In Japanese that is called *zōbō*, "the dharma of the semblance (era)." Lastly, there is a period in which conditions have so obviously deteriorated that there can no longer be even the pretense that understanding, praxis, and spiritual achievement are possible. That is *mappō*, the Degenerate Age. Pure Land Buddhists who accepted the three-phase theory believed they were living in that final phase.

Having explained those general facts about the Pure Land tradition, I now return to the related Japanese historical events of philosophical significance. Although popular Pure Land practices were prevalent in Japan by the ninth or tenth century, philosophical reflection within the tradition did not mature until the late twelfth century. When it did, it drew on Tendai and Shingon ideas that had arisen in the interim. So let us see what was happening in those traditions after Saichō and Kūkai.

TENDAI AFTER SAICHŌ

In the ninth century both Saichō's Tendai Buddhism and Kūkai's Shingon Buddhism continued to flourish. The most significant Tendai trend was toward increasing esotericism. As I briefly mentioned in Chapter 4, while in China, in addition to his focused study of exoteric Tiantai Buddhism, Saichō had fortuitously happened upon a teacher of esoteric Buddhism who initiated him into some practices before his return to Japan in 805. Upon returning home, Saichō's immediate goal was to expand his temple on Mt Hiei in northeastern Kyoto, transforming it into a major monastic center for study and praxis. But the emperor had a different priority.

Emperor Kanmu (737–806) so fancied the esoteric strain of Buddhism Saichō had introduced to Japan that he almost immediately constructed on Mt Takao in northwest Kyoto an ordination platform for Saichō to use in esoteric rituals. Furthermore, in granting Saichō two annual imperial ordinations for Tendai, Kanmu stipulated that one would be for Tendai exoteric meditation practice and one for esoteric rituals devoted to Dainichi Buddha, the Great Sun Buddha at the center of most Japanese esoteric practices. Hence, the incorporation of esotericism into Japanese Tendai Buddhism might have originally been accidental, but by the time of Saichō's death, it became a defining characteristic of the tradition.

Tendai Esotericism

After Kūkai's return from China, Saichō (unlike the court), quickly saw the value of Kūkai's unique training. Saichō befriended him, making copies of his esoteric texts and ritual implements as well as receiving instructions about higher-level rituals. Saichō also sent students to Kūkai for personal instruction when Kūkai set up residence in Kyoto at Mt Takao. Relations between the two monks eventually soured, though, perhaps because Kūkai had realized that bolstering the esoteric profile of Tendai would only hinder the flourishing of his own esoteric Shingon school. In any case, Tendai would have to turn elsewhere to further its esoteric aspirations.

One of Saichō's disciples, Ennin (794–864), played a key role in that effort. Saichō died in 822, followed by Kūkai in 835. Three years later, Ennin ended his three-decade sojourn on Mt Hiei to go to China, where he spent nine years. Ennin divided his time among mastering the practices of esoteric Buddhism, studying Tiantai exoteric doctrine, and trying to stay out of jail.[124] Returning to Japan in 847, Ennin advanced Tendai esotericism by putting its teachings on equal status with those of the *Lotus Sutra*. He argued that the *Lotus Sutra* and esotericism both teach a single, universal vehicle or path, avoiding the distinctions among the vehicles or branches of Buddhism important to other schools. In other words: both Tendai and Shingon excelled at systematizing and relegating all other traditions. Ennin even admitted that when it came to praxis, the esoteric was superior to Tendai's exoteric methods.

Saichō himself had placed no special emphasis on Amida in either doctrine or practice, but that was not the case for his successors. In fact, Ennin introduced Pure Land practices to Mt Hiei, bestowing them with the prestige of the monastic center's approval. In particular, Ennin established there a select form of meditation that involved chanting the *nenbutsu* while circumambulating a statue of Amida. As the practice became institutionalized on Mt Hiei, it required a monk to spend ninety days[125] of continuously circling the image, visualizing the Pure Land, and chanting the *nenbutsu* formula. The practice became so popular on Mt Hiei that all three precincts of the temple complex built their own halls for the express purpose of that practice.

Enchin (814–891) advanced Tendai's esoteric agenda even further. During his visit to China (853–858), he not only studied exoteric Buddhism at the Tiantai monastery, but also went to Chang'an specifically for esoteric ordinations. Upon his return, he wrote a commentary on the *Dainichi Sutra*, claiming its doctrines and teachings superior to all exoteric sutras, even those of the *Lotus Sutra*.

The relegating of the exoteric under the esoteric reached its apex when Annen (841–?) replaced the traditional Tendai ranking of the four teachings that had placed the *Lotus Sutra* in the highest position with a five-tiered list that placed esotericism above the *Lotus Sutra*. Annen even suggested the esoteric teachings be called *Shingon*. Obviously, if Tendai were to remain true to the balance between exoteric and esoteric that Saichō had imagined, it would have to rein in esotericism's rise to supremacy. As abbot of Mt Hiei, Ryōgen (912–985)[126] undertook that task.

Ryōgen's Reforms

Ryōgen's reforms broadly influenced the subsequent evolution of Japanese philosophy in various ways. Most notably, he reestablished and made more rigorous the Tendai tradition of public examinations and debates, mastery in that area being requisite to promotion in monastic rank.[127] That brought Tendai training out of the one-on-one environment of the secretive esoteric master-student relation to reemphasize the exoteric teachings on which those examinations and debates focused.

With that change, Tendai's main temples became, on one hand, centers of learning attractive to nobles seeking an alternative to the Confucian-based academies of the aristocratic families or the imperial college for training government bureaucrats. On the other hand, for commoners enrollment in a Tendai monastery became one of the few options for a high-quality education. Therefore, without demeaning esotericism, Ryōgen reinvigorated the exoteric roots of the Tiantai teachings Saichō had brought from China, transforming the Mt Hiei monastic complex into an institution within which one could undertake almost any kind of Buddhist study or practice.

The result was that by the late Heian period, Mt Hiei was a preferred site for the education of bright young men with the requisite talent and ambition regardless of whether they were aristocrats or commoners. In light of those developments, it is not surprising that the major philosophical thinkers in the ensuing Kamakura period typically began their careers as Tendai monks training on Mt Hiei. Of the topics commonly chosen for examination and debate, that of radical enlightenment had perhaps the greatest impact on subsequent Japanese Buddhist thinking.

The doctrine of radical or inherent enlightenment ("hongaku"). As explained in Chapter 2, from its origins in India some twenty-two centuries ago, Mahayana Buddhism has insisted on the inseparability between the realm of enlighten-

92–103

ment (nirvana) and the realm of delusion (*saṃsāra*). As this notion made its way from India into China and beyond, the East Asians added two corollaries.

First, if this world is already the world of enlightenment, the problem is not gaining enlightenment, but rather realizing enlightenment as already present while deactivating delusions that constrain our engaging the world as it is. The Japanese term for this "inherent (original, primordial, or radical) enlightenment" is *hongaku*,[128] whereas the term for coming to realize what has been there all along is "initialized (or acquired) enlightenment" (*shikaku*). Defining the relation between the two became a priority for Tendai philosophy and praxis.

The second corollary to the inseparability between enlightenment and delusion was that because delusion is a product of *human* thinking, all other beings must be free of it, suggesting that all nonhuman beings are intrinsically enlightened or, in more precise terminology, all beings have *buddha-nature*. After centuries of debate, Tendai doctrine explicitly stated this to be true even of nonsentient natural objects such as grasses and trees or mountains and rivers.[129]

This conclusion may at first seem odd, but it is not really surprising given what we have seen so far. On one hand, according to Mahayana exoteric teaching, the triple embodiment theory entails that the entire cosmos is the reality-embodiment of buddha. Therefore, the cosmos as a whole is enlightened in some respect. On the other hand, in esoteric teaching, everything is the expressive activity of the cosmic Buddha, Dainichi. So, in that context as well, as self-expressions of Dainichi, all things are aspects of Dainichi's enlightened function.

The discussions concerning inherent enlightenment and universal buddha-nature in East Asian Buddhist history are diverse and often technical, so I will touch on them only as needed when explaining the philosophers we are considering.[130] It is not difficult, however, to see the sweeping philosophical implications. To put it simply: humans are the only glitch in the perfection of the universe. If enlightenment is a way of engaging the world, we—not the world—hinder that engagement by failing to initialize the enlightenment within us that makes authentic engagement possible.

How and why does that happen? What does this tell us about our human situation? Those would be central questions for many Japanese philosophers during the twelfth and thirteenth centuries. The queries about human nature, the particularities of the human predicament, and our failure to achieve enlightenment echo the aforementioned Pure Land concerns. That overlap between Pure Land and Tendai brings us to Ryōgen's second important contribution to the climate of Heian-Kamakura philosophy.

Ryōgen and Amidism. Ryōgen had a personal affinity for Amidism and Pure Land practices. For him, *nenbutsu* meant visualization more than the vocalization stressed by Kūya. So, he reemphasized the Amida-centered walking meditation originally brought to Mt Hiei by Ennin. In general, for Ryōgen *nenbutsu* was merely one aspect of a complex Tendai praxis involving an array of techniques, texts, and buddhas. Still, partly because of Ryōgen's reaffirmation of Pure Land practices on Mt Hiei, anyone who trained there and followed the standard regimen would have contact with Amidism, forging a connection between a high-church praxis among the mountain monastics and the everyday praxis of many common people in the cities and rural areas. That synergy would drive Pure Land developments in the Kamakura period.

Building the socioeconomic network for Tendai dominance. Ryōgen's third contribution was not itself philosophical, but did have a long-range impact on the context in which later philosophers worked. Specifically, he successfully aligned Tendai with secular political and economic power. From Saichō's first attempts to secure patronage for his fledgling school of Buddhism, Tendai had always claimed its existence directly benefited the country. For example, Saichō had argued that his Mt Hiei temple's location northeast of Kyoto could defend the city from the evil spirits who normally attack from that direction. Along those same lines, since its inception, Tendai had routinely performed rites to protect the state, to restore health, to foster prosperity, to ensure fortunate rebirth, and even to give one a thaumaturgical advantage in court politics. Tendai's ever-growing repertoire of esoteric rituals only enhanced its offerings.

Tendai's political influence continued to grow through the ninth century as Ennin and Enchin had allied themselves with the aforementioned Fujiwara, an aristocratic family on the rise. By the end of that century, the Fujiwara had become the most powerful political force in Japan, ruling the country through a regency system that allowed them to manipulate the throne almost at will. Their family temple in Nara, Kōfuku-ji, was a center for the Hossō school.

Of the six Nara schools, Hossō kept the strongest profile throughout the Heian period, being a major rival to Tendai. In response, Ryōgen undertook the effort to cement stronger relations with the Fujiwara and soon many ordained members of the Fujiwara held positions of authority within the monastery on Mt Hiei. By massaging those connections, Tendai's monasteries received as gifts extensive, tax-free landed estates throughout the country, guaranteeing them a generous annual income and national influence.

A darker side of Tendai's good fortune was that the accumulation of wealth and power obliged the need for armed security. As a result, the larger temple complexes formed brigades of armed monks who could defend it from attack. After a while, it became clear that the warrior monks could construe "attack" and "defense" rather loosely to include taking military action to settle doctrinal differences and mounting preemptive strikes against just about anyone else with an army, whether secular or clerical. At one point, Mt Hiei's clerical army swelled to over 10,000 men and other temples, regardless of sectarian affiliation, often followed suit. As we will see later in this chapter, the resultant secular, materialist, and domineering climate often disheartened the Kamakura philosophers who eventually left Mt Hiei and initiated religious movements of their own.

97–101

Genshin

Genshin (942–1017), like his master Ryōgen, strengthened Mt Hiei's profile in multiple areas. First, the rigors of Ryōgen's open examinations and debates inspired Genshin to write a treatise aimed at training students in logic and argument, in part to make them more competitive against their Hossō rivals in public debates.[131] Second, Ryōgen's political connections helped Genshin secure an appointment as a court monk, giving him access to the highest echelons of secular power. Third, and historically most significantly, Ryōgen's interest in the Pure Land set the stage for Genshin's own, even more intense, commitment to that tradition. A sign of that commitment was that despite his stellar career in scholarship and politics, Genshin eventually retired from the center of activities on Mt Hiei to live in a small hermitage on the mountain. While residing there, his study and praxis of Pure Land Buddhism culminated in the work for which he is most famous, *The Essentials for Attaining Birth in the Pure Land*.

Essentials not only details the bliss of Amida's Pure Land for his devotees' rebirth, but also vividly describes the torments of hell, the site of rebirth for those who turned their backs on Buddhist teachings and praxis. The bulk of the work, though, analyzes specific practices leading to rebirth in the Pure Land. Following the Tendai penchant for hierarchical categories and heuristic expression, Genshin outlined a spectrum of practices from the most sublime for those of highest spiritual talents to the most simple for those of limited abilities.

Even within the practices for the spiritually more gifted, Genshin rated them from the most transcendent and rarefied methods of meditating holistically on Amida down to lower practices focused on only one of the Buddha's characteristics. Ranked lower than all visualization practices was the vocal recitation of the *nenbutsu,* a technique so simple Genshin thought anyone could follow it. Accordingly, Genshin followed his teacher Ryōgen in considering the vocalized *nenbutsu* as inferior to the visualized *nenbutsu*: to simply chant "*namu amida butsu*" was only for those lacking in self-discipline or spiritual acuity.

The Heian court community quickly embraced Genshin's *Essentials*, especially for its splendid accounts of the Pure Land. Yet, the book was also a hit among the general populace, especially when illustrations were added as street-corner preachers devised sermons around the work while unrolling the picture scrolls. For the common people, the simplicity of the Pure Land teachings was an appreciated relief from the abstract doctrines of other Buddhist traditions. Moreover, like Dante's *Divine Comedy,* Genshin's *Essentials* attracted the attention of the commoners more for its depictions of hell than paradise, adding a fire-and-brimstone dimension to some Pure Land preaching such that many likely practiced the *nenbutsu* as much to avoid hell as to ensure rebirth in the Pure Land.

In summary: for the Heian courtiers, Genshin's portrayal of the Pure Land held out the hope of an afterlife in the most exquisite spiritual circumstances. Genshin's *Essentials* let them imagine a transition from the court of Genji, the Shining Prince, to the Pure Land of Amida, the Buddha of Infinite Light. For the general populace, meanwhile, Genshin's book held the prospect for a better existence after this life, one certainly better than hell, but also better than the circumstances of many ordinary people in this world.

The plight of those ordinary people worsened as the Heian period progressed from its latter stages into the Kamakura period (1185–1333). Before turning to those turbulent events, however, we will examine what was happening within Shingō Buddhism during the Heian period after Kūkai.

SHINGON AFTER KŪKAI

Shingon's trajectory during the Heian period resembled Tendai's in some ways: forging alliances with the court and aristocracy, amassing wealth through landed estates, mustering armies, and competing with rival religious groups. The major difference was the cult of personality that had coalesced around Kūkai's charisma, lending Shingon cultural capital to exchange for political influence and wealth. For understanding this phenomenon, the final sixteen years of Kūkai's life are particularly important. By the time Saichō died in 822, Kūkai was already becoming Japan's most prominent Buddhist celebrity. The court esteemed him as an artist, poet, intellectual, and wonder-worker, as well as religious leader. Furthermore, unlike Saichō, who spent the final two decades of his life in contestation with the Nara Schools, Kūkai wooed the Nara Buddhist leadership to Shingon's advantage.

For example, in 822 Nara's Great Temple to the East (Tōdai-ji) built Shingon-in, an esoteric subtemple, and in the following year the emperor appointed Kūkai abbot of Kyoto's most prominent urban temple, the Temple to the East, Tō-ji. In doing so, the emperor also took the unusual action of deeding the temple to Shingon in perpetuity. In 827 Gomyō (750–834), the most prominent Hossō scholar from Nara and one of Saichō's severest critics, received a prominent post at Tō-ji, thereby strengthening even more the link between Kūkai and the Nara Buddhist elite. Throughout that period, with imperial approval Kūkai continued work on his major mountain complex on Mt Kōya to which he retired in 832 until he passed on in 838.

As a result, by the end of his career Kūkai had fostered three major Shingon centers: the massive isolated complex on Mt Kōya, the urban Temple to the East in Kyoto, and the mountain temple outside Kyoto on Mt Takao (which had originally been given to Saichō for esoteric initiations). In the immediately ensuing centuries, the former two centers competed over which would be Shingon's main headquarters. In that rivalry the Temple to the East had the advantage of proximity to the court, whereas Mt Kōya had the advantage of including Kūkai's mausoleum, a site of inestimable spiritual potency.

Kūkai's thaumaturgical powers were legendary even in his own time, but his reputation only escalated after death. In fact, as explained in the last chapter, in the subsequent centuries, a mythos around Kūkai's enduring status arose, the popular account being that Kūkai never died, but instead entered permanent meditation waiting for the age of Miroku, the buddha of the future. Miroku is a bodhisattva who will come into the world in the distant future when all the followers will be able to achieve enlightenment together. Over time the faithful came to believe that Kūkai himself was an incarnation of Miroku and as the centuries passed, many of Japan's elite wanted to be associated with Kūkai even in death. Consequently, Mt Kōya's cemetery became a premier resting place for the ashes of Japan's rich and famous.

75–80

Kakuban's Shingon Amidism

Perhaps as a side effect of his unparalleled charisma even in death, Kūkai had no immediate major successors that would expand his Shingon teachings as Ennin or Enchin had done for Tendai. Furthermore, since Shingon, unlike Tendai, was from the start esoteric to its core, it felt no urgency to develop further in that direction. Probably the most important thinker after Kūkai in Heian-period Shingon was Kakuban (1095–1143), also one of the most creative thinkers on Amidism during that era.

We saw that earlier in the Heian period there had been an increasing number of practices that blurred the distinction between buddhas and *kami*. In response, the aforementioned metapractical theory of *honji suijaku*[†] emerged as an esoteric Buddhist strategy for relegating *kami* practices into a subordinate position under the umbrella of esoteric Buddhism. Now at the end of the eleventh century, we find an emphasis on various Amidist practices that begged for

[†] See pages 145–6.

more formal explanation and justification. Was there a way to relegate Amidism into the two dominant traditions of Tendai and Shingon?

Whereas Ryōgen and Genshin had both strongly advocated *nenbutsu* practice, they did so only as one of an array of different Tendai practices. In effect, Tendai had relegated Amidism to being just one of its many visualization disciplines. For Kakuban that would not suffice and in response he created a Shingon metapraxis, a theory justifying the praxis of Amidism that superseded any Amidist theory that Tendai had devised up to that time.

Such a Shingon metapraxis would have to answer questions like the following: What is the precise relation between Amida and Dainichi? If a particular Amidist devotional practice is spiritually effective, how can Shingon explain that efficacy? How far can one progress by focusing on Amida instead of on the multiplicity of buddhas in the Shingon pantheon represented in the traditional mandalas?

For the question about the relation between Amida and Dainichi, Kakuban offered a simple metaphysical explanation. Given the mandala system, all the buddhas, including Amida, emanate from, and are grounded in, Dainichi. Since the holographic paradigm demands the part contain the configuration of the whole, we can just as well state the relation from the opposite direction: as part of the cosmos, each buddha also contains, or *is*, the cosmic buddha in some way.[132] Therefore, by becoming intimate with Amida through a suitable praxis, one fathoms the source of Amida, namely, Dainichi.

That traditional Shingon understanding served as Kakuban's philosophical point of departure. Specifically, he stressed that Shingon has always taught that Amida is one of Dainichi's "five wisdoms" and, as is usually the case in Shingon holographic logic, to grasp completely one part is to comprehend the whole. This had critical implications for praxis.

As a Shingon Buddhist, Kakuban obviously believed all praxis should be esoteric rather than exoteric and so his Amidist praxis would necessarily involve the three intimacies of mind, speech, and body; the three acts of thought, word, and deed; the three practices of visualizing, vocalizing, and gesturing. In particular, Kakuban's Amidist praxis was a tripartite ritual performance: picturing Amida, intoning a special mantra, and enacting the gesture of a secret mudra. One might assume the mantra would be the standard vocalized *nenbutsu: namu amida butsu*. Not so. In the Shingon esoteric system, Amida already had his own mantras.[133] In fact, Kakuban took pains to explicate the various layers of meaning and significance in the three syllables of Amida's name to demonstrate that the name itself constitutes a mantra.[134]

The form of the praxis advocated by Kakuban allowed him to argue metapractically that the validity of *nenbutsu* praxis (broadly defined here as "being mindful of Amida") depends on its being esoterically, not exoterically, interpreted. The ordinary, that is exoteric, notion detaches the practitioner from Amida. Distinguishing own-power from other-power, imagining the Pure Land as a place distant from this world in which one can be born after death, enumerating Amida's forty-eight vows—all these were for Kakuban exoteric teachings that treat Amida as separate from us and his Pure Land as detached from this realm in which we currently live.

In Kakuban's esotericism, by contrast, the characteristic Shingon concepts apply to Amidism. That is, the buddha enters me and I enter the buddha (*nyūga ganyū*); the only "power," whether self or other power, is the dynamic of empowerment (*kaji*); and the Pure Land as the site of enlightening activity is available right here and now in this very body (*sokushin jōbutsu*). To the extent invocation practice has any value, Kakuban insisted, is by reason of its mantric efficacy. By intoning it, one gains access to the common ground where Amida and the practitioner are inseparable and, since Amida is inseparable from Dainichi, Amidism amounts to being an alternative route to the basic Shingon experience of merging self and Dainichi.

In some respects, Kakuban's approach paralleled the Tendai Pure Land thought found in Ryōgen and Genshin. Both Mt Hiei and Mt Kōya were seeking ways to integrate Pure Land practices and Amidist devotion into their greater Tendai and Shingon doctrinal syntheses. There are important differences, however, in their respective approaches. First of all, because of the emphasis on mantra as one of the three intimate practices, Kakuban's Shingon Amidism gave equal weight to invocation and visualization, whereas Ryōgen and Genshin stressed the latter.

Second, and more philosophically significant, were strategic differences in how Tendai and Shingon tried to assimilate Amidism. In the Tendai case the integration was a matter of finding within Tendai theory and praxis an appropriate niche into which one could relegate Amidism. In Kakuban's case, by contrast, his argument was that, if it is practiced esoterically, Amidism is— like any other part of the Shingon system—the whole system. When properly understood, Amidism is not part of Shingon; it *is* Shingon.[135*] This is a direct application of the whole-in-every-part thinking Shingon associates with the mandala. As we will now see, that holographic way of thinking was central to much philosophy in the Kamakura period as well.

NEW RELIGIOUS MOVEMENTS IN THE KAMAKURA PERIOD (1185–1333)

A suitable term for characterizing the transition from Heian to Kamakura is *de-centering*, a process that began with upheavals in the social and political spheres. Through the latter part of the Heian period, the aristocrats resided for increasingly long periods at the court, leaving their provincial estates in the hands of stewards who would guard them and collect taxes from the peasants. Those stewards formed the basis for the later *samurai* ("those who serve") or *bushi* ("military gentry") class. As time passed, the samurai assumed almost complete management of the estates' financial and military responsibilities and by the early twelfth century, the court aristocrats had become so politically effete that the newly risen samurai started seizing the estates and then fighting among themselves for territory. During the Genpei War in 1185 the Minamoto clan destroyed its major competition, the Taira, and seven years later, Minamoto no Yoritomo (1147–1199) was granted by imperial decree the hereditary title of *shōgun*, the general in charge of governing the country.[136]

The Kamakura Zeitgeist

Yoritomo ruled from his military base in Kamakura, about fifty kilometers southwest of what is today Tokyo and 350 kilometers from Kyoto's imperial court. In its competition with the court, the Kamakura shogunate (*bakufu*, literally "tent government") may have had the power of the sword, but it lacked the cultural charisma and authority of the emperor. It also lacked the funds to support its military allies well enough to guarantee stability. So, the Minamoto shogunate, even under the Yoritomo, continued to show deference to the throne. To acquire the accoutrements of cultural sophistication, the shogunate looked to scholars, intellectuals, and Buddhist priests to lend the former military outpost of Kamakura some polish and a luster of cosmopolitanism.

When Yoritomo died in 1199, rule was turned over to his eldest son, but the boy was no leader, a point immediately clear to Yoritomo's widow Hōjō Masako (1157–1225) and to her father Hōjō Tokimasa (1138–1215), who had been one of Yoritomo's closest advisors. Masako had taken tonsure as a Buddhist nun after her husband's death, a common practice for widows at the time, but she remained active in politics, which was not so common.

The family relations reveal something of the delicacy in the dynamics of power. The Hōjō clan was of the Taira lineage, the losers in the decisive Genpei War to the Minamoto. In an earlier skirmish between the two families, however, the Taira had defeated the Minamoto and Yoritomo's father had been executed. The rest of his family was exiled to Kamakura and held hostage by the Hōjō branch of the Taira, Tokimasa being charged with holding Yoritomo in custody. But Tokimasa was not the only Hōjō keeping an eye on the young Yoritomo. So did his daughter, Masako, who on her wedding day abandoned her intended spouse to elope with Yoritomo. Tokimasa apparently had little objection since he had already been impressed with Yoritomo's abilities and when total war between the Minamoto and Taira broke out, he fought on Yoritomo's side against his own Taira family.

Thus, the Minamoto and Hōjō families came to be bound by blood, love, and power. When Masako and her father saw the weakness of her first son as the new shogun, they replaced him with the second, eventually making Tokimasa regent. This initiated the Hōjō regency which controlled the Kamakura shogunate until it fell. The end result was that the Minamoto victors over the Taira ended up under the control of a scion of the Taira family, namely the Hōjō. Yet, Masako did not hesitate to intervene in the name of her own legacy. At one point, she caught wind of a plot that her father was going to replace her son with his own second wife's son and Masako promptly had her father exiled. She clearly deserved her sobriquet, "the nun shogun."

Meanwhile, for about a century before, the power of the seated emperor was itself mitigated by "cloistered emperors," that is, emperors who abdicated the throne only to exercise greater power from behind the scenes. In 1221, the then current cloistered emperor, Go-Toba (Toba II), thought he saw the chance to snatch back the power from the shogunate. Many regional warlords, especially those from the Kansai area surrounding Kyoto rather than the Kantō area surrounding Kamakura, had previously tried in vain to wrestle power from the Kamakura shogunate, but Go-Toba calculated that the tipping point had been reached and he could forge an alliance that would succeed. He had miscalculated, however, and his armies were crushed in record time, Go-Toba being exiled to an island in the Sea of Japan. As a result, the shogunate became stronger than ever by confiscating the lands of the rebellious aristocrats and regional warlords, turning them over to allies.

The problems of the central government were just the tips of the iceberg, however, as the stability of the religious institutions also started to deteriorate. The armies from various Buddhist temples were periodically inflicting havoc on one another in the form of raids, assassinations, and arson. The armed conflicts on both the religious and political fronts brought brutal hardships to the disenfranchised in rural and urban areas alike. Japan has little arable land and unfortunately, those flatlands are good sites not only for farming and urban development, but also for staging large battles. As centers of wealth and power, the cities, of course, were also vulnerable targets for marauders.

As if the wreckage from human violence was not enough, plagues, famines, fires, volcanoes, typhoons, tsunami, and earthquakes were unusually devastating during this period as well, making everyday life all the more precarious. Vivid accounts from the time describe Kyoto with rotting corpses piled up along the street to be taken away. It was as if people no longer needed a picture scroll to see Genshin's hells; they needed only to look out their windows. A vignette from Kamo no Chōmei's *An Account of My Hut* concerning the famine of 1181 vividly portrays the horror of living in Kyoto at the time:

> The number of those who died of starvation outside the gates or along the roads may not be reckoned. There being no one even to dispose of the bodies, a stench filled the whole world, and there were many sights of decomposing bodies too horrible to behold. Along the banks of the Kamo River there was not even room for horses and cattle to pass....
>
> In the case of husbands and wives who refused to separate, the ones whose affections were the stronger were certain to die first. This was because whether man or woman, they thought of themselves second and gave to their beloved whatever food they occasionally managed to get. With parents and children it inevitably happened that the parents died first. Sometimes an infant, not realizing that its mother was dead would lie beside her, sucking at her breast.[137]

So began the Kamakura period and the need for a new set of philosophical and religious orientations. There was little time for, or comfort in, metaphysical speculations. To many people, esoteric Buddhism's promise of being absorbed into and absorbing the cosmos through the ritualistic empowerment of Dainichi seemed pathetically irrelevant. People were too preoccupied with their own survival to construct grand metaphysical schemes that purported to be theories of everything. Instead, the philosophers turned their analyses to the problems of this world, their speculations to wondering what failing in humanity had caused such suffering, and their innovative thinking to devising spiritual strategies to rescue themselves. Pure Land, Zen, and Nichiren Buddhism—what scholars call the "new Buddhisms of the Kamakura period"—were the major philosophical-religious responses to the crisis.

The Heian religions of Shingon and Tendai had highlighted comprehensiveness and inclusiveness. Tendai, probably the more powerful of the two at the time, used the metaphor of the circle (*en*) to represent its all-embracing character that included all teachings and practices whether exoteric or esoteric. Rather than Tendai completeness, rather than Kūkai's complex system for understanding everything, the founders of the new Kamakura religious movements would stress instead simplicity in both doctrine and praxis. Urgency inculcates focus. Complexity was an intellectual and spiritual luxury the reformers felt they could no longer afford.

As young men or even as boys, many of Japan's brightest males had gravitated to the center of the circle, the point from which all intelligibility and insight seemed to emanate—the Tendai monastery and learning establishment on Mt Hiei. Some stayed for decades; others for only a few years. But a significant number of the gifted left discouraged when they found that centrifugal forces of social, cultural, economic, and political fragmentation had shattered the Tendai

Lecture Hall of Mt Hiei's Enryaku Temple

circle of wholeness. Without a circle, there could be no center, the Tendai synthesis now seeming no more than a will-o'-the-wisp. In light of their abandoning Tendai to found new religious groups, we find something surprising if we today take the cable car and ropeway from Kyoto up Mt Hiei to visit Enryaku-ji, the headquarters of the Tendai sect. There we can visit the Lecture Hall in the main Eastern Precinct of the temple complex.

In the original of the building pictured above, the monks gathered to hear lectures on Tendai doctrine, both esoteric and exoteric. Philosophically speaking, this hall was the intellectual center of the center. In today's building, we find portraits and sculptures of the great Kamakura-period religious figures who studied there such as Hōnen, Shinran, Eisai, Dōgen, and Nichiren. The presence of those images is startling in that they depict men associated with the founding of religious traditions that split off from Tendai. It is as if one were to visit Vatican City and find images of Luther, Calvin, and Knox in Saint Peter's Basilica.

How can this be? The obvious answer is economic: tourist-pilgrims by the tens of thousands visit the site each year and most are not Tendai Buddhists. Yet, entering this hall, seeing the image of their religion's founder alongside the other famous religious leaders, they come to appreciate this temple's prominence in the history of Japanese Buddhism and may drop a coin or two in the offering box beside the image of that founder. There is a deeper philosophical point behind the presence of these images, however.

Many years ago I asked a Tokyo University-educated Tendai monk about the images, pointing out that Saint Peter's includes no representations of Protestant reformers. Almost as an afterthought and with the hint of a mischievous smile, he did mention the economics of the pilgrim factor. His main explanation, though, was more doctrinally based. He noted that none of the religious leaders introduced into Japanese Buddhism a doctrine or practice that was not already part of Tendai at the time. It is as if "they selected one part of the tradition and made it their entire focus, bringing the most profound insight to it. In so doing, they enriched our own Tendai tradition." He had put his finger on the crucial point: *selection* was indeed the hallmark of the Kamakura new religions.

Although the Kamakura reformers' trajectory of thinking would ultimately diverge from the Tendai orthodoxy of the time, their Tendai training did give them one point that inoculated them against utter despair, namely, the holographic notion that every part contains the pattern of the whole. That idea is central to both the exoteric and esoteric dimensions of Tendai. On one hand, in exoteric Tendai doctrine, it inspired the teaching that "all three thousand worlds are in one thought moment" (*ichinen sanzen*). On the other hand, in esoteric Tendai doctrine (like Shingon), the teaching was that every point on the mandala allows one immediate access to the center and, therefore, to the whole. The shock waves of the explosive late Heian events had left the Tendai image of the perfect circle in shards. Yet, as Tendai itself had taught, the perfect circle is not a mosaic: it is not that each part had its own discreteness and assumed meaning only when put side by side with other pieces in the right way. Instead, Tendai's circle of completeness is holographic: the whole repeats itself fully in each of its parts, a fractal image of complexity deriving from recursivity's utter simplicity.

In theory, therefore, if you could just pick up a piece of the shattered image of the whole and delve into its detail correctly, you would have the image of whole again without needing a master template, indeed without needing any other piece at all. All the teachings are in one teaching; all the practices are in one practice. All one needed was the right "selection" (*senchaku* or *senjaku*): getting the right single teaching, the right single practice, and looking at it in just the right light. That procedure of making the key selection and finding the whole within it defined the agenda for the reformist thinkers in abandoning the Tendai center on Mt Hiei. In paring down Buddhism to a single teaching, text, or practice, the new religions of Kamakura were, in effect, excluding nothing. Instead there were laying out a different route to the whole.

That way of thinking also explains how the present-day Tendai monk could see their religious insights as leading back to the Tendai ideal of completeness. The inspiration behind the vision of the Kamakura religious thinkers and the present-day monk's affirmation of their contributions to Tendai are grounded in the same holographic paradigm.

For my narrative of Kamakura philosophy, I will begin with the Buddhists we have already been tracking, the followers of Amida and the Pure Land tradition.

New Pure Land Religions

Since we will engage a Pure Land philosopher, Shinran, in our next chapter, my present concern is to explain the larger context of Pure Land thought at the end of the twelfth century. Along the lines favored by Ryōgen and Genshin in Tendai, and by Kakuban in Shingon, Pure Land practices continued their popularity among elite practitioners from both major traditions. For Tendai, *nenbutsu* generally meant the visualization and meditation on Amida and, only secondarily, the invocation of the phrase *namu amida butsu*. Like Tendai, Shingon, especially outside Kakuban's followers, considered Amidism to be only one aspect of a more comprehensive praxis. Among the general populace, however, the voiced *nenbutsu* defined the praxis, as it had for Kūya in the tenth century. This popular version of Amidism was a praxis requiring no meditation teacher and no textual study, but only a wholehearted immersion in the chanting itself. It was a practice well-suited to an illiterate farmer facing a drought or to an impoverished city-dweller living amidst the stench of corpses.

The praxis of the early twelfth-century Amidist, Ryōnin (1073–1132), illustrates how the vocalized *nenbutsu* tradition continued to develop after Kūya, lending the praxis a metapractical justification and a new twist in its performative format. Trained on Mt Hiei as a Tendai monk but disillusioned with the corruption created by the political and economic rivalries, Ryōnin retired to a small valley temple in the northeastern outreaches of Kyoto. There he recited the *Lotus Sutra* and the *nenbutsu* day and night. In response to a vision, he formulated what he called *yūzū* ("interpenetrating") *nenbutsu* for which he drew explicitly on holographic thinking.

Ryōnin's reasoning was as follows. If, as Tendai teaches, one (*ichi*) moment of thought (*nen*) contains the configuration of everything, then one recitation of the *nenbutsu* (*ichinen butsu*) must be equivalent to *all* recitations of *nenbutsu*, and it is not only for oneself but also for everyone.[138*] This led to a communal *nenbutsu* praxis in which groups would chant in harmony to bring about rebirth not only for themselves, but also for humanity as a whole. Gifted in musical composition, Ryōnin used the patterns of Tendai chants to create harmonious intonations of the *nenbutsu* that were both spiritually and aesthetically edifying. Thus, like his contemporary Kakuban, Ryōnin's metapraxis relied on holographic thinking. Although their standpoints and goals differed sharply, their common use of the holographic model of the whole-in-every-of-its-parts foreshadowed the influential role that paradigm would play in the transition from Heian to Kamakura Buddhist philosophy.

242–8   *Hōnen and the revolution in Kamakura thinking.* The most important Kamakura Pure Land thinker before Shinran, and the inspiration for a new orientation in Japanese religious philosophy, was undoubtedly his mentor Hōnen (1133–1212).

Because their lives and teachings are so intertwined, I will return repeatedly to Hōnen in our next chapter's engagement with Shinran and so for now, I will consider him briefly on his own as representative of the zeitgeist that inspired Kamakura Buddhist innovation.

Hōnen was an erudite scholar schooled in Mt Hiei's Tendai teachings and textual studies. (In fact, until his death Hōnen always considered himself a Tendai monk.) Although an unrivaled master of the Buddhist canon, he felt he was making no personal spiritual progress until he surrendered wholeheartedly to the Way leading to the Pure Land. For years he had tried the visualizing and walking meditation practices for Amidism recommended by Genshin, but had found them ineffective. This is how he expressed his transformative spiritual experience:

> What can I do, what can I do! A person like myself is absolutely incapable of following the precepts, meditation and wisdom.... Is there a practice I can pursue? Although I sought answers from countless wise teachers and although I called on all the scholars, there was none who could teach or show me the way. Thus, with a heavy heart full of dejection and pain, I turned to the sacred texts, and as I turned the pages, I came upon the following passage in Shandao's *Commentary on the Meditation Sutra* which reads: "Exclusively repeat the Name of Amida with a single-hearted devotion... never ceasing for even one moment..." I realized that ignorant beings such as ourselves should revere this passage, rely exclusively upon this truth, practice the uninterrupted recitation of the Name, and thus prepare the karmic cause which assuredly determines rebirth [in the Pure Land]. Then, we not only shall believe in Shandao's teaching, but we also shall accord with Amida's vow.[139]

According to tradition, from that point on, Hōnen turned exclusively to the vocalized *nenbutsu* practice.

In the just quoted passage Hōnen mentioned Shandao (613–681), a Chinese Pure Land commentator whom he regarded as one of three great Chinese thinkers from the Pure Land heritage. The other two were Shandao's teacher Daochuo (562–645) and Tanluan (476–542). In developing an independent Pure Land sect in Japan with its own praxis and metapraxis, Hōnen drew heavily on their ideas. Since their teachings so inspired Hōnen and Shinran, I will begin by discussing a few of their key points.

Tanluan lamented people's inability to follow the Buddhist Way and achieve enlightenment through its standard practices, drawing a distinction crucial to all later Pure Land thought: the difference between "one's own power" or "self-power" (*jiriki*) vs. "other-power" (*tariki*). The "difficult practices," sometimes referred to collectively by Daochuo as the "Gate to the Path to Self-perfection,"[140]* rely on the individual's own efforts: the person undertakes a practice, resolving to continue it until attaining enlightenment. By contrast, the so-called *easy practices* which Daochuo classified as the "Gate to the Pure Land" require the practitioners to entrust themselves to a power outside themselves. In that case, it involves people's surrendering to the power of Amida's vow to bring them to enlightenment. According to Tanluan, any attempt to achieve enlightenment by our own effort is subject to the prideful and counter-productive influence of the ego. By posing the argument in that way, Tanluan brought the Pure Land tradition in line with the general Buddhist doctrine of no-ego even as he was claiming the usual Buddhist path was no longer effective.

Daochuo intensified Tanluan's distinction. According to Daochuo, since the Buddha's true teachings had entered a degenerate era of human history, the Gate to the Path of Self-perfection is no longer available and the only option remaining is the Gate to the Pure Land. Where Tanluan believed the distinction between easy and difficult practices was chiefly a difference in attitude while performing any of a variety of practices, Daochuo insisted there is just one true practice for us. That practice is to recite the *nenbutsu*, to call on Amida's name through the verbal formula: *namu amida butsu* ("I take refuge in Amida Buddha").

Shandao, Daochuo's direct disciple, brought a psychological dimension to the doctrines by highlighting the incorrigible character of human nature as it has been karmically corrupted through the accumulation of negative propensities. He insisted, however, that (as the narrative of the Pure Land Sutras had explained) Amida's vow and his Pure Land alternative were designed precisely for that situation. Only practices reliant on Amida's power are productive and of those, one excels over all others, namely, the recitation of Amida's name.

Besides supporting Daochuo's focus on the *nenbutsu*, Shandao also elaborated on the nature of the entrusting faith assumed by the practices of other-power. The eighteenth, nineteenth, and twentieth vows all refer to the Pure Land Buddhist's state of mind or attitude as represented in such phrases as "sincere mind" or "sincere wishing." Shandao claimed the proper attitude of entrusting involves "three mindful hearts:" sincerity, profundity, and a wish for rebirth in the Pure Land achieved by accumulating spiritual merit with the right kinds of practice.

Shandao's teaching sparked Hōnen's turn to the Pure Land path to enlightenment. Esteemed for his mastery of many hundreds of Buddhist sacred texts, Hōnen had come to recognize that his own personal spiritual development ultimately hinged on the significance of a single line from a Chinese commentary and the commitment to the single practice it entailed. At that point Hōnen became the first Kamakura philosopher to make *selection* the core of his religious thought and praxis. For Hōnen, reading that line from Shandao was finding what I call the *holographic entry point*, that is, a key experience in which we discover that by fully engaging a single part, we encounter the whole. For Hōnen the whole of Buddhism distills into the single-hearted recitation of the *nenbutsu.*

In his major work, *Passages on the Selection of the Nenbutsu of the Original Vow,*[141] Hōnen elaborated on his principle of selection. In defense against a charge of heresy (and presumably as guidance to his followers), the work is largely quotations from sutras and commentaries: mainly the three Pure Land sutras and the three Chinese commentators, especially Shandao. Hōnen applied his erudition to selecting passages proving the authenticity of his interpretation.

His selections were more than proof texts in the sense of enumerating citations of scripture to prove his orthodoxy. As with Kūkai's citation of sacred texts, Hōnen was not simply interpreting texts he thought inerrant. He accepted *all* the sutras as legitimate. His breakthrough came from his ability to point to the single lines that could open one to the deepest meaning of *all* the scriptures. For Hōnen, selection itself was a practice of religious insight.[142*] If scholarship does not lead us to praxis, does not help us find the one practice that works in today's situation, it is counterproductive. Thus, Hōnen famously asserted, "When scholars are born, they forget the *nenbutsu.*" Or, perhaps more fully representing his views:

> Even if you study Shakyamuni's whole teaching, you should still become an ignorant man who doesn't know a word and regards himself as ignorant as a nun[143*] or layman. Never behave as a wise man, but single-mindedly recite the *nenbutsu.*[144]

Selecting the right texts, therefore, was no more than a preliminary to selecting the Gate leading to the Pure Land, the Way of reaching spiritual liberation by depending on an other power. That was in contrast with the Gate for the Path to Self-perfection, which depends solely on one's own power. Hōnen's justification followed Daochuo's interpretations and arguments, stressing the inadequacy of the Path to Self-perfection during this Degenerate Age. Lastly, even within the Pure Land path itself, we still must select the right practice. In stressing the vocalized *nenbutsu* as the sole practice, Hōnen deviated from the Amidism of Ennin, Ryōgen, and Genshin, his Tendai predecessors. In defending himself against accusations of heresy, Hōnen developed innovative interpretations to show his view was not only consistent with Shandao, but also with the Pure Land sutras, even those passages that seemed to stress visualization over vocalization.

Behind Hōnen's various textual and doctrinal discussions was what he viewed as the most crucial act of selection in all of Buddhism, the *selection involved in Amida's vows* themselves. The traditional Amida narrative, as explained earlier, says that Hōzō surveyed all the universes, pointedly choosing precisely those characteristics for his pure land that would best help those in most need.[†] Based on that choice, he took his vows and, upon realizing them, became Amida Buddha. Thus, Hōnen reasoned, because Amida's vows were specifically intended to help those least able to help themselves, they were meant for those who could not follow the Path to Self-perfection.

Hōnen had identified a flaw in Genshin's view. If Amida's vow and his Pure Land itself were for those who could not earn rebirth and eventual enlightenment by their "own power" (*jiriki*), then Amida's vow was precisely for those who could not perform Genshin's visualization *nenbutsu* (a practice more like the Gate to the Path to Self-perfection). Amida designed his Pure Land specifically to serve only those who had to abandon the Path to Self-perfection and could do no more than voice the *nenbutsu* while trusting the power of Amida's vow to bring them to liberation. Hence, by that line of reasoning, Genshin's Pure Land praxis is incapable of effecting birth in Amida's Pure Land.

Furthermore, Hōnen believed that when scholars like Ryōgen and Genshin claimed the vocalized *nenbutsu* was only an expedient for those unfortunates who were incapable of any other practice, they did not realize this was the Degenerate Age and those "unfortunates" were actually *everyone*. As Daochuo had argued some five centuries earlier, the effects of the Degenerate Age were the *raison d'être* for Hōzō's taking the vows in the first place. Too self-effacing to be strident in his criticisms of Genshin and Ryōgen, and fearful lest charges of heresy would be leveled against his followers which included laypeople and clergy, women and men, and people from all classes, Hōnen expressed his views cautiously and with nuance. However subtle the rhetoric, though, this quiet, intelligent, and pious man had set into motion a revolution in Buddhist thinking within Japan.

Hōnen's Pure Land Sect (*Jōdoshū*), despite periods of persecution and exile, gained wide acceptance and became a major religious force both in his time and in centuries to follow. In the next chapter, we will engage the philosophy of his student Shinran, who became the founder of a spin-off school, Shin Buddhism (*Jōdoshinshū*, literally, the "True Pure Land School"), the most popular form of Japanese Buddhism today. Taken together, the followers of the various Pure Land sects presently total about 60% of the population of the whole country. Before concluding this chapter, though, we need to consider the two other major Buddhist traditions to arise from the de-centering process of the Kamakura period, namely, Zen and Nichiren.

† See pages 147–8.

Zen Buddhism

As we have seen, Hōnen made the theory of the Degenerate Age pivotal in his analysis of why we need to entrust ourselves to the "other power" of Amida's vow. In explaining his teachings, I did not refer to the other afore-mentioned major theme from the late Heian period, the theory of inherent enlightenment (hongaku). Hōnen considered the doctrine of inherent enlight-enment irrelevant to the crisis of the Degenerate Age, assuming that even if we are inherently enlightened, we cannot realize it, manifest it, or initialize it while in our present situation of corruption, distraction, and decline. The immediate and pressing need, according to Hōnen, was to be reborn in the Pure Land, where the conditions of enlightenment can be met and until which theories about enlightenment are moot. The Zen Buddhists disagreed.

For most Zen Buddhist thinkers, it was the Degenerate Age theory that was irrelevant. If people could not realize their inherent enlightenment, then they were either misguided or lazy. Zen Buddhists held that anyone can real-ize enlightenment in this world even under its present circumstances, but it takes discipline, focus, and—contrary to Hōnen and his followers—self-effort. The name Zen (C. Chan) traces back to the Sanskrit Buddhist term, dhyāna, a form of meditation that quiets the mind through deepening concentration and absorption. In that sense, zen is common to many traditions of Buddhism and often functioned as such in China. I mentioned already that even Saichō had studied zen meditation in China, incorporating it into the larger system of exoteric Tendai praxis.

Chinese Buddhist communities tended to coalesce around charismatic teach-ers. With the benefit of hindsight, traditions constructed lineage trees defining their particular branch of Buddhism, typically naming the school for a pre-sumed founder or for the locale where the founder taught, often the name of a mountain where a temple was located, for example.[145] Using such reconstruc-tions of the past, Chan gradually identified itself as an independent Chinese Buddhist school with a lineage tree of what they called buddha-ancestors aligned into branches and sub-branches.[146]

As a school, Zen or Chan claims distinctiveness in its highlighting the meditative technique of clearing the mind of concepts, usually subordinating or even excluding all other practices, even contemplative ones such as visual-ization or esoteric ritual. The Zen tradition punctuates that point with a canon of jarring, iconoclastic narratives about the great masters of the past. Those buddha-ancestors reportedly burned buddha images or sutras for firewood and kindling, violated all interpersonal etiquette and formality even toward their teachers, ridiculed the study of sacred texts, and so forth. Those narratives signal an important shift in how Chan Buddhists understood meditation and enlightenment, often called in Japanese "realization" (*satori*).

In its early stages Chan enlightenment implied detachment from the world in favor of absorption into an emptied psychological state: so-called no-thought or no-mind. As the centuries passed, though, Chan and Zen Buddhists reconstrued their ideal and its terminology, taking meditation not to be an escape or form of detachment, but rather a prelude to engaging the world in a new and more direct way. Thereafter, realization came to require expression in the everyday world as behavior, words, and even artistic expression.[147]

To train their students to break free of fixed, routinized ways of thinking and acting so that they could become capable of truly spontaneous behavior, the masters devised innovative techniques for linking praxis to a test for spontaneous expression. The kōan (C. *gong'an*) practice was one such technique. In that training method, the master assigns a puzzling phrase or anecdote (often culled from the Zen canon of master-student exchanges) as a focus for the student's praxis. For example, the eighteenth-century Japanese Zen master Hakuin Ekaku (1686–1769) devised the kōan "what is the sound of one hand clapping?" as a barrier for the student to "break through." The point is not to answer the kōan in a rational or preconceived way, but to use it as a prod to shatter habitual responses and to display the ability for spontaneous expression in thought, word, and deed.

Viewed from the larger context of Buddhist thought, the metapraxis justifying the kōan technique is that if you face a problem that cannot be solved when filtered through previous experience, you can obliterate temporarily all the psycho-physical propensities[†] by which you ordinarily establish meaning. Then you will no longer be subject to the effects of negative ("unskillful") propensities and will open yourself to engage reality as it is. The final test is whether you engage that reality with only the propensities necessary for creative expression in the present context (such as mastery of your native language, artistic skills, memories of exemplary behavior from the buddha-ancestors, etc.). There is no restriction therefore on *what* the expression may be. It could be a gesture, lines from a poem given a new context, a shout, drawing an ink wash circle, or whatever. The true test is in *how* the expression arose in the specific master-disciple encounter. Was it truly spontaneous, without premeditation?

Eisai and the Rinzai Zen Tradition. Zen Buddhism came to Japan in full force only in the late twelfth century, initially by the efforts of Eisai (or Yōsai 1141–1215). A Tendai monk his whole life, Eisai made two trips to China in hopes of revitalizing his own Japanese tradition. His five-month journey in 1168 con-

† See pages 58–61.

centrated on Tiantai sites, but his trip in 1187, which lasted four years, focused on Zen training in the tradition of Linji (J. Rinzai). Zen's rigorous stress on meditation and kōan practice seemed to Eisai an excellent vehicle for bringing a renewed, more disciplined emphasis to his own Japanese Tendai tradition. Maybe then, one could reverse the trends toward materialism and militarism plaguing the Buddhist establishments of his time.

Although Eisai found no incompatibility between Zen and Tendai, the Mt Hiei establishment certainly did and as a result he had to defend himself against charges of heresy.[148] Despite his efforts, the imperial court ruled in favor of his opponents and forbade him from promoting Zen in the capital. So he went to the other center of power, Kamakura, the home of the military government, where he was warmly welcomed by the Minamoto shoguns. With his erudite mastery of Chinese culture, Eisai could perhaps help the shogunate establish its own base of high culture in Kamakura to compete with the court in Kyoto.[149] The Kamakura samurai may also have relished the aggressive, confrontational style of Rinzai Zen discipline and praxis.

In any case, when the aforementioned nun shogun, Hōjō Masako, built Jufuku-ji (Temple for Longevity and Good Fortune) in honor of her deceased husband, she appointed Eisai to head it as a temple for his combined Zen-eso-tericism praxis. Minamoto no Yoriie, Masako's eldest son and shogun in 1202, then also built for Eisai a temple in Kyoto, Kennin-ji, again combining Zen with Tendai and Shingon esotericism. (Apparently, the imperial injunction against teaching Zen in the capital could not stand against the will of the shogun.) Despite his success in building Zen temples, throughout his life, Eisai kept his formal affiliation with Tendai and maintained his original project of integrating the Zen practices with esoteric ones.

During the thirteenth century more Tendai monks went to China to study Linji-style Zen and set up new temples on their return. Enni (1202–1280) founded what would become one of the most influential and important early Rinzai Zen temples, Tōfuku-ji (Eastern Temple for Blessings). Built with sup-port from the Heian court, its name stems from the two most prestigious temples from Nara: Tōdai-ji (Great Temple to the East) and Kōfuku-ji (Temple for Extending Good Fortune), thereby affirming heritage while heralding a new era. The latter of the two older temples was the aforementioned Fujiwara family temple, the center of the powerful Hossō school.

Enni's connections with the court, including the imperial family, made Tōfuku-ji Rinzai Zen's first solid foothold in the capital. Yet, following Eisai's precedent, Enni made it inclusive (and politically more secure) by integrating Zen with Tendai and Shingon esotericism. Throughout the eleventh and twelfth centuries, therefore, Rinzai Zen built its base by securing support from both centers of power, Kamakura and Kyoto. Philosophically, though, there was little systematic, creative thought in Kamakura-period Rinzai.[150*] For that, we have to turn to the other Zen tradition in Japan, Sōtō.

141-62

Dōgen and Sōtō Zen. The founder of Sōtō Zen in Japan was the thirteenth-century Zen Master, Dōgen (1200–1253), often considered along with Kūkai to be Japan's most astute premodern philosopher. Since we will engage him in Chapter 6, I will here only situate him and his school in its broader historical setting. Disaffected with Mt Hiei where he was undergoing training as a Tendai monk and seeking alternatives, Dōgen found himself at Eisai's Kyoto temple, Kennin-ji. He studied under Myōzen, abbot of the monastery after Eisai's death, and then eventually accompanied him on a trip to study and practice Zen in China. His teacher there was Rujing, a master of the Caodong (J. Sōtō) as contrasted with the Linji (J. Rinzai) branch of Zen associated with Eisai. Like most of his contemporaries now considered founders of schools that broke away from Tendai, Dōgen also did not intend to start a new sect but only to revitalize Buddhism in his homeland. In accord with the Kamakura-period stress on selection, Dōgen focused on the single practice of Zen meditation (*zazen*) as the true foundation for all Buddhist praxis. Through *zazen* alone, he argued, one could achieve the realization all Buddhists sought. The key point for this book is that he *argued* his philosophical standpoint, undertaking a penetrating analysis of consciousness, forms of thinking, and creative expression. Along the way, he wrote sidebars on such issues as temporality, language, karma, ethics, and the unity of bodymind.

Like other Kamakura figures, Dōgen probably began his writing as a defense against charges of heresy, but later his motives were more philosophical, an attempt to work out a detailed metapractical justification for his emphasis on Zen meditation alone. In his mature writings from the early 1240s, it seems that Dōgen, like many philosophers throughout history, was often writing more for himself rather than to defend his position against some external criticism. Our concern for this chapter is not those philosophical ideas, but instead the historical impact of both him and his school of Sōtō Zen.

Like Eisai, Dōgen met almost immediate resistance from Mt Hiei and had to leave Kennin-ji, where he had settled after returning from China. He moved away from the city proper of Kyoto to the outlying region of Fukakusa, eventually founding Japan's first truly Zen temple, Kōshōhōrin[zen]-ji ([Forest [Zen] Temple Upholding the Sacred Treasures). As his upstart temple attracted more monks, it also garnered negative attention from Mt Hiei and the court.

Aware of Eisai's earlier success, Dōgen appealed to the Kamakura military government, but failed to win its support. Nor could he secure any financing from the court. Then Ennin built his impressive Rinzai-affiliated, Fujiwara- and imperial court-supported temple, Tōfuku-ji, in the same neighborhood as Dōgen's Kōshōhōrin[zen]-ji. Squeezed by hostile forces around him, Dōgen left his little temple and accepted the offer of Hatano Yoshishige to build a new mountain temple complex in isolated Echizen, today's Fukui province. Dōgen moved there in 1243 and remained until just before he died a decade later. At the Temple of Eternal Peace (Eihei-ji), as he eventually named it, he devised a comprehensive monastic training regimen in line with the strict Zen discipline he had encountered in China.

Although Dōgen failed in his lifetime to secure either imperial or shogunal patronage, in the end his institution thrived. This was because it reached out to other constituencies, mainly ordinary people, starting with those rural regions near the Temple of Eternal Peace. Instrumental to that expansion of Sōtō Zen was Keizan (1268–1325). Born about fifteen years after Dōgen's death, Keizan originally studied esotericism as well as Zen at Tōfuku-ji. When he turned his focus to Sōtō Zen, he wove into its fabric of praxis both esoteric and folk religious practices, creating a pattern that would eventually allow it to attract a broad membership of commoners throughout Japan. By that process, Sōtō gradually grew to be much larger than Rinzai Zen in its number of followers, but only at the cost of diluting Dōgen's emphasis on Zen meditation alone.

Nichiren and Nichiren Buddhism

86-91

Named for its founder, Nichiren Buddhism is the third new religious movement from the thirteenth century we will consider. Nichiren (1222–1282) was from eastern Japan, close to the Kamakura shogunate's center. Initially trained as a monk in a Tendai temple from that area he, like so many other of his contemporaries, felt the need to study at Mt Hiei's center of education and training. Unlike most of the other figures we have discussed, however, he never found a suitable mentor, either on the mountain or elsewhere. Inspired by a saying of the historical Buddha, Shakyamuni, Nichiren decided to follow the teachings (the Dharma), rather than a personal teacher.

In his formative years, Nichiren had been familiar with both Pure Land and esoteric teachings. Hōnen's Pure Land followers were numerous in the region where he grew up and the oldest extant version of Kakuban's major work, *The Illuminating Secret Commentary on the Five Cakras and the Nine Syllables*, is a copy in Nichiren's hand. Yet, early in his career, Nichiren decided to make his sole focus the *Lotus Sutra*. That was his version of "selection."

From what I have said previously, it should not be surprising that Nichiren was convinced that the *Lotus Sutra* had fallen into neglect. On one hand, at the dawn of Japanese cultural history, the *Lotus Sutra* was arguably the most important single scriptural text in Japan. Prince Shōtoku, we have seen, allegedly wrote Japan's first commentary on it; it contributed to the ideas of heuristic expression, the universal availability of enlightenment, and the meta-physics of the eternal Buddha Shakyamuni as the source of all buddhas; it supported various popular religious devotional practices, especially those for Kannon (the bodhisattva of compassion); and it served for Saichō as the cen-tral text of his Japanese Tendai sect (as it had for the Chinese Tiantai tradition). Since Saichō, whom Nichiren admired, the prominence of the sutra in Tendai had gradually faded, however.

As explained earlier, Ennin, Enchin, and Annen had all consigned it to status equal to or below esoteric teachings. Although the *Lotus Sutra* continued to be a popular text for chanting, it functioned as only one of a battery of differ-ent scriptures in the Tendai canon. Also, because the sutra itself says it is the highest teaching meant only for the most gifted of listeners, many assumed it inappropriate to their own Degenerate Age. In sum: Nichiren had solid evi-dence to support his claim that the *Lotus Sutra* had been deprived of its former preeminence.

For Nichiren, the calamities of the times, both natural and human made, were signs of eroded devotion to the *Lotus Sutra*. Like many of his contempo-raries, he believed the Degenerate Age had begun in 1052, but unlike most of his cohort group, he also thought the Degenerate Age was the ideal time for proclaiming the *Lotus Sutra*. How can the *Lotus Sutra* be simultaneously the most wondrous teaching for elite listeners and the sutra specifically directed to the problems of the Degenerate Age? Nichiren based his interpretation on the traditional Tendai distinction between the two halves of the text, its first fourteen and final fourteen chapters, the so-called *manifestation gate* and the *essential gate* to the teachings.[151*]

Nichiren claimed the historically manifest Shakyamuni of the first half of the sutra used heuristic expression in adapting his teachings to his audience. That served the previous epochs well, but in the Degenerate Age, the situation has become so corrupt that even with such heuristic aids, Shakyamuni cannot lead people to enlightenment. Therefore, it is now the time of the Eternal Buddha, the Shakyamuni of the last half of the sutra, who directly brings followers of the wondrous teaching (*myōhō*) so they can "attain enlightenment in this very body" (*sokushin jōbutsu*).[152] That is why, Nichiren explained, the *Lotus Sutra* also states that in the Degenerate Age when all other teachings have faded away, it alone will be propagated everywhere.

Yet, despite its timeliness, the sutra warns that the wondrous teachings will often fall upon deaf ears, those of people with deluded, entrenched commit-ments to the old teachings. So fixed are they in their psycho-physical propensi-ties that they no longer understand those classic teachings and certainly cannot practice them. They will even resent any suggestion the former doctrines have been superseded. Nichiren surmised that was why the *Lotus Sutra* predicts its proponents will face resistance and persecution. There will be a clash of world views between those committed to the no longer effectual doctrines and practices against those who challenge the old ways with something new. Confrontation between the two groups is unavoidable and fully in accord with the *Lotus Sutra*'s own predictions, at least as Nichiren understood them.

The nature of that conflict had, for Nichiren, implications for the rhetoric to be used in teaching the new ideas and practices. For bringing the ignorant and deluded to enlightenment, Nichiren distinguished two styles of engagement: "embrace and accept" (*shōju*) and "break-down-and-subdue" (*shakubuku*). The former, Nichiren said, was suitable to previous times when heuristic expressions were still effective. The pedagogical theory behind the embrace-and-accept method was to start from the standpoint of the wrongheaded people to lead them gradually to a more inclusive understanding that would eventually dissolve their previous, deluded position.

The break-down-and-subdue method, by contrast, directly attacks the ground on which the opponents stand, forcing them into a sudden and radical paradigm shift. To sit down with them and calmly reason would be to accept the very premise that Nichiren wanted to reject, namely, that the heuristic style of the old teachings—adapting to time and place, adjusting for audience, allotting for insight to blossom gradually—could still work in this Degenerate Age. Such a premise was itself a delusion to be eradicated because we obviously cannot use the techniques of heuristic expression to teach the ineffectiveness of heuristic expression. For Nichiren, the contrast between embrace-and-accept versus break-down-and-subdue is as sharp as the difference between leading people by the hand versus slapping them in the face. As Nichiren put it, it is like the "difference between the two worldly arts of the pen and the sword."[153]

Nichiren followed the break-down-and-subdue method his whole career, spewing *ad hominems* and virulent rhetoric in every direction, even writing the shoguns and chastising them for supporting the wrong teachings. Not surprisingly, the response was exile, imprisonment, beatings, and attempted assassinations. For Nichiren this only confirmed that indeed this was the Degenerate Age and that he was right in shaking the system to its foundations.[154] A new era had dawned and people needed to open their eyes.[155]

For Nichiren, that his were both the best of times and worst of times was not an oxymoron, nor even a paradox; it was a tautology. Its being the worst of times proves it is the best of times: only in the most adverse circumstances is it possible to overthrow old, no longer effective, ways of thinking. Nichiren's confrontational style produced writings that often seem more inflammatory than philosophical, more rant than reason. Behind the rhetoric, however, I believe we can detect a philosophical metapraxis. To outline the character of that metapraxis, though, I need first to describe the praxis Nichiren advocated.[156]

The centerpiece of the praxis is the *daimoku* ("focus on the title [of the *Lotus Sutra*]"): intoning with an entrusting mindful heart (*shinjin*) the phrase: *namu myōhō renge kyō* ("I take refuge in *The Lotus Sutra of the Wondrous Truth*"). Nichiren's practice of intoning a phrase with an entrusting mindful heart fundamentally differed in its significance from the seemingly similar Pure Land tradition of intoning a phrase with an entrusting mindful heart. However much the praxes might appear similar formally, their metapractical understanding was radically different.[157*] For many centuries, going back to India, people believed the title of the *Lotus Sutra* had mantric power. In Japan, Kūkai was among the first to advance this idea in terms of his own esoteric system. Moreover, given his intimate knowledge of Kakuban's writings, Nichiren knew how he had treated the name "Amida" as a mantra, breaking it into its three syllables, analyzing each individually.[158*]

The mantric-like praxis in Nichiren Buddhism uses for its focal point an altar in front of a hanging scroll with the *daimoku* inscribed on it. For the purposes of the practice, Nichiren designed a special mandala, totally in calligraphy. The *daimoku* runs down the middle vertically and is surrounded by the names of buddhas, bodhisattvas, and *kami*. The real focus of the praxis was not the simple incantation or any visual representation, but rather the "single thought moment" (*ichinen*) of devotion the practitioner performs. Note that we find again the typically Kamakura-period stress on selection.

The mention of the "single thought moment" brings us to the metapractical justification for the praxis. Nichiren follows the whole-in-every-part form of analysis by elaborating on the classic Tendai doctrine of "three thousand realms as a single thought moment" (*ichinen sanzen*). Assuming the interfusion and interdependence of all things, Tendai claims that to engage perfectly in one thought moment is the holographic entry into the entirety of all thought, all dharmas (phenomena), and all realms of existence ("the three thousand realms"). According to Nichiren, the Eternal Buddha and the practitioner interfuse through the *daimoku* praxis. The Eternal Buddha's full expression, the self-expression of reality, is holographically inscribed in Shakyamuni's single expression, the *Lotus Sutra*. That whole wondrous truth of the *Lotus Sutra* is, in turn, holographically inscribed in its part, the title of the sutra (*myōhō renge kyō*).

When the practitioner chants the title with an entrusting mindful heart (*shinjin*), the word *namu* ("I take refuge in") merges with the *daimoku*. Expressed in the Tendai exoteric doctrine of "three thousand realms in a single thought moment," we have the metaphysical and experiential equivalent of the esoteric *nyūga ganyū* ([the Buddha] enters me and I enter [the Buddha]). By that process, for Nichiren as for Kūkai, one "becomes Buddha in this very body" (*sokushin jōbutsu*). Rather than saying enlightenment is impossible because it is the Degenerate Age, by focusing on the last half of the *Lotus Sutra*, Nichiren

87-8

shows how this singular path to enlightenment is possible precisely because this *is* the Degenerate Age.

Furthermore, because of Nichiren's commitment to the holographic paradigm, he cannot conceive of a personal transformation without a world transformation, an individual transformation without a national transformation, a present thought moment (in me) without an eternity (in Shakyamuni). The Degenerate Age is not, spiritually speaking, the last epoch; it is the complete collapse of diachronic or historical time. It is not enough to simply believe in this, nor enough to simply argue on its behalf. You must perform it. That is why Nichiren called himself and his followers "enactors" (*gyōja*)[159] of the *Lotus Sutra*. If one's very body is here and now the Buddha, there can be no concern for life and limb. You prove your faith by enacting it in a way that challenges directly and vehemently every supposition of the old way of thinking. The rhetoric in the break-down-and-subdue method is itself evidence of your devotion to the "wondrous truth" that is the *Lotus Sutra*.

Moving Forward from Detached Understanding to Engaged Knowing

In this chapter I have presented an overview of some five centuries of Japanese philosophy, covering a range of events and individual thinkers. We have gone from the court of the Shining Prince to the Pure Land of the Buddha of Light, from the Heian attempts to be all-inclusive to the Kamakura stress on selection, from the privileged and cloistered world of the Heian court and monastic centers of learning to the violence and devastation typical of Kamakura turmoil and disorder, from the wish for cosmic immersion to the desperate hope for personal emancipation.

To appreciate the contexts of Japanese philosophizing, I have taken in this chapter a detached standpoint, but now we return to engagement. In the next two chapters the focus will narrow to two Kamakura philosophers: one chapter engages Shinran and the other Dōgen. Now knowing something of their social, political, and historical context, you are prepared to come face to face with the individual thinkers themselves, to engage with them in their intensely personal analyses and reflections. As we did with Kūkai, we will initially encounter them in moments of crisis.

We first met Kūkai as a young man in a young culture with a bright future, an ambitious philosopher on a quest to systematize all known ideas and practices, a thinker determined to make sense of it all. He knew his goal and he was working on how to achieve it. In the next chapter, we meet another young man but one from a decaying culture on the brink of spiritual, political, and economic dissolution. Unlike Kūkai in his cave in the wilds of Shikoku, this is not a man with a plan. In an ancient little temple in the center of Kyoto, we find instead a young Tendai monk, despondent and distraught, a self-proclaimed failure ready to give up on any hope of spiritual breakthrough. Adjust to the shadows of the temple hall and to the growing darkness drowning the man's spirit. He is about to have a vision that will change his life.

The Medieval Period

5. SHINRAN 親鸞 (1173–1262)

Naming What Comes Naturally

When I ponder the compassionate vow of
Amida, ...it was for myself, Shinran, alone.
SHINRAN

The year is 1201. An outline of a dozing monk haunts the shadows and smoke of Hexagon Hall (Rokkaku-dō), a small temple in central Kyoto. A statue of the bodhisattva Kannon, the embodiment of compassion, glimmers in the candlelight while the incense infuses the air, the walls of the building, and the fabric of the monk's robes. Exhausted, he is in day ninety-five of his hundred-day retreat. Although just twenty-eight years old, he recently marked the beginning of his third decade as a Tendai monk from Mt Hiei. He has dedicated almost his whole life to the Buddhist path, but where has it gotten him? He is not even on Mt Hiei anymore, having abandoned that grand citadel of learning and practice to withdraw to this humble sanctuary.

Tradition claims Prince Shōtoku himself had founded Hexagon Hall some five centuries earlier and perhaps the lingering charisma of that saintly Buddhist patron could somehow breathe new spiritual life into the monk. With nagging awareness of his own limitations, heartsick over the worldliness and materialism of life on the holy mountain, the monk came to this retreat on no one's advice, drawn here out of desperation.

For years he had been assigned to a subtemple on Mt Hiei dedicated to Amidism, a place where Tendai monks practiced the *nenbutsu* as Ennin had introduced it more than three centuries earlier: continuously invoking the name of Amida, visualizing his Pure Land, and circumambulating Amida's image for

181

days on end without rest.† The monk had himself undertaken various practices and poured over copious sacred texts to no avail. More despondent than ever, he had withdrawn to this lonely spot, far removed from all he had called home for so long. He came to beseech help from Kannon, just some spark of hope amid the external chaos and the internal turmoil.

Now his eyelids are subtly twitching with the rapid eye movements accompanying a dream. This monk is known to history as Shinran (1173–1262) and a new chapter in Japanese Buddhism is about to be written. After his vision, he leaves the temple and commits himself exclusively to the Pure Land Gate. According to an account written later by his wife Eshin-ni, Shinran had been visited by the spirit of Shōtoku, whom he considered an embodiment of Kannon (the bodhisattva of compassion), advising him to find a master in the Pure Land tradition.[1] Upon completing his retreat, he slid open the door and went out the temple gate to reenter the city. Shortly after, he met Hōnen.

Committed to giving Shōtoku's counsel a chance, Shinran vowed to spend one hundred days in Hōnen's company, as he had just spent one hundred days in the hexagonal temple. Then he would know one way or the other whether Shōtoku's advice was authentic or just the dream of a crazed washout. He listened attentively to Hōnen's teachings day after day and as time passed, Shinran realized he had found his master.

INSPIRED BY HŌNEN

Corroborating Shinran's own experience, Hōnen claimed no one in this Degenerate Age can achieve enlightenment through one's own efforts: the Path to Self-perfection as practiced on Mt Hiei no longer works. Shinran took solace in learning that one of the most eminent and pious Tendai scholars had also abandoned the study centers and practice halls of the mountain. If the Tendai doctrines and practices had not worked for Hōnen, no wonder they had failed Shinran as well. But Hōnen had apparently discovered an alternative, namely, the Gate leading to the Pure Land.

By surrendering our own efforts, Hōnen taught, we can let the power of another, the salvific potency of Amida's vow, assure a heavenly rebirth that ultimately results in enlightenment. He maintained that by reciting the *nenbutsu* and keeping our focus on Amida, we ready ourselves for the moment of death when Amida will come to guide us to his Pure Land. Shinran spent the next six years with Hōnen as a close disciple.[2]

In 1207 the imperial government issued a ban on preaching the "Nenbutsu" religion in the capital, beheading four of Hōnen's followers, two of whom had

† See page 150.

The Hexagon Hall Today

apparently become too influential on a pair of the emperor's ladies-in-waiting.[3] The emperor also exiled key figures in the movement, including both Hōnen and Shinran, banishing Hōnen to the island of Shikoku and Shinran to the Echigo area in northern Honshū.[4] The teacher and student never saw each other again.

Around the time of his exile, it seems Shinran again encountered the apparitional Kannon: this time Kannon promised to take the form of a beautiful woman who would satisfy Shinran's lustful desires, transforming them into expressions of compassion. *The Account of Shinran's Dreams* (*Shinran muki*) relates Kannon's words as follows:[5]

> When due to the retribution of previous karma the practitioner [Shinran] is involved in sexual experience, I will incarnate myself as a striking woman and become the recipient of the act....[6]

That dream apparently precipitated Shinran's decision to abandon his monastic vows of celibacy and take a wife,[7] an act that together with his banishment made him in his own words, "no longer monk, no longer layman."[8] The exile order had stripped Shinran of his ordination names, Shakkū and Zenshin, granting him a secular name as a replacement. Refusing that alternative, Shinran instead called himself "Toku" ("the stubble head"), a pejorative term for monks who were slackers in following the strict rules of monastic life, not even maintaining the simple regimen of shaving their heads frequently enough to prevent stubble. Later, he added a prefix to his self-imposed name, making it "Gutoku," the *foolish* stubble-head."

The expulsion of Hōnen and his disciples may have temporarily cleansed the capital of his movement, but it also inadvertently dispersed the Pure Land teachings broadly across Japan. That is, exile led to widespread conversions, especially among rural populations. When the banishment ended after five years, Shinran had adapted so well to living simply among the peasants that he did not immediately return to Kyoto, but instead moved to the rural Kantō area, near present-day Tokyo and Kamakura. Unlike the Zen and Nichiren leaders discussed in Chapter 4,[†] he did not try to garnish the support of the military government, but instead remained among the commoners and outcastes,[9] not returning to Kyoto for another two decades. Just a couple of years after his departure from the region, the military government banned the Pure Land religion in Kamakura, presumably alarmed by its increasing popularity.

While out of touch with Hōnen, Shinran started developing his own spiritual ideas, making him a creative Pure Land philosopher in his own right. Although he thought he was merely amplifying rather than modifying Hōnen's teachings, it soon became evident that Shinran's thought had diverged sharply from that of Hōnen's other disciples, creating differences that triggered a schism in which Shinran's supporters called themselves the "True Pure Land Sect" (*Jōdoshinshū* or just *Shinshū*) to distinguish themselves from Hōnen's "Pure Land Sect" (*Jōdoshū*). In this book, I will refer to Shinran's religion as "Shin Buddhism," the preferred name among its English-speaking members today.

Shinran himself did not intend to create a new school, certainly not one that would seem to set his teachings apart from Hōnen's. In fact, perhaps as an outgrowth of his experience on Mt Hiei as well as in the capital, Shinran remained distrustful of religious institutions throughout his life. To his way of thinking, there was no distinction between clergy and laity or teacher and disciple. Ironically, Shin Buddhism eventually became, and still is, the largest Buddhist denomination in Japan.

SHINRAN'S QUESTIONS

To engage Shinran's philosophy, it would help if you imagine his philosophical questions like ones you might ask yourself. The problems that concerned him and even the source of his frustration are perhaps not as alien to our situation today as you might first imagine. Mt Hiei confidently asserted that the Way to enlightenment, the procedure for engaging the world realistically and effectively, was clearly laid out for anyone having the mettle,

† See pages 172, 173, 175.

intelligence, and diligence to follow its regimens. The Tendai promise was that if you could dedicate yourself to its psycho-spiritual praxis and course of study, then the peace, compassion, and insight of enlightenment would surely be yours.

Shinran had followed the Tendai protocol, but to no avail. He acknowledged his own limitations, confessing he could not maintain the rigor of praxis to which he aspired nor master the overwhelming corpus of Tendai teachings. But Hōnen! He was one of those extraordinary geniuses that appears once in a generation. Everyone on Mt Hiei marveled at his command of the canon and the seriousness with which he engaged every discipline. If that extraordinary man, forty years his senior, could not follow the Path to Self-perfection, what hope was there for someone like Shinran? Perhaps it was indeed the era of *mappō*, the Degenerate Age in which enlightenment was no longer attainable.

250-1

Yet, as we saw in Chapter 4, Hōnen did finally discover a path, the Gate to the Pure Land. Unlike the Path to Self-perfection that focused on the pinnacle of human achievement and mapped the route of its staggeringly steep ascent, the Pure Land alternative focused on how things are right here and now, even if it be amid the anguish of self-despair. What could be more Buddhist than that? Instead of dreaming and striving for what is not, you could engage what is. Would it work for Shinran? He didn't know, but he felt he had no choice:

> As for myself, Shinran, I simply receive the words of my dear teacher, Hōnen, "Just say the *nenbutsu* and be saved by Amida," and entrust myself to the Primal Vow. Besides this, there is nothing else.
>
> I really do not know whether the *nenbutsu* may be the only cause for my birth in the Pure Land, or the act that shall condemn me to hell. But I have nothing to regret.... The reason is that if I were capable of realizing Buddhahood by other religious practices and yet fell into hell for saying the *nenbutsu*, I might have dire regrets for having been deceived. But since I am absolutely incapable of any religious practice, hell is my only home.[10]

The Problem in Trying to Figure Things Out

Of course, in the long run, taking the Gate leading to the Pure Land did work for Shinran. Being exiled to the backwoods of Echigo was a small price to pay for having become Hōnen's follower. Separated by such a distance from his master and fellow disciples, however, Shinran brooded over what had happened and how to understand it. The question that puzzled him was *why* the Path to Self-perfection had failed. If it could not work for even someone like Hōnen, that seemed strange. Was it simply the external circumstances of the Degenerate Age or was there something else, something inherently wrong with the prevailing Buddhist regimen of study and self-discipline?

Shinran came to identify the problem as one of *hakarai,* the calculative thinking and weighing of logical alternatives that characterized the philosophical reasoning behind the Path to Self-perfection. Being egoless and free of distortions and delusions, a buddha can engage in *hakarai* effectively. But we ordinary people, bound up as we are with karmic afflictions and crippled with delusions, cannot.

Hakarai is not simply reasoning, but also an attitude toward reasoning, a self-confidence that you are on top of things and if there is something you don't yet understand, you can figure it out eventually. For ordinary delusional human beings, *hakarai* functions as a form of intellectual hubris, a lack of recognition for the karmic circumstances and delusions preventing us from experiencing reality as it is. If we cannot encounter reality without our delusions, our thinking about reality will be no more than the reinforcement of those delusions. (Recall Kūkai's admonition about how difficult it is to break out of a fixed mindset.[†])

Still, if we want to engage Shinran, we must at least imaginatively share with him a time and place. So let us invite him for a moment to our world. Where would he likely find *hakarai* active in our world today?

I think Shinran could see *hakarai* in those people today who effuse a naïve scientism, the theory that the detached knowing of science is the only valid source of knowledge. There are those who believe what we really know is what science tells us; and what we do not yet know, science will figure out soon enough. Technology will solve all our problems, even those that technology spawned.

Or perhaps Shinran would find *hakarai* in present-day evangelists and gurus who claim special knowledge of the spiritual dimension—the insider information about which is the right book, the right doctrine, or the right religious leader. (Remember that despite his profound admiration for and commitment to Hōnen, Shinran admitted he could not *know* Hōnen was right—Hōnen and his followers might all end up in hell.)

Or maybe Shinran would find *hakarai* in today's self-help industry that promises you are only one program away from finding psychological, spiritual, physical, social, and financial well-being. In our self-confidence that we can solve our own problems, figure out things for ourselves, and reach our goals through our own efforts, Shinran would likely find the seeds of a self-delusion lying at the heart of the Path to Self-perfection.

By identifying *hakarai* as the problem, Shinran's reflections had taken a decidedly philosophical turn that gives his writings a relevance beyond his

† See page 133.

situation in medieval Japan. *Hakarai* is not a medieval Japanese problem; it is a human problem. Prepared now to engage Shinran on those terms, let us turn to the details of his critique.

Critiquing the Metapraxis of the Path to Self-perfection

The limitation in the Path to Self-perfection, according to Shinran, is how it leads you to understand your "self." On one hand, for its praxis, the Path to Self-perfection involves devoting yourself to a disciplined regimen leading to enlightenment, a focused task achieved through your own efforts. That is what the Pure Land tradition calls relying on "self-power" or "one's own power" (*jiriki*), which Daochuo[†] had in China earlier identified as a spiritual danger. The Path to Self-perfection assumes you can study and analyze the traditional texts and doctrines so as to determine the truth for yourself.

Shinran's insight was that *jiriki* and *hakarai* share a common characteristic: you can participate in neither without first isolating your self from either its goal of praxis or its object of thought. In other words, in both praxis and theory, the Path to Self-perfection assumes a discrete, detached self. That, says Shinran, is the fatal flaw in any system trying to follow the Path to Self-perfection. Shinran thinks the impulse to isolate the self in such a way derives from *bonnō*,[11] a term variously translated as "blind passions," "afflictions," or "defilements."

However translated (I will use "afflictions" or "karmically determined afflictions"), *bonnō* has three characteristics central to Shinran's analysis. To start with, they are examples of the aforementioned "unskillful" or harmful "psychophysical propensities,"[‡] habitual tendencies that can cripple our ability to achieve enlightenment on our own. Quite simply, they are spiritually bad habits of mind and body. Second, emerging from the basic drives of repulsion, desire, and foolishness, they are so thoroughly human that Shinran doubts they can ever be completely rooted out, at least during these corrupt times that lack a cogent system of spiritual support. Third, however much they may permeate the human situation at large, the afflictions are not innate but karmically generated. They are not only the cause of spiritually unproductive actions, but they are also the result of such actions from the past, a "karmic residue" as Shinran calls it. In short: in the deepest sense, our afflictions are self-inflicted.

Shinran's argument can be summed up as follows. The Path to Self-perfection, the Path to enlightenment undertaken through my own efforts (*jiriki*), assumes that *I* can know and *I* can undertake the self-liberating praxis leading to enlightenment. Because of karmically determined afflictions, any appear-

---

† See pages 165–6.
‡ See pages 58–62.

ance of the *I* is tainted by egocentrism and selfishness—the only *I* one can have is an ego-based *I*. Yet, enlightenment is by definition egoless (*muga*). Therefore, by its own logic, the Path to Self-perfection cannot result in enlightenment.

The Alternative: The Gateway to the Pure Land

This brings us to the second step in Shinran's analysis: the posing of an alternative for the Gate to the Path to Self-perfection, namely, the Gate to the Pure Land.[12] In terms of praxis, we have seen that Shinran believed the root problem with the Path to Self-perfection is its dependence on your own-power or self-power (*jiriki*). The alternative is to eradicate any pretension whatsoever that by your own effort or design you can successfully undertake a praxis ending in enlightenment. The way to give up dependence on your own power, Shinran says, is to surrender yourself to the "power of another" (*tariki*), namely, to the power of Amida's vow.† Tradition calls this an "easy" path, but Shinran found it to be fraught with traps by which self-effort can subtly insinuate itself back into the practice.

Before turning to the details of Shinran's praxis, comparing it with Hōnen's, let us review what is at stake in Shinran's argument up to this point. In refuting the Path to Self-perfection, Shinran demonstrated its ineluctable contradiction: you have to depend on the ego's efforts in order to eliminate the ego. In the second step of his argument, Shinran explained an alternative: the Way of the Pure Land and its total dependence on other-power. If he is not going to fall into the same contradiction as the Path to Self-perfection, however, he must demonstrate that the Pure Land Path does not in any way rely on the ego. If there is even a modicum of ego, or the slightest sense that a discrete self is an agent in the praxis, the analysis slips back into own-power. Then Shinran's argument would fail. That prospect led Shinran's to scrutinize the details of Pure Land praxis.

HŌNEN'S PRAXIS AND SHINRAN'S PRAXIS COMPARED

Isolated from the rest of Hōnen's group, Shinran's analysis began to follow its own course. Although I think Shinran honestly believed he was only working out corollaries to Hōnen's teachings, we cannot know whether Hōnen would have agreed. It is fair to say, in any case, that most of Hōnen's closest disciples interpreted their master's teaching quite differently from how Shinran did

† We surrender not to Amida but to the power of Amida's Vow. When we consider Shinran's metaphysics later in this chapter, the importance of that distinction will be clear.

and so the schism between the two forms of Pure Land teaching was perhaps inevitable. Concerning points of divergence, I will focus on four interconnected issues: (1) the radicalization of the distinction between own-power and other-power; (2) the change in the meaning of the *nenbutsu*; (3) the de-emphasis on the deathbed visitation; (4) the dehistoricizing of tradition. On all four points, Shinran's final position grew directly out of his philosophical agenda of proving the Gate to the Pure Land contains absolutely no residue of self-effort.

Own-power vs. Other-power

In critiquing the Path to Self-perfection, Shinran extended the doctrine of other-power to its logical endpoint. I have already mentioned that Hōnen had emphasized the invocation of the *nenbutsu* as a *continuous* practice[13*] leading up to the moment of death when Amida would accompany the faithful to be reborn in his Pure Land. For Hōnen, to vocalize the *nenbutsu* while holding Amida in mind is a practice that accumulates spiritual merit. That merit qualifies the individual for such rebirth and ultimately for enlightenment itself. Yet, Hōnen explicitly stated that any merit we might acquire via Pure Land praxis is not the result of our own effort, but is the working of Amida's compassion.[14]

Shinran argued, however, that any activity with the *goal* of achieving merit is not authentically the Pure Land Way since the intention of acquiring merit presumes a belief, however subtle, that we can help ensure our own rebirth in the Pure Land and, by extension, our own enlightenment.[15] Such thinking taints the purity of our entrusting ourselves to other-power.

To sum up the difference: Hōnen, at least as interpreted by most of his disciples, believed you could not achieve enlightenment *totally* on your own power. Shinran's analysis was more radical. He believed you could not achieve enlightenment by resorting to your own power *in any way whatsoever.* That difference in interpretation influenced their views of *nenbutsu* as well, a second point of contrast.

Nenbutsu

For Hōnen, the *nenbutsu* is a species of practice, but unlike most other practices it relies on other-power. That is, in saying the *nenbutsu*—for Hōnen, a merit-producing activity—we are not acting on our own, but doing something only through the assistance of power from elsewhere. Yet, there is no denying we are participating in a *joint activity* with Amida Buddha, an inherently meritorious performance leading to birth in the Pure Land. The recitation of the *nenbutsu* is in fact a prerequisite for the emission of Amida's light. "The light of Amida Buddha shines because one recites *nenbutsu*. If the recitation of *nenbutsu* ceases, upon what would Amida Buddha shine his light?"[16]

To clarify Hōnen's distinction between own-power and other-power in relation to the *nenbutsu*, consider this analogy: the difference between an ordinary electric motor, for example one in an electric fan, and an engine in an automobile. To run, the electric motor needs to be connected continuously to an external power supply, that is, it must be plugged into a wall outlet outside the fan. When not plugged in, it has no power. Conversely, if the motor is not operational, the power from the wall outlet does nothing.

An automobile, on the other hand, contains its own power source, igniting the gasoline with sparks, and using its own power to "move itself" (automobile) while transporting its own fuel without needing a constant external connection. At least until it runs out of fuel, the car engine is self-sufficient.

For Hōnen, practices performed through one's own efforts are like engines—they are self-contained. The other-power practices, however, are more like motors needing external links to a continuous power source to keep running. Insofar as either kind of practice "works," it accumulates merit. To continue the analogy, in this Degenerate Age, the own-power practices have run out of fuel and cannot get us to our goal, namely, rebirth in the Pure Land and the enlightenment to which that leads. Only the continuous, externally powered, practices can generate the merits to make such rebirth possible.[17]

Shinran's opposing view is that reciting the *nenbutsu* is like neither a motor nor an engine because the *nenbutsu* does nothing at all. It is a "nonworking" (*mugi*). For him, the problem with the view attributed to Hōnen is that it really distinguishes two kinds of agency in which you might engage. In both, however, you still *do* something. Whether it is an electric motor or a car engine, the machine is still doing the work. For Shinran the *nenbutsu* shows rather than does something. The *nenbutsu* is more like a pilot light indicating you are plugged in to an external power source rather than a merit-producing machine. The saying of the *nenbutsu* is for Shinran not a means to an end, but the sign that you have achieved the end, that rebirth in the Pure Land is already assured or settled (*shōjō*). In other words: for Hōnen, the *nenbutsu* is a necessary cause for attaining rebirth in the Pure Land, but for Shinran it is the result of one's rebirth as being assured.[18*]

Given that interpretation, Shinran eluded the debate among his contemporaries about how many times the *nenbutsu* had to be uttered: since the *nenbutsu* itself is a sign, not a practice, the point is moot. The true *nenbutsu* is uttered neither once nor many times. Rather, it is significant only when it is made to be uttered by Amida, that is, the "pilot light" goes on when we are engaged with the power source of Amida's vow.

For Shinran the quality of the entrusting mindful heart is crucial. It is a spontaneous utterance of awe and gratitude accompanying the moment of fully entrusting yourself to the power of Amida's vow.[19*] Rather than a mantra[20*] chanted to accomplish some end (whether that chanting is understood to be ultimately from ourselves or from a buddha), Shinran's *nenbutsu* is more like shouting "Hallelujah!"—a spontaneous ejaculation of fulfilled faith.[21]

> True and real entrusting faith [*shinjin*] is unfailingly accompanied by the *nenbutsu*. The *nenbutsu*, however, is not necessarily accompanied by [the] entrusting faith that is the power of the Vow.[22]

Deathbed Visitation

In stressing the *nenbutsu* itself, rather than the deathbed visitation from Amida, as the verification of entrusting faith, Shinran again diverged from many of Hōnen's other followers. Shinran was critical of the Pure Land teachers who emphasized the point of death because it seemed to suggest we must *do* something at that moment in order to be assured rebirth in the Pure Land.[23] For Shinran, the moment of import is when we completely entrust ourselves to the power of Amida's compassionate vow. Although that moment might occur at the approach of death, it could as readily occur at any other time as well.

Hōnen as well de-emphasized the moment of death when he assured his followers that Amida would come to take them to the Pure Land even if they were unable to say the *nenbutsu* at that moment, as long as they had accumulated the merit of saying the *nenbutsu* repeatedly throughout their daily lives up to then.

> Through the merit of *nenbutsu* frequently recited in daily life, Amida Buddha is certain to come to take us to his Pure Land at our time of death.[24]

Hōnen's language suggests the deathbed visitation of Amida to take the dying person to the Pure Land serves as the capstone of a life dedicated to spiritual deepening. By contrast, Shinran's view of temporality, as I will now explain, precludes such a model of gradual progress in the accumulation of merit.

Personal History, Human History

Shinran radically reinterpreted the traditional Pure Land accounts of both personal and human history. I begin with the former. As already mentioned, unlike those emphasizing the moment of entrusting faith as the culmination of a lifetime praxis, Shinran stressed the abruptness of the experience:

> Contemplating the true and real entrusting faith, I find there is the one thought-moment.[25] One thought-moment expresses the ultimate brevity

of the instant of the realization of entrusting faith and manifests the vast, inconceivable mind of joyfulness.[26]

Or:

In the space of an instant, one swiftly transcends and realizes the supreme, perfect, true enlightenment. Hence, [it is called] "transcending laterally."[27]

The odd phrase "transcending laterally" (ōchō) needs explaining, but it turns out to be an alternative expression for distinctions already introduced. Practices based in our own power are said to be "forward," presumably because in them we set a goal and direct our effort toward it. Those based on other-power are, on the contrary, "lateral" because their result comes to us from outside any path we have intentionally set for ourselves. In addition, in either the forward or lateral path, we can progress to enlightenment either step-by-step (the "departing" traditions) or all at once (the "transcending" traditions).

So Shinran understands Hinayana practice to be "departing forward" because it is both gradual and based in one's own power. Mahayana practices such as Shingon, then, are "transcending forward" because they are based in our own power and achieve enlightenment suddenly. Among lateral practices, Shinran labels "departing laterally" those which understand the nenbutsu as a path of accumulating merit with Amida's help, a path laid out by Amida's Vow (hence a "lateral" path). It is cultivated throughout life and culminates at the point of death and rebirth. As I just characterized it, Hōnen's purported view of spiritual evolution might fit that model (although Shinran, of course, does not think that view accurately represents Hōnen's and so does not mention him).

True other-power nenbutsu practice, according to Shinran, is "transcending laterally" since there is a sudden and complete transformation once you totally surrender yourself to the power of Amida's vow. All steps of achievement are traversed at once. To ignore this always available possibility of sudden transformation in favor of an emphasis on the time of death, Shinran believed, was an unnecessary restriction on the power of Amida's ever-present, timeless vow.

As he looked askance at the idea that the Way of the Pure Land involves a step-by-step spiritual progress through time, Shinran was equally skeptical of the diachronic history implied in the narrative of the Degenerate Age. Viewed from the cosmic standpoint, Amida's vow is not an ancient event that has become relevant only in recent centuries. Shinran says instead that the "true lineage of the Pure Land teachings" is for all people regardless of whether they lived in the Buddha's time or in any of the three subsequent periods of the Dharma.[28] His inspiration for that cosmic view likely derives first of all from the seventeenth vow: all buddhas praise the name of Amida.

Secondly, as we have also seen, the Amida narrative began by remarking on the historical Buddha's joy in recognizing the realization of Amida's vow. For Shinran, when taken together, those two points imply that all buddhas—all enlightened beings—insofar as they have attained enlightenment, have also participated in the power of Amida's vow.

> Even holy masters of the Mahayana and Hinayana entrust themselves to the power of the Vow to attain birth, without calculating in any way.[29]

From Shinran's vantage point, the Degenerate Age (*mappō*) is not so much a matter of gradual historical decay, but more primarily a universal characterization of the human condition. That is, it has always been the Degenerate Age and Enlightenment has always involved entrusting ourselves to Amida's vow, even when it was not formally described as such. Actually, Shinran's critique of the Path to Self-perfection already entailed that conclusion because his criticism was logical, not historical. That is, because the Path to Self-perfection depends on a discrete self or ego for its agency, it cannot *by definition* result in enlightenment which is without ego. Moreover, what is precluded by definition could *never* have been true. Therefore, for there to have been enlightened buddhas in the past, they must have achieved enlightenment via other-power not their own power.

Let us now look more closely at Shinran's metapractical theory, his argument for why the Pure Land option is effective. That theory will take us more deeply into his psychology of both entrusting faith and morality.

SHINRAN'S METAPRAXIS

In the last chapter, I cited Hōnen's self-description of the despair he felt before he read Shandao's commentary.[†] Earlier in this chapter, I also quoted Shinran's description of his own attitude of having nothing-to-lose. Since that attitude is relevant to entrusting faith, I suggest we examine Shinran's words again, this time gleaning from it different themes.

> As for myself, Shinran, I simply receive the words of my dear teacher, Hōnen, "Just say the *nenbutsu* and be saved by Amida," and entrust myself to the Primal Vow. Besides this, there is nothing else.
>
> I really do not know whether the *nenbutsu* may be the only cause for my birth in the Pure Land, or the act that shall condemn me to hell. But I have nothing to regret, even if I should have been deceived by my teacher, and, saying the *nenbutsu*, fall into hell. The reason is that if I were capable of realizing Buddhahood by other religious practices and yet fell into hell for saying the

† See page 165–6.

nenbutsu, I might have dire regrets for having been deceived. But since I am absolutely incapable of any religious practice, hell is my only home.[30]

The Psychology of Entrusting Faith (shinjin)

In the passage quoted immediately above, Shinran is no longer arguing against something—the Path to Self-perfection—but is instead describing the personal and experiential nature of entrusting faith, taking up two possible criticisms of his position along the way. First, someone might argue that to entrust oneself to other power is a choice and choice involves a self who makes the decision. If that is so, the arising of entrusting faith is not completely free of ego or one's own power. Put simply: to *choose* to entrust in other-power by surrendering one's own power is itself an act of one's own power. In the just quoted passage, however, Shinran explains that to entrust in other-power is not a choice, but a response to having no alternative, precisely the situation of *not* having a choice.

A second possible criticism of Shinran's position is that he had to "figure out" that the Pure Land path is right, an apparent act of the kind of *hakarai* that is an earmark of depending on one's own power. Shinran's response in the passage makes it clear, however, that he does not claim to have figured out anything. Having given up, he just follows what he heard from Hōnen. Shinran himself *does not claim to know he is right*. Therefore, he did not arrive at the Pure Land Gate through any reasoning process. No *hakarai* was involved.

To be consistent with his own theory, Shinran could not come to his conclusion through logical argument. Yet, he could nonetheless describe and analyze his (and our) situation. Shinran's psychological insights arise from his analysis of the "karmically determined afflictions" (*bonnō*) permeating the human condition. We habitually become attached to the objects of ordinary life, yearning to keep them even as they pass away. Haunted by ignorance concerning the impermanent nature of reality, by greed for material and psychological accomplishment, and by desire to prolong our existence, we do not even seek the peace of enlightenment. And if we come to desire it, we approach it through "calculating" (*hakarai*), the self-centered cost-benefit analysis of our actions. We do not realize that the ego which wants to control our spiritual release from attachment is itself the cause of attachment: the desire to be free of desire subverts its own mission precisely because it is a desire by the ego to improve its own situation. Upon recognizing the catch-22, we quit trying.

What Hōnen discovered and Shinran elaborated, however, was that in giving up we can be saved from our delusions. But only if we give up entirely, without the least trace of doing it as a means to save ourselves. In that case we are liberated from our delusions not *because* we have given up, but the *giving up itself* is being liberated. Put more boldly, salvation (namely the assurance of rebirth in the Pure Land) is not the response to despair; salvation is another name for despair, at least despair of the right sort. In that way, Shinran recast the entire problem of delusion and enlightenment.

As I explained in Chapter 2, Mahayana Buddhism generally teaches that nirvana is samsara and samsara is nirvana, that is, that enlightenment and delusion are inseparable. Expanding on that assumption, Shinran applied a second universally accepted Buddhist principle: delusion is the source of human anguish. From those two premises, it follows that enlightenment is inseparable from anguish: in anguish itself, we should be able to discover enlightenment. In other words, enlightenment does not escape anguish; it *engages* it.

Shinran did not mean that we have one foot in delusion and one in enlightenment. Nor that we are really one (enlightened) but superficially the other (deluded). Rather, our delusion itself is the proof of enlightenment and enlightenment itself is the proof of our delusion. Such an extraordinary claim, a formulation so apparently alien to much of the accepted Buddhist tradition, is worth reading in Shinran's own words

> When I consider the matter, my birth in the Pure Land is settled without doubt for the very reason that I do not rejoice at that which should have me bursting with joy.[31]

> I know truly how grievous it is that I, Gutoku Shinran, am sinking in an immense ocean of desires and attachments and am lost in vast mountains of fame and advantage, so that I rejoice not at all at entering the stage of the truly settled [those for whom rebirth in the Pure Land is assured] and feel no happiness at coming nearer the realization of true enlightenment. How ugly it is! How wretched![32]

Shinran knows Amida's power intimately not because he feels bliss or enjoyment, but precisely because he does not. In trying to convey this psychological description of delusion and the enlightenment of entrusting faith, the English

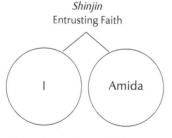

Entrusting as External Relation
Connecting I and Amida

Entrusting/Anguish as Internal Relation,
the Overlap of I and Amida

terms *own-power* and *other-power* do not capture the dynamic very well. As Kakuban had argued,† such terminology is intrinsically dichotomous and binary, almost as if the person and Amida were individual beings linked by the external relation of entrusting faith.

From the standpoint of true entrusting faith, however, the relation between self and Amida is internal, not external. Hence, to fathom the working of one's own karmic afflictions and the resultant anguish is to fathom the working of Amida's vow. (See diagrams below, the one on the right representing Shinran's view.) Where there is anguish, there is the working of Amida's vow. Where there is no anguish, there is no working of the vow. So, it is literally impossible to feel joy—the lack of anguish—over the fact that Amida's vow has assured our rebirth in the Pure Land. The working of the vow only exists where there is anguish.

Furthermore, since our own personal anguish is the only anguish we can truly know (knowledge here assumes an internal relation between knower and known), we experience the working of Amida's vow only within ourselves. That explains one of Shinran's famous passages from the epilogue to *Lamenting the Deviations*:

> When I ponder on the compassionate vow of Amida, established through five eons of profound thought, it was for myself, Shinran, alone. Because I am a being burdened so heavily with karma, I feel even more deeply grateful to the Primal Vow which is decisively made to save me.[33]

It is fitting that the popular Pure Land tradition in later years sometimes refers to Amida as *Oyasama*, "our parent." Shinran himself said Amida's name is our father and Amida's light our mother.[34]* Because the Sino-Japanese character for "parent" (親) also means "intimacy," we could say Amida is "the intimate one." Through our anguish, Amida intimates what is most intimate, the compassionate and wise working of his own enlightenment on our behalf. In engaging our anguish instead of ignoring or trying to transcend it, we experience the power of Amida's vow.[35]*

From this description of entrusting faith, it follows that reflection is crucial to Shin Buddhist spirituality. Every action is to be examined in terms of its source: is it being performed out of our own efforts or out of Amida's power? Genuine entrusting faith allows for no self-delusion. We must not secretly take pride in the quality of our faith. Nor may we seek the goal; the goal must come to us of its own. Hence, we can take no credit for spiritual attainments—they are all

† See pages 157–8.

Amida's doing. Even our entrusting ourselves to Amida's vow is itself only the working of Amida's vow in us.

Furthermore, since entrusting faith requires reflection, the fathoming of our own karmically determined afflictions and anguish, we cannot teach it to someone else. At most, all we can do is express our own experience. Hence, Shinran claimed to have no disciples.[36] Likewise, since the path to the Pure Land is by definition open to anyone who reflects on his or her own human situation, it can make no distinction between men and women, educated and uneducated, clergy and laity.

> In reflecting on the ocean of great entrusting faith, I realize that there is no discrimination between noble and humble or black-robed monks and white-clothed laity, no differentiation between man and woman, old and young. The amount of evil one has committed is not considered, the duration of any performance of religious practices is of no concern. It is a matter of neither practice nor good acts, neither sudden attainment nor gradual attainment, neither meditative practice nor non-meditative practice, neither right contemplation nor wrong contemplation, neither thought nor no-thought, neither daily life nor the moment of death, neither many-calling [of the *nenbutsu*] nor once-calling. It is simply entrusting faith that is inconceivable, inexplicable, and indescribable. It is like the medicine that eradicates all poisons. The medicine of Amida's vow destroys the poisons of our wisdom and foolishness.[37]

The Psychology of Moral Action

The emphasis on rebirth in the Pure Land as being independent of good and evil actions flirts with antinomianism, the theory that we are free of moral norms, beyond any concerns about good or evil. That is, if Amida's presence is known through the awareness of our own wickedness, does it not follow that the stronger the wickedness, the stronger the working of Amida's vow? Indeed, Shinran at times seemed to have said as much:

> Even a virtuous person can attain birth in the Pure Land, how much more readily someone plagued with bad karma.... The reason is that when people sow good karmic seeds by what they perceive to be their own self-power efforts, they are not putting their complete trust in the other-power and, as such, they are not in accord with the original vow. On the other hand, as soon as someone's commitment to self-power practice is turned over, because that person truly trusts in the other-power, he or she attains birth in the True Land of Reward.[38]

258

From such statements, it was easy to misconstrue Shinran as saying we should commit evil so we could entrust ourselves more fully to Amida's vow. After all, if Amida's enlightenment is intimately intertwined with our delusions and karmic afflictions, does it not follow that strengthening the passions causing those delusions would only increase the power of Amida's presence? Although Shinran certainly did not intend to be understood that way, such a misreading of his intent did occur even in his own day:

> Once there was a man who fell into wrong views proclaiming that he would purposefully do evil as a way for attaining birth, since the Vow is directed to those who commit evil. Thus saying, he performed many evils. When Shinran heard about this, he admonished in a letter, "Do not take poison just because there is an antidote."[39]

Shinran's response refers us to the cause of evil, namely, the ego. If we try to do evil, just as when we try to do good, the action is construed in terms of an "I" acting as agent of the deed. That ego—that sense of an "I" independent of Amida—obstructs the arising of entrusting faith and detaches us from Amida and the working of his vow.

Let us look more closely at Shinran's own explanation in the above mentioned letter concerning the evil-doer. After the poison and antidote analogy, Shinran continued:

> When people begin to hear [Amida] Buddha's vow, they wonder, having become thoroughly aware of the karmic evil in their hearts and minds, how they will ever attain birth [in the Pure Land] as they are. To such people we teach that since we are possessed of karmically determined afflictions, the Buddha receives us without judging whether our hearts are good or bad.
>
> When, upon hearing this, people's trust in the Buddha has grown deep, then he or she comes to abhor such a self and to lament their continued existence in birth-and-death. Such people then joyfully say the Name of Amida Buddha, deeply entrusting themselves to the Vow. That people seek to stop doing wrong as the heart moves them, although earlier they gave thought to such things and committed them as their mind dictated, is surely a sign of having rejected this world.[40]

That is, the person of entrusting faith "abhors" in his or her old self the ego who thought it could neatly distinguish and choose between good and evil. Shinran seems to mistrust our rational capacity to determine morality because he believes that although good is stronger than evil, evil is smarter. If we resort to figuring out moral choices, trying to be good on our own power, we subtly capitulate to the working of the ego. Ignorance, hatred, and desire will generate self-deceptive rationalizations to hide our real motives from our verbalized intentions, even those spoken only to ourselves.

Rationalizing is the greatest obstruction to doing good. Our problems begin when we think we can figure out what is good and what is evil:

I am at a total loss when it comes to fathoming good and evil. The reason is that if I could understand what is considered good in the mind of a buddha, then I could claim to understand good, and if I could understand what is considered evil in the mind of a buddha, then I could claim to understand evil. But as an ordinary person beset with the defilements living in a world as transient as a burning house, everything I see is just a wide variety of lies and nonsense—there is no truth to any of it. The only thing genuine in my world is *nenbutsu*.

259

Since the process of figuring things out (*hakarai*) needs the ego for its agency, even when we try to do good, we subconsciously also feed the source of evil, the valorization of the ego. We congratulate ourselves for winning the moral battles, but in reality we have already lost the moral war because as long as ego is the general, even an apparent victory only makes the true enemy stronger.

According to Shinran, if we can instead entrust ourselves completely to Amida's vow, we will gradually undo the negative psycho-physical propensities, the bad habits, that we have formed through the years when our egos dictated our behavior. As the ego dissolves through the other-power of entrusting faith, no new negative conditioned responses will form and the power behind the old behavioral patterns will not recharge.[41] There may still be some harmful, long-range karmic effects of previously committed ego-based actions, but these effects (so-called *akugō* or karmic evil) will eventually play themselves out and only Amida's enlightened working (*gi*) will remain. Once entrusting faith opens us to an internal rather than external relation with Amida, the overlap between Amida and us can become ever greater until the two, in theory, merge. Then Amida's compassion will express itself through us as spontaneous moral activity.[42]

Shinran's theory of ethics does not fit neatly into either of the two traditional camps of western ethical theory, consequentialism or deontology. The consequentialist maintains the goodness of an action lies in whether its outcome is beneficial (in the sense of overall well-being, happiness, or pleasure, for example). To an extent Shinran agrees insofar as he judges goodness of results in terms of helping other people, relieving their suffering, and bringing them closer to enlightenment.

Yet, that is not all that is involved in a good act for Shinran. The intention, not just the consequence, is critical and that brings him closer to the deontologists. For Kant, the goodness of an action depends on the actor's sense of duty in following a moral principle, regardless of consequences. ("It's the principle of the thing.") Shinran would agree that Kant is correct in addressing the intention of the action, but wrong in his stress on duty. In fact, Shinran would assert almost the exact opposite from Kant: *if you perform an action for the sake of doing the right thing, then you are not a good person.* Shinran's position is that the good action is done with no calculated purpose at all. If I do something only because I think it is right, then I am acting on my own power—my own power to distinguish correctly right from wrong and to act according to that distinction.

> The reason is that since the person of own-power, being conscious of doing good, lacks the thought of entrusting the self completely to other-power, he or she is not the focus of the Primal Vow of Amida.[43]

Shinran's psychology of moral action sheds light on a persistent moral issue: can we truly perform a good deed with no involvement of the ego at all? Sometimes we may think we perform such a deed, but if the circumstances are right, we catch ourselves in our self-deception. An example might be when we anonymously do something kind for someone. Apparently egoless, we seek no credit or token of gratitude, acting out of pure altruism, or at least we think so at the time.

Suppose, however, that the anonymously performed good deed comes to be publicly praised, but attributed to the wrong person who deceitfully accepts the compliment. How do we feel then? In such cases we may discover that although we thought the action egoless, we secretly took pride in our anonymity, enough that when praise for the action is erroneously attributed and fraudulently accepted, our ego is stung. For Shinran that implies that the deed was performed by an ego-driven "bad person" (*akunin*) after all. Although we may have rationally deluded ourselves that our preference for anonymity was egoless, we secretly delighted in our "virtue," thereby feeding our own egos in the process. In summation: if I perform an act, however altruistic my self-avowed motives might seem, if I understand it as *my* altruistic act, it is not egoless after all.

What would be a good act that occurs "naturally" without self-conscious intention, without agenda? I was thinking about this some years ago while I was waiting in an airport boarding area, where my usual modus operandi has been to read a book or newspaper to "have something to do" to pass the time. On the occasion I am now recounting, however, I let myself have nothing to do; I was without agenda. I did not simply pass over into a "zoned out," self-absorbed state of inactivity, but instead opened myself to what was happening around me.

Having nothing to do is not the same as doing nothing. The former allows for responding quickly to a situation of need; it is being poised to act without any conscious agenda about what specifically to do. In the midst of all the activity around me, I saw a woman with a small child, a baby carriage, and two carry-on bags standing on the moving walkway in the middle of the concourse. She looked like she might have some problem negotiating everything when the moving walkway ended. As a result, I felt uncomfortable foreseeing her being unable to handle everything quickly and safely. So, I spontaneously got up and walked toward her. Arriving at the moving walkway as she was about to get off,

I helped her with her empty carriage, allowing her to concentrate on her child and carry-ons. She thanked me and I said, "It was nothing."

It *was* nothing, the kind of nothing that makes impromptu helpful action possible. If I had had an agenda, as in reading a magazine, I would not have seen her problem in time to help, if indeed if I would have seen it at all. Yet, because I had nothing to do, I saw her difficulty and identified with it. When the problem worked itself out naturally, I was grateful for the relief from *our* hassle. (I was uneasy foreseeing her upcoming difficulty so I was in that sense helping myself as well as her.) Consciously trying to help others by figuring out moral principles or devising some plan of moral action would be, according to Shinran, only another obstruction to the working of spontaneous, natural compassion.

We can say, then, that Shinran condemns not people who do good, but rather, "do-gooders," people who are always trying to do good by weighing (*hakarai*) their behavioral options, by figuring out ahead of time the best thing to do. According to Shinran, although ostensibly humble, such people really act out of a form of egoism and arrogance: they believe that they always know what is best for everyone else. They have made doing good deeds into a practice they undertake by their own power, precisely what Shinran says we should avoid. Since the *nenbutsu* is practiced without calculation, Shinran says it is "not a practice."[44]

There is another wrinkle to Shinran's analysis, however. Referring back to my experience in the airport, I represented it here as a good deed. In picking that example, I was therefore indirectly taking pride in performing an egoless, unpremeditated act. Perhaps the original deed was egoless, but in giving the account here, was I not taking some credit for being egoless? So it seems that ego entered into my *memory* of the egoless act after the fact. That egoism is, according to Shinran, the residue of karmic evil. Because of previous experiences (such as being praised by others for good deeds), I have formed a psychophysical propensity to take pride in such actions, thereby feeding the ego even when trying to act without ego. If that is correct, how should I have reflected on that event at the airport so that even its memory would be egoless? I would have to see it as not my act at all, but rather the working of Amida's compassionate vow. What kind of agency has no "I" for its agent? That raises the issue of the precise nature of Amida and the vow.

THE NATURE OF AMIDA: SHINRAN'S METAPHYSICS

What does it mean that Amida acts through the person of entrusting faith to perform acts of compassion? To answer that, we need to ask first about the metaphysical status of Amida. For example, of the three embodiments—historical, celestial, and cosmic—which applies to Amida? For both Shingon and

Tendai Buddhism, Amida is only a celestial embodiment, an appearance of the deeper reality that is the whole cosmos as Buddha.[45] We might assume Shinran would reject the idea of Amida as being derivative in such a way. In at least in one respect, however, he does not:

> The four lands are: first, the land of the cosmic embodiment; second, the land of the celestial embodiment; third, the land of the historical embodiment; and fourth the land of transformation. The "Pure Land of Peace" of which we are now concerned [as the land of Amida] is a celestial land.
>
> The three embodiments are: first, the cosmic embodiment; second, the celestial embodiment; and third, the historical embodiment. The Amida Buddha with which we are now concerned is a celestial embodiment.[46]

So, Shinran apparently conceded that at least in some contexts ("the Amida Buddha with which we are now concerned"), Amida is a celestial rather than a cosmic embodiment. Yet, it does seem peculiar that Shinran would advocate absolute faith in a non-absolute form of the Buddha and so, as we might expect, his theory is more complicated than what I have explained so far. Following the pattern found in other traditions such as Kūkai's Shingon Buddhism,[†] Shinran at times speaks of the cosmic embodiment as having variegated forms.[47]

Amida and the Two Kinds of Cosmic Embodiment

Let us begin with the following trenchant passage in which Shinran speaks of Amida Buddha as a cosmic embodiment with two forms.

> [We] know buddha-nature to be this mindful heart of entrusting faith (*shinjin*). The buddha-nature is the true nature of reality, and the true nature of reality is the buddha's cosmic embodiment. Therefore, we speak of two cosmic embodiments of "[Amida] buddha," the cosmic embodiment in itself as the nature of reality and the cosmic embodiment as heuristic expression. The cosmic embodiment in itself as the nature of reality has neither form nor color; ... words fall short in attempting to describe it.
>
> From this cosmic oneness, however, a form of expression emerged that is called "the cosmic embodiment as heuristic expression" and this took shape as the monk Hōzō. In his practice he put forth forty-eight great vows of an inconceivable nature, expressing what he hoped to accomplish as a bodhisattva. Among them are the "original vow of light immeasurable" and the "universal vow of life immeasurable." ... And it is in this manifestation that we speak of him as the Buddha of Unimpeded Light in All Directions.... Thus you should understand that Amida Buddha is light and, as light, is the form that wisdom takes.[48*]

257

† See pages 110–11.

Thus, Amida has two cosmic embodiments: the cosmic embodiment in itself as the nature of reality (*hosshō hosshin*) and the cosmic embodiment as heuristic expression (*hōben hosshin*). For convenience, I will henceforth refer to the first as Amida-in-itself and the second as Amida-for-us. The Amida-in-itself has neither color nor form, an Amida that concepts and words cannot really describe. The Amida-for-us, on the other hand, manifests the compassionate self-expression of the Amida-in-itself and appears as Hōzō, the bodhisattva who took the forty-eight vows and became the Amida that has concerned us in this chapter thus far. Shinran finds the link between the two in the vows themselves.†

For Hōzō's twelfth vow to be fulfilled (which indeed has been fulfilled or we would be speaking of the Bodhisattva Hōzō instead of the Buddha Amida), Amida must also be the Buddha of Immeasurable Light. As the universal light of wisdom shining everywhere, Amida can no longer have a form, color, or personality. From that absolute standpoint, then, through the fulfillment of the vows, Hōzō not only becomes Amida but more specifically becomes the Amida-in-itself.

256–7

To address our human needs and to give us an escape from our self-generated karmic afflictions, however, Hōzō also becomes Amida-for-us, giving us an objectified source of power outside our own ego-centered agency. That other-power is engaged through entrusting faith.

Yet, if we become fully engaged in entrusting faith, the ego and all its projected delusions disappear, so there is no longer any need for the heuristic of the Amida-for-us. That would seem to imply that to the extent we completely entrust ourselves to Amida's vow(s), the personal Amida-for-us disappears into the Amida-in-itself. But if that is correct, what happens to the entrusting faith when its object disappears into the formless?

Shinran seems to be saying that once the entrusting faith has been fully realized, Amida as the personal object of that faith disappears into the cosmos as light. In other words, once our entrusting faith (*shinjin*) loses both its subject (since we have surrendered the ego) and its object (since the personal Amida who took the vows has disappeared into formlessness), that entrusting faith *becomes another name for the compassionate universe itself.*

On the metaphysical level, the Amida in-itself is an entrusting of itself to itself, an unfolding as the world in which we can (heuristically) distinguish Amida from ourselves. But insofar as we participate in that entrusting process, both Amida and we as separate entities disappear again into the cosmic

† See pages 147–8.

embodiment's self-expression. This metaphysical process will be clearer if I describe its experiential implications.

Try thinking about Shinran's vision in these personal terms: your karmic afflictions—your negative habits of mind and body—isolate you from reality so that you think of yourself as an independently existing "I" who looks at things from afar so as to gauge them, manage them, and figure them out. Whenever you establish an external relation, a bridge of calculations and ideas spanning the gap between that "I" and "reality," you commit yourself to knowing reality as something outside you. That attempt to know through detachment is precisely the *hakarai* function Shinran so adamantly rejects. As long as you are a subject while reality is an object on which you act, your ego remains intact, functioning as the nucleus of delusional attachments, and enlightenment becomes impossible. Therefore, Shinran maintains that you need to discover an agency for engagement other than the "I," namely, the power of Amida's vow to which the person of entrusting faith surrenders.

That Amida of the vow, however, only exists as a way for your "I" to get outside itself. It is the heuristic Amida, the Amida-for-you. If your entrusting faith is profound enough, however, the external relation between your "I" and "Amida" transforms into an internal relation of intimacy, even a unity, between yourself and Amida. When that occurs, Amida's agency and your agency merge. By making the object of your entrusting faith an agent, by making the object of faith the only subject, the distinction between your "I" and "Amida" disappears. But then, there is no longer an "I" on whose behalf Amida takes the vow.

So, the Amida-for-you disappears as your "I" disappears. Then, there is only, as Shinran puts it, Amida's "working (*gi*)" that is "nonworking (*mugi*)." Neither Amida nor you cause things to happen; they just happen of themselves. Shinran identifies this spontaneous function as "happening of its own accord" (*onozukara*), or as a "naturalness" or "spontaneity" (*jinen*).[49*] There is no longer even a discrete person to be enlightened so there is no need for a heuristic Amida. That is true enlightening—Amida as reality's universal self-illumination.

Given that metaphysical explanation of entrusting faith and the two forms of Amida, the question remains of how Amida's compassion is present in the human world. That is an ethical as well as metaphysical issue usually expressed in terms of the so-called *transference of merit*.

The Coming and Going of Merit

All Mahayana traditions share the idea of the bodhisattva vow, the oath of the advanced compassionate person to put the spiritual progress of others ahead of one's own. Since spiritually skillful actions result in positive karmic effects, those actions are considered to have "merit" and the bodhisattva vow allows that karmic merit to be transferred to others. This will seem less mystical and magical when we consider an analogy with an example from the secular world. We all know people who sacrifice their prospects for personal wealth for the sake of serving others. The energy and its fruits that might have been used for their own personal enrichment are transferred to the betterment of others. The bodhisattva transfer of merit is analogous except that it is targeted specifically at the *spiritual* well-being of others. In Pure Land Buddhism, the twenty-second vow† refers to this transfer of merit to help others as "turning back" (*ekō*).

The merit transfers in two directions. First, in taking his bodhisattva vow, Hōzō-Amida has transferred his own merit to help lead us to his Pure Land. He could have achieved nirvana simply for himself, but instead he placed his priority on establishing a Pure Land for those who most needed spiritual help. Our benefiting from that transfer of merit is known as *ōsō ekō*, "transfer in the going (to the Pure Land) aspect." The other direction is *gensō ekō*, "transfer in the returning (from the Pure Land) aspect," that is, the Shin Buddhists' leaving the Pure Land to act as bodhisattvas in spiritually assisting others. That returning aspect of merit is, of course, still Amida's merits at work, but those who have been reborn in the Pure Land are, as it were, carried in that stream of Amida's reentry into our world. In that way, the person of true entrusting is a carrier, or even embodiment, of Amida's compassion.

That theory of the dual transfer of merit serves as the metaphysical backbone of Shinran's ethics. If our compassion for others is to be fulfilled, our attempts to help others must be entrusted not to ourselves but to Amida's power. So, the truly compassionate person is not compassionate by one's own efforts, but rather, is made so by Amida's compassion. That said, Amida's power is really only a phase in the self-expression of the Amida-in-itself, that is, Amida's compassion is really a spontaneous (agentless) naturalness or, more literally, a being "made to be so of itself," *jinen hōni*. Here we find the most profound level of Shinran's metaphysics.

> "To be made to become so" means that without the practitioner's slightest calculation, all one's past, present, and future karmic evil is transformed into the highest good.[50]

In other words, by entrusting oneself completely to Amida (the Amida-for-us), we become part of the natural process of the Buddha's self-expression. That pure act of entrusting faith takes us beyond the Amida-for-us to the Amida-

† See page 148.

in-itself. As such, we dissolve into Amida's universal light of compassion and wisdom.

My interpretation of this dynamic is that the coming and going of merit between the Pure Land and this world can be a continuous oscillation between the two, rather than two steps in a one-time-only event. I will begin with an explanation of the latter possibility so the contrast will be clear. The one-time-only theory would imply that when a person of entrusting faith dies, he or she goes to the Pure Land, makes great spiritual progress there, and then to complete one's enlightenment, returns to the world as a bodhisattva to help others. Such an interpretation remains close to the narrative of the original Indian Pure Land Sutras. and a conservative literalist might leave it at that. But not Shinran. Not the Shinran who rejected the historicity of the Degenerate Age in favor of its psychological meaning for his philosophical anthropology, not the Shinran who extended Tanluan's analysis of the two forms of Amida to serve his radical reinterpretation of *shinjin* as dissolving the Amida-for-us into Amida-in-itself, and not the Shinran who used the concept of "naturalness" to formulate a new theory of agency. Shinran was no conservative literalist.

As we have seen in a previously quoted passage,[†] Shinran construes entrusting faith as equivalent to the working of the cosmos (based on his formula: entrusting faith = buddha-nature = nature of all things = cosmic embodiment). Since, furthermore, Shinran understands entrusting faith as occurring in daily life, it follows that a person of entrusting faith can experience the true nature of things even before dying and going to the Pure Land. Because of that dynamic, we are capable of good deeds, but only when our entrusting faith has eradicated the agency of the action as deriving from our own power.

The easiest way to make these views coherent, I believe, is to think of Shinran's theory about rebirth into the Pure Land as an oscillation rather than a one-time-only event. To help us think through that interpretation, I will take the standpoint of someone inside the experiential and philosophical framework Shinran has constructed.

Because of the negative karmic consequences of past deeds, my psychophysical propensities have separated me from the way reality is. Despite all attempts to free myself of the constructed ego that creates that separation, because my cognitive, emotional, and intellectual habits are so entrenched, I continuously fall prey to egocentric thoughts, words, and deeds. Even when I attempt to be altruistic, the ego lurks in the background, poised to enter my self-understanding once the action is completed. I secretly take credit for being so altruistic.

† See page 202.

In response to that vicious cycle, I relinquish all attempts to figure out and fix the situation, releasing myself to the other-power of Amida's vow which was designed precisely for people in my situation. As I do so, I assume an attitude of having nothing to do and, by a natural responsiveness, compassionate actions occur. At that *moment* (what Shinran calls the "one thought moment" or *ichinen*), the entire world is Amida's working, happening of itself without individual agency, either my own or Amida's. In that sense Amida's merit has taken me to the Pure Land and transferred merit back into this world through the responsive, compassionate acts of which, we might say, I am the "carrier." (Recall my earlier anecdote of how my having nothing to do at the airport expressed itself in a selfless act of compassion.)

Yet, as Shinran said, though my birth in the Pure Land is assured, I find myself unable to rejoice in that fact because as soon as I do so, that rejoicing would be affected by the "residue of karmic evil," the still present propensities that lead my ego to congratulate myself for my piety or virtue (as I did when I recounted my "selfless" act in the airport). That falling back on my own capacities—bedevilled with delusions, desires, and ignorance—re-creates my need for Amida to become the "other" to which I can give over my "I." And the process starts over.

I understand this as an oscillation: going to the Pure Land as the result of relinquishing the ego and returning from the Pure Land to compassionately help others are not single, but *recurring*, events. The experience of entrusting faith and the persistence of karmic afflictions are such that, at least in this world, I can at best only oscillate between selfless engagement and self-delusion.

In support of that interpretation consider first these comments from Shinran's major technical treatise *The Teaching, the Practice, the Entrusting, the Enlightenment* (*Kyōgyōshinshō*). Therein Shinran quotes Tanluan on the distinct, but fundamentally inseparable, functions of the two cosmic embodiments.

> All Buddhas and Bodhisattvas have cosmic bodies of two dimensions: the cosmic-embodiment-in-itself and the cosmic-embodiment-for-us. The cosmic-embodiment-for-us arises from the cosmic-embodiment-in-itself; and the cosmic-embodiment-in-itself emerges out of the cosmic-embodiment-for-us. These two dimensions of cosmic-embodiment are different but are not separable; they are one but cannot be regarded as identical.[51]

Of course, that also implies that the real basis of the universe is the simultaneous act of Amida's compassion and of human entrusting (entrusting faith) in that compassion. As Shinran put it:

> This Amida pervades the countless worlds and the minds of all those in the ocean of being. Thus, plants, trees, and our land all attain buddhahood. Since in their mindful hearts, all sentient beings entrust themselves to the vow of

the Amida-for-us, this entrusting faith is itself buddha-nature; buddha-nature is itself the true nature of things; the true nature of things is itself the cosmic embodiment.[52]

In short: entrusting faith is the cosmic embodiment. Everything is the cosmic embodiment's self-expressive act. The Pure Land is not something separate from this world, but is rather the dynamic of Amida's presence within this world and as this world. When we consider this point of view, the functions of Amida begin to appear similar to the functions attributed to that buddha by Shingon, not only by Kakuban but also to some extent by Kūkai. So let us take a look at the similarities and differences.

Shinran's Amida and Shingon's Amida Compared

Although the details are somewhat different, the overall structure of Shinran's metaphysics resembles Kūkai's theory of *hosshin seppō*, "the cosmic embodiment preaches the Dharma (true teachings) through the dharmas (all phenomena)." Like Kūkai, Shinran believed that all things are enlightened. Furthermore, the cosmic embodiment assumes the form of particular buddha personalities to teach the Dharma more explicitly. All phenomena and all buddhas are expressions of the cosmic embodiment's own enlightened self-expression.

The critical divergence between Shinran and Kūkai is that, in Shingon's terms, Shinran places a special emphasis on one particular manifestation of the cosmic buddha, namely, Amida. If Shinran were to debate this point with Kūkai, he could give two philosophical reasons in defense of this position, one metaphysical and one metapractical. Metaphysically, Shinran would argue that Kūkai had only fathomed one dimension of Amida's ontological status, namely, Amida as a celestial form of the buddha-for-us. By the twelfth vow,[†] however, we know that Amida is also the infinite light associated with wisdom and, Shinran might have added, by the thirteenth vow, the infinite life associated with compassion. Those formless, depersonalized characteristics of Amida identify him also as the buddha-for-itself.

In one respect, and this makes Shinran somewhat closer to Kakuban, Shinran maintains that Amida is indeed a celestial buddha, but not just any celestial buddha. Amida's character is such that once we become intimate with him, he and we together disappear into the formless, nameless ground of enlightenment itself. Amida is a signified reality that dissolves as soon as it is grasped, thereby eliminating any possibility of our becoming fixated on a finite manifestation of the infinite, a form of the formless but not the formless itself. Put that way,

† See page 148.

Shinran could go beyond Kakuban's stance to claim that there are no meta-physical grounds for holding Dainichi as understood in Shingon Buddhism to be superior to Amida as understood in Shin Buddhism. Indeed, in broad metaphysical terms, Shinran's metaphysics is only a variation of Kūkai's, much as Kakuban thought his own was.

The deeper philosophical difference between Shinran and either Kūkai or Kakuban is metapractical, rather than metaphysical. Since Shin praxis varies so sharply from Shingon praxis, that is to be expected. Metapraxis explains how the praxis is suitable for gaining insight into reality, reality as explained by the metaphysics. If the metaphysics of Shin and Shingon Buddhism are similar and the praxes wholly different, the metapractical theories must diverge. The key variant between Shinran and the Shingon thinkers lies in their religious or philosophical anthropologies, that is, their theories about the nature of our humanity and its situation.

Given his sense of the Degenerate Age, his encounter with the human suffer-ing around him, and his acute sensitivity to psychological limitations, Shinran found the esoteric version of the cosmic Buddha to be too distant, abstract, and impersonal. According to Kūkai, as I explained in Chapter 3,[†] Dainichi expresses himself out of his own "self-enjoyment" as the universe. Unlike Shin-ran's statement about Amida's having taken the vow for Shinran alone, Kūkai's Dainichi only "deigns to let itself be known" to us.

Feelingly hopelessly deluded and ego-driven, Shinran tried but could not find that primordial enlightenment within himself, even with the aid of esoteric ritu-als. In that despair, however, he was inspired by Hōnen and discovered Amida's vow reaching out to him, making enlightenment available to him via the Pure Land Gate. Amida stood there in the midst of Shinran's anguish, indeed as Shinran's anguish, to call him, and to be called through, the power of the Name, the *nenbutsu*. The parent came for the child. In returning to the parent, Shinran found himself empowered by and through the cosmic embodiment. Carried aloft in Amida's love, Shinran found himself again in the world, but in the world as part of Amida's compassionate expression. At that point, truly selfless acts of compassion become possible.

As soon as that happens, unfortunately, the alienation of self from Amida again takes form as the karmically afflicted ego once again asserts itself. At that point, Shinran must again relinquish any sense of self-power, making every act (*gyō*) Amida's act. Despairing at the loss of naturalness into a corrupted and corrupting sense of ego, Shinran again turns to the vow of the Amida-for-us. The power of Amida's vow reestablishes an internal relation with Shinran until

---

† See quotation on page 113.

the two eventually merge, disappearing together into the cosmic-embodiment-in-itself. Then the cycle is repeated again and again. At least, that is how I understand the dynamic when we view it through the oscillation rather than one-time-only interpretation.

So, in a sense, even from Shinran's perspective, Kūkai was right. Our inherent enlightenment is readily available to us. But for Shinran, Kūkai is wrong about how it is available. Shinran's and Kūkai's religious experience only meet at that moment when Shinran disappears with Amida into the formless cosmic embodiment and when Shinran is brought back into the world as a carrier of Amida's compassion. Immediately after that, however, Shinran loses the intimacy with Amida, an intimacy that can only be reestablished through the power of Amida's vow to generate entrusting faith. Although Amida is, on one hand, the source of entrusting faith, Amida (as Amida-for-us) also can be said to exist only insofar as we ourselves are the expression of that entrusting faith. Amida and we are in internal relation with each other, interdependent in such a way that without us Amida cannot be fully Amida and without Amida, we cannot be fully ourselves.

CONCLUSION

This concludes our engagement with Shinran. We have seen how his critique of the Path to Self-perfection had three steps. First, he revealed the logical contradictions in any Buddhist philosophy or praxis that assumes a discrete self or ego as agent of either thought or action. His critique was framed by his rejection of the detached form of knowing he called *hakarai*. Second, he explained an alternative, the Pure Land Gate of other-power, a Way of knowing and engaging the world without the slightest hint of ego. Finally, Shinran developed a metaphysical system and metapractical justification for entrusting faith, explaining how and why the Pure Land Gate is effective in leading to enlightenment.

In his writings Shinran uses the ocean as a metaphor in two ways. On one hand, the ocean is the ocean of desires in which we find ourselves awash and drowning, the realm of birth-and-death plagued by our karmic afflictions.[†] On the other hand, the ocean is the power of the vow of Amida that offers rescue from our despair.[‡] Shinran frequently alternates between the two significations of the ocean metaphor, but in the following passage he juxtaposes them:

---

† See, for example, the quotation on page 195.
‡ See, for example, the quotations on pages 197 and 208.

Let's consider the term *ocean* [from this text we are analyzing]. Since time immemorial, there have been the streams of practices, both those of ordinary people and those of sages. So also have there been the infinite ocean waters [drowning] the ignorant and various transgressors. Together they have been transformed into the waters of the great treasure ocean of all virtues true and real—the waters of the great wisdom-compassion of the Primal Vow. Truly, as the sutra says, "The ice of karmic afflictions melts, becoming the water of virtues."[53]

In other words, the same ocean in which we are drowning through our own ignorance also has within it the buoyancy to keep us afloat and save us—if only we let it. When we see the ocean as a threat to overwhelming our ego-existence, we flail against it, trying to push it away lest we go under. As long as we do so, we will be drowning in that reality. When we see the ocean and ourselves—reality and egoless self—not as oppositional but interlinked, however, we and the ocean become joined in our buoyancy, allowing us to float to safety with no self-conscious effort.

In our next chapter, we will engage Shinran's contemporary, Zen Master Dōgen. Like Shinran he addressed many of the Kamakura period's major philosophical and spiritual concerns, but he marked out a different path. Dōgen rejected the idea of the Degenerate Age; he stressed achieving enlightenment by our own efforts; and he advocated meditation rather than voicing the *nenbutsu* or taking the standpoint of entrusting faith. Despite those differences, we will also find continuity between the two thinkers even though, as far as we know, they knew nothing of each other. In Dōgen and Shinran, we will find two alternative responses to the challenges of the Kamakura situation, two spiritual options that frame much of subsequent Japanese religious experience and philosophy.

Shinran never left Japan, but our encounter with Dōgen begins on an ocean voyage. Unable to find what he needs at home, he gambles on taking a hazardous journey to China to find answers to his questions.

6. DŌGEN 道元 (1200–1253)

Nothing Doing; Everything Counts

The buddhas profoundly realize their
delusions, while ordinary people are
profoundly deluded in their enlightenment.

DŌGEN

We find Dōgen as a young monk on a ship headed for China in 1223, a man on
a mission in the company of his Kyoto mentor, Myōzen (1184–1225). Peering out
at the sea around him, a great empty circle of water in all directions, watching
the ship's keel cut through the waves, he pondered the confluence of past causes
and future hopes that put him on this ship, at this time, going to that place. The
sea breeze on his shaved head reminded him of what he had sacrificed: casting
off the markings of his aristocratic origins—the garb, headgear, even his birth
name—to assume the classless status of Buddhist monk. The scent of the brazier
swept him back to his mother's funeral when he had first resolved to become a
monk as he watched, through the tearful eyes of an eight-year old, the smoke
from the incense stick curl up into the air dissolving into oblivion. After some
years of badgering, Dōgen had prevailed on his family to enroll him in the Mt
Hiei monastery, where he had become a Tendai novice around the age of eleven.

Dōgen had immediately put his elite literary education to good use by pouring over the sacred texts and by focusing his physical energies on completing
the demanding regimens of the mountain. Dōgen was nothing if not earnest.
Yet, here he was on the way to China with no intention of visiting Mt Tiantai,
the international home base of the Tendai tradition in which he had trained,
and no intention of pursuing the esoteric ordinations so valued on the mountain. No, he was going to China to study Zen or, as it was called in Chinese,
Chan Buddhism.

But what did he know of Zen? He looked over at Myōzen squatting on the deck, darning a small tear in his monk's robe. On a trip down from the mountain into Kyoto, Dōgen had met Myōzen some six years earlier at Kennin-ji, the aforementioned monastery founded by the Tendai monk, Eisai, who had twice gone to China, bringing back techniques and texts from the Chan tradition.[†] Dōgen had little time to train with Eisai before the master's death, but he stayed on to become a disciple of Eisai's chosen successor as abbot, Myōzen.

Dōgen had gone to Kennin-ji out of frustration with his Tendai praxis on Mt Hiei, especially because its metapractical system did not quite make sense to him. The formal debates on the mountain sometimes centered on the topic of inherent enlightenment: the idea that all of us are essentially or radically already enlightened or awakened; that this world of delusion is no different from the world of enlightenment; and that all beings—even the grasses, trees, mountains, and rivers—are enlightened.

Yet, if that is so, Dōgen kept wondering why Buddhist practice remains so complicated and grueling. Why did he have to learn the complex esoteric Buddhist ritual system: the plethora of mantras, the mudras, and the mandalas? Why did he have to study and chant the sutras? Why did he have to sit for hours in the Tendai style of tranquil meditation? Why did he have to train so hard to become enlightened when he supposedly was already enlightened?

There seemed, therefore, to be an inconsistency between the arduous praxis to initialize enlightenment (*shikaku*) and the ideal of being already innately enlightened (*hongaku*). Why struggle to achieve what we already have? Although Myōzen didn't have a solution to this paradox either, there was something alluring in the directness and simplicity of Zen praxis, even as Kennin-ji's regimen intermixed it with Tendai practices, both esoteric and exoteric. So Dōgen had stopped his wandering and stayed on at Kennin-ji, finding Myōzen to be a sympathetic listener and insightful advisor.

In their six years together, their personal quests grew so intertwined that when Myōzen decided in 1223 to fulfill a long-standing wish to visit China, he invited Dōgen to come along so the teacher and student could practice together. Dōgen considered China under the Song dynasty to be a repository of literary treasures and spiritual achievement. Surely, if there were any place he could find answers to his questions, if anywhere he could indeed realize his dream of enlightenment, it would be there.

The ship landed in China at Qingyuan, Dōgen remaining aboard until he got a better sense of where he wanted to go, while Myōzen immediately set out to explore on his own. One day an elderly Chinese Chan monk came to the ship

† See pages 170–2.

to buy Japanese mushrooms. Dōgen could not wait to bombard the visitor with questions. What was Zen Buddhist practice like in China? What exactly was this enlightenment experience all about? The ensuing discussion was not what Dōgen had expected, though. The monk was the chief cook (*tenzo*) for a monastery some twenty kilometers away and, despite Dōgen's urging him to stay and talk about Buddhism, he had to return to his temple to prepare the meal for the next day's special festivities.

Here is Dōgen's own account of the exchange, written some years after the event:

> I further asked the cook: "You who are so advanced in years, why don't you sit in meditation to pursue the Way or contemplate the words of the ancients? It is troublesome being cook; all you do is labor. What good is that?"
>
> The cook laughed and said, "My good man from a foreign country, you don't yet understand the pursuit of the Way and do not yet know about written words."
>
> When I heard him speak like that, I suddenly felt ashamed and taken aback. I asked him, "What are written words? What is the practice of the Way?"
>
> The cook said, "If you don't slip up and lose sight of what you are talking about, how could you not be that man [you aspire to be]?"
>
> At the time I didn't understand. The cook said, "If you still don't understand, come to Mt Yuwang some time. On that occasion we can discuss the Way of written words." Having said that, the cook got up, saying, "It is late in the day and I am in a hurry, so I am going back now."[54]

Dōgen had ventured to China to engage the true Buddhist teachings about practice and enlightenment. Now this strange Chan cook had come along, confirmed Dōgen's confusion, and then set off into the sunset without explanation. Fortunately, that would not be their only encounter.

Some time later, the cook was planning to retire to his distant home province, but before he left the region, he thought of the earnest Japanese monk from the ship and sought him out. He found Dōgen on Mt Tiantong. Delighted to see him again, Dōgen offered refreshments and the discussion started where it had left off aboard the ship. As Dōgen later told his own students:

> The cook said, "To study written words is to understand their provenance.[55] To exert yourself in pursuit of the Way requires an affirmation of the provenance of pursuing the Way."
>
> I asked him, "What are written words?" The cook answered, "One, two, three, four, five." I also asked, "What is pursuit of the Way?" He said, "In the whole world, it can never be hidden."
>
> Although there was a great variety of other things that we discussed, I will not record them at this point. The little I know about written words and understand about pursuing the Way is due to that cook's great kindness. I told

my late teacher Myōzen about the things that I have just related here and he was so pleased to hear of them.

Later I saw a verse that Xuedou (980–1052) wrote to instruct the monks:

> One letter, seven letters, three letters, or five;
> Investigating myriads of images, one reaches no basis.
> In the depth of night, the moon sets into the dark sea;
> Seeking the black dragon's pearl, one finds there are many.

What that cook said some years before and what Xuedou expresses in this verse clearly coincide. More and more I understand that the cook was a true man of the Way. But in the past what I saw of written words was one, two, three, four, five. Today what I see of written words is also six, seven, eight, nine, ten.

You disciples who come after me, thoroughly contemplate there in accordance with here and thoroughly contemplate here in accordance with there. If you make this kind of effort, you will be able to obtain in written words the Zen of a single [true] flavor....[56]

ENGAGING DŌGEN'S QUESTIONS

To engage Dōgen's philosophy, you need to try to make his questions your questions. So, pause and consider how you yourself might approach the following line of inquiry. How do you know reality and what praxis is involved in attaining that knowledge? On one hand, the issue might seem simple enough. After all, reality never takes a leave of absence; it is always right there ready for us to engage. On the other hand, once you scrutinize the matter, you stir up a hornet's nest of philosophical problems. For example, *who* is trying to know reality? Your simple answer might be "I am." But is that "I" real? "Of course," you might say. As Descartes pointed out some four centuries ago, even when I doubt I am real, what is doing the doubting must be real. So I must exist ("I think; therefore, I am"). If that is right, though, consider the peculiar problem arising next.

If you are real, when you know reality, reality (or at least part of reality) is what knows reality. If so, how can a part of reality ever be mistaken about what really is? Since reality is always present, it must be present to itself. If the reality of which you are a part is self-conscious, your knowing reality should be easy; if it is not self-conscious, even reality cannot know reality and knowledge must be impossible. Here we can find our own version of Dōgen's puzzle: how can knowing reality (enlightenment) be both manifest and so difficult to attain?

To make this metaphysical and epistemological puzzle even more familiar to the idiom of our age, it can be posed in our popular psychological terms. Suppose a friend or advisor says that you are "out of touch with reality" or that you need "to face reality." What exactly does that mean? First, the statement assumes that reality is patently accessible to any of us. Second, it implies that you are living your life according to some irreality or delusion and that, for your own good, you should somehow change how you engage the world. Psychotherapists are fond of saying that such a change is "hard work." The puzzle is why being in touch with reality is such "hard work" if that reality has been available to us all along. Today, in the modern western world, theories about the unconscious, the effects of trauma, and the mechanism of biochemical imbalances all attempt to shed some light on this matter, but let us now consider how the problem and its answer would be framed in Dōgen's world.

As I have noted, one Buddhist conundrum was the relation between *hongaku* (inherent awakening) and *shikaku* (initialized awakening). On one hand, Tendai Buddhism, like virtually all other forms of Mahāyāna Buddhism, teaches that phenomena appear "just as they are," that is, reality does not veil itself in "illusion" (what orthodox Indian philosophical texts refer to as *māyā*[57*]). This is the heart of the *hongaku* teaching: because of this direct accessibility to reality in its undistorted form, all of us are in this sense somehow already enlightened. If things are such as they are (how could they be otherwise?) and if we are such as we are (how could we be otherwise?), then on some fundamental level, that which is necessary and sufficient for enlightenment is already present.

On the other hand, Tendai Buddhism, again like most other forms of Buddhism, teaches that achieving enlightenment requires a demanding program of praxis: the inherent awakening has to be initialized as *shikaku* and we have to align how we are with how things are. The philosophical paradox is how the two Tendai teachings fit together. For Dōgen, this problem boiled down to the relationship between enlightenment and practice. The Chinese cook had given Dōgen two clues during their second meeting. First, he said that the key to understanding practice is to understand the *provenance* of praxis. Second, the cook suggested that understanding the provenance of praxis relates to understanding the provenance of words. With that reminder, let us return to the narrative of Dōgen's trip to China to pursue further his final position on this question.

FROM ZEN STUDENT TO ZEN MASTER

The second conversation with the cook occurred in a Zen monastery on Mt Tiantong where Dōgen had already joined a Chinese monastic community there. After Dōgen had left the ship, he visited prominent Zen teachers at various locations in China, staying in touch with Myōzen all the while. Only upon meeting Zen Master Rujing (1162–1227) in 1225 did Dōgen feel he had at last found the teacher he was seeking and he joined Rujing's monastic community on Mt Tiantong. Rujing, a master of the Chinese Caodong (J. Sōtō) tradition, emphasized *zazen* (seated meditation) as Zen's core practice. A famed disciplinarian, Rujing insisted his students spend long hours in *zazen* every day. During one session, an exhausted monk next to Dōgen fell asleep and Rujing chastised him for sleeping by shouting, "In *zazen* bodymind drops away." We do not know how Rujing's words affected the drowsy meditator, but Dōgen experienced an awakening. Henceforth, the phrase "bodymind dropping away" (*shinjin datsuraku*)[58] would be a principal term in Dōgen's Zen vocabulary.

After his two-year apprenticeship with Rujing, Dōgen returned to Japan a credentialed Zen master. Although Japanese Sōtō Zen historians consider him the founder of their sect, Dōgen's original intent was not to create a new form of Japanese Buddhism, but to offer a corrective and enhancement to the Buddhism already in place. Since Dōgen believed *zazen* to be the foundation of all Buddhist praxis, not just Zen praxis, his first task was to explain the correct method for *zazen* and to give a metapractical justification for his exclusive emphasis on *zazen* as "just sitting" (*shikantaza*).

Like most other major Kamakura-period thinkers, Dōgen was intent on *selecting* the one practice that opens to the benefits of all practices. For the physical side of *zazen*, his instructions were simple: find a suitably quiet and comfortable place to sit, assume a stable full-lotus position, sit quietly with the eyes opened slightly, calm the breath, and so forth.[59] The notable part of his otherwise pedestrian instructions was an allusion to a provocative Zen *kōan*:[60*] "Think of not thinking. How do you think of not-thinking? Without thinking."

In initially introducing the distinction among thinking, not-thinking, and without-thinking, Dōgen probably intended it as no more than practical instruction. Specifically, he was prompting the correct psychological state appropriate to *zazen*: don't think and don't try to not think; just let go of the whole distinction. That is, Dōgen originally used the kōan to prescribe a state of awareness that releases the practitioner from both the activities of thinking, fantasizing, or daydreaming as well as any conscious attempt to empty or blank the mind. Dōgen's *zazen* is alertness to what is happening as it is happening without fixating on any moment as a point of analysis, conceptualization, or affect. To reflect on any moment or even to intentionally try not to make any such reflection prevents us from being aware of what is happening in the moment at hand, that which is presencing here and now.

Dōgen was advocating neither a "stream of consciousness" nor a frozen blankness, but rather something akin to a "stream of awareness" in sync with the stream of ever-changing phenomena. Simply stated, Dōgen was teaching a form of full engagement in which self and reality overlap and (ideally) fully interpenetrate. Note, however, that Dōgen's original use of the kōan was as an instruction in how to practice, not a justification for the practice. At this point, he was using the kōan practically, not metapractically and, to that extent, it had only minor philosophical significance.

It is not that Dōgen initially offered no metapractical justification at all for his exclusive focus on *zazen,* but his original defense of the practice was mainly an appeal to history and tradition. He argued that seated meditation has been fundamental to Buddhism since its origins. The historical Buddha, Siddhartha Gautama, had achieved nirvana while sitting in meditation under the bodhi tree and all Buddhist schools depicted seated buddhas and bodhisattvas in their paintings and statuary. Since the Japanese word for "seated meditation" is *zazen,* it might seem Dōgen had made a good case justifying his exclusive emphasis on that one practice since seated meditation did seem to be universally emphasized in a wide array of Buddhist traditions.

If that is as far as it goes, however, the argument is spurious and Dōgen had to know that. Just because Buddhists have always engaged in seated meditation does not mean that the *technique* of seated meditation has not varied. Not all Buddhists (indeed probably no other Buddhists at all in Japan at Dōgen's time) thought of seated meditation as "just sitting" (*shikan taza*). During his training on Mt Hiei, Dōgen himself had undoubtedly sat in meditation, but when doing so, he was performing esoteric ritual meditations with mudras, mandalas, and mantras or he was doing the exoteric Tendai meditation, "calming and insight" (*shikan*[†]).

In the final analysis, to justify his exclusive emphasis on *zazen,* Dōgen had to prove not only that seated meditation was Buddhism's most fundamental and universal practice, but also that his "just sitting" practice was the purest form or basis of *all* forms of seated meditation. He had to move from practical instruction to metapractical justification, a shift that entailed his being a Zen philosopher as well as a Zen master.

DŌGEN THE PHILOSOPHER

Why was this emphasis on *zazen* alone so important to Dōgen and his audience? I have already explained the dark mood of many Kamakura Buddhists, often characterized in terms of the Degenerate Age, *mappō.* In such despondent times, when it came to praxis, simpler was better. Yet, the simpler still had to be efficacious as there was no point in simplifying praxis if the result was a second-rate or lower-level insight.

Suppose, however, Dōgen could demonstrate the new praxis was not only simpler, but also the one element common to all effective Buddhist praxes?

† This Tendai term *shikan* (止観) is not the same as the *shikan* (只管) of Dōgen's *shikan taza.*

Then, he might argue that the new distilled praxis was not only necessary, but also sufficient, for attaining enlightenment because the *zazen* part of Buddhist praxis would holographically contain the whole of Buddhist praxis.

Dōgen's "just sitting" obviously met the simplicity criterion. After all, what could be simpler than just sitting without thinking? The nub of the issue was the other criterion: how could Dōgen defend "just sitting" as the foundation, the holographic entry point containing the pattern of all efficacious praxes? How could *zazen* alone generate perfect enlightenment? A justification, Dōgen realized, would require an analysis of thinking itself. That realization led him to consider the "without thinking" kōan to be not merely a guide for how to practice *zazen*, but also a key to a metapractical argument justifying his selection of *zazen* as the sole focus of praxis.

What Is Thinking?

As I have explained, Dōgen's practical instructions in how to do *zazen* stressed without thinking. (Henceforth, I will use *zazen* to refer specifically to Dōgen's "just sitting" as a "without thinking" form of *zazen*.) It follows then that *zazen* itself cannot yield knowledge of anything: knowing involves concepts, but without-thinking does not conceptualize. To that extent, *zazen* per se cannot even yield truth in the usual meaning of the word because truth usually implies that what we think or say matches or expresses the way things are. In an important sense, because it lacks concepts, without thinking's engagement with reality is *meaningless*. Then with what does *zazen* present us and how can that be considered the foundation of all Buddhism?

> The cook said, "Exertion in pursuit of the Way requires an affirmation of the provenance of pursuing the Way."

Dōgen came to realize that although *zazen* does not give us the truth, it does give us what we need to be able to see the truth, what Zen sometimes calls the "eye for the truth" (*shōbōgen*). As an analogy consider the function of our physical eyes. Our eyes do not themselves know the empirical facts of physical reality. Yet, they generate the visual sensations on which cognition and concepts operate, operations that in turn produce empirical knowledge. So our eyes are the basic source, the provenance, for all visual knowledge of the world. Yet, in themselves the eyes yield no meaning.

Analogously, the eye for the truth does not know the truth, but is a prerequisite to seeing it. As without thinking, *zazen* lacks conceptualization, and intrinsically cannot present us with the meaning of reality. Hence, truth must arise through some additional process that forms meaning. Still, without-thinking is as foundational to grasping the buddha's truth (*buppō*; S. *buddha dharma*) as opening the physical eyes is to grasping visually accessible truth (visual dharmas). Following the cook's challenge, we can say opening the eye for the truth is "the provenance of the practice" for engaging and expressing how things actually are. That is what the Zen tradition preserves and treasures; it is the "repository of the eye for the truth," *shōbōgenzō*, the term Dōgen selected for his collection of philosophical essays.

What, then, does the eye for the truth see? On one hand, it does not see any *thing* at all, that is, it discriminates nothing through labels or concepts. In Buddhist terminology, it is "outside names and forms." Any naming and conceptualizing is the product of thinking, not without-thinking. On the other hand, although devoid of meaning, without-thinking does not experience a simple void. Only not-thinking generates in consciousness a pure void, a complete vacuity, a pervasive nonexistence. Without-thinking, by contrast, is immersed in a presence, but a presence without verbal identification.[62] As the idea of inherent awakening suggests, things are accessible "just as they are" or, to use the more technical terminology, they are "thusness" or "suchness" or "as-ness."

Nyoze and *inmo* are the two Zen words for as-ness that Dōgen commonly used in his writings. The word "thusness" or "as-ness" sounds odd in English because it makes a noun out of an adverb. English commonly nominalizes adjectives ("happy" into "happiness," for example), but not adverbs (English lacks the noun form "happily-ness"), but that inability is no more than a quirk of English grammar. We certainly could imagine a noun form derived from an adverb. That is, if "happiness" is the state of "being happy," then "happily-ness" is the "way of acting happily." The distinction is that "happiness" is a "whatness" whereas "happilyness" would be a "howness." Sanskrit allows such linguistic constructions and so the adverb *tathā* ("thus," "as," or "such") can be nominalized into "thusness," "as-ness," or "suchness" (*tathatā*). The Japanese term *nyoze* or *shinnyo* is commonly used to translate that Sanskrit word.

It is critical to remember that as-ness is never a thing, but a *way* things work or function. Most importantly, it is not what makes things as they are nor a substrate beneath or behind phenomenal existence. As I explained in Chapter 2's overview, in Buddhism phenomena (*dharmas*) are events, not substantial things and, as events, they are always in flux.[†] Given the central Buddhist doctrine of impermanence, "as-ness" refers to the manner in which the interdependent flow of events occurs. In his essay from the *Repository of the Eye for the Truth* entitled *Busshō* (Buddha-nature), Dōgen insists on the importance of this point by making two linked claims. First, that phenomena do not *have* buddha-nature,

† See pages 56–7.

but rather, all being *is* buddha-nature. And second, that impermanence is itself buddha-nature.[63]

The other Japanese term, *inmo,* gives this notion of as-ness a distinctively East Asian, especially Zen, spin. Unlike *nyoze,* this term did not come into Chinese as a translation for any specific Indian Buddhist term, but originated instead in the Chinese slang of the Song era. In Chinese, it was a modifier originally meaning something like "that kind of ..." or "such a...." The Chan (Zen) Buddhists gave this phrase a technical sense, "the way things are," making it almost synonymous with "as-ness."

To acquire some sense for the linguistic play in this term, imagine a community of people who took the "how is it" from phrases like "how is it good? how is it delicious? how is it awful?" and elided it into "howzit." Then they used howzit as a noun for "the way things (really) are" using locutions like "howzit is the ground of insight" or "you need to penetrate the howzit," or "you have to go beyond the thing to its howzit." Again, it is crucial that *inmo* refers to an ever-changing flow that is in itself without meanings attached. At the most, we can say *inmo* is not what things mean, but *how* they mean. Let us now see what Dōgen says about *inmo* in his essay of the same name in *Repository.*

Dōgen's commentary begins with a reflection on the words of the Chinese master, Yunju Daoying (?–902) on as-ness or suchness:

> If you seek to attain things as such (*inmo*), you must be a person as such (*inmo*). But of course you are already a person as such (*inmo*). So why be anxious about things as such (*inmo*)?[64]

Yunju's saying is much like my earlier queries to you about knowing reality. If you are real, how can you not know reality? Surely if any kind of knowledge is at all possible, what is real must be able to know what is real. Why, then, is there a problem of "attaining things as such"? Dōgen says the problem arises when we think of ourselves as physical beings (as a stable "I") separate from the flow of things as such. That sense of self would distort how we experience without-thinking.

> We are just figures in that world extending in all directions. How does one know there is as-ness? I know it is so because my bodymind appears along with the whole world and I know that it is not an I [separate from the inventory of the world]. My body is already not [an isolated] I: life is carried along in the passage of time, hard to encapsulate for even a moment.
> The blush of youth has left for somewhere else, not a trace to be found. There are many things of the past we can never encounter again. Even the innocent heart doesn't last, but comes and goes. Even if we might speak of there being truth (*makoto*), it is not something persisting in the purview of an individuated ego (*goga*).[65]*

This passage may seem filled with resignation about the flux of things, a darker version of the Heian courtiers' appreciation of impermanence as a source of *aware*. Yet, Dōgen's perspective is actually not at all pessimistic. Only when we think of ourselves as separate from, rather than within, the flow of phenomena do we feel regret: the blush of youth gone from our cheeks, we think, is something that happens *to us*. In the spirit of Master Yunju, Dōgen puts his emphasis on the fact that we are as much as-ness as are the other processes of the world around us.

When we recognize that fact, the individuated ego—that conceptualized sense of "I" as distinct from the world—disappears into the flux of the way all things are, the impermanence that is itself buddha-nature. Aging, for example, is not something that happens to me; aging is *how* I am. Without aging I would not be such as I am. Even dying is not something that happens to me, but is how I am at a certain time. The only I is an impermanent I, inseparable from the flux comprising reality.

The Way of Engaging Presence

Dōgen uses a distinctive word for the as-ness engaged in without thinking, namely, the compound term *genjōkōan*, "the presencing of things as they are."[66] The first half of the term, *genjō*, means to be complete in its presence. As the cook said, "In the whole world, it can never be hidden," that is, there is no veil of illusion hiding the secrets of true reality. Furthermore, the completeness in that presence harks back to Xuedou's poem cited by Dōgen, "Seeking the black dragon's pearl, one finds there are many." The singular or particular opens into the whole; the provenance of enlightenment is always accessible. To find it, you need only have the eye for the truth. As for the second half of the term, in Zen parlance *kōan* means the focal point of praxis. As such, Dōgen gives the term a dual significance.

On one hand, Dōgen uses *kōan* to refer to how phenomena are present in without-thinking, each phenomenon being fully as it is in its own time and place.[67] Using a term from the *Lotus Sutra*, Dōgen says, "each phenomenon fully exhausts itself" (*ippōgujin*) in its self-presentation. This notion of *kōan*, therefore, underscores the fact that thinking or evaluation inevitably rearranges phenomena, making something foreground, something else background.[68] In the pure presencing of *genjōkōan* characteristic of without-thinking, however, each phenomenon is as it is, how it is, without the involvement of human purpose or preference.

In ordinary consciousness—what Dōgen calls "thinking"—we select our focus, we establish a center of attention, and leave the rest to the periphery. Through that selective focus, meaning arises. Yet, from the standpoint of the phenomena rather than from the standpoint of the ego with its agendas both patent and hidden, each event is equally present, exhausting itself in being fully what it is with nothing concealed.

Consider this simple example from my experience as it is right now. If I look at this page in front of me, the window across the room loses its intensity as a phenomenon, blurring off into minimal awareness. If suddenly there is a "thud" at the window, my whole attention focuses on that and the page blurs away. Did the window assert its presence at first less, and then later more strongly? No, it was always exhausting itself as all it could be, but *my* thinking moved it front and center or into the margins. While I was reading, the window did not mean much, but with the thud, it acquired urgent significance.

The term *kōan* has a second meaning in Zen that is also relevant to Dōgen. Namely, it can refer to the traditional exchanges between Zen masters and their disciples that become focal points in Zen praxis.[69] The *kōan* about thinking, not-thinking, and without-thinking fits that category, for example. Such a *kōan* often served as the theme or topic for one of Dōgen's talks or essays, a practice common among Zen masters even today. In this second context, then, the full term *genjōkōan* suggests that the focal "issue at hand"[70] in Zen dialogues is how to engage the presencing of things as they are. The practical purpose of studying the traditional *kōan*s of the Zen tradition is not to focus on what they are about, but rather, to see *how* the great masters' engaged the issue at hand. The key is not *what* was expressed, but *how* the expression occurs. We will return to this point later when examining how Dōgen demystifies the interaction between masters and disciples.

This discussion of *genjōkōan* leads to Dōgen's *Repository* essay by that name, one of the most famous Buddhist essays in Japanese philosophical and religious history. Dōgen himself seemed to have valued it highly because when he started compiling his essays into the *Repository* collection, he placed it first. Let us begin with how the essay characterizes the relation between the *zazen* practitioner and phenomena.

144–7

> To practice-authenticate the totality of phenomena by conveying yourself to them—that's delusion. To practice-authenticate yourself by letting the totality of phenomena come forth—that's realization.[71]

145

The statement draws a clear distinction between two kinds of self-understanding. In the first, one thinks of oneself as someone who goes out into the world to confirm what is real. This form of knowing by a detached observer is akin to the method of an ordinary empiricist or scientist. The other mode, the one Dōgen associates with realization, is someone whose identity is inseparable from the presencing phenomena. That is: you know yourself as engagement within the midst of events rather than as external observer. It is a difference between understanding yourself as a person who *has* experience and as a person who *is* experience. Dōgen gives an apt analogy:

> Suppose a person travels aboard a ship. If she turns her eyes to look back at the coast, she mistakenly thinks the shore is moving away from her. But if she fixes her eyes close by the ship, she knows it is the ship that is moving forward. Analogously, if she has a confused notion of her own bodymind, when she tries to sort out the totality of phenomena, she mistakenly assumes her own mind and her own nature are permanently fixed. Yet, if she returns inward, engaging her daily tasks intimately, she will have clarified the pattern in the way of things[72]—the totality of phenomena is there without an "I."[73]

145

Those alternative views of the self-world relation expressed in the example of the moving boat take us from a paradigm of external relations to one of internal relations. That is, in the delusional paradigm, one sees the self and the world as two independent entities related through experience or knowledge: I experience reality; I know reality. In the enlightened paradigm, by contrast, one understands self and world as interpenetrating aspects of a single process. The experience and the knowledge arise from the interfusion of self and world.[74]

My second comment about the passage on page 223 concerns the odd compound verb "to practice-authenticate" (*shushō suru*). The first term in the compound is *shu*, a common Buddhist expression for self-cultivation or, simply, praxis. In this case, it means specifically the practice of *zazen*. The second term in the compound is *shō*, that is, "authenticating," "witnessing," or "verifying." It is one of Dōgen's favored terms for enlightenment and it relates specifically to what the cook had called the "provenance of practice." In *zazen*, according to Dōgen, I can directly authenticate how things are, including how I am, without thinking.[75]*

Therefore, the compound term *shushō* (affixing *suru* makes it into a verb) undercuts the common tendency to think of practice as a means to authentication. For Dōgen, that would be as wrongheaded as thinking one practices medicine in order to *become* a doctor. To practice medicine is to *be* a doctor. Analogously, for Dōgen, to practice without-thinking is itself to confirm the presencing of things as they are. To practice *zazen* is to be enlightened, at least enlightened in the sense of actively and directly engaging as-ness. *Zazen* is an end in itself, not a means to the goal. Already in his first philosophical essay, *Bendōwa* (*Discussion on Pursuing the Way of Praxis*), Dōgen was explicit about this:

> You are off-track when you think that practicing-authentication is not one. From the standpoint of the buddha's truth, practicing-authentication is a single event without separation.[76]

Indeed, Dōgen even holds that to sit properly in *zazen* (to be just sitting without thinking) is at that moment to be a buddha. That is not as strange as it might at first seem. Suppose you and a buddha are for a moment both sitting properly in *zazen:* without thinking, without separation between "I" and "world," just authenticating or witnessing the presencing of things as they are in their as-ness without generating any specific meaning. In what significant sense would your experience and the buddha's experience differ at that moment? Without expression—whether in thought, word, or deed—there is nothing to distinguish the two experiences. They are both meaningless; no conceptual overlay has been superimposed on the experience. Indeed, they are meaningless in exactly the same way for exactly the same reason.

Here we have reached the "provenance of practice" to which the cook referred and perhaps also to the doctrine of inherent awakening (*hongaku*) insofar as it assumes we are all already buddhas. The difference between enlightenment and delusion arises when we go beyond that experiential moment and express it either authentically or inauthentically in thoughts, words, and deeds. It may be true that all of us are buddhas, but the sad fact is that most of us are deluded buddhas.

Deluded buddhas—what could that possibly mean? Although a peculiar turn of phrase, it is consistent with Dōgen's way of speaking. For example, again in the essay *Genjōkōan,* he wrote:

> The buddhas profoundly realize[77] their delusions, while ordinary people are profoundly deluded in their enlightenment. Those who are greatly deluded in their realization are ordinary sentient beings. And there are those who attain further realizations based on their previous realizations, while there are also those who keep on deluding themselves further while in their delusions. When buddhas are truly buddhas, they have no need to acknowledge themselves as buddhas. They are, nevertheless, authentic buddhas, and buddhas go on authenticating.[78]

145

Dōgen resorted to such descriptions because there are multiple paths by which the inherent enlightenment (*hongaku*) gets "initialized" through expression in thought, word, and deed. For a buddha who is not deluded, the initialization is an awakening (*shikaku*). Yet, an expression can also be deluded. In that case there is (initialized) delusion in the (inherent) enlightenment, leading Dōgen to say those people are "greatly deluded in their enlightenment."

This discussion about expression brings us to the second intimation from our friend and mentor, the cook: "The study of written words is to understand the provenance of written words."

Language and Meaning

You might have assumed Dōgen's emphasis on without-thinking as the provenance of Buddhist praxis would mean he had little concern for words. That is not at all the case. There would be little point to having the eye for the truth if you never got around to expressing the truth. That would be like having an eye for design without ever designing anything. In his *Repository* essay *Mitsugo*, Dōgen affirmed the importance of words. In general Buddhist parlance, the term *mitsugo* means "esoteric language" along the lines analyzed by Kūkai and esoteric Tendai Buddhism, for example. The Zen Buddhist tradition often uses the term *mitsugo* more specifically to mean the inexpressible, trans-verbal transmission between the mind of the master and the mind of the disciple.

A case in point: Zen's myth of origins recounts the transmission from the historical buddha, Shakyamuni, to the first Zen disciple, Mahākāśyapa. The story goes as follows. One day Shakyamuni sat before the usual assemblage of monks, laity, and divinities who dropped by to hear the buddha's sermons. This time, however, Shakyamuni did not speak, but only twirled a flower and winked. Of all those present, only Mahākāśyapa responded—by smiling. Recognizing that engaging smile, Shakyamuni then praised his disciple, saying he is bestowing on him "the repository of the eye for the truth" (*shōbōgenzō*).

That event marked the beginning of Zen as an ongoing tradition handed down from one generation to the next. The traditional Zen explanation had been that the twirling of the flower and wink functioned as the transmission of "Zen mind" that is "outside words and letters," an insight defying expression in ordinary words. For expressing enlightenment, only "esoteric language"— words or gestures transcending discursive meaning—appertains.[79] Dōgen considered that interpretation a wrongheaded mystification and his essay presented an alternative.

Dōgen starts by characterizing what he considers the faulty analysis of the narrative:

> Those who have not heard a genuine master's instructions, though they may sit on a meditation seat like a buddha, have not even dreamed of the way things really are. They cavalierly say the twirling of the flower and winking at the great assembly of monks are Buddha Shakyamuni's "esoteric language" (*mitsugo*). By that reasoning, the Buddha's verbal exposition would be only superficial, as in what can be conveyed by matching (verbal) names and forms (of things). Twirling the flower and winking in nonverbal exposition—that, they think, would itself be an occasion of using the technique of esoteric language....

160

Then Dōgen gives his corrective to that commonly accepted interpretation:

> Yet, the Buddha says after seeing Mahākāśyapa's smile, "I have the repository of the eye for the truth and the wondrous mind of nirvana. I transmit these to Mahākāśyapa." Is such an utterance verbal or nonverbal? If Shakyamuni dislikes the verbal and prefers to twirl the flower, he should have saved the twirling for after speaking.[80]

160-1

Note that Dōgen's interpretation embraces the utterance as well as the silent gestures, considering them two parts of a single act. After all, if this is a narrative about the transmission of enlightenment, the salient point is that the transmission itself occurs verbally ("I transmit these to Mahākāśyapa"), only *after* the nonverbal exchange. In addition, the pivotal verbalization does not refer to something, but instead does something. It is performative. If one wants to say the Zen transmission is *mitsugo* that term should, Dōgen reasons, apply to the verbal as well as nonverbal expressions in the story.

Dōgen concludes, therefore, that the *mitsugo* is in the expressive exchange taken as a whole.

> Yet, if you regard verbalization as superficial, then twirling the flower and winking must also be superficial. If you regard his verbalization as just matching names and forms, then you are not engaging the Buddha's truth. Although you have known verbalization to be names and forms, you do not yet know that there are no names and forms for the Buddha—your unenlightened feelings have not yet dropped away. The buddhas and ancestors, having completely penetrated their bodyminds and having let them drop away, expound the dharma, do so verbally, and turn the dharma wheel. Many are those who see or hear them and who derive benefit from them.... 161

Through that characterization, Dōgen has transformed the ordinary understanding of *mitsugo* from being a form of secretive language to being a verbal performance expressive of engagement. *Mitsugo* is not a subset of language, whether verbal or nonverbal, but is instead a way of using language. Its focus is not just what is said, but also *how* it is said. As the narrative says, it is not a simple matter of matching words (names) with externally existing things (forms). That is, Dōgen distinguishes two ways of using language, not two kinds of language. To understand his point, we need to consider three facets of Dōgen's theory of language and meaning. These facets are equally relevant to language in one's own private thinking as to language in interpersonal communication. Those three facets are: the experiential origin of words and concepts, the fluidity of meaning, and language as a way of engaging the present.

The origin of words and concepts. The first facet of Dōgen's theory deals with how words and concepts arise and how they accrue meanings that are right or wrong, true or false. A good point of departure for exploring this aspect of his theory is another passage from his *Genjōkōan* essay. As before, Dōgen refers to an experience of being at sea:

> When we have not yet fully engaged phenomena with the bodymind, we think that is all there is to the phenomena. If we sufficiently engage them with the bodymind, however, we sense there is something more left out.

For example, suppose I board a ship and go out to sea beyond the sight of land. When I look around in all directions, what is visible is a circle of water with no distinguishing marks, nothing else. Yet, the ocean is not simply a circle or a square—you cannot exhaust all the other things the ocean can be. The ocean is like a palace [to a fish] and like a glittering string of jewels [to a deity looking down at the glistening water from the heavens]. It is just that what reaches my own eyes as an individual is, for the moment, nothing but the visible circle.

The totality of the phenomena is like this. Whether it is a delusion-perme-ated realm or something beyond, the world takes on many aspects. Yet, we see and grasp only what reaches our eyes in our praxis. If we are to inquire into the manner and style of the totality of phenomena, we should know that beyond their being visible as circularity or angularity, there is no limit to the other things the ocean or the mountains can be. We should bear in mind that there are many worlds everywhere. And it is not just that the all-encompassing world around us is like this, but you should know that it is the same right here at your feet and in [the aforementioned] single drop of water.[81]

The passage depicts an ordinary experience of being out at sea and character-izing the ocean around us as a great circle, its circumference being the empty horizon in all directions. This is obviously not describing a *zazen* (without-thinking) experience, however, because one is *conceptualizing* the presence—the ocean—in a certain way, namely, as a "great circle." Dōgen accepts that the ocean-as-circle is what our physical eyes accurately see. Yet, of course, as Dōgen himself points out, "the ocean is not circular" and "not square."

Up to that point, any empiricist would agree. Although empirical knowledge takes sense data for its basis, it requires for its standard of knowledge more than an ever-changing flow of sensory input. The empiricist organizes the data, modifying it in light of previously perceived data, piecing it together into a picture of reality.

For example, an empiricist on Dōgen's boat would know the ocean is not a circle—however it might appear at this moment—because she has a memory of her perception of the shoreline before the boat left its dock. She knows the shore of the ocean is full of irregularities: inlets, promontories, deltas, and so forth. Consequently, being a good empiricist, she is able to reason that the present appearance notwithstanding, the ocean is not a circle. Its apparent circularity is due to the curvature of the earth and the limits of human vision—other facts acquired by the processing and interpreting of earlier empirical data.

Yet, Dōgen is not an empiricist, at least of the sort just described. Admittedly, like an empiricist, Dōgen believes that reality is more than mere mental con-structions.[82] He believes things show themselves for what they are—the Bud-dhist position on as-ness commits him to at least that much. Still, his reasons for saying the ocean is not a circle differ from those of the empiricist. To recognize the ocean is not circular is not for him a matter of connecting the present event to previous empirical data and knowledge, but rather, Dōgen's point is that what appears in any moment depends on one's standpoint. And that standpoint—positioned as it is in the experiential flux of phenomena—could change. This is what we might call Dōgen's form of contextualism or perspectivalism.

You can find that view expressed in the opening sentences of the paragraph under consideration. Things do not appear (to an undeluded person) as something other than what they really are. Yet, as-they-appear is not *all* that things are: in any appearance there is "something more left out." The circular ocean is simply "what reaches my own eyes as an individual...for the moment."

In comparing the ocean to a glittering palace or jeweled necklace, Dōgen is perhaps alluding to a well-known Yogācāra Buddhist doctrine of the "four views of one water" (*issuishiken*).[83] According to that theory, because of their respective karmic circumstances, different kinds of beings view the "same" body of water in a different way. To a deity in the heavens looking down at it sparkling in the sunshine or moonlight, it will look bejeweled. To a starving ghost looking at it from its hellish existence, it will appear as a pool of pus and blood. To a fish swimming in it as its home, it will be a palace. To a human being, it will be water. So, the perceptual appearance varies according to the mental constructions of the being looking at the same item. By speaking of the "palace" and the "jewels," therefore, Dōgen may have the Yogācāra example in mind, but if so, his emphasis is actually quite different.

Rather than stressing the psychological and karmic differences in the viewers of the water, Dōgen limits his discussion to three perspectives with differing spatial locations: beneath the water (as for a fish), on the water (as for human beings in a boat), and from the sky above the water (as for a deity or a bird flying overhead). The main point for Dōgen seems to be not—as it was for Yogācāra philosophers—that the meanings of the ocean are mental constructs[84] but rather that each characterization of the ocean is necessarily within a given physical or experiential locus. For Dōgen, therefore, experiencing the ocean as a "great circle" is appropriate to a person far out at sea looking around in all directions. Similarly, it is appropriate to a fish swimming about in its oceanic home with the light filtering through the shimmering water to view the sea as a translucent palace. Lastly, to a celestial being, it is appropriate to see the light reflected off the waves as a sparkling string of gems.

In sum: in characterizing Dōgen's theory of meaning, the first point is that *meaning always arises from a context*. It is always situated; it arises in a particular time-place or locus. In discussing meaning we need to specify that locus, what Dōgen sometimes terms the "occasion" (*jisetsu*[85*]). When meaning arises, it is only out of a particular occasion.

The fluidity of meaning. The second facet of Dōgen's theory of meaning in the passage now under discussion is the idea that *meaning is as fluid as the contexts in which it is embedded*, that is, the meaning of phenomena in a situation is only for *that* occasion. If we think at any time we have sufficiently captured the full significance of some phenomenon, that only proves, as Dōgen said in the first sentence of the passage, that we "have still not fully realized the phenomena in bodymind." If instead the phenomenon "fills the bodymind," then we will know that whatever meaning we attribute to it, there will also be something else left out. On another occasion's shift in situation or standpoint, there will be new meanings beyond what we now think.

As Dōgen said in the passage, "Whether this delusion-permeated realm or beyond it, the world takes on many aspects. Yet, we see and grasp only what reaches our eyes in our praxis." Here we see the necessity for continuous praxis. As without-thinking, *zazen* will always take us back to the point where the specifics of the situation dissolve back into the meaningless flow, the as-ness or presencing. That flux is a boundless, infinite resource out of which new situations and new meanings can arise.

Again, lest we forget, we are not detached onlookers who take the flow of phenomena to be the object of our experience. For Dōgen the "I" is lost in the same as-ness as all phenomena experienced in *zazen*. Situations call for response, but we can only respond appropriately when we are open to what each situation calls for. Whenever we have given meaning to a situation, we know we have in some way given form to the formless presencing and, in so doing, limited its possible expressions to just the one at hand. Even in the fullness of the moment, we know there is something missing. No meaning is ever *the* meaning sufficient to all occasions. As soon as they have served their purpose, the meanings should disappear back into the flow of meaningless presencing.

Engaging the present. The third facet of Dōgen's theory of meaning seems to lead in almost the opposite direction from the previous one. *We realize meaning through complete engagement with the present context.* Both the situation and the person are actualized through performative expression. For Dōgen, the occasion that gives rise to meaning is a moment to live. The vitality of immersing ourselves in the occasion and expressing it fully is to have "realization beyond the great realization." It initializes the inherent enlightenment: one realizes *hongaku* as *shikaku*, inherent awakening as initialized awakening. Dōgen discusses this idea in terms of a fish swimming in that same sea and a bird flying above it.

A fish swims through the water and however much it swims about, there is no limit to the water. A bird flies through the sky and however much it flies about, there is no limit to the sky. Yet, the fish has never yet left the water; nor the bird the sky. It is just that when the task at hand is great, the use of the water or sky is great; when the requirements are small, the use is small. The bird and fish neither fail to utilize completely each opportunity, nor fail to flit about everywhere.

Yet, if the bird leaves the sky or the fish leaves the water, it will immediately die. You should certainly know that the fish lives because of the water and the bird lives because of the sky. Conversely, the water has life because of the fish and the sky has life because of the bird: by means of this vitality, it is the bird; by means of this vitality, it is the fish. We can take this further: there is the oneness of authentication and praxis as there is the oneness of life and longevity.[86]

146–7

Dōgen's provocative image suggests that to live is to engage and express fully each situation as it arises. Each contextual situation—each occasion—is enough to meet the needs of meaningful life. It can be as small in scope as the taste of cool water on a hot day or as grand as a spectacular sunrise seen from the highest mountain peak. Whatever the occasion may be, in its own terms it is limitless. We cannot exhaust the meaning of any moment any more than the fish in sea can run out of water or the bird out of sky. Yet, although inexhaustible, any situational context is just that—a delimited context. The present occasion may be infinite, but it is not everything—something is always "left out."

Commentators on Zen sometimes say the goal is to participate in the infinity of the "absolute present." Dōgen's emphasis on infinity is more nuanced, however. Dōgen does indeed maintain that the richness of the present occasion is infinite—the expressed meaning always leaves something out to be further expressed. No number of expressions or interpretations can exhaust the possible meanings of a single moment. Yet, the meaning at any moment is still always *only* contextual.

For the fish, the ocean is a shimmering palace, full of infinite possibilities, but shifting in scope. It can be the smallest space while the fish is motionless or a vast expanse in any direction when the fish swims its course at full speed. Yet, as with a camera's zoom lens, however small or however large its field, on every occasion the image completely fills the frame. The ocean would not be the ocean without the fish (its vitality would disappear); the fish would not be the fish without the ocean (it would die). They are actualized together through the occasion of the fish's living in the sea as its shimmering palace.

Of course, the total engagement with the present (the "whole working" *zenki*) can itself lead to a deluded expression of the situation. The fish might think the ocean is *nothing but* a shimmering palace, that a shimmering palace is the only meaning the ocean can have. That is, the infinitude of the present occasion might be mistaken for an absolute beyond which there is nothing else. To be infinite is not the same as being all inclusive. For example, consider the domain of real numbers between 2 and 3. Since that domain is infinite (2, 2.1, 2.11, …, 2.2, 2.21, …, 2.3, 2.31, etc.), one might mistakenly think there can be nothing else outside it. Yet, of course, there is an infinity of real numbers outside that domain (1, 4, 5, 6, …). Just because the series is infinite, it does not mean that there is not something more beyond it.

That was the thrust of Dōgen's second point: that meaning is necessarily contextual. The present is open to an infinity of possible meanings but there is still an infinite number of meanings that do not fit the present occasion. To claim the present is open to infinite interpretations is not to say it is open to *any* interpretation. Like the domain of real numbers between 2 and 3, the number of possible meanings can be infinite but nonetheless limited. Not every interpretation is true, not even possibly true.

Howzit?

To help you engage Dōgen's philosophy and not merely think about it, I will summarize Dōgen's three points about the origin of meaning by examining the occasion of your reading this book right here, right now. First, what is the *meaning* of the thing you are presently looking at. Your answer presumably is "a book." Is that really all that it is, however? As it appears in its present context, this object before you is, in various important ways, not just a book like any other book. It is different from other books on your shelf, for example, because it is a "now-being-read book."

The books on the shelf, even if you glance at them right now, are external to you in ways that this book is not. The books on the shelf are only there in your visual field of experience, but as this book is being now read, it has intellectual meanings beyond the merely visual; it is internally related to you in a way that the other books are, for now at least, not. This book is more than just the shapes and colors of the books across the room. Even if you are close enough to the other books on the shelves that you can read their titles, that is still different. There is reflexivity when you are engaged in reading this book. As you are reading these sentences, you are concurrently reading about reading these sentences at this moment. No other book on your shelves has that special significance right now.

Now I ask: *where* are you in relation to this book? The books on the shelf are "over there" and you are sitting "over here," but where are you in relation to this book right now as you are reading this very sentence? You could say you are here with the book in your hands, perhaps propped up in your lap or on a table or desk, but is that *all* that you can say meaningfully about where you are as you read these sentences? If you think it is, try the following experiment.

First, read the following instructions in full so you can carry them out without having to refer back.

> Take a deep breath, relax, and without otherwise moving, continue looking where you are now looking on this page. *But stop reading.* Just calmly let the presencing of the sensations be there without bestowing any meaning whatsoever on the event, even for just a second or two. Don't change your position; don't think about anything and don't fight against thinking. Just for a moment do nothing but be aware of what is in front of you as it blurs out of focus. Do this for a few moments and then come back to read the next sentence.

Now that you have come back, who or what came thus? Howzit? When I asked where you were a few moments ago, if you thought you had said everything meaningful with "I am here with the book in my hands (perhaps propped up at a desk or table)," then where did you just now go and come back from? Again, based on the assumption that Dōgen is writing about meaning as *how* rather than what, the issue is *how* you changed without moving from your reading chair. If who you are is *how* you are, then in realizing how the book is, you cannot help but realize how you are. The meanings of you and the book interfuse.

Furthermore, when you took a moment to do nothing but be aware without establishing any focus or meaning, there was just the "presencing of things as they are." While without thinking, you were an intimate part of that presencing. If for that brief moment, you were indeed without thinking, then you were doing *zazen* (even if you were standing up). You were for that moment, Dōgen says, indistinguishable from a buddha. In asking you, right after that moment, "who or what came thus?" the question was summoning the buddha from your inherent awakening. A title for a buddha is *nyorai* (S. *tathāgata*)—the "one who has thus come." Depending on your expressive response to the question, therefore, you could either realize the situation and thereby initialize awakening or you could be deluded in your realization and be merely a "deluded buddha."[†]

So, our little experiment in meaning-formation teaches two lessons. First, you can begin to see the multiplicity of meanings that come out of the realization of what is happening in any experience, however common or simple. Second, with your few moments of *zazen*, you can better understand how without thinking can take you out of the field of fixed meanings to open you to further meanings available to you in your situation. That is why in his first philosophical essay, *Bendōwa*, Dōgen wrote that *zazen* is the "touchstone." Without thinking, *zazen* escapes the rigid confines of a reality in which we think we have exhausted the meaning of what is happening right here and now. *Zazen* does not itself generate any meaning, but it opens us to the provenance of words and concepts. It

† See page 225.

does not give us truth, but it opens our eye for the truth. In doing so, we open up the "virtues" (*toku*)[87] of the situation—its range of possible meanings.

We are not finished, however. In our experiment, you found multiple meanings arising from your engagement with the book in front of you. Yet, is that *all* it means? What if, for example, the context or occasion radically shifts? The book has infinite meanings beyond the infinite meanings of any one context. Suppose a wind blows through your room and important papers on your desk begin to fly away. You slap the book down on the papers and run to close the window. That is the occasion of *Engaging Japanese Philosophy* as paperweight and the rich array of meanings that can flow out of that occasion if we fully engage it. Or perhaps you are hungry and find yourself short of funds. You can stop by the used bookstore, sell your book, and buy a hotdog from the vendor down the street. Then we have *Engaging Japanese Philosophy* as lunch money. Or perhaps you have had enough of my prodding and when you happen to see me across the room, you throw the book at its author. Then it would be *Engaging Japanese Philosophy* as assault weapon. As Dōgen says, "there are infinite worlds" of meaning for this book and whatever meanings it might have right now, we should be aware that there is still something more left out.

THE INTERPERSONAL

Yet, as rich as our discussion of Dōgen's theory of meaning has been, even this is only half of Dōgen's response to the cook's intimation about the source of words and concepts. In Dōgen's characterization we have now the "one, two, three, four, five" but have not yet fathomed the "six, seven, eight, nine, ten." To do that, we need to consider Dōgen's understanding of interpersonal communication. The wondrous flow of meanings we have examined in relation to your engagement with this book occurred only through the interaction between me as writer and you as reader. That is a reminder that we cannot have an adequate theory of language and meaning without explaining the social dimension. To begin, then, let us return to Dōgen's theory of *mitsugo* and the essay by that name.

Communication

As I already explained, Dōgen expanded on the traditional interpretation of Zen transmission from master to disciple by arguing that *mitsugo* ("esoteric language") includes both verbal and nonverbal expression. In doing so, he expanded the meaning of the *go* ("language") part of the term. Now let us consider what he says about the *mitsu* ("esoteric") part.

On the occasion when you meet someone, you hear and express *mitsu* words (*mitsugo*). When you know yourself, you know *mitsu* activity (*mitsugyō*†).[88]

......

> This word *mitsu* means the pattern in the way of things as intimacy (*shin-mitsu*).... Intimate action does not know self vs. other, as if I alone can know my intimate self and do not understand any other person's intimate self. Because "intimacy is what is near you," everything exists through intimacy; each half exists through intimacy. Personally investigate this pattern in the way of things with clarity and diligence in your practice.[89]

161

In that passage Dōgen demystified the notion of *mitsu* by taking it out of a transcendent plane of reality where disembodied minds directly transmit the buddha's truth to other disembodied minds. Instead, Dōgen immerses *mitsu* in the most ordinary domains of life, at least when that ordinary life is lived with intimacy. Dōgen has made *mitsugo* to be no longer an obfuscating, nondiscursive form of expression. Instead he sees *mitsugo* as the way language arises in life's intimate contexts. *Mitsugo* is using language as intimation. An intimation is a hint that, on one hand, expresses all that needs to be said in order to be understood, but yet, on the other hand, is so subtle or indirect that only one's intimates are likely to get it (as was the case with only Mahākāśyapa's responding to Shakyamuni's twirling the flower). *Mitsugo* is in the glance between lovers, in the elliptical sentences between lifelong friends, in the little asides or jokes that only insiders get.

In arguing for language as intimation, Dōgen has undermined the paradigm in which external relations define the interpersonal. We often think of language as a communicative bridge that connects one individual to another. In that paradigm, language is the external relation that forms a link between two separate people: we communicate in order to connect with others. For the kind of communication in which Dōgen was interested, however, there is no place for discrete individuals living in the integrity of their private, self-contained lives. For Dōgen, intimation is not the language that bridges my independent self with your independent self. Rather it arises in the discovery of our overlap, in the internal, intimate relation by which each of us brings our half into the whole. This theory of language as intimation influences Dōgen's understanding of both the master-disciple relation and the relation between reader and text. Let us start with the former.

---

† The term *gyō* 行 can mean either "praxis" or "activity." In Dōgen's use those two meanings are often inseparable because in Zen to practice is to act as a buddha. Since there is no single English term that quite covers the appropriate semantic range, multiple terms will be used as befit the particular English context, e.g., *practicing, praxis, activity, action, conduct, in-action*, and so forth.

Master and Student

A popular understanding in Dōgen's time as well as today is that the Zen master is an authority figure who stands apart from the disciples, judging their progress or insight from the perspective of his or her[90] own enlightened standpoint. The other side of the coin in that relational model is that the disciple sees the master as the embodiment of enlightenment, the ideal to which one aspires and submits. In short: that well-established model assumes a strict differentiation and fundamental separation between teacher and student. Given his preference for intimacy over integrity as the paradigm of ideal interpersonal communication, however, it is not surprising that Dōgen rejected that paradigm of the master-disciple interrelation.

Dōgen elaborated his position in his discussion of *kattō*, a Zen term customarily referring to the student's deluded entanglement in concepts or words. The term itself refers to the entangling vines or branches of kudzu or wisteria, a metaphor for complications and internal conflict. The traditional understanding is that the master uses any technique available (kōan practice, meditation, shouting, hitting, and so forth) to cut through the student's entrapment, triggering an enlightenment experience. The disciples are ensnared in words or concepts and the master is the savior who cuts them free.

In his *Repository* essay "*Kattō*," however, Dōgen reshaped the meanings of the key terms so that *kattō* suggests something more like "intertwining" than "entanglement." For Dōgen, *kattō* is not the students' problem alone. Nor does the master's expertise cut through their *kattō* for them. Instead Dōgen took *kattō* to be a form of engagement that intertwines the master, the disciple, and the problem in an internally related way so that they cut through the entanglement together.

> Generally, saints set out in their personal practice to cut off the roots of *kattō*, but they do not personally practice this as slicing through *kattō* with *kattō*. They do not know about entangling *kattō* with *kattō*, to say nothing of knowing how to inherit *kattō* through *kattō*. Knowing the inheritance of the dharma itself to be *kattō* is rare—no one has heard of this. It has yet to be uttered. So few have authenticated it....[91]

Dōgen recommends, therefore, a procedure in which the master and the disciple lose their discrete standpoints and grapple together with the problem of entangling words and concepts by using words and concepts. In characterizing the dialogue between student and master, Dōgen wrote:

> Therefore, the very utterances are lines that leap out of themselves; student and master personally practice together. The very listenings are lines that leap out of themselves; student and master personally practice together. The

common personal investigation of master and disciple is the ancestral inter-twining [*kattō*]. The ancestral intertwining is the life of the skin-flesh-bones-marrow.[92*] The very twirling of the flower and winking [by Shakyamuni in front of Mahākāśyapa] are the intertwining.[93]

162

Thus Dōgen envisioned dialogue as a mutual engagement among student, master, tradition ("the ancestral intertwining"), and words. The mention of tradition allows me to return to something Dōgen said earlier in his story about his encounters with the cook. When Dōgen asked the cook, "What are words?" the cook replied, "one, two, three, four, five." From our discussion of the origin of words, there are three things we can say about this characterization.

First, the sequence of *five* numbers signifies the discreteness of each moment. For something to be countable, it must stand alone in some way. That is, enu-meration is predicated upon individuation. Second, as a *sequence,* it is a single event of interrelated parts. Something can be "three" in a sequence only if there is first a "two," for example.[94] Third, the words of the cook were in a specific language: Chinese. Words and thoughts are always embedded in a language. That is part of the occasion of their expression in every instance.

What, then, can we say about the "six, seven, eight, nine, ten?" It is significant that Dōgen mentioned that sequence only after he had discussed the poem by the earlier master, Xuedou. The point then may be that tradition adds to, fills out and fills in, the expression. Just as the cook had available to him the Chinese words for his expression, his expression was also embedded in a tradition. So, even in talking about the origin of words in terms of numbers, the cook's state-ments resonate with the words of the buddhas and ancestors preceding him. The question may then be how Xuedou was present in Dōgen such that Dōgen could express the experience as "six, seven, eight, nine, ten." It seems that not only were teacher and student (the cook and Dōgen) practicing together, but somehow Xuedou was there, too.

Therefore, however striking Dōgen's phrase that "student and master practice together" may be, even more revolutionary is his claim that the master and stu-dent are also practicing together with all the great buddhas and Zen ancestors. He sometimes refers to this phenomenon as the "comportment of buddhas-in-action" (*gyōbutsuigi*). Dōgen gave his own special interpretation of this term in the *Repository* essay with that title. At the beginning of the essay, Dōgen makes it clear that *buddhas-in-action*[95] is not a category among the usual typology of buddhas and buddha-embodiments. *Buddhas-in-action* refers not to a kind of buddha, but to a *way* of being or practicing buddha. He writes:

Buddhas invariably conducting themselves with comportment—that is bud-dhas-in-action. Buddhas-in-action are neither celestial buddhas nor historical buddhas, neither buddha embodiments-in-themselves nor embodiments-for-others. They are not (characterized by) inherent/initialized awakening, nor are they naturally awakened/unawakened. You can't compare such buddhas alongside buddhas-in-action.[96]

According to Dōgen, the way to engage buddhas-in-action is to be one. Otherwise, we place those various characterizations of buddhas as externalized ideals to which we aspire or which we revere. By putting them on a pedestal in that way, we make them into false idols that hinder our own realization.

> If you are not a buddha-in-action, you cannot be free yet from the constraints of "buddha" and "dharma," and the buddha-demons and dharma-demons will enlist you [into their fold].[97]

Because of the dangers of idolatry, whether real or ideal, Dōgen says we must "go beyond buddha" (*butsukōjō*) and only a buddha-in-action can do so.

> Know this: buddhas don't wait around for awakening while treading the buddha path. Only the buddhas-in-action go about their daily tasks while on the path that goes beyond buddha.[98]

"Going beyond buddha" means, therefore, that Buddhists should get past the reified, idolized notion of the buddha as something beyond them to which they should aspire. After all, as we have seen, according to Dōgen's analysis of the inherent enlightenment doctrine, we are all already buddhas ourselves. Dōgen writes:

> Now let's go a step further in investigating this "comportment of the buddhas-in-action." When the phrase "this very buddha is I myself" (*sokubutsu sokuji*) comes up as such, the comportment of (Master Huineng's phrase discussed earlier in the essay) "I am so; you are so"[99] is only about my own capacities. Yet, in truth the buddhas everywhere are dropping away and this is no one-way process.[100]

In other words, when we immerse ourselves completely in the everyday, losing all sense of ego, we are not becoming *like* a buddha, but instead are *being* a buddha. Since the buddhas are immersing themselves in the same way, they do not have ego-identities either. Because we cannot be *like* something if we lack our own identity, if we disappear, the buddhas disappear.[101] Such is the comportment of buddhas-in-action. Dōgen continues:

> So, an old Buddha [Hongzhi Zhengjue (1091-1157)] said, "Get ahold of that there, and bring it here into your daily tasks." When you take this to heart as such, the various dharmas, bodies, practices, and buddhas are already intimate with you. These practices, dharmas, bodies, and buddhas—they are only distracting when we take them that way one after the other. Since they are distracting, they just drop away in your taking them so.

Don't let anyone convince you that the eye blinded by the glitter of the phenomenal world doesn't see any phenomenon, doesn't see one thing. The blinded eye reaches this phenomenon over here, that phenomenon over there. It flits about here and there, going in and out of the same [sensory] gateway, and nothing is hidden away from it in the whole world. Because of that, there is [everywhere] the Buddha's intimate language, intimate authentication, intimate practice, and intimate entrustment.[102]

Dōgen has in those passages worked through the full implications of the oneness of practicing-enlightenment. To express the truth, we have to first ground ourselves in the openness of without-thinking. By practicing *zazen*, we are authenticating the way things are in the meaningless flow. To mesh with that flow we have to stop trying to emulate buddhas and just be buddhas-in-action ourselves, thereby losing ourselves and all sense of buddhas or enlightenment. That is not yet expression, but the provenance of expression. It is our return to what we are in our inherent awakening. As he states it in the *Genjōkōan* essay:

To model yourself after the Way of the buddhas is to model yourself after yourself. To model yourself after yourself is to forget yourself. To forget yourself is to be authenticated by the totality of phenomena. To be authenticated by the totality of phenomena is to completely drop away one's own bodymind as well as the bodymind of others. All traces of enlightenment are depleted and those depleted traces of enlightenment go on and on. When you first seek the dharma, you actually distance yourself from its environs, but when the dharma is already correctly transmitted to you, you are immediately what you really are.[103]

145

Although *zazen* is in itself a kind of enlightenment, it lacks the expressive quality found in the fulfillment of initialized awakening. It would be like having a word processing program on your computer, but not initializing it and then never using it to write anything. We cannot live in a world without meaning anymore than a fish can live without water. We find ourselves in cruxes of time and being, in the nexuses that are the occasion for meaning. If we respond to the occasion appropriately, we realize the fullness of the moment and its infinite capability to assume new forms of meaning.

If, instead, we fixate on the situation of something outside us or surrounding us, if we simply replay old interpretations from former occasions, we fall into delusion. But even then there is the possibility of that delusion's being realized for what it is—delusion. By fully realizing the delusion, we can return to the touchstone of *zazen*, dissolving our preconceived constructions of reality into the meaningless flux of phenomenal awareness. And the process can begin anew with new expressions arising from new occasions.

The idea of the praxis outlined by Dōgen is relatively simple, but hard to perform. The slightest slip and we construct a self-standing ego or "I" separate from reality or "the world." Such an ego is painfully out of touch with the ebb and flow of the shifting occasions for expression and has lost contact with the enlightenment inherent in all of us. Once we construct an artificial reality out of meaning, it becomes rigid and we assume that we have explored the full meaning of phenomena. We forget that there is something left out, forget that there are further worlds of meaning to engage.

Fortunately, we are not alone. According to Dōgen, we have, first of all, the teachers who will entangle themselves in our entanglements and practice together with us. Secondly, we have the Zen tradition itself with its models of how masters in the past have expressed themselves on their own occasions. This brings us to the last topic in my treatment of Dōgen's philosophical system: how to engage the tradition and its teachings.

Tradition and Values

For Dōgen, tradition is nowhere more important than in the area of ethical standards. With its insistence on the fluidity of meaning and the newness of each occasion, Zen runs the danger of antinomianism, the flagrant disregard of all rules, including those of morality. (Shinran's Shin Buddhism, we saw in the previous chapter, also had to address the charge of antinomianism.†) Therefore, Dōgen's account of good and evil is an important antidote to this tendency. The locus classicus for his discussion is his *Repository* essay, "*Shoaku-makusa*" [Do No Evil].

156–60

Dōgen's focus in the essay is on a moral dictum with a long history in Buddhism. The statement is found, for example, in the early popular South Asian Buddhist moral classic, *Dhammapada* (*The Footsteps of Rightness*), and has a special history in Japanese lore as supposedly the last words quoted by Prince Shōtoku on his deathbed in 622. The Japanese reading of the Chinese verses and the usual way of understanding them are:

Shoakumakusa	Not doing evils,
Shuzenbugyō	Devoutly practicing every good,
Jijōgoi	Purifying one's own mind:
Zeshobukkyō	This is the teaching of all buddhas.[104]

156

On first glance, we can hardly imagine a simpler, even more insipid, statement of morality. It might seem beneath Dōgen's intellect to even cite it, let alone write an essay on it. Yet, he did. As if to eliminate any chance that one

† See pages 197–201.

of his disciples might not take the lines seriously, Dōgen begins by discussing the last line first: "This is the teaching of all buddhas." He claims that all the buddhas have transmitted this precept to each other through the ages. One can feel his gravitas when he writes about this line: "This truth must be investigated with concentrated effort."[105] Even more severely he writes a bit later, that "If you do not hear *not doing evil*, you are not hearing the buddhas' true teaching but the talk of devils."[106] So much for Zen's supposed antinomianism.

But this is Dōgen we are considering. We have repeatedly seen how he takes an ordinary understanding of a term and, like Shakyamuni's flower, gives it a twirl to mean something else in hopes we will finally get it (wink, wink). Surely, for a philosopher who interpreted meaning as contextual and fluid, the phrase *shoakumakusa* cannot be a simplistic, rigid imperative "do no evil." So what does this phrase *shoakumakusa* really mean for Dōgen?

> Ordinary people at first construe this as "do no evil."[107] Yet, it is not like what they make it out to be; rather, it is like what it is when one hears it as the preaching of enlightenment. So heard, it is an expression in the words of unexcelled enlightenment. Because it is already the language of enlightenment, it is the enlightenment of language. As the preaching of the unexcelled enlightenment gets turned around into the [heedful] listening to it, the resolve to do no evil comes to be the conduct of doing no evil. In the evils' (*shoaku*) becoming no longer produced, the power of one's praxis is immediately presencing. This presence exhaustively presences all the earth, all worlds, all times, and all phenomena as its domain. This domain takes nonproduction (*makusa*) for its own domain.[108]

Dōgen's point was that we should not focus simply on what *shoakumakusa* means. Instead we should investigate more deeply *how* it means. If one takes it as just a moral imperative handed down by some authority, it will have some value, but only in a limited way. At most, it might lead to a resolve to be a good person. If one takes it to be an expression of enlightenment itself, however, the phrase has extraordinary transformative power. The resolve to do no evil becomes internalized so that one actually becomes a person who does no evil, indeed can do no evil.

The nondoing of evil changes from being a moral prescription to become a description of a moral person. The shift is from reading a statement as a prescription to discovering it as a description of an already-existing relation. Such a shift often signals a transition from external to internal relations. That is again the case here.

First, I will put this into the words from a different tradition to illustrate in more familiar English the rereading Dōgen is proposing. Take the biblical mandate "Thou shalt not kill." If one hears that as a moral imperative from an authoritative source, one might develop the resolve to never violate that command. If one goes further in nurturing that resolve, however, one realizes and appreciates ever more deeply that it is based in a mandate from God. When we see the commandment as no longer just a good moral maxim, but instead as God's words, we may be transformed in our relation not only to God, but to all humanity, that is, to all of God's other children. That deepened sense of religious brotherhood and sisterhood becomes then part of what we are. As such, killing our fellow human beings is unthinkable, not to mention undoable. Then the phrase has changed its sense and "Thou shalt not kill" becomes not a simple imperative from God—"do not kill"—but instead a description of what we are, people of whom one can say "you will not kill."

Now let us put this in Dōgen's terms. For him, the pivotal point is in the phrase "not do" of "do not do evil." Again, Dōgen's focus is on the *how* of the verb, not the *what* of the object. The Sino-Japanese word for "do" in this "not do" (the *sa* of *makusa*) literally means "to produce." Hence, in heeding the words of the buddhas, the practitioner realizes that evils exist because they are produced or created. In particular, they are produced by the delusional sense of an independent ego. If that ego drops away, dissolving back into the meaningless flux of phenomena, there is only nonproduction (*makusa*). So, naturally, there will be no evil. If one grounds one's expressions in their proper basis—without thinking—and if one responds to occasions appropriately—without ego—there is no way for evil to be produced.[109*]

In the rest of his essay, Dōgen fleshes out the complementary details for the other two phrases.[110] He concludes with an analysis of a Chinese Zen story. The famous Chinese poet Bai Juyi went to master Daolin (741–824) to ask the meaning of the buddha's truth. Daolin responded with *shoakumakusa shuzenbugyō*. Taking that to be inane, Bai Juyi said that "even a three-year old" could say that. Daolin retorted "Maybe a three-year child could say it, but even an elder in his eighties cannot practice it."[111] Dōgen's analysis is that because Bai Juyi did not take the words seriously, he never formed the resolve to follow the mandate. If he had, he would have seen that the dictum was no simple mandate at all, but instead another gateway into the presencing of things as they are and the egoless expression of them in their shifting occasions of meaning.

A important consequence of Dōgen's interpretation is that even a fixed statement from a traditional text is open to shifts in meaning as the reader's situation changes, including as the reader's spirituality deepens and matures. Is the phrase *shoakumakusa*, therefore, really an imperative or really a description? Dōgen's answer is that it can be both; the present context of the reader is critical to the text's meaning. A book, including the great master texts of the Buddhist tradition, are therefore as much an opening into different worlds of meaning as was the ocean in his aforementioned analysis from "*Genjōkōan.*"[112]

Conclusion

This concludes our engagement with the philosopher Dōgen. Dōgen's philosophy suggests that it is not a matter of what you know, but instead a matter of how you know. It is not a matter of whom you meet, but of how you meet. It is not a matter of what you express, but of how you express. In this chapter, I focused on the development of Dōgen's basic metaphysical and metapractical positions. Significantly, in his final years, his writings focused more on praxis than philosophical issues, establishing the rules of monastic life and the proper way to carry out daily activities. It is as if once he established the metapractical argument for the primacy of how over what, he could concentrate on the practical details of life lived as a buddha-in-action. He made the move from metapraxis back to praxis.

In his emphasis on *how* over *what* and on the necessity of having an open mind so one could continuously respond to the fluidity of changing circumstances, Dōgen is in the mainstream of the earlier Japanese philosophers we have already examined. Dōgen's distinctiveness lies in his ability to shape his language for the purpose of expressing the most complex ideas in light of the most everyday experiences. Dōgen's *Repository* is his country's first sustained philosophical treatise written in Japanese rather than Chinese.

Why did Dōgen choose to write such a sophisticated and erudite text in Japanese? When his contemporaries like Shinran and Nichiren wrote in Japanese, it was mainly in letters to laypeople, many of whom could not read Chinese. That is, Dōgen's contemporaries wrote in the Japanese language primarily to make their work more accessible to the laity. Dōgen's *Repository*, however, is not written in ordinary Japanese. It is full of neologisms, twists in syntax, and arcane references to other texts. It relishes double meanings and paradoxes, tossing in images like walking mountains, the wagging tongue of the cosmic buddha, and pictures of rice cakes you can eat.

What then is the significance of such an unusual writing style? There are many approaches to answering that question, but here I will suggest one that reinforces the interpretation I have been developing in this chapter. Dōgen wants us to live in the world with a sense of openness. Meanings for him do not fix reality, but emerge from reality's self-expression. By engaging in that self-expression, we discover ourselves as well as the world. No item is *simply* what it seems, even though it *really* is as it appears. Every phenomenon has multiple meanings to be discovered as its contexts and situations undergo constant change. Dōgen's is a world of changing realities and ever new meanings.

That is *what* he says about language. However, the key to being a buddha-in-action always lies in *how* not *what*. By using Japanese, his native language, he could capture that moment when meaning comes into being within the present scheme of things as they are. In that respect, Dōgen did not write *Repository* to make his ideas accessible to others, but rather, he wrote it as the ideas expressed themselves. Dōgen wrote the book as an expression of himself, leaving his half of the intimacy while inviting us to engage him with our half of the intimacy. In reading Dōgen we discover ourselves as well as Dōgen. Like the student and the master, the reader and the writer must "practice together." Perhaps an anecdote will help clarify.

Some four decades ago when I was just beginning my career of engaging Dōgen, I called on Professor Tamaki Kōshirō, a renowned professor of Buddhist Studies from Tokyo University and a Dōgen scholar whose works I admired. In our first meeting I ventured a few straightforward questions to break the ice including "Why did Dōgen write *Repository* in Japanese?" In a matter-of-fact tone of voice, he replied, "*Repository* is not written in Japanese."

Startled, I felt a flush of embarrassment. For the preceding months, had I been so foolish as to be reading some Japanese translation of a Chinese original? How could I have missed *that*? Fortunately, Tamaki continued. "Dōgen did not write in Japanese; he wrote in his own language. No one had ever written in such a Japanese language before him." I then pressed the issue, "Does that mean Dōgen was in some respects writing *Repository* not for an audience, but instead for himself?" Tamaki nodded affirmatively.

I then shared my difficulties in reading Dōgen, my puzzling over curious phrases and odd words. I asked Tamaki which dictionaries or commentaries of the many available would be the best guide. He then leaned forward, looking straight into my eyes and said (in English this time), "Forget commentaries. The Dharma is in *you*." It took me many years to appreciate that Tamaki was not being idiosyncratic or radical in his statements, but that the position he outlined was in fact firmly anchored in Dōgen's own text. Dōgen's text is his half of the intimacy; as his reader you must bring your own half.

In wrapping up our engagement with Dōgen, I will offer a couple of simple points of comparison and contrast with our two previously engaged Buddhist philosophers: Kūkai and Shinran. Like Kūkai, Dōgen believed that the cosmos is self-expressive, showing itself at all times as it is. Yet, unlike Kūkai, Dōgen did not believe we needed an esoteric key to decode its intimations. Dōgen's Zen maintains that engagement with reality is available with directness, without the need to master how to read Dainichi's "expressive symbols" (*monji*). That difference in focus between Kūkai and Dōgen reflects the disparity between the Heian and Kamakura philosophical mentalities. Whereas Kūkai's interest was cosmic and all-inclusive, Dōgen's, like Shinran's, was *selective*, existential, and personal.

Turning now to Shinran, if we limit our focus to the content of Shinran's and Dōgen's writings, they seem to radically diverge: other-power versus self-power; the Degenerate Age (*mappō*) versus the Age of Correctness (*shōbō*); anti-institutionalism versus monastic discipline; a rhetoric of egoless humility versus a rhetoric of egoless assertiveness. That, however, is only the *what-they-said* kind of analysis. We might instead look more closely at their commonalities: disappearing buddhas; an antinomianism that is not an antinomianism; reading old texts and terms in radically new ways; a reverence for teachers; and a valorization of naturalness and spontaneity. When we shift to the *how-they-lived* and the *how-they-experienced enlightenment*, the differences between the two Kamakura philosophers begin to dissolve.

Now that we have engaged Shinran and Dōgen, we can turn to the historical events following them. What happened to the traditions they founded? How did Shinran's Shin Buddhism and Dōgen's Sōtō Zen Buddhism become so popular among ordinary people, especially given the philosophical complexity of their most central ideas? What new ways of philosophizing came on the scene? That will be our concern in our next chapter as we leave the engagement mode to return again to historical narrative.

7. Refuge from the Storm
Muromachi to the Warring Domains (1333–1568)

> The most precious thing in life
> is its uncertainty.
>
> YOSHIDA Kenkō[113]

As explained in Chapter 4[†] in the late twelfth century the samurai seized control of the country and established their military government (shogunate) in Kamakura, some 450 kilometers east of the capital[‡] in Kyoto. Although this marked a formal transition from aristocratic to military rule, the Kamakura shogunate still often deferred to the court for its political connections and charismatic authority. Philosophically, there was more at stake than a political change in the center of power, however; there was also a subtle cultural shift.

Suggestive of that shift are the two images of Amida Buddha pictured on the next page, one from the eleventh century in the Fujiwara family temple at Uji (south of Kyoto) called Byōdō-in, the other the mid-thirteenth-century "great Buddha" of the temple Kōtoku-in in Kamakura. The late Heian-period buddha is an Amida for aristocrats, a celestial buddha presiding over the paradisiacal Pure Land, a buddha whose compassion can bring the end of suffering to all who entrust themselves to his Vow. The face is kindly, the shoulders a bit narrow, the arms soft and thin, and the fingers delicate. Strings of glistening glass balls, a technological marvel of the age, hung in jewel-like streams around the original golden gilded statue, surrounded by images of Amida's heavenly entourage.

By contrast, the brawny Amida from Kamakura is a soldier's buddha with powerful shoulders, massive chest, mustache, and strong hands. He not so much presides over a paradise as sits firmly and squarely among us, anchored

---

† See pages 158–9.

‡ In Japan the capital is the city in which the emperor officially resides. As was the case in the Kamakura period, the capital does not necessarily function as the center of government administration.

Amida of Byōdō-in   Amida of Kamakura's Kōtoku-in

to this world by both gravity and gravitas. In the fourteenth and fifteenth centuries, this Amida's temple was twice destroyed by typhoons and a tsunami once obliterated the building entirely, but the image remained unscathed. Then the temple building was again destroyed in 1495—that time by fire—but the Buddha again survived. Since then the Great Buddha has sat unperturbed in the open air, as solid and immovable as the shogunate had hoped it itself would be.

It turned out, however, that the medieval[†] shogunates were neither immovable nor solid. In Chapter 4 we saw how tenuous was the power of the Kamakura shoguns, under the control of the Hōjō regents and plagued with nagging dissension from both the court and samurai power bases in central Japan and Kyoto.[‡] Although cloistered emperor Go-Toba's plan to overthrow the shogunate in 1221 had failed miserably, the court had secured enough economic and political clout to remain a threat.

A little over a century later, the emperor Go-Daigo (1288–1339) redid Go-Toba's calculations and decided this time the throne could succeed in restoring imperial power. The Hōjō regents uncovered his plot, thwarting the coup before it really got underway. But Go-Daigo continued scheming. In 1331 he was under such surveillance that he tried to leave the capital for Nara, was captured, and forced into exile. In 1333 he escaped and started raising his army anew. The Kamakura shogunate again made a preemptive strike, sending its general, Ashikaga Takauji (1305–1358), to wipe out Go-Daigo's armies and to take the

† In this book, for the purposes of simplicity, "medieval" designates the span from the beginning of the Kamakura period through to the beginning of the Edo (Tokugawa) period, that is, from roughly 1185 to 1600.

‡ See pages 159–61.

capital, but the general switched sides and occupied the capital on behalf of the emperor. Then the shogunate dispatched its other chief general, Nitta Yoshisada (1301–1338), to remedy the situation, but like Takauji, he also betrayed the shogunate and occupied Kamakura for the imperial forces. Thus ended the Kamakura period in 1333: the Hōjō leadership along with several hundred allies committed suicide, Takauji put Go-Daigo on the throne, and the Kenmu Imperial Restoration was complete.

The emperor's samurai allies were quickly disenchanted with the arrangement, however, as Go-Daigo did not reward them with the patronage, power, and money they felt their loyalty had earned. As a result, four years later Ashikaga Takauji again switched allegiances and overthrew Go-Daigo. Nitta Yoshisada's last minute efforts to come to the emperor's defense having failed, Takauji forced Go-Daigo to vacate the capital and move south to Yoshino. Takauji then installed a new emperor on the throne. That was the beginning of the "Northern and Southern Courts" period of imperial succession that lasted about 55 years until 1392. To keep a closer eye on court politics and to have his troops ready at hand where he thought he might most likely need them, Ashikaga Takauji made the Muromachi district in Kyoto the home of his new government. This raised the curtain on the Ashikaga or Muromachi Period (1338–1573).

MUROMACHI AESTHETICS

The shogunate's presence in Kyoto enkindled a new cultural synergy among the military government, major Buddhist temples, and the court. Politically, the early Muromachi shoguns concentrated on securing and maintaining alliances with the various regional land-owning military lords (daimyō). They only partially succeeded, and that for only a rather short time. The Muromachi shogunate's political achievement reached its apex with the famous third shogun, Ashikaga Yoshimitsu (1358–1408), who ruled from 1369 to 1395. Yoshimitsu's reign gives us a thumbnail sketch of the Muromachi convergence of culture, politics, and economics.

Financially strapped after paying off his allies in the coup, Yoshimitsu realized that if he were to reestablish trade relations with China, he could increase the flow of money into the capital and thereby stabilize his fragile military government. Such a relation with China was not, of course, unprecedented and so it is instructive to review the medieval history of the interaction between Japan and the continental empire.

Back in the twelfth century there had been extensive exchange between Japan and (Southern Song) China, partly because the shogunate had wanted greater access to the cultural riches of China to burnish the image of Kamakura as a center of cultivated life rivaling the Kyoto court. It was under those conditions that Zen monks like Eisai, Myōzen, and Dōgen were able to travel freely to China, and Chinese monks were heartily welcomed into Japan as teachers and abbots of newly established (mainly Rinzai Zen) temples. The renewed cultural exchange also triggered a revival of Chinese scholarship, an enterprise that had lost some of its cachet in the latter Heian period when many courtiers seemed to prefer cultivating more "native" aesthetic sensitivities.

Relations with China soured with the fall of the Song in 1279. Under the Yuan Dynasty Kublai Khan had offered affiliate status to Japan, but only in return for Japanese concessions: Japan would have to pay tribute, accept the Chinese dynastic calendar, and assume the status of an independent satellite country (like Korea) under the umbrella of the Chinese "Middle Kingdom." In return, China would send Japan gifts, trade freely, and formally recognize Japan's ruler as a "king" within the Chinese imperial sphere.

Japan refused the Khan's offer and the result was the two failed Mongol invasions in 1274 and 1281. The Mongols attacked the southern island of Kyushu with superior forces and advanced weaponry, but accounts say that both times typhoons devastated the attack forces and the Japanese were saved. Given the almost miraculous nature of their victories, the Japanese deemed the storms divine acts, dubbing them *kami kaze* ("sacred winds"). Those late thirteenth-century hostilities ended significant official relations between China and Japan.

When a new Chinese dynasty, the Ming, came to power in 1368, there was again a chance to affiliate with the Empire of the Middle Kingdom under stipulations much like those of the Khan a century earlier. This time Ashikaga Yoshimitsu jumped at the opportunity. To him, a little tribute and some mild kowtowing would be more than rewarded by the economic and cultural benefits of an alliance. Not surprisingly, Ming China designated the "king of Japan" to be not the Japanese emperor, but the shogun.

Kyoto underwent a new economic and cultural boom, and the shogun's coffers and prestige swelled. The Kyoto court—finally reunited by Yoshimitsu during the latter years of his tenure as shogun—actively participated in the new cultural vitality of Muromachi Japan. As a result, Kyoto enjoyed a vibrant and refined city life that cut across classes: aristocrats (including those disenfranchised as big losers in any of the many struggles for power), the samurai, the newly risen urban merchants and money lenders, and even the craftsmen now organized into guilds. With the infusion of Chinese influence, the arts began to flourish.

Yoshimitsu himself received court titles, rising to the highest rank by 1380, eventually receiving imperial appointment as chancellor (*daijō daijin*). This meant that Yoshimitsu could legitimately consider himself both shogun and courtier. Befitting his newly acquired aristocratic associations, he became a renowned patron of the arts as consumer, financial backer, and participant. He engaged in a full spectrum of aesthetic production: poetry, calligraphy, painting, music, drama, dance, and gardens. As an example of the latter, across from the imperial palace, he built his own shogun's residence, the "Palace of Flowers" (*Hana no gosho*), the site of garden parties that were a highlight of the Kyoto social calendar.

THE GOLDEN AND SILVER PAVILIONS

In 1395, feeling his political work complete and aching to enjoy his final years in aesthetic self-indulgence, he abdicated in favor of his capable son, Ashikaga Yoshimochi (1386–1428). Yoshimitsu retired to his grand retreat today known as the Golden Pavilion, Kinkaku-ji, nestled in Kyoto's Kitayama (Northern Hills) district, thereby leading historians to name the span from the beginning of Yoshimitsu's rule in 1369 until his death in 1408 as the "Kitayama epoch." Those decades are famous for a renewed, Chinese-influenced sense of elegance called *fūryū*, "stylistic refinement." Although Chinese in origin, by this time in Japan the term was used more broadly to signify a cultivated appreciation of landscape art, gardens, architecture, calligraphy, and nature poetry.

The design of the Golden Pavilion discloses Yoshimitsu's self-evaluation of his accomplishments as shogun. The tiers integrate different architectural motifs: the lowest is in the palace style of the court; the upper two, gilt in gold leaf, are in the architectural manner of samurai estates and Zen Buddhist temples, respectively. The surrounding ornamental pond evokes Amida's Pure Land and a Chinese-style phoenix sits atop the roof. Hence, Yoshimitsu's pavilion symbolizes the cultural and political elements he had tried to integrate. It serves as a trophy for his victories.

For contrast, let us go eastward crosstown in Kyoto to the Silver Pavilion (Ginkaku-ji) built by the eighth Muromachi shogun, Ashikaga Yoshimasu (1436–1490). There we can glimpse the nadir rather than the zenith of Muromachi political power as well as signs of a different aesthetic.

The fact that the eighth Muromachi shogun, Yoshimasu, was the grandson of the third shogun Yoshimitsu, bespeaks the brevity of the Ashikaga shoguns' reigns. And Yoshimasu did not seem inclined to change that pattern. He had been so enthralled with the aesthetic aspects of his courtly upbringing that from the outset he disdained the office of shogun and planned early abdication. Not having a son of his own, he brought his brother out of monkhood to be prepped as his successor. Before the transition of power occurred, however, Yoshimasu's wife bore him a son and he reneged on the promise to his brother, triggering a catastrophic dispute over succession.

Yoshimasu eventually distanced himself from the issue to let the interested forces fight it out. And fight it out they did for over a decade (1467–1477) in the Ōnin War (named for the Ōnin era 1467–1479). Military lords from across the

The Golden Pavilion

country came to the capital with their armies in the contest for power. At the end, Kyoto lay in waste with nearly every major building in the city destroyed. Nero is said to have watched while Rome burned; Yoshimasu retreated from the conflagration to the Eastern Hills (Higashiyama), the eventual site of his Silver Pavilion. The Ōnin War ended in stalemate, its legacy being the almost complete erosion of the shogunate's political power, the impoverishment of the court, and the levelling of the cultural and spiritual capital of Japan.

The center had once again dissolved, a recurring theme in the medieval age: first the Heian court, next the Kamakura shogunate, and now the Muromachi shogunate. Returning home from the capital, the various *daimyō* found themselves battling factions within their own families as well as waging wars against their regional neighbors. Japan had entered a century of armed conflict that historians call the Period of the Warring Domains (Sengoku). It lasted a full century from the outset of the Ōnin War in 1467 until 1568.

Befitting the mood of unrealized dreams, Yoshimasu's Silver Pavilion never received its silver adornment—there was no money for it. Perhaps, though, it is better that way. When we visit the Silver Pavilion, we find it a lonely, rustic place, the raked lines of its gravel garden suggestive of deeper movement beneath the cool, white surface. Whereas the Golden Pavilion is a glittering trophy to political accomplishment, the Silver Pavilion is a retreat—a withdrawal away, within, and below. Those senses of withdrawal drew on and nourished

The Silver Pavilion

the distinctive aesthetic sensitivities of the medieval age from late Kamakura to the end of the Warring Domains Period. Let us examine them in a bit more detail.

1224–6   *Withdrawal from—"wabi."* Yoshimasu's retreat into the Eastern Hills was a withdrawal from the court: both its remnants of Chinese-style grandeur and its political machinations. As the Golden Pavilion oozes opulence, the Silver Pavilion exemplifies plainness and simplicity, what is known as *wabi*. The term derives from words meaning "to pine away for" or "to be without material comforts." The word's earlier provenance was Japanese poetry, but *wabi* became especially popular in such areas as the aesthetic of tea ceremony with its love of nature, calligraphy, poetry, and landscape—interests shared by the aesthetics of *fūryū* but *wabi* stressed naturalness rather than elegance.

The founding theorists of tea ceremony, Takeno Jōō (1502–1555) and his disciple Sen no Rikyū (1522–1591), identified the following two poems as expressive of the classical poetic tradition of *wabi* that they aspired to bring to the Way of Tea.[114]

Chosen by Jōō	*Chosen by Rikyū*
When I look afar	To those waiting
Beyond the cherry blossoms	Only for the flowers to bloom,
Or tinted leaves—	Show them spring

Only huts by the harbor
In the autumn dusk
(Fujiwara no Teika [aka
Fujiwara no Sadaie], 1162–1241)

In a mountain village,
Its grass sticking up amidst the snow.
(Fujiwara no Ietaka, 1158–1237)

The first poem advocates abandoning the fixation on the splendor of cherry blossoms and the scarlet maple leaves so often acclaimed in the Heian aesthetic of courtly elegance (*miyabi*). To foreswear such aristocratic elitism opens one to a more profound aesthetic represented here by the earthy plainness of fishermen's huts fading into the monochromatic twilight. In the second poem, the lesson of *wabi* is that the true lover of nature can appreciate not just the brilliance of spring blossoms, but also the subtlety in life's taking form within the featureless snowy desolation of early spring in the mountains.

Withdrawal within—"sabi." The second key aesthetic term, one often associated with *wabi*, is *sabi*, a word whose derivation means *lonely*. *Sabi* is not merely a subjective state, but pertains more to a field of ideas and value containing both persons and objects. The English word *lonely* can have this sense as well when we speak of a "lonely place," for example. A lonely place is not only isolated, but is also internally related with the loneliness in anyone who happens to be there. One's personal loneliness and the place's loneliness resonate as a field of loneliness where subject and surroundings blur into, and reinforce, each other. The Japanese often refer to such a field of affect, idea, and meaning as *kokoro*, a notion I will explain more fully in Chapter 10's engagement with the philosopher Motoori Norinaga. *Sabi* is a quality that may at times pervade *kokoro*.

The *sabi* aesthetic has nuances not only of loneliness, but also of being left alone, of being allowed to grow old. A tarnished silver implement may have lost its luster, but the aesthete should also be able to appreciate the beauty in its patina. The same can be said of a tombstone partially hidden in moss. In modern times, the meanings of *sabi* and *wabi* have developed such that the two terms have become nearly interchangeable. If pressed to make a distinction based on the words' classical use, however, I would venture the following.

As it stands, unadorned and without its intended silver coating, the Silver Pavilion suggests *wabi*. It is rustic, plain, and simple. If the original plan had been carried out, however, and if the silver were then left to tarnish to a patina, the Silver Pavilion would become *sabi*, an artifice left alone and benignly neglected so that it begins to fade into its natural surroundings. *Wabi* is more an aloneness resulting from choice; *sabi* more one resulting from accepting, or even being enthralled by, natural decay.

A comparison between the medieval aesthetic of *sabi* and the earlier Heian aesthetic of *aware*[†] elicits further features. *Aware* had the sense of poignant appreciation for things' impermanence, such as the cherry blossoms whose bloom might last for only a week. The idea was that the blossoms are most striking when we value their beauty as transient. The *sabi* aesthetic, by contrast, finds aesthetic value not in the passing, but in the presence of the past. Yoshida Kenkō's (*ca.* 1283–*ca.* 1352) early fourteenth-century "jottings," *Tsurezuregusa* (often translated as "Essays in Idleness"), captures well this difference:

> Are we to look at cherry blossoms only in full bloom, the moon only when it is cloudless? … People commonly regret that the cherry blossoms scatter or that the moon sinks in the sky, and this is natural; but only the exceptionally insensitive would say, "This branch and that branch have lost their blossoms. There is nothing worth seeing now."
>
> In all things, it is the beginnings and ends that are interesting. Does the love between men and women refer only to the moments when they are in each other's arms? The man who grieves over a love affair broken off before it was fulfilled, who bewails empty vows, who spends long autumn nights alone, who lets his thoughts wander to distant skies, who yearns for the past in a dilapidated house—such a man truly knows what love means.[115]

So, *sabi* involves not so much a retreat from the glitter of the world, but rather, a deepening in signification born of aging—the aging of the object and the aging of the person. When Kenkō esteems a now-ended love, the sensitivity is an echoing memory, memory both of what was and of the unfulfilled hope of what could have been. Such mature sensitivities arise most naturally in solitary reverie. To continue to call the hermitage the "Silver Pavilion" when it has never had any silver on it is an homage to *sabi*.

1170–1   *Withdrawal below—"yūgen."* At the ground of both *wabi* and *sabi* is a more profound value driving medieval aesthetics. Consisting of two sinographs respectively meaning "dim" or "hidden away" 幽 and "mystery" 玄, *yūgen* connotes a hazy, unfathomable mystery lying beneath surface appearances. In Chapter 4[‡] I quoted Kamo no Chōmei's twelfth-century account of the devastation during the early Kamakura period. He retired to his "ten-foot hut" in the hills where he could live simply, so simply he could pack up his hermitage—the sticks constructing the hut as well as his few possessions—and tote them away at the spur of the moment. Obviously, his intentions befit the self-imposed austerity of *wabi*, but in characterizing his poetic response to the challenges of his life in

† See pages 140–3.
‡ See page 161.

1212, Chōmei spoke instead of *yūgen*. Asked its meaning, he responded that the term itself is confusing, but went on to explain:

> [A]ccording to the views of those who have penetrated into the realm of *yūgen*, the importance lies in the "left over," which is not stated in words and an atmosphere that is not revealed through the form of the poem....
>
> On an autumn evening, for example, there is no color in the sky and no sound, and although we cannot give a definite reason for it, we are somehow moved to tears. A person lacking in sensitivity finds nothing particular in such a sight, but just admires the cherry blossoms and scarlet autumn leaves that are visible to the eye.†

1207

Chōmei's description of *yūgen* is primarily a form of aesthetic sensitivity, but his elder contemporary, the founder of *waka*‡ aesthetics Fujiwara no Shunzei (aka Fujiwara no Toshinari), claimed that the engagement with *yūgen* should arise out of a state of mind disciplined through meditation, the attitude achieved in the aforementioned Tendai Buddhist seated meditation called *shikan*,[116] "calming and contemplation." He described the consequent awareness of profundity as follows:

> Now, if we pay attention to this [clarity and tranquility of calming and contemplation] at the outset, a dimension of infinite depth as well as profound meaning will be discovered. It will be like listening to something sublime and exalted while trying to understand the poetic sensibility—its fine points, weak points, and its depths. This is to say that things that otherwise are incapable of being expressed in words will be understood precisely when they are likened to calming and contemplation.

1173

In his art of Nō (Noh) drama, Zeami (1363–1443) considered *yūgen* to be the "foremost" art of the performer, claiming we encounter it when an actor achieves a depth regardless of the role being portrayed, whether demon or bodhisattva. In 1424 he discussed its rarity:

> In a sense, [*yūgen*] is something you can see, and members of the audience take particular delight in it, but an actor with *yūgen* is not all that easy to find. This is because few truly know the savor of *yūgen*. When that is the case, no actor crosses into its realm.

1210

As Chōmei had referred to *yūgen* as a "dimension," Zeami called it a "realm" in which the actor and the character portrayed become one. Zeami associated this plummeting of profound meaning and performance with the Zen Buddhist

---

† Note the similar sentiment expressed in the two previously quoted *wabi* poems, roughly contemporaneous with Chōmei's comments.

‡ Traditional poetry written in Japanese.

ideal of "no-mind," seeing in it a link between the actor's art and the meditative aspect that carries over into the everyday.

> In their critiques, members of the audience often say that the places where nothing is done are interesting. This is a secret stratagem of the actor.... When you consider why it is that this gap where nothing is done should be interesting, you will find that this is because of an underlying disposition by which the mind bridges the gap. It is a frame of mind in which you maintain your intent and do not loosen your concentration in the gaps where you've stopped dancing the dance, in the places where you've stopped singing the music, in the gaps between all types of speech and dramatic imitation, and so on. This internal excitement diffuses outward and creates interest. However, should it be apparent to others that you have adopted this frame of mind, that is no good. If it becomes apparent, then it is likely to turn into a dramatic technique in itself. Then it is no longer "doing nothing...."[†]
>
> In the most general terms. you should not limit this to the actual occasion of performance. Day after day, night after night, whether coming or going, sitting up or lying down, you should not forget about this intent; you should bind your experiences together with a resolute mind. If you employ your creativity in this way without negligence, your performance will improve evermore.

1211-12

1216-19

In his classic 1939 study, the aesthetician Ōnishi Yoshinori wrote that *yūgen* is (1) hidden, (2) dim, (3) still, (4) profound, (5) complete, (6) mystical, and (7) inexplicable. His characterization of the third and fourth elements summarize what we found in the medieval understanding of the term:

> A third and no less very closely related element in the meaning is the sense of *stillness* that accompanies what is dimly hidden within the general notion of *yūgen*. But along with this sense is an indication of a state of mind that reaches sentiments of beauty as well, as when one is absorbed in the tearful feelings of abandon to the colorless, voiceless sky of an autumn evening of which Kamo no Chōmei speaks, or "a lonely thatched dwelling in a late-autumn shower" that Shunzei praised for its poetic spirit of *yūgen*, or the fleeting sight of snipes flying out of a swamp in an autumn nightfall.
>
> The fourth sense of *yūgen* is what is called *profundity*, a sense of "depth and distance." This element is, of course, related to the foregoing, but even in general notions of *yūgen* it does not have to do with mere temporal or spatial distance. There is a particular, spiritual meaning here, as in the case of a profound and abstruse idea like the "deep and mysterious buddha-dharma" (*Rinzairoku* 1.18[‡]). We may consider part of *yūgen* the corresponding sentiments of beauty

---

† The term "doing nothing" derives from the Daoist notion of agenda-less activity (C. *wuwei*), an ideal highly valued in Zen Buddhism as well.

‡ *The Record of Linji*, a text associated with the Chan master considered to be the founder

that have been given particular emphasis by those like Shōtetsu and Shinkei, what is often referred to in theories of poetry as "depth of heart" or as Teika and others put it, "having heart.†"117

1217

In general, then, in the Muromachi aesthetic, *yūgen* can assume an ontological dimension beneath the surface, whereas *wabi* and *sabi* tend to refer more to the phenomenal level, although they may be anchored in *yūgen* as well. The end result is that the three terms can work together and blur into each other rather than remaining distinct. In their discussions of *yūgen,* Shunzei, Zeami, and Ōnishi all pointed to a common element: the link between *yūgen* and Buddhist meditation.118 This link bring us to the question of how religion evolved during the latter medieval era.

Medieval religion

Medieval Shintō

At its outset the Kamakura period had no major discrete religious institution or coherent set of practices and doctrines that could be distinctively designated "Shintō" as we know that tradition today. Yet, the characteristics of what I have called proto-Shintō continued to be highly visible in Japanese culture. Mark Teeuwen has identified four elements that would later amalgamate into the formation of Shintō from the eighteenth century up through the modern period: *kami*-worship, valorization of the ancient Japanese language, stress on the mythohistorical chronicles *Kojiki* and *Nihonshoki,* and the imperial lineage rituals directed to various *kami* in local or regional shrines.

457

In the early medieval period Shintō shrines were usually managed under the auspices of Buddhist temples or at least Buddhist clergy. Moreover, the esoteric theory of *honji suijaku*‡ continued to incorporate the *kami* into Buddhism by relegating them to being trace manifestations of buddhas and bodhisattvas. During the medieval period, though, some philosophical and institutional developments began to shape proto-Shintō themes into a more coherent and distinctive profile.

Kitabatake Chikafusa (1293–1354). First of all, the schism into the Northern and Southern courts in the latter half of the fourteenth century led to theorizing about the Shintō spiritual, historical, and philosophical justification for imperial

---

of what is in Japan called "Rinzai Zen."

† The word "heart" here is the aforementioned *kokoro.*

‡ See pages 145–6.

succession. In fact, the pronunciation of the term 神道 as "Shintō" (rather than *jindō* or *kami no michi*) seems to have begun around this time.[119]

A fervent advocate of the imperial system and of Go-Daigo's rightful place as sole emperor, Kitabatake Chikafusa wrote in the early 1340s his *Chronicle of Gods and Sovereigns*,[120] tracing the imperial succession from its mythic origins described in ancient chronicles up to Go-Daigo. The following lines are typical of his tone:

> It has simply been my intent to discuss some of the principles behind the fact that there has been no disruption of the legitimate line of imperial succession from the time of the age of the gods. Our country is the divine land, and thus the succession has been followed in accordance with the will of Amaterasu Ōmikami. Nevertheless, when sovereigns within that succession have made errors, their reigns have been brief. Although the succession invariably returns to its direct course, there have been temporary aberrations. These aberrations, however, have always been the fault of the individual sovereigns themselves and have not occurred because of any failing in divine aid.

1019

In Chapter 2 I examined the religiophilosophical ideology of imperial authority up through the Nara period, drawing as it did on Buddhist, Confucian, and proto-Shintō ideas. Of the three, proto-Shintō was the least philosophically developed at that time. Chikafusa's text tried to reverse that situation, referring to Japan as the "divine land" or "land of the *kami*" (*shinkoku*), a phrase previously used only infrequently. In so doing, he accentuated the proto-Shintō assertion that Japan was created by the *kami* and that the *kami* of the imperial family—the Sun Goddess Amaterasu—serves as protector not only of the emperor but also of Japan at large.

From antiquity, the Japanese had understood the celestial *kami* as protectors: first of the clans and villages, then of the whole land of Japan. We have already come across the *kami kaze* interpretation of the typhoons that had repelled the Mongols in the thirteenth century. Buddhism assigned *kami* the role of safeguarding the Dharma, the true teachings and practices of Buddhism. But how do the *kami* have such might? Chikafusa's answer was that their power depended on their primordial creative energy. His earlier work, *Collection on the Beginnings of Beginnings* (*Gengenshū*),[121] had argued that by focusing on the *kami*, we return to the origin of everything, thereby grounding both proto-Shintō and the imperial lineage in primal generative energy.

Watarai Shintō. Based in the Outer Shrine of Ise, the medieval Watarai Shintō school as well appealed to the primordial character of the *kami*. By the medieval period, the esoteric Buddhist relegation of the *kami* to a derivative status had become so deeply engrained in the culture that even Ise's Inner Shrine of Amaterasu and Outer Shrine of Toyouke were described in terms of the Womb and

Diamond mandalas, respectively. And Amaterasu, the Sun *kami,* was explicitly identified with the Great Sun Buddha, Dainichi. Hence, a "dual Shintō" (*ryōbu shintō*) system mirrored the "dual mandala" (*ryōbu mandara*) Shingon Buddhist tradition introduced by Kūkai.

Concerned that the Outer Shrine Ise was considered of lower status than the Inner Shrine and denouncing the idea that *kami* were mere projections of buddhas, the Watarai priests formulated a new interpretation based on the principle of *origins.* They claimed, first of all, that as the primordial creators, the first *kami* are intrinsically superior to later *kami.* The Watarai scholars then contrived an argument and produced a secret oracular text showing that Toyouke, the *kami* of the Outer Shrine, was actually the primordial creator *kami,* Amenominakanushi no kami, the "Lord Kami of Heaven's Center."[122]

No one had ever claimed that the Sun Goddess was the oldest *kami*—the *Kojiki* and *Nihonshoki* unequivocally described her as one of the later *kami* to come into existence. Until the appeal to origins became the criterion for superiority, however, that fact had made little difference: though not the oldest, Amaterasu could still be the most important *kami.* Starting with Kitabatake's claim that the essence of *kami* is their creative energy, the Watarai philosophers argued that what comes earlier in the act of creation must be superior to what comes later. Unlike Kitabatake, however, they rigorously applied the criterion of priority to make distinctions among the *kami* themselves and not just between the *kami* and other beings such as buddhas.

Following that line of thought, the Watarai School philosophers could buttress their claim for the superiority of Toyouke over Amaterasu and, by extension, the superiority of the Outer over the Inner Shrine at Ise. Moreover, the appeal to origins allowed them to argue that the esoteric Buddhists were right about the interfusion of the *kami* and buddhas, but that the Buddhists had reversed the true relation. After all, the *kami* were creators and the buddhas were not.[123] Therefore, the *kami* must have existed prior to buddhas or bodhisattvas and the latter must be manifestations of the former, rather than vice versa.

Western readers may find nothing remarkable in the Watarai argument: what comes first is most fundamental; historical priority entails ontological priority; the creator is greater than the created. Such claims have been part of the discourse of western philosophy from the beginning of pre-Socratic speculation and they are equally central to Jewish, Christian, and Muslim doctrines about creation, teleology, and history.

In fact, those premises are so basic to most western thinking that we often must take pains to remind ourselves that logical priority does not entail temporal priority: "if x, then y" does not necessarily mean x must *preexist* y. For example, "if it is raining, then it is precipitating" does not mean the rain existed before the precipitation. So logical inference need be neither temporal nor causal. For that reason, most Buddhists maintain that just because the Buddha's cosmic embodiment is logically and metaphysically primary, it does not necessarily mean that the cosmic buddha existed in a time before other buddhas or that the cosmic buddha *created* the cosmos. In addition, classical Confucianism, with its emphasis on human virtue and social harmony, also showed little interest in cosmogonic theories.

To summarize: an argument that historical priority entails ontological or metaphysical importance was not a major part of the standard Japanese philosophical repertoire previous to these medieval Shintō thinkers. From that point forward, however, appeals to primordiality or historical priority became a dominant motif in Shintō philosophy.[124]*

Yoshida (Yuiitsu) Shintō. The seed that Kitabatake Chikafusa and the Watarai theorists had sown in the fourteenth century eventually bore fruit as Yuiitsu or Yoshida Shintō in the late fifteenth and early sixteenth centuries. Adjacent to today's Kyoto University is the Yoshida Shrine, originally established in 859 by Fujiwara no Yamakage. Our interest is an octagonal building erected by Yoshida Kanetomo (1435–1511) on a hill within the Shrine precincts. It is the "Shrine of Great Foundation" (*Taigenkyū*), now officially designated by the Japanese government a "National Treasure." The shrine includes 3132 pebbles in its central font fed by rainwater, each representing one of the *kami* mentioned in the early tenth-century *Engishiki*, a textual foundation for many ancient *kami*-related rituals. Moreover, along the walls of the shrine compound each *kami* has a

The Shrine of Great Foundation

respective point of veneration. By going to the Shrine of Great Foundation, therefore, one can simultaneously worship all the major *kami* of Japan.

That ritual site is the heart of "The One and Only Shintō," Yuiitsu Shintō, also called Yoshida Shintō, since it was the accomplishment of Yoshida Kanetomo and his successors. In creating Yuiitsu Shintō, Kanetomo had two goals. First, he hoped to give Shintō a philosophical foundation as not only a discrete but also an all-inclusive tradition. Second, he wanted to make his own Yoshida Shrine the central shrine for all Japan. Let us see how he pursued both aims.

Like his Shintō-theorist predecessors, Kanetomo claimed to be going back to *original* and *primordial* events for understanding the activities of *kami* and our appropriate personal, political, ritualistic, and social relations with them. For his metaphysical account, he drew heavily on Chinese *yin-yang* theories of cosmic process along with esoteric Buddhist forms of ritual praxis and metapraxis. He called his theoretical standpoint "Fundamental and Original Shintō" (*Genpon Sōgen Shintō*) defining the nomenclature as follows:

> The term *gen* 元 designates the beginning of beginnings before the appearance of yin and yang. The term *hon* [*pon*] 本 designates the state before the appearance of thought processes…. The term *sō* 宗 designates the original spirit before the diversification of energy. All phenomena return to that single origin. The term *gen* 源 designates the divine function referred to as "mingling with the dust and softening one's radiance" [i.e., the divine function softens its brilliance by mingling with this human world and its needs, manifesting itself appropriately and heuristically]. This provides the basis of benefit for all living beings…
>
> ……
>
> There are two broad interpretations of the two [sinographs making the term *shintō*]…. The term *shin* denotes the foundation of the totality of things in Heaven and Earth. Therefore, it is also qualified as unfathomable *yin* and *yang*. The term *tō* [C. *dao*] denotes the rationale of all activities. Therefore, it is said [in the first chapter of the *Daodejing*], "The Way is not the constant Way." As a consequence there is nothing in the material world, nor in the worlds of life, of animate and inanimate beings, of beings with energy and without energy, that does not partake of this "Shintō." Hence the verse:
>
>> *Shin* is the mindful heart of the totality of things,
>> *Tō* is the source of all activities.
>> All animate and inanimate beings of all realms of reality are ultimately nothing but Shintō only.[125]

The logic of Kanetomo's disputation in favor of Yuiitsu Shintō is worth tracing for how it relegates other positions by invoking the principle of origins. The passage just quoted begins with a discussion of mechanisms of creation, taking the appeal to origins to even more radical extremes than that envisioned by most Watarai thinkers. Rather than merely claiming the *kami* of his tradition to be the first *kami* among all the *kami* or that the *kami* preceded the buddhas historically, Kanetomo constructed an entire cosmogony about the beginning of *everything*, even of the *kami* themselves. That is, Kanetomo took Chikafusa's "beginning of the beginnings" to its logical endpoint, back to before even the bifurcation into *yin* and *yang*, not to mention the appearance of *kami*.

On one hand, Kanetomo was trying to "purify" Shintō of its distortions by what he considered various misinterpretations over the centuries. To that extent, his project was not unlike that of the Watarai school or even of Kitabatake Chikafusa. On the other hand, since the term "Shintō" itself was still in the process of being authoritatively defined, Kanetomo used the openness of the term to embrace the broadest possible semantic range, making it "the *kokoro* (mindful heart) of all things" and the "source of all activities" even "preceding the appearance of thought processes." From his stipulated definition, it was relatively easy for him to deduce that *all traditions* (Buddhism, Confucianism, Daoism) are outgrowths of Shintō, and that all creation and all thought are rooted in Shintō (see Kanetomo's definitions of *gen, hon,* and *sō* in the above quotation). He cites a metaphor that legend attributes to Prince Shōtoku:[126]

> Japan produced the seed, China produced the branches and leaves, India produced the flowers and fruit. Buddhism is the fruit, Confucianism is the leaves, and Shintō is the trunk and the roots. Buddhism and Confucianism are only secondary products of Shintō. Leaves and fruit merely indicate the presence of the trunk and roots; flowers and fruit fall and return to the roots. Buddhism came east only to reveal clearly that our nation is the trunk and roots of these three nations.[127]

In that passage Kanetomo shifts the argument from simply claiming Shintō is *distinct* from everything else to claiming it *includes* everything else, basically a shift from allocating a central place for Shintō to relegating everything else under it. Kanetomo's philosophical enterprise effectively mirrored the architectural function of the Shrine of Great Foundation, which relegated the *kami* of all traditions into itself as its center, making worship at the shrine a way of engaging all sacred reality through a single experience (a means of participating in the holographic part that contains the structure and pattern of the whole). Now, on the philosophical level, he aspired to make Shintō the entry point into all traditions and all spiritually significant functions by claiming Shintō to be the origin of them all. That strategy legitimized his naming Yoshida Shintō as "One and Only Shintō."

Scholars have commonly characterized Kanetomo's Yuiitsu Shintō as "syncretistic" or "combinatory." That is indeed *what* he did, but the philosophical significance lies in *how* he did it. He was attempting to develop an alternative metaphysical and metapractical *system*, going so far as to characterize esoteric Buddhism as the ancient Indian form of Shintō. What he seemed to have realized is that if Shintō were to be free of Shingon esotericism, it would have to *replace* how Shingon esotericism had functioned in the dominant Japanese world view. But the only way to do that philosophically would be to prove Shintō is as all-inclusive and as all-relegating as Kūkai's secret mandala of the ten mindsets.

In response, Kanetomo also organized his theory into "exoteric" and "esoteric" aspects. The accounts of *Kojiki* and *Nihonshoki*, for example, were to be considered exoteric and public, while the esoteric narratives were those handed down secretly within the Urabe-Yoshida kinship group "from the beginning." Furthermore, in characterizing Shingon Buddhism as "Indian Shintō," Kanetomo could claim that Kūkai's achievement was to bring Shintō rituals back to their proper home and origin, namely, Japan. In Kanetomo's own mind, he was not borrowing from or combining with Shingon esotericism, but rather was discovering or revealing the Shintō origins of Shingon. Admittedly, Kanetomo's arguments and system lacked the philosophical nuances and sophistication of Kūkai's, but to his credit he saw whence the philosophical force of esoteric Buddhism derives—its ability to relegate, that is, to be simultaneously all-inclusive and hierarchical.

As suggested by the design of the Shrine of Great Foundation, Kanetomo's achievement was much more than philosophical. Indeed, his lasting historical impact was more in the areas of Shintō ritual and institutional development. The Ōnin War had left Yoshida Shrine, like almost every other major Kyoto building, in ruins. At the time, it might have seemed its reconstruction could be most efficiently effected if it were made a subsidiary of one of the larger institutions of *kami*-worship, most obviously the nearby Kamo Shrines. Kanetomo would have none of that, however.

Instead he cultivated his personal relations with both the court and the military to solicit their support in ensuring Yoshida Shrine would not only continue to be independent but would, in fact, also become the hub of its own nationwide system of Shintō shrines. Kanetomo even claimed that the *kami* of both the Inner and Outer Shrines at Ise had miraculously come to reside in the Shrine of Great Foundation.[128] Through the efforts of Kanetomo and his successors, by the beginning of the sixteen century, Yoshida (Yuiitsu) Shintō had become the premier Shintō institution in Japan, a status that would last into the nineteenth century.

Part of Yoshida Shintō's spiritual charisma lay in its ritual praxis. Patently derivative of Shingon esotericism, Kanetomo's One and Only Shintō offset that fact by his aforementioned claim that Shingon praxis derives (via India) from the "source" that is Fundamental and Original Shintō. Thus, Kanetomo could unapologetically not only adopt the Shingon praxis system (with some appropriate shifts in terminology), but he could also borrow Shingon metapractical theories such as the three intimacies of body, speech, and mind to explain the efficacy of mudras, mantras, and various ritual implements and images.

If we compare Kanetomo's and Kūkai's vision of esotericism, however, we find a key difference. Kanetomo used "esotericism" to mean primarily "secret" in the sense that he had access to a cosmogonic account handed down covertly in his sacerdotal lineage over the generations. That secret narrative could only be shared with other members of the One and Only Shintō priesthood who had vowed never to reveal its mysteries to the uninitiated. In other words, Kanetomo's version of Shintō used esotericism to maintain exclusivity. By contrast, we saw that the thrust of Kūkai's esotericism was toward inclusivism: the engaged knowledge of the three intimacies of body, speech, and mind was available to everyone who "understood their own mind." Because of that inclusivism, Kūkai had envisioned art, for example, as a way of communicating Shingon to the illiterate and he established a school in Kyoto's Temple to the East for children of both genders and all classes. In his shift to making esotericism mean exclusivism, Kanetomo was by no means unique, however. Indeed, his attitude toward esoteric secrecy was the norm rather than the exception in medieval Japanese religious thought and practice. In Buddhism, for example, esoteric initiations had become not only a way of preserving elite power, but also a source of funds—laypeople could sometimes pay fees to access the secret doctrines and associated rituals.

We have already seen two early attempts to restrain secrecy within Buddhism. In the tenth century, the Tendai leader Ryōgen, had instituted the public debate system on Mt Hiei not only to compete with the Hossō sect in logic and argumentation but also to undermine the secrecy of private teacher-student transmissions.[†] By making spiritual and intellectual progress open to public display, Ryōgen had tried to nip the secrecy movement in the bud. Three centuries later, Dōgen also felt the need to undermine esoteric exclusivism, insisting that the "esoteric" (*mitsu*) in Zen should mean "intimacy" (*shinmitsu*) not secrecy. Such intimacy, he claimed, is not restricted to private, translinguistic encounters between master and student, but to the contrary, is part of the fabric of the most everyday and universal aspect of our experience.[‡]

Obviously, Ryōgen's and Dōgen's attempts to bridle the exclusivist secret practices enjoyed only limited success. Secret transmissions of texts and practices, including secrets for sale, were not only at the core of esoteric Buddhist

† See pages 151–2.
‡ See the discussion and quotations on pages 234–5.

and Yoshida Shintō institutions, but they permeated the practice of the arts as well. For example, even Zeami's system of training Nō actors included private initiations and oaths of secrecy. Artistic troupes and guilds devised secret lineages to pass down the ideas and practices distinctive to their tradition.[129] As we will now see, the rise in secrecy corresponded with the prominence of affinity groups during this period, an organizational structure important to the growth of Buddhism in the late medieval period.

LATE MEDIEVAL BUDDHISM

The new forms of Buddhism developed by the great Kamakura religious thinkers such as Hōnen, Shinran, Dōgen, and Nichiren did not have much of an immediate impact on the overall Japanese religious milieu.[130] The Tendai, Shingon, and the Nara Schools (especially Hossō) continued to constitute the most visible and politically potent Buddhist presence throughout the thirteenth and much of the fourteenth centuries.[131*] The popular ascent of the Kamakura religious groups was gradual but constant—so much so that today the vast majority of Japanese Buddhists belong to denominations affiliated with the Kamakura founders.

Contributing to that transition were the class and regional alliances that loosely corresponded with religious affiliation. In the face of the late medieval period's lack of a strong social, intellectual, and political center, affinity groups of people with similar backgrounds, interests, and values coalesced for the purpose of commerce, self-governing, and self-protection. Such groups flourished in all sectors of Japanese society. Although those coalitions first became visible in the early medieval period, they rose to prominence with the Ōnin War, a conflict that drew many regional landowners and samurai warlords to the capital.

With the war's ending in stalemate after a decade of strife, the regional lords returned to their home provinces to face local uprisings and competition from their neighbors. Military alliances among regional landowners were one kind of affinity group, meeting the need to maintain control over areas no longer successfully administered by the shogunate through its provincial governors (shugo).

A second type of affinity group involved the peasants from those outlying regions. Overtaxed into impossible debt, their lives continually disrupted by the military exploits of their landlords, the peasants united to protest taxation, to demand forgiveness of debt, and to be a force with which the regional lords, the constables, and the central government—at least what was left of it—had to contend. At times military and peasant groups, both often called ikki, allied with each other against either the shogun or aggressors from neighboring provinces. As common interests shifted, so did the composition and function of the *ikki*.

Meanwhile, in the cities, especially Kyoto, the shogunate's decaying ability to guarantee law and order spurred the creation of neighborhood (*machi*) affinity groups. The *machi* were not only smaller than the previous units of local government, but they also increasingly functioned more or less independently of the former chains of command that had linked smaller units to larger ones all the way up the shogunate bureaucracy. Overlapping those neighborhood units were guilds (*za*) of artists and craftsmen who collaborated in protecting their property and in preventing domination by other constituencies. The guilds often joined forces with their neighbor merchants who, although functioning in a different domain, nevertheless shared many interests and concerns. Thus, the denizens of the neighborhoods (*machishū*) became social units unto themselves, allowing pockets of merchants, craftsmen, and artists to survive or even thrive.

Not surprisingly, some affinity groups also shared religious affiliation, especially with the "new religions" of the Kamakura period who themselves needed protection from the establishment sects. Depicting the situation with broad strokes, we can say Hōnen's followers were concentrated in the Kyoto region with strong representation among both aristocrats and commoners. Shinran's adherents were mostly peasants from rural areas, originally especially in Kantō (Eastern Honshū). The Nichiren sect was strongest among lower-level samurai along the Eastern Honshū coast and, later, among merchant groups in Kyoto. Rinzai Zen attracted mostly the elite: aristocrats and higher-level samurai from Kyoto, Kamakura, and other urban areas. Dōgen's Sōtō Zen appealed to samurai outside those cities and eventually spread among the more general populace in rural areas along the Japan Sea coast. Therefore, as affinity groups expanded their influence, so did the Kamakura new religions, the two often functioning as two sides of the same coin.

Shin Buddhism

As an example, let us consider more closely how affinity groups interacted with one particular sect from the Kamakura period, Shinran's Shin Buddhism. As we saw in Chapter 5, Shinran was not interested in building religious institutions. To the contrary, he rejected the very idea of establishing a Buddhist sect with ordained clergy, temples, and a central administration, even to the extent of claiming he personally had no disciples. With the passing decades, though, Shin Buddhists found the need to organize, as least for self-defense against the repeated attacks from the Tendai warrior monks.

In the early fourteenth century, Kakunyo (1270–1351) tried to make Shinran's mausoleum in Kyoto into a Shin Buddhist headquarters. Hongan-ji (Temple of the Primal Vow), as it came to be called, was not able to defend itself from the Tendai assailants effectively, however, mainly because most Shin Buddhists resided in rural areas, many in eastern Japan where Shinran had spent so many years in exile far from the capital. Kakunyo's successors read the situation astutely and started to coordinate those widespread groups as much as possible. The full integration coalesced in the fifteenth century under Rennyo (1415–1499) who, almost against his will, found himself at the center of a new peasant political consciousness.

I have already mentioned the peasant affiliate groups (*ikki*). When the Ōnin War broke out in the mid-fifteenth century, the situation in the provinces worsened as the provincial governors and constables, losing their military forces to the battle in Kyoto, became unable to enforce administrative control. Rennyo had earlier abandoned Kyoto for the Kaga region (see map on page 697) in 1471 to escape the wrath of the Tendai militia from Mt Hiei, which had burned Hongan-ji to the ground in 1465. In doing so, he increased his missionary efforts to the region's peasantry on behalf of Shin Buddhism (or the *Ikkō*[133] Sect as it was commonly called at the time). He also wrote a series of pastoral letters that were copied and distributed to leaders of Shin Buddhist groups scattered throughout the country. Those widely read epistles became the centerpiece for Shin Buddhism's revival. For the most part, Rennyo remained rigorously faithful to Shinran's teachings, but he did add two emphases that might have been responses to competition from other traditions.

First, to be more receptive to popular Amidism, he brought a more pietistic orientation to Shinran's teaching. For example, Shinran had prohibited prayerful supplication to Amida, explicitly criticizing the use of the phrase "please save me" (*tasuke tamae*). Insisting that Amida's help is offered spontaneously and is already available to us if we only depend on it, Shinran believed any such supplication smacked of self-power because it implies *my* asking for help is a *cause* of Amida's helping me.

Resorting to the ocean metaphor so central to Shin Buddhism, we could put the distinction in the following way. Suppose I am drowning in the ocean and I call out for help. If I am then saved by a passing boat I hailed, my rescue was at least partly the result of my effort—my calling out. My rescue was admittedly carried out through the intercession of others, but that rescue might not have occurred it I had not shouted my plea for help. Suppose instead I did not call out but just ceased struggling so hard and let the buoyancy of the water keep me afloat until I drifted to safety. In comparing the two options, the first alternative is initiated by self-power—I *do* something to *make* something happen *in the future*. (I shout to get someone to help me). In the latter alternative, by contrast,

I *give up* my struggling, merely *depending* on the assistance (the water's buoyancy) that is *already* there. The analogy makes Shinran's rationale for rejecting the phrase "please save me" clear enough. It is so subtle, though, that it is not surprising his distinctions were lost on the general populace.

By Rennyo's time, the phrase "please save me" had become immensely popular in the praxis of Pure Land followers, including Shin Buddhists.[134] Rather than excluding them or letting them join other Pure Land groups that allowed the practice, Rennyo came around to allowing the phrase's use. But he did so if and only if the phrase were uttered as an expression of fully trusting Amida's Vow, rather than *asking* for Amida's grace. That is, what counts is the state of faith, not the words. I would say it is more like a child who is injured and a parent comes over, bending down to help. The child's reaching toward the parent is not a gesture of *asking* for help but rather a gesture of *accepting* the help that is already coming. Such a distinction was probably as lost on Rennyo's constituency as Shinran's logic would have been, but at least Rennyo had found a way to accept a widespread practice of Amidist pietism without technically violating Shinran's philosophical position. In so doing, he removed an obstacle to Shin Buddhism's growth.

A second new twist that Rennyo brought to Shinran's teaching was his claim that passing through the Pure Land Gate could lead to material benefits in this world besides the later assured rebirth in the Pure Land.[135] The promise of material as well as spiritual benefits was a hallmark of the Nichiren tradition but had never been accepted by Shinran. In fact, Shinran's view on the human situation in this world was so bleak that, as mentioned in Chapter 5, he had actually said that although his birth in the Pure Land was assured, he could not even feel joy over that fact.†

To sum up: Rennyo had established a strong Shin Buddhist institutional structure with a nationwide network, had allowed his followers to ask Amida for help, and had suggested that entering the Gate to the Pure Land would bring benefits in this world as well as after death. On one hand, Shinran would likely have frowned upon all those developments, seeing them as inconsistent with both the spirit and letter of his teachings. On the other hand, without Rennyo's modification of Shinran's position, Shin Buddhism would likely have ceased to exist or would have, at best, been a marginal religious group always struggling to survive against encroachment by outsiders. Instead, Rennyo brilliantly succeeded in spreading Shin Buddhism throughout Japan, beginning with the Kaga region to which he had fled and which had formerly been a stronghold of Tendai.

† See pages 195–6.

With the power vacuum caused by the Ōnin War and the displacement of troops from the provinces to go fight in the capital, the Shin Buddhist (or Ikkō) peasantry, against Rennyo's wishes,[136] rose up against the Kaga provincial governor and local representative of the shogun's government, Togashi Masachika (1455?–1488). With the help of the region's samurai gentry, many of whom had also become Shin Buddhists, the rebels took control of the region and forced the governor to suicide. This was the first major "*ikkō ikki*" rebellion, its success emboldening the Shin Buddhist peasantry throughout rural Japan. Class consciousness now went hand-in-hand with religious commitment, political action with sectarian affiliation.

The peasant uprisings both reflected and inflamed the volatility of the social order on several fronts. Not only did the shogunate and the Tendai establishment feel threatened, but so did some affiliate groups in the capital as well. To them it seemed a rebellious Shin Buddhist peasantry could endanger the security and economic détente among the various urban constituencies. Not only government officers, but also merchants and moneylenders, would fear the prospect of peasant armies invading the city, demanding forgiveness of all debts. Indeed at one point a crowd of angry peasants had done exactly that. They marched into Kyoto and burned down the offices where records of tax debts were recorded.

Since the Nichiren followers, generally called the "Lotus Sect" (*Hokke shū*), had a strong constituency among merchants and lower-order samurai in the southern sector of the capital, they repeatedly engaged in hostilities with Shin Temples in Kyoto and its environs. Moreover, both Shin and Nichiren Buddhists continued to be targets of Tendai aggression from Mt Hiei. As a result, skirmishes among Tendai, Nichiren, and Shin temples in the environs of Kyoto continued throughout the remainder of the medieval period.

Sōtō Zen. Meanwhile, the Sōtō Zen Sect founded by Dōgen was expanding its base among commoners as well, especially in rural areas and towns. The successful proselytizing was mainly due to Keizan Jōkin (1268–1325). Keizan was a student of Dōgen's student, Gikai (1219–1309), but he also trained in Kyoto at the aforementioned Tōfuku-ji (Eastern Temple of Blessings), a Rinzai Zen temple that had integrated esoteric elements into its teachings and practices. Keizan eventually returned to his Sōtō Zen roots, helping the tradition expand its following by introducing esoteric and folk religious elements.

Because that strategy was not consistent with Dōgen's original emphasis on "seated meditation alone," Sōtō Zen ended up softening the rigors of Dōgen's austere praxis, at least for the laity. The same can be said for its attitude toward Dōgen's philosophy: his *Repository of the Eye for the Truth* (*Shōbōgenzō*) came to be treated as an arcane text meant only for the most sophisticated scholar-monks. Only snippets of it, not much more than an isolated few lines here and there, were known to most Sōtō Zen Buddhists. The sect continued to revere Dōgen as its founder, of course, but not until the modern period did his writings receive the philosophical attention they enjoy today.

Thus, as Rennyo had done with Shinran, Keizan found it pragmatically necessary to dilute the philosophical purity in the philosophy of his sect's founder. He lectured to the emperor Go-Daigo and established his own major Sōtō Zen monastery, Sōji-ji, which would quickly eclipse Dōgen's Eihei-ji as the most influential Sōtō temple in Japan, a status it maintained until the modern period when the two temples adopted a cooperative sister-temple relationship.

Rinzai Zen. Given the conflicts endemic to the late medieval period, there was not much opportunity for the Shin, Nichiren, or Sōtō sects to refine their philosophical systems. Rinzai Zen Buddhism was, however, above the fray to a great extent, enjoying both an intellectual and cultural flowering. As mentioned earlier, in the Kamakura period Rinzai Zen had been especially attractive to the shogunate, partly because the stern discipline of Rinzai Zen practice and its master-apprentice hierarchy evoked images of military training.

Yet, that love of discipline could not have been the only appeal because the court aristocrats soon joined those elite samurai in their attraction to Rinzai Zen. What the elite samurai and courtiers shared was an admiration for Chinese high culture. With the travels of Rinzai monks to China and the immigration of Chinese Zen monks to Japan, Rinzai Zen temples became major sites of education in Chinese language and literature. Since official government documents were written in classical Chinese, the shogunate depended on clerics for their linguistic skills and knowledge of Chinese texts.

In return, Rinzai Zen enjoyed government patronage, including the underwriting of several major temples in Kamakura and eventually also in Kyoto. With income from gifts of land, Rinzai Zen could establish a nationwide network of temples and by the end of the Kamakura period, the government felt the need to exert some control over this Rinzai expansion. Using Chinese precedents, it established the so-called Five Mountain system for ranking temples as well as individual monks within the Rinzai institutions.

The system gave the government direct control over the Rinzai Zen institution and its cultural capital. Depending on shifting political alliances and the personal relations between the shogunate or court with specific abbots, the rankings of the temples varied somewhat in the ensuing decades. (Sometimes the five highest ranked temples were from both Kamakura and Kyoto; sometimes there were five from each city; sometimes there were more than five in the list.) It was not until around 1386 that the hierarchy was fixed.[137] Musō Soseki

163–71

(1275–1351) was the Rinzai monk generally credited with being the spiritual cornerstone of the system that eventually emerged.

Austere in temperament and rigorous in praxis, Musō was celebrated for both his spiritual insights and cultured sensibilities. His preference to be left alone to live as a hermit and his wariness of secular politics only increased his charisma, making him all the more irresistible to the elite. He was a mentor and confidant to the most influential figures of the era including the Kamakura regent Hōjō Takatoki (1303–1333), Emperor Go-Daigo, and the two founders of the Muromachi shogunate, Ashikaga Takauji and Ashikaga Tadayoshi. In short: in the transition from the Kamakura shogunate, to the Kenmu Restoration, to the Muromachi shogunate, Musō was in the inner circle of all three regimes.

Through the patronage gleaned from his associations with the elite, Musō was able to build temples, most notably the Temple of the Heavenly Dragon (Tenryū-ji) and to renovate or redesign others, including the famous moss garden of the Temple of the Fragrance from the Western [Paradise], Saihō-ji. Musō gave the Five Mountain system an institutional reputation that made it a permanent fixture in the spiritual and cultural landscape of Japan.[138] In particular, he helped forge a link between Rinzai Zen and the arts such as poetry, painting, and landscape design. That long-range impact of Rinzai Zen culture helps explain the elements of Zen architectural style in the Golden and Silver Pavilions, for example.

Philosophically, Musō maintained the Zen tradition of focusing on the "original nature" that precedes and transcends such distinctions as pure or defiled, sacred or ordinary. Such distinctions, he said, are like those of a dream: even if a master teaches you about original nature in a dream, you still do not get the point as long as you continue dreaming. The point is to wake up, not to have a dream about waking up. This original nature is available in each and every daily experience, but ordinarily we are so wrapped up in the objects, thoughts, and desires of life that we do not see what is behind them.

164-5

Musō compared delusional existence to that of a fisherman who lived amidst the extraordinary natural beauty of West Lake near Mt Fuji but was so consumed by the details of daily life that he never noticed it and wondered why some monks would come to his vicinity just to see the scenery.

169-70

> The difference between the monks and the old man had nothing to do with the mountains, trees, water, and rocks that they were seeing, but with whether or not they were moved by the sight of them. The experience of being moved is not something that one learns through explanation. When the time is ripe and one's heart [kokoro] is open to being moved, then the experience comes naturally.
>
> The same is true of original nature. One knows this ground only when one proceeds directly to it. Although crystal clear to the person who knows it, it

cannot be picked up and shown to anyone else. Thus, although it is inherently possessed by all, when one is not in accord with it, then everything one does simply generates more samsaric karma. This is what an ancient master [Dahui Zonggao (1089–1163)] meant when he said that one either knows it completely or knows it not at all.

In other words, the goal is not to acquire knowledge or eliminate delusions, but rather, as we say in English, to "get it."

To get it is a form of engaged knowing in which the point becomes clear on its own—completely and all at once. For example, after pondering some problem over and over, we may suddenly see the solution and what that once hindered our insight becomes supporting details in what we have grasped. Many of us have sometimes worked on a problem intently for a long period without "getting anywhere." Then, when we took a break, the solution suddenly dawned on us. We got it. Musō's sense of engaged knowing seems like that.

To engage original nature, we must first let go of what we think we need to know, the dichotomies that lock us into what the Chinese Daoist sage, Zhuangzi (369–286 BCE), called "the this and the that."[139] By freeing ourselves from the pull of two exclusive alternatives, by waking from the dream, we can fully engage the profound oneness behind it. Then we can again address everyday problems. The dichotomies that had so entrapped us become just elaborations on the original nature. Then we can carry out our daily affairs without disengaging from our deeper spiritual sensitivities; we can fish without missing the beauty of West Lake.

For a contrast, consider the legend of Alexander the Great and the Gordian Knot. When his conquests brought him to the city of Gordium in Phrygia, he was led to the chariot that had belonged to the regal founder of the city. The chariot was tied with a huge knot so intricate that its own ends were not showing. Only the man who could untie the knot, Alexander was told, would be worthy to rule Asia. Examining the rope, its intricate intertwining strangling itself into a solid ball, Alexander took out his sword and cut through it in one stroke. He solved the problem by not engaging it in the everyday way.

There is a crucial difference between Alexander's approach and Musō's, however. Alexander's sword solves the problem by cutting the knot in two, whereas Musō's Zen sword cuts the knot in one. The treasury of phrases used in Rinzai Zen praxis includes *ittō ichidan*, "one slash of the sword cuts into one piece."[140]* That is, the Zen approach is to cut through the distinctions to access the oneness that is their source. Once that source is reached, the rope, as it were, is still intact and one can use it as appropriate.[141]

It is at that point that Musō saw the relation between art and Zen praxis. Artistic creation is not itself a Zen practice, but once one "gets it," once one fathoms the source of distinctions, including artistic distinctions, then one can engage artistic activity. The resultant artwork can then serve as a cue to a more novice Zen practitioner, not as an aesthetic object, but as a prompt to discover for oneself the source of the artistry that produced the artwork.[142]*

We have seen earlier in this chapter that the medieval aestheticians, Shunzei and Zeami, had linked the aesthetic of *yūgen* with Buddhist meditation, Shunzei with Tendai *shikan* meditation and Zeami with Zen's no-mind. There is clearly similarity between Musō's theory of original nature and the aesthetics of *yūgen*. They share an appreciation for a profundity that resists expression, that must be engaged contemplatively, and that must be brought back into the affairs of daily life.

That Shunzei identified with Tendai Buddhism and Zeami with Zen Buddhism is significant, however. Some two and a half centuries separate the two. During that interim, the Five Mountain system of Rinzai Zen flourished, in many ways superseding the prominence of Tendai. That shift permanently affected the dynamic between Buddhism and the arts. In accord with Musō's contributions, the Five Mountain system of Rinzai Zen became a center of Japanese cultural accomplishment in the fourteenth through sixteenth centuries. The Rinzai production in arts and letters became so well known that it acquired its own name: *gozanbungaku* "Five Mountains Literature," a movement steeped in Chinese learning as well as poetic and artistic expression.

As I explained earlier, Rinzai monks had served the Kamakura shogunate as experts in Chinese language and texts, a highly valued skill in government circles where Chinese remained the official language of legal documents. This continued and even intensified with the Muromachi elite's renewed interest in Chinese cultural achievements while monks like Musō benefited from the relation. Through the nationwide network of Rinzai temples, monks also served as instructors in regional samurai centers of learning far from the capital.

When the Warring Domains Period came to a close, however, there would be the need for a new philosophy to serve a re-centralized state. Some Rinzai monks were positioned to present that philosophy, but it would not be Buddhist—it would be Confucian. To understand how it came about that Zen monks would advocate Confucianism, we will first have to see how the period of warfare ended, giving birth to a new political and social order. We take up that narrative in the next chapter.

The Edo Period

8. The Open Marketplace of Ideas
Unification and Edo Thought (1568–1801)

9. Ogyū Sorai (1666–1728)
The Present Wisdom of the Past Perfect

10. Motoori Norinaga (1730–1801)
In Touch with the Spirit of Words

8. The Open Marketplace of Ideas

Unification and Edo Thought (1568–1801)

There is no way to humaneness
except through understanding
human feelings.

HORI Keizan

1175

With the dissolution of the military and political center of the Muromachi shogunate, the regional military powers competed for control of the country, the leadership being drawn from multiple sources. Some descended from old shogunate offices such as the deputy constables; others were samurai warriors who had broken off from the central government to form armies of their own; still others were landed gentry with enough wealth to answer to no one but themselves. The most direct route to the reunification of Japan would be to find a new military leader, cunning in political strategy, astute at warfare, and able to take full advantage of breakthroughs in military technology. Reunification required someone who could bring all the daimyō and warlords in line, someone who could recognize martial talent and negotiate alliances with his most powerful competitors, someone strong enough and ruthless enough to annihilate anyone who stood in the way of national unification. Oda Nobunaga (1534–1582) fit the job description.

STEPS TO UNIFICATION: THE THREE HEGEMONS

The new weapons serving Nobunaga's ambitions were muskets and cannons. When the Portuguese first landed at an island off Kyushu in 1543, the local daimyō marveled at their weaponry. News of the game-changing technology spread quickly and within decades firearms and cannon were manufactured at sites throughout Japan. Wood-framed palaces with paper doors would no longer suffice and the major daimyō started building stone castles with the requisite walls, towers, moats, and drawbridges. Nobunaga's hub of power was central Japan and he efficiently set into play his awesome military machine, now augmented with deftly deployed fire power, to expand throughout the central region. Then he moved westward to take the capital and advance beyond. Aided by his astute general, Toyotomi Hideyoshi (1537–1598), victories were swift, meting out death and devastation to anyone who resisted.

Nobunaga realized that if he were going to expand further westward, he would need to protect his eastern flank where Tokugawa Ieyasu (1543–1616) was beginning to overrun that region's warlords. At the same time, Ieyasu wished to secure his western flank so he could safely expand his domain eastward. The result in 1561 was an alliance, basically ceding the eastern regions to Ieyasu's ambitions and leaving Nobunaga free to target the more powerful central and westward warlords. Nobunaga successfully brought central Japan and much of the West to its knees, establishing his castle on Mt Azuchi on the eastern shore of Lake Biwa just east of Kyoto. Because Ieyasu's first wife had family ties to an enemy's family, Nobunaga suspected her of treason and in 1579 ordered Ieyasu to kill both her and his eldest son. He did. That act of loyalty was enough for Nobunaga to let Ieyasu pursue his plan of dominating the East.

In 1582 Nobunaga and his own son Nobutada were killed in Kyoto during a coup led by his vassal, Akechi Mitsuhide (?–1582). Nobunaga's right-hand man, Hideyoshi, was at the time some 100 kilometers away in what is today's Himeji area. Having just taken a castle through the creative tactic of flooding out the inhabitants by diverting the flow of a river, Hideyoshi raced to Kyoto with his army and in less than two weeks avenged Nobunaga's assassination, thereby becoming his successor.

Despite initial mutual wariness, Hideyoshi formed an awkward alliance with Ieyasu, helping him completely secure the East by defeating one of his last remaining rival warlords in Kantō. In so doing, Hideyoshi attained control of almost all Japan, seizing most of Ieyasu's former holdings, but ceding him some territories in deference to their alliance. Displaced from his former castle, Ieyasu needed a new headquarters and Hideyoshi picked out for him a fishing village called Edo in the backwaters of a bay in Kantō. Today we know it as Tokyo.

Meanwhile, Hideyoshi established his government to the south of Kyoto at Momoyama ("Peach Mountain"), absorbing in short order the rest of western Japan and the southern island of Kyushu. Then he set his sights beyond the Japanese archipelago. He attacked Korea in 1592, the only attempt by a Japanese ruler to invade the mainland in premodern times. Hideyoshi's venture, which continued until his death in 1598, was a dismal failure, sapping both his resources and those of the daimyō he coerced to join him in his folly. Tokugawa Ieyasu managed to stay out of the disastrous affair, thereby growing his economic and military base while others in Japan were depleting theirs. Hideyoshi was succeeded by his boy, Hideyori, to whom Ieyasu, like the other major warlords, had sworn allegiance before Hideyoshi had died.

The reality, however, was that the country was on the verge of degenerating again into warfare among the various daimyō and Ieyasu was not about to let his hard-won gains be undone. In 1600, he brought his unified armies of eastern Japan to Sekigahara in present-day Gifu province about one hundred kilometers northeast of Kyoto. Seeing the threat of being overrun one by one, most western daimyō combined their forces to meet Ieyasu in full strength. The battle of 100,000 men on each side ended in a decisive victory for Ieyasu, making him supreme military ruler of all Japan and recipient of the imperially bestowed title of *shōgun* in 1603, a title held by his descendants until the Meiji Imperial Restoration of 1868. The period 1600 to 1868 is, therefore, known as the Edo or Tokugawa period.

As for Hideyoshi's son Hideyori, he held the hereditary claim to being his father's successor, but Ieyasu's success at Sekigahara had reduced Hideyori's military power to about the level of a daimyō. Ieyasu continued to be suspicious of Hideyori's intentions, however, and showing outrage at a temple bell inscription commissioned by Hideyori that supposedly slighted his status, Ieyasu besieged Osaka Castle in 1614–1615. The result was Hideyori's defeat and suicide. With that victory, Ieyasu was then not only the most powerful man in Japan, but also had eliminated the only other competitor who might have had enough political connections to mount a successful rebellion against him.

In the remainder of this chapter I will focus on the period of unification from Nobunaga's Azuchi epoch to the beginning of the close-out of the Tokugawa period, altogether roughly the span 1568 to 1800. Before turning to the philosophical developments, I will comment on the nationwide changes in the social, political, and cultural climate that accompanied Edo's transformation from fishing village to metropolis, a change in milieu that would radically alter the course of Japanese philosophy.

A POST-MEDIEVAL SOCIETY

Compared with the preceding Warring Domains period (1467–1568), the ascendancy of the Tokugawa shoguns heralded a time of comparative peace and stability. The Edo period did witness sporadic rebellions, mainly peasant revolts protesting oppressive taxes and the government's feckless policies against famine.[1] Until the nineteenth century, however, there was no organized effort on the part of regional lords to support an all-out coup. The Tokugawa peace resulted from strategies aimed at regulating religion, politics, and economics. I will discuss the religious dimension in more detail later in this chapter, but will only mention in passing here the ban on Christianity, the eradication of

religious military forces, and the establishment of a Buddhist temple registra-
tion system that served simultaneously as a census-taking apparatus necessary
for taxation and a way to root out religious fanatics, especially Christians. All
those actions were designed to reign in any possible sources of religious unrest.

In terms of politics and economics, the Tokugawa administration allowed the
daimyō some autonomy over their domains and a portion of local revenue, but
always under vigilant military surveillance. Guns were banned throughout the
country, the daimyō could no longer build their own ships or engage in international trade, and they had to turn over significant revenue to the shogunate.
Most striking was the policy of alternate attendance (*sankin kōtai*), requiring
every daimyō to leave his regional domain in alternate years to be in attendance
at the shogun's court in Edo. Furthermore, the law required the daimyō, when
returning to their home domains, to leave behind their wives and children in
Edo, making them effectively hostages.

The alternate attendance policy had broad implications. First, it remade the
transportation system into an effective national network of roads leading to Edo
with the accompanying support system of wayside inns. The daimyō, for the
sake of prestige as much as safety, traveled to and from Edo with a retinue of
guards, attendants, vassals, retainers, consorts, and banner bearers numbering
in the hundreds, often many hundreds. Added to the cost of maintaining a secondary residence in Edo befitting their social station, those journeys consumed
a large portion of the daimyō income, income that was in part distributed along
the roadways throughout Japan.

Of course, a large amount of daimyō wealth went into the economy of Edo
itself, along with other key cities on the route, especially Osaka and Kyoto.
That, in turn, supported a vibrant economy in those cities for merchants, artists, tradesman, and the entertainment industry. A new culture, both urban
and urbane, would blossom in those cities, affecting every sector of the newly
unified Japan. City populations swelled to the extent that by the end of the
seventeenth-century, for example, Edo had become larger than any European
city while Kyoto and Osaka each approached the size of Paris.

Economics and Class

With money flowing more freely across the country, the shogunate
saw the need for a coherent economic policy, devising a single monetary system and standardizing weights and measures. Furthermore, for adjudicating
contracts and achieving consistency in civic and penal law, the shogunate put
into place a nationwide judicial system.[2] As part of its social restructuring, the
Tokugawa regime formally divided the populace into a hierarchy of four classes,
each with its own duties and privileges: samurai, farmer, artisan, and merchant.

(The aristocracy was above the class hierarchy, the clerics outside it, and the outcastes below it.) In sum: the shogunate's modification of the transportation, economic, legal, and class systems collectively nurtured a national identity among the people, especially among the upper and middle echelons of society.

The shogunate never did have in practice the economic or political power it had in theory, though. The more wealthy and powerful daimyō formally signed oaths of allegiance to the shogunate, with the silent acknowledgement that the shogunate could only continue to survive as long as their loyalty remained solid. The shogunate's authority flowed through councils consisting of the most potent daimyō, the daimyō collectively owning three-fourths of the land in the country. Despite the limitations imposed by the councils, the shogunate did succeed in centralizing and stabilizing the government well enough that it was, for the most part, in everyone's interest to buy into the new social-political-economic system of a unified Japan.

I used the term "buy into" advisedly. The economic implications of the Tokugawa peace become clearer if we examine more closely the dynamics of the new four-class social and political system. Each class had its own economic profile and challenges, but their interaction provided Japanese philosophizing with a new context and new audiences.

The samurai enjoyed the rights and privileges befitting their newly attained place in the social order. For all intents and purposes, the class system in urban settings came down to the samurai (between five and ten percent of the population) and everyone else, the so-called townspeople (chōnin). Despite their prestige, however, the samurai were not necessarily affluent. In peacetime, there was little demand for their warrior skills and many found themselves rōnin, that is, samurai without masters, or as the etymology of the sinograph suggests "men battered by waves (of fortune)." They may have had the cultural capital of belonging to an elite, well-educated class, but the samurai were light on material capital.

Meanwhile, the merchants and moneylenders had the opposite problem. Although at the bottom of the four-class totem pole, even lower than a farmer or craftsman, the merchants did have money, often lots of money. A cunning businessman in an urban center could strike it rich by capitalizing on the Pax Tokugawa and its commerce-friendly infrastructure. So, in contradistinction to the samurai, what the merchants lacked in cultural capital they more than made up for in monetary capital.

As for the farmers, their comparatively high status derived from their actually producing something of intrinsic worth—rice. The Tokugawa economy was not on the gold standard, but the rice standard: the benchmark for the value of a monetary unit or a tract of land or the determination of tax responsibility was measured as its equivalence in rice. In that sense, the peasant rice farmers literally made money, but the catch was that they didn't own what they made. If ever there was a group of laborers alienated from the means of production, it was the Tokugawa peasantry. The peasants owned neither the land they worked nor the rice they raised. Indeed, it was often illegal for peasants even to eat rice at all, being forced to subsist on buckwheat, barley, and vegetables. So, for the most part, despite their elevated social status, the peasants of the Tokugawa period were as bad off as they had been in the medieval era, resulting in the aforementioned peasant uprisings that periodically plagued the Tokugawa peace.

That leaves the artisans. No longer supported solely by patrons, in the new economy the artisans brought their wares to the open market as commodities to be bought by urbanites of any class. In the exploding urban economy, they could make a decent living either by targeting high-end goods to the moneyed or by selling their wares in quantity to the general public.

The Floating World

City-dwellers captured the mood of their lifestyle with the epithet "the floating world"—*ukiyo* (浮世). The term itself was a play on words. During medieval times, imbued with its Buddhist sensitivity to transience, the lonely sadness of *sabi*, and the call to plumb the depths of *yūgen*, the Japanese term *ukiyo* was written in different sinographs meaning "the melancholy world" (憂世). The shift in the sinographs indicates that both the medieval and Edo mentalities recognized the impermanence of things, but they differed in their response to it.

As we found in the last chapter, the late medieval agenda was to recognize the pain of the world, to withdraw from it, or perhaps to fathom a profound serenity beneath it. The Edo response, on the other hand, was not to plunge below the currents, but to go with the flow: to float along the surface of the stream of change, tantalized by the glittering lanterns of the city reflected on its ripples. It engaged the sensate, material, and superficial over the ascetic, spiritual, and profound.

The floating world of the samurai and townspeople reveled in the enchantments and titillation of its pleasure quarters, courtesans, entertainers, bath houses, sexual exploits, and swashbuckling samurai. These became the stuff of floating-world pictures (*ukiyo-e*), first in painting and then soon after, and more famously, in the woodblock medium designed for mass production and popular consumption.

The Edo-period Japanese publishers often preferred the woodblock technique of printing to that of moveable type, which had been introduced from China via Korea in the late sixteenth century. The medium of the woodblock print allowed for a rich collaboration among writer, calligrapher, artist/illustrator, and printer, a collaboration echoed today in the medium of *manga* (graphic novels and comics), for example. With the availability of mass publication, basic literacy among city dwellers skyrocketed, creating a profitable market for copies of old classics, picture books, nonfiction works such as travel guides or religious texts, and new literary works written explicitly for the townspeople of all classes.

The townspeople were a new breed of city-dweller quite different from the neighborhood affiliate groups represented by the *machishū* of the Muromachi period.[†] The *machishū* had formed their allegiances in private or even in secrecy, motivated partly by fear and self-protection. The *chōnin*, by contrast, were more often a free association of urban denizens, often with little more in common than the quest for a good time. Hence, the Tokugawa shogunate, a most totalitarian and autocratic form of government, had given birth to an oddly open urban culture that cut across the very class distinctions it had invented. Certainly, class restrictions remained in force, but except for the distinction between samurai and everyone else, they were not as constraining as they appeared in theory.[3*]

In the literary realm, the floating world was expressed in the fiction of such writers as Ihara Saikaku (1642–1693). His *Life of an Amorous Man* (1682), for example, depicted the lifelong sexual exploits of a man from age six (!) to sixty, chronicling his seduction of 3,742 women and 725 boys. Saikaku embellished the book's irreverent and satiric tone with backhanded allusions to Murasaki's medieval classic, *The Tale of Genji*. For instance Saikaku's protagonist shared some character traits with Prince Genji as did some of the amorous adventures in the two books, and Saikaku impishly wrote his novel in 54 chapters, the same number as in *Genji* (in its contemporaneous form). The profitability of such books as Saikaku's testifies to the rising levels of literacy, reaching the point where even a townsperson might imaginably appreciate a satirical reference to a medieval classical text.

All in all, it would seem the din of the hedonistic, frivolous, materialistic, and raffish Edo-period culture had drowned out the subtle tonalities from the Heian world of the shining prince. And it might seem the medieval aesthetic had washed away in the ebb tide of the floating world. Or had it? The floating world, it turns out, had cross-currents.

If we see Saikaku as overturning the elitist values of *Genji*, the literary style of his contemporary, the famous haiku poet Matsuo Bashō (1644–1694), worked in the opposite direction, bringing depth to the mundane. Trained in Zen and relishing the rustic *wabi* aesthetic implicit in the life of the itinerant poet, Bashō's trademark literary expression took the form of the *haiku* or *haikai*. In his time

† See page 266.

the *haikai* was strictly a light, playful verse style engaged by clever wordsmiths at drinking parties in the company of coquettish courtesans and playboy rascals. Its cultural status was akin to the English-language limerick of today, a poetic form more for the pub than the literary guild. Bashō transformed *haikai*'s 17-syllable poetic expression into an art form, displaying at times the spiritual sensitivity, creativity, and depth of earlier elite poetry, but stripped of its precious self-conscious intertexuality and ubiquitous literary allusions.

His *haiku* also often abandoned urban sophistication to tease out the poetic and spiritual nuances of everyday life. Bashō's *haiku* were attuned less to the trendy fashions and artifices of the cities and more to the seasonal variations of nature. His poems were sparks arising from the field of sensitivity (*kokoro*) available right here and now, especially in the overlap between the human and the natural. In those sparks, Bashō sought both elegance in style (*fūga*) and a naturalistic undermining of artifice (*sabi*). In Chapter 4, I differentiated the engaged subjectivity in the aesthetic of Murasaki Shikibu with the detached subjectivity in the aesthetic of Sei Shōnagon. Applying that same distinction here, I would say Bashō was more on the Murasaki end of the spectrum and Saikaku on the Sei end.[†]

The Yen for Philosophy

Critical to our philosophical concerns, the urban centers spawned a novel form of educational institution: secular academies supported by student tuition.[4] Previously, most formal instruction had occurred in Buddhist temples (or in some cases, Shintō shrines), in the imperial academy (for the aristocrats), in academies run by the regional daimyō for educating their own samurai and village heads, or in a private tutoring arrangement for the family of a rich patron. Those sites of learning continued in the Edo period, but the newly established urban academies became the breeding-ground of innovative philosophizing, representing a swing toward the commodification of knowledge and culture.

Certainly, as in the medieval world, secrets continued to be for sale by various religious groups and artistic guilds, but the Edo academy was generally more open and public. In contrast to the previous centers of learning, the academies were usually designed as income-producing enterprises in competition for student tuition with other academies. Advertising, publishing for profit, admission policies, and the reputation of the teachers were all as much a part of the Edo-period Japanese academic scene as they are in today's competition among colleges, schools, and universities in the United States, for example. The first

† See page 144.

question for us to consider, then, is demographic: what sectors of the society produced the new teachers and students?

My previous discussion of the four classes suggests part of the answer. The samurai had status and sometimes a good education from their daimyō schools. With the Tokugawa peace, however, many were unemployed and financially strapped. Meanwhile, the merchants had wealth, but little formal education and low social status. The urban secular academy brought the two together for their mutual benefit: the samurai became teachers and transmitters of high culture to the merchants. As the system evolved, of course, former students regardless of class could become the next cohort of teachers, and those who could afford tuition regardless of social status could enroll in the next pool of students.

As another alternative some students gravitated toward the small private schools called *terakoya*[5] in which a teacher or husband-wife teaching couple would house, feed, and educate a group of students in a more home-like setting. The *terakoya* could often offer a student a more intimate master-apprentice model of learning than what a student could find in the large academies. In addition, the daimyō, now with a new pool of scholar-teachers for hire, continued to run their own schools in the provinces. The collective impact of those varied forms of schooling was significant. Especially in its cities and large towns across the country but also in pockets of other areas, Japan achieved a literacy rate as high as, and possibly higher than, any other place in the world at the time. In some regions, even the peasants possessed an unusually high rate of literacy, at least at the basic level.[6*]

The Edo-period social transformation gave philosophy a new forum away from the monastic centers,[7] the court, or the shogun's offices. Philosophy could become secular and more populist, attending more directly to the practical needs and interests of the townspeople. In fact, for the most part, to ensure fiscal stability it *had* to address that new audience. If people did not want to read their books, if students did not want to pay tuition to study with them, the teachers' families could starve. If necessity is the mother of invention, it is also the sire of diversification. If two academies were competing for the same students, they would underscore, even exaggerate, their differences in order to increase their market share. As any college admission officer will attest today, branding and defining a market niche are crucial to success in student recruitment.

As a result, in the Edo-period intellectual landscape, to claim philosophical uniqueness and superiority was not just for ego-aggrandizement or the love of truth; it was also often a tactic for financial survival. The result is that in the Edo period we find a proliferation of schools of thought and varieties of philosophical theories. It was in the interest of every thinker to stress his philosophical differences from others since establishing uniqueness is a first step to claiming supremacy.

The contrast with the classical and medieval rhetoric is striking. Unlike the Edo-period's demand to brand one's own philosophy as unique, when the medieval Buddhist monastery had been the main site of scholarship and creative philosophical thinking, the pressure was to dodge accusations of heresy. The meme was one of tradition, not innovation. In the Kamakura period, for instance, Eisai and Dōgen insisted they were not trying to establish a new sect, but only bringing clarity to Tendai Buddhism (in Eisai's case) or to Buddhism in general (in Dōgen's case). Shinran's philosophical praxis, ontology, and metapraxis differed markedly from Hōnen's at various points, but he maintained he was only repeating what Hōnen had said and meant. And Hōnen in turn claimed he was doing nothing more than reflecting the Pure Land texts and commentaries by his Chinese Pure Land predecessors. Even Nichiren, who relished rather than shied away from the charge of heresy, said his goal was no more than to return Japan to its earlier reverence for the *Lotus Sutra*.

It is also possible that many medieval Buddhist thinkers might have saved their more revolutionary ideas for preaching, often to the illiterate or barely literate. There would then be no written record of what they said (as perhaps the philosophers themselves would prefer, given the fear of heresy charges). My speculation on this point derives from the limited extant copies of informal Kamakura religious writings we do have. Among them we often find some of the most thought-provoking philosophical discussions—in the letters of Shinran and Nichiren, in Yuien's compilation of Shinran's sayings in *Tannishō*, in Ejō's record of Dōgen's oral teachings in *Shōbōgenzō zuimonki*, and so forth.

How many medieval texts aimed at a general audience have been lost? We cannot know. Furthermore, the fear of accusations of heresy and the penchant for secrecy likely prevented them from being widely shared publicly, thus decreasing the likelihood of their survival over time. When we consider that even Yuien's collection of Shinran's sayings in *Tannishō* ended with a cautionary note to be careful with whom one shared that text, the wonder is that today we have access to such a text at all.

In short: in the classical and medieval period, the most creative philosophers adopted the rhetorical conceit of claiming they were not being innovative. It was quite the opposite of the Edo-period rhetoric. Even those Edo philosophers who argued for a return to the wisdom of ancient China or Japan did so as a direct criticism of their contemporaries' enthusiasm for new or newly imported ideas. That is, they wore their conservatism as a badge of honor making them unique.

Signifying the public and commodified nature of philosophy in Edo Japan, plaques and broadsides from booksellers organized the Edo-period Confucian

Section of Program Ranking Scholars by Sumō Classes

scholars into a format mimicking sumō programs (*sumō banzuke*). As in sumō, they divided the competition between the philosophers of eastern Japan (Edo) and western Japan (Kyoto - Osaka). In the section of a *Gakusha kakuryoku shōbu tsuki hyōban* (*Reputation Attached to a Sumō Match of Scholars*) shown above, the philosophers are ranked by the grades used to rank sumo wrestlers (from highest to lowest: *ōzeki, sekiwake, komusubi, maegashira*, etc.).[8] For example, in the section of the program depicted above, Kumazawa Banzan is the *ōzeki* and Ogyū Sorai the *sekiwake* of the East, while the equivalent ranks in the West are filled by Arai Hakuseki and Itō Jinsai. Clearly, Edo-period readers were encouraged to consume philosophical debate as spectacle.

That commodification, competition, and dissemination make the philosophical materials of the Edo period all the more difficult to organize and evaluate. Soon after the period ended, Inoue Tetsujirō (1856–1944) tried to classify the Confucian philosophers from that era into three groups: the school of Zhu Xi, the school of ancient texts, and the school of Wang Yangming. His categorization is helpful in many ways but, not surprisingly, also limiting in others. We should be cautious in grouping people into "schools" that they themselves did not recognize.[9*] Yet, if we are to avoid this problem by treating each philosopher as a unique thinker (as many wanted to present themselves), we drown in detail that is neither philosophically interesting nor reflective of what was actually happening.

Consequently, because my approach will be more general than detailed, I will necessarily, like Inoue, draw my distinctions with broad strokes and include some of my own groupings of the philosophers. But unlike Inoue, I am not claiming that these categories were necessarily reflections of how the Edo thinkers regarded themselves. Rather they represent how they appear to me (and I hope to us) from a perspective distant in time and place. Furthermore, because the next two chapters in this book will engage two single philosophers of this era, one Confucian (Ogyū Sorai) and one Shintō (Motoori Norinaga), I hope the richness of engaged knowing will absolve me of some of the sins of overgeneralization to which I might fall victim in the detached survey undertaken in the rest of this chapter. Before turning to my overview of Confucian, Buddhist, and Shintō developments in the Edo period, however, we need take account of a new philosophical competitor to come upon the scene: Christianity and various forms of western knowledge.

WESTERN LEARNING AND CHRISTIANITY

I have already mentioned the introduction to Japan of western technology (including weaponry), science, and medicine. Until then, the Japanese sciences had been based almost entirely on Chinese models, but we should remember that in many fields (astronomy, pharmacology, physiology, ship building, navigation, some areas of mathematics, book printing, etc.), at least until the sixteenth century, Chinese science and technology were equal and often superior to the West's. Even the gunpowder used in western muskets and cann+ons had been invented in China, though it was not put to military uses there (the Chinese used it mostly for fireworks). In the sixteenth century, however, the West enjoyed revolutionary breakthroughs in physics, modern mathematics, cartography, chemistry, medicine, and the applied technologies associated with them.

When that new science and technology entered Japan, it immediately caught the attention of key Japanese intellectuals who became the core specialists in "Dutch Learning." It acquired that name as a side effect of the Japanese National Seclusion policy. From about the third decade of the seventeenth century, the Tokugawa shogunate banned all trade with westerners except the Dutch and even that was highly regulated. The result was that most of what the Japanese learned of western science in the seventeenth through mid-nineteenth centuries was via books written in Dutch.

554–5

Dutch Learning (Rangaku)

Among the imported Dutch scientific texts, the Japanese were most intrigued by those in the fields of medicine, cartography, and astronomy. The interest was primarily practical. It was hoped that new medical information could impact health and longevity while cartography could give the Japanese a better understanding of world geography as well as improved navigation techniques. Even Japan's concern with astronomy was more practical than theoretical, mainly involving the attempt to develop more accurate calendars which would help improve agricultural planning.

Of the three fields, the western medical texts presented the greatest culture shock because Chinese medicine had been for the most part the unchallenged norm in Japan since ancient times. When the Japanese doctors saw the Dutch anatomical charts, however, they were stunned that they bore so little resemblance to those of China. Could western bodies really be that different from Chinese bodies? The bewilderment changed to amazement in 1771 when Sugita Genpaku (1733–1817) with a few other medical colleagues observed an autopsy (a rare event in Japan at the time) with the specific intent of comparing what they saw with what was depicted in the Dutch and Chinese anatomical charts. Confirming the accuracy of the western version, they immediately undertook the project of translating the Dutch book of anatomy, an event which created a ground swell of academic interest among physicians.[10]

That said, for the most part, Chinese medicine continued to dominate Japanese practice well into the modern period. In fact, it still has a significant presence in Japan today where it exists alongside western medicine. The inability of western (Dutch) medicine to supplant Chinese medicine suggests two general points about the status of Dutch Learning in Japan during the Edo period.

First, there seems to have been no concerted effort to fully assimilate Dutch Learning into Japanese culture in the way that, for example, Buddhism and Confucianism had been a millennium earlier. That is, Edo Japan made no sustained attempt at hybridization, nor a blending of western ideas with eastern ideas so as to create something intellectually new. Nor was western science at this point relegated under one of the existing philosophical systems as, say, proto-Shintō had been relegated to a subordinate place in early Heian esoteric Buddhism. Admittedly, some lip service was paid to the idea that the western scientific empiricism was consistent with neo-Confucianism's "investigation of things" and its call for the "expansion of knowledge," but no one to my knowledge made a serious effort to integrate western empiricism and neo-Confucianism into a single system. For the most part, western science was left as a reserve of possibly useful technical knowledge and skills, but not something to be philosophically fostered.

Still, as an exotic import, western scientific thought enjoyed cachet among a niche of Japanese philosophers. As the eighteenth century drew to a close, some gained access to western books other than those in Dutch. In response, they learned the appropriate languages so they could translate the western texts into Japanese. Consequently, the term "Dutch Learning" started to fall out of use in favor of the new term "Western Learning" (yōgaku).

The other conclusion about Dutch Learning is that however limited its impact on Edo philosophy might have been, its very presence reminded Japanese that although they may no longer have significant dealings with the West while the program of National Seclusion was in effect, the flourishing of western technological and scientific prowess might someday threaten Japan's isolation. At the very end of the Edo period it did exactly that. The western scientific and technological books that trickled into Japan in the early and mid-Edo period likely set an intellectual and pedagogical foundation for the rapid modernization of Japan in the latter half of the nineteenth century.

Certainly western science and technology were still alien to Japanese culture in many ways, but their achievements and potential for practical application were known to some well-informed groups of Japanese intellectuals. Those intellectuals would engineer in the mid- and late nineteenth century one of the great social transformations in history, converting Japan from a quasi-feudal to a modern technological state in just a few decades. It seems improbable that the transformation could have been as fast and effective were there not some key influential intellectuals who knew of the western scientific context and what would be required to educate a generation of Japanese in the needed skills.

I will address Japanese modernization more fully in Chapter 11. For now, I will turn to another kind of book brought to Japan by the cargo ships of the sixteenth century: the bibles carried by Roman Catholic missionaries. Despite its short-lived presence in Japan of just a century, Christianity's immediate impact would be much more visible than that of Dutch Learning. In fact, that we speak of *Dutch* Learning in the Edo period rather than Spanish or Portuguese Learning is already a hint about how Christianity interacted with Japanese culture during their initial encounter.

A Century of Christianity

In the sixteenth century the West brought to Japan a new religion: Roman Catholic Christianity. Headed by the famous Spanish Jesuit Francis Xavier (1506–1602), the first religious mission to Japan landed at Kagoshima on the southern island of Kyushu in 1549 via a Portuguese trading ship. For the next half century there followed a stream of missionaries, Jesuit and Franciscan (and toward the end of the period some Dominicans), both Spanish and Portuguese. Initially, the missionaries enjoyed a warm welcome in Nobunaga's castle at Azuchi and then Hideyoshi's at Momoyama. The missionaries were treated somewhat like the aforementioned Rinzai Zen monks who had served the shogunate and court as experts on Chinese arts and letters,[†] except in the case of the missionaries, of course, their expertise was about the West rather than China.

† See page 270.

In other words, Oda Nobunaga and Toyotomi Hideyoshi were more interested in the missionaries' secular knowledge than their spiritual gifts. Since part of the Jesuit global agenda was to master as quickly as possible the native languages of the people they were trying to convert, they made a cottage industry of studying Japanese and translating Christian texts.[11] That also qualified them as handy interpreters for the Japanese government in its negotiations with European traders.

Although unsuccessful in converting Nobunaga, Hideyoshi, or even their highest officials, the missionaries capitalized on the hegemons' permission to preach freely among the people. Usually targeting the local leaders or regional daimyō first, the missionaries hoped for top-down conversions: win over the leaders and their people would follow. The strategy worked quite well and Roman Catholicism made significant inroads into various regions, first in the southern island of Kyushu, and then in various locations on the main island of Honshū, especially in areas a little distant from the capital such as the affluent merchant city of Sakai, near what became Osaka.

Nobunaga's use of Christianity to check Buddhism. For the most part, Nobunaga delighted in the success of those conversions, not out of piety, but out of appreciation for how they were undermining the dominance of Buddhist institutions. To Nobunaga's way of thinking, any rival of the Buddhists was a potential ally. He had repeatedly found the various Buddhist affinity groups as well as the old-guard religious establishment of Tendai and Shingon to be impediments in his efforts at unifying and controlling the archipelago.

Meanwhile, the Buddhist affinity groups, especially those of Shin Buddhism, were ever suspicious of the centralized government and its penchant for exorbitant taxation policies. So, they were not inclined to surrender the regional political gains they had made during the chaos of the Muromachi and Warring Domains periods. As a result, Nobunaga felt the need to stamp out the Ikkō Ikki[†] uprisings once and for all. In service to the unification alliance, Ieyasu had squelched a major Ikkō Ikki rebellion in 1563 and by 1580, Nobunaga had divested the Shin Buddhist affinity groups of any real military power.

By the same token, the Tendai Buddhist establishment had successfully maintained its political influence for eight centuries and was no more willing to concede to a military general than they had been to the populist Kamakura religions. Centered on Mt Hiei, with a bird's-eye view of the capital in the valley below, Tendai controlled a key land route to Kyoto from regions adjacent to the Japan Sea. Not friendly to Nobunaga, the Tendai temple on Mt Hiei sometimes served as a safe house for those plotting to overthrow the regime, occasionally

† See pages 269.

even acting as a rendezvous point for rebel troops. In addition, the Mt Hiei Tendai temple had its own army of ten thousand warrior monks. On September 13th, 1571, Nobunaga took decisive action.

Some years ago I was on Mt Hiei and I noticed that a towering Japanese cedar (*sugi*), some thirty or forty meters high, was being cut down, presumably because of disease. It was located on a hill just behind the Tendai temple's main hall. On a hunch, I hiked up to examine the stump. Sure enough, as clear as a thumbprint at a crime scene, the stump corroborated that Nobunaga had been there and what he had done. The tree stump had about four hundred annual growth rings, indicating it had started its life as a sapling in the natural reforestation of the hillside after Nobunaga's attack. When Nobunaga took the mountain in 1571, he had destroyed all three thousand temple buildings, annihilated the army of warrior monks, and killed everyone else he could find. Then he burned to the ground the entire top of the mountain.

In the four centuries of that tree's growth, Tendai Buddhism had never regained the political, economic, and military power it had enjoyed before then. That tree stump marked not only Nobunaga's destruction of Mt Hiei, but also the end of the era when Tendai, Shingon, and Hossō Buddhism would hold sway over the Japanese Buddhist world. After reunification in the late sixteenth century, the primary focus of Buddhist spiritual life would permanently shift to the religions that had their origins in the thirteenth century: Pure Land, Zen, and Nichiren.

Against that background, it is clear why Nobunaga trusted neither the old Buddhist establishment nor the new Kamakura religions. If Christianity could undermine Buddhism's influence, Nobunaga would happily tolerate the new religion. Besides, the missionaries, with their European connections and language skills, could expedite trade relations with the West and keep him abreast of innovations in military technology. To a man who had gained control of most of Japan through the strategic use of musket and cannon, no information was more valued.

Hideyoshi's ambivalence toward Christianity. At the beginning of his rule, Hideyoshi followed the model of his mentor, Nobunaga, in how to treat the foreign missionaries. Fascinated with what lands lay beyond the Japanese archipelago, Hideyoshi mused over how much of it he could make his own. He poured over maps of a world the Japanese had only begun to realize existed, seeking information from his Catholic missionary advisors and European trading partners.

Hideyoshi's treatment of the Christians was hardly consistent, however. In 1587, just five years after his rise to power, Hideyoshi became uneasy about the flourishing of Christianity on Kyushu and he issued a proclamation ordering all missionaries to exit the country, though he never really pushed to enforce the edict. Then, to learn more about the Spanish empire as research for his own dreams of global conquest, in 1592 he sent a diplomatic mission to meet with the Spanish governor in the Philippines. A year later Hideyoshi permitted a group of Spanish missionaries from the Philippines to build a church near Kyoto. In 1597, however, he executed all the church's priests and parishioners. Then in Nagasaki, a major port city on Kyushu, he publicly executed a diverse group of twenty-six Christians: both priests and laity, both Japanese and Europeans, both adults and children. For their execution he employed another technological innovation recently introduced from the West—crucifixion.

What accounts for Hideyoshi's erratic policies toward Christianity? For each incident of Christian persecution, historians can identify a probable precipitating event, but Hideyoshi seemed most motivated by one persistent concern. Whereas Nobunaga had relished the Christians' animated intellectual attack on Buddhism, Hideyoshi worried that the Christians were too fanatic and that their loyalties were to an alien god and foreign institution. His emissaries to the Philippines had witnessed the collusion between the church and armed forces of Spain, joined in lockstep to build an empire, a kingdom of God and monarch. Hence, always paranoid (sometimes for good reason), Hideyoshi could at any moment be easily persuaded his suspicions were valid and then erratically lash out. All it would take was an isolated populist uprising, or an unauthorized foreign galleon mysteriously shipwrecked offshore, or a comment by one of the newly arrived (Protestant) Dutch traders who delighted to recount the sins of Catholicism and its empire.

Ieyasu's suppression of Christianity. When Tokugawa Ieyasu came to power in 1600, he was at first tolerant of the Catholic missionaries because they gave him access to Portuguese trade. As the number of Dutch and English traders increased, however, Ieyasu had new options. His Dutch and English suppliers were not only Protestant rather than Roman Catholic; they also did not seem much interested in any missionary work or conversions. So, in 1614, Ieyasu ordered all missionaries deported. Unlike the impulsive Hideyoshi, once Ieyasu made a decision, he stuck with it, putting ever-greater pressure on any missionaries who tried to remain or any Christians who tried to practice their faith openly. By 1637, Ieyasu had killed thousands of Christians and only a few handfuls of missionaries were still at large in the country. That was the year of the Shimabara Uprising, a rebellion of peasants, former vassals, and masterless samurai.

When Ieyasu put down the rebellion, he killed its teenage leader, Amakusa Shirō (1622?–1638) and over 35,000 of his followers. Because the uprising had started in an area under Christian influence, Ieyasu held the foreign religion responsible. In reality, though, the revolt was triggered by frustration over taxation, exorbitant debt, famine, and by anger against the unresponsive central government. In other words, it was much like the earlier Ikkō Ikki uprising with similar complaints and a similar amalgamation of affinity groups. The only significant difference was that the religious common denominator in the Shimabara *ikki* had been Christianity, not Shin Buddhism.

In any case, the entire country came under Tokugawa Ieyasu's control and having none of Hideyoshi's dreams of world conquest, Ieyasu slammed the door to the West. The proclamation of National Seclusion, which was in effect from 1639 to 1854, banned from the country all Roman Catholic missionaries or traders, proscribed the practice of Christianity, and banned all Japanese from foreign travel. The only exception was limited commerce with the Chinese and Koreans and highly restricted trade with the Dutch who were relegated to living on an artificial island built for them off Nagasaki called Dejima (or Deshima). Except for a small underground group of "hidden Christians" mostly from the Nagasaki area, the Roman Catholic era of Japan was essentially over.

The Refutations of Fukansai Habian (Fabian)

The question for this book is whether those eight or nine decades of a Christian presence in Japan had any lasting influence on Japanese philosophy. What kinds of arguments did the missionaries develop against Buddhism? How did the Buddhists try to refute those arguments? Oddly enough, for a spirited defense of both sides of the debate between Christianity and the traditional Japanese religions, we can examine the writings of a single man, Fukansai Habian (1565?–1621?) or, as he is better known to the West, Fucan Fabian.[12] A native Japanese educated as a boy in the Kyoto Zen monastery Daitoku-ji (Temple of Great Virtue), he converted to Christianity and joined the Jesuits in 1586 as a lay brother and applicant for the priesthood. Trained in theology and rhetoric, he wrote a stylistically engaging and philosophically sophisticated defense of Christianity, *Myōtei mondō* (*Dialogue between Myōshū and Yūtei*) in 1605. It portrays a philosophical discussion between Myōshū, a distraught, recently widowed young Buddhist woman and Yūtei, a female Christian recluse.

1038–46

The theological core of Fabian's Christian apologetic in the dialogue is the nature of creation. We have seen that the medieval Shintō philosophers had already introduced into Japanese thinking the appeal to origins as the basis for criticizing Buddhism, drawing on the cosmologies of Chinese process narratives found in Daoism or Confucianism. Chikafusa† had associated the *kami* with their primordial creative energy and a century later Kanetomo character-

† See page 258.

ized the original source, the beginning of beginnings, in his "Fundamental and Original Shintō" doctrine as preceding the dynamic interplay of *yin* and *yang*, the process of thinking, and even the differentiation of energy.[†]

From the standpoint of Fabian's Christian scholasticism, however, even those ideas of creation were inadequate because they did not allow for an infinitely wise and caring *creator*. Without God ("Deus") as the creator of everything, there would be no explaining the presence, even the limited presence, of knowledge and love in the world. How do we know there is such a creator? Fabian drew on the traditional Christian argument by design: when we see the intricate harmony and order in nature, it is like seeing an extraordinary architectural edifice. Such a monument could not come about by chance, but was clearly created by an intelligent being. Such an insight into design and its origins, Fabian argued, is missing in the religious philosophies of Japan, whether Shintō, Buddhist, Confucian, or Daoist.

Moreover, Fabian contended that the founders of those eastern traditions were either mere human beings (Shakyamuni Buddha, Confucius, Laozi) or celestial *kami* who are finite, fallible, and historical beings much like humans. Fabian argued that the true source of creation, the genuine beginning of beginnings, must be that which created the human and which itself transcends all limiting human characteristics. God is an immaterial, pure spirit (not a physical being like the buddhas or *kami*) who creates and orders the material world. Thus, God is "principle" (*ri*; C. *li*) not matter.

To look for creation in material processes alone, as Fabian claimed the East Asian traditions do, is to believe mistakenly that the created must be of the same essence as the creator. He suggests that would be like nonsensically asserting that the blossom of a tree must already exist in its roots because the roots cannot produce something unlike themselves. Yet, the roots do produce something unlike themselves: the blossom. No matter how much we search, we cannot find the blossom in the roots. The blossom exists in the roots not materially but "in principle." Analogously God, although immaterial, is the principle behind and within all material creation.

Three years later in 1608 Fabian left the Jesuit order, his explanation being that European racism had blocked his rising from the rank of lay brother to that of priest. (Jesuit accounts claim he was expelled for breaking his vow of chastity.) Fabian's polemical writings continued, however, but he now directed them against Christianity in favor of the East Asian traditions he had formerly renounced. In 1620 he wrote his famous treatise, *Ha Daiusu* (*Refuting the Deus*

---

† See pages 261–2.

Adherents). In that work he argues that it is the Christians who have the simplistic view of creation.

The problem with Christianity, Fabian now claimed, is precisely its anthropomorphic conception of God, the creator. Fabian focused on the Christian argument, one that he himself had used some fifteen years before, that the only way to explain the goodness, virtue, and wisdom in the world is to assume they reflect the qualities of the creator. Flipping the import of his former no-blossom-in-the-roots analogy, Fabian now argued that since we cannot know the roots by knowing the blossom, we cannot know the nature of the creator by knowing the nature of the created.

Furthermore, Fabian contended that by attributing anthropomorphic qualities like wisdom and intelligence to God, the Christians overlook that wherever there is intelligence, we find conceptual binaries that serve as alternatives: bad as well as good, hate as well as love. Thinking cannot proceed without the interplay of opposites. Thus, God's intelligence entails the possibility that evil and hate are real alternatives for God, even if they happen to be unchosen alternatives. Yet, since God is presumed to be perfectly good, evil and hate cannot be true divine alternatives. Hence, the idea of an intelligent, all-good God is self-contradictory. Indeed, to attribute *any* qualities to God is to limit a supposedly infinite being. So, even if God exists, that Creator cannot be anything like a human agent with qualities like intelligence or goodness. In conclusion, even if there were a God, Fabian believed he had proven it could not be the God of the Christians.

Fabian's second major objection was that the Christians misrepresented the East Asian traditions either out of ignorance or deception. Following on his previous point and having rejected the idea of an anthropomorphic creator as being self-contradictory, we are left with an idea of creation as an agentless process—exactly what the Buddhist theories of conditioned coproduction, the Chinese *yin-yang* accounts, and Shintō accounts of *kami* as creative energy have maintained all along. The agentless process of reality that Christianity mocks is actually more logical than the idea of an anthropomorphic creator, he argued.

The Christians (including Fabian himself in his earlier spiritual incarnation) had also renounced Buddhism and Shintō on the grounds that their most spiritually advanced beings were no more than human (Shakyamuni) or barely more than human (the celestial *kami*). Hence, they could not be the creators of a universe. Fabian retorted that the Christian argument focuses only on the historical embodiment of the Buddha, ignoring the cosmic embodiment† (which is not an agent but rather a set of spontaneous functions).[13] Dusting off

† See pages 81–3.

the hoary Buddhist *honji suijaku* theory† Fabian asserted that the Shintō *kami* are really all grounded in the cosmic buddha as well. So, it is simply not true to say that the highest form of spiritual being in the Japanese religions is no more than human.

Moreover, Fabian noted that the Christians did indeed know of the cosmos-as-buddha theory, but whenever confronted with that fact, they rejected it out-of-hand because the Buddhists say this cosmic buddha is "nonwise" (*muchi*) and "nonvirtuous" or "without qualities" (*mutoku*). How could the Buddhists be so deluded, the Christians snorted, to think the universe to have been created by an ignorant, evil God! Fabian replied (correctly) that the prefix *mu* (無) in Japanese does not mean "not," but rather "outside the distinction of." Hence, the Buddhist point is logical: the source of everything (*mu* as "emptiness") must be the source of all characteristics and cannot have characteristics itself. Fabian claimed that unlike the Christians, the Buddhists realize it is a contradiction to attribute *any* qualities—even positive ones—to what is infinite or unlimited. The real is the *original mind*, a term Fabian likely learned from his early Zen training and in usage much like the *original nature*‡ for Musō Soseki.[14]

As a final touch to his anti-Christian polemic, Fabian referred to lessons from recent history. He pointed to how the fortunes of many wealthy and powerful families in western Japan had fallen once they converted to Christianity. This was because, Fabian maintained, Christianity was a foreign religion in the "land of the *kami*," a term that harks back to Chikafusa. The *kami*, he claimed, would retaliate against any Japanese who did not show them due reverence, a claim at least as old as the sixth century when Mononobe used it against the pro-Buddhist Soga.‡ Of course, Fabian made no mention of the role that Hideyoshi and Ieyasu might have played in the downfall of those Christian families, but even if he had, the hegemons would likely not object to having their actions associated with the *kami* that protect Japan.

There is another aspect in Fabian's argument that perhaps even he lacked the reflective capacity or external standpoint to see. Namely, Christianity had tried to achieve hegemonic spiritual and intellectual authority in Japan by using refutation rather than an assimilative strategy such as relegation. Buddhism had succeeded in Japan in part because it had found, through the *honji suijaku* theory, a way to find a place, albeit a subordinate place, for the indigenous *kami* in its system. Kanetomo's Shintō philosophy did not try to refute Buddhism and all forms of Chinese thought, but rather to relegate them to the margins of a more inclusive system. Fabian—was it a sign of his European-based Christian

---

† See pages 145–6.

‡ See page 55.

training?—had no place for relegation in his polemics, however. When a Christian, he unreservedly rejected all Japanese religious doctrines and practices; later, after rejecting Christianity, his view of Japanese religions unconditionally rejected all Christian elements. No compromise, no reinterpretation of basic ideas or symbols, no borrowing of practices, no allocation, no hybridization.

But did it have to be so? Could not Christianity have found a way to coexist with native Japanese spiritual elements?[15*] I mentioned previously that the merchant city of Sakai near Osaka had a strong Christian presence in the sixteenth century. Sakai was also the home of the aforementioned Sen no Rikyū (1522–1591), famous for his aesthetic theory of tea ceremony.[†] So it is not far-fetched to think Catholic ritual may have influenced Rikyū's gestures for tea ceremony: how the bowl is wiped with a cloth in tea ceremony mirrors how a priest wipes the chalice at Mass, for example. If the two new traditions in Japan—Christianity and tea ceremony—could have flourished alongside each other in Sakai for some period of time, might the story of Christianity in Japan have turned out differently?

As we will see in Chapter 11, moreover, there are also possibly Christian elements in Hirata Atsutane's (1776–1843) revision of Shintō teachings about the afterlife. And lastly, in the modern period, Christianity reentered Japan as part of the western philosophical and cultural tradition as well as a missionary movement. When political circumstances permitted the free exchange of ideas, philosophical dialogue between Christians and representatives of traditional Japanese religions thrived and continues today. As a result, in twentieth-century Japan, even when state ideology was stressing a Shintō spirituality and warrior ethic, Japanese academic philosophers still often tried to explain the place of God in their philosophical systems.

Admittedly, as the Whiteheadian American philosopher Charles Hartshorne once noted, the God of the philosophers is not the same as the God of religion. In the final analysis, Christianity's impact on Japan has generally been more intellectual than religious. Still, from the interaction with Christianity, Japanese philosophy was exposed to at least three new ideas. First was the possibility of a God who (unlike the *kami* of the ancient Japanese myths) created the material world *ex nihilo*. A second contribution was a refinement of argumentation by refutation. And lastly, Christianity brought a paradigm of a pure transcendence that is both ontologically beyond this world and yet interactive in it.

Now let us turn to the most significant philosophical development in the Edo era: the resurgence of Confucianism.

† See pages 252–3.

CONFUCIANISM IN THE EARLY EDO PERIOD

As I explained in Chapter 7, in the fourteenth century the third Muromachi shogun, Ashikaga Yoshimitsu, had reestablished full diplomatic and trade relations with China, triggering a surge of Chinese imports: ideas, texts, and artwork as well as both practical and luxury goods.† That influx of culture from abroad fostered a renewed fascination with "things Chinese" (*kara no mono*) expedited by a resumed two-way flow of Buddhist monks between China and Japan. In terms of enduring philosophical impact, the most important development was that by the late fifteenth century, the Japanese monks, mainly Rinzai Zen monks, were bringing numerous texts from the then dominant philosophical tradition of China, what the West calls *neo-Confucianism*. At the same time, the spoils of Hideyoshi's military misadventures in Korea included not only new texts but also some Korean neo-Confucian scholars/officials taken as prisoners. As the Japanese studied this newly imported form of Confucianism, they realized it differed significantly from what they had previously associated with that tradition.

The Confucianism of Buddhist Monks

Before the sixteenth century, Japanese Confucianism did not have its own creative thinkers comparable to Buddhism's Kūkai, Dōgen, or Shinran. Since the Nara period, Confucianism in Japan had been mainly a fixed canon of classical arts and letters studied either for self-edification or as preparation for the civil service exam. In addition, Confucianism furnished an array of ideal forms for social relations and it (along with Chinese Legalism[16]) inspired the system of laws and bureaucratic government.

Neo-Confucianism, by contrast, expanded that range of topics to include sophisticated metaphysical speculations about the nature of physical reality, analyses about the basis for human knowledge, and metapractical theories concerning the role of meditation. Even more surprising to the Japanese monks was that the neo-Confucian canon had mounted intricate arguments against Buddhism. Since the eighth century, except for aesthetics and a smattering of Shintō thought, Japan's constructive philosophy had taken place almost entirely within Buddhist contexts, but this new wave of Confucianism would eventually supplant that Japanese Buddhist intellectual hegemony.

The obvious question is why the Rinzai monks who visited China would not only tolerate, but actually abet, this intellectual revolution, a shift in thinking

† See pages 248–9.

that would seemingly be against their own interests as Buddhists. There were undoubtedly many factors, but here I will discuss just a few.

First, with their new contacts abroad, some monks were undoubtedly shocked to find that the current Chinese Confucianism was so much more than the classics and commentaries the Japanese had been reading for the preceding millennium.[17] To preserve their standing as Japanese custodians of Chinese culture and as influential advisors to the hegemons, the monks were expected to keep abreast of intellectual and cultural movements of contemporaneous as well as classical China. After all, Chinese neo-Confucianism was hardly a new continental fad: it had by this point been steadily growing in influence in China and Korea for some five centuries. Now competing with the Christian counselors to the hegemons for the government's favor, it was all the more important for the Japanese advisors to be well informed about what seemed to them to be a rapidly changing intellectual landscape in East Asia.

Furthermore, the aforementioned Five Mountain tradition of Rinzai Zen had become increasingly aestheticized and secularized, enough so that the praxis of the Confucian literati might have seemed to many monks more attractive than the rigors of Zen praxis. Indeed, many studied the Chinese arts and letters at Rinzai temples without even bothering to be formally ordained as monks.

Lastly, since the hegemons' support for Buddhism was, to say the least, often fickle, the persecution of targeted Buddhist groups remained a possibility. Thus, the Rinzai Zen establishment was in jeopardy of losing its privileged position if the newly introduced Confucianism appealed to the new regime. It thus seemed prudent to be in the vanguard of the new Confucianism rather than be its reactionary opponent.

On a deeper intellectual level, as the Japanese monks fathomed the details of this new species of Confucianism, many admired how it had assimilated and relegated major aspects of Buddhism and Daoism—their theories as well as their practices—into a new comprehensive scheme. The early Confucian tradition, in both China as well as Japan, had lacked systematic formulation and philosophical justification, its persuasive power residing in its utopian vision of an ideal community with regularized and harmonious human interactions. Daoism's emphasis on cosmogony and on how to live in accord with the ways of nature were only a muted and tangential concern in early Confucianism as were the Buddhist interests in logic and in the internal dynamics of the self (emotions, the psychological mechanics of thinking, yogic practices for analyzing and controlling predispositions, distinctions among kinds and levels of consciousness, and so forth).

The new Confucianism introduced to Japan in the sixteenth century, however, addressed many of those traditionally Buddhist and Daoist preoccupations. Before turning to its impact on Japan, I will set the background by sketching a few key ways neo-Confucianism had developed its grand synthesis in China.

Chinese Neo-Confucianism

The Chinese neo-Confucian movement is often considered to have started with the eleventh-century brothers, Cheng Hao (1032–1085) and Cheng Yi (1033–1107), and to have been epitomized in the next century by Zhu Xi (J. Shushi; 1130–1200). By expanding Confucianism to incorporate Buddhist and Daoist streams of metaphysics, philosophical psychology, epistemology, cosmogony, and psycho-spiritual discipline, it became the most comprehensive and inclusive philosophical system in East Asia.

The comprehensive character of the new system enabled Zhu Xi and his fellow neo-Confucians to formulate a devastating philosophical attack on Buddhism and Daoism as discrete traditions. Relying on argument by relegation, they claimed that what was right about each of those traditions was now shown to be a part—albeit a subordinate part—of Confucianism.

Furthermore, the neo-Confucians claimed, Buddhism and Daoism *per se*, with their inadequate pragmatics of social ethics and politics, are intrinsically incapable of establishing the social milieu necessary for human flourishing and personal self-cultivation. In other words: neo-Confucianism was said to be superior because it had assimilated the best ideas and practices of Buddhism and Daoism, while preserving something the other two philosophies had always lacked, namely, a rich engagement with the social aspect of human existence.

A pivotal idea in Zhu Xi's system was that of "principle" or "pattern" (C. *li*; J. *ri*). Found in venerable texts as ancient as the *Book of Changes* (*Yijing*), this ancient Chinese view of nature was that reality, driven by the *yin-yang* dynamism, was in a perpetual state of flux with ever-changing balances or imbalances between the two. Yet, that change was not chaotic. At any given time, reality has a discernible pattern and this pattern permeates all events of the moment. Hence, through holographic praxis and analysis, a person could discern the pattern in all things at any moment by discovering it in any one thing. [1260-1]

That theory became a metapractical justification for various forms of prognostication. If you wanted to determine whether the present was a propitious time for some enterprise, for example, you needed to know the dominant "pattern in the way of things" (C. *daoli*; J. *dōri*) at that time so you would know if your intended action would go smoothly. In fact, some scholars surmise that the sinograph for principle or pattern (理) might have originally represented the cracks on a tortoise shell that appear after it is thrown into the fire (a fortune-telling practice similar to reading the tea leaves after drinking a cup of tea in parts of Eastern Europe, for example).

In ancient China, the *Yijing* and its associated praxis were the most systematized manifestation of this idea: to discover the pattern of things in the present, you manipulated yarrow sticks randomly in a way that would yield one of sixty-four major hexagrams. For each hexagram, the *Yijing* provides an accompanying poetic, highly stylized, and imagistic passage that would not itself yield a direct answer to your query, but would serve as the focus of contemplation until a propitious course of action became clear. Presumably, the idea was that to interpret the passage, you had to attune your own mind to the pattern of the moment as well. We can understand the neo-Confucian theory of principle or pattern as a sophisticated elaboration and systematization of that ancient Chinese world view, shaping it into a comprehensive philosophy.

In Zhu Xi's neo-Confucianism, although empty of content in itself, principle supplies the primary ordering of reality, determining the flow of generative force (C. *qi*; J. *ki*) in the universe as the interaction of *yin* and *yang*. On the epistemological level, the goal for the neo-Confucian, therefore, is to quiet the emotions through meditation and to refine the sensitivities through the study of the classics, thereby enabling one to "investigate things" in the world until their principle is clear. Knowledge occurs when the patterns or principles in the mind correlate with the patterns and principles in things.[18]

Even that brief sketch of Zhu Xi's system reveals how it expanded traditional Confucian social theory to include both Daoist and Buddhist sensitivities. Drawn from Daoism is the emphasis on being in accord with the patterns of nature as well as analyzing the dynamics of natural energies like generative force and *yin-yang*. Derived from Buddhism is the emphasis on calming the mind and opening oneself to the engagement with phenomena.

Moreover, the idea of principle as an ordering function in all things was itself undoubtedly influenced by the Huayan (J. Kegon)† Buddhist metaphysics going back to one of its Chinese founders Dushun (557–640). Lastly, the Zhu Xi school held that principle itself and the dynamics of *yin* and *yang* were grounded in the *supreme ultimate* (*taiji*; J. *taikyoku*), a unitary and unifying ground within limitless potential and becoming, an idea that had roots in Zhuangzi's Daoist philosophy of creativity and perhaps also in the Buddhist notion of the void or emptiness.

Of course, the last thing the neo-Confucians would want to do is abandon the strength of traditional Confucianism: its emphasis on the binary social relations, cultivation of the virtues, and scholarly study of the classics. The connec-

† See pages 92–5.

tion was able to be maintained because it was assumed that the virtues based in the principles or patterns of heaven (C. *tianli*; J. *tenri*) were the same patterns in the way of things (C. *daoli*; J. *dōri*).

In fact, even benevolence or humaneness (C. *ren*; J. *jin*), which earlier Confucianism had limited to interpersonal relations, could also be construed under neo-Confucianism as a Buddhist-like empathy linking people not only with each other but also with all other beings. In that respect Zhu Xi's epistemology contained at least a dimension of the affective along with the intellectual. In this expanded version of benevolence that emphasizes engagement or even immersion into its object, one could, for example, imaginatively empathize with bamboo as a way of understanding it. As a result, the neo-Confucian sense of principle—whether we consider its function in the metaphysical dynamic, the epistemological relation of knower and known, or in the ethical relations within society—is the ground of goodness and truth.

By the time Zhu Xi's system arrived in Japan in the sixteenth century, another neo-Confucian philosophy accompanied it, that of Wang Yangming (J. Ōyōmei; 1472–1529). The Wang Yangming School (J. *Yōmeigaku*), strongly rooted in Chinese Zen ideas, reasoned that since principle exists in the mind as well as in reality, it could be accessed first through introspection and then applied to the external world, rather than in the opposite direction as Zhu Xi had argued. Moreover, since as Zhu Xi himself suggested, principle is inherently good and only corrupted through the disharmonious working of the generative force, it follows, argued Wang Yangming, that the mind is inherently good and contains innate knowledge. It need only be tapped and *put into action* for it to be complete.

The rationale of Wang Yangming's position is notably similar to that of the inherent enlightenment/initiated enlightenment dynamic found in such Zen thinkers as Dōgen, for example. That is, Wang Yangming's theory of inherent knowledge and goodness resembles Dōgen's claim that to be enlightened is to enact or practice enlightenment—knowing and doing cannot be separated. Given their similar orientation, it is hardly surprising that the followers of Zhu Xi, in China as well as Japan, accused the Wang Yangming School of being closet Zen Buddhists.

Having briefly surveyed the thrust of neo-Confucian thinking in China, let us turn to its impact on Japan.

The Ascent of the New Japanese Confucianism

The Edo-period Japanese philosophers were immediately attracted to a few key ideas in the two neo-Confucian traditions. With regard to the Zhu Xi School, many admired its quasi-empiricism: we can discover natural laws by engaging the patterns discoverable in natural phenomena. This naturalistic approach not only correlated with what an elite group of intellectuals were gradually discovering about western science, but its naturalism also undermined the secrecy typical of the medieval Buddhist world view.

As I have said, compared with the medieval city dwellers, the denizens of the Edo-period cities were more public than private, especially when it came to marketing ideas and exchanging information. Befitting the new intellectual climate, Zhu Xi's philosophy suggested the mysteries of the world were actually readily knowable if you would recognize the patterns. Although his idea of principle may seem transcendent, it was reassuring to many Japanese of the time that even this highest reality was in some way accessible on the surface of the phenomenal realm. There was no need to plummet the depths for the hidden reality of *yūgen*, for example, if principle or pattern could be discovered right here in the empirically available world.

As for the Wang Yangming School, its introspective, idealist tendencies might have seemed too contemplative for many townspeople, but they appreciated its pragmatic claim that knowledge without action is not really knowledge at all. The tendency toward withdrawal typical of the medieval world view had been replaced in Edo Japan by a valorization of action: whether the warrior's decisiveness, the merchant's manipulation of market forces, the kabuki actor's swashbuckling swagger, the scholar's commodification of philosophy, Saikaku's characters' playboy antics, or Bashō's pilgrimages into the back country. Even the ordinary townspeople enthusiastically pursued fun and entertainment.[19]*

Yet action should be virtuous. Wang Yangming's philosophy reaffirmed the inherent goodness of human nature. Through introspection, you could discover that moral core within you, a core that was manifest both in virtuous action and in knowing. Since you could discover the source of morality and knowledge by introspection rather than investigating things or studying texts outside yourself, virtue and insight were available to anyone regardless of class or education. The practicality of that idea appealed to the ordinary people of the Edo era even if they did not consider themselves to be formal followers of Wang Yangming.

Japanese Confucianism's challenge to Buddhist supremacy. By the late sixteenth century, the signs were clear: Japan was about to undergo a reversal in its intellectual evaluation of Buddhism vis-à-vis Confucianism. Up to then, Kūkai's treatment of Confucianism, his relegating it to being a product of the second lowest of the ten mindsets,[†] represented the dominant philosophical view. For Kūkai, Confucianism was a legitimate first step, but only a first step, away from our animal natures, allowing us to form a civil society of harmonious interpersonal relations. In the final analysis, Kūkai had believed that classical

† See pages 132–6.

Confucianism had almost nothing significant to contribute to metaphysics, epistemology, or psychology. Now, toward the end of the sixteenth century, Confucianism returned to Japan in a new form, this time relegating Buddhism to a subordinate position within its new, more comprehensive schema.

Given the status of Japanese Buddhist philosophy at the time, no school of Buddhist thought was initially poised to mount an intellectual counteroffensive against the neo-Confucian criticisms. Because neo-Confucianism's argument was one of relegation, a successful Buddhist response would likely have to develop an even more comprehensive scheme that would relegate neo-Confucianism to a subordinate position within it (as Kanetomo's One and Only Shintō had to relegate Shingon Buddhism into his system to supersede Shingon's earlier relegation of Shintō within its own system, for example).

At the time of neo-Confucianism's entrance into Japan, the two most comprehensive and all-encompassing forms of Japanese systematic Buddhist philosophy, Tendai and Shingon, were waning in influence. Of the two, Tendai—with its mix of exoteric and esoteric systems of thought—was probably better suited intellectually to take up the philosophical challenge, but just about the time when Confucianism was starting to establish its new foothold on Japanese shores, Nobunaga was incinerating Mt Hiei, the center of Tendai intellectual teaching and praxis.

Moreover, the now ascendant Kamakura religions (Pure Land, Nichiren, and Zen) were not particularly interested in developing a new comprehensive vision of the whole, as they had already forsaken that enterprise when they splintered off from Tendai in favor of the principle of selection, of identifying the holographic entry to the whole through a single practice or single text. In addition, for reasons already explained, some Kamakura religions of the sixteenth century were occupied by social and political insurgencies that drew their energies away from philosophical issues.

Ironically, the only Kamakura Buddhist tradition with the intellectual training, social prestige, scholarly resources, and contemplative space capable of taking on neo-Confucianism was Rinzai Zen. But Rinzai Zen, infused with the sinophilia characteristic of the Five Mountain tradition, had become enamored of neo-Confucianism. So the path was clear for Confucianism's ascent in the world of Japanese philosophy.

A still further advantage in favor of neo-Confucianism was attitudinal. The Kamakura religions, now becoming dominant in Japan, had arisen at a time when the ideology of the Degenerate Age was at its height. In one way or another, they all tried to develop a form of Buddhism suitable to an era in which, they believed, the social welfare net and religious education system were at their weakest, when the fabric of social harmony and spiritual education was fraying to the point of disintegration. For Zen, the response to the Degenerate

Age was to retreat into monasticism; for Pure Land, to depend on the transcendent power of Amida's vow; for Nichiren, to lose oneself in the single-minded devotion to the miraculous powers of the *Lotus Sutra*.

From the new Japanese Confucian world view, by contrast, the Kamakura analysis correctly identified the degeneration of society's knowledge and norms of behavior, but the Buddhist response was wrongheaded. The goal, the neo-Confucians argued, should not be to find a way of escaping the social degeneration, but instead to engage society's ills directly so as to reverse the social degeneration itself.

The Confucians believed the theory of the Degenerate Age had deluded the Buddhists into thinking human beings were helpless in the face of their social and intellectual problems. That is, in their quest for personal enlightenment (whether through *zazen, shinjin,* or the *daimoku*), the Buddhists had underestimated the potential of the social interdependence that defines human nature. Buddhism not only lacked the Confucian value of humaneness but, the Confucians argued, its philosophical anthropology—its theory of what it means to be fully a human being—was inadequate.

The Confucians agreed with the Buddhists about the importance of purifying your mind, but they insisted that was not enough: such a goal must be embedded in a larger project of returning to the social harmony inspired by the humanistic paradigms of the Confucian classics. The center of that praxis was not meditating, not praying, not chanting, but the scholarly study of the right texts until their virtuous paradigms became second nature and manifest in your activities as a member of society.

As we will see later in this chapter and the next, much of Edo-period Confucianism's scholarly study focused on unpacking central concepts, expanding on Confucius' idea that political and social harmony derives from understanding the key terms of human interrelationship and enacting them as the fundamental virtues. That was the ideal of the "trueing up of terms" or, as it is also commonly translated, "the rectification of names" (C. *zhengming*; J. *seimei*). When Chen Beixi's (1159–1223) Chinese treatise, *The Meaning of Confucian Terms*, was brought to Japan in the late sixteenth century, it became a template and inspiration for several Japanese Confucian thinkers.

293; 304

This focus on language was especially attractive to the Rinzai monks of the Five Mountain system, which had given them an excellent education in Chinese studies, including an appreciation of the classical Chinese lexicon. The Rinzai monks were not only literate but also literary. The traditional Confucian emphasis on music and poetry as models of harmony to be carried over into social affairs of the everyday world had already influenced their training. Indeed, in many cases they relished that aspect of their Rinzai Zen education over more traditional Zen practices.[20]* Living a privileged lifestyle with access to the court and shogunate, already steeped in the classical Chinese arts and letters, some Rinzai monks undoubtedly gravitated toward the ideal of the erudite Confucian scholar as teacher and sagely political advisor. To them, it might have seemed not so much something new as an improved version of what they were already doing.

From Zen to Confucianism: The Case of Fujiwara Seika. An early example in the transition from Rinzai Zen Buddhism to Confucianism, Fujiwara Seika (1561–1619) blazed the trail for the Japanese Confucian revival. He started his career as a Rinzai Zen monk at Shōkoku-ji, one of Kyoto's Five Mountain institutions. Disaffected with what he perceived to be the degeneration of Buddhism from a tradition focused on spiritual cultivation to one emulating courtier culture fixated on the arts and ostentation, he started reading more widely in the Chinese intellectual tradition. The turning point was when he had the opportunity to become a student of the Korean neo-Confucian official-scholar, Kang Hang (1567–1618), a prisoner captured and brought to Japan by Hideyoshi's invasion force.

298-303

Although Seika became a major proponent of Confucianism in Japan,[21]* he did not entirely abandon Buddhism. The issue for him was whether to interpret neo-Confucianism as an improved form of Zen or Zen as a subordinate part of neo-Confucianism. In other words: could Zen relegate the new Confucianism or could the new Confucianism relegate Zen? If we look at the extended following passage, we can see how Seika's rhetoric negotiated that issue.

> If you have any plans of your own in [mind], no higher wisdom will emerge. We may compare this to a mirror. Things are dust. If the inside of the mirror is clean and bright, a speck of dust can be wiped away immediately so that you can see clearly. The clarity and brightness in this mirror is called the [void]. Within it there is spirit or what we may also call supreme goodness. *The Doctrine of the Mean* speaks of it as an equilibrium before the stirring of feelings (i.4) and [Confucius'] *Analects* as an "all-pervading unity"(iv.15). Where there is clean and limpid lucidity within the mirror, there also are void and spirit.
>
> If one devises ways to dispose of things, those devices themselves become things. It only takes a single speck of darkness or murkiness in the mind for all kinds of thoughts to appear. Without these thoughts, clear knowledge would be born naturally as void and spirit, and as a result one would in all things "hit what is right without effort" (*Mean* xx.18). Thinking about not having thoughts entails having thoughts. It is not that thoughts are to be despised, only that thoughts should come to the fore naturally. This is what is called the great working of the whole.

298-9

In the passage Seika's emphasis on mind, void, and even the metaphor of the dusty mirror are all classically Buddhist themes and would have been familiar to him from his Zen training. So would have been the emphasis on naturalness, which has origins in Daoism as well as Buddhism. Even his distinctions among thoughts, thinking about not having thoughts, and thoughts arising naturally correlates well with Dōgen's analysis of thinking/not-thinking/without-thinking.[†] Therefore, much of Seika's terminology could be considered not especially Confucian at all.

Yet, the rhetoric of the passage is revealing. The citations are not from Buddhist but Confucian texts (the *Analects* and the *Doctrine of the Mean*). Although on the surface Seika's passage is conceptually syncretistic in integrating Buddhist, Daoist, and Confucian ideas, the rhetorical structure makes the Buddhist and Daoist ideas seem like interpretive glosses on classic Confucian points. And the final goal of the praxis is framed in terms of "supreme goodness," a Confucian rather than a Buddhist term (such as "enlightenment," for example). If Seika was consciously doing this, it was an extraordinarily subtle and sophisticated move toward relegating Buddhism to a subordinate position within Confucianism: Zen's role is merely to support Confucian ideas and values.

Of course, if one wanted to relegate Buddhist ideas into a greater neo-Confucian philosophy, the most obvious way to do so would be to work from the already completed system of the Chinese philosopher, Zhu Xi. By the end of the sixteenth century, Zhu Xi's philosophy had become preeminent in both China and Korea, having withstood its critics for four centuries. Why reinvent the wheel in Japan if one could just import it from China? That was the approach of Hayashi Razan (1561–1619), who also started out as a Zen Buddhist, then studied a bit with Seika, and finally specialized in the thought of Zhu Xi, making full use of commentaries he acquired from the scholarly Korean prisoners of war. Razan is often considered the founder of the Japanese Zhu Xi tradition of philosophy, the refinement of which became the Hayashi family business for generations as they tried to make their philosophy attractive to the new Tokugawa shogunate.

304–17

Shushigaku: The Japanese Zhu Xi School.[‡] Razan brought neo-Confucianism to the shogun at least partially in the guise of Buddhism—literally. Using his acquaintance with Tokugawa Ieyasu, Fujiwara Seika had secured a position for his student Razan as one of the many advisors to the shogunate, but there was a condition. Following what had by then been a centuries-old tradition, the shogunate would accept only Buddhist monks as advisors and Razan had only a couple of years of Zen training, and even that only as a young boy. Not dissuaded,

---

† See pages 217-19.

‡ In this book *Zhu Xi School* and *Wang Yangming School* refer to the philosophical traditions found broadly in China, Korea, or Japan. The Japanese *Shushigaku* and *Yōmeigaku* refer specifically to the respective schools as developed in Japan.

Statue of Confucius
at Yushima Seidō

he shaved his head like a monk and took to wearing Buddhist robes. Would the strategy succeed? How would the Tokugawa shoguns respond to a neo-Confucian in Buddhist clothing? Part of the answer can be found at a serene site sequestered within today's pulsating Tokyo book district.

Our specific destination is Yushima Seidō, an artifact of Japan's golden age of Confucianism. Yushima Seidō (the Yushima[22] Hall of Sages), located in Tokyo's Ochanomizu[23]* ("Tea Water") area, is nestled in an enclosed, park-like grove of trees along the banks of the Kanda River. The proper entrance is at river level below the heavily trafficked Hijiribashi ("Bridge of Sages"). After descending the stairs to the river, we pass an outdoor statue of Confucius, some four-and-a-half meters high, a gift from the Lion's Club of Taipei in 1975. In today's Japan such Confucian monuments are not prevalent, so its presence alerts us to the distinctive character of the place we are about to enter. We come to a stairway that starts from the Apricot Gate labeled with its lacquered plaque reading "The Gateway for Entering Virtue." Passing through, we climb the stairs until we reach the next gate that opens to the courtyard in front of the building called *Taiseiden,* the Temple of Great Accomplishment.

Once inside, we find a Confucian temple of learning, with offerings to

Interior of Hall of Great Accomplishment

Confucius and images of the great Confucian sages of history, including the generations of the academy's headmasters, most of whom were members of the Hayashi family. Although the building has been rebuilt and relocated several times, it goes back to the original Confucian shrine and school founded by Hayashi Razan in 1630 with support from the third Tokugawa shogun, Iemitsu. Toward the end of that century, it was moved by the fifth Tokugawa shogun to its present site, where in the late eighteenth century it served as the official academy of the shogunate under the direction of the Hayashi family. In many ways Yushima Seidō's role paralleled that of the court academy (*daigaku*) in ancient times, except its purpose was classical training for the retainers of the shogunate instead of the court.

After the fall of the shogunate in 1867, Yushima academy, the temple, and its lands transferred to imperial control. It served variously as headquarters for the National Museum, the Ministry of Education, and what later became two major national universities, Ochanomizu Women's University and Tsukuba University. Today the surrounding Ochanomizu district in Tokyo is also home to several colleges and universities (some built on lands formerly held by the academy), the largest book-selling district in Japan (Jinbōchō) especially famous for its used and antiquary books, and shops selling musical instruments (today mostly electric guitars and synthesizers rather than the bamboo flutes, koto, and shamisen of olden days). Ochanomizu abuts Kanda, the home to many of Japan's most prestigious publishing houses. With such a history, Yushima Seidō clearly symbolizes a center of learning, not only for the Edo period, but for the modern as well. It also proves that Razan's stratagem had worked, but as I will now explain, only to a certain extent.

We have seen why the Rinzai monks and the townspeople might have admired neo-Confucianism, but why would the Tokugawa shoguns underwrite its study? Before going further, it need be said that despite appearances, Shushigaku Confucianism was not the "official ideology" of the Tokugawa regime that many scholars had once thought.[24] In fact, it seems the shogunate did not have any dominant ideology but rather dealt with matters on an *ad hoc* basis. Admittedly, Yushima Seidō with its adjoining official academy of the Tokugawa retainers, was under the direction of the Hayashi School of Shushigaku, but the school was not as prominent nor as lavishly supported by the Tokugawas as the Hayashi family accounts boasted.

Furthermore, the shogunate's respect for Confucianism was certainly not religious—the Tokugawas generally belonged to the Pure Land Sect, the tradition of Hōnen.[25] Indeed, despite the altar and offerings found at Yushima Seidō, this Japanese Confucianism was not particularly religious in either its beliefs or rituals, the formal observances of note being only the semi-annual *sekiten* rite celebrating the Confucian masters.

Indeed, I suspect an attractive feature of neo-Confucianism for the shoguns was that it was *not* religious in the way Buddhism and Christianity were. With the troubles it had with religious fanatics from those groups, the Tokugawa shogunate was not about to endorse any religion as a path to national unity and social harmony. If they could successfully secularize Japanese values and knowledge, however, the people might be loyal to the secular center of power—the shogunate.

In fact, if there was a dominant ideological theme throughout the period, especially in the samurai way of thinking, it was *loyalty*, a traditional Confucian virtue elevated to new heights in Japan.[26] As the tablet on the Apricot Gate suggests, the Confucian focus was on virtue, particularly civic or social virtue and the shogunate had a vested interest in its people's expressing those virtues as loyalty to the regime. Perhaps the highest loyalty, certainly spiritual loyalty, was directed to the emperor, but Tokugawa Ieyasu had been officially appointed by the emperor to run the state. (The hereditary title "shogun" could only be conferred by the emperor, an honor that had been withheld from Ieyasu's predecessor Hideyoshi, for example.)

So the Tokugawa regime with its hierarchy of classes, its extensive bureaucracy of law and commerce, its complex coordination and supervision of daimyō across the land—that whole system assumed a culture based in loyalty. The Tokugawa state depended on people's loyalty to society and to the state, not to some sutra or buddha or *kami* or Zen tradition and certainly not to a foreign Christian God. How could such loyalty and virtue be instilled in the people? Through education in the proper relational paradigms of human community. By engaging the right virtues as displayed in exemplary classical Chinese didactic texts, a person would become virtuous, and if everyone were virtuous, society would be harmonious.

In the end, the rise to eminence of the Hayashi house is not the true significance of Yushima Seidō. After all, even among neo-Confucian academies, Yushima Seidō was not large: Yamazaki Ansai (1618–1682) had established a tuition-paying academy with some 6000 students, for example. Instead, that isolated complex on the banks of the Kanda River best exemplifies something larger than the fate of a single family. It represents a historic shift in Japanese intellectual culture—education would henceforth move primarily from the religious monastic centers to secular academies. Some academies, like Yushima Seidō, would be run by the shogunate or at the regional level by local daimyō. Those academies trained their own samurai bureaucrats as well as the heads of peasant villages. Many more, like Ansai's, were urban schools supported by student tuition.

The Tokugawa shoguns had decided that social order and efficient political administration require the dissemination and administration of laws and that, in turn, required at least pockets of literacy. No tradition in Japan valued literacy and the appreciation of classic moral texts more than Confucianism and the secular academies became part of a cultural movement that, as I mentioned earlier, made Japan in the late seventeenth century one of the most literate, perhaps *the* most literate, country in the world. Of course, as one might expect in the competitive marketplace of ideas, there were significant points of philosophical contention.

Confucian Critiques of Neo-Confucianism

Yamaga Sokō (1622–1685). Sokō had two lasting tracks of influence on Edo thought which put him at odds with the most prominent Shushigaku philosopher of the era, Satō Naokata (1650–1719). The first was Sokō's sharp critique of the Zhu Xi School and the second was his valorization of the medieval warrior ethos. I will address both vectors of Sokō's influence, indicating some of the implications for various later philosophers. Let us begin with his critique of Zhu Xi neo-Confucianism, deferring discussion of the samurai warrior ethic to a subsequent section of this chapter.

335–46

First, although trained as a Shushigaku scholar, in the last third of his life Yamaga Sokō abandoned the Chinese Song and Ming commentaries to focus on the original ancient classics and the early Confucian thinkers, especially Confucius and Mencius. In 1665 he wrote *Essential Records of the Sagely Teachings,* a text interpreted by many Shushigaku thinkers to be such an impudent affront to Zhu Xi's thought that they successfully conspired within the shogunate to get Sokō exiled from Edo for ten years. That event signaled a major rift among the Japanese Confucians between those who favored the neo-Confucian metaphysics of principle against those who argued for a return to the nonmetaphysical moral and social orientation of "original Confucianism."

The term *original* was variously defined by the anti-Shushigaku critics, but none understood it to extend later than the three classical Confucian philosophers—Confucius, Mencius, and Xunzi—the last of whom lived more than a millennium before the neo-Confucian tradition is considered to have begun. Sokō's classicist critique was elaborated by such later luminaries of the age as Itō Jinsai, Kaibara Ekken, and the subject of our next chapter, Ogyū Sorai.

347–59

Itō Jinsai (1627–1705). Perhaps the first townsman of neither Buddhist nor samurai background to establish himself as a major Confucian philosopher, Jinsai's classicist tradition argued for a re-emphasis on the ideas and values preceding the neo-Confucian innovations, his school being known as Kokigaku (Learning the ancient meanings). He criticized Zhu Xi's philosophy for being based in detachment rather than engagement. The Shushigaku philosophers, he claimed, had metaphysically grounded their whole system in something transcendent and static: principle or, even more problematically, a ground at the basis of principle called variously the supreme ultimate (*taikyoku*), the ultimate of nonbeing (*mukyoku*) or simply the void (*kyo*).

1265, 1267

Epistemologically, Jinsai objected to the Shushigaku claim that to know principle one had to achieve a mental quietude detached from affect and permeated with what Zhu Xi had called *seriousness* or *reverence* (*kei*). Jinsai instead argued for a more vitalistic image of reality as based in generative force (*ki*; C. *qi*). For him "principle" was no more than an empty abstraction distilled from the dynamics of *ki*: "Obviously [principle] did not exist first and then *ki* come later. Principle is simply the rationale existing within *ki*." Jinsai saw principle as something "dead" and, therefore, incapable of influencing the vital flow of *ki*.[27] Moreover, such vitalism could not be known through detachment, but had to be engaged.

348

Jinsai found the key to that engagement in the primary traditional Confucian virtue of humaneness or benevolence (C. *ren*; J. *jin*), which Jinsai believed clashed with Shushigaku's pursuit of transcendent principle carried out through the dispassionate "investigation of things." Humaneness, he claimed, is not embedded in objective, dispassionate observation, but rather in active engagement through *love*. Along those lines, Jinsai claimed that the neo-Confucians wrongheadedly tried to exclude all "feelings" from the function of pure "mind."

> Human feelings are the desires of human nature; they are what activate people.... If compassion, shame, deference, and right and wrong do not belong to the mind, where do they belong? If one calls them feelings rather than parts of the mind, then what is mind? One might as well abandon the notion altogether and speak only of human feelings.

355

The problem with neo-Confucianism, as Jinsai saw it, was its assimilation of Buddhist ideas, even if ultimately only to relegate them to a subordinate position. Through the influence of Buddhism, he argued, Confucian had lost its emphasis on the practicality of rightness in favor of transcendent concerns more akin to the Buddhist pursuit of Dharma. As a result, they had abandoned "the great Path of the world" to "travel among the thorns and bushes" of Buddhism that will "get them nowhere." He claimed the neo-Confucians viewed the primary Confucian virtue of benevolence "abstractly, as if it were unimportant" and "they seem not to realize that they have fallen into a bitter, heartless teaching."

353

Kaibara Ekken (1630–1714).[28] Like Jinsai, Ekken was a vitalist who rejected the neo-Confucian priority given to principle, believing it led to a false bifurcation between principle and generative force.[29] Perhaps because he was a physician and naturalist (he wrote a pioneering work on botany called *Plants of Japan*),

360-73

Ekken argued that there is one basic elemental reality which any form of knowledge must engage, namely, generative force, a vital energy surging through all things (not only what we normally consider living things).

Unlike Jinsai, however, Ekken never formally left the fold of Shushigaku. Indeed he wrote the first Japanese commentary on Zhu Xi's *Reflections on Things at Hand*. Still, he sharply criticized the impractical, intellectualist trend his tradition had undertaken, sometimes using Zhu Xi's own ideas to refute what Shushigaku had become. We see the ambiguity in his position in the following passage. In it he clearly disapproves of the way that Shushigaku had developed and calls for a return to the classical Confucian insights. His blanket censure of "Song Confucian scholars" would technically include Zhu Xi. Yet in referring to the model of learning from "things close at hand," he seems to be referencing Zhu Xi against the other neo-Confucians.

> ...Confucius considered filial piety, obedience, loyalty and sincerity as fundamental, and he regarded learning as involving both study and practice.... This means we learn from things close at hand and progress to higher levels.
>
> Song Confucian scholars, however, felt it was urgent to make it their first priority to pursue the truth by understanding the supreme ultimate and the nonfinite, to pursue practice by quiet sitting and purifying the heart, and to pursue scholarship by detailed analysis. Being both lofty and abstract, trivial and impractical, this learning of the Song Confucians came to be regarded as difficult to understand and to put into practice. Yet Song Confucian scholars took these useless and unimportant issues as their first priority.

363

For Ekken, the proper approach is to engage what is near at hand—the vital phenomena of the physical world—and to discover their workings. Philosophical reflection should always serve the practical betterment of society.[30] Keeping to that commitment, Ekken wrote an influential book on the proper education of women according to Confucian standards, *The Book of Great Learning for Women*. By today's standards, the book is fraught with the customary sexist prejudices, but it does represent Ekken's idea that for society to be harmonious, the Confucian teachings must be explained in an accessible way that anyone can understand and follow.

We might wonder how Ekken might respond today to the question of education for women. Would he narrow-mindedly stand by his reading of the tradition or would he learn from the immense changes in gender roles that have evolved since his time? I raise this question because Ekken spoke out against rigid dogmatism, one of his guiding insights being that all humans are susceptible to error and bias. So we must always doubt our results and submit them to further "investigation of things."

With regard to his naturalism, Ekken's philosophy was not so positivistic and empirical as to lack a sense of spiritual wonder. He called heaven and earth the "great parents," arguing that we should show the filial piety toward the natural world that we show our own parents. Therefore, although he did not share Jinsai's emphasis on love, Ekken nonetheless did recognize the role of the affective in engaging both the natural and social worlds.

Ogyū Sorai (1666–1728). Since our next chapter will engage Ogyū Sorai's thought in detail, I will not here go into his critiques of the neo-Confucians except to point out that he, too, made a call to return to the classical tradition, expunging all the Buddhist and Daoist influences introduced by the neo-Confucians. As a classicist Confucian, Sorai was such a purist that he believed no texts after Confucius's *Analects* constituted true Confucianism and even the *Analects* was important only because it points back to the wisdom of the ancient classics that had preceded it. 393–410

As for the relation between principle and generative force, Sorai had a different take on the issue from Jinsai or Ekken. Specifically, he believed the entire discussion of generative force (including its relation to principle) was spurious since the word does not occur in the *Analects*. Lastly, Sorai worried that a samurai mentality was developing in Japan, one that threatened to confuse martial loyalty with the more classic Confucian virtues. That object of concern leads into our next topic: the theorization of the samurai's role in Edo society.

THE WARRIOR ETHOS OF THE EDO PERIOD

As I already explained, the Tokugawa shogunate imposed a four-level class structure in which the samurai enjoyed status above that of farmers, tradesman, and merchants. Since there were no longer major wars but only isolated and intermittent skirmishes, there was no longer the need for a substantial military force. That raised an identity problem for the samurai: if they were no longer primarily warriors, what were they? Without the opportunity to apply their skills in warfare, what practical purpose could they serve in the new Pax Tokugawa? The first philosopher to seriously address those questions was the aforementioned Yamaga Sokō, whom I have treated so far as a classicist critic of neo-Confucianism.[†] His valorization of the samurai character is his second track of influence in Edo-period thinking, the topic to which I now turn.

---

† See page 312.

Theorizing the Samurai

Yamaga Sokō's role for the samurai. Yamaga Sokō was the son of a masterless samurai (*rōnin*) and in his displacement, his father relocated the family to Edo to seek better opportunities. Although Sokō, as we have seen, ended up rejecting the Shushigaku Confucianism he had studied in his early and middle years, there was one philosophical constant throughout his life, namely, his commitment to the art of the warrior. He was a brilliant strategist, publishing his influential *Anthology of Martial Strategies* in 1642 when he was only twenty. Throughout this chapter we have been attentive to the market forces at play in the commodification of knowledge during the Edo period. So, the question is: what market was Sokō's martial philosophy serving? To a great extent, it was the almost desperate need for the samurai to justify their existence and their superior class status in a time of peace.

Sokō led the movement to transform the samurai from being simply a warrior to a person with a warrior *mentality* and, beyond that, to define a role for such a person in the newly evolving peacetime society of the Edo period. According to Sokō, besides duty to his lord, the samurai should be a contributing member of society at large. As he put it, the samurai "will not be able to avoid involvement in parent-child, sibling, and spousal relationships." Furthermore, unlike the lower classes who are so busy with their jobs,

> the samurai puts aside the tasks of the farmers, artisans, and merchants to make the Way his exclusive duty. In addition, if ever a person who is improper with regard to human morality appears among the three common classes, the samurai quickly punishes them, thus safeguarding true heavenly morality on earth.

1109

In explaining the samurai function in the social system, Sokō introduced a contrast between the inner and outer dimensions of duty. Outwardly, the samurai was trained in the martial skills, but inwardly, he focused on his role in the binary relationships. "In his mind, he pursues the civility of letters, while outwardly he is prepared martially." If the samurai succeeds in both directions, the "three common classes make him their teacher and honor him, and by following his teaching come to know what is essential and what is insignificant...."

1109

To summarize: Sokō was not so much developing a Way of the Warrior (*bushidō*) as defining how the Confucian Way applies to samurai. As I will explain in Chapter 11, the idea of a distinctive Way emerging from the warrior mentality does not fully come into its own until there is a romanticized reconstruction of the tradition in the early twentieth century. Sokō further insisted that the standards of morality for the samurai are higher than those of the other three social classes precisely because the samurai, not at war, have time to study and cultivate the five Confucian relations. And lastly, he maintained that the samurai are not only moral exemplars to be held in high regard by others, but also the enforcers who punish those who deviate from the Way and disrupt social harmony.

Nakae Tōju (1608–1648). The most prominent philosopher of Yōmeigaku (the Japanese neo-Confucian School of Wang Yangming) was Nakae Tōju. Following the Yōmeigaku emphasis on the inseparability of thought and action, Tōju argued that a true Confucian should not isolate the cultural arts of the scholar from the martial arts of the warrior. "Originally, letters and arms were a single virtue, and not a thing that could be separated...." Like his contemporary Sokō, he advocated a policing role for the samurai against those "with malicious intent" who would go against the Way. In 1651 he articulated the two dimensions as follows:

> "Letters" means correctly practicing the way of filial piety, brotherliness, loyalty, and sincerity. "Arms" means striving to eliminate things that obstruct filial piety, brotherliness, loyalty, and sincerity.

Tōju's analysis arose from his concern that the unbridled warrior mentality could easily get out of control and therefore needed to be restrained with Confucian training as a scholar. He had explicitly warned against developing martial skills so as to "become fond of killing people" and for that reason, the samurai had to train in the "learning of the mind as well." He was particularly cynical about ostentatious displays of the warrior mentality in times in peace. "In peaceful and uneventful times, being obsessed with displays of bravery and courage for the sake of preparing oneself for battle is to be obsessed with an ignorant and useless pursuit."

Sokō's and Tōju's attempts to bridle the martial aspects of the samurai were not completely successful. Within a few decades, a competing popular characterization of the samurai mentality emerged, one in which virtue arose from within the martial rather than as an externally imposed constraint. A good example is Yamamoto Tsunetomo (1659–1719) and his 1716 martial classic *Hagakure* (*In the Shadow of Leaves*[31]), which begins:

> The Way of the warrior is to die....This is the strength of the martial Way. Every morning and evening, one should die again, and when one has entered a state in which one is constantly living in a body that is already dead, one will grasp the freedom of the martial Way. One will be able to fulfill the duties of his position without error throughout his life.

The fixation on a mentality focused on death, as we will see later in this chapter, drew on a particular rhetoric used in Rinzai Zen earlier in the Edo

318–23; 1110

1110–11

321

321–2

1106

period,† but I suspect this new type of romanticized, extremist language and sentiment was also fueled by an increasingly powerful obsession with loyalty. From the standpoint of the new ideology of the samurai, loyalty was a virtue steeped in the martial way rather than a virtue learned from Confucian texts. Concerning loyalty, *Hagakure* says:

> If one is devoted to service, forgetting reason and forgetting his own self, and places greatest importance on his lord without consideration for secondary or tertiary matters, everything will become clear and settled…. By being excessively devoted to service and placing utmost importance on one's lord, it is possible that one will make mistakes, but this is the truly desirable approach.
>
> Although it is said that excess is bad in all things, if one is a retainer, excessive devotion to one's service that results in mistakes is actually an expression of true desire. People who look at things through reason will generally become hung up on minor details and live their lives in vain.

1108

When viewing together the two passages from *Hagakure*, the ambiguity becomes clear. The first passage tells us that if we think of ourselves as already dead, we can perform our duties "without error." Yet, the second passage says that it is better to err out of an emotional excess of loyalty than "to look at things through reason." Philosophers like Jinsai and Ekken had argued for the recognition of Confucian feeling to complement Confucian reason. But now, in this more militant ideology, feeling was trumping reason itself. What had changed? The tension between duty and loyalty or between principled behavior and emotion lay at the heart of the famous Akō Incident and the frenzy of debate swirling around it.

The Akō Incident and the Issue of Loyalty

Loyalty was a well-established value in Japan, its having been mentioned as far back as Article 6 of Shōtoku's *Seventeen-Article Constitution*. Moreover, the Tokugawa state ideology, I have been arguing, coalesced around that sense of loyalty. Although it lacked the status of being one of the five Confucian "cardinal virtues"—benevolence, rightness, ritual propriety, wisdom, and trustworthiness—loyalty did play a role in the classical system's analysis of the five dyadic relationships insofar as loyalty was the virtue to be shown by the minister to the ruler, just as filial piety was to be displayed by the child in relation to the parent. In Japan, though, amid the upheavals of the medieval period

37

† See pages 337–8.

with its ever-shifting alliances, affinity groups, and acts of treachery, loyalty also accrued a distinctly military sense: loyalty of the samurai retainer to one's lord.

That samurai loyalty was not merely recognizing and deferring to authority or hierarchy, but also involved a deep affective tie to your lord and the house you served. In the Edo period, the Tokugawa shogunate hoped to direct that loyalty to itself, away from the samurai's traditional ties to regional lords. As I will explain in Chapter 11, loyalty (this time to the emperor instead of the shogun) would play a key role in the downfall of the Tokugawa regime. In short: the particulars in the social and cultural construction of loyalty as a virtue played a key role in times of political change throughout the Edo period. Since the Akō Incident and the controversy crystallizing around it exemplifies so well the search for an ideology of loyalty at a critical time in Japanese history, I will begin with a summary of the key events.

The incident. Our story begins late at night in early January 1703 in the Ichiriki tea house, still standing today in the Gion section of Kyoto. (See photo below.) Our interest is in a samurai, passed out in drunkenness, huddled in the corner of the room where he has spent the night—as he has done for many months now—drinking, gambling, and carousing with the geishas. His name is Ōishi Yoshio (aka Kuranosuke, 1639–1703), a samurai formerly under the employ of Asano Naganori (1667–1701), lord of the powerful Akō domain.

Lord Asano had been forced to commit suicide in the spring of 1701 for the crime of pulling his sword and drawing blood while on the premises of the shogun's castle. He had been there as part of his alternate residence service requirement in Edo and had been charged with supervising a highly ritualized visit of

Ichiriki Teahouse Today

the emperor's emissaries from Kyoto. In such refinements, Asano was no expert and he had to learn proprieties from Lord Kira Yoshinaka (1641–1703), the shogunate's authority for such affairs. Kira apparently enjoyed treating Asano as a country bumpkin and may have intentionally misled him on points of protocol so that Asano would appear a rube. In any case, unable to tolerate the perceived humiliation any longer, in violation of all regulations about behavior in the shogun's court, the fiery Asano drew his sword and wounded Kira, cutting him on the forehead and shoulder. Asano was immediately restrained before he could complete his murderous intention.

Justice for Asano was harsh and swift: that same day Asano was tried by the shogun's officials, found guilty, stripped of his title and holdings, and forced to perform *seppuku*, ritual suicide. Kira, on the other hand, was praised for not drawing his own sword in defense. Though injured, he was well enough to return home, where he put his guards on alert should Asano's retainers, now masterless *rōnin*, attempt to retaliate.

When Ōishi relocated to Kyoto some months later, Kira kept him under surveillance. After many more months passed, it was clear to Kira's men that the derelict Ōishi had neither the will nor wherewithal to be a threat. Kira relaxed his security.

Toward the end of January in 1703, Ōishi abruptly stopped his nightly visits to the tea house and nobody seemed to know his whereabouts. Then word came that he had rendezvoused with his fellow former Asano retainers to carry out their revenge against Kira. It seems that forty-seven of Asano's former retainers had about a year earlier taken an oath to kill Kira, but seeing the tactical difficulties, assumed the guise of moral laxity and physical decrepitude as a ploy inducing Kira to drop his guard. The plan worked perfectly and forty-six[†] of the "loyal retainers" killed Kira on January 31, presenting his decapitated head to Asano's grave at Sengaku-ji, a temple in Edo. They then turned themselves over to the shogun's authorities who tried them and ordered them all to commit *seppuku*. Today at Sengaku-ji in Tokyo near the Shinagawa train station, one can visit their graves alongside that of their master.[32] (See photo on facing page.)

The Edo period's newly installed media infrastructure circulated news of the exploits of the "forty-seven loyal retainers" throughout Japan and almost immediately spawned a public controversy involving many leading intellectuals of the day. So much so, the shogenate imposed a gag order on publications. Yet, the event still became the stuff of both literature and stage, including Takeda Izumo's classic 1748 puppet (*bunraku*) play, *Treasury of the Loyal Retainers*

---

† Forty-seven retainers had taken the oath of revenge but only forty-six were tried. A nonsamurai member of the group was apparently ordered home to Akō to keep him out of the trial and presumably to inform families about the deed. Hence the discrepancy in numbering.

Tombstones of the 46 *Rōnin* at Sengaku Temple

(*Chūshingura*), the paradigm for countless dramatic productions on stage and film up to the present.

For our philosophical interests, it is significant that so many Japanese were no longer bound to the medieval media of oral accounts, secrets, and rumors. They could now *read* about the event, and the intellectuals—always vying for publicity in the era of the commodification of knowledge—could *write* about it, knowing their views could be dispersed across the country to colleagues and students. Hence, we have a classic instance of a philosophical debate made public through the medium of print. If we look at the range of philosophical responses the event provoked, we will not only better understand the ideology of loyalty, but we will also get a much broader picture of the intellectual scene than just what neo-Confucianism as an academic school represents.

The philosophical controversy. The Akō Incident spurred a debate over two conflicting interpretations of loyalty. Hayashi Hōkō (1644–1732), Razan's grandson and the head of the shogun's academy in its new location at Yushima Seidō, was politically astute in voicing both sides of the argument:[33]

> ...First, I will view their vendetta from the perspective of the hearts of the forty-six men. It was imperative that they "not share the same sky with their master's enemy" and that they "sleep on reeds, using their sword as a pillow" [*Record of Rites*]. ...To hang onto life by enduring shame and humiliation is not the Way of the samurai.
>
> We must also consider the vendetta from the perspective of the law. Anyone who sees the law as his enemy must be put to death. Although the forty-six

men were carrying out the last wishes of the deceased lord, they could not do so without committing a capital crime in the process.[34]

Hōkō's citations were all from Chinese Confucian texts, but he did refer to the "Way of the samurai," hinting it might have a code of its own.

On one side of the debate conservative Confucians maintained that the original meaning of loyalty was loyalty not to one's lord, but to the ruler, which in this case meant the shogun and his court's juridical sentence. The aforementioned Confucian classicist, Ogyū Sorai, followed that line of argument:

> Forgetting his ancestors and acting no more courageously than a common fellow, Lord Asano yielded to a moment of anger that morning and thus failed in his attempt to kill Lord Kira. Lord Asano's behavior must be deemed not-rightness (*fugi*). At best, the forty-seven men can be said to have deftly carried out their master's evil intentions. How can that be called rightness (*gi*)?[35]

In other words, how can two wrongs make a right? To twice defy the law is certainly worse than to defy it once.

The prominent leader of the neo-Confucian Shushigaku tradition, the aforementioned Satō Naokata, was normally at odds with Sorai on various issues but on this point they saw the situation eye-to-eye. Naokata was, first of all, critical of Lord Asano's original violent action because he had shown no sense of ritual propriety. Specifically, even if he felt honor required him to attack Lord Kira, Asano should have restrained his anger until the ritualized visit of the emissaries had concluded.

Naokata was equally critical of the *rōnin* for not respecting the legal judgment of the shogun's court. Indeed, after they had flouted the law by killing Kira, the *rōnin* pleaded their case to the judicial system as if there could be some excuse for such disrespect.

> If later they had reflected on the nature of their crime [in killing Kira], a violation of the shōgun's law, and committed suicide at the temple of Sengaku-ji, their intentions would have merited sympathy despite the wrongness of their deed. Instead they reported their deed to the inspector general and waited for a verdict from the shogunate.... But was not such behavior part of a scheme meant to win them praise? Having committed a capital crime and blatantly having disobeyed the authorities, there was no need for them to report anything, nor was there any need to wait for a verdict. These were not the acts of men who had readied themselves for death....

Naokata wondered how such a mad distortion of the virtue of loyalty could come about and placed the blame on the retainers' teacher in the Akō domain, his old rival and neo-Confucian apostate, Yamaga Sokō (1622–1685).[36]

As the *rōnin* were being immortalized in literature, philosophy, and on the stage, the interpretation arose that their deeds were valorous precisely because they were irrational. Even a young philosopher who would later become one of Sorai's most prominent students, Dazai Shundai (1680–1747), succumbed to that clearly un-Confucian sentiment. After giving the appropriate Confucian reasons for condemning the actions much along the lines of Sorai or Naokata, Shundai then added an ethnic qualifier:

> Moreover, for samurai of this Eastern country [Japan] there is an indigenous Way: if a samurai sees his lord murdered, he will immediately lose all self-control and become crazed for revenge. Without thought about what is right or wrong, he will leap into the fray believing it is only through death that he can demonstrate his righteousness. Humane men inevitably see such self-sacrifice as a vain waste of life, but they also realize that the state depends on this Way, and thus they strive to preserve it. They also know that this Way is effective in maintaining morale among the samurai. Therefore, it cannot be abandoned.[37]

In effect, Shundai was saying the *rōnin* did not follow Confucianism, did not act rationally, did not act legally, and did not act morally, but what they did was *Japanese* and necessary to the fighting spirit of the samurai and ultimately to the protection of the Japanese state. That emotional and ethnocentric apologetic, one that would fuel the militarism of the nineteenth and twentieth centuries, was not the only way to defend the *rōnin,* however. One could also try to defend them on purely rational, Confucian grounds.

Asami Keisai (1652–1711) was, like Naokata, a Shushigaku neo-Confucian. Yet, he responded to Naokata's criticism of the *rōnin* almost immediately, rejecting the claim that they had not acted in accord with Confucian virtues. Noting that the Confucian tradition in China did indeed allow for the rightness of a son's revenge against the murderer of his father, one only has to recognize further that the relation between lord and retainer is parallel to that of father and son. Therefore, argued Keisai, the *rōnin* were displaying a kind of "filial piety."

384-6

As for Naokata's claim that the *rōnin* were defying the law and therefore not acting with rightness, Keisai said that, to the contrary, they complied with the law and authority of the shogun by voluntarily turning themselves in immediately after the completion of their deed. Their actions were always directed against Kira, never against the shogunate.

Giri and ninjō (duty vs. human feelings). In the Shundai and Keisai apologetics on behalf of the *rōnin*, we have seen that one defense was on the grounds of having the right "human feeling" or "emotion" (*ninjō*) whereas the other was on the grounds of correctness in relation to "duty" (*giri*). *Giri* and *ninjō* were part of the axiological dialectic of the time, a tension between two fundamental human values that was played out not only in philosophical forums but also in literature and on the stage. The tension between *giri* and *ninjō* is, for example, especially highlighted in the some of the puppet plays of Chikamatsu Monzaemon (1653–1724).[38]

Both *giri* and *ninjō* are terms imported from China, both used in Confucian philosophy. In fact, the *giri/ninjō* binary can be seen as parallel to the tension between principle and feelings in the debate among Confucians concerning epistemological issues. For a Confucian like Naokata, the *giri* aspect was dominant because of his focus on Zhu Xi's *seriousness* or *reverence* (*kei*), whereas as we have seen, a Confucian like Itō Jinsai emphasized a central role for affect.[†]

In general, a popular perception was that the Confucians, especially the neo-Confucians, were stern, passionless adherents to a list of virtues strictly governing human behavior. They envisioned in that respect a society ordered by rule-governed relations, a society where duty to the social hierarchy was to be preserved above all else to avoid public scorn and possible legal sanctions. In other words, the popular opinion was that Confucianism, especially Shushigaku, emphasized external relations and detachment.

Some neo-Confucians were aware of that perception of Confucianism as unfeeling and argued that the tradition needed to be more sensitive to the vital role of emotions in its traditional framework. Hori Keizan (1688–1757) was one proponent of that interpretation:

> Now if the highest of all is what the *Analects* call the pursuit of humaneness, this humaneness is the core of human beings and there is no way to seek it except through understanding human feelings.... One must know of what Confucius speaks when he says:
>
>> You want to turn your own merits to account; then help others to turn theirs to account—in fact, the ability to take one's own feelings as a guide—that is the sort of thing that lies in the direction of humaneness. (*Analects* VI.28).
>
> Without understanding human feelings, how can one compare one's own situation with that of another?

As we will see in Chapter 10, Keizan was one of Motoori Norinaga's mentors and his sensitivity to the affective aspect of human nature may have influenced his student's valorization of the emotions in his Native Studies philosophy. It is also noteworthy that Keizan's emphasis on knowing human emotions through emotions echoes Murasaki's argument in defense of fiction in *The Tale of Genji*.[‡]

---

† See page 313.

‡ See pages 141–3.

1261
1175-6

In discussing the debate between Satō Naokata and Asami Keisai over the meaning of loyalty and rightness in the Akō Incident, I noted they were both from the Shushigaku tradition. Their connection was actually closer than that and it points us in the direction of another, as yet unmentioned, intellectual stream of the Edo period. Both were students (among the six thousand) of the aforementioned Yamazaki Ansai, but they left the fold for different reasons. For Keisai the rift arose from some of Ansai's Confucian interpretations,[39*] but in the case of Naokata, it was because Ansai had begun to synthesize neo-Confucianism with Shintō. Naokata was a purist who would not countenance any diluting of the Confucian tradition. This brings us to the position of Shintō in Edo-period Japanese philosophy.

SHINTŌ AND BUDDHISM IN THE EDO PERIOD

As we have seen in previous chapters, Shintō (or at least proto-Shintō) had started to develop some ideology of its own back in the Nara period with the publication of the chronicles, *Kojiki* and *Nihonshoki*. Yet, as an independent philosophical tradition, Shintō's maturation was subsequently stunted by its being relegated to a subordinate position within the system of esoteric Buddhism. In the medieval period, some schools of thought began to emerge, the Yoshida tradition of One-and-only Shintō (Yuiitsu Shintō) being the most comprehensive and probably most influential. Still, compared with Buddhism, Shintō philosophizing had not yet come into its own, a situation that would change in the Edo period.

Japanese Confucianism and Shintō

I begin with a few comments about how the Edo-period Confucians in general viewed Shintō. Not surprisingly, like most other topics of the time, they took a variety of positions. From the beginning of the Japanese neo-Confucian movement, Fujiwara Seika insisted there was nothing in the newly introduced philosophy that would exclude either Shintō practice or the idea that the *kami*, Amaterasu, is the foundation of imperial legitimacy. "The Way of sincerity [the Shintō virtue of 'genuineness' (*makoto*)] is the sincerity of heaven's own Way," noting further in reference to the ruler: "If, however, one is honest and compassionate to the people, then regardless of whether one prays to the *kami*, one will gain their protection." Thus, Seika saw Confucianism as complementary to Shintō or even interchangeable with it: "The names may differ, but the spirit is the same."

300

300-1

301

Yamazaki Ansai, by contrast, emphasized the virtue of "reverence" (*kei*) in the Confucian tradition, but did so in a way that included reverence toward the Shintō *kami*. In the end he developed a syncretism between the two so strong that out of it developed a new variety of Shintō, what was called Suika ("grace and protection") Shintō. It not only affirmed that, if appropriately revered, the *kami* would protect Japan but also explicitly stated that the grace and protection from the *kami* would be filtered through the emperor.

In making the argument for Suika Shintō ("Suika" was an ordination name conferred upon Ansai by a Shintō priest with whom he studied), Ansai undertook an extraordinarily elaborate rereading of the ancient Japanese creation myths to develop a system whereby neo-Confucian ideas and Shintō values could harmonize. This was basically an example of assimilation through hybridization rather than allocation or relegation, that is, something new was emerging from the cross-pollination of Confucianism and Shintō. For a stalwart traditionalist like Naokata, that hybridization was destroying the integrity of Confucianism itself and so he abandoned Ansai's academy and its teachings.

From the other direction, there were attempts by Shintō thinkers to try to make use of neo-Confucian ideas and terms to recast the traditional Shintō world view. From the end of the sixteenth century, as Confucianism reappeared on the Japanese philosophical stage (this time as a protagonist instead of a backdrop), various Shintō philosophers had tried to enhance Shintō's own intellectual profile by borrowing Confucian terms and ideals.

Dating from the early Heian period, as we have seen, Shintō had been relegated to a subordinate position within the most comprehensive Shingon and Tendai Buddhist systems, using most notably the algorithm of *honji suijaku*,[†] an algorithm turned on its head by Watarai Shintō to place Shintō above Buddhism. Furthermore, Yoshida Kanetomo, as we saw in Chapter 7, blatantly used Shingon ideas and practices to build his Yuiitsu system.[†] Such events exemplify the complex interactions between Buddhism and Shintō over the centuries. Now that it seemed likely that a new philosophical system—neo-Confucianism— might displace Buddhism's intellectual hegemony in Japan, it is not surprising that Shintō thinkers would try to form a new series of correlations, relegations, and alliances. One such thinker from the Yoshida (Yuiitsu) tradition was Yoshikawa Koretari (or Koretaru) (1616–1694).[40]

Koretari, who had achieved the highest rank of esoteric initiation in the Yuiitsu system, followed the lead of Razan on several points such as identifying the primal *kami* to be Kuninotokotachi and then correlating that *kami* with neo-Confucianism's *supreme ultimate*. Admittedly, to personify the supreme ultimate in that way is unconventional, but the correlation allowed the claim that a *kami* nature resides in every person and can be manifested by clearing the mindful heart of obfuscating desires.

† See pages 262–4.

That direct manifestation of the pure mindful heart is *makoto,* the central Shintō term meaning directness, genuineness, and sincerity. Koretari then identified that "sincerity" with the neo-Confucian virtue *cheng,* written with the same sinograph (誠). Like Ansai, Koretari emphasized prayer and reverence, identifying the latter with the Shintō rituals of purification and exorcism such as *misogi.*

Koretari's attempt to assimilate neo-Confucian ideas into the philosophical system of Yuiitsu Shintō spun off another hybrid, Yoshikawa Shintō. The parallels with Ansai's Suika Shintō are not accidental. Yoshikawa Koretari, although about the same age as Yamazaki Ansai was at one point his teacher. That the two ended up founding two different Confucian-Shintō traditions rather than cooperating to establish a single new one may reflect not only the different directions from which they came to their conclusions, but also possibly the competitive intellectual spirit of the times.

In general, then, the attempt to synthesize neo-Confucianism with Shintō occurred from both the direction of Shintō and of neo-Confucianism. Neither option ultimately succeeded over the other in becoming the hegemonic Shintō ideology or praxis, however. Since the time of Kūkai, Shintō had maintained its intellectual place in Japanese thought by first interacting with Buddhism and now by interacting with neo-Confucianism. Perhaps it was time to rethink the tradition on its own terms, to create a Shintō philosophy from the ground up, so its legs would be planted firmly on its own native turf without the crutch of imported ideas. At least that is the direction proposed by some members of another highly influential group of Edo-period philosophers, the so-called school of Native Studies (*kokugaku*).

Edo-period Native Studies

Although the philosophical story of the Edo period began with the ascent of the newly fashioned Confucianism, its ending and sequel are, to a great extent, the tale of Native Studies. Throughout the nineteenth and much of the twentieth century, the dominant issues driving Japanese culture became increasingly related to Shintō rather than Confucianism. Even Buddhism came to have more effect on twentieth-century Japanese academic philosophy than did Confucianism. Details of that transition will be the topic of Chapter 11, but here I will focus on the inception of the Native Studies tradition.

To understand the impetus and philosophical agenda behind Native Studies, we need to understand what it opposed. The sinophilia of the Japanese, that mania for "things Chinese" starting at the end of the sixteenth century and continuing into the next, was almost overwhelming. Some Japanese were so committed to looking at the world from the standpoint of China that they referred to themselves and their fellow Japanese as "barbarians." The Rinzai Zen monks' love of Chinese arts and letters spread rapidly throughout the country and, as key residents of the Rinzai temple study centers were won over to neo-Confucianism, the infatuation with China became an infatuation with Confucianism.

We have witnessed the captivating quality of Chinese thought and culture previously in the history of Japanese philosophy, starting with the Asuka and Nara periods, then the late Heian and early Kamakura, and again in the Muromachi. There is a critical difference when we come to the Edo-period, however. In those previous eras of the Japanese enthrallment with things Chinese, the carriers of Chinese culture were often Chinese *people*. The court and shogunate dispatched emissaries to and received emissaries from China. Moreover, they attracted Chinese Buddhist monks to emigrate and head major Japanese temples.

Yet, in the Edo period, if you wandered the corridors of culture in Edo, Kyoto, or Osaka, you would be inundated with things Chinese but would find not very many Chinese people (and any Korean scholars you might come across would have as likely as not been prisoners captured during Hideyoshi's mainland exploits). Partly because of altercations between Japanese and Chinese diplomats in the early sixteenth century, political relations between the two countries had degenerated to the point of ceasing official diplomatic exchanges by the mid-sixteenth century. With piracy in the Japan Sea making both trade and travel hazardous and with the fall of the Ming dynasty to the Manchu, the situation reached the point aptly described by Peter Nosco:

> There were, in short, no more Japanese pilgrims to China like those who in earlier centuries had returned home with tales of the magnificent empire of Japan's continental neighbor; and those Chinese who did come to Japan were mostly merchants in pursuit of a quick profit from what was often a clandestine trade.[41]

So, the China of Edo-period sinophilia created for the most part an *imagined*[42] China, not inhabited or embodied by actual living Chinese. Consequently, in vigorously pushing a nativist agenda by criticizing the "Chinese mentality" (*kara no kokoro*), declaiming the "filth" of Chinese arts and letters and their effect on Japan, the Native Studies scholars were for all intents and purposes targeting sinophilic Japanese more than the Chinese themselves. Of course, they made no effort to make clear the distinction between the two and there is little evidence that most would have even wanted to do so if they had thought of it.

Yet, with some important exceptions, if a Japanese ever did meet a Chinese, it was far more likely a profiteering trader or black-marketeer than a Confucian scholar.[43]* That, of course, only added fuel to the offensive caricature and egregious hyperbole. My point is not to exonerate the inflammatory rhetoric of some of the Japanese nativists, but instead to give it a proper context. The conflict between the Confucians and the nativists was primarily confrontation *in Japan* between an *imagined* China pitted against an *imagined* archaic Japan. It was a confrontation of opposing imaginaries, not opposing realities that could be evaluated on the grounds of empirical evidence and reason. The initial battlefield was, strangely enough, philological.

Keichū (1640–1701). As with many real wars, the conflict between the imaginaries can be traced to a fortuitous event. A Shingon monk called Keichū had a penchant for scholarly pursuits and liked to dabble with ancient Japanese texts and writing systems, perusing erudite studies and examining the ancient texts himself when he had a chance. Among the very small circle of scholars interested in such things, Keichū's skills as a philologist were well regarded.

As far as we know, he was a practicing Shingon priest his entire life, which would include the regular chanting of mantras. At the same time, as a lover of the ancient *waka* (classical Japanese poems), he was expert in medieval poetics and agreed with those who believed the *waka* were expressive of the deepest human feelings. He also believed that, like mantras, part of the spiritual power of words (*kotodama*) in *waka* lay in their sounds. By his time, there was already a long-standing tradition from medieval poetics of valorizing the *waka-darani*, the idea that *waka* are much like *darani* (S. *dhāraṇī*), the mantric phrases of esoteric Shingon Buddhism.[44]* With those interests and skills, Keichū was aptly prepared to further a nativist agenda against the sinophiles, but it took happenstance to get him personally involved. A precipitating cause was the founding of the so-called Mito School.

Tokugawa Mitsukuni (1628–1700), grandson of Ieyasu and daimyō of the Mito domain, was an avid patron of research projects, particularly those concerning Japanese history and letters. In 1657 he established a research center of more than a hundred scholars to undertake a massive project of writing a full political history of Japan (including, importantly, a major section on Shintō-related materials). The study, called the *Great History of Japan* (*Dai Nihonshi*), would span the centuries from Japan's origins up to the early fifteenth century. He relocated the enterprise from Edo to Mito in 1698 where it became the heart of what is known as the Mito School (*mitogaku*), about which I will say more in Chapter 11. The 397-volume history reached completion only in 1906.

A committed neo-Confucian, Mitsukuni recognized the vital importance of histories in the classical Chinese tradition as the basis for understanding the ideal of ruler-vassal relations. The Mito School history was consequently written in Chinese in the classical style of Chinese histories. That said, Mitsukuni was no starry-eyed sinophile. He admired the Chinese tradition as much for the template it supplied as for its content. He would like to see a Japan fitted into that template but in a way that maintained, even highlighted, its distinctive Japanese character.

Along with histories, another key part of the Chinese template was the admiration and collection of ancient poems such as the classic *Book of Odes*. Looking for a native parallel, Mitsukuni turned to the oldest collection of poems written in Japanese, *Man'yōshū*.† After a sputtering start, in 1673 Mitsukuni turned over to Shimokōbe Chōryū (1624–1686) the project of assembling a critical edition from extant versions and then writing a commentary. Because of failing health, Chōryū eventually realized he would not be able to finish and suggested Mitsukuni invite his friend, Keichū, to help. In 1683 Keichū began his research, although declining to join Mitsukuni's institute, preferring to work at his temple home.

Keichū, it turns out, was a better philologist than some had imagined. He brought to his study of the *Man'yōshū* text a sensitivity for the orthography of sounds, making several breakthroughs in determining how the text used sinographs phonetically. (Was his knowledge of the Sanskrit *siddhaṃ* phonetic script in Shingon mantras a factor contributing to that sensitivity?) At the same time, in his commentary Keichū did not restrain his pious admiration of ancient Japanese culture, marveling at how the ancients were able to govern themselves harmoniously without the help of mainland-derived ideas from Confucianism or Buddhism.[45]

The Confucians of the seventeenth century, Itō Jinsai for example, had already turned to philology to study the ancient Chinese texts and language. Keichū proved the same could be done with ancient Japanese. A key difference was that the Chinese scholarship obviously focused on the philology of Chinese writing, but Keichū's interest was on penetrating the writing of *Man'yōshū* to do a philology of the *spoken* sounds of the ancient Japanese language. Again his daily exposure to mantra practice may have spurred that interest.

Later Keichū turned his attention to *The Tale of Genji*, working through the language and script meticulously but also noting along the way that the content of the text itself had been misconstrued. Up to then, literary studies of *Genji* had pigeonholed it as a didactic text, that is, scholars had assumed it exemplified the Confucian dichotomy of good and bad, judging its characters accordingly. Keichū found, however, as we found ourselves in Chapter 4† when we analyzed the exchange between Prince Genji and Lady Tamakazura in the "Fireflies"

† See pages 53–5; 77–8.

chapter of the work, *Genji* is more about exploring human feelings than prescribing proper human behavior.[†]

Thus, Keichū had discovered that philology can do more than teach us about the ancient Japanese language; it can also give us interpretive insights into the ancient Japanese world view. [46] With his studies of *Man'yōshū* and *Genji*, Keichū had identified two of the classics at the heart of what would become the Native Studies movement. He had established a perspective and methodology of sorts, but not an agenda. For Native Studies to develop into a school of thought, however, it needed not only a basic orientation, but an institutional presence and vision.

Kada no Azumamaro (1669–1736) supplied that institutional presence. The Kada were a family of Shintō priests who had overseen for centuries the famous Fushimi Inari Shrine in the south edge of Kyoto. Having spent time in Edo and noting the shogunate's support of Yushima Seidō, Azumamaro dreamed of establishing a similar institution for the study of the classics written in the ancient Japanese language. In 1778 he wrote the "Petition for the Establishment of a School of Native Studies," a formal request to the shogun to support the founding of an academy somewhere in Kyoto, possibly at Fushimi itself.[47] His prospectus was to build an institute for research and teaching that would include a library of ancient texts and a curriculum in the philological study of ancient Japanese. The shogunate apparently completely ignored the petition, little interested in having Shintō replace Confucianism as the dominant ideology. But the vision lived on.

Azumamaro had already established on his own a prototype for the school in his Fushimi Inari Shrine, using it not only to train Shintō priests but also to research the language of the ancient Japanese texts. We can deem the school a success if for no other reason than it was where the first major Native Studies thinker seriously studied classical poetry for the first time. His name was Kamo no Mabuchi.

Kamo no Mabuchi (1697–1769). Mabuchi expanded on some ideas only implicit in earlier Native Studies scholars like Keichū and Azumamaro. Native Studies arose, he said, from reverence for the awe-inspiring emperor and the imperial line that in the ancient past brought peace, prosperity, and harmony to the land. To recapture that charismatic power, he argued, we need to return to the ancient texts—the ancient *words*—produced in antiquity. Then we may assimilate them until they become our own, the mindful heart (*kokoro*) of antiquity merging with our own mindful heart. In doing so we will not only discover the ancient *Japanese* virtues such as genuineness or sincerity (*makoto*), directness, vitality,

466–71

[†] See pages 141–4.

and "manliness" (*ooshiku shite*), but also those virtues will come to define our own character.[48]

According to Mabuchi, the ancient texts were not read, but recited. Then the poems will of themselves (*onozukara*) "color one's mindful heart and may even enter and become part of one's speech" until "only one's body is left behind in this later age as one's mindful heart and speech return to the distant past."[49] Mabuchi generally rejected all Chinese-derived texts as deviations from the ancient Way, allowing but one exception, Laozi's *Daodejing*. He admired Laozi's idea that morality flows naturally once one is removed from the Confucian rationalistic reflections on virtues.[50]

Mabuchi focused his efforts on analyzing the language and style of *Man'yōshū* poems, stressing their unadorned, direct expression of the human mindful heart (*kokoro*). He associated that plainness with the "masculine" (*masurao-buri*), making it clear that he was using the term in the sense of gender, not sex. Whether male or female, the poet displayed the same masculine style, he claimed.

The issue of gender would be, as we will see in our engagement with Motoori Norinaga in Chapter 10, central to many Native Studies thinkers. One purpose of the gender distinction was to criticize the samurai mentality so admired in the popular media since the time of the Akō Incident. Mabuchi advocated a masculinity that was direct, natural, and sincere, but not one shaped by principles defining one's loyalties. Norinaga, as we will see, thought masculinity an ideological construction designed to serve the military state and turn men against their inherently "feminine" (*taoyameburi*) nature shared by all people regardless of sex.

Yet, despite their unconstrained esteem for the imperial Way, both Mabuchi and Norinaga were cautious not to speak out directly against the shogunate. Of course, their ideas could certainly lead one in that direction and indeed did so in the nineteenth century as we will see in Chapter 11.

472-92 *Motoori Norinaga* (1730–1801). The last Native Studies philosopher I will consider in this chapter is the aforementioned Motoori Norinaga, a disciple of Mabuchi. Since he will be the focus of Chapter 10, there is no need to go into his philosophy here in any detail. However, one point should be mentioned: the way he explicitly brought religion into Native Studies.

Norinaga's primary focus was not on *Man'yōshū*, but instead on *Kojiki*, the ancient mythicohistorical chronicle partially written in an almost unintelligible hybrid Japanese, a result of there being no standard orthography for Japanese in the early eighth century.[†] Using the powerful philological tools inherited

---

† See pages 75; also see About the Japanese Language, pages 685–7.

from his Native Studies predecessors, Norinaga tried to read through the hybrid Japanese to unearth a layer of the pure ancient Japanese beneath it. The connection between Shintō and the study of the ancient Japanese language had always been in the background—after all, the "school" of Native Studies had started in Azumamaro's Shintō academy—but the precise nature of the connection was not explicit until Norinaga. He made it so by treating *Kojiki* as the language of the *kami,* its narrative being not only *about* creation, but also the *enactment* of creation as voiced by the gods themselves. For Norinaga, there is no creation without genuine language and no genuine language without creation.

That purported connection between language and creation was not totally new in Japan. We could trace it back to Kūkai, for example, in what I termed the "conference" rather than "reference" relation between word and reality, an idea that continued into the *waka-darani* theory of medieval poetics. For esoteric Buddhism, however, that relation applied to all languages and even in the thirteenth-century collection of tales, *Sand and Pebbles* (*Shasekishū*), the claim was merely that since it applies to all languages, it should apply to the ancient Japanese of *waka* as well.

The Native Studies philosophers, by contrast, claimed that the co-creative function of word and reality was the special province of the ancient Japanese language alone. By bringing *Kojiki* into the heart of the Native Studies canon (even Azumamaro had favored the Chinese-language *Nihonshoki* for discussing the ancient myths), Norinaga succeeded in linking Shintō religion with the poetics of the *waka.* That is, to study the ancient Japanese language became simultaneously a poetic, spiritual, and ethnic enterprise.

Later developments in the Native Studies movement will take us into the early nineteenth century and the events leading to the deposing of the shogun and restoration of the emperor. As such I will be able to address them more aptly in Chapter 11. Before leaving the discussion of the history of philosophy in the Edo period, however, I need to mention Buddhist developments, though they were neither as pioneering nor as striking as what we have seen in Edo-period Confucianism and Shintō.

Edo-period Buddhist Philosophy

From the seventh century when Shōtoku politicked for its having the status of a state religion, Buddhism gradually established itself as the dominant religious and philosophical institution in Japan. By the early seventeenth century, however, Buddhism found itself in a somewhat precarious position. Although the three Kamakura traditions of Zen, Pure Land, and Nichiren were becoming a challenge to the dominant Tendai, Shingon, and Hossō sects, they nonetheless found themselves in a similar defensive posture with respect to the shogunate, especially after the hegemons had attacked the Shin Buddhist institutions for their role in the Ikkō uprisings. To maintain a strict administrative oversight, the Tokugawa regime imposed on the temples a rigid system of institutional hierarchy, allowing each sect to have only a few main temples, the rest being subordinated as branches.

Intellectually and spiritually, Buddhist monastic centers shifted in focus as they increasingly created their own parallel to the Confucian academies, namely, seminaries for textual studies. The scholarly output was prodigious: critical editions of texts, series of commentaries, compendiums of teachings, hagiographies of founders, and institutional regulations. In the age of the commodification of knowledge and the rise of non-Buddhist competition for scholarly studies, a question is how all that activity was funded.

What the shogunate took away in political or military power, it gave back in a new system for financial support. After purging Buddhism of groups it considered politically dangerous, the shogunate needed a systematic way to dissipate any future Buddhist tendencies toward political fanaticism. Its solution was both creative and effective: it simply required every Japanese to become at least nominally Buddhist. Specifically, every Japanese family had to enroll in the registry of a local Buddhist temple. For the government, this had the initial benefit of rooting out any remaining Christians as Christians generally felt obligated not to ally with any other religion and the new regulation would force them to reveal their religious allegiance.

Moreover, since those temple records became the data for the census and hence the basis for setting taxation rates, it also made Buddhist temples complicit in the shogunate's collection of revenue. Note the irony: after wiping out the Buddhist peasant revolts against taxation, the shogunate transformed Buddhism into an arm of the taxation system. In that process, the temples received a small share of the revenue stream, but even more importantly gained regular access to families so as to be able to pitch special services, especially rituals related to funerals and death memorials.

As self-sustaining institutions, the Buddhist scholars in the temple seminaries had little to do with the larger intellectual issues of the day. Admittedly, through much of the Edo period, there were exceptions to that generality, but from the standpoint of philosophical creativity rather than scholarly exegesis or editing, the Buddhist tradition entered a period of relative inactivity. The exceptions are, however, noteworthy and I will briefly discuss two, one an individual named Jiun Sonja, the other a cluster of thinkers from a single tradition—not surprisingly, Rinzai Zen.

104–9   *Jiun Sonja* aka *Jiun Onkō (1718–1804)*. Jiun was an ordained Shingon monk (having affiliations with Sōtō Zen as well) whose career ran counter to the typical pattern in Edo Japan in that he was first a Confucian and then became a Buddhist, initially to follow his father's wishes, but then as a lifetime commitment. Once it became clear that Jiun wanted to argue the superiority of Buddhism over Confucianism, his Buddhist master advised him to study Confucianism further, this time at Itō Jinsai's academy where there was a strong emphasis on philology, on trueing up the terms by going back to the early Chinese texts.

That philological training inspired Jiun to investigate the roots of Buddhism, but the relevant texts were in Sanskrit, a language barely studied in Japan. Undaunted, he took up the study mainly on his own, becoming Japan's premier authority on Sanskrit in the premodern period, writing a 1000-volume study. In that respect, Jiun represents yet another example of an Edo-period thinker who used philology as a means of unearthing the origins of a tradition—in his case Buddhism—in much the same way as his contemporaries did in Native and Confucian Studies. That same impetus to go back to when things were done properly also prompted him to develop a new form of monasticism based on what he understood to be the original principles of Buddhism that preceded and transcended the various sectarian forms of Buddhism known in Japan.

Jiun's philosophical acumen was well displayed in his arguments in favor of Buddhist over Confucian ethics. In particular, against the Confucian charge that Buddhism was antinomian, Jiun pointed to the ten precepts practiced by all sincere Buddhists. These were prohibitions against ten specific acts of wrongdoing that would hinder one's progress toward enlightenment: "killing, stealing, adultery, lying, frivolous language, slander, equivocation, greed, anger, and wrong views."[51] Comparing those negative prohibitions to the Confucian virtues, Jiun underscored their specificity. The Confucian virtues were far more general and abstract and, hence, open to extensive interpretation. While those interpretations might lend fuel to philosophical treatises, they are hardly the kind of practical, everyday guidance needed by most people. Thus, argued Jiun, contrary to the Confucian critiques, it is Buddhism not Confucianism that better serves ordinary people.

Jiun also maintained that through its teaching and praxis of the precepts, Buddhism is, contrary to the typical Confucian argument, acutely aware of the social dimension of human existence. The difference, according to Jiun, is that Confucianism did not recognize from where its virtues derived, namely, from the same ground of reality—the same Buddha nature or "dharma-ness" (S. *dharmatā*)—from which the ten precepts emerge. Whereas Confucianism based its virtues in the authority of the ancient Chinese sage kings, Buddhism found morality to have a universal metaphysical and psychological basis. Hence, in the final analysis, Jiun accepted the Confucian virtues but only by *relegating* them to being an incomplete and not fully realized expression of the more comprehensive Buddhist truth.

In short: whereas Jiun appealed to origins to reform Buddhism from within, he used relegation to argue for the superiority of Buddhism over Confucianism. As I noted already, when neo-Confucianism entered Japan in full force some two centuries earlier, it gained philosophical potency from the way it relegated Buddhist and Daoist ideas into its system, and at the time, there was initially no significant Japanese Buddhist response reversing the order of that relegation. By the end of the eighteenth century, Confucians were publicly criticizing Buddhists for neglecting their duties of filial piety, supporting their claim by remarking that Buddhist monastics were those who took a vow to "leave home" (*shukke*). Perhaps such criticism stirred Jiun to make his argument of relegation in Buddhism's defense. However sophisticated his critiques might have been, however, they came too late to block the Confucianism ascent to a level of hegemony in Japan.

Edo Rinzai Zen. In Edo-period Japan, not all Rinzai Zen Buddhist monks became Confucians and the Rinzai tradition underwent notable transformations from within. I will here highlight two: the Zen link with the warrior mentality in the early Edo period and the attempt to revitalize Zen spirituality against the elitist aestheticism of the Five Mountain movement toward the latter part of the period.

I have already explained how the end of warfare and the unification of Japan at the close of the sixteenth century created a large pool of masterless samurai, all seeking a way to make a living as something other than a soldier. Some, I noted, went into the business of academia, becoming teachers in their own academies. Others became functionaries in the new Tokugawa bureaucracy. Some even went so far as to swallow their pride and enter the mercantile world, dropping from the highest to the lowest social class.

Still others became Buddhist monks, usually Rinzai Zen monks. At least, that career path did not involve a demotion in social rank because, like aristocrats and outcastes, monks were outside the four-class system. Furthermore, for many samurai with at least some education in the old daimyō academies, the arts and letters emphasized in the Five Mountain culture were both familiar and attractive. Of course, the former warriors did have to be acculturated into at least the basic spiritual principles of Zen. As a result, Zen leaders found creative ways to help the samurai make the transition. One strategy was to bring martial arts into the monasteries—the study of the Way of archery or of the sword, for example.

Another, more philosophically interesting, option was to try to link the warrior mentality with the Zen mentality. Thus, at about the same time as the Confucians Sokō and Tōju were theorizing the meaning of the samurai in Edo secular society, Zen thinkers were finding a conceptual home for former samurai in their religious communities. Three Zen philosophers that explicitly

made that connection between Zen and the former warriors were Takuan Sōhō 178–82
(1573–1645), Suzuki Shōsan (1579–1655), and Shidō Bunan (1603–1676).

In letters to the shogunate's master swordsman, Yagyū Munenori (1571–1646), Takuan developed his idea that the focused, undisturbed, and flexible mind of the Zen Buddhist is akin to the mental disposition required in master swordsmanship. Neither should "get stuck" on any objectified thought, but remain consistently in the flow of events as they emerge. Only then can spontaneous responsiveness be maintained.

Suzuki Shōsan, by contrast, was a samurai warrior by training, but one who 183–9
retired to become a Zen monk, trying to live a serene temple life. Not content with the quietude of that lifestyle, he brought his combined Zen and warrior mentality back into the world of action. He saw a link between the Buddhist resignation in the face of the cycle of birth-and-death and the samurai idea of not fearing one's own mortality. True freedom for either the samurai or Zen Buddhist, Shōsan claimed, derives from the "death energy" generated out of the confrontation with one's own mortality and then pushing beyond it without anxiety. Through that engagement with mortality, one discovers the true self, the egoless buddha-nature. Thus, the Zen student should bring the "warrior's glare" to *zazen* practice and the warrior should practice *zazen* as a way of developing focus and the action of "no-mind." In the focus on death as a spiritual discipline, Shōsan's Zen set the stage for the valorization of death in martial texts such as the aforementioned *Hagakure* a century later.[†]

Shōsan did not go so far as to claim that being a warrior was as good as being a Zen monk, however. The superiority of the Zen mentality over the warrior mentality, he claimed, rests in the fact that the warrior's focus in battle dissipates when the battle is over, but Zen is continuous and fills every moment of the monk's life-as-death. Again, however, the later martial tradition would turn that point around by insisting the warrior mentality should be brought into daily life.

In Bunan (also pronounced Munan) the warrior connection was less blatant, 190–4
but he shared with Shōsan the emphasis on "dying while alive," again a phrase that would find echoes in the later *Hagakure*. Like Shōsan, Bunan emphasized the importance of attentiveness and immediacy over reflection or conceptual rumination.

> The teachings of Buddhism are greatly in error. How much more in error it is to learn them. See directly. Hear directly. In direct seeing there is no seer. In direct hearing there is no hearer. 191

In stressing how immediacy is more fundamental than even Buddhist teachings, Bunan was underscoring the Zen Buddhist focus on experience over the study of texts. Yet, unknowingly he was also presaging the later move among some thinkers to place the direct experience of loyalty over the cooling effect of reason.

The other notable aspect of Edo-period Rinzai was its attempts at institutional reform, the effort to return the Rinzai monasteries to being training centers for buddhas, not literary aesthetes. A factor in the reform movement was the introduction of a new tradition of Zen, namely, Ming Dynasty Chinese Rinzai. Although it is true that the presence of a live Confucian scholar from China was a rather rare sight in Edo-period Japan, there remained pockets of Chinese Zen Buddhist monks residing in the country, including one group centered in Nagasaki on the island of Kyushu. Their efforts to bring more Chinese masters to Japan resulted in the arrival of the Rinzai master, Ingen (1592–1673) in 1654.

After some effort, Ingen managed to gain the sponsorship of the shogun, Tokugawa Ietsuna (1641–1680), who granted him the land to build a temple complex south of Kyoto in Uji. Because it was so different from the Rinzai traditions introduced earlier to Japan (Ingen's Ming-period Buddhism represented mixed Pure Land and Zen practices, for example), it was treated as a separate Zen sect in Japan called Ōbaku (C. Huangbo) after the mountain in China that was the site of Ingen's temple there. It did not seem to engage much in the philosophical developments of the day, but had a strong influence on the arts, especially calligraphy. Yet, it was a challenge to the Rinzai monastic establishment and helped trigger a revitalization of Zen praxis within the temples.

The most influential Rinzai leader in the transformation of Zen monasteries back to being more like centers for Zen practice instead of Chinese cultural study centers was Hakuin Ekaku (1685–1768), a man so valorized in the present-day Rinzai tradition that almost all of today's Rinzai Zen masters trace their lineage of transmission back to him. Hakuin resuscitated the intensity of Rinzai Zen training in line with its ninth-century Chinese founder, Linji Yixuan (J. Rinzai Gigen).[52] Hakuin's dynamic training tactics were all-or-nothing: every minute of every day was to be an intense focus on practice so as to realize a sudden breakthrough into realization.[53] We could say, following the slogan of Bunan (who was Hakuin's teacher's teacher), it was "dying while living." Hakuin claimed that no master could bring a student to enlightenment, but through the master's badgering, yelling, hitting, presenting kōans, and intimidating, the disciple could reach the point of the "Great Doubt" in which all conceptual discourse and analysis would freeze up. Then, only then, could the student break through into the "Great Death" which would be the opening into the "Great Joy" of enlightenment.

Hakuin was equally critical of the aesthetic and literary practices that could interrupt the true praxis, even though he himself wrote poems, painted, and engaged in calligraphy. As Musō Soseki had said centuries before, such artistic endeavors were by-products of the creativity that would arise from enlighten-

202–10

ment and not techniques used to gain enlightenment. Hakuin also reached out beyond the temples to the ordinary people in sermons in which he explained techniques of breathing and chanting that anyone could do "in the midst of the everyday activities." While such practices might not lead to the breakthrough achievable in a monastic setting, it could deeply enrich the lives of ordinary people. In that concern for the people, Hakuin was akin to an earlier Edo-period Rinzai Zen philosopher to whom we now turn, Bankei.

Bankei Yōtaku (1622–1693) was in some ways the most disarming of the Zen philosophical masters. Unlike the later institutional reformer Hakuin, Bankei had tried to distance himself from the Rinzai monastic centers, instead tending to the spiritual needs of his rural community. Preferring to stay out of the limelight, his spiritual attainments were nonetheless so legion that he was eventually called on to be a major teacher in the great monasteries of both Edo and Kyoto. His insights were profound and his training thorough, yet he preferred to speak in a down-to-earth language understandable to anyone. Bankei's message was the same whether speaking to a group of illiterate farmers or to advanced monks under his charge, thus undercutting the distance between the monastery and the family home. His premise was that all experience is grounded in what he called "buddha-mind" or, more famously, the "unborn."

195–201

In using the term "the unborn" (*fushō*), Bankei assumed its technical Buddhist use. In that context, the word does not imply (as one might assume from the language) something eternal, but more specifically refers to being "unborn of karma." That is, it most precisely indicates what our mindful heart is without the "karmic afflictions" (*bonnō*; S. *kleśa*) accrued through our past "unskillful" actions of thought, word, and deed. (We encountered the concern about the karmic afflictions previously in Chapter 5's discussion of Shinran's Shin Buddhism.)

For example, when we ordinarily think, our thoughts depend on our previous thoughts. We think in words we have previously learned, words affected by a variety of contextual and personal distortions fueled by hatred, ignorance, and desire. Therefore, in its technical Buddhist sense, anything that is *born* is born of, and colored by, those distorting influences. To engage the original mindful heart or the buddha (enlightened) mindful heart is, therefore, to engage that core of ourselves that has *not been born* of those negative ego-driven influences. It is to be egoless and uncalculating. Hence the term *unborn*.

Bankei criticized the intensity of the discourse in both the Zen and neo-Confucian traditions that stressed an effort at achieving a focused contemplative serenity that quelled all emotions. Bankei countered that if the unborn is the basis of all experience, we can manifest it as enlightenment naturally. That is, he wanted focused attention to be not something we try to do, not something we put on our agenda, not an aspiration for intense training, but instead something completely natural and ordinary. The point, then, is not to try to focus, but rather to not fall into distraction. Typical of his rhetorical style, he explained the point in light of a most everyday kind of event:

> Suppose a woman is engaged in sewing something. A friend enters the room and begins speaking to her. As long as she listens to her friend and sews in the unborn, she has no trouble doing both. But if she gives her attention to her friend's words and a thought arises in her mind as she thinks about what to reply, her hands stop sewing; if she turns her attention to her sewing and thinks about that, she fails to catch everything her friend is saying, and the conversation does not proceed smoothly. In either case, her buddha-mind has slipped from the place of the unborn. She has transformed it into thought. As her thoughts fix upon one thing, they're blank to all others, depriving her mind of its freedom.

195-6

In other words, Bankei is advocating a simple praxis of engaged knowing that simply merges into or overlaps with the object of attention. Furthermore, his theory of the unborn yields the basis for a metapractical justification of why the best way to focus is not to try to focus.

Before leaving this discussion of Edo-period philosophizing, I will mention one other cluster of thinkers outside the privileged world of Confucianism, Buddhism, and Native Studies. The mission of those teachers, like that of Bankei, was to enhance the everyday lives and spiritual awareness of not the elite, but the general populace, in their case, specifically the townspeople of the new urban centers.

Philosophies for the Townspeople

The literacy of urban society and the public nature of knowledge as a commodity in the marketplace of ideas enabled those with a basic education to acquire more if they so wished. There were publications, scholarly lectures open to the general populace, and public debates over the topics of the day.[54] When knowledge becomes a commodity sold on the open market, it acquires not only commercial, but also cultural, value. A significant sector of the population lacked the time, inclination, or resources to become full-time scholars but many nonetheless wanted to benefit from this new, publicly available knowledge. The *Shingaku* (literally, "study of the mindful heart")[55] movement was one vehicle by which that market niche was served.

411–15
436–40

Shingaku. Founded by Ishida Baigan (1685–1744) and developed by his disciple, Teshima Tōan (1718–1786), *Shingaku* distilled the complexity of neo-Confucian teachings and blended them with key Zen ideas and practices gleaned mainly from the teachings of Zen master Bankei. The result was a school of thought and praxis appealing to a large sector of the townspeople, especially merchants and artisans. As the movement grew, it also made inroads into rural areas where it served modestly educated peasants as well.

The teachings of *Shingaku* functioned on two levels, as a practical ethic and as a spiritual path for achieving wisdom.[56] For lectures, Tōan would sometimes divide his audience into two groups depending on their interests and capacities: a practical morality for everyone and spiritual training for those who earnestly sought it. Of course, and this was the philosophical achievement of the movement, the two were ultimately interdependent because the two projects were grounded in a common agenda, namely, to come to "know our original mindful heart."

The claim was that if we could achieve that goal, we would naturally act properly in all five Confucian dyadic relations, that is, the virtues would emerge spontaneously without the need for a detailed scholarly study of the classics. The key for us to know the "original mindful heart," *Shingaku* claimed, was to recognize that the ego-centered, ordinary mindful heart that we usually think of as "mine"—*my* ideas, *my* intentions, *my* efforts—is an overlay disguising a deeper and purer level of thought and affect. Certainly, their term *original mindful heart* (*honshin*) invokes a range of associations from the East Asian philosophical tradition, but since *Shingaku* itself explicitly connected the word to Bankei's notions of the unborn and buddha-mind, I will begin there.

Bankei's theory of the mindful heart is redolent of a variety of Buddhist theories and traditions, including the previously analyzed idea of *hongaku* ("radical," "inherent," or "original" awakening) from the medieval period.[†] Following a few suggestive statements by Bankei, *Shingaku* thinkers realized that the theory is also not at all inconsistent with Confucian teachings. For example, Mencius had argued for the innate goodness of human nature that, were it not for distorting external factors, would express itself naturally as benevolence or humaneness. Neo-Confucianism used the meditative technique of "quiet sitting" (*seiza*; C. *jingzuo*), undoubtedly influenced by Chinese Zen, to access one's true nature as inherently good, what was called *bright virtue*.

In *Shingaku* praxis the novices begin by engaging in simple experiments to show their experience is not simply the construction of an ego-centered "I." By simply being reflective and aware when they see or hear an object, they come to realize that "my mind" or "I" is not controlling the experience. *My* mind can decide not to listen, but it cannot stop hearing, for example. In effect, my experience occurs in a conscious field that is bigger than "me." That larger field is the "original mindful heart." When students relinquish all sense of ego, they will feel more naturally connected and engaged with other people and other things:

† See pages 151–2.

benevolence toward others, for example, will occur of itself without the need to study about benevolence.

For the student with a proclivity to go deeper, *Shingaku* offered more advanced contemplative techniques for engaging that same original mindful heart in even more profound ways. *Shingaku*'s hybrid philosophy included elements of Zen and Confucianism, but blended in such a way that it was no longer simply one or the other, but a unique philosophy of its own adapted to the various needs of the ordinary city dwellers instead of the scholars in the academy.

Although the most celebrated case, *Shingaku* was not the only attempt at developing a hybrid philosophy for the townspeople. For example, one syncretistic thinker who was particularly aware of how his teaching was the product of hybridization rather than allocation was Ninomiya Sontoku (1787–1856). He claimed to have developed a philosophical "medicine" for the health of the Japanese nation and its people, a "round pill" consisting of one-half the "essence" of Shintō, one-quarter of Confucianism, and one quarter of Buddhism. When asked the function of each (as if they had been allocated discrete roles), Sontoku laughed and said, "When I mentioned that the pill was round, I meant that it well combines and harmonizes the ingredients so that one does not know what the pill actually contains." Sontoku realized that hybridization creates a new species.

Critics and skeptics. When we analyze the Edo period's philosophical activities, some perhaps directed as much to securing a niche in the marketplace of ideas as to securing the truth, it comes as no surprise that there were critical thinkers who stood enough outside the intellectual establishment to view it with a jaundiced eye. Two examples of such observers were Tominaga Nakamoto (1715–1746) and Andō Shōeki (1703–1762), both of whom wrote pointed critiques of all three mainstream traditions: Confucianism, Buddhism, and Shintō.

Tominaga's analysis was the more scathing.[57] Like some postmodern critics in the West today, he argued that philosophical systems are no more than contingent conceptual constructions. Their rhetoric and theories disguise their real purpose, namely, to serve various historical and cultural agendas. According to Tominaga, each tradition has its own proclivities: Buddhism a penchant for "sorcery," Confucianism for "high-flown language," and Shintō for "mysteriousness, esoteric and secret transmission, and the bad habit of simply concealing things." In competition with each other, each Way claims it is *the* Way and the others are false.

Beneath them all, Tominaga maintains, lies the true Way, which is simply the direct engagement with the affairs of everyday life. "We should simply strive in all matters for what is ordinary." Reading scholarly texts, devising speculative

447–53

451

430–5

433-4

431

philosophies, and forming complicated schools of thought only obfuscate matters. Unlike Buddhism, Confucianism, and Native Studies respectively, the true Way "has not come from India, has not been transmitted from China, and it is not something initiated in the age of the [*kami*]...." The true Way is to live life as daily affairs present themselves without taking lofty excursions into abstract thought or fantasizing about escapes to romanticized times and places other than our own. It is to "write in today's script, to speak today's language, to eat today's foods..." as well as "to follow today's customs, to respect today's rules, to mingle with today's people," all the while being "perfectly sincere." Tominaga was not so much anti-intellectual as he was, in the spirit of Zen Master Bankei, arguing that the wisdom we seek is found in the direct engagement with the affairs of daily life, rather than in abstract, scholarly reflections on the nature of reality or romantic valorization of some nonexistent past. 431

Andō Shōeki was a utopian thinker who could in one respect be said to have drawn on the available traditions—Confucianism, Buddhism, Shintō, and (especially) Daoism—to develop his own vision of a more natural, what we would today call ecologically simpler and more responsible, way of life. His guiding insight was that the natural world is a single system of which we are a part. The same energies (what he called the eight kinds of generative force or *ki*) that compose the cosmos also compose us. From that premise he argued in a direction radically divergent from the metaphysical analyses of many of the aforementioned philosophical traditions. 416–29

Shōeki maintained that since the Way of the natural world is immediately accessible to us as the functions we find in ourselves, there is no need for philosophical schools, academies, or the scholarly study of texts. In fact, those institutionalized systems of thought and those who nurture them are part of a scam, a process of artificially constructing knowledge so as to make oneself the expert in it. Once the scam is underway, the so-called sages and scholars can then command the adulation and financial support they feel they are owed. In other words, to put his point in the jargon of our day: the traditional philosophical systems are constructed for no reason other than to acquire authority and power. One of his more animated critiques:

> Written characters are no more than arbitrary and capricious constructions contrived by the ruling sages of old to make books and scholarship, which they then use to set themselves higher than others and, on the pretext of teaching those below them, to establish self-serving laws. This enabled them to eat their fill of the food of others without having to work themselves.... 428

When challenged as being a hypocrite since he himself was writing books, Shōeki responded that he had to write himself to expose the sham, but only as a heuristic device allowing him

...to destroy the ancient books that are the roots of thievery and strife.... It takes a thief to point out a thief. To destroy the mistaken writings and books that are the roots of thievery, we must use those very characters and books that are the root of thievery.

428

Shōeki compared his use of writings to using wedges to deconstruct a building. Once the building has come down, you throw away the wedges along with the rest of the rubble.

His characterizing scholars and sages as "thieves" is a good example of how he drew on, but then dismantled, the traditional philosophical systems. Shōeki noted that Chinese Daoist masters, Laozi and Zhuangzi, also described themselves as thieves, but then, he says, they proceeded to regard themselves as sages, "failing to see that they were cut of the same cloth" as those they criticized. The point is not to develop a new school of philosophy, not even a school that criticizes other schools. Instead Shōeki urges us to return to the direct participation in everyday life as everyday life, harmonizing with the generative forces both within the self and in all things. It is as simple as finding the Way that is "apparent in the hearth and in the human face," without falling into rationalization or study.

428

CONCLUSION

In the newly risen urban environments, the secrets typical of the medieval centers of learning and culture were brought into the open for the public to engage. Ever larger numbers of people were included in the discourse, as audience if not participants. Competing ideas coalesced into a rich mix of theories from a variety of traditions. Judging from the sumō ranking of philosophers, even witnessing the arguments had entertainment value for some people, and few aspects of life were more highly valued by the Edo Japanese than entertainment.

From the entertainment standpoint, I cannot help but see a parallel with today's televised talk shows that pit proponents of one view against another to capture the sparks of disagreement on tape. Some viewers I imagine watch such programs not so much to learn or even to be intellectually stimulated, but rather to be entertained. Everyone likes a good fight, even a fight with words. Certainly not all Edo-period philosophers were motivated by the quest for celebrity, but the commodification of philosophy forced competition, typically public competition. The diversity of theories, even if we recognize it was a diversity constructed in part to secure a niche in the marketplace of ideas, is staggering. If we stand back far enough from the foray, however, a few recurrent themes emerge.

First, there was often the construction of an ideal past, a world of either Confucian sage-kings or simple, pre-sinicized folk who communed with the *kami*. Second, there was a sustained focus on language, its origins, its semantic and syntactic structures, and even its orthography. Third, there was the idea that through the right methodology, we could study texts to recapture that pristine past, to once again see the world from the standpoint of the ancient sages or the *kami*. Fourth, there was the assumption that deep within us as people, just as deep within our history, there is an original goodness that can somehow be engaged and put into action. It was accessible via an array of approaches: the philological study of ancient texts, the contemplation of metaphysical principles, or the uncontrived, direct engagement with the everyday.

Of the two great philosophical traditions spawned from the Edo-period milieu—Confucianism reborn and Native Studies matured—each had a major thinker who embodied those qualities. They are the Confucian philosopher Ogyū Sorai and the Native Studies Shintō philosopher Motoori Norinaga, the topics for our next two chapters. In this chapter we have observed and mapped the course of philosophy in the Edo-period's floating world, tracing the flow and eddies of its waters. That is not the same, however, as knowing those waters by navigating them ourselves, feeling the tugs and jolts of its currents. To do that, we will now engage those two philosophers, joining them in their philosophical journeys. We start with a young man who as a kid owned but one book.

9. Ogyū Sorai 荻生徂徠 (1666–1728)

The Present Wisdom of the Past Perfect

Thereby you will be able to sit at the same
table and exchange civilities with the
ancients without an interpreter.... Can
there be anything more joyful than this?
Ogyū Sorai

A man in his mid-twenties in a coastal village of the province of Kazusa, 115 kilometers from Edo, is packing his possessions in preparation for his move to the city, a wish fulfilled after years of anticipation. He examines a wooden box, the edges smooth with wear. It contains a book he has owned since a young teenager, a cherished copy of a commentary on the Chinese Confucian classic, the *Book of Great Learning*. Ogyū Sorai (as he would later call himself) has been living in Kazusa neither by birth nor by choice, but because the shogunate had exiled his father, Ogyū Hōan (1626–1706), thirteen years before. Now that the shogun, Tokugawa Tsunayoshi (1676–1709), has released Hōan and his family from banishment, they are moving back to the city. Sorai recalls vividly how in his early teens, his family had left Edo in shame and disbelief (we do not know what prompted the exile order; in his later years, Sorai said only "it was for cause").

What a life he had lived as a boy before the exile, though. Edo was a metropolis of over a million people and still growing. Because his father had been physician to Tsunayoshi, the heir apparent to the shogun at the time, Sorai had sometimes accompanied him to the castle, once even glimpsing the shogun's wife. The youngster had found himself amid the hustle-bustle of city life with its townspeople, merchants, literati, artisans, samurai, and residents of the entertainment quarters. For a little while, at least according to some accounts, he had enjoyed the good fortune to attend a fine Confucian academy affiliated with the Hayashi family. There he found the books and the scholarly conversations he loved so much.

As a boy, Sorai knew the family expected him to become a physician like his father, but even then Sorai had known what he wanted: he yearned to be a scholar. His father, like most physicians of Chinese medicine, was trained in Chinese Confucian philosophy himself and Sorai knew he would likely let him chase his dream. Then the dream withered in the face of exile, an exile as much intellectual and emotional as geographical. As he wrote years later:

> I lived for thirteen years there [in Kazusa]. Since every day I met only farmers and other country people, there is no need to ask whether I had teachers or friends. The only thing I had to educate myself with was one book, the *Daigaku genkai*, which my father had stored in a box. It actually bore the smudges of my father's hands. I attended to its study and exerted my strength on it for a long time. In the end, I could completely understand a host of books without needing exposition.[58]

In repeatedly reading that text, not having access to the libraries of commentaries available in Edo, Sorai would memorize passages of the original Chinese classic and likely copied and recopied portions for calligraphy lessons. By means of that practice, he had not merely studied the book; he had internalized it, incorporating it into his bodymind. Yet in the end, the most influential aspect of his study was not its content, but instead his approach to reading it. It was less a matter of what he learned and more a matter of how he learned it.

HOW TO READ A CHINESE CLASSICAL TEXT

In his later years as a philosopher, Sorai did not especially highlight that commentary on the *Book of Great Learning*, nor did his references to it go beyond its title to discuss either its interpretation or even its author. What had impressed him in his study were the *words*: their sounds, their rhetorical rhythms as revealed in the ancient Chinese writing style, and their plain meaning. How different this was from the way he had originally learned to read such documents.

By Sorai's time, there was a long-established method among Japanese scholars for reading a classical Chinese text, what he referred to as the *wakun*[59]* method. In that technique, one pronounces every Chinese character as if it were Japanese, twisting the syntax around to fit Japanese word order, and inserting prepositional particles and inflections which Japanese grammar requires, but Chinese does not.[60]* The result is neither Chinese nor quite Japanese, but to Sorai's mind, a bizarre and contrived hybrid.

Furthermore, since that *wakun* reading method had originated some half a millennium earlier in the Heian period, the original Chinese was being transformed into an antiquated Japanese most ordinary people could not understand. The only ones to speak it, Sorai sniped, were intellectuals who liked to pretend they knew the Chinese classics even though they could not read a word of Chinese in Chinese. Sorai considered that no more than a ploy to gain respect and authority. That is, because the *wakun* method produced an artificial language known only to scholars, nonspecialists would think the scholars must have been saying something deep and esoteric.[61]*

Yet, the original Chinese classics were, Sorai insisted, as straightforward, simple, and down-to-earth as any text could be. Their content was something his fishing and farming neighbors in Kazusa could understand if they only knew the Chinese. Accordingly, Sorai concluded that if you want to explain a text to someone who does not know Chinese, you should translate it into simple contemporary Japanese, thereby mirroring the directness of the original. He called this the "translation model" (*yakubun no gaku*). To use the academic *wakun* method not only leads to pretentious scholarship, but it also disguises the most significant point about the Chinese classics: they are not intricate or arcane, but forthright and plain. Before you can presume to explain what the text says, you must know *how* to read such a text. Sorai believed a whole tradition of Chinese, Korean, and Japanese commentaries had obscured that vital fact.

As he developed this line of thought later in life, Sorai insisted that education should focus on the Six Classics, the texts preceding even those of Confucius. In Sorai's matured viewpoint, Confucius was the completion of Confucianism, not its point of departure. Sorai's isolation in exile had led him to find an alternative way to read the Chinese classics without translation, what came to be called the "Nagasaki model" (*Kiyō no gaku*). As mentioned in the last chapter, the Tokugawa shoguns closed Japan to all intercourse with the rest of Asia, except for some trade with China and Korea in the Kyushu port of Nagasaki. As a result, in Nagasaki various Japanese negotiated with Chinese traders and sailors, learning to communicate with the foreigners in their native tongue.

Building on this idea of talking to Chinese in Chinese, Sorai argued that to engage the ancient Chinese classics authentically, one had to learn the Chinese pronunciations of words and attune the ear to the rhythms of the language. Then, one should study the ancient classics themselves—directly without the use of scholarly explications from later eras—until one could read them naturally in their native syntax without the distortions imposed by the *wakun* system.[62] This would make possible a dialogue with the ancients, a way to engage them without the burdens of commentaries and twisted prose.

...It is by no means sufficient just to read archaic-literary-style works. You should try to reproduce the style with your own hand. Once you acquire facility in writing in that style, you will come to feel that the classics flow out from your own mouth.

......

Thereby you will able to sit at the same table and exchange civilities with the ancients without an interpreter. How different the situation would be from when you just wandered about in front of the gate, waiting for the beck of others [the commentators]. Can there be anything more joyful than this?[63]

With his radical perspective and rare skill of being able to read Chinese as Chinese both in its modern and ancient forms, Sorai founded his own school upon returning to Edo.[64]

From the passages just quoted, we can imagine the excitement he caused as a teacher with his innovative Nagasaki method. Studying under Sorai, students could feel they were meeting and talking with the ancient sages, rather than merely studying about them. In contrast with the other academies, Sorai's curriculum offered an engaged rather than detached way to glean the wisdom of ancient Chinese texts. Word of this bright young scholar from the outlands began to spread through the city.

Sorai's prestige was no doubt enhanced by his father's renewed service as physician to Tsunayoshi, who had become shogun. Within a few years, Yanagisawa Yoshiyasu (1658–1714), the shogun's chamberlain, offered Sorai an official position with his family. Serving as an advisor as well as a Confucian scholar, Sorai became a counsel to Yoshiyasu and sometimes even to the shogun himself on matters of state and governance as well as philological or literary matters.

On the death of Tsunayoshi in 1709, however, there was a shift in political orientation as the new shoguns, Tokugawa Ienobu (1662–1712) and later his son Ietsugu (1709–1716), assumed office. Ienobu was Tsunayoshi's nephew and, since Tsunayoshi had no sons of his own, became his adopted son. Ienobu had a close relation with the samurai Confucian scholar, Arai Hakuseki (1657–1725).[65]   387–92
As attaché to Ienobu's chamberlain, Hakuseki became tutor and confidant to both Ienobu and his son, who reigned as a child shogun from the age of three until his death a few years later.

Hakuseki attacked Sorai's scholarship and the Nagasaki method, ridiculing him for taking the modern language of sailors from South China to represent the eloquent language of the sage kings.[66] In the political arena, Hakuseki convinced Ienobu to change many fiscal and foreign policies that Tsunayoshi had put into effect, policies that Sorai had originally endorsed.[67*] Because of that transition in power, and in fear of surveillance or recrimination from the new shogun and his tutor, Sorai took his master's advice, retiring from his position with the Yanagisawa house and opening with its support a new private school, the Miscanthus Patch Academy (Ken'en juku).

During this final period of his career, Sorai developed his philosophical ideas most fully, especially in his *Distinguishing the Way* (*Bendō*) and *Distinguishing Names* (*Benmei*). Both books sharply criticized most other schools and teachers of Confucian studies, including the neo-Confucian Shushigaku and Yōmeigaku, as well as many details of Itō Jinsai's Kogigaku philosophy. In 1714 Sorai became a controversial public figure when *Jottings from the Miscanthus Patch* (*Ken'en zuihitsu*) appeared in print, a work pointedly critical of Jinsai.[68]

In light of his father's exile experience, Sorai was likely wary of further confrontation and his two most developed works, *Distinguishing the Way* and *Distinguishing Names,* did not see publication until 1737, nine years after his death. As he was writing those two works, however, a new shogun from a different branch of the Tokugawa family, Yoshimune (1684–1751), came to power. He wanted to restore Tsunayoshi's policies and commissioned Sorai to write two treatises on the theory and practice of government with special attention to issues of current concern. Those two works, *A Proposal for Great Peace* (*Taiheisaku*) and *Discourse on Government* (*Seidan*),[69] went beyond practical advice on current political matters, developing an ideology supporting a totalitarian feudal form of governance under shoguns, rather than either imperial rule or something more egalitarian.

Lastly, just a year before he died, Sorai published his several-year correspondence with two feudal warriors on various matters of political and moral practice. Those letters, *Master Sorai's Responsals* (*Sorai sensei tōmonsho*), give us further insights into Sorai's thinking at this most active philosophical time in his life. That collection of texts—*Distinguishing the Way, Distinguishing Names, A Proposal for Great Peace, Discourse on Government,* and *Responsals*—represent Sorai's philosophy as I will discuss it in the rest of this chapter.

SORAI'S PHILOSOPHICAL QUESTIONS

To engage Sorai, we need to be clear about the questions he wanted to address and the previous approaches available to him. Like most other Confucians, Sorai inquired into the means to a peaceful, harmonious, and prosperous society built on appropriate interpersonal relations. In western categories, we could say his primary interests were ethics and politics. Putting the issue in those terms, we can pose our first philosophical question this way: assuming an intimate connection between personal normative behavior and political harmony, should we go from ethics to politics or from politics to ethics?

Ethics and Politics

One alternative assumes social harmony begins with developing the character of individuals. That is, we need to cultivate sagely leaders, accomplished scholar politicians, who can properly set the foundations for a harmonious society. Mere laws, however well formulated, would be worthless unless the people could understand and dedicate themselves to the values behind them. In Sorai's time, most Confucians accepted that premise, placing their priority on the self-cultivation of the five classical virtues: wisdom, benevolence, filial piety, rightness, and trustworthiness. Before being capable of ruling, the rulers had to undergo thorough training in the Confucian Way.

However much the philosophers ranging from Jinsai to the neo-Confucians agreed on that long-range goal, as we saw in Chapter 8, they vigorously debated the practical means to getting there: studying the classics or carefully investigating physical phenomena or turning inward in contemplation. Those disputes generated an array of metapractical philosophies, each based in its own assumptions about human nature, the structure of the natural world, and the pedagogy for teaching virtue.

Sorai rejected the very premise underlying those debates. For him, the proper Confucian Way is to go in the opposite direction, that is, to go from politics to ethics or from social to individual virtue. In making his case, he attacked the fundamental assumptions of his opponents about sagehood, human nature, and the scope of reason. In particular, he claimed that it is impossible to become a sage today, that there has not been a sage since Confucius, and that there will never be another. Hence, the efforts of philosophers who hope to cultivate sageliness as a precursor to cultivating a harmonious society are futile. Even more radically, Sorai argued that human nature is not a constant across individuals: people are not the same in their potential for moral development or wisdom.

Sorai was dismayed that so many of his contemporaries did not recognize that fact. He surmised their blindness was a consequence of Buddhism's corrupting fantasies about universal buddha-nature and inherent awakening. That misguided Buddhist egalitarianism had seeped into the Confucian traditions of China, Korea, and Japan, turning them away from the original insights of Confucius and the sage kings of ancient China. According to Sorai, one can do nothing to transform the character with which one is born. Some people are simply born with better character than others.

408–9

In the ancient Chinese classics, unlike Buddhist texts, Sorai could find no trace of egalitarianism: not political, not metaphysical, and not spiritual. Put bluntly, Sorai asserted some people are *by nature* better than others, an idea contrary to most of the preceding two millennia of Confucian philosophy.

Indeed, that innate difference justifies why there must be those who rule and those who are ruled. Unless we accept that fact, Sorai claimed, we cannot ever hope to establish a harmonious society.

Lastly, Sorai agreed with his contemporaries about how Confucian philosophy had evolved over the centuries. Namely, it sprouted from its roots in the ancient Six Classics to then develop through the contributions of Confucius, then the early commentators like Mencius and Xunzi, the Chinese neo-Confucian schools and their Japanese offshoots, Shushigaku and Yōmeigaku. As it evolved, Confucianism engaged in increasingly intricate forms of analysis, systemization, and rational argument. Yet, Sorai (and to a lesser extent Itō Jinsai and Yamaga Sokō before him) evaluated that historical trajectory as one of degeneration rather than progress. As Sorai says in *Distinguishing the Way*:

> Now, the Way is the Way of the early kings. Yet from Zisi [the reputed author of the *Doctrine of the Mean*] and Mencius on down, it must said that Confucians have only belittled [the Way] ever since they began debating about it with the hundred schools.[70]

All commentaries after Confucius were, to Sorai's understanding, no more than arguments to persuade critics and disbelievers, arguments necessary only because the audience had lost its trust in authoritative leadership. According to Sorai, trust is the foundation of the Confucian Way, a tradition based not on disputation, but on evaluating how a person behaves, or on respecting what a person is.

Sorai concluded, therefore, that the rational debates that had become so prominent in the Confucianism of his time were actually deviations from the Way of the sage kings. He maintained that Confucian commentators had become so entrenched in their disputes that they mistook argumentation for the Way itself, thereby undermining the very tradition they assumed they were defending. As we saw with his system for reading classic texts, Sorai always favored a direct, unconvoluted approach to acquiring wisdom.

Sorai's theory of textuality led him to rethink the nature of discourse and its role in establishing the social harmony associated with the ancient Chinese sages. His theory of language was the connective tissue between his early philological work and his normative vision of society.

Philosophy of Language

An underlying premise in Confucianism of any form is that social harmony depends on people's treating one another properly. The first question, then, is how to understand the moral concepts supporting such appropriate behavior.

Trueing up the terms. As I explained in Chapter 2's discussion of Chinese thought at Shōtoku's time,[†] Confucianism argues for the convergence between terms we use to describe human relations and those we use to prescribe how those relations should be enacted. For example, if I understand what it *is* to be a husband, I do not then have to ask how a husband *should* behave. In the modern West, parting company with most ancient and medieval traditions, philosophers like David Hume (1711–1776) introduced a strong distinction between *is* and *ought*, between facts and values, between the descriptive and the prescriptive. For Hume those binaries are separated by an unbridgeable gap. Hume's bifurcation lies behind today's familiar claim, for example, that science's task is to gain factual knowledge about how the world *is*, not to judge how we *ought* to use that knowledge; science describes but does not prescribe.

Such a sharp separation of fact and value runs counter to the basic Confucian world view. Confucianism maintains that the descriptive is inextricably linked to the prescriptive. Because the is-ought distinction is so deeply engrained in modern western philosophical thinking, the Confucian view might at first seem counterintuitive to readers from that tradition. Yet, our everyday way of speaking belies Hume's strong distinction.

For example, we would not normally say "Be an *adult*! And furthermore, act as an adult *should* act!" or "She was a *real* teacher. But, more than that, she was a *good* teacher." When we speak of a person as acting in some interpersonal role, it is natural to assume that a person who is *really* performing in that role is acting as one *should* behave in that role. Accordingly, the Confucian response to the problems of social disharmony is that we would all be better off if parents were really parents, children were really children, husbands really husbands, wives really wives, friends really friends, rulers really rulers, subjects really subjects, and so forth. This is the aforementioned doctrine of the "rectification of names" or, as I prefer to translate it, "trueing up the terms" (*seimei*).

Following that ancient insight, Sorai insisted on getting the terms right and his book, *Distinguishing Names*, is a philosophical lexicon in which each critical term has its own heading and explication. Viewed in its proper Confucian context, the book is much more than a mere glossary of key expressions, though. In accord with the principle of trueing up the terms, a Confucian discussion of a word's meaning, however historical or philological, always has a prescriptive edge as well as a descriptive core. To know fully what a term describing human relations means is to know how human relations should be lived. In short: Confucian lexicons are intrinsically normative; the study of words is inherently linked to the study of ethics and politics.[71]

† See pages 49-51.

395–6

In his Preface to *Distinguishing Names,* after stressing the importance of understanding the true meaning of words, Sorai inquires into how words first arise. Obviously, for many ordinary words we match word and reality straightforwardly by what philosophers today call ostension or "showing." If you do not know what the word *sun* means, I can simply point to the sun. It is easy to imagine how such words could take form and, as Sorai notes, such naming of physical objects requires no particular genius.

Still, how can we explain the origin of names for abstractions toward which we cannot gesture? Or, more to the heart of Sorai's concerns, how could a name develop for a virtue such as "benevolence" or for a regulative ideal like "the Way" (*dao* in Chinese) or for a model relation like "friend"? For that to happen, Sorai reasoned, someone had to manifest the referent before there was a word for it: there had to be a virtuous person before one could make a name for the virtue, an actual friend before there was a word for "friend."

Yet, if the first virtuous person wished to teach others about virtue, she would need to name the virtues, the virtue of "friendship," for instance. To teach the word, she would need to point to what the word "friend" refers. How? By *being* a friend and *showing* how a friend acts. Analogously, we can fully understand benevolence, for instance, only by encountering a truly benevolent person. And we can become benevolent only by modeling ourselves after such a person. Learning the Way derives not from detached analysis, but from a form of engagement, namely, the emulation of those who follow the Way. A word naming a virtue or a human relation points not to a thing, but to a mode of interpersonal behavior. In the final analysis, therefore, moral terms like "benevolence" refer to a *how* not a *what*.

In Sorai, then, we find an intriguing mix of detached and engaged knowing at the heart of his system. On one hand, his general theory of language relies on ostension, even for words referring to abstractions or to virtues. That is, he assumes there must be a preexisting reality to which words are subsequently devised to refer. To that extent, Sorai's view is strictly a theory of language as *reference,* which in contrast to a theory of language as *conference,* involves a detachment between the speaker and the object.

On the other hand, according to Sorai, to really understand the meaning of a word, at least a word referring to a virtue, one must engage it by enacting it. That is because the referents of moral terms are performative behaviors, not static objects like the sun which can be designated by the word "sun." Since the way to know the meaning of a named virtue is to perform it, once one knows the word, one has already enacted the word's meaning. In summary, Sorai's theory of the nature of language involves external reference and detachment, but when he describes the process of learning a key term, the aim is to achieve a form of engaged knowing.

A major question, however, is how such a system of meaning-performance could ever have started. It seems we have a chicken-and-the-egg problem. Without the performance of a virtue to emulate, we cannot have the word for the virtue. Yet, without the named virtue, there is nothing to emulate. For Sorai, the answer to the conundrum lay in correctly understanding the role played by the ancient sage kings whom Confucius considered to be the prototypes for a harmonious society. As we will see, Sorai's ultimate solution to the problem resembles a *deus ex machina*.[72]

The role of the sage kings. If we follow Sorai's line of thought back to its theoretical starting point, we come to his most fundamental premise. In the beginning, there had to be someone or some group of people who somehow just became virtuous. Then, after exemplifying the virtues, they could name them appropriately. Subsequently, other people could learn to act virtuously as they came to understand the terms and to model themselves after how the prototypes exemplified them. According to Sorai, those paragons of virtue "at the beginning" of human civilization were the sage kings of ancient China, the ones whose terminology and conduct fill the pages of the Six Classics (the *Books of History, Odes, Rites, Music,* and *Changes* as well as the *Spring and Autumn Annals*).

For Sorai, we humans can never fully fathom the source of life and meaning, that cosmic force called "heaven" (*ten;* C. *tian*). Heaven is beyond human comprehension. Yet, as the basis of all harmony, it demands of us that we preserve harmony in our own lives. Through some extraordinary event at the dawn of human civilization, a few remarkable people—the sage kings of ancient China—felt this call to concord. Being merely human, to them the call itself was inexplicable; they could not describe, explain, or even understand what engulfed them. Yet, they felt this heavenly mandate (*tenmei*) in every fiber of their being.

400–1

The ancient sage kings responded to that mandate by devising a system within their own repertoire of human feelings, thoughts, and actions. In so doing, they could exemplify how to live in the world harmoniously. The sage kings did not teach about heaven or how it works: how could they express in philosophical doctrines what they did not fully understand themselves? Still, they could perform the ideal of social harmony by the style of their behavior and attitude. They could exemplify the basic binaries needed to comprise an ideal society: parent and child, senior and junior, husband and wife, ruler and subject, friend and friend. Their paradigms of virtue gave us the Way (J. *dō* or *michi;* C. *dao*). This Way is the mode of human relationship expressing and preserving harmony, for both now and for future generations.

This grand vision of origins has mystical undertones, but our task today, according to Sorai, is not to be mystical. There is no need for the contemplative praxis of the Buddhists, the Daoists, or the Yōmeigaku Confucians or even that followed by some Shushigaku Confucians. The mystic moment of revelation, if we want to think of it as that, only occurred at one time in the distant past and need not occur again. We no longer need sages and surely by no efforts of our own can we make ourselves into sages.

Even the sage kings did not train to become sages; it just happened to them as part of heaven's call. This mandate from heaven may suggest intention, and Sorai does not criticize the occasional references in the ancient classics to a personified Lord of heaven called *Shangdi*.[73]* In the final analysis, though, Sorai was not concerned with whether there is a being in charge of heaven. For him, the pivotal point was only that the call to harmony issues from heaven. That call to harmony is our common vocation as human beings living between heaven and earth.

There is one further crucial step in the progression toward a harmonious society, however. With all the books available to us, how can we know which to choose for guidance? How can we be sure the Six Classics are the proper foundation? Sorai saw in this question the need for one more sage, a second-order sage or "meta-sage," we could say. There must have been a wise person who lived close enough to the times of the ancient sage kings and their texts to understand their unique value and to point this out for all future generations. Such a second-order sage did not create virtues and words himself, but knew where to look for them. That sage was Confucius.

Sorai understood the contribution of Confucius's *Analects* to lie in its citations from, and its extolling the significance of, the Six Classics. There will be no further sages after him not because of decadence or *mappō*, but simply because there is no longer a need for any more sages. The sages have already epitomized all the virtues and all we need do is emulate and adapt those models. If the vocabulary of the virtues already points ostensively to their referents, that is, to the performance of the sage kings, the process of developing an ethic has already reached its completion. We need only adapt those prescriptive behaviors to our present circumstances. That word *adapt* does raise a further issue, however.

Organicism. If the sage kings really got it right, there would presumably be no need for later adjustments. Yet, Sorai did not think that to be the case, partly because he accepted an organicism articulated by some of his contemporaries such as Kaibara Ekken. As I noted in our last chapter,† Ekken had highlighted

† See pages 313-14.

the omnipresent flow of the life force, the matter-energy field known as *ki*. Sorai followed Ekken in saying that "things" (*butsu*) were "living things" (*katsubutsu*), that is, life is a not a physical phenomenon, but instead physical phenomena are life. As a vital power that is both matter and energy, *ki* has its own patterns of ebb-and-flow, give-and-take, *yin*-and-*yang*. If one wants to map that flow abstractly, one can identify its "pattern" or *ri*.

Many latter-day Confucians, according to Ekken (and Sorai agreed with him on this point), had made the error of taking the abstraction as the primary reality and saying the physical world of matter-energy conformed to it. They misconstrued this pattern to be a "principle" that defines and orders the stuff (*ki*). From the organicists' view, however, that way of thinking is backward—like saying the Mississippi River follows the map in making its way from Minnesota to New Orleans. In reality, of course, the map (if it is a good one) conforms to the flow of the Mississippi River. The Mississippi River determines its own course, the path that the map later depicts. Analogously, *ri* does not control or direct *ki*, but only represents—after the fact—the patterns *ki* has followed in life's ever-changing circumstances and shifts in historical context. For those reasons, Ekken insisted the proper object of study was the physical world as this omnipresent, pulsating reality.

Sorai agreed that things, as living things, are always in transition. He differed from Ekken's naturalism concerning what to study, however. Instead of focusing on the fluctuating things themselves, Sorai stressed the study of change longitudinally through human history. Therefore, although the sage kings embodied and named the key virtues and patterns of human relations, how to enact those virtues must adjust to changing historical circumstances. Although the sage kings displayed how to be benevolent or how to act in the right way, they did so in the context of ancient China, not of the Edo Japan of Sorai's contemporaries (with its heavily populated urban centers, for example). The virtues remain constant, but their practical expression must adapt to the flux of events.

As for historical change, Sorai taught that after fathoming the Way of the sage kings, you should then study later history for its insight into how present affairs came about. Without that knowledge, you cannot effectively adapt the Way to our current situation. Just as *ki* changes in its manifestation, so must the performance of the ancient virtues. The virtues cannot be, Sorai reasoned, fixed principles that dictate the same behavior in every possible, ever-changing circumstance. In effect, Sorai shifted his focus from how the sage kings actually *did* exemplify the virtues in ancient China to how they *would* do so in the present situations. Clearly, such speculation necessarily involves interpretation. So, the question now is this: who determines how the sage kings would act today and what is the basis for such a judgment?

38–9

Sorai deemed the typical answers to such questions in his day to be inadequate. One wrong approach would be to let people individually decide for themselves, a situation Sorai believed would end in chaos. To his mind, such a democratic idea likely derived from the Buddhist mistake of thinking everyone can be equally good, can be both wise and virtuous. Indeed, the Shōtoku *Constitution* had said as much.[†] Yet, human history, Sorai insisted, disproves that assumption. When it comes to acting suitably, most people have to be led or at least trained because they are unable to become virtuous on their own.

Another erroneous approach to answering the question of how sage-kings would conduct themselves today, Sorai believed, would be to analyze the behavior of the sage kings in hopes of uncovering the principles behind their actions. Many neo-Confucians would take such an approach, hoping to unearth the ancient precepts and then apply them to our present-day context. Yet, the sage kings did not use principles for guidance any more than the river uses a map to plan its course. If the sage kings had acted according to principles, Sorai asked, then why did they not say so? Indeed, the ancient texts make no mention of the word principle (*ri*) at all. It would be folly to presume we could understand what the sages would do in our context, if the way we understand the sages' actions were unlike the way the sages would have understood their own conduct. (Remember, understanding involves emulating the ideal behavior of the sages. We cannot do so by superimposing our ideas on their actions.)

A third misguided response, Sorai felt, would be to let things just be: the natural Way will be clear when we stop trying to impose our ideas on the situation. That is basically the agenda-less spontaneity (C. *wuwei*; J. *mui*) that Daoists promote.[74] According to Sorai, the Daoists are right not to use fixed, absolute rules to govern action in an ever-shifting world, but they are mistaken if they think the conduct of the sage kings was simply "natural" or "spontaneous." The virtues were consciously developed by the sages after being inspired by heavenly mandate. Hence, it would be a mistake to return to Daoist naturalism. The conduct of the sage kings, not nature, teaches us how to act.

TRAINING THE RULERS

If Sorai rejects those three options, in his view who does make the necessary adaptations in performing the virtues and on what basis do they decide? For Sorai, the answer to "who" is simple: those with the talent (the virtue) to lead and to teach, those known in Confucian terminology as the "accomplished ones" (*kunshi*; C. *junzi*). These accomplished ones are not sages and therefore cannot establish the Way for communal life, but they have learned

---

† See pages 64–5; 71–2.

the Way of the ancients and have matched their demeanor to it. Supplemented by their study of history, they have acquired the expert knowledge for conducting human affairs appropriate to shifting circumstances.

Not everyone has the native capacity to perform such a crucial role, however, since it involves, for one, the ability to see and do what is good for the whole and not just oneself. According to Sorai, this is an innate quality found in the samurai: they can see the forest for the trees, while the general populace or plain people (*shōjin*)[75] can only attend to the details of making a living. The farmer concentrates on the single task of "cultivating the fields and feeding the people"; the artisans on "making household goods for the people to use"; the merchants on "keeping produce and goods circulating so as to benefit the people of the world." The samurai, however, "oversee all of this and prevent disorder."

That fourfold class system, Sorai claims, "did not exist naturally in heaven and earth" but was the doing of the ancient sages (and presumably in putting the class system in place, the Tokugawa shogunate had just revived an ancient practice).[76] All four classes must perform their respective roles in a harmonious society. To that extent each person has an appropriate role to play in society, functioning in effect as "officials" of the state:

> Although each class performs its own duties, each assists the others, and so if any one class were lacking, the country would be the worse for it. Because people live together, they are all officials helping the ruler become the "father and mother of the people." Seen in this way, things should be clear. This is why knights are called "accomplished ones."[77]

Sorai assumed that those selected for training as accomplished ones would come from the samurai class since nature has endowed them with the innate talent to rule.[78] That claim of special innate virtue distinguished him from Yamaga Sokō and Nakae Tōju who, as we saw in Chapter 8, argued that the status of the samurai relieved them of the onus of having to earn a living as a farmer, tradesman, or merchant. That freedom, in turn, allowed them the time to concentrate exclusively on studying the Way and cultivating virtue. That is, for Sokō and Tōju, being a samurai was more a matter of privileged birth entailing a sense of social responsibility or *noblesse oblige*, whereas Sorai believed samurai were intrinsically superior human beings whose virtue should be nurtured as a valuable resource of the state.

Given that class bias, some translators render Sorai's use of the term *kunshi* as "prince," rather than the more general "accomplished person." The translation as "prince" is highly suggestive in other ways as well. In light of Sorai's political ideas, the rendering as "prince" calls to mind the Italian Renaissance political treatise, *The Prince*, by Nicolo Machiavelli (1469–1527). The juxtaposition of the two thinkers makes for a provocative comparison as we shall now see.

The Machiavellian Sorai

Maruyama Masao (1914–1996), arguably Japan's most prominent postwar intellectual historian, was able to find several significant correlations between the two thinkers.[79] For example, he pointed out both Sorai and Machiavelli[80*] directed their political treatises to ruling dictators (Sorai assumed the shogun, not the emperor, was the *de facto* ruler of Japan). Both suggested techniques for maintaining and executing absolute power. Both insisted that the ruler's success lay in developing an effective state that could, above all, protect its own sovereignty. Both argued that behavior supporting political stability and the preservation of power takes priority over the need for the ruler to live a personally moral life. That last point particularly interested Maruyama.

Maruyama's reading along the Machiavellian line of comparison is that Sorai drew a sharp wedge between the public sphere of politics (which was left to the discretion of the rulers) and the private sphere of morality (where the scholarly goal was to master the classics).[81*] In Maruyama's interpretation, Sorai believed that the scholar's role in society, as contrasted with that of the political leader, was only for the development of that private sphere and self-cultivation.

> But for Sorai, who had broken the continuity between private morality and politics, ... the scholar's work is at most to gain an understanding of the Way and explain it. Inventing the Way or putting it into practice is a task left to political rulers.[82]

Maruyama musters support for his position from such Sorai quotations as "learning is different from public duties; after all, it is a private matter" and "the task of Confucian scholars is to preserve phrases and sentences and pass them on to future generations.... This is their only duty."[83]

Maruyama sees such statements as signaling Sorai's departure from the former Confucian ideal in which the private morality and public authority of the ruler were inseparable. As such, Sorai becomes a harbinger in Japan for a more modernist view of the state, one which separates politics from the dominance of religio-moral systems. Writing in the immediate postwar period, Maruyama was interested in exploring the history of Tokugawa political theory in search of factors leading to Japan's disastrous ethnocentric totalitarianism as well as of ideas, however undeveloped, that might be used in building a historical foundation for a postwar Japanese democracy. In his comparison with Machiavelli, Maruyama believed he could demonstrate that Sorai's philosophy could contribute to both parts of his agenda.

Yet, my agenda in this book is not Maruyama's. So I think it critical for the sake of understanding Sorai's place within the larger framework of the history of Japanese philosophy to elaborate another profile of his thought, one in which the political and scholarly are not so sharply separated. I can most easily define that profile of Sorai's philosophy by explaining in more detail Sorai's pedagogical theory in relation to the "princes." Sorai's ruminations about how a scholar should train rulers was not simply an idealized thought experiment. He had designed a specific curriculum for transforming rulers into accomplished ones. And for those who did not complete that curriculum, he advocated that they keep the scholars close at hand as advisors.

In the end, my analysis will be that the wedge Maruyama saw Sorai insert between the private and the public does not cut all the way through. In fact, as we examine more closely the pedagogical profile of Sorai, I will argue he begins to resemble Plato more than Machiavelli.

Sorai's Educational Agenda

What training do the samurai need to become effective rulers? For Sorai, as already noted, the Way of the sage kings is not a product of nature or even the direct activity of heaven, but rather the design put into place by ordinary human beings, however remarkable. As is by now a familiar move to us in studying the history of Japanese philosophy, Sorai makes it clear the Way is not a "what," but a "how." Consequently, when the latter-day Confucian philosophers explained heaven as "principle" or "pattern," they were committing a double error.

First, they were asserting we can know what heaven is. Sorai sees that as the height of human arrogance and folly. The Way is not a factual knowledge about heaven, but instead the result of the sage kings' devising ways to bring about the harmony mandated by heaven. We can know only how the sage kings responded to heaven; we cannot know heaven itself. The neo-Confucian quest for the "pattern of heaven" (*tenri*) is a fool's errand.

Second, Sorai believed the later Confucians were also mistaken in their obsessive "investigation of things" that attempts to discover principle or pattern (*ri*) in physical objects and then to match them with patterns in their minds. According to Sorai, that whole project was destined to fail as well since we cannot fathom the intricacies and mysteries of the natural world any more than those of heaven. We have enough of a challenge in just trying to understand and manage the human world.[84]

Besides, the sage kings did not give us principles or explain patterns, but instead, simply showed us how to act, creating names for the values they exemplified, the virtues that Confucius himself latter praised so highly. Those traditional values, not the natural world, should be our focus. To learn the Way is to copy those patterns of behavior, to enact them ritually, which is to say, to perform them repeatedly until they become second nature.

The educational praxis for the accomplished ones, therefore, is to internalize the Way of the sage kings, following their paradigm of conduct. To do that the student must engage the ancient texts with their whole selves, mind and body. As Sorai says in *Distinguishing the Names*: "Contrasting the body and mind comes from Buddhist texts" and is alien to the Way of the sage kings, a praxis based in ritual action (*rei; C. li*), which is to say, the praxis of bodymind.[85]

That Way applies to four domains: "There is not something called 'the Way' apart from [the sage kings'] rites, music, penal laws, and administrative systems of government."[86] In that list the first two—rites and music—are required of everyone insofar as they are part of a society. No one lacks the capacity to practice music and the rites of appropriate behavior. Because such practice involves attention to detail, even commoners can understand what is required. Through music they will learn harmony; through the rites of appropriate behavior, they will learn the proper way to perform their binary human relations.

The latter two domains of the Way—laws and administrative institutions— are different in that they require the aptitude to discern what is best for the whole rather than just oneself, and to act in the interests of a harmonious society serving everyone. Those domains of praxis are available only to those possessing the innate talent to appreciate and perform them: the "accomplished ones" or at least "princes"-in-training.

Mastering the Six Classics and the Ancient Literary Style

Because the most important quality of rulership is achieved by internalizing the Way of the sage kings, the next question is how to do so. Sorai says you must absorb the words of the Six Classics so they become the core of your feelings and sensitivities. This involves the ability to not just read the words, but to internalize their style, to make them your own. He calls this ancient literary style "*kobunji*" and Sorai's school of philosophy is, therefore, known as *kobunjigaku*, "the learning of the ancient literary style."

To understand what Sorai means by that nomenclature, we can break down the term *kobunjigaku* into the four sinographs comprising it. *Ko* means "ancient" or "archaic" and for Sorai it refers specifically to the styles of language beginning with the Six Classics and continuing in most Chinese texts up to around the beginning the Common Era. That includes works like *Daodejing* and *Zhuangzi*, for example, even though their content is Daoist and on most points mistaken according to Sorai. He did recommend studying them, however, for mastering their ancient literary style.

The *bun* of *kobunjigaku* refers to "culture," especially literary culture. So, it means for Sorai something like "cultured expressions" which in turn connects with the third part of the compound term *ji,* which normally means words or verbal expressions. Sorai insists on distinguishing these from ordinary words (*gen*), however, and to be explicit sometimes adds a prefix to *ji* meaning "cultivation" or "mastery," thereby giving us the term "mastery words" (*shuji*).[87] For Sorai, ordinary words, like those of everyday speech and uncultured prose, are sloppy and imprecise, falling prey to a verbosity that erodes the direct link between word and fact.[88]*

By contrast, Sorai maintained that the ancient literary style avoids superfluous words and has a sense of "rightness" (*gi*). Such language not only successfully "conveys the meaning" (*tatsui*) but also uses just the right expression to do so, the "mastery words." Sorai believed this combination gave the ancient literary style a unique dual function. On one hand, in its straightforward communicative capacity, it had the precision to speak what is genuine and true (*makoto*). On the other hand, in its cultivated mastery of nuance, the ancient literary style also displays an openness or suggestiveness (*ganchiku*).

That openness makes the ancient language more adaptable to changing contexts as they arise. Since all things are "living things" (*katsubutsu*), they are forever in flux, but the openness of the ancient words allows them to shift in meaning in accord with the changing realities. Sorai was one of the first Japanese thinkers to address the importance of the historical development of language and its relevance to truth. His insight is that language must change because the state of affairs to which language refers is always changing.

Finally, *gaku*—the last term in the compound *kobunjigaku*—is the now familiar sinograph meaning "study" or "learning," especially through emulation. In developing his emphasis on the ancient literary style, Sorai's inspiration was the Chinese poetics of Li Panlong (1514–1549) and Wang Shizhen (1526–1590). In their own writings, they modeled their style on that of the ancient poets whom they studied. Although Sorai's primary interest was philosophy, ethics, and politics rather than poetry, he heartily endorsed the notion of studying as emulating. Perhaps it resonated with his childhood experience in Kazusa of reading and rereading the book in the box.

In accord with his theory of learning, Sorai had his students study the ancient literary style until they could easily express themselves in it, a pedagogy that led his critics to mock his school for doing no more than training imitators. Sorai responded in a letter that although it may start out as mimicry, his idea of engaged reading does not stop there.

> However, once you get accustomed to those models, the habit becomes your nature, and even what came from the exterior becomes your own flesh. Hence, those who carp at imitating do not yet know the true meaning of studying.[89]

Sorai further explained that in assimilating the ancient literary style as their own, students must distinguish its two rhetorical forms: descriptive (*joji no bun*) and argumentative (*giron no bun*). For learning syntax, both are beneficial, but Sorai insisted his students follow only the former as a model for their own writing. He believed the descriptive fits his praxis of emulation because it conforms word to reality whereas he deemed the argumentative, as I explained earlier, to be a form of persuasion directed toward someone who, at least initially, does not trust what we have to say.

When trying to be convincing to a skeptic, we tend to adopt for the sake of argument our opponent's categories. Because those categories arise not from our direct relation with reality, but from a mistaken perspective (the wrongheaded point of view of the person with whom we are arguing), the words lose their capacity to directly match things. As a result, we distance ourselves from the truth even as we "win" the argument.[90] Sorai's system obviously does not consider refutation or reductio arguments to be reliable means for arriving at the truth.

Not only does argument lack trust, but it also creates metaphysical ideas such as "principle" or "universal human nature" that have no correlates in the vocabulary of the ancient classics. According to Sorai, we do not serve Confucianism well if in defending it against the metaphysical arguments of its critics, we develop our own metaphysical way of speaking that is alien to the Way of the sage kings. Grounded as he was in praxis, Sorai judged metaphysical categories to be of no practical benefit. Indeed, they are outrightly counterproductive.[91]*

Surprisingly, Sorai concurred with the Confucian maxim popular in his day (and favored especially by the Shushigaku philosophers) that the accomplished ones should engage in *kakubutsu*, which usually means the "investigation of things." He gave the phrase a new twist, however, by reinterpreting the two constituent terms *kaku* ("investigating") and *butsu* ("things"). Let us begin with the second sinograph, *butsu*. As suggested in his criticism of the metaphysical strains of neo-Confucianism, Sorai held that the "things" to study are the forms of social behavior. In so doing, he clearly disassociated himself from those who identified *kakubutsu* with what we might today think of as empirical natural science.

For Sorai, the category *butsu*[92] includes the two subcategories of "performative events" (*ji*) and the aforementioned "verbal expressions" (*ji*).† In linking those terms with the classics of the ancient literary style, Sorai suggests the content of the *Book of Music* and the *Book of Rites* exemplifies the proper forms of ritual behavior (*rei*; C. *li*), that is, physical performance. By following the practices in those books, you can grasp the meaning of harmony (*wa*) in music and the

---

† Despite identical pronunciation, these are different words. The *ji* (事) I translate here as "performative events" usually refers broadly to just "events" of any sort, but Sorai almost always restricts the term to human affairs. The *ji* (辭; in modern form 辞) meaning verbal expression is the same *ji* from *kobunji*, that is, the term for "(mastery) words."

meaning of centeredness (*chū*) in the ritualized conduct. The *Book of Odes* and *Book of History*, by contrast, concern rightness (*gi*) and are thereby associated with correct verbal expression. Putting these together, by studying the "things" (*butsu*) in the classics, you can enact the Way of the sage kings both behaviorally and verbally. This brings us to Sorai's interpretation of the *kaku* of *kakubutsu*.

Sorai understands *kaku* to mean not the "investigation" of things (which smacks of detached knowing), but rather, being open to letting the things come forward and becoming part of us (a more engaged paradigm of knowing).[93*] As he states in *Distinguishing the Way*:

> "Things" [*butsu*] refer to the good things associated with the rites [*rei*]. *Kaku* refers to "coming...." When the good things associated with the rites come to us completely, then our knowledge of them becomes naturally clear. Such were the methods of the sage kings' teachings.[94]

That passage enhances Sorai's previous point about the meaning of "learning" (*gaku*), an educational model more intimate and engaged than what he took to be the usual understanding among neo-Confucians. For Sorai, to learn is to emulate and to emulate means to follow an instance of ideal behavior.

To learn from the sage kings, therefore, is more like learning a dance step from someone than learning something from a book or from our own inner reflection. After learning the step, though, we will not simply ape it on the dance floor, but will instead inevitably adapt the movements to our circumstance and particular needs, just as the accomplished ones will make the adjustments needed to suit the practice of the Way of ancient Chinese sages to the context of Edo Japan.

Sorai, therefore, advocates what modern-day educators sometimes call "learning by doing," or perhaps even better, "learning *in* doing." That is, the learning is not the result of the doing, but is the doing itself. Despite his cynicism about Buddhism, on this point at least, Sorai (perhaps unwittingly) is in agreement with Kūkai's understanding of ritual praxis as well as Dōgen's view that practice is itself enlightenment. In all three cases, the praxis is an end in itself, not a means to something else.

Classical Style, Ritual, and Political Leadership: A Modern Western Analogy

To some readers Sorai's links among ancient literary styles, ritualized behavior, and political harmony might seem exotic. So, I suggest considering an analogy from a western setting: the speeches of Martin Luther King, Jr., in the American civil rights movement of the 1960s. For King, the classic text was, of course, the Bible, particularly in its King James English translation. Raised as a devout Christian and trained as a minister, Dr. King studied that text with its archaic English expressions until its words, its rhythms, and its style became part of his own style. He studied the rhetoric of the Bible by absorbing it as his own.

He also evoked the lyrics of African-American spirituals, modern-day odes that embellish biblical words with the plaintive and hopeful expressions of the downtrodden. Because of his innate talents and years of training, King articulated the disharmony in his racially segregated society through the biblical language of enslavement, captivity, exodus, and liberation. He did not so much argue as *perform* his philosophy.

For example, King did not try to persuade through scientific studies that blacks are equal to whites. Nor did he often present his case in terms of formal law or principle. (King's ideal of justice was more biblical than constitutional.) Instead, applying Sorai's terminology, we could say he used descriptive discourse (*joji no bun*), not argumentative discourse (*giron no bun*). He described and presented himself as a black man, a Christian, and an American, embodying for his audience all the tensions those identities entailed in his society.

Using the Bible's venerable literary style (*kobunji*), King expressed discord, injustice, and the thirst for freedom. Instead of an argument, he had a "dream" and he orchestrated the harmony (*wa*) envisioned in that dream with the ritual of singing—blacks and whites together—"We Shall Overcome." Through the ritual (*rei*) of freedom marches, harking back to the exodus of the ancient Jews out of Egyptian captivity, he displayed the centeredness (*chū*) of avoiding the extremes of either passive resignation or violent opposition. Multitudes of ordinary folk (*shōjin*) did most of the singing; they did the marching; they worked the communication networks. Yet, what pulled the people together were the words of an accomplished person (*kunshi*) who brought the style and power of ancient words into a new situation. The result was eventually a step toward a more harmonious society, which is what heaven, whether Christian or Confucian, mandates.

Although we could obviously find many fundamental differences between Sorai's description of the accomplished one and the case of Martin Luther King, Jr., the comparison is nonetheless illuminating. King was certainly no samurai, by either privileged birth or martial temperament. Yet, through his educational training, he attuned himself to the biblical text and adjusted it to his modern circumstances just as Sorai says an accomplished person should. The comparison with King shows how the training in the words of a classic can be so internalized they become, in Sorai's words, part of the "flesh." When King spoke the words of the prophets, his audience could, as Sorai said, "feel that the classics flow out from his own mouth."

The Accountability of the Rulers and the Role of Scholars

Admittedly, as history teaches us and as it taught Sorai as well,[95*] political power can disrupt as well as harmonize. If the rulers have the innate virtue to see the whole and if they have access to the ancient prototypes of how to bring about harmony, then they are also accountable for any social disharmony their policies may cause.

In Sorai's early days as an advisor to the Tokugawa shogun Tsunayoshi, a defendant was brought before the shogun's court on charges of abandoning his mother, leaving her to fend for herself. The man's excuse was he had tried to take care of her, but his dire poverty made it impossible. When Tsunayoshi asked for Sorai's advice, Sorai noted the defendant's situation was by no means unique, since poverty was ravaging the countryside throughout Japan. Sorai contended the real responsibility lay first with those in charge of the economic and social welfare of the people, that is, the local magistrates and other officials (and ultimately the shōgun as well?). Compared with their failure to rule properly, the man's crime was insignificant.[96]

Thus, however much Sorai supported the samurai rule, especially that of the shogun, we can see he also insisted that such power to rule carries with it the moral burden of following the heavenly mandate to establish harmony. As samurai, the rulers have the innate talent to rule properly, but they need to nurture that talent through education, a process in which Confucian scholars (*ju*) play a critical role.

The accomplished ones cannot be self-taught when it comes to learning from the ancient sage kings. They need experts, the Confucian scholars, to guide them through the classics. In his political treatise, *Proposal for Great Peace* (*Taiheisaku*), Sorai complains about the lack of education among the samurai.

> Although they are called warriors (*bushi*), so long as they are concerned with the task of governing the state and the world, the samurai are rulers of the people. When they become commissioners or occupy other official positions, they are equivalent to a chief minister or high official,... but they fail to realize they are accomplished ones.... They fail to realize that talent and intellect are to be developed and broadened by learning and that the state is to be governed by letters. It is stupid in the extreme to think that the land can be governed by thrusting out one's elbows and glaring at the people, and by repressing the entire population by terrifying it with the threat of punishment.[97]

As a solution Sorai recommended the shogunate establish a number of schools with the curriculum Sorai designed.[98] Clearly, he thought it best if all government officials underwent his program, but he recognized that many samurai would not have the time or will to attain the education he wished for them. In that case, scholars like himself should be there as close advisors to rulers in administering the state. As Yoshikawa Kōjirō explains:

> Sorai firmly believed that the Way of the sage kings, which had primarily been the methods or techniques of government for rulers, could be attained through the study of classics, including the writing of prose and poetry as well as the performing of music. He regarded it as a duty of scholars to achieve [the learning of the Way] on behalf of politicians and to advise them on the basis of it if they were too occupied with their administrative work.[99]

Those pedagogical comments bring us to the Platonic, rather than Machiavellian, profile in Sorai's view of morality and politics.

The Platonic Sorai

In the *Republic,* Plato developed his ideal image of the state. Like Sorai, Plato believed people are born with different natures, talents, and proclivities. Consequently, he linked his ideal vision of the state to take those differences into account, speaking of three tiers in the social and political order. At the bottom were the producers (which would be the farmers, artisans, and merchants in the Edo society, that is, the townspeople). Motivated mainly by physical appetites, they look to the state to tend to their physical well-being in the form of food, shelter, and clothing. Plato's second tier consisted of the auxiliaries, the protectors and peacekeepers (analogous to most of the samurai in Edo society). Motivated mainly by spirit and emotions, they keep order in society and personally aspire to be courageous, holding honor or respect most dear.

At the top in Plato's scheme are the guardians or philosopher-kings (similar to Sorai's accomplished ones). They have an intuitive insight into the Good that they bring into overseeing the affairs of the state. Motivated only by the idea or form of the Good, they wish to regulate society for the harmony and well-being of all without any concern for personal wealth, honor, or power.

As he aged, Plato realized his ideal society run by philosopher-kings was not to be and in his later years became a political advisor to a dictator in Sicily. That did not go as he had hoped and so he returned to writing after abandoning his misadventure in practical politics, this time focusing on a more pragmatic approach to political theory in his works, *The Statesman* and *The Laws.* Even in his unfinished and longest work, *The Laws,* however, Plato still upheld the critical role of virtue in a ruler. He rejected the idea that just governance is ever simply a matter of law. A virtuous ruler, if not a philosopher-king at least someone trained in the Way of philosophy, must know how to interpret and, even sometimes, when to overrule the law. Plato might well have assented to Sorai's sentiments in *Responsals* when he wrote :

People are more important than laws. Even if laws are bad, considerable benefits accrue from them if the ones enforcing them are good. It is useless to examine the laws if evil people prevail.[100]

To sum up this comparison: there is evidence in Sorai's writings to support a Platonic, as well as a Machiavellian, reading of his political philosophy. At least at times, Sorai did write as if his goal was not simply to support the shogunate's authority to rule (as one might expect of a Machiavellian), but instead to show the way to a harmonious society by developing the virtue of leaders (as a Platonist would argue).

One aspect of Sorai's thought that does not mesh well with Platonism was his insistence that the ruler remain attuned to the needs of the people. For Plato, ideal rule was straightforwardly a top-down affair with the philosopher-kings coordinating all the social tiers below them. Though no supporter of democracy in any form, Sorai did recognize that it was in the best interest of the state for its rulers to be "attentive to people's concerns." He wrote in *Responsals*:

> For example, no matter how much one regulates one's mind and refines one's person and no matter whether one is as polished as the most perfect gem, if one is not attentive to the people's concerns and livelihood and if one does not know how to govern the country, what difference will all this make? Thus, if one does not see things in terms of "the father and mother of the people," no matter how beautiful or persuasive one's language is, what one does will be as different as clouds and mud and will be ten thousand miles away from the Way [of the sage kings].[101]

Being attentive in that way requires an affective dimension in rulership, bringing human feelings to bear in making the adjustments appropriate to the fluidity of conditions.

> What do I mean by adjustments? I mean the attempt to conform with human feelings [because] in establishing the Way, the sage kings were guided by human feelings.[102]

In summation: to develop the innate talents of the samurai for rulership requires learning the Way of the sage kings, the study of history in service of understanding present circumstances, and a continual, affectively charged engagement with the needs of the people. Only then can the ruler wisely adjust the Way of the ancient sage kings to the present situation.

SORAI'S IMPACT

Given when Sorai lived, it is not surprising that we can have two such different readings of him, one Machiavellian and one Platonic. The early

Edo period was a time of ambivalence and ambiguity: a new social order was taking form. The country was making its first step into what we think of as modernity: rapid urbanization, the spread of literacy, the first murmurings of nation-building, the beginnings of a centralized bureaucracy, and the economics of a mercantile culture. Probably not since the era of Shōtoku had there been such a conscious concern for nation and society. Sorai's position, including his privileged access to the highest echelon of political power in Japan, kept him engaged in those practical realities.

Yet, those changes also challenged earlier formulations of personal identity. Most forms of Buddhism and even some of the neo-Confucian movements found personal identity in an introspective or contemplative self-cultivation. To Sorai's Confucian sensitivities, many Buddhists focused too much on a blissful afterlife and not enough on building a harmonious society in this life. A classical Confucian to the core of his being, Sorai looked for a model in which personal harmony was inseparable from social harmony, developing a romanticized nostalgic view of the ancient Chinese classics. His ultimate goal was to bring the model of the sage kings into the social and political concerns of his day. That is, Sorai himself was looking in two directions: to the ideal past and to the practical present. It is understandable, then, that we can read him in multiple ways.

Moreover, we should not forget the teenager in Kazusa. Political dynamics had brought exile to his family, his only escape being immersion into the book in the box. That experience yielded an innovative vision of learning and a new feel for how to make the past present. He learned that if you could incorporate the past, assimilating it into your very flesh, you can bring it with you to your encounter with the practical issues in your new circumstances. His calling was to teach others how to do that as well.

As we continue in this book, we will make further comparisons with Sorai. Some of the most pertinent will be with another Edo-period philosopher, one also struggling with similar issues about traditional values and new circumstances, Motoori Norinaga, the chief architect of the Native Studies movement. Let me introduce him to you. We will find him in an inn, having a animated conversation with an elderly gentleman about ancient Japanese language and literature.

10. Motoori Norinaga 本居宣長 (1730–1801)

In Touch with the Spirit of Words

People cannot help telling others what has profoundly touched their mindful hearts.[103]

Motoori Norinaga

We are in an inn on the twenty-fifth day in the fifth lunar month of the year
1763. Two men are huddled over the table, sipping warm sake and involved
in intense discussion. The older man is a scholar in his mid-sixties and as his
garb suggests, a traveler who will be spending the night at the inn. The town
is Matsuzaka (or Matsusaka), a popular stopover for pilgrims to the nearby
shrines of Ise, including the shrine to the Sun Goddess, Amaterasu, progenitrix
of the imperial family. The elderly man had, in fact, been at the shrines earlier
that day, one of the last legs of a nationwide lecture tour he had been taking
for five months with a few students, a tour underwritten by Tayasu Munetake
(1715–1771), a former shogun's son and a *waka* poet in his own right. This old
gentleman is clearly no ordinary scholar.

He is the aforementioned[†] Kamo no Mabuchi (1697–1769), the country's
leading authority on the classic Japanese poetry from the eighth-century collection, *Man'yōshū* (*Collection of Ten Thousand Leaves*). To study *Man'yōshū* is a
triply difficult task. Preserving some of the oldest poems in the archaic Japanese
language, its interpretation requires an appreciation of the Japanese world view
from over a millennium earlier. Moreover, it is philologically intricate, with
grammatical forms and even vowel sounds long ago fallen out of use. Finally, at
the time of *Man'yōshū* the Japanese writing system had not yet developed into
its final form: it used the Chinese-derived characters in ways that sometimes

458–9;
466–71

† See pages 331–2.

have to be decoded before they can be read. To be the country's leading expert on such a work is obviously the fruit of a lifetime of focused study and it is not surprising that Mabuchi has acquired a sizable number of students.

The younger man involved in the conversation is in his early thirties, a local pediatrician and aspiring scholar with as yet no significant reputation. An ardent admirer of Mabuchi's philological work and literary criticism, the young man is, on one hand, self-deprecatingly respectful; on the other, bubbling with enthusiasm over his projected scholarly enterprise. This man is Motoori Norinaga and his goal is to carry out the kind of philological work Mabuchi has been undertaking, but to direct it not to the poems of *Man'yōshū*, but to the slightly older, linguistically more complex ancient chronicle, *Kojiki* (*Record of Ancient Matters*). As explained in Chapter 2,[†] *Kojiki* is a repository of ancient prayers and grand mythic narratives about the *kami*'s creation of the world along with its more historical accounts of ancient emperors and empresses.

Norinaga then continues, expressing his fascination with the poetics of later narratives like *The Tale of Genji* and the poems collected in the medieval anthologies, the early ninth-century *Kokinshū* (*Collection [of Japanese Poems] from Ancient and Present Times*) and the twelfth-century *Shinkokinshū* (*New Collection...*). Mabuchi urges the young man to narrow his focus. He advises the ebullient Norinaga to forget about everything from later periods and to spend another couple of decades mastering *Man'yōshū*—its world view, its language, and its writing system—before turning to the more complicated *Kojiki*. Since Mabuchi had himself studied *Kojiki* and even written a little about it, he knows firsthand the challenges of the text. Though impressed with Norinaga's talents, Mabuchi still considers such a project beyond the skills of such a young scholar.

As he talks with his impassioned companion, it is likely that Mabuchi sees something in Norinaga besides his imposing intellectual talents, namely, his religious zeal. For Norinaga, *Kojiki* is clearly more than a chronicle of Japan's early history; it is more than the first book to be written (at least in part) in Japanese; it is more than the supreme challenge for any Japanese philologist. It is also the textual foundation for knowledge about the *kami*.

Compared to Norinaga, Mabuchi is more an aesthete, a sensitive classicist with nostalgia for a bygone era, than a religious devotee. Even earlier that day at Ise, it would have been hard for him to miss the fervor in some pilgrims, an ardor that might have reminded him of his own introduction to Native Studies at the school of Kada no Azumamaro (1669–1736).[‡] Azumamaro was a Shintō

† See pages 75–7.
‡ See page 331.

priest, teaching at an academy on the grounds of a Shintō shrine with many students who also were Shintō priests. So, Mabuchi feels he knows whereof he speaks when advising Norinaga to defer his religious interests until after he becomes much more familiar with *Man'yōshū*. We do not know the details of their discussion in that inn,[104] but we do know the consequences, consequences so important that the meeting came to be known in Japanese cultural history simply as "the evening in Matsuzaka."

NORINAGA: SCHOLAR IN TRAINING

The first consequence of the meeting was that Norinaga enrolled in Mabuchi's academy in Edo. That formally aligned him with the Native Studies movement, a literary and philological lineage he would himself trace as starting with Keichū, continuing through Azumamaro and Mabuchi, and reaching to himself. Norinaga would go on to become the most influential critic of Japanese literature in premodern times, helping define the classical literary canon and the terminology for interpreting it. After the evening in Matsuzaka, however, he never met Mabuchi again face-to-face, his further tutelage amounting to a correspondence course.

As he did with his other students, Mabuchi insisted that Norinaga write to him in the classical manner of *Man'yōshū*, including writing *Man'yōshū*-style poems of his own. Reminiscent of Sorai's pedagogical approach to the classic Chinese texts, Mabuchi believed students should so immerse themselves in the style of the ancient Japanese poems that they could freely express their deepest feelings in it. He described the result he desired:

> Unconsciously, the verse will color one's mindful heart and may even enter and become part of one's speech...[until] only one's body is left behind in this later age as one's mindful heart and speech return to the distant past.[105]

From Mabuchi's letters to Norinaga, we know he was sometimes impressed with Norinaga's questions about *Man'yōshū*, but at other times unhappy or even frustrated.[106] Furthermore, at the very outset of their correspondence, Norinaga asked Mabuchi to lend him his annotated copy of *Kojiki* as a first step in his grand project: to compile a critical edition based on the best available manuscripts. Mabuchi initially ignored this request, but finally relented after several subsequent appeals. It had by then become clear to Mabuchi that, first of all, Norinaga was only going to take his advice partially. Yes, he would study *Man'yōshū* more thoroughly, but he would do so simultaneously with his research into *Kojiki,* not as a precursor to it. Second, as he could tell from Norinaga's unimpressive *Man'yōshū*-style poems, his heart was not in it. It was in *Kojiki.*

Norinaga's relation to *Kojiki* is the second consequence of that fateful evening in Matsuzaka. Norinaga, a philologist, would change the face of Shintō and position it as a centerpiece in a new Japanese nationalist identity. Later in this chapter and in the next, we will see how and why that happened, but we will first examine the literary side of Norinaga's career, starting with the extensive training and experience he brought to the table that evening in Matsuzaka.

Norinaga was the first-born natural son of Ozu Sadatoshi (1695–1740) and his wife Katsu (1705–1768). "Norinaga," the pen name he later adopted, grew up in a strongly religious family with both Buddhist and Shintō sensitivities. The family was affiliated with Pure Land Buddhism, the school founded by Hōnen, and several family members were tonsured at some point in their lives, including Katsu in her senior years. At the same time, although the Ozu family already had an adopted son and heir, Sadaharu (1711–1751), when they wished their own natural son, they prayed to a local Shintō *kami,* Mikumari. They promised Mikumari that if a son were born to them, they would take him in thanksgiving to the shrine when he was thirteen years old. Norinaga was the answer to that prayer and as an adult, he took this indebtedness to the *kami* seriously, facing in the direction of the Yoshino shrine every morning in prayer.[107]

Since the Ozu family already had an heir, Norinaga was initially spared the responsibility of having to run the family mercantile business. This was just as well because his interests were never economic, even in difficult financial times. At eighteen, for example, he was temporarily adopted into another merchant family, the Imaida, but showing no skill or interest in that family's business activities, he was relieved to have the adoption dissolved two years later. Norinaga's elder step-brother died unexpectedly in 1751 at the age of 38, making Norinaga the head of the house. Not wanting any further involvement in the mercantile world, he liquidated the family business, investing the proceeds in a fund for the financial care of his brother's family. His passion was always for the literary, scholarly, and philosophical.

Still, the Ozu family was not so prosperous the burgeoning scholar did not have to earn a living. So, he made a compromise to satisfy both his own personal desire to study in the capital and his family's need for him to find a steady source of income: he decided to become a physician. He moved to Kyoto in 1752 and shortly thereafter changed his family name from Ozu to Motoori, the name of a samurai branch of his ancestry which had been obliterated by Oda Nobunaga in the sixteenth century. The two events, dissolving the family business and taking a new name, evidence his formal break with his family's mercantile history.

While studying Chinese medicine in the capital, Norinaga was also able to study Chinese philosophy. In fact, for half of the five years he studied in Kyoto, he lived in the house of his Confucian philosophy teacher, the aforementioned

Hori Keizan (1688-1757).† Since Keizan had been Sorai's friend, it is probable 1174-6
that Norinaga received some instruction in Sorai's philosophy at the same
time.[108] Perhaps even more importantly, though, Keizan also had interests in
Japanese poetry and literature, areas well represented in his library.

At some point during his time in Kyoto, Norinaga first came across the
writings of Keichū. His philological approach to the ancient *Man'yōshū* poems
fascinated Norinaga and permanently moved him in the direction of native,
rather than Chinese, studies. With Keizan's decease in 1757 and his studies as a
pediatric physician completed, Norinaga moved back to Matsuzaka, setting up
his medical practice. From there, he increasingly pursued both his Pure Land
and Shintō heritage, becoming more actively involved in his family Buddhist
temple and the major Shintō shrines at Ise.

NORINAGA'S POETICS

Once back in Matsuzaka, Norinaga joined the local literary circles,
giving lectures on such Japanese works as *The Tale of Genji*, *The Tosa Diary*,
Man'yōshū, *The Pillow Book*, and Keichū's commentary on the *Hyakunin isshu*, a
collection of one hundred classical poems by one hundred poets. In fact, about
the time he returned to Matsuzaka, he had already written his first significant
work, a theory of Japanese poetry and poetics called "A Small Boat Cutting
through the Reeds" (*Ashiwake obune*). Already in this work, we find in place the
fundamentals of Norinaga's philosophy of language and its link to both communal harmony and creativity. That theory drove Norinaga's philosophy for the
rest of his life, providing the critical link between his poetics and his religious
theory about the prehistoric Age of the *Kami*, a theory that would profoundly
affect Shintō's future role in history.

As an entrée into his theory of language, we begin with this extended statement about poetry from *A Small Boat*:

A poem is not merely something composed to describe one's feelings when
one can no longer bear the *mono no aware*. When one's feelings are extremely
deep, one's heart still feels dissatisfied and unresigned, even after having
composed a poem. In order to feel comfort, one must read the poem to someone else. If the other person hearing the poem finds it has *aware*, this will
greatly comfort the poet. ... And since this is the intent of poetry, it is a basic
principle and not an accident that poem must be heard by others. Someone
who does not understand this might say that a true poem describes one's
emotions exactly as they are, whether bad or good, and it has nothing to do

† See page 324.

with whether or not people hear it. Such an argument sounds plausible, but it betrays ignorance of the true meaning of poetry.[109]

We note, first of all, the key term *mono no aware*.[110] I treated the ideal of *aware*[111] in my analysis of Heian aesthetics where I described it in terms of the capacity to be touched by things.[†] *Aware* was part of the sensitivity underlying the courtly elegance (*miyabi*) so highly respected in the world described in *The Tale of Genji*. Norinaga wrote "When people speak of what they feel in their hearts, this is an awareness of *mono no aware*."[112] Norinaga insisted that authentic poetic speech arises not from simple emotion, but from an *awareness* of that emotion. That is, poets speak when they realize that they have been in touch with things and are touched by them. Mabuchi's analysis of the *Man'yōshū* poems was that they were often a *direct expression* of emotion, but for Norinaga there was that additional moment of reflection before the poem arises.

A second emphasis in the quote is that if the *mono no aware* is genuinely felt, the outpouring of words is itself not enough—the experience has to be *shared*. That claim also diverges from what Mabuchi admired so much in what he called the "manliness" in the *Man'yōshū* poems: the frank, direct, and unrefined expression of the unadorned "genuine mindful heart (*magokoro*)." Norinaga agreed with that characterization, but where Mabuchi saw only purity, Norinaga saw also the raw and undeveloped.

In the final analysis, Norinaga disagreed with Mabuchi's claim that *Man'yōshū* was the highest phase of Japanese poetry, using an analogy stating the difference between a pure white and a tastefully patterned, colored kimono.

> The ancient style is a like a white robe, and the style of later years is like a robe dyed with a variety of colors such as crimson, purple, and so on. The white costume is beautiful precisely because of its whiteness. Yet the dyed one is similarly beautiful in its own way because of the dyeing. Just because you consider the white robe beautiful, you do not have to be narrow-minded and consider the dyed one as unsightly.[113]

Each kimono has its appropriate place, but the elegance of the latter is the more sophisticated and artistic; it displays a depth of feeling, an acquired tastefulness, as well as purity. Analogously, Norinaga believed the refined, decorative poem can accomplish more than the plain:

> If one has to say what makes poetry unique for the expression of otherwise inexpressible feelings, then it is because of the sophistication [*aya*] applied to the words. It is this sophistication that enables one to express an infinite range of *aware*.[114]

† See pages 140–1.

The term *aya* suggests figure or design, Norinaga's idea being that the creative expression may start with the primitive, uncultured, "masculinity" that Mabuchi finds in *Man'yōshū*, but it need not be just blatantly expressed as it is. It can be further refined by being responsive to an aesthetic audience with which it is shared. This extra step in sensitivity and responsiveness to others makes it, in Norinaga's terms, more "feminine."

Accordingly, the ideal poetic expression is not only pure in its genuine mindful heart (*magokoro*), but it also resonates with its particular time and place, expanding its capacity to touch and be touched by the responses of others. This implies a poem for the Heian courtiers should not have the same figure or design as one for the medieval period or for the Edo period. Similar to other creative fashions, the form of poetry must fit its times. In that regard, Norinaga most admired the early tenth-century *Kokinshū* and the early thirteenth-century *Shinkokinshū* collections not only for their sophistication but also because they best suited their era (and Norinaga thought his own time as well). That explains why, despite Mabuchi's instructions to write poetry in the early eighth-century *Man'yōshū* style, Norinaga found himself repeatedly drawn to those later poetic patterns.

Such aesthetic considerations led Norinaga to think more deeply about *kokoro,* the mindful heart, than Mabuchi's theory would allow. For Norinaga, the aim of a poetic text is not so much to match up with already existing facts (as Sorai's referentialism might imply), but instead to be a direct expression of *kokoro. Kokoro* is a term ordinarily embracing both heart and mind, the seat of personal intentionality both emotional and intellectual. Yet, in Norinaga's philosophy, this term is not restricted to the experiencer as if it were no more than the source of personal subjectivity. Norinaga thought it was much more than that.

According to him, things and words have *kokoro* as well (called respectively *mono no kokoro* and *koto no kokoro*). In this broader sense *kokoro* means more than just the human mindful heart, but instead indicates something's ontological openness to being involved in internal, overlapping relations. *Kokoro* embraces an intimate form of knowing and expressing, a form engendered by engagement within a semiotic field of words, patterns, things, and community, instead of detached observation. Poetic expression occurs when the *kokoro* of the thing, the *kokoro* of the poet, and the *kokoro* of words resonate harmoniously in a shared field of meaning.

If we return to Yamanoue no Okura's poem about the widower's grief and the rising mist of Mount Ōno analyzed in Chapter 3,[†] we can say that what cre-

---

† See pages 53–5.

ated the poem was not the poet alone, but rather the harmonious resonance among the mist, the words of the poem, and the poet's grieving heart. The poem emerged from the resonant field in which the three are inseparable. The mutual resonance established a field of engaged knowing in which both the knower and the known are transformed. That parallels the poem's merging the mountain mist with the widower's grief. If a person has sensitivity (*kokoro ga aru hito*—a person with the mindful heart), he or she will be aware of the *kokoro* of things and of words as well. An affective knowledge will be creatively expressed through the poetic medium.

> *Waka* [classical Japanese poetry], though a means to express one's feelings, is different from ordinary language in that it is accompanied by embellishment [*aya*] and a beautiful musical tune. It has been so even from the ages of the deities.[115]

In such passages, we find Norinaga urging an engagement with reality that goes beyond what can be expressed through the ordinary, ostensive language stressed by Sorai. The difference between Sorai and Norinaga is not merely a matter of whether one prefers Chinese or Japanese cultural forms. The real point of contention between the two thinkers concerns how language and reality are related.

LANGUAGE PHILOSOPHIES: SORAI AND NORINAGA COMPARED

Sorai: Language as Reference

393-410

I will begin by reviewing Sorai's ideal of philosophical language and adding a few further points that will be helpful in our comparison with Norinaga. Rightly or wrongly Sorai finds the ancient Chinese of the Six Classics to represent the ideal, a language in which he thinks words point to already existing realities with few surplus words serving any other function. For Sorai, language theoretically has one primary task: to tell it like it is. Sorai applauded the ancient Chinese language for its lack of superfluous verbiage: even the preposition-like Chinese particles that grew in number as the language evolved over the centuries were, to his mind, not needed. As much as possible, he wanted each word to match up with one referent. In that respect, he came dangerously close to being the equivalent of a twentieth-century western logical positivist like the early Ludwig Wittgenstein, Rudolf Carnap, or A. J. Ayer. I say "dangerously" close because logical positivism leads to a conclusion Sorai could not possibly accept.

In logical positivism, the word's referent must be empirically verifiable. This is not a problem for words such as *dog* or *apple* because in cases like those I can link your word *dog* to the animal I am petting or the word *apple* to the fruit I am biting into. For most logical positivists, however, there is a serious problem with phrases like "good apple" or "good dog." We cannot perceive that to which the word *good* refers. What does good feel, taste, or look like?

A. J. Ayer argued in *Language, Truth, and Logic* that when we say, for example, "truth-telling is good," we are just verbally emoting and not asserting anything knowable, that is, anything empirically verifiable.[116] For him, "truth-telling is good" boils down to be something like exclaiming "truth-telling—hurrah!" Such an exclamation is neither true nor false; it is just an expression of a feeling. In the logical positivist's sense of proper philosophical language, therefore, we really cannot speak of "good" at all and as the student Wittgenstein wrote at the end of his *Tractatus Logico-Philosophicus,* we must therefore "pass over [nonscientific statements] in silence."[117] The normative, the realm of oughts and shoulds, falls outside the domain of philosophical discourse.

That philosophical amorality is a danger Sorai would certainly want to avoid since it is precisely the goodness of the virtues that he hopes to accentuate. In fact, as we saw in the last chapter, Sorai is barely even concerned about language as referring to things like apples or dogs. When he talks about "things," he is talking almost always about human affairs and relations as they are appropriately performed. How can Sorai keep his tight correspondence between word and reality without falling into the logical positivists' black hole of amorality?

The sage kings came to Sorai's rescue. Sorai could respond to the logical positivists by pointing to the descriptions of the sage kings in the Six Classics and saying "You want to know to what 'good' refers? It refers to *them* and *their* way of acting." As we saw when we discussed Sorai in relation to definition by ostension—that is, defining a word by pointing to what it refers—in the beginning, only someone who was benevolent could give us the word "benevolence" by performing it and then naming it. By being an ideal ruler, a sage king showed us how a ruler performs and then gave us the word "ruler." Because of that unique and unreplicated event, the word "ruler" becomes both descriptive and prescriptive, that is, it tells us what a ruler *is* simultaneously with showing us what a ruler *should* be. So, the phrase "good ruler" becomes almost a tautology or redundancy like "unmarried bachelor."

In that precise sense, Sorai resembles the logical positivists insofar as he rids himself of having to use the word "good." He does so, however, not by excluding the normative, but by finding the normative in the correct use of descriptive words about human relations. For Sorai, the good is empirically knowable, at least if we know where to look for it, namely, in the Six Classics. In that respect, Sorai's affirmation of the Way of the sage kings is prerequisite to his formulating an ideal philosophical language in which words match with realities on a near one-to-one basis but yet also designate how things *ought* to be.

Norinaga's Expressive Theory of Language

Norinaga's view of the ideal philosophical language is radically different. If Sorai wants to tell it like it is, Norinaga wants to express it as it happens. Sorai puts his speakers at a distance from human events so they can see the full picture and line up the words descriptively with the realities. In that respect at least, Sorai's ideal philosopher resembles a detached, externally related observer.† In his view, the samurai is an accomplished-person-in-the-making, one capable of seeing the whole and what is best overall. That distinguishes the inherent capacity or virtue of the samurai over other classes of people.

By contrast, Norinaga's speakers find themselves in the midst of a creative event in which there is a reverberating internal relation among words, things, and the speaker. In fact, as we have seen for Norinaga, the audience is part of the event as well, their heritage contributing to the *aya* that gives verbal expression its form, pattern, and design. Poetry is written in "lived words" that emerge out of *kokoro*, unfolding like a blossom. The analogy of flowers with words was widespread in East Asian literary theory, but Norinaga took the comparison unusually seriously. For example, he analyzed the process of verbal inflection as the blooming of the root word.[118*] I will try to explain how Norinaga thought about that analogy while trying to avoid too technical a discussion of classical Japanese grammar and sentence structure. To do so, I will focus on a simple example of a single Chinese sentence from the *Analects*, noting how it might be expressed in both English and modern Japanese, pointing out the differences I think Norinaga would see among them.‡

Analyzing a sample sentence. Let us take for our example *Analects* 2:11, a famous passage that has been translated as "*Reviewing* the old as a *means of realizing* the *new*—such a person *can* be *considered* a *teacher.*"[119] The original Chinese is written in just ten sinographs, very roughly corresponding to the English words I italicized.[120] We can see even in the translation from Chinese to English that English syntax requires additional words and, just as importantly, extra context. This would be even more true in a translation into modern Japanese. Yet, Sorai's point is that the ten sinographs say all that is really needed to communicate the meaning. (Try reading only the italicized English words—"Reviewing old means of realizing new can considered teacher." The meaning is still intelligible

---

† In other respects, however, we have seen that Sorai does stress engagement. For example, when explaining how to read a classical text, he says we should immerse ourselves in it until it becomes part of our "flesh." See page 363.

‡ For a brief discussion of some fundamental aspects of the Japanese language that are mentioned by philosophers in this book, see in the reference material "Pointers for Studying Japan," the section on "About the Japanese language," pages 685–95.

even though it is not standard English.) So, according to Sorai, nothing is gained by the embellishments one would find in rendering it into English, or even more so, into Japanese.

Norinaga's response would be that the ten sinographs of the original Chinese sentence are just a bud that has not bloomed into a full linguistic event. For example, an on-line study guide for Japanese middle-school students studying classical Chinese interprets the meaning of the original into a modern Japanese sentence with eighteen sinographs and twenty-six syllabary characters. A somewhat literal English rendering of the Japanese would be: "If one inquires into the affairs and ideas of the past and discovers new things through the present, one could probably get to be in a position to instruct."[121] Some of this verbiage is obviously more fully unpacking the context for a Japanese teenaged student, but a few points about that modern Japanese version would capture Norinaga's special attention.

First and perhaps most importantly, the modern Japanese sentence ends with *ni nareru darō,* "could probably get to be." That locution specifies the nature of probability, making the neutral Chinese word for possibility or capability more explicitly hypothetical ("could" rather than "can"). The importance of that difference, Norinaga would point out, is that the *darō* expresses something of the speaker's attitude (doubting, speculating, wondering). In the original Chinese, the speaker's psychological state is invisible. Norinaga would also point out in introducing the speaker's psychological state, the Japanese does not *refer to* the speaker's state of mind (it is not ostensive), but rather *expresses* it.

Second, the copula *darō* is a plain form of the verb which might not be appropriate in a less straightforwardly informational context. If the speaker were speaking in a slightly more formal context, for example, the verb form might well have been *deshō.* Thus, the *darō* reveals something of the social context in which the statement is made. Furthermore, if the person addressed were of especially high status in relation to the speaker, the verb form might even have been *de gozaimashō.* That inflection is not only more formal but also expressive of the speaker's humble status in relation to the listener. Thus, unlike the simple classical Chinese statement that Sorai so admires, the Japanese statement expresses a social space within which the statement is made. Importantly for Norinaga, the verb form does not so much refer to the social situation as it *performatively* establishes it. The language does something as well as designates something.

Lastly, although in this particular sentence, the significance is not as obvious as it would be in others, Norinaga also wrote extensively about the Japanese syntactic "particles" (*joshi* or *te-ni-wo-ha*) that indicate the case of the noun preceding it, telling us whether it is the subject or object in the sentence, a location in which something exists or at which something happens, and so forth. Such particles (since they typically come after rather than before the word they qualify, they are sometimes called "*post*positionals" as contrasted with "*pre*positions"), Norinaga explains in detail, often render more than mere grammatical information, suggesting such nuances as the speaker's affect or the relation between the speaker and the listener. Again, such particles have a diminished role in ancient Chinese, although (to his dismay) Sorai notes that as the Chinese language developed over the centuries, they increased in number.

For Norinaga, the bottom line is that the crucial part of the statement is not in the bud but in the blooming, not in the simple referential core we find in the minimalist ancient Chinese sentence with its ten sinographs, but in the "extra" units of the Japanese language Sorai thinks expendable. When Sorai criticized the *wakun* reading of Chinese texts with all the tiny marginal notations used to convert the Chinese into a quasi-Japanese reading, he ridiculed those notational marks as "cat whiskers" that clutter up the page. For Norinaga, we could say, behind those whiskers is a living cat eliciting our response, waiting to be petted. Norinaga maintains that those "extra" units place any particular statement into a specific time, place, attitude, and interpersonal relationship. It communicates the entire self-expressive semantic field (*kokoro*) that is the poetic-spiritual element of any genuine speech act. To Norinaga, Sorai's ideal ostensive sentence is a bud of meaning that has not yet fully blossomed.

A parallel from western philosophy. If we take this debate between Sorai and Norinaga out of the Japanese context, the philosophical issue may be more starkly outlined. In twentieth-century western philosophy there arose a movement, which included the aforementioned logical positivists, that understood the philosopher's task as analyzing ordinary spoken and written utterances for their propositional content. Propositions are devoid of feeling and simply make a claim as to what is the case. Then, using whatever means the particular philosophy accepts as veridical such as empirical verification, you could determine whether the proposition is true or false.

An advantage of isolating the propositional aspect of language is that it explains how different words could be saying exactly the same thing. For example, the English "it's raining" asserts the same proposition as the German "*es regnet.*" They are logically equivalent: when one is true, the other must be true; when one is false, the other must be false. This is because spoken or written words themselves are not true or false, but rather, the propositions they assert are true or false. Thus, two different utterances may express the same proposition. Through the use of formal logic, philosophers can then develop valid linkages among true propositions to construct immensely rich and complex pictures of the world. Computer modeling for forecasting the weather or for exploring marketing strategies are concrete applications of this type of thinking.

Norinaga alerts us to the price we pay in making this transition from oral or written expressions to propositions. Let's consider the following two statements. It is her wedding day and the bride-to-be jumps out of bed in the morning and looks out the window. She turns and says to her mother, "It's raining." Meanwhile, across the state where there has been a crop-crippling drought for weeks, a farmer gets up, looks out the window, and says to his wife, "It's raining." Propositionally, the two statements are identical; they are both making assertions about the state of affairs outside the window. Yet, the two utterances are hardly the same. We need only look at the tears in the mother's eyes and the joyous smile that breaks across the face of the farmer's wife.

For Norinaga, the propositional analysis misses the human element, the *kokoro,* the ability to be in touch and touched by things and the need to share that sensitivity with others. If we had tape recordings of the two spoken remarks about the rain, we could hear the difference—sense the disappointment or joy—even without seeing the people involved. In speaking we use intonation and stress to intimate the *kokoro,* a complex signal system that English writing unfortunately reduces to merely a few punctuation marks.[122*]

What is at stake. From this extended comparison, we can see that the difference between Sorai and Norinaga is not simply a Sinophile's fondness for ancient Chinese and a nativist's ardor for ancient Japanese. The real debate has little to do with ethnicity, but more about the nature of language and what in language is most philosophically important. For his case, Sorai extols the virtues of the ancient writing style in the Six Classics because it most approximates his idea of a philosophically perfect language, a language that tells us accurately without elaboration or theorizing just what a harmonious society looks like and the human relations it includes.

Of course, Sorai knows Chinese speakers use their language to express their anger and their joy, to court a lover, or to curse an enemy. He knows the spoken language includes all sorts of locutions not found in the ancient texts. As we saw in the last chapter, he also knows the Chinese language has been used to argue against theoretical positions of various types, thereby relinquishing pure description for persuasive rhetoric. Yet, he can leave all that aside for his philosophical purposes, much as an advocate of propositional analysis would do in our philosophical world today. Sorai seeks a purely factual, descriptive language that accurately portrays the proper way for people to behave toward one another so as to attain social concord.

Norinaga instead sees the ideal language as something that allows people to engage their world and their community, allowing them the means to intimate their personal sensitivities and sensibilities. Sorai's ideal language refers; Norinaga's confers. Whereas Sorai is a referentialist, Norinaga is an expressionist.

Their debate is about what language is for, and what functions of language best reveal our human qualities. The disagreement between Sorai and Norinaga is as much about philosophical anthropology (the philosophical analysis of what it means to be human) as it is about linguistics.

That philosophical anthropology leads us to now examine more closely the form of self-cultivation and community Norinaga's ideal implies.

NORINAGA ON THE COMMUNITY OF PRAXIS

As we have seen, unlike his teacher Mabuchi, Norinaga believed that the pure *magokoro* (genuine mindful heart) has to be cultivated by being engaged in a praxis within a community of similarly sensitive people, people who can recognize and respond to *aware*. The impulse to express one's feelings is natural and universal; what is intimately known cries out to be intimated to others: "People cannot help telling others what has profoundly touched their mindful hearts."[123] For there to be greatness in poetic expression, however, that impulse of the genuine *magokoro* must be restrained until it can acquire the sophistication of the embroidered figures of speech. That sophistication is engendered by the aesthetic training of emulation, sharing, and performance. Through that regimen, the poetry becomes more than just a universal expression of the human spirit; it also reveals the particular time and place of the community that bestows the words with polished figure or form.

In his "First Steps into the Mountain" (*Uiyamabumi*), a methodological handbook written for his students, Norinaga explains:

> Words, behavior, and mind generally coincide in all human beings.[124] For example, a wise person is wise in words and behavior. Also, men think, speak and behave in a manly way, while women think, speak, and behave in a womanly way. This also applies to the differences in historical periods. The words, behavior, and mind of the ancient people are by definition those of remote antiquity. Those of middle antiquity are those of middle antiquity, and those of later ages have their own later manner. The words, behavior, and mind of the ancient people are similar within their respective categories. In the present era, if you wish to study the words, behavior, and mind of the ancient people, their words are found in poetry, and their behavior, in historical writings.
>
> There is no way of recording history except in words; similarly, the nature of people's minds may be known through poetry. Since words, behavior, and mind coincide, what you need to know in later years about the mind and behavior of the ancient people and the conditions of their society is preserved in ancient words and ancient poetry.[125]

Admiration for the Culture of the Heian Court

Poetry is necessarily artifice, an artifice of communication in a specific community. Seen from that vantage point, the poems of *Man'yōshū* recorded in the eighth century may be a genuine, even spontaneous, expression of the human heart, but Norinaga still considers them primitive in comparison with the cultivated, more "feminine" poetry to follow in later periods such as that of *Kokinshū* and *Shinkokinshū* or even the great prose fiction like the eleventh-century *The Tale of Genji*. Norinaga found in the later works the highly refined, developed, and elegant (*miyabi*) articulation of the genuine heart of sentimentality, a sentimentality nurtured in and directed toward an audience of equally accomplished aesthetes. Since Norinaga was already lecturing on *The Tale of Genji* by the time he met Mabuchi, it is relevant to see how Norinaga approached Murasaki's work.

Written by a woman, *The Tale of Genji* exemplified to Norinaga the feelings of an artist allowed to verbalize publicly her unrepressed sentimentality, thus achieving a highly sophisticated, nuanced level of expression. According to Norinaga, Lady Murasaki as a woman felt no pressure to moralize or rationalize in the form of what Norinaga called the "Chinese mentality" (*kara no kokoro*), liberating her to write about human events and emotions as actually lived in the court without resorting to ethical considerations. She did not, for example, have to judge the virtue of Genji's numerous extramarital affairs, including a relation with an emperor's wife. Norinaga believed no Chinese-influenced, "masculine" *kokoro* could describe such events and feelings with such accuracy and depth: the urge to structure, rationalize, and moralize would eventually distort the simple report of what had actually happened.

Concerning the dangers of over analysis, Norinaga shares Sorai's preference for description over argumentation,[†] using here the analogy of the lotus flower.

> The impure mud of illicit love affairs described in *The Tale of Genji* is there not for the purpose of being admired but for nurturing the flower of the awareness of sorrow in human existence. Prince Genji's conduct is like the lotus flower, which is happy and fragrant but has its roots in the muddy water. But *The Tale of Genji* does not dwell on the impurity of the water; it dwells only on those who are sympathetically kind and who are aware of the sorrow of human existence, and it holds these feeling to be the basis of the good man.[126]

According to Norinaga, not all societies in all historical periods equally repress what he calls the *feminine* (*taoyameburi*). He believed the Heian court, for example, was somewhat free of the "Chinese" tendency to repress the emo-

† See pages 363–4.

tions for the sake of Confucian morality and so he deemed it the high point of Japanese cultural development. As mentioned in Chapter 4,† that many Japanese still see the Heian period in that light is at least in part the direct impact of Norinaga's analysis. For Norinaga, the Heian period was an age in which even males could write poems, openly shed tears, love intensely, and value nothing more highly than the capacity to be in touch with and be touched by the world. In short, it was an aesthetic age in which *mono no aware* flourished.

The Heian period was also the period in which there was an explicit praxis for cultivating that sensitivity to *mono no aware*. The praxis in this case, according to Norinaga, centered on the term *miyabi*, the Heian word for courtly elegance. "Every person has to have the sense to appreciate *miyabi*. Without this, one will not be able to appreciate *mono no aware*."[127]

Norinaga's stress on *miyabi* set his aesthetic apart from Daoist naturalism.[128]* Norinaga understood the Daoists to be abandoning society and culture to escape into nature. For him, by contrast, humans are being most natural precisely when we develop such "artifices" as society and poetry. Sharing our sensibilities with a sensitive community is the highest and most natural expression of our basic humanity.[129] "If it is proper to leave things in their natural course, it is nothing but nature to leave artifice as artifice."[130] Norinaga believed that by embracing the primitive and unrefined, the Daoists were, like Mabuchi and the *Man'yōshū* poets, privileging the masculine over the feminine, cutting themselves off from the praxis of courtly elegance.

Poetry and Society

Norinaga rejected the common Confucian claim that poetry was relevant to governance.[131] Yet, his aesthetic does posit a vision of ideal community by way of what Peter Nosco calls the "indirect" value of poetry for governing self and the social order.[132] For Norinaga, poetry must be social: the aesthetic cannot limit itself to the private, but must resonate with community. In terms of modern western sociological terminology, poetry does not serve *gesellschaft* ("society" as ruled by legal agreements through government institutions), but it plays a crucial role in serving *gemeinschaft* ("community" as a gathering of people through kinship and bonds of feeling).

Norinaga opened this line of thought by drawing a distinction between two facets of the ancient poems. On one hand, there was the poem's *raison d'etre* as the sincere expression of a person's innermost, welled-up feelings. This he called the "root character" or "essence" (*hontai*) of poetry. This is an important aesthetic and even psychological function, but it has little practical usefulness

† See pages 144–5.

in directly enhancing either political stability or the development of individual character. It is basically an unvarnished, spontaneous voicing of sentiment.

Yet, if we had a community in which people wrote *and shared* such poetry, people's innermost feelings would be understood and appreciated by others. This would make the society easier to harmonize and govern. Then poetry can be said to have a "usable aspect" (*mochiyuru tokoro*). By sharing in the poetic process as both performers and audience, a community acquires an interpersonal knowledge. Such a mutual understanding among people can be the foundation for a harmonious society.

Norinaga's take on poetry is neither moralistic nor didactic, but intimate. The poet intimates to her intimates what is most intimate. When Norinaga sees a political and social usefulness in this, he is envisioning a society held together not by principles or laws, but by feeling and sensitivity, a community of intimacy instead of a society of integrity. This is a core value in his vision of the "way of the ancients" (*inishie no michi*).

> Although the study of poetry is of no use for understanding the principle of things, it has the power to develop one's heart and reasoning faculties naturally, because it uses words artfully and expresses human feelings effectively.…
> It is further beneficial in that it naturally enables one's heart to experience human feelings extensively; it enables those of high standing to acquire knowledge about matters concerning those of low standing; it enables men to understand the feelings of women, and the wise to understand the thoughts of the foolish.… It is of considerable benefit to those who stand at the head of the people to understand elegant literary matters.[133]*

NORINAGA'S FIXATION ON *KOJIKI*

Mabuchi and Kojiki

Before he ever met Mabuchi, Norinaga had already formulated the outline and much detail for the views we have been examining: his basic theories of language, creativity, and cultural community. That is what he brought to the table that evening in Matsuzaka. Given this prodigious philosophical analysis and clarity of vision, the real question may be not why Norinaga dared to ignore Mabuchi's admonition to focus exclusively for two decades on *Man'yōshū*, but instead, why Norinaga felt it so important to affiliate with Mabuchi in the first place.

First of all, as sophisticated as his literary theories might have been, before his association with Mabuchi, Norinaga was not credentialed as a scholar. His teacher in Kyoto, Hori Keizan, had but a modest scholarly reputation, certainly almost none in the field of Native Studies. So, Norinaga needed a mentor, a lineage, and a school with which he could identify. Mabuchi represented access to just what Norinaga needed at the time.

Furthermore, there is no doubt that Norinaga admired Mabuchi as a great scholar of the ancient Japanese language and world view. A few years before their meeting, Norinaga had read Mabuchi's *Study of Poetic Epithets* (*Kanjikō*), a work so innovative in its interpretations that Norinaga initially found it "alien and strange." Rereadings convinced him, however, that Mabuchi's work was a major contribution to researching ancient Japan and its literature. Furthermore, Mabuchi's work had proven that, contrary to what his own teacher Azumamaro had said, *Kojiki* was more valuable to Native Studies than *Nihonshoki*.†

So it is obvious on that level why Norinaga would be excited to meet such an eminent scholar who shared with him an interest in *Kojiki*. In the end, Mabuchi may have counseled Norinaga not to study *Kojiki*, at least not yet, but Norinaga also knew Mabuchi had realized there was something important in that text to be unearthed. Rather than taking Mabuchi's advice to defer his study of *Kojiki*, Norinaga zealously jumped into the project with no delay.

Norinaga spent half his life writing the commentary on the *Kojiki* he had discussed that evening in Matsuzaka. The final work, *Kojikiden*, made *Kojiki* intelligible for the first time in over a thousand years.[134] Even more importantly, it transformed *Kojiki* itself into a canonical text for Shintō, especially in its portrayal of the creation of the world and the role of the celestial *kami*.

As we have seen with a variety of Edo-period philosophers including Sorai and Mabuchi, the rapid social, economic, and intellectual changes of their era often triggered a romanticized pining for more ancient and simpler times. The fantasy was of a golden age (whether in China or Japan) when people lived together so harmoniously that governance was nearly automatic. Without reflection or analysis, people had understood their respective roles.

From what we have discussed so far, Norinaga was enthralled with his idealized picture of the Heian court as a community permeated with emotive sensitivity and aesthetic expression. Yet he also emphasized that the Heian world was a deliberate human invention refined over centuries of Japanese cultural history. If the Heian culture was an embroidered pattern appropriate to its own time and place, two questions beg clarification. First, what was the ideal Heian culture a refinement *of*? On that point, Norinaga generally agreed with Mabuchi: the raw material was the genuine mindful heart, *magokoro*, so well expressed in the *Man'yōshū* poems.

The second question has a less obvious answer: why is this nonrationalizing, emotive, and sensitive mindful heart "genuine?" For example, why is it more

† For more comparisons between *Kojiki* and *Nihonshoki*, see pages 75–7.

authentically human to respond to the *aware* of things than to find the intellectually accessible pattern (*ri*) common to the natural world and the human
mind? More specifically, what justifies the claim that a *Man'yōshū* poet is acting
in a more authentically human way than a Shushigaku philosopher? Or, for that
matter, on what basis can Norinaga claim that his ideal of language as intimate
engagement is better than Sorai's ideal of language as detached ostension?

The determining factor for Norinaga in all these questions boils down again
to his philosophical anthropology: the theory of what it means to be human.
Never wavering in his conviction that human beings are fundamentally spiritual or religious, he believed that understanding our humanity begins with
understanding the process of divine creation and the human role within it.

Norinaga's line of thinking was as follows. To justify why Heian society was
the epitome of human creativity, we have to know how humans themselves
were created; to know why expressive language is more valuable than ostensive
language, we have to know where language itself came from; to understand how
we should act in present circumstances, we must know how everything began.
(Note the by now familiar Shintō appeal to origins.) Such were Norinaga's
motivating inquiries that led him, after that night in Matsuzaka and against the
advice of Mabuchi, to direct so much of his energies toward penetrating *Kojiki*
and the Age of the *Kami* it depicts.

Reading Kojiki as cryptology. For Norinaga the significance of *Kojiki* is not only
what it says, but also how it says it. *Kojiki* includes sections in Japanese, making it the oldest extant example of the language, at least in any extended form.
So, if one wants to reconstruct "original Japanese," the so-called language of
Yamato, *Kojiki* contains valuable information not found elsewhere. A major
obstacle, however, is that the text, unlike the somewhat later *Man'yōshū,* is not
exclusively in Japanese. Some sections are in standard Chinese; some use Chinese sinographs to write Japanese in something like the *wakun* fashion Sorai
discussed but in reverse so that the original is a Japanese sentence contorted
to fit Chinese word order; some use Chinese characters only for their phonetic
sounds without any regard for their Chinese meaning; and some use Chinese
characters for their meaning, but pronouncing them as the Japanese word with
the same meaning. Furthermore, these different sub-languages and multiple
orthographies can be intermixed into a near unintelligible garble. All we see
is a sequence of Chinese characters that looks superficially like a Chinese text
until we try to read it.

Since the reader can only tell from context what type of writing a given
sentence represents and the context can only be determined by knowing the
meaning of the surrounding sentences, there is a vicious circle that makes interpretation more like cryptology than hermeneutics: one can only understand the

part if one understands the whole, but to understand the whole, one needs to understand the parts first. For that reason, to get the context right, one has to have interpretive moorings outside the text itself.

One obvious source of such information is *Nihonshoki,* another historical chronicle written just a few years later than *Kojiki. Nihonshoki* presents none of the problems just discussed because it is written entirely in Chinese. Since some of its content overlaps with *Kojiki,* Norinaga could use it as one external aid in reading. Whenever the two texts disagree on some matter, however, Norinaga always favored *Kojiki* since it was a bit older, it contained original Japanese, and its format and style was not modeled on the chronicles of China and Korea. Hence, he believed it better represented the oral tradition before the major impact of mainland literary forms.

A second, in some ways better, source of information for reading *Kojiki* is *Man'yōshū.* That was, of course, Mabuchi's point in Matsuzaka. *Man'yōshū* was compiled only a few decades after *Kojiki* and, compared with the orthography used in *Kojiki,* is somewhat more uniform and coherent. Thus, *Man'yōshū* could give Norinaga good clues for determining what Chinese character was being used for which Japanese phonetic sound. In fact, Norinaga's attention to pronunciation of the ancient language led to philological discoveries that changed the mainstream interpretation of some key concepts.

For example, Mabuchi and others had assumed the word *kami* meaning "sacred presence or deity" was linked to the word *kami* meaning "upper or above." Hence, Mabuchi surmised that the *kami* in the religion of the ancient Japanese people (what I call "proto-Shintō") were the gods who were "above" humans in either status, physical location, or both. Norinaga's philological studies proved, however, that the two words were not pronounced the same in ancient Japanese. Specifically, there was a vowel difference in the second syllable that no longer existed in Japanese by the time the *kana* syllabary was developed in the early ninth century and has been in use ever since. Hence the popular etymology endorsed by such scholars as Mabuchi was simply wrong.

Even those two external sources would not suffice, however, in developing an adequate key for deciphering *Kojiki*'s mysteries. So, Norinaga felt he had to go beyond the limits of what philology could offer. Basically, he needed a heuristic, a way of looking at his data that he could not justify in itself, but which would allow him to generate working hypotheses about what a textual passage means, hypotheses that themselves could be gradually tested against the text at other places. This is a little odd as a literary interpretive device, but not so unusual if we consider the comparison with cryptology.

Suppose a police investigation intercepts a coded message from an underworld drug ring under surveillance. To crack the code, the police cryptologists will make some heuristic assumptions such as the original language of the message before it was encoded and the likelihood of its contents. For example, they might assume the message is in English and it is about the time and place of an impending drug shipment. So, the police investigators would look for encoded English words, local place names, and numbers representing time—all assumptions that can be verified only when and if the meaning of the message becomes clear.

In a parallel way, Norinaga assumed the base language of *Kojiki* was archaic Japanese, basically like the language of *Man'yōshū*, but in some respects even older. Except for the passages obviously written in Chinese and to be read as Chinese, Norinaga's assumption was that *Kojiki*'s orthography represented the formerly unwritten archaic Japanese. His task was to break through the written surface layer to get back to the sounds beneath. Those would be the words of the original Japanese archaic language harking back to the time of creation itself.

The creation myth. This brings us to his heuristic assumptions about the content. The *Kojiki*, especially the first section entitled "Age of the *Kami*," is the narrative of the creation of Japan (or by extension, of the world) through the activities of the celestial *kami*. That part of *Kojiki* is least like the Chinese-language twin chronicle, *Nihonshoki*, which devotes far fewer pages to that prehistorical or mythological account. Furthermore, *Nihonshoki* sometimes presents multiple versions of events rather than a single narrative like *Kojiki*'s. To Norinaga that suggested that the first section of *Kojiki* was the most Japanese section of the book and that the later sections were more likely influenced by Chinese models of dynastic chronicles, as indeed *Nihonshoki* certainly was.

Like the other thinkers of his era who longed for a lost archaic way of life, Norinaga assumed that the qualities he found "genuine" in the Japanese poets of later times emerged out of qualities descending from the Age of the *Kami*. He called this "the ancient Way"(*inishie no michi*).[135] Let us see now how this interpretive template led him to his analysis of the ancient Japanese language in *Kojiki*.

Norinaga's theory of the Yamato language meshed with his theory of poetic expression. The world in which we live includes a web of intimately related affects, a claim having spiritual as well as aesthetic implications. The world was born of intimacy. I mean that not only in the sense of the physical acts of love that sometimes contributed to the world's creation, but also in the sense that creation itself was the fortuitous expression of the gods' inner selves. Parts of what we know as the world were originally sometimes no more than pieces of the gods that fell off while bathing, as in the case of the birth of the sun and moon recounted in *Kojiki*, for example.[†] For Norinaga the key point is that

† See page 53.

there was no rational cosmogonic plan, but rather, out of the gods' being in touch with each other—both physically and emotionally—the world took form spontaneously.

That cosmogonic creativity resembles the moment of poetic creativity in which the words-things come into being through their spontaneous expression in the poet. Applying that principle to his reading of *Kojiki*, Norinaga found no problem with the inconsistencies in the stories: consistency is the criterion of "the Chinese mentality" (*kara no kokoro*) and its logic, not the criterion of the sentimentality in the "genuine mindful heart" (*magokoro*). The ground of creative expression, like other forms of engaged knowing, is not open to the analyses of intellectual reflection, that is, it cannot be described in the discursive terms appropriate to a rationally devised metaphysical system. To understand creation, one must engage it; one must participate in it. It is critical, of course, that we reenact the original creation in its own linguistic and ontological form. Such was the task of Norinaga's philology, making it in effect a form of epistemic and spiritual praxis.

If the original words preserved in *Kojiki* are the intimations of the time of creation itself, they are words-things (*koto*) that constitute us as part of that creation. Like all poetic expressions, the resonance of their sound is inseparable from their meaning and this primal resonance continues to reverberate in today's (Japanese) language. Unlike Mabuchi who insisted his students write poems only in the *Man'yōshū* style so as to preserve the spiritual power of the language (*kotodama*), Norinaga believed we should write our poetry in the context of our own aesthetic communities. It is the creative act of poeticizing that taps the spiritual power of the words, not adherence to the archaic forms themselves. Norinaga was well aware that mere mimicry of form easily degenerates into dilettantism.[136] For him, the point was to be genuinely responsive to one's own affectively known context. Only then can the aesthetic and the religious be intimately connected.

Norinaga's philosophical anthropology. For Norinaga, what then does it mean to be a human being? As already mentioned, it means to have a "genuine heart" (*magokoro*), to be in touch with things and to be touched by things. The ability to be touched by the world is innate, but an individual may deny that innate capacity and thwart its natural function: one can become a "heartless person" (*kokoro naki hito*) rather than a "person with heart" (*kokoro aru hito*). Since it is natural for human beings to be people of heart and it is a distortion of our true selves to be heartless, we can speak of the genuine mindful heart as the true manifestation of our humanity.

The creation myth of *Kojiki* depicts a beginning of things in which there is no sharp separation between *kami*, things, words, and human beings. All came into being out of a single field of interdependence, what we might consider the *kami* field of *kokoro*. For Norinaga the basic mechanism for the creation of a poem is the same as that for the creation of the world. Hence, we are most ourselves when we are most like our origin, that time of creation when all came into being. (Might we not call this, as the medieval Shintō theorists did, "the beginning of the beginnings?") And more crucially, we are most like our origins when we participate in the creative expression of poetry with our own genuine mindful heart (*magokoro*). Sometimes scholars treat Norinaga as if he had two discrete personas: the Norinaga of poetics and the Norinaga of Shinto (including politics). But there was one Norinaga and his theory of creativity is the connective tissue within all his writings.[137]

In his own time, the greatest challenge to the *magokoro*, Norinaga maintained, was the increasing dominance of the sinophiles' "Chinese mentality" (*kara no kokoro*) in Japanese culture. To help us get a better fix on Norinaga's understanding of *magokoro*, it will help to examine more closely how Norinaga contrasted it with the Chinese mentality.

According to Norinaga, the Chinese mentality, as opposed to Japanese sentimentality, thrives on abstraction, rationalism, moralism, and intellectual *hubris*. It assumes the world can be penetrated by logic. Rather than touching and being touched by the heart of things, it looks for principles (*ri* or *kotowari*) that instill reality with rational order and pattern. The Chinese mentality is interested in *what* texts say *about* principles and rules of conduct, not for *how they express* (*mono ii [no] sama*) the mindful heart. The Chinese mentality, Norinaga concluded in agreement with Ogyū Sorai, is "masculine" rather than "feminine." That raises the issue of Norinaga's view of gender and its relation to Japanese culture.

For Norinaga, the genuine heart of sentimentality is fundamentally the same in men and women, but social norms generally require males to hide their true selves under the veneer of rationality and a public display of courage.[138*] In the society of his time only women, he maintained, are allowed to express their feelings spontaneously and publicly. Although men have the same feelings as women, they repress their expression by means of their philosophizing as Confucians or Buddhists, presenting only the stoic demeanor dictated by the samurai code or the rule of Buddhist asceticism. Moreover, males are taught that feminine sensitivities are inferior and should be surrendered to the masculine.

Yet, as Norinaga points out, however brave and loyal a samurai may be, as he lies dying on the battlefield, who does not think of mother, wife, and family?[139] No intellectual theory can ever explain everything; no process of austerity can ever completely eliminate human feeling. Since there will always remain the nonlogical and the sentimental qualities that only women are allowed to show openly, the attempt to be completely virile will ultimately fail. Still, the so-called Chinese mentality or ideal tries, said Norinaga, to suppress the feminine as much as possible and thereby turns males against their own inherent natural tendencies, making them willing soldiers in loyal service to the abstract principles of the state.

ENGAGING NORINAGA'S PHILOSOPHY TODAY

As we did with Shinran, let us try to engage Norinaga more intimately by imaginatively—creatively—inviting him to leave his world for a moment to visit ours. Let us imagine that his opponent was not the Chinese mentality of eighteenth-century Japan, but instead the modern emphasis on detached knowing so prevalent in our world today. Since there is little doubt that he would find the two similar in their emphasis on empiricism, logic, referential language, and rationality, it is not difficult to make this adjustment. If Norinaga were to speak with us directly, what might he say? Perhaps something like the following.

> Let us start with poetry. Anyone who has ever read a poem with any sensitivity already knows the inherent power of words. The poetic words express the harmony in the interresponsive field of poet, reader, and subject matter. Anyone who has ever written a poem, written a poem mindfully with a sincere heart and not as an academic exercise, knows that the poet does not write about feelings, events, or things, but rather, the entire context of world and poet at that moment expresses itself through the words. A poem is not *about* anything; it is the self-expression, an intimation, of that total context including poet, words, and things.
>
> Assuming we do have such experiences, we may ask how such remarkable moments come to be. The presuppositions of detached knowing and empiricism cannot satisfactorily explain how poetry is possible. For there to be poetry, the world cannot be something forever outside us to be observed from an external, value-free, emotion-free standpoint. Nor is rationalism of any help here. For there to be poetry, the world cannot be merely a set of mathematically and logically discernible laws to be fathomed through the mind alone without the heart. Both empiricism and rationalism insist on seeing the world in an external relation to us, making knowledge into a third thing, a relating quality that brings two independent realities—world and self—into a relationship.
>
> Poetry, by contrast, reveals a reality of internal relationships. The world and we are inseparable, at least inseparable without loss. Without world, we would not be what we are; without us, the world would not be what it is. The first part of the statement is clear enough: without the world we could not even exist. But why is the second part true?
>
> As the species which feels, humans play a key role in nature's self-expression. Note that the emphasis is on feeling, not rationality. Rationality is not the defining character of our humanity; sensitivity, affectivity, and respon-

siveness—the ability to be in touch and to be touched—is what defines our humanness. While all animals are in their own way sensitive and responsive, only humans can feel the *mono no aware* in a poetic and communal way. The eagle may soar above the forests and waterfalls, but only humans go into those forests expressly to do no more than feel awe and maybe, like Ansel Adams, express that awe in a photograph to be shared with others. The bee may flit from cherry blossom to cherry blossom, but only a human being can feel the fleeting beauty of the flower petals and express it in a poem or even just a tear. The world would not be the same without us. Without us the world would lose a part of itself, something internal to the meaning it has evolved. Without us the world would no longer be creatively, poetically expressive. It would not lose only its tongue; it would lose as well its mindful heart.

Your reaction to such a Norinagan riff might be that it is aesthetically and spiritually edifying, but is there really a philosophical point? That very question reveals the influence of our modern western version of what Norinaga called the Chinese mentality. Why is philosophy—the *love* of wisdom—about reason but not emotion? What strange quirk of the imagination has led us to be convinced that the world has rational principles holding everything together, but not ties of affectivity and intersensitivity as well? Against Norinaga's challenges, we could, of course, marshall empirical evidence to prove our belief. We could point to the accomplishments of our scientific understanding and its success in allowing us to adapt to the world and to adapt the world to us.

Yet, could not Norinaga argue that the poetic view of the world also works? It works not so much in helping us to change or even to know about the world, but it does help us feel at home in it. And when are we most human? When we manipulate the world? A beaver can do that. When we accumulate and process facts about the world? A mechanical, computerized space probe can do that. No, we are most human when we feel at home in the world—being in touch with it and being touched by it—in such a way that we can express the mutual sensitivity (*kokoro*) that make self and world a whole.

Let us follow Norinaga's vision a bit further. Suppose for a moment that the bond of reality is an internally interactive pattern of getting in touch and being touched. Suppose that words are not ciphers for external realities, but part of the self-expression of those contextual realities in which we find ourselves. Why should we assume the dog's bark is a spontaneous, natural part of its fear, but for us to yell "Go away!" is not? Why is the bird's song a natural part of what it is, but language for us is a product we developed so we could talk about external realities? Perhaps the world, at least the only world known to us humans, is held together by a field of feelings-significations-thoughts (*kokoro*). Within that field are the internally related things-words (*koto*) simultaneously taking form as the world and as our expressions.

Given such suppositions, what purpose would be left for rationality? Rationality would not be what defines us, but only a tool, albeit a critically important tool. Even poets must house themselves, find a stable source of food, and plan ahead as a means of survival. Without rationality there would be for us no subsistence. To survive we think and designate; to be human we feel and express. In such a view, we would have to take care lest the servant become the master: our reason should always serve our sensitivity, our thoughts should serve our capacity to be interresponsive, but not vice versa.

Norinaga did not believe that to be human, we have to be good poets, but we do have to be poetic. In fact, starting with Mabuchi, most Japanese critics have not deemed Norinaga's poetry to be of high quality. Yet, for Norinaga, that is besides the point. For him, spirituality resides in the ability to know the creative power of poetic language by participating in it, not by appreciating it from outside. Poetic forms will undergo transformation as the sociohistorical contexts of poetry change. The *waka* of the Heian court may be today's hip hop of the urban streets. The rapper is not talking *about* life in the streets, but is an outpouring of that life itself. In that respect, poetry is not just a spiritual event in which one engages in creation; it is also an expression for a community of listeners in a given time and place. The purpose of the poet is to reveal the *mono no aware*, the affectivity of life in the present context, not the context of a time and place long gone.

For Norinaga, the purpose of poetry, like the purpose of religion, is to bind us together as a community without having to rely exclusively on formal contracts, laws, and discursively designated rules of behavior. If we can only express our fundamental humanness, our ability to be responsively in touch, we would naturally form a harmonious community. We would have a world of intimacy in which we would each intimate to each other what is innermost to ourselves as human beings. In such a community, artistic expression would be the way we come to know each other so that we can live together in some semblance of harmony. We would live in the land of the gods, speaking their language, echoing their intimations. At least that is how Norinaga saw matters and how, I believe, he would advise us in our situation today.

Yet, however much we might be attracted to Norinaga's point of view, it is impossible to read much of him without being struck by his ethnocentrism. Romanticism can sometimes be a universal celebration of humanity transcending geographical, ethnic, or political boundaries. At other times, however, it takes root deeply within a particular soil, celebrating the specialness of a particular place, a specific people, and an individual language. Although Norinaga showed at times signs of the former, for the most part, he was a romantic of an ethnocentrist hue. Now that Norinaga's visit to our world has ended, we must return him back to his. If we do not, we will not be able understand how his philosophy was taken in a direction that he did not anticipate and, I believe, he would have viewed in horror.

NORINAGA'S ETHNOCENTRISM

Where we find Norinaga the universalist, we also find Norinaga the Japanist, his academic discipline of Native Studies blurring into an ideology of nativism. Because he was a fundamentalist who took the words of *Kojiki* literally, Norinaga found himself in an ambivalent position. On one hand, his natural proclivity was toward universalism. What he was saying about language, human nature, and the character of spirituality were meant to be true for everyone in every country. Yet, the very text he used for his inspiration was anchored in ethnocentric claims: Japan is the center of the world, the Land of the Gods; only the Japanese have the story of creation correct; only the emperor of Japan is a direct descendant of the *kami* who created the world.

To some extent, Norinaga tried to mitigate the ethnocentrist implications of his theory by maintaining, for example, that all countries once had the original story of creation. All of us were created from the same source, descended from the same stock. He thought the ethnic differences in creation narratives was due to the late arrival of literacy to the Japanese archipelago. Being illiterate for so long, the Japanese had preserved the cosmogonic account as an oral tradition and when they did finally write it down, they did so in an orthography that virtually no one could read. Therefore, the true, full story of creation was kept intact, whereas elsewhere it underwent changes as people tried to bring rational criteria to it in an effort to improve on it or to serve their own political purposes.

As a result, only fragments of the original story remain in other lands: Norinaga pointed, for example, to myths in other countries about the importance of the sun. And does not Amaterasu, the Sun Goddess, shine equally on all nations in the world, not favoring Japan? So, if Japan is the only country to have the complete story of creation right, that was ultimately a matter of chance, not the sign of the inherent superiority of the Japanese people. If the Japanese had not been foolish enough to write the narrative in a system almost no one within a few decades would be able to read, they too would have lost parts of the story.

Norinaga's efforts to be universal could only go so far, though: his theories were glued to a literalist reading of an ethnocentric text. Although he himself on some level may or may not have had an inclination to consider the Japanese people to be superior to other races, *Kojiki* unmistakably affirms the unique stature of the Japanese emperor not only as descended directly from the *kami*, but also as someone with a specific mission to rule over the human domain. In his defense of nativism and based on his reading of *Kojiki*, Norinaga regarded Japan as the Land of the Gods and Japanese, among all extant languages, to be the closest to the original sounds of divine creativity. Poetry could be written in various styles (*Man'yōshū*, *Kokinshū*, and so on), but to have the spiritual power of *kotodama*, its words must be the words of ancient Yamato.

With historical hindsight, we can see where this type of thinking could, and in fact did, lead. If all the world has a common source and we are all really brothers and sisters, if our common bond is through the *kami*, and if there is only one family in the world descended directly from the *kami*, should not that family reign over the world? Norinaga himself did not work out the syllogism. If he had, the first corollary would be to return the emperor to his proper place in Japan.

Yet, Norinaga did not want his premises to lead to such a political conclusion. In fact, he had taken pains to show that the Tokugawa family was also descended from the *kami*, though from a lesser deity than the imperial progenitrix, the Sun Goddess. As the descendants of that *kami*, the Tokugawa were to rule the country as the agents of the emperor. Norinaga abhorred war and, to his way of thinking, no principle was worth dying for. Still, whatever his own view might have been, in his ideas were the seeds of revolution and, ultimately, of imperialism and jingoism as well.

NORINAGA'S PHILOSOPHICAL CONTRIBUTION

How, then, are we finally to interpret Norinaga's philosophy and its place in the development of Japanese values? First, we should note that Norinaga was unequivocally a philosopher of engaged knowing. He envisioned a reality in which world, humanity, and verbal expression were internally related in a single field of interresponsiveness. A romantic to the core, he stressed the affective as being more reliable than the intellectual, however beneficial the latter might be. As a philosopher, he directly confronted the challenges to intimacy found in Tokugawa Japan, in particular, the challenge of what he called the Chinese mentality found in the Japanese Confucians (and Buddhists). In meeting those challenges, he played in his own time and place a role similar to what we have seen in Kūkai, Shinran, and Dōgen. That is, his writings aimed to center or re-center Japanese philosophy on engagement rather than detachment. Unlike those three, however, Norinaga's philosophy was Shintō rather than Buddhist.

Shintō as a tradition had always emphasized internal relations in its praxis. Yet, not until the development of Native Studies did it have a philosophical rationale for defining that emphasis on intimacy, for articulating its ground, and for analyzing the social and cultural methods for achieving it. Through the contribution of philosophers like Norinaga, Shintō became, for the first time, a full-fledged philosophical tradition, albeit an intellectual tradition with a strong anti-rationalist bent.

Since Shintō was now philosophical, it could also become blatantly ideological in support of a new image of the state and society. As a Shintō philosopher, Norinaga had valorized the affective side of our humanity. His teacher Hori Keizan had also praised feelings as a universal human characteristic central to Confucianism.[†] Against those universalizing trends, though, we have also seen the ethnocentricism of Dazai Shundai. In defending the actions of the samurai involved in the Akō Incident, Shundai had said the *Japanese* passions were especially volatile, a characteristic he believed essential not only to samurai loyalty but also ultimately to the defense of the nation.[‡]

Does Native Studies entail a claim that emotionalism and sensitivity are somehow uniquely Japanese? Does the romanticized emphasis on responsiveness include the responsiveness of the warrior in his act of killing? Norinaga the poet, the pacifist, and the proponent of the "feminine" (*taoyameburi*) certainly did not think so. But the questions remained. Would some future nativists with a different agenda weaponize Norinaga's ideas into a jingoistic, militarist ideology? The short answer is yes; the longer answer is found in our next chapter.

[†] See page 324.
[‡] See page 323.

The Modern Period

11. Black Ships, Black Rain
The End of Edo to the End of War (1801–1945)

12. NISHIDA Kitarō (1870–1945)
Putting Nothing in Its Place

13. WATSUJI Tetsurō (1889–1960)
Philosophy in the Midst

14. Aftershocks and Afterthoughts
Postwar to the New Century

15. Conclusion

11. Black Ships, Black Rain
The End of Edo to the End of War (1801–1945)

> There's no way out of this hole.
> We have to be ready to die, and
> we have to put a good face on it.
> TAYAMA Katai (1908)[1]

To specify when the "modern" begins in a cultural history can be a knotty problem. In the West, for example, modern philosophy starts with Descartes in the early seventeenth century and involves philosophy's detachment from the Church and scriptural authority, the development of scientific thinking, and the rise of individualistic humanism. Yet, in that same western cultural history, modernism in literature and the arts does not begin until the late nineteenth and early twentieth centuries, heralded by a focus on form and the challenge to long-standing stylistic conventions of beauty, diachronic narration, and historical positivism.

For Japan, scholars have agreed that the *modern* period in philosophy means post–1868, the date of the shogunate's fall and the restoration of the emperor to power.[2*] It is the era when Japan founded modern universities based on western models and established philosophy departments within them. In this chapter I survey the period from approximately 1800 to 1945, setting the context for the rise of modern academic philosophy in Japan. My treatment of the end of that period will be somewhat sketchy in some details because it will be covered again in Chapter 14 when I deal with the postwar period. As I mentioned in the Introduction, some historical events are best described as a capstone to a sequence of earlier events, whereas others are best understood as setting the stage for subsequent events. In Chapters 12 and 13 we will return from the historical narrative to the engagement approach as we will enmesh ourselves in the theories of two of Japan's most significant twentieth-century philosophers, Nishida Kitarō and Watsuji Tetsujirō.

To begin, I recount the events and ideas that led to the overthrow of the shogunate, focusing especially on those that intersected with philosophical concerns.

THREE IDEOLOGIES FOR IMPERIAL RESTORATION

By the late 1700s, the fabric of Tokugawa shogunate was no longer merely fraying at the edges, but had started unraveling so much the center was in danger. To make the shogunate operate effectively at its outset, the Tokugawa leadership had reconstituted the country's domains, often putting new daimyō in charge of designated regions. Those most supportive of Ieyasu at the Battle of Sekigahara, for example, were kept close to Edo; those whose loyalty was not beyond a shadow of a doubt, at a distance. That was initially a shrewd strategy. If some daimyō or group of daimyō wanted to move against the government, they would have to travel some distance, giving the shogunate, with its significant system of surveillance, time to prepare.

In the long run, though, as the power at the center weakened, it became easier for distant domains to operate with increasing autonomy. This was especially true of the domains of Chōshū at the southwestern tip of the main island of Honshū and Satsuma on the neighboring island of Kyushu (see map page 697). Those two provinces were particularly threatening to the shogunate since they had access to sea routes by which they could import weapons. Trade with the outside world was, of course, forbidden to the daimyō, as was the compiling of a private military arsenal. Yet, once the shogunate lost its tight grip on the distant provinces, it was possible to get away with the crime.

The Warrior Ideology of Loyalty

The coalescence of loosely connected samurai ideas and values into the ideology of loyalty was one of the three intellectual supports for the overthrow of the shogunate and was especially strong in Chōshū and Satsuma. The samurai in such regions idealized the warrior mentality that had been gathering momentum throughout the Edo period so that loyalty became a primary, perhaps *the* primary, virtue. The open question was only to whom the loyalty was directed: one's lord, the shogun, or the emperor. Certainly, as we found in the case of the forty-seven loyal retainers,[†] the samurai were often most loyal to their daimyō, but toward whom did the daimyō direct *their* loyalty: the imperial court or the shogunate? Competition between the court and shogunate for the allegiance of the daimyō dates back, as we have seen, to the first shogunate in the twelfth century, but for much of the Edo period, the Tokugawa had the upper hand. Once Ieyasu had secured the official title of "shōgun" for himself

† See pages 319–23.

and his heirs in the early seventeenth century, the emperor's role receded ever further into the background.

Ieyasu, as we have seen, built up his home base in Edo competing with Kyoto not only as a center of power, but also of culture. Moreover, to cultivate the charisma of the house of Tokugawa, Ieyasu's son constructed an opulent mausoleum for him. The site was a holy mountain some 120 kilometers from Edo known as Nikkō ("Light of the sun"). In addition, Ieyasu acquired the posthumous appellation, Tōshō Daigongen. Tōshō means "East Illuminating," the shō written with the same sinograph as the second sinograph in the name of the Sun kami, Amaterasu, the progenitrix of the imperial family. As for daigongen, in Buddhism it refers to a primary physical embodiment of a buddha or bodhisattva.

So, the Tokugawa were playing the same semiotic game that emperor Shōmu had played at the establishment of Great Temple to the East in Nara almost a millennium earlier: using the symbols of Shintō, Buddhism, and the sun to bring luster and gravitas to their rule.[†] As Shōmu had built monasteries and nunneries in each province, the Tokugawa constructed hundreds of Tōshō-gū (shrines to Tōshō) throughout Japan, the main one, of course, being at Nikkō. To reinforce the status of the Nikkō mausoleum and its enshrined deity, imperial emissaries were compelled to travel from Kyoto annually to pay homage. It seems even the emperor's men had to submit to their own version of alternate attendance.[‡]

Thus, the long-range goal of the Tokugawa seems to have been to overshadow the status of the emperor: politically, culturally, and spiritually. If that indeed was the plan, it failed. A by-product of the reemergence of Confucianism in Edo-period Japan was that the Chinese classics clearly directed loyalty to no feudal lord or general, but to the emperor alone.

Admittedly, in those same Chinese classics, the emperor only ruled by the "will (or mandate) of heaven," but in Japan the authority for imperial rule had, as we have seen, long before shifted to the blood relation between the imperial family and the creator kami. Thus, there was a solid basis for an argument, based in both Chinese Confucianism and in the ancient mythicohistory associated with proto-Shintō (including, thanks to Norinaga, the newly resurgent status of Kojiki) that one's warrior loyalty should be directed to the emperor. Since the Satsuma and Chōshū daimyō held an age-old grudge against the Tokugawa for being assigned to territories so far from the capital and bakufu, they relished

† See pages 96–7.
‡ See page 280.

the prospect of arming themselves in preparation for the next inevitable confrontation with their old adversaries.

The Mito School Imperialist Ideology

A second intellectual justification for restoring imperial power arose not from those having a blood feud with the Tokugawa but, strange to say, from those with a blood-tie to the Tokugawa, namely, the Mito branch of the house. The Mito was one of the three major scion-producing families (*Gosanke*) in the Tokugawa family tree. Should the main line of the family not produce a male heir, for example, one would come elsewhere from within the *Gosanke*. They were to assist the shogunate against hostile daimyō and their domains had special status of being *shinpan* ("intimate" or "parent" domains).

As I already explained,[†] early in the Tokugawa reign, the Tokugawa daimyō of Mito had established a historical research institute to write the mammoth *Great History of Japan*. The resulting Mito School of thought (Mitogaku) had started much as advertised: it was a research group of some hundred scholars representing various points of view. As the end of the eighteenth century approached, however, the school assumed a new complexion: it increasingly became a think tank for developing an argument supporting imperial restoration. Did the evidence compiled for the *History* produce an argument that Japan's uniqueness and spiritual strength resided in the imperial succession, a dynasty existing unbroken since the Age of the Gods? Or was the political turn a response to the increasingly obvious failure of the shogunate to successfully run the state— a call for imperial restoration as a way of shaking the government out of its doldrums to inspire a new beginning? It is difficult to say. In any case, the Mito School set the ideological underpinnings for a revolution.

The Mito School held three phrases in high regard that enjoyed a wide circulation during the waning years of Edo and beyond. The first was *sonnō* ("revere the emperor"), a rather self-explanatory exhortation, but terms related to reverence, as we have seen,[‡] had accrued resonances both Confucian and Shintō.

Second, beginning with the Russian and British fleets illegally intruding into Japanese waters at the outset of the nineteenth century, Aizawa Seishisai (1782–1863) expanded the phrase to create a second slogan *sonnō jōi*: "revere the emperor and expel the barbarians." This call to arms resonated with those wishing to preserve Japan's closure policy, even if it meant military action against encroaching foreigners. The belligerent samurai of Satsuma and Chōshū, for example, let it be known they were armed and ready for such a confrontation.

1020–2

† See pages 329-30.
‡ See, for example, pages 297; 313; 325-7.

By the mid-nineteenth century, it became clear to most informed observers that such military action would be futile and self-destructive, however. The West's military technology had far outstripped Japan's over the preceding two centuries of the closure policy.

The third term from the Mito School, one that would influence Japanese thinking through 1945 and even up to today, is *kokutai*, a Chinese political expression for *state formation* which accrued special meanings in Japan. The word *kokutai* (meaning literally, the "essence" or "body" of the "country" or the state) came to designate a form of polity considered distinctive, perhaps unique, to Japan. It referred to the specific political structure of a state ruled by an emperor like Japan's (and perhaps found nowhere else). That is, *kokutai* involves a monarch who is directly descended from the creating deities, is the head or father of the (Japanese) people (all of whom are themselves more distant descendants of those deities), and is bestowed with charisma embodying the spirit of the nation. Using my terminology, the emperor had become a political holographic entry point, a focal object in which the pattern and connectedness of all Japan could be engaged.

1255–6

The description of *kokutai* may be vague, but in some ways, it is supposed to be. One knows *kokutai* not be analyzing it, but by participating in it, by playing a part in, as it were, the body politic. During the Pacific War, the allies spurred on their armed forces with the slogan that "the Japanese think their emperor is a god." What is true in that caricature derives in part from this special meaning of *kokutai*. The emperor is the source of Japanese wholeness, but is not (as one might expect of a god) omnipotent, transcendent, or possessing the power of creation.

The Native Studies of Hirata Atsutane

509–22

To appreciate the third philosophical ideology supporting imperial restoration, it is important to know the shogunate was not only becoming militarily feeble; it was also in financial straits. Despite their capacity and willingness to use force, the shoguns also appreciated that steadfast loyalty needs to be rewarded with more than honor. Two centuries earlier Emperor Go-Daigo had learned that lesson† and the Tokugawa were astute readers of history. Once the curtain had been drawn shut on the era of the Warring Domains, the victorious Tokugawa shogunate no longer had significant spoils to distribute. So it rewarded loyalty by letting the daimyō keep a significant portion of the wealth produced from their lands. The alternate residence rule did drain much of those

---

† See pages 247–8.

funds, but those proceeds went to merchants, hospitality services, and artisans, not into the shogunate coffers.

The Edo Period's boom years—cultural as well as economic—were the latter half of the seventeenth and the early decades of the eighteenth centuries, an epoch generally known as the Genroku era (although the formal Genroku period was technically only the years 1688–1704). The shogun during much of that time was Tokugawa Tsunayoshi, whom I briefly mentioned in relation to our engagement with Sorai.[†] The sparkling culture of the era—with its literary luminaries like the aforementioned Saikaku and Bashō, artistic achievements in painting (the resurgent Tosa and Kanō schools topped off by the lustrous Rinpa style with its extensive fondness for gold and silver), and the theatrical blossoming of both kabuki and *bunraku* (puppet theater)—led the extravagant Tsunayoshi to reduce the shogunate treasury to a permanent state of near bankruptcy.

The national indebtedness spurred runaway inflation throughout the land and, with the stranglehold on foreign trade, there was almost no outside money coming in. That left little cushion for times of hardship and when those hardships hit, such as the Kyōho Famine of 1732–1733, there were riots in the streets of Edo. Fifty years later, the Tenmei Famine of 1782–1787 took hundreds of thousands of lives and after that, the Tenpō Famine of 1833–1836 led to major revolts in 1837 in both Osaka and what is now Niigata prefecture. The latter two reverberated with philosophical resonances.

The Osaka riot was led by Ōshio Heihachirō (1793–1837), a Yōmeigaku Confucian. As earlier explained, Yōmeigaku derived from the teachings of the Chinese neo-Confucian, Wang Yangming, who emphasized the innate character of goodness and the inseparability of knowing and doing.[‡] Morally outraged at the hoarding of rice by the government and wealthy merchants while people died of starvation, Ōshio and his followers took to the streets of Osaka, burning down a quarter of the city.[3] Finally cornered by the authorities, the rebel had to commit suicide.

In the other 1837 revolt, the rural uprising led by Ikuta Yorozu (1801–1837) in Echigo (see map page 697), the precipitating cause was the same: government collusion in hoarding food for profit during a time of widespread starvation. The end result was also the same—the suicide of the rebel leader. But the philosophical background was different: Ikuta Yorozu was not a Confucian, but rather a student and teacher of Native Studies within his rural community.

As the example of the Ikuta Yorozu Rebellion illustrates, Native Studies participated practically as well as theoretically in supporting the overthrow of

† See pages 346-9.

‡ See pages 303–4; 317.

the shogunate. Such a militant attitude might seem anomalous. From what we have seen so far, Native Studies was an elite philological and literary movement, hardly something targeted to farmers and resulting in a violent attack on the government. Furthermore, Norinaga himself was a pacifist for whom death was always a tragedy with no promise of reward in an afterlife. He was the last person to urge others to die for a principle or a cause. What happened to account for such a radical change in the tenor and audience of the Native Studies movement? Hirata Atsutane (1776–1843) is what happened.

Atsutane considered himself the prime disciple of Norinaga and the true heir to the leadership role of the Native Studies movement, a bit surprising since he never met Norinaga nor even corresponded as Norinaga had with Mabuchi. Furthermore, although a reputable philologist, Atsutane's real strengths lay elsewhere.

Like Norinaga, Atsutane aspired to defend native sensitivities against an ever-encroaching "Chinese mentality," but on one point he could not agree with his self-designated master.[4*] Namely, he could not accept Norinaga's claim that at death all people, regardless of how they lived their lives, go to the underworld, the Land of Yomi, to rot forever. Norinaga had claimed that the only mention of afterlife in *Kojiki* concerned the story of Izanagi's journey to the hellish defilement of Yomi in hopes of rescuing Izanami. Norinaga reasoned that if even a *kami* like Izanami would be banished to Yomi after death, no better fate could befall people like us.

Fascinated by supernatural phenomena, Atsutane believed the world of spirits and of the afterlife had to be more complicated than what Norinaga had envisioned. Yet, based on the evidence in *Kojiki* alone, he could not disprove it. So Atsutane made a radical departure from Norinaga's methods by rejecting the idea that the study of ancient texts and their language was the only approach to discovering and reengaging the Ancient Way.

If we want to neutralize all residues of the "Chinese mentality" on Japanese culture over the centuries, there was, Atsutane argued, another valid source for insight besides *Kojiki*, namely, the values and oral traditions of rural Japanese. Atsutane reasoned that since those people were both illiterate and isolated, they must have been untouched by Chinese influences. At that point, we might say, Atsutane created the field of Japanese folk ethnology. He traveled among the remote mountain people and peasants collecting their stories and explanations about "the other world" and "afterlife," discounting what he could identify as nonnative influences from China or Korea.[5]

Without detailing all the differences between Norinaga and Atsutane,[6] two points are relevant to our philosophical narrative. First, in line with his reinterpretation of the other world and its spirits, Atsutane introduced into Native Studies a new conception of the afterlife. In Atsutane's version, people would be judged after death by the *kami* Ōkuninushi based on how well the deceased had followed the Way of the *kami*. That *kami* meted out the reward of heaven or the punishment of hell accordingly. Buddhism had its own theories of heaven and hell, of course, but the idea of a divinity judging one's actions in the afterworld seems more Christian than Buddhist. Perhaps not coincidentally, Atsutane was acquainted with both Christianity[7] and western scientific thought, the afore-mentioned Dutch Learning.[†]

Whatever the inspiration for Atsutane's vision of the afterlife, it had an unmistakable political ramification: since the emperor, as the descendant of the *kami,* is the proper ruler of Japan, if someone were to die in service to the emperor, that would automatically guarantee rebirth in paradise. Unlike Norinaga, Atsutane believed that there *was* an upside to death if one lived one's life and died in service of the Ancient Way.

The other point about Atsutane's approach is that it philosophically enfran-chised, even esteemed, the Japanese commoner. This contributed to the success of his movement—Atsutane's followers far outnumbered those of Norinaga— and indirectly supported the aforementioned uprising led by Atsutane's student, Ikuta Yorozu. Atsutane had convinced his followers that the ancient Japanese spirit was alive not only for the highly educated scholars who had first-hand knowledge of the ancient texts, but also for commoners who had assimilated the Ancient Way through folklore. His formal inclusion of peasants into the Ancient Way movement enlarged the pool of recruits who might be enlisted in the revolution.

It is noteworthy that from the era of Warring Domains throughout the Tokugawa regime, peasant uprisings against unfair taxation and exploita-tion could draw on divergent religiophilosophical sources. Shin Buddhism had inspired the medieval *Ikkō Ikki,* Christianity the Shimabara Uprising in the early Edo period, Wang Yangming's neo-Confucianism in the Osaka riots of 1837, and Native Studies in the Ikuta Yorozu rebellion also in 1837. The fabric of Tokugawa power and authority was being pulled apart by a variety of constituencies, in this case by those with economic grievances.

Demise of the Tokugawa

From the end of the eighteenth century, the Tokugawa shogunate was feeling distress on multiple fronts: economic, political, ideological, and military. The last thing it needed was another major challenge, especially from outside, a world from which it had tried so hard to isolate itself. European imperialists had started testing for chinks in the armor of the shogunate's seclusion policy

† See pages 288–90.

since the early nineteenth century when English and Russian ships cruised the outskirts of Japan's harbors only to be turned away.

The shogun's advisors panicked. Fight or negotiate? Seemingly unaware of the long-term risks for internal affairs, in an almost painfully effete act, the shogunate suspended the alternate residence requirement, urging the daimyō to use the savings to start building up their own military forces. Apparently, it hadn't occurred to the Tokugawa brain trust that those newly armed troops could just as easily turn their sights on the shogun as on the barbarians from abroad.

When the United States dispatched Commodore Matthew Perry to force trade relations with Japan, he arrived in Edo Bay in 1853 with a letter from President Millard Fillmore demanding a trade agreement. He said he would return again in a year with his "black ships" (steamers billowing black smoke, a new and horrifying sight to many Japanese who witnessed it). When he did, Japan had no choice but to sign an agreement officially ending Japan's seclusion policy and giving the U.S. a highly advantageous trade agreement (no tariffs on American goods; the right to establish U.S. ports of trade in Japan; Americans in Japan being exempt from Japanese laws, etc.). The British and the Russians were quick to follow the American lead and make their own, equally lopsided, trade agreements with Japan. By 1860 Japan was experiencing a desperate trade imbalance of more gold leaving the country than coming in, which in turn triggered even more financial instability and riots.

As tremors of fear and desperation continued to shake the nation, the shogunate continued its errors and miscalculations. First, it tried to punish all daimyō having pro-imperialist leanings and in so doing, increased its number of staunch enemies. It even undertook an ill-advised assault on Chōshū to quell its critics there, but the exploit was a disaster as the shogun's troops were routed as soon as Satsuma joined Chōshū's side. Finally the Mito daimyō, Tokugawa Nariaki (1800–1860), devised a stratagem to resolve the situation. Nariaki's fortunes for decades had alternated between serving on the shogun's innermost council to being placed under house arrest for falling from grace for some reason or other. In accord with his long-range plan, Nariaki managed to get his son, Tokugawa Yoshinobu (1837–1913), named shōgun in 1867. There were strings attached, however.

Noriaki's idea was Yoshinobu would relinquish power to the emperor, but with the understanding that Tokugawa land holdings remain intact and a Tokugawa chaired the potent council of daimyō. Following the plan, Yoshinobu officially dissolved the shogunate offices in November 1867 with the emperor's formal approval coming in early January 1868. For the fiery pro-imperial loyalists from Satsuma and Chōshū, however, that was not enough. They wanted to strip the Tokugawa of all power, to turn over their land holdings to the emperor, and to install a full imperial restoration. So, in late January they stormed and seized the imperial palace in Kyoto.

In a *coup d'état* that could only make sense in the surreal political climate of 1868, the rebels kidnapped the reluctant emperor in order to force him to become fully emperor. After sporadic resistance from pro-shogunate forces for the next year and a half, the hostilities finally ended and the new era of Meiji ("enlightened rule") had begun, spanning the years 1868–1912.

When the emperor Meiji moved to Edo to take residence in the newly christened imperial palace (the former Tokugawa castle), the city officially became Tokyo, the "Eastern Capital." One of his first acts upon arrival was to send an envoy to pay respects at the Sengaku-ji cemetery, the aforementioned resting place for the forty-seven samurai from the Akō Incident.[†] In the face of all the complex events I have just described, the sixteen-year-old emperor knew in the end to what his rise to power was most indebted: the warrior mentality and its sense of loyalty, a loyalty now no longer directed to daimyō or shoguns, but to him. He and his senior advisors would have to rely on such single-minded dedication if they were going to refashion Japan into a modern nation, safe from aggression foreign or domestic.

BUILDING A NEW JAPAN

The decades leading to the demise of the Tokugawa shogunate was a tragi-comedy with bad casting, a performance with the wrong actors on the stage of history at precisely the worst time. By contrast, the Meiji period (1868–1912) was a whole new production. A group of extraordinary leaders, both political and intellectual, took control of Japan's destiny and within an amazingly short time made Japan not only the most technologically advanced and modernized country in Asia, but also a world power in its own right. A price was paid for that rapid progress, but there seemed to be no palatable alternative. The senior leadership advising the teenaged emperor saw Japan as having two options: either become a colonizer or become a colony.

From the first incursion of the western imperial powers, Japan was acutely aware of its vulnerability. Western technology had grown so rapidly during the period of national seclusion that the Japanese had fallen disastrously behind. During seclusion, some books from the West, especially those on science and medicine, had made their way into the country either legally or via the black market. So some intellectuals did have a sense of the technology gap, but even they must have been stunned to discover how great the gap had become. If the Japanese could not catch up and build a military force of their own that

---

† See pages 319–23.

would stave off the western forces of expansion and domination, the future was bleak. Japan would become another Philippines, another India, another Africa, another Indonesia, another Indo-China, another South America. Another western colony.

As if the insufficiency of advanced science and engineering was not enough, to industrialize Japan would require extensive natural resources beyond the meager deposits buried in the volcanic rock of the archipelago. Where would Japan get the needed oil, coal, rubber, and iron? Initially, it had to buy its resources by selling whatever products it could to western markets. Silk and other textiles were one such export and hordes of young women were shipped off from family farms (which were unable to support them anyway) to factory towns in the mountains where they worked long hours for poor pay under horrendous conditions.[8] Locked into their workhouse dormitories where tuberculosis was often rampant, some young women even longed to escape to the cities, where, if worse came to worst, they could make better money as prostitutes. Farmers were already sometimes selling daughters to (mostly legalized) brothels where they would be indentured servants for a few years until their debt was paid.

To make ends meet, many poor families depended on income from their children's labor in the new factories sprouting up throughout the country. Their plight was so bad that when the government made free public elementary education compulsory for all girls and boys while increasing taxes to help pay for the expense, some parents took to the streets in protest, bewailing the loss of needed income.[9] In the long run, Japan's leaders concluded that the only hope for the country seemed to be to do what the western powers had done: colonize countries that had the requisite natural resources.

Early Military Success

Consequently, the highest priority was placed on military development, with an attendant boost in its allocation within the national budget (up to 40–50%) and a program of male conscription starting in 1873. Time was of the essence. It had taken five or six decades of sputtering starts to create the political revolution culminating in the imperial restoration. Now Japan would have only a decade or two to carry out its industrial revolution. No price would be too great to pay as the sovereignty of the nation was at stake.

Japan succeeded in its mission. It took control of the northern island of Hokkaidō in 1869 and the Ryūkyū Islands (Okinawa Prefecture) in 1879. In 1895 Japan defeated China in the first Sino-Japanese War and took Taiwan as part of its spoils. By 1904 it felt ready to challenge Russia, a nation that had struck fear into the Japanese when its ships had started testing its seclusion policy a century before. An issue of contention was that with its victory over China, Japan felt entitled to complete control of Korea, but Russia threatened military intervention to prevent that from happening.

By 1905 Japan had initiated a naval attack on Russian vessels in the Japan Sea and had landed one million forces on the continent, alarming the Russians, who were dealing with increasing internal unrest and a threat of revolution in Moscow some 9000 kilometers to the west. Through the initiative of U.S. President Theodore Roosevelt, the two countries underwent negotiations and Japan won control of Korea and some railway lines in Manchuria. Further negotiations over the next decade granted Japan control of some railway rights in China as well. Together those spoils of war enabled Japan to build a permanent military presence in Manchuria and to occupy a large section of Inner Mongolia. Although the general populace showed signs of battle fatigue (the war with Russia in particular had taken its toll on Japan's personal and economic resources), there was no denying the Japanese Empire was well underway.

THE BIRTH OF MODERN ACADEMIC PHILOSOPHY

Transforming the Social Institutions

Japan underwent a major overhaul culturally as well. The government dissolved the Tokugawa scheme of four social classes, put into place a compulsory public school system for both boys and girls on the elementary level, started up a series of "higher schools" for the most capable students as a preparatory system for university education, and founded national ("imperial") universities. A new breed of educational innovators founded private universities, including even some colleges serving only women.

In the Charter Oath of 1868 inaugurating the new era, the Emperor Meiji had pledged to have "deliberative assemblies ... and all matters decided by public discussion." This did not turn out to be what some had hoped. Even when a parliament (the National Diet) was established in the 1889 Constitution, it may have been the first national assembly in Asia, but its democratic constituency was severely limited. By 1900 only 2% of the population was allowed to vote, for example, and the emperor, not the legislature, controlled most of the power.

More important to our narrative, however, the Charter Oath also promised that "knowledge shall be sought throughout the world so as to strengthen the foundations of imperial rule."[10] That pledge, unlike the political one, was wholeheartedly pursued and it transformed the character of Japanese philosophy. The universities assumed the responsibility of training Japan's first generation of academic philosophers, housing them in newly established departments of philosophy.

Finding the Words: Nishi Amane

The Meiji intellectuals quickly perceived the West was not all engineering and technology but also, like Japan itself in the Edo period, had a set of core philosophical ideas and values. Since modernity is not merely a way of doing but also a way of thinking, the Japanese sought to understand those thought processes as part of its plan to compete with the West. To that end the study of philosophy played a significant role in the new system of higher education.

The Charter Oath's call to seek knowledge "throughout the world" sprouted programs for sending Japan's brightest young people to the West to study specific fields in the countries the Japanese perceived to be leaders in that area. For example, some studied public education and agricultural science in the United States, others medicine and science in Germany. (And yes, baking in France.) As an alternative, especially in the early decades of the modern period, professors from Europe or the U.S. were brought to Japan to teach in the institutions of higher learning. To make this possible, English was studied in schools at all levels and at Tokyo Imperial University it was the most common foreign language of instruction. But that is not all: not only was there a further study of other modern languages such as German and French, but also, where relevant, Greek and Latin. All higher education required at least a functional knowledge of classical Chinese and the hybrid *kanbun* language, still the literary style of choice for official documents at the time.

This posed an initial problem: how to express the newly introduced western philosophical ideas in Japanese. It was one matter to expect university students to be able to study western philosophy in its original languages, but if the ideas were to have any impact on the larger Japanese populace, it had to be rendered into Japanese as soon as possible. As the Catholic missionaries of the sixteenth century had stressed the importance of dictionaries in their attempt to understand and work through cultural differences,[†] the Japanese now needed a new vocabulary for translating the western philosophical lexicon into Japanese. In that enterprise the pioneer was Nishi Amane (1829–1897).

555-9

Sent to Leiden to study law and political theory in 1862 even before the Meiji Restoration had occurred, Nishi acquired there his first intense taste of western philosophy. He was personally attracted to positivism and utilitarianism as they were the dominant stream in the Netherlands at the time. Yet, despite his limited exposure, he also acquired an unusually broad grasp of the western tradition. Thus, in the first years of Meiji, he was perhaps uniquely well qualified to create Japanese neologisms for key western philosophical terms.

† See page 291.

In devising a western philosophical vocabulary for Japanese thinking, Nishi almost always constructed new compound words out of sinographs, rather than, for example using either phoneticized European words or words taken from or constructed out of the lexicon of native Japanese words. A side effect of that decision was that his newly minted terms were easily transferred to other countries that use the sinograph system of writing, notably China and Korea. So Nishi influenced the philosophical vocabulary of modern Korea and China as well.

Perhaps most important of all, Nishi had to decide how to render the term "philosophy" itself into Japanese. After some experimentation, he decided on *tetsugaku* (study of wisdom), the word still used today (in its alternative pronunciations) throughout East Asia. The choice was controversial since it raised a fundamental question for the Meiji Japanese intellectuals: is this western enterprise called "philosophy" essentially different from intellectual traditions in Japan before the modern period? Should it be explicitly linked, for example, to neo-Confucianism by calling it *rigaku* (study of principle)? In fact, for some time the two terms competed, but when the philosophy department was established at the newly founded Tokyo Imperial University, it was called the department of "*tetsugaku*." That ended the discussion.

There remained the issue of scope. Was *tetsugaku* limited to the West or was there *tetsugaku* in Japan before the modern influx of western thought? For example, was Shinran a philosopher in the way Augustine was a philosopher? How about Dōgen and Schopenhauer? Sorai and Machiavelli? Norinaga and Kierkegaard? Is the difference between Kūkai and Thomas Aquinas greater in fact than the difference between Thomas Aquinas and Nietzsche? Is Kantianism or positivism as a school of thought appreciably different from a school like Shushigaku or Native Studies? Even Nishi Amane himself wavered on such issues.

554–69

There were many subplots in this controversy such as whether western philosophy could or should function in modern Japan as Confucianism had done in the Edo period. Another issue was that if Japan isolated western philosophical thinking from Japanese philosophical thinking, that could confine the imported "philosophy" to halls of academia where it might interact with, say, science and history, but not touch the spiritual (ethical, religious, aesthetic) dimension of the traditional "Ways" of Japan.[11*] Such an approach would line up well with one of the more vociferous slogans of the time to characterize the goal of modernization: *wakon yōsai* "Japanese spirit; western ingenuity." But was such a bifurcation between spirituality and philosophical thought really such a good idea? The controversy would continue for decades. Indeed, as I will explain in the Conclusion of this book, it continues today.

Buddhism and Western Philosophy

In the early years of Meiji, Buddhism came under attack in various ways by nativist, pro-Shintō ideologues of various ilk.[12] Predictably, the suppression was strongest in the most pro-imperialist strongholds of the country, especially Mito and Satsuma. Mito set the basic anti-Buddhist ideology in motion and Satsuma methodically shut down almost every Buddhist temple in the province by 1877.[13] Nationwide the government forced the physical separation of Shintō shrines located in the precincts of Buddhist temples and Buddhist clergy were no longer allowed to preside over Shintō rituals, which had been more or less the norm before then.

Anti-Buddhist treatises appeared everywhere and gangs prowled the streets at night desecrating Buddhist cemeteries and even raiding people's homes to smash their Buddhist images. Many officials treated Buddhism as a "foreign" and therefore suspect religion. Naturally, the state support of Buddhism, including the Edo-period requirement that every family be registered in a Buddhist temple, was terminated. Buddhism had to adapt quickly to fit the newly hostile environment. For example, it allowed or even encouraged its clergy to marry (formerly only Shin Buddhist priests did so). Then the clergy could participate in the family and population-growth programs advocated by the state.

As we saw in Chapter 9, Buddhist Studies as an academic discipline had been restricted during the Edo period to seminary-like schools for each denomination. Starting in the Meiji period, it became an academic discipline in the imperial universities covering all Asian manifestations of the tradition, not just those of Japan. To avoid the appearance that the universities were teaching a "religion," especially one other than the newly ordained state religion of Shintō,[14] Buddhist studies were fitted into departments of Indian studies (*Indogaku*) where the study of Sanskrit was required.

Influenced by the then current models of religious studies in the West, those departments heavily favored history and the philological study of texts. If the West was in a quest to find the "historical Jesus," Buddhist studies could try to find the "historical Buddha" in India. Psychological, ethical, sociological, political, and sometimes even philosophical issues in Buddhist studies were attenuated in those programs within the self-avowedly secular universities.

As a counter, just as Protestant and Catholic organizations had started modern universities of their own in the U.S., so did some Buddhist sects in Japan. To a great extent, the Buddhist Studies curricula in their universities resembled the public and major private universities that stressed the study of Indian Buddhism as the necessary foundation. That said, perhaps because of their direct links with practical religion (many scholars in Buddhist universities also held ordinations in their own denomination, for example), philosophical and ethical issues were not as markedly excluded.

In Shin Buddhist settings, for example, this led to a tradition of Japanese Buddhist philosophy that interacted explicitly with western ideas, a phenom- enon that included such major thinkers as Kiyozawa Manshi (1863–1903), Soga Ryōjin (1875–1971), Kaneko Daiei (1881–1876), and Yasuda Rijin (1900–1982). Such figures functioned as the Shin Buddhist equivalent of philosophical theologians from the Christian or Jewish faiths in the West. Another thinker arising from the Shin Buddhist tradition, Inoue Enryō (1858–1919), took his philosophical skills in a somewhat different direction.

262–72

273–9; 280–5

619–30

Inoue Enryō and the Landscape of Global Philosophy

One of the most inclusive approaches to philosophy as a global phe- nomenon was outlined by Inoue Enryō. Trained in Shin Buddhism—several of his family members were Shin Buddhist priests—Inoue was deeply steeped in Buddhist philosophy. In addition, as part of its modernization efforts, the Shin Buddhist administrative center at Hongan-ji sent Inoue to study philosophy at Tokyo Imperial University. Early on, perhaps sensitive to the attacks on Bud- dhism in the early Meiji period, including intellectual criticisms coming from

Hall for the Four Sages

Christian quarters, Inoue wrote apologetic defenses of Buddhism, arguing it was the least superstitious and most "scientific" of religious traditions.[15]

Later, however, Inoue turned his attention increasingly to the more general problems of philosophy. His view was that the three basic philosophical orientations in philosophy up to his day were idealism (the theory that reality is fundamentally a product of spirit or mind), materialism (the theory that reality, including even mental events, is fundamentally matter), and "only principle-ism" (the neo-Confucian theory that "principle" is the basis of reality and is more basic than either the material or the mental). Inoue maintained that philosophy had enmeshed itself in irresolvable problems by taking only one of the facets of true reality—ideas, matter, principle—and theorizing it as if it were the whole.

Thus he argued for "principle *qua* matter-mind" (*ri soku busshin*). In other words, matter and mind are two sides of the same coin and principle is inseparable from them in such a way that if you look into principle, you find matter-mind and if you look into matter-mind you find principle. Unlike the idea of principle in the Shushigaku neo-Confucian system, Inoue's "principle" is not transcendent to the dynamic of the material-mental world, but *is* it.[16] *Soku*, the term I translated "*qua*" in Inoue's catch phrase, is borrowed from Chinese Buddhism and became a crucial term among some modern Japanese philosophers.

Pagoda of the Six Wise Men

I will discuss it more fully below when we consider Inoue Tetsujirō. For now, though, let us pause to appreciate an aesthetic representation of Inoue Enryō's philosophical world view.

In the Nakano Ward in the western extremity of Tokyo we find the Hall of Philosophy Park, a temple to philosophy designed by Inoue Enryō in the early twentieth century. The design of his temple/garden compound gives us a three-dimensional picture of how the terrain of philosophy looked to at least one well-informed thinker from that first generation of Meiji philosophers. The temple grounds are on two levels, the lower one divided into two gardens, one in the shape of the sinograph for "matter" and

627-30

the other for "mind," thereby representing the two foundational perspectives for philosophical development: materialism and idealism.

Of more relevance to us is the upper level of the complex which one can enter by either of two gates: that of "philosophical reason" (*tetsuri*) or that of "commonsense" (*jōshiki*). The former is a Buddhist-style temple gate framed by two statues. Where we would normally expect Buddhist guardian deities on each side of the gate, in this case we find a ghost and a forest goblin (*tengu*). The alternative entrance is a rather simple bamboo gate in the style typical of many traditional Japanese gardens. Either gate leads to an area with several structures, including the Hall for the Four Sages (containing images of Socrates, Kant, Confucius, and the Buddha); the Pagoda of the Six Wise Men (with Shōtoku and Sugawara no Michizane from Japan; Zhuangzi and Zhu Xi from China; Nāgārjuna and Kapila[17] from India); and the Arbor of Three Teachings (Shintō, Confucianism, and Buddhism—represented respectively by Hirata Atsutane, Hayashi Razan, and Shaku Gyōnen[18]).

627   According to Inoue, Jesus was not one of the sages because he was a religious figure rather than a philosopher, whereas the Buddha Shakyamuni was both.[19] Interestingly, and consistent with the Japanese view of Confucianism throughout history, Inoue does not mention Confucius as a religious leader, but only as a philosopher.

My first observation is that altogether thirteen figures are included, but only two are from the West, selected deliberately to represent the classical period (Socrates) and the modern (Kant). In that respect, Inoue may be implying that in the West there was a founding sage for each period, whereas China and India only have a continuous tradition, at least as of the beginning of the twentieth century. Also, Inoue's selecting Kant rather than Descartes as the founding "sage" of modern western philosophy reveals the German bias in his training. That is, for Inoue real modern philosophy began not with philosophy's breaking free of theology, but rather, with philosophy's becoming a critical, transcendental philosophy. As we will see, German Idealism, which could be considered to have emerged out of Kantian thinking, became a cornerstone of the Japanese university curriculum for many decades.

Inoue also explained that the Pagoda of the Six Wise Men and Arbor of the Three Teachings were added, in part, because visitors had been "disappointed

628 not to find a Japanese sage in the Hall of the Four Sages." When he had first thought of his scheme, he had considered philosophy as existing only in India, China, and the West. Yet, responding to popular sentiment, he changed his mind and considered Japan to have had a philosophical tradition of its own as well.

The Impact of Inoue Tetsujirō 611-18

One impression Nishi Amane had garnered while in the Netherlands was that the hotbed of western philosophy was not there, but in Germany. As academic philosophy developed in Japan during the late Meiji (1868–1912) and Taishō (1912–1926) periods, the early enthusiasm for French positivism and British utilitarianism cooled, giving way to an ardor for the German tradition, both German idealism and also the German perspective on the history of western philosophy with its stress on the Greek and medieval periods. An important figure in that Germanic turn within Japan was Inoue Tetsujirō (1855–1944). Not related to Inoue Enryō and also very different in temperament, Inoue Tetsujirō was a giant in the early history of modern Japanese philosophy, if not for the breadth of his intellect, at least for the length of the shadow he cast on much of its development.

Inoue Tetsujirō's credentials and accomplishments were truly impressive. He was a member of the first class to graduate from Tokyo Imperial University in 1880, the premier institution of higher learning in the country. He studied in Germany from 1884 to 1889 encountering such figures as Eduard von Hartmann (who developed a pre-Freudian theory of the unconscious), Wilhelm Wundt (a founder of experimental psychology), and the early neo-Kantian psychologist Otto Lipmann. Inoue tried to get von Hartmann to come to Japan to teach, but he declined and instead recommended and arranged for Raphael von Koeber (1848–1923) to fill the position. Koeber became an important influence on two generations of Japanese philosophers studying at Tokyo Imperial University, bringing not only a special knowledge of Schopenhauer, but also a passion for classical and medieval philosophy.

Inoue Tetsujirō himself became the first native Japanese professor of philosophy at the university. He had assisted Nishi in the early efforts to settle the translation of key western philosophical terms and then made it his own special interest in serving as the chief editor of a sequence of new and comprehensive philosophy dictionaries over the years. He was at one point chair of the philosophy department and also served as the dean of the school of literature. In 1925 the emperor appointed him to the House of Peers, although he resigned the position after serving for one year. Thus, he was intimately implicated in the political events of his day, influencing national politics as well as the development of the academic study of philosophy.

As a philosopher Inoue Tetsujirō's major contributions included his dictionaries,[20] his comprehensive taxonomies of western philosophical traditions, and importantly, his assumption that philosophy was not a tradition unique to the West. In fact, his teaching was mostly not about western philosophy as much as about Asian traditions, including Indian philosophy and Chinese philosophy (especially the latter). He wrote three volumes on Edo-period Confucian philosophy, one each on Yōmeigaku, Shushigaku, and what he called *Kogaku* "School of Ancient Studies" (what I have called the philosophers of "classical Confucianism" such as Itō Jinsai and Ogyū Sorai). Thus, Inoue lent credibility to the study of Asian traditions of thought by applying the term "philosophy" (*tetsugaku*) to them.[21]

Inoue Tetsujiro's epistemology. Inoue Tetsujirō did not contribute much in the way of an enduring, creative philosophy of his own, but did present a philosophical problem that would in some ways haunt Japanese philosophers for much of the early and middle years of the twentieth century.

As we will see, that concern arises from some issues that Inoue Enryō had also posed. Inoue Tetsujirō articulated the problem in the 1890s as part of his taxonomy of philosophical positions, the general outline of which is as follows. What is the relation between things as we experience them (the world of phenomena) and things as they are in themselves without our experiencing them (the world of reality)?[22] Some say we cannot know the relation (a position called skepticism), but Inoue rejected that on the grounds that we cannot *know* that we cannot know, so skepticism is unfounded and gets us nowhere philosophically. He turned then to the nonskeptical options. One theory is to say what we call "reality" is actually just our *experience*. To nonphilosophers, that may seem a perplexing position. If so, I suggest you undertake a little experiment.

> Pause a moment and try to name one reality that you in no way experience, remembering that *experience* here includes not just empirical sensations but also thinking, imagining, wishing, fantasizing, and so forth.
>
> You can't. Even a logical impossibility—a square circle—is conceptualized (experienced) as a logical impossibility. Therefore, when we speak of "reality," this perspective claims we are really speaking of the field of all our experiences. We cannot, by definition, even think of anything falling outside it.

That philosophical position is generally considered a species of *idealism* (in the sense of idea-ism, not ideal-ism).

The opposing theory, called *realism*, is that reality does indeed exist independently of experience: experience is always an experience of *something*, something "out there." For example, no one ever experienced the planet Neptune until it was seen in a telescope in the mid–nineteenth century. Yet, common sense would seem to dictate Neptune was real—it was out there—long before there was any experience of it. So, realism maintains that experience has to be an experience of *something* and that something is reality. Inoue Tetsujirō correctly notes, by the way, that the positions of idealism and realism are found in various Asian and western philosophies alike.

Inoue thought that a fundamental breakthrough in philosophy would occur when we resolve the nature of the relation between the realm of phenomena and the realm of reality. Like Inoue Enryō, Inoue Tetsujirō believed the problem is that the two domains are considered to be mutually exclusive and so we create philosophies that deal with only one or the other: either idealism is right and realism wrong, or vice versa. The solution, he believed, would be evident if we could somehow demonstrate how the two realms are the same, the difference arising only when we take different *standpoints* or *perspectives* on that same realm.

For example: if I look out my window at the leaves in the tree glistening green in the sunlight, I can take two perspectives on that event. One is in the direction of analyzing "the leaves look green" as a phenomenon in my experience and the other is in the direction of analyzing it independently of my experience "the light is reflecting off the surface of the elliptical shapes at a wavelength of 510 nanometers." In either case, Inoue would maintain, the descriptions express the same event. Here he uses the word with Buddhist resonance that Inoue Enryō had earlier used: *soku*. He says that his theory can be characterized as "phenomena *soku* reality" (*genshō soku jitsuzai*). In terms of my example, it would be a matter of "looking green *soku* reflected light of 510 nanometers."

In Chinese Buddhist texts the term *soku* (C. *ji*) functions somewhat like a copula establishing not exactly an equivalence, but rather, an interchangeability between two terms, *a* and *b*. Hence, "*a soku b*" is often translated into English as "*a* as *b*," or "*a*, that is to say, *b*," or "*a qua b*," or "*a sive b*" (as in Spinoza's famous Latin dictum, "*Deus sive natura*"). The occurrence of this term is particularly striking in many Chinese Mahayana Buddhist texts, especially those from the Perfection of Wisdom tradition emphasized in Nāgārjuna's Indian Mādhyamaka tradition (the Japanese Sanron School of the Nara Period). Therein we find famous formulations that use *soku* to link an *a* and *b* that are often commonsensically seen as mutually exclusive.

The *Diamond Sutra* famously says, for instance, "form *soku* emptiness; emptiness *soku* form." If Inoue could *explain* and not merely use that *soku* relation in his "phenomena *soku* reality" formulation, he would have penetrated a philosophical problem of truly universal significance, one that would relegate both idealism and realism into his new, more comprehensive philosophical system. Unfortunately, he could not find any such explanation, at least not one that would stand up to philosophical scrutiny. But he did make the problem a quest, a Holy Grail, for some modern Japanese philosophers.

How could one even begin to go about resolving such a problem? One approach makes it a topic for logic. What kind of logical connection is this *soku*? Can it be an operator as in formal symbolic logic, a new operator that can be placed alongside the others already familiar in western thought such as *or, and, if-then,* and *if-and-only-if?*[23] Or perhaps it is a logical connection in a less formal way such as a dialectical relation that involves some form of transition from *a* to *b*. (If you are thinking of Hegel when you hear that, you are thinking what many Japanese philosophers also thought.) Or perhaps, staying close to the East Asian tradition, maybe *soku* indicates a dynamic interrelation of opposites as in *yin-yang*. In short: one might explore a variety of logical venues for explaining *soku*.

Another possible strategy for explaining the *soku* relation would not be through logic at all, but by means of an analysis of what was sometimes called by Japanese philosophers "subjectivity." What Inoue Tetsujirō could not explain in examples like ours of "looking green" *soku* "the 510 nm wavelength of light" is *who* or *what* takes the two different perspectives. When *I* say it "looks green" and *I* say it is light of a certain wavelength, is the *I* making those judgments the same? For this point, it might be helpful to go back to the example we explored when engaging Dōgen in Chapter 6: the different meanings of the ocean to a fish, a person in a boat, and a deity looking down from the heavens.[†]

As we recall, expanding on a venerable Buddhist interpretation, Dōgen said the fish would understand the ocean surrounding it as "a translucent palace" and would be right in doing so; the human being out at sea in a boat would understand the ocean as the "great circle" all around the boat and would be right in doing so; the deity in heaven would understand it as "a glittering string of jewels" and would be right in doing so. They are all correct insofar as they each understand the ocean from their own contextualized experiential standpoint. They would only go wrong if they were to say that their characterization is the one and only one true meaning of the ocean. As Dōgen said, "there are many worlds" here.

On the surface this may resemble my explanation of Inoue Tetsujirō's theory in terms of the "looking green" and "being a ray of light of a certain wavelength." But is it? In Inoue's case it is the same subject who takes either of two perspectives; the same subject looks at the same event from either of two directions or two contexts. That is, Inoue's analysis seems to be assuming an "I" or a "subject" that remains constant across the perspectives, something that takes the two perspectives consecutively, whereas Dōgen's Zen view rejects the idea of such a constant, detached subject or ego. For Dōgen the one who makes the judgment about the ocean in each case is part of the context, not something that stands outside and chooses the context.

Hence, Dōgen's philosophical position is neither a simple idealism nor a simple realism. It is like an idealism in recognizing that meaning has to be

146

---

† See pages 228–30.

mentally constituted—it is not simply something given in the direct experience of the world. But it is unlike idealism because it lacks a fixed subject, an "I" that constitutes the meaning. Dōgen's view is also like realism in that there is "something out there"—what he called *genjōkōan* (presencing of things as they are) or *inmo* (as-ness).[†] But Dōgen's is not a naïve realism in that he does not assume that the "something out there" is a discrete substance that stably exists on its own without anyone's experiencing it. For naïve realism, meaning already resides in the reality and our expressing it is no more than putting a name on what is already fully presented.

When we reflect on the Japanese philosophical tradition as we have seen it unfold so far, Dōgen's view that the subject and object are not separate is by no means unique. We have other Buddhist portrayals such as Kūkai's *nyūga ganyū* (the buddha-as-cosmos enters me and I enter the buddha-as-cosmos) and Shinran's *shinjin* as a process wherein the person of faith and the object of faith both disappear into the naturalness of *jinen hōni* (happening of itselfness). Moreover, in aesthetic theories and the poetics of Norinaga, we find *kokoro* represented as a single field that includes the object, the artist or poet, and the medium— all constituting meaning together in a single act. In the terminology I have been using in this book, the type of problem Inoue articulates only applies to detached models of knowing. In engaged knowing, by contrast, there is no such original chasm separating (phenomenal) experience and knowing (reality).

To sum up this point: when modern Japanese philosophers address the problem of idealism vs. realism, or the problem of the relation between subject and object, they are inevitably doing so in a cultural context that includes a traditional world view in which those problems do not have the same valence as they have in the modern West. Modern Japanese philosophers may even deny that they are trying to justify the Japanese world view or trying to articulate a specifically "Japanese" philosophy. Yet, I believe their culture's intellectual background leads them to believe *there must be an answer* to the types of riddles Inoue Tetsujirō's philosophy presented. There must be an answer because the idea of the inseparability of subject and object is deeply embedded in so many aspects of Japanese culture.

The conservative political thought of Inoue Tetsujirō. I previously said that Inoue Tetsujirō cast a large shadow on later Japanese philosophy and I also noted that the emperor had appointed him to the House of Peers in 1925. My two observations are connected. Why would the emperor (or his advisors) even know about, not to mention honor, a philosopher in such a blatantly political manner? Certainly no one in the imperial chambers would have the slightest

---

† See pages 220–2.

interest in resolving the conflict between idealism and realism. Nor would they be dazzled by Inoue's philosophical dictionary. Rather, they admired Inoue because he used his philosophy to serve the educational, moral, and political agenda of the imperial state. His interventions in support of the national ideology were specific and voluntary. He even at times seemed to go out of his way to collaborate.

In 1890 the government promulgated the Imperial Rescript on Education, a nationalistic statement of how education is to serve the state in loyalty and filial piety directed toward to the emperor. Every school in the land enshrined a copy of the emperor's portrait and a copy of the Rescript was to be read aloud on special occasions, parts of it to be memorized by the students. In 1890 loyalty to the emperor and the imperial link with divine forces were not yet firmly entrenched in the minds and hearts of the ordinary Japanese, especially those distant from the pro-imperial ideologies cultivated in Mito, Satsuma, and Chōshū. The Imperial Rescript and its attendant rituals were a deliberate attempt to educate the next generation in the proper attitudes.

In the first place we see the document consists of rather pedestrian Confucian moralisms about maintaining the proper dyadic relations, but some rhetorical points stand out. For example, the Rescript begins with the founding of the empire by the "imperial ancestors" on a "basis broad and everlasting" and into which they "firmly planted virtue." Here we have the now familiar Shintō appeal to origins and the apparent claim that the imperial ancestors set a ground that was not itself virtuous but in which virtue was planted by imperial fiat.[24] Thus, imperial power is not subject to virtue, but rather, is only responsible for instilling virtue. When it comes to the emperor, morality is for other people. This attitude, as we have seen, goes back to the early centuries of Japanese political thought in which no one ever argued in Japan, as they did in China, that the emperor's authority or behavior was subject to what Confucianism called the "will of heaven" or "mandate of heaven."

Next we note that the Rescript maintains that the state is sustained by the subjects' loyalty (*chū*) and filial piety (*kō*). The linking of these two is the continuation of the vector redefining loyalty in Japan that we have been monitoring since its appearance in Shōtoku's *Constitution* where it simply meant, as it usually did in ancient China, loyalty to the state as headed by the emperor. The first real change occurred in the medieval period when loyalty came to be primarily directed to one's lord. During the Edo period, it was transferred (problematically, as we saw in the Akō Incident) increasingly to the shogunate. Toward the end of the Edo period, following the Confucian ideal again, it started to shift back to the emperor.[25] At the turn of the nineteenth century, the Mito and Native Studies Schools, argued that the loyalty to the emperor was more than just a Confucian virtue; it was also a loyalty based in the divine succession of the imperial line going back to the Age of the Gods. By that understanding, the emperor is also the father of the Japanese people and is due filial piety from his subjects.

In other words, we find a convergence of the two virtues: loyalty to the emperor and filial piety toward the spiritual father of the Japanese people, a combination sometimes found in traditional Chinese thinking as well. In Japan's case, however, the tie between the paternity of the emperor and the filial nature of the people was a direct racial or blood tie reinforced by Shintō mythology. This combination of loyalty and filial piety would be the dominant ideology supporting imperial rule throughout the war years,[†] all the more powerful because it combines a virtue of rationalized social hierarchy with an affective component usually reserved for one's own parents. In this context, it is not surprising that the Rescript used the Mito School's favored term for the imperial system—*kokutai*—when it characterizes the "source" of Japanese education. As we will see later, debates over the meaning of *kokutai* will be another recurring theme in modern Japanese political philosophy.

We need to bear in mind, however, that the Rescript was originally a hard sell to the newly westernized intellectual elite who, without tight regulation, had read widely among western books on democracy, freedom, and individual rights. Some intellectuals, ecstatic with the spirit of the Japanese Enlightenment promised in the Charter Oath, had assumed Japan could at least follow the ways of modernity defined by the western Enlightenment: its separation of church and state, its emphasis on reason over affect, and its vision of the state as dependent on the "consent of the governed." Perhaps after that, some dared to hope, Japan could "evolve" as a "civilization" to go beyond what the West had done. A good example of such an intellectual was Nakae Chōmin (1847–1901).

604–10, 563–4

Chōmin (the sobriquet he gave himself meaning "the masses," literally, the "trillion people") was a journalist, French language teacher, and politician (he was elected to the first Diet under the 1890 Constitution). A liberal, leftist thinker steeped in Rousseau (he had translated Rousseau's *Social Contract*), he despaired over the broken promise of the Japanese Meiji enlightenment. Religiously an atheist, philosophically a materialist, and politically a socialist, in 1887 he wrote a popular little dialogue on political theory, *A Discourse by Three Drunkards on Government*. In it Chōmin argued against the right-wing, impe-

---

† In this book, I use the term "war years" to refer to the period from the Sino-Japanese War in 1894 up through the end of the Pacific War in 1945. That span of half a century includes not only those two endpoints, but also the Russo-Japanese War, World War I, the incursion into China, and the attack on Pearl Harbor. In other words, from 1894–1945, Japan was either at war, going to war, or preparing for war. It was also a period of internal strife with frequent political assassinations.

rialist direction being taken by the conservatives who seemed to have seized control of the Meiji Restoration.

For his efforts in writing such a book and for his work on behalf of founding the Liberal Party (*Jiyūtō*), Chōmin was officially expelled from Tokyo for two years. In their attempt to establish an authoritarian imperial state, the conservatives recognized Chōmin and his comrades as a lost cause. Indeed, Chōmin continued to be a thorn in their side until his death. Since no intellectual imbued with the western ideals of freedom and liberty would readily embrace the retrograde (that is, premodern) ideology of the Mito or Satsuma imperial loyalties, was there no one who could nonetheless win over at least some of those intellectuals to the spirit of the Imperial Rescript? Enter stage right: Inoue Tetsujirō.[26]

Inoue was by nature and training a conservative Confucian moralist and he was outraged at what he perceived to be the lax education and miscreant behavior of the "modern" Japanese populace. Now that the samurai class was officially dissolved, who would take over their role, bestowed on them by Yamaga Sokō: to be moral sheriffs ensuring the virtuous behavior of the people?[†] The Imperial Rescript seemed the answer, but how could it be packaged in a way attractive to the increasingly modernizing and westernizing intelligentsia?

Inoue Tetsujirō's strategy was simple, perhaps even simplistic, but it did successfully fulfill his agenda. He knew he could not convince the new intellectual elite to return to Confucian virtues on the grounds that it was the ancient Way of the sages as, for example, Sorai had argued. For Inoue, the Edo-period Confucian systems would have to be somehow reintroduced if they would have traction in the new Japan. Because of its complexity, however, he deferred that plan until a decade later when he wrote his aforementioned three-volume series on Edo-period Confucianism. For the time being, Inoue sought a more immediately available resource to support the Rescript in the face of the Japanese modernists enamored of western thought.

Since the utilitarianism of philosophers like John Stuart Mill was still in vogue (Nakae Chōmin, for example, considered him the greatest of all philosophers), Inoue Tetsujirō turned to it as a new source of justifications for a national morality. He argued, for example, that filial piety is utilitarian since the young will eventually get old and the respect shown elders now would then be directed toward them when they most need it. That is, in the long run the greatest happiness for everyone would result if we were all always filial. Inoue's defense of the Rescript on utilitarian grounds is all the more striking when we consider he disliked utilitarianism and even lambasted it in his

---

† See page 316.

later writings.[27] By then, however, the bulk of the populace had already been indoctrinated in the new national morality and so he no longer needed the utilitarian rationale.

In subsequent years Inoue wrote several more right-wing works on "national morality" and *kokutai*. To assist in that agenda, he nurtured an allied ideology: *bushidō*, the Way of the warrior. Basically, he tried to make the warrior mentality of the imperial loyalists more philosophically credible by transforming it into a full-blown system of ethics.

Inoue Tetsujirō and the Way of the warrior. I mentioned that the dissolution of the samurai class, the presumed enforcers of public virtue, created a need for a new national morality system. People like Inoue wondered who could fill that void. His answer was again straightforward and simple: *everyone.* That is, if a national morality system could raise everyone to revere and enact "samurai values," the moral foundation, the "moral energy" of the state (as the right-wing German ideologues would call it), could push Japan through its present transition to evolve into an ideal, self-policing society.

Inoue's inspiration for this turn to the Way of the warrior came from an unlikely source: a book by Nitobe Inazō (1862–1933). Given Inoue's background, the book's impact on his thinking was surprising for several reasons. First of all, Nitobe was a Christian, having converted after spending six years as a student in the United States and Germany. Before Nitobe's book, Inoue had argued that Christianity undermines Japan's national morality because its values are not national but universalist (everyone is treated equally) and because it directs loyalty toward a transcendent God rather than the emperor. So Inoue would not normally be expected to look to a Christian to further his agenda.

Moreover, Nitobe's wife was American. His wife's illness led him to suspend his civil service and educational responsibilities to escort her to her family home in Malvern, Pennsylvania. There in 1899 Nitobe wrote in English a book called *Bushidō: The Soul of Japan* in hopes it might help his foreign friends gain some insight into traditional Japanese culture. Thus, Inoue Tetsujirō's Japanism was being influenced by a book not only written by a Christian but also written in English and published in the United States.

Lastly, although he held three doctorates (plus two honorary degrees), Nitobe's specialties were agricultural science, economics, and English literature. He was not in any way an expert on Japanese history or thought, as he himself openly admitted. He merely hoped that by comparing the Way of the warrior with western medieval chivalry, he might offer his English-reading audience a helpful analogy for understanding his homeland. International understanding was Nitobe's mission in life: he later became the under-secretary general of the League of Nations.

1103–12

In summation: Nitobe's book was written in English by a Christian who was an avid internationalist and not in the least a Japanologist. Inoue Tetsujirō would nonetheless use that book as his point of departure in developing an anti-westernizing, anti-modernizing, nationalistic, and ethnocentric code of ethics. Nitobe probably never dreamt that an avid reader of his English book would be Inoue Tetsujirō, the eminent philosopher of ethics and philosophy at Tokyo Imperial University.

Still, it is not difficult to imagine how Inoue would react to Nitobe's edifying, romantic flourishes such as we find at the very opening of the book:

> Chivalry ... is still a living object of power and beauty among us [Japanese]; and if it assumes no tangible shape or form, it none the less scents the moral atmosphere, and makes us aware that we are still under its potent spell....
>
> The Japanese word which I have roughly rendered chivalry, is [bushidō] ... Bushidō, then, is the code of moral principles which the knights were required or instructed to observe. It is not a written code; at best it consists of a few maxims handed down from mouth to mouth or coming from the pen of some well-known warrior or savant. More frequently it is a code unuttered and unwritten, possessing all the more the powerful sanction of veritable deed, and of a law written on the fleshly tablets of the heart.

1104

Just two years later, in his own Japanese book entitled *Bushidō,* Inoue Tetsujirō would take those ideas in the following direction:

> And if one were to identify the content of this thing called *bushidō*, its primary principle ultimately comes down to the spirit of the Japanese race....
>
> However, *bushidō* developed gradually, aided by Confucianism and Buddhism, and in this way gradually came to be perfected. Because of this, in its fully finished form *bushidō* is the product of a harmonized fusion of the three teachings of Shintō, Confucianism, and Buddhism.
>
> ......
>
> It is not possible to say with accuracy in what age *bushidō* arose.... If one goes further and further back, it is possible to discover some of the principles of *bushidō* already in the tales of the Japanese gods.... The Japanese race has a spirit that primarily respects the martial, and it must be said that this is the source of *bushidō*. In other words, it would certainly be safe to say that *bushidō*

1104–5

has existed since ancient times.

Through such rhetoric, Inoue hoped to make the Imperial Rescript and its agenda of national morality intellectually more palatable. To reject the Rescript or the implicit *bushidō* values behind it, Inoue believed, would not be just an error in thinking, but also an act of disloyalty or even a renunciation of one's own essential Japanese identity.[28] Nonetheless, some dared to do so.

Resistance to Ideological Conservatism

Uchimura Kanzō's Christian protest. Opposition to the conserva- 1032–4 tives came from various quarters, Christianity being one. Uchimura Kanzō (1861–1930) brought his personal religious reservations to national attention in 1891 when the First Higher School in Tokyo held a special ceremony honoring the Imperial Rescript. After a formal reading of the document, each teacher and student was to walk up and bow to the signature of the Emperor at the bottom.

The third person in order was a teacher, Uchimura Kanzō. Years earlier while a student in college in the northern island of Hokkaidō, he had converted to Christianity, a commitment that only deepened years later when he studied at Amherst College in the United States. When it was his turn, he walked up to the copy of the Rescript, but refused to bow because it seemed to him at the time an act of worship and not merely everyday respect. In conversations with upset colleagues, he challenged them to mention one incident where he did not personally behave in exactly the ways stipulated by the virtues and ideal dyadic relations mentioned in the Rescript.

Nonetheless, the "disrespect incident" (*fukei jiken*) eventually led to Uchimura's dismissal as a teacher at the school. The event proved the Rescript was being read as not merely a moral document but also one based in a spirituality that included viewing the emperor as *kami*. Uchimura became an independent writer who established the Christian "no church" (*mukyōkai*) movement that involved Bible study in people's homes with no formal clergy and no institutional affiliation. He wrote extensively: both books and hundreds of articles in popular media. He argued throughout his life that there was nothing inconsistent in being both a loyal Japanese and a devoted Christian. He famously wrote: "I love two Js and no third; one is Jesus, and the other is Japan." 1033

Ōnishi Hajime's critical philosophy. To properly address a position like the one put forward by Inoue Tetsujirō would take more than an act of courage and a confession of patriotism, however. It demanded a philosophical critique. That is precisely what Ōnishi Hajime (1864–1900) set out to do. Although he died at the 631–5 age of thirty-six, he can arguably be considered the most astute critical thinker of the Meiji period. He was a Christian, a graduate of today's Dōshisha University in Kyoto and he supplemented that education at Tokyo Imperial University with training in Kantianism, the English Hegelianism of T. H. Green, and the German idealist tradition of personalism going back to Kant.

Ōnishi bristled at the suggestion by people like Inoue that Christianity was incompatible with Japanese virtues or loyalty to the state. When Inoue criticized Uchimura Kanzō's act of "disrespect," Ōnishi responded not with inflammatory rhetoric or defensive apologetics. Instead, he meticulously picked apart in an analytic manner the basic assumptions behind the Rescript as the basis for a "national morality." In his 1893 essay "Loyalty, Filial Piety, and the Foundations of Morality," he interrogated what a "foundation of morality" could mean. Ōnishi's argument is too detailed to present more than its gist here.

Basically, Ōnishi pondered what it could mean for loyalty and filial piety to be presented as a *foundation* for ethics. In a deontological ethics such as Kant's, there is an appeal to universal reason, the categorical imperative for example. In a utilitarian ethics such as Mill's, on the other hand, the foundation is the maximization of benefits, something that can be measured. By comparison, loyalty and filial piety would seem to be unquantifiable ethical *attitudes* or *behaviors* that arise from some foundation, but what could that foundation be? Moreover, why should the foundation be only national and not universal?

In posing such questions, Ōnishi was directly addressing Inoue Tetsujirō's claim that Christianity, precisely because it is universal, must work counter to a national morality.[29*] Ōnishi pointed out that the "national morality" theory assumes that all Japanese without exception have the same nature. On what basis would it make sense to say all Japanese have the same nature, but not all human beings have the same nature? By definition, human nature cannot be a cultural product. In other words, Ōnishi was pointing out that even a "national morality" is universalizing, but it just does not go far enough. It universalizes only enough to embrace all the Japanese people, but not enough to include all human beings.

Ōnishi also turned his critical skills to the other Inoue, specifically, to Inoue Enryō's syncretism and its use of *soku* as a term. He noted that without a strict logical and philosophical foundation, syncretism could amount to no more than "mixing oil and water." Opposing ideas in themselves cannot be synthesized. He believed Inoue Enryō's attempt to bring opposites together by using some unexplainable *soku* relation was the death knell, not the culmination, of philosophy.[30]

1115–64

The Women's Movement. Another angle of criticism against the reactionary, militaristic and anti-modernist ideology arose from a burgeoning women's movement. Even from the evidence we have already seen, there was a glaring paradox in Meiji thinking about gender. First, I mentioned the horrific conditions of life and work imposed on women, but at the same time, new educational opportunities were opened to them (mandatory public education at the primary level and even the establishment of women's-only colleges). The spirit of the new sensitivity to gender was plainly evident in such prominent Meiji intellectuals and educators as Fukuzawa Yukichi (1835–1901), an icon of those who argued for westernization and modernization. A pioneer in calling for the education of women, Fukuzawa soon realized that education alone is not enough. A broader social change is necessary. In 1885 he wrote:

A woman may become well versed in science or in literature, even well informed in law. Such a woman may well compete with men in the classroom, but when she returns home from school, in what position does she find herself?

At home, she owns no property of her own, and in society she cannot hope for a position of any consequence. The house she lives in is a man's house and the children she brings up are her husband's children. Where would such a person, without property, without authority of any sort, and with no claim on the children she bears, and herself a parasite in a man's house, make use of the knowledge and learning she acquired? Science and literature will be of no use. Even less would her knowledge in law serve her.

601-2

Thus, access to education must be only a prelude to full rights for women. As he wrote fifteen years later:

In the Imperial Restoration of thirty years ago people did away with the oppression of the feudal Tokugawa regime.... Had people hesitated at the time for fear of disturbing the peace, we Japanese would still be wallowing under the feudal caste system today. Therefore, to have women claim their legitimate rights and to create equality between men and women would be like discarding the old feudal regime and establishing the new constitutional system of the Meiji government. People were daring enough in the political revolution. I cannot see why they should not be the same in a social revolution.

1115

Of course, powerful men arguing for the rights of disenfranchised women can be no more than the first step. And even the education of women could be subverted into a yet new twist on gender inequality. Like Fukuzawa Yukichi and Nishi Amane, Nakamura Masanao (1832–1891) was a leader of a group of prominent thinkers and politicians from the Meiji Six Society, a think tank dedicated to "promoting civilization and enlightenment." He translated John Stuart Mill's *On Liberty* and was the head of what became Ochanomizu Women's College. Yet, he also popularized the phrase "good wife; wise mother" (*ryōsai kenbo*) to describe the proper role for women in the modernization movement. He believed education for women was important, but mainly because it would aid them in fulfilling their household roles.

Still, with the new educational opportunities available, Japan produced a group of highly talented, intelligent, educated women who could criticize the inequalities of the age and unveil the suffering of women disguised as the advance of modernization. Through their efforts some improvements materialized. For example, as the Meiji era ended, like men, women were beginning to organize unions such as those for office and textile workers.

Yet, just as women were beginning to make breakthroughs that could bear fruit as a new, less sexist society, a counter movement harking back to the need for a national morality, maintained that Japan must never forget the traditional value of "good wife, wise mother." The internationally acclaimed poet, Yosano Akiko (1878–1942), could not help but point to the hypocrisy as she wrote in the last full year of the Meiji period, 1911:

> Recently the question of the liberation of women has come to the fore. It was not the women who initiated the discussion but rather a group of men who took an academic interest in the question, all the while opposed to the actual liberation of their own wives and daughters. They felt sorry for women and thought it would be good for them to have a decent education. None of this attracted much attention among the women themselves. Of late a counter-reaction to this view has arisen with many men now proclaiming that women's training should be in the practical matters, such as sewing and embroidering, and not in higher education. Women, they say, should be educated to become docile creatures....

For Yosano, the situation called for raising the consciousness of women so that they liberate themselves from the male-dominant views. She wrote:

> It is laughable to see Japanese men forget their joy at their own liberation, then suppress the liberation of women, and revert back to old misogynist ideas.... But Japanese middle-class women are not even aware of these issues that stare them in the face.
>
> It is up to women to wake up and deal with the problem of women's liberation, regardless of what men say. If we are not to accept the old-fashioned position of "glorified maid-servants," middle-class women must take the lead by opening their eyes, reforming themselves, and securing the necessary qualifications to solve women's issues. What is urgently needed here is for women to become thinking women, women with brains, in addition to being working women.

In that same vein Hiratsuka Raichō (1886–1971) organized a feminist literary movement, *Seitō* (The Bluestocking Society).[31] Highly accomplished in Zen meditation, she turned to the secular world as one of modern Japan's greatest social reformers. True to her Zen sense of freedom and commitment to dismantling the archaic laws and customs oppressing women, she refused to be personally shackled by the unequal marriage laws. So she entered into a common law relation, giving birth to two children.

In her manifesto of 1911 inaugurating the birth of the Bluestocking Society, Raichō argues that true women's liberation must be a spiritual as well as social transformation. In her opening lines, she cleverly resorts to Shintō symbolism, pointing out the gender bias in the State Shintō movement. If Japan were going to return to the Age of the Gods, is that not when the earth was ruled by a female, the Sun *Kami*, Amaterasu?

1138–45
1140
1140
1148–58

In the beginning, woman was truly the sun. An authentic person. Now she is the moon, a wan and sickly moon, dependent on another, reflecting another's brilliance.

Seitō herewith announces its birth.

Created by the brains and hands of Japanese women today, it raises its cry like a newborn child....

Passion is the power of prayer. The power of will. The power of Zen meditation. The power of the way of the gods. Passion, in other words, is the power of spiritual concentration....

Each and every woman possesses hidden genius, the potential for genius. And I have no doubt that this potential will soon become a reality. It would be deplorable, indeed, if this tremendous potential were to remain untapped and unfulfilled for lack of spiritual concentration....

Our savior is the genius within us. We no longer seek our savior in temples or churches, in the Buddha or God.

We no longer wait for divine revelation. By our own efforts, we shall lay bare the secrets of nature within us. We shall be our own divine revelation. 1148–9

By contrast, Yamakawa Kikue (1890–1980), argued that the real change must 1159–64 not be a change merely for women, but rather an economic change that sees the root of social injustice, including the oppression of women, as lying in capitalism. Thus, liberation must be for all workers, men as well as women. She wrote in 1928:

We do not regard the differences between men and women a major factor compared to the essential characteristics that unite us in being human. We understand that, just as men are subject to the social environment, so, too, are women swayed by their environment. On the surface it may seem that men control the forces moving society. But in point of fact, the more fundamental power lies in the social conditions that move the way we think. It is for this reason that women's liberation, and at the same time that of all humanity, should not be directed at men as opponents in the struggle. We must turn our attention to the social conditions that control their thinking. As long as there is no change in these conditions, women will never attain more than what current government and economics allow them when they assume the same position as men; for when the same societal conditions prevail, the same results will emerge. 1162

Like so many other Japanese movements fighting for social change, the long-range effects of the women's movement would go into slumbers until after the Pacific War had ended and Japan could rebuild its society yet again. An indicator of that postwar progress is that Yamakawa Kikue was named Japan's first head of the Women and Minors Bureau of the Ministry of Labor in 1947.

The personal introspection of the I-novel. New genres of literature took form, most notably, the so-called I-novel (*shishōsetsu*), which reached its greatest popularity in the Taishō period (1912–1926). A branch of the literary naturalism that strove to describe reality as it is, the I-novel relinquished the ordinary narrative of a distinct plot line to present the world from inside the experience of the protagonist (who could be portrayed in either the first or third person). Sometimes confessional in form, the protagonists could be presenting the secret of their inner self—exposing the deepest feelings and motivations within the experience of everyday events. At other times, the I-novel could flow like the *zuihitsu* ("following the flow of the brush") style from the classic tradition of Sei no Shonagon's *Pillow Book,*[†] except less a comment on events and more a record of the responses themselves, akin to the stream-of-consciousness genre of the West.

In the I-novel we can detect a new Japanese sense of self, one that perhaps could only emerge after the ambivalence over the Russo-Japanese War with its tragic losses and seemingly minor gains. The novels represent a first serious questioning of whether Japan was on the right path after all and that all the modernization was really worth the price. The outwardly directed, ambitious spirit of the Meiji Restoration had turned inward and exposed a neglected, wounded sensitivity.

Although the economic and personal costs of the Russo-Japanese War had darkened the national mood, the next war, World War I, brought an economic boom. It generated a vibrant market both at home and abroad for arms and other materiel, products the Japanese industrial infrastructure was always ready to supply. As a result, industrial production skyrocketed, the economy tripled, unemployment dropped, unionization brought modest gains for labor, and the parliamentary monarchy was showing signs of effective governance. Yet, the progress was fragile.

With the war's end, the economy began to fizzle and social unrest to rise. The 1923 Kantō Earthquake had leveled the city of Tokyo and its environs, creating an additional strain on the economy. Universal male suffrage in 1925 increased democratic participation, but also led to a rise in leftist, socialist, and communist political groups, energized by what seemed at the time a successful communist state in Russia. By the time of the death of the Taishō emperor and the installation of Hirohito, the emperor for the Shōwa period (1926–1988), Japan was at a decisive point: should it pursue further westernization and modernization or return to the retrospective vision of the Rescript?

† See pages 144–5.

The country was becoming increasingly polarized along a rural-urban axis. On one hand, in rural areas the Imperial Rescript was generally successful in raising two generations of school children indoctrinated with the vision of *kokutai* and feeling of the loyalty-filial piety directed at an emperor *kami*. On the other, in the cities, with their intellectuals and social reformers, there was open debate between the conservative elements in government and calls for more populist freedoms.

Then, with the devastating impact of the Great Depression, the economic and political system collapsed. By the end of the 1920s, Japan had reached a fork, with one path bearing sharply to the left and further modernization, the other sharply to the right, even to the extent of a call for a "Shōwa Imperial Restoration" that would dissolve the Diet. The issue was decided not by debate but by guns. The early 1930s are sometimes referred to as the period of "government by assassination." From 1930 to 1932 two prime ministers were assassinated and there were also two failed *coups d'état*. The military was taking over.

The Military on the Move Again

World War I had allowed Japan to move aggressively into China, seizing railway lines, military bases, and several islands that had formerly been held by the Germans. With the government failing at home, the military was free to put into action its aggressive agenda abroad. In September 1931 the Japanese Guandong Army, stationed in Manchuria to protect the Japanese-controlled railway lines there, staged a fake attack on the railroad and then retaliated against the "Chinese aggressors." By January 1933, the Guandong Army had taken all of Manchuria. The entire exploit had involved two years of planning, all without knowledge of either the military headquarters or the civilian government in Tokyo.

The League of Nations went into conniptions, but did nothing concrete. The Japanese people were mostly ecstatic—the empire was on the move again. Yet, there were more political assassinations and more failed *coup* attempts. A bizarre example was the attempted coup in 1936 led by Kita Ikki that tried (to the horror of the emperor) to accomplish a Shōwa Imperial Restoration that would bring all control back to the emperor while simultaneously establishing a socialist revolution on behalf of peasants and factory workers. After killing several political leaders, the revolt was quickly put down by troops headed by Tōjō Hideki (1884–1948). Kita was executed. 1022–3

Tōjō was then dispatched to Manchuria to head the Guandong Army, where he forged alliances with its key leaders, a group that had already shown its disdain for the democratic government back in Tokyo. Tōjō returned to Tokyo after the start of the second Sino-Japanese War (1937–1945) to be army vice minister in charge of the Chinese campaign. The Japanese military campaign in China included the demonic frenzy known as the "Rape of Nanjing" at the close of 1937 in which many tens of thousands of civilians—including women and children—were victimized and murdered. That triggered even more alarm in the West, but by 1939 Europe was embroiled in its own major war and seemingly little could be done.

Out of exasperation, the United States coordinated an oil embargo on Japan in July 1941, an embargo that would only be lifted were Japan to withdraw from China. The hope was if the military machinery could be starved of energy, the onslaught would cease. By international law, a naval embargo can be considered an act of war and Japan-U.S. relations were on the brink of dissolution.

In 1941 Tōjō had risen to be both chief general of the army and prime minister, taking control just in time to be involved in the decision to bomb Pearl Harbor in December. Tōjō was convinced the United States. would soon capitulate and negotiate an end to hostilities (much as the Russians had done at the beginning of the century). The Japanese military hoped the United States would hand over most of East and Southeast Asia as well as the western Pacific to Japan. That was obviously a miscalculation.

Instead, after Pearl Harbor, the United States regrouped what was left of its Pacific fleet and in June 1942 won a resounding victory at Midway, an aerial naval battle fought with aircraft carriers, the ships never being close enough to fire on each other. All four of Japan's carriers were destroyed and the Japanese were never again able to go on the offensive for the rest of the war. For all practical purposes, the tide had changed and the outcome was now inevitable. As the U.S. forces relentlessly moved across the Pacific fighting ferociously for control of one island after the other, Japan's final all-out strategy for defending its homeland crystallized.

The *kamikaze* attacks against Allied warships, a modern mechanized version of the legendary sacred winds that had defended Japan from Mongol invasion in the thirteenth century, were the last hope against invasion by sea. On land, the army coordinated hundreds of thousands of civilians to defend Okinawa once the U.S. forces landed. The Battle of Okinawa in spring 1945 persisted for almost three months. The civilians joined in the fight with no more than rocks, bamboo spears, and their bare hands, retreating ever more deeply into the mountains until there was nowhere to go. Then against the pleas from the American translators speaking over loudspeakers, and often forced at gunpoint by the remaining Japanese troops, the civilians killed themselves rather than surrender, many jumping over the cliffs onto the rocks below. In total, 250,000 people on the Japan side died in a failed attempt to defend Okinawa, about half of them civilians.

The loyalty instilled by the Imperial Rescript had turned out to be a weapon of last resort. The fanatics had hoped the sacred wind of the *kamikaze*, the fighting spirit of the military, and the loyalty-to-the-death of the citizenry would be a defense against any material force conjured by modern western technology. The bombs of Hiroshima and Nagasaki were the final dashing of that hope. As the radioactive black rain fell over those cities, there was no longer any doubt that an immediate unconditional surrender was necessary.

The political events from the late 1930s through to the end of the war in 1945 had created a tense and unhealthy atmosphere for free and creative philosophical thinking. The militarist state ideology became ever more strident and the thought police were scrutinizing the academic world as well as the public media for crimes of treason and lese majesty. Philosophers, journalists, and political activists of the wrong stripe were jailed, often never to be heard from again.

One scholar, I was told, was incarcerated for giving the wrong pronunciation for an ancient emperor in one of his academic papers. Others lost their academic positions, with measures taken to ensure they would be unable to secure a new one. Given the events described in this chapter, much of the immediate philosophical effects were unsurprising and predictable: the erosion of trust among scholars fearing a colleague might be working for the police, the universities' buckling under pressure from the central government to squelch freedom of speech, a predictable cadre of thinkers working as collaborators in the promulgation of the official state doctrines, and professors not knowing what to say to their students who would soon be conscripted into military service, all too likely to be killed or maimed.

The generalities are obvious enough, but the specifics complex. The long-range effects of those events during the last decade of the war years affected Japanese philosophy well into the postwar years, probably even more than they affected events of the time when they occurred. Therefore, I will pick up that part of the historical narrative in Chapter 14. Before leaving the topic of the birth of modern academic philosophy in Japan, however, I will conclude with some summary remarks about how the period as a whole should be viewed.

THE MODERN PERIOD AS CONTEXT FOR JAPANESE PHILOSOPHY

Because of the tumultuous changes depicted in this chapter, most interpreters of modern Japanese philosophy—in Japan as well as the West— tend to think of it as an almost totally new species of Japanese thought. Because the social tapestry of society was ripped apart and rewoven into a new design, it is natural to think of there being an accompanying rupture in the flow of philosophical thinking. Indeed, as we have seen, some modern Japanese philosophers even denied that there was any philosophy at all in Japan until the modern period, and Nakae Chōmin wondered if there was any philosophy even then.

There was indeed something new afoot in Japanese thinking beginning with the Meiji period. How could there not be with the sudden influx of twenty-five centuries of western philosophical texts along with a series of scientific ideas and technological innovations that had already totally transformed the West in the preceding couple of centuries? Japanese schoolchildren were coming home speaking words from languages unheard before in Japan except perhaps in muf-fled negotiations within the shogun's inner sanctum. A new government was set in place—a weird mix of western constitutional monarchy and a throwback to the ancient imperial ideals of the Nara period. Families were split and relocated to serve the smoking dragon of industrial production as other children were sent off to far-away institutions of learning to be trained as leaders in the new Japan. And then there was war after war after war after war.

In light of such events, philosophy in Japan would certainly have to be some-thing new, a radical departure from what had gone before. Yet, I have already recounted other ruptures in Japan's earlier history: the dissolution of the cul-tural and political center, upheavals in the social order, and the demise of tra-ditional educational institutions, for example. In those cases, the Japanese had managed to maintain some continuity even within the disruption. Although there may have been radically new theories and terminologies introduced from abroad, although the focus of the thought might have shifted in stunningly new directions, I find that in modern Japanese philosophy the basic patterns of thinking and the modes of analysis changed much less drastically. *What* was thought about was certainly different, but *how* it was thought did not change nearly as much.

Internal relations still tended to dominate over external relations. Opposi-tion was usually not considered concrete or foundational, but understood to arise from abstraction. Argument by relegation continued to be an aspiration of most sophisticated philosophical systems. Holographic relations generally interlinked whole and part so that they contain each other. Knowing and acting were typically so intertwined that one would be incomplete without the other. Thinking and feeling were characteristically described as part of a single field in which self-world-expression occurred of itself without the activity of an external, discrete agent. In short, the model of engaged knowing, even when challenged with twentieth-century western models of detached knowing, would maintain its prominence. We will see some clear evidence of this in the next two chapters as we engage two modern Japanese academic philosophers, Nishida Kitarō and Watsuji Tetsurō.

Of the two, Nishida presents in some ways the greatest challenge to the claim for continuity because he makes so few direct references to previous Japanese thinkers. It is easy to see him as a western philosopher that the fortunes of fate had somehow dropped in Japan, as if he were one of those European or American philosophers like Koeber or Fenellosa who found themselves teaching philosophy in English at the newly established Tokyo Imperial University.

But we should know by now to be suspicious of a study of Japanese philosophers that stops at the level of what is being discussed. The process of engaged knowing is at least as much about how as what, and if we allow ourselves to join in with Nishida's philosophizing we will be able to get a better feel for what he is doing and why. The more we engage Nishida's thinking, the better we will be able to appreciate his remarkable craft, creativity, and insight. We may also find he is more Japanese than he might have let on or perhaps even knew himself. So, let us now meet Nishida. We engage him as a student sitting at a desk in Tokyo Imperial University.

12. Nishida Kitarō 西田幾多郎 (1870–1945)
Putting Nothing in its Place

> It is not that there being the individual,
> there is experience; but instead, there being
> experience, there is the individual.
> Nishida Kitarō

A student sits in a hallway at Tokyo Imperial University in 1891, pouring over a book at a small desk outside the main reading room. As a special student in the limited-access program (*senka*), he is not allowed into the library's main reading room with those enrolled in the regular philosophy program and does not have the privilege of entering the open stacks. Nor will he be able to earn the regular graduate degree from the university but only a certificate stating he completed the required number of elective courses.[32] A slight shadow is cast over the book he is reading as a professor walks by. Showing deference, the student rises partially from his chair and gives a slight nodding bow. The professor keeps a straight face and shows little sign of having noticed. He proceeds to the main reading room where the other students are gathered and he smiles wanly as they all bow to acknowledge his presence.

The professor is the aforementioned Inoue Tetsujirō[†] recently returned from eight years in Germany, the first native Japanese to be named a professor in the philosophy department. The student in the hallway is Nishida Kitarō. Inoue has no clue how special this special student would be: Nishida would become the most highly regarded and influential Japanese philosopher of the twentieth century and the only philosopher in modern Japan to have a school of thought develop around him.

† See pages 421–30.

Nishida had started his academic career on the fast track to success. Bright and hardworking, he had been admitted to the Fourth Higher School in his home city of Kanazawa. As I mentioned in Chapter 10, the higher schools comprised a national system of preparatory academies that fed its students into the universities. Graduating from one usually meant automatic admission into a degree-granting program at one of the Imperial Universities, the first and greatest of which was Tokyo Imperial University.

Nishida was a talented student, especially in mathematics and philosophy, and he excelled in both English and German as well. Yet, full of bravado, his attendance was irregular and when he was held back a year, he resented taking classes in fields that bored him (such as chemistry). Moreover, he certainly did not relish studying alongside students who had been a year behind him. In a rash move, he decided he could do better studying on his own and dropped out of school.

An eye disease sabotaged his self-study program and after a hiatus he decided to return to the formal study of philosophy. Lacking a degree from the higher school, the best he could do was pass the entrance exam to Tokyo Imperial University and enroll in the limited-access program.

NISHIDA'S RISE TO FAME

With his special student status, every course for Nishida was an elective, but he opted to follow the curriculum of the regular philosophy program. Like most of his contemporaries, he studied a range of western works, from the classics up through German idealism. He read widely not only in Japanese translation, but also in German, English, and a little in French. Because initially his English skills were better than his German, he immersed himself in the history of the British and American traditions, writing his university thesis on Hume's theory of causality. Tokyo professors Ludwig Busse, Inoue Tetsujirō, and later Raphael von Koeber had already begun their push to make German idealism the western tradition of choice for the next generation of Japanese philosophers, and so Nishida became well acquainted with Kant, Fichte, Hegel, and Schopenhauer as well.

Nishida did not focus his studies exclusively on western philosophy, however. He took a course on Indian philosophy from Inoue Tetsujirō and enthusiastically continued his study of Chinese classics. Like all other advanced students of the time, Nishida was proficient in reading traditional Chinese, including Buddhist texts. The latter enhanced his Rinzai Zen Buddhist meditation praxis, which he first undertook through the encouragement of D. T. Suzuki (Suzuki Daisetsu, 1870–1966), a lifelong friend going back to his schoolboy days in Kanazawa. Nishida may not have been as absorbed in Zen practice as Suzuki, but neither was he cavalier about it. In his early teaching years, he often participated in supervised periods of intense meditation (*sesshin*), an experience that likely sensitized him to the complex and subtle workings of consciousness in ordinary experience.

After graduating from university, Nishida found employment first as a teacher of English and then of German in various preparatory schools around Japan, also teaching ethics and history. Without a chance to study abroad, he polished his German by writing his daily journal in that language, all the while continuing his philosophical writings. His essays were perspicacious enough to secure him a position in the philosophy department of the newly established humanities division of Kyoto Imperial University in 1910. He held that position until his retirement in 1928, using it as a fulcrum for leveraging change in the field of Japanese academic philosophy.

The essays that won him his position in Kyoto were compiled into his maiden and ultimately most famous book, *Inquiry into the Good*. When it appeared in January 1911, it gathered only modest attention and that mainly from specialists. However, when it was later reviewed in glowing terms by the celebrated writer and critic, Kurata Hyakuzō (1891–1943), it attracted not only philosophers but also a much wider audience interested in ideas.[33] Part of the excitement was the general opinion that only now, at the very end of the Meiji era, had Japan found its own philosophical voice. Free of the pedantic style of much traditional scholarly works in Japan, *Inquiry* displayed a western style of writing, but without the rigidity of many western works that had been translated into Japanese. Intellectuals also detected that the book suggested at least a subtle appreciation of traditional Japanese values and ideas.

THREE PROFILES OF NISHIDA AS PHILOSOPHER[34]

I have said that Nishida was the most eminent philosopher of twentieth-century Japan. Not only was his own philosophical achievement noteworthy, but he was also a direct influence on a group of prominent philosophers who came to be known either as the "Nishida School" or, more commonly, as "the Kyoto School."[35] Although a prolific writer, the succession of his works often followed a tortuous path. Throughout his career, Nishida held steadfastly to a few deeply held philosophical convictions. Yet, in articulating them he developed philosophical systems that underwent frequent major revision, even reconstruction. Often his own severest critic, Nishida seldom settled long in a particular formulation of his philosophy without tinkering with it and eventually scrapping at least part of it. Many commentators recognize Nishida as having advanced as many as three full-blown systematic philosophical theories, any of which alone might have secured him a place of prominence in twentieth-century Japanese thought.

The popularity of Nishida's *Inquiry into the Good*, when combined with his status in the history of Japanese philosophy, suggests three factors to consider if we want to engage him in his philosophizing. First, we can safely assume that he was doing something fairly significant within the field of academic philosophy as it was taking shape in Japan at the end of the Meiji era. After all, it had secured him a faculty appointment at Kyoto Imperial University despite the fact he was a drop-out of the higher school in Kanazawa, had no regular degree from Tokyo Imperial University, and had never studied abroad (a prized credential at the time).[36]

So Nishida had earned his appointment in Kyoto based primarily on the quality of his work, his reputation as a teacher in his early positions, the impression he had made on his fellow students while at Tokyo, and his activities in professional philosophical societies. Even more remarkably, Nishida had assumed his position at Kyoto before his work had caught the public's eye, that is, before *Inquiry* had even been published.

Our first task for engaging Nishida, therefore, is to identify what topics he was addressing and why Japanese philosophers trained in the western tradition would find his work so compelling. Generally speaking, his main target of analysis was the self-world relation in our experience. Although he made no mention of their work, that theme clearly paralleled the concerns of the two Inoues.[†]

The second issue for us to explore is why, once it was introduced to the public, Nishida's *Inquiry* stirred so much enthusiasm among non-philosophers. *Inquiry* became probably the best-known work in Japanese philosophy of the twentieth century. However profound or interesting his philosophical ideas might have been, they never would have inspired such a following unless they were also timely. The book had clearly struck a chord for the educated readers of the time, but what exactly was it? As I will explain, it involved the nature of self-awareness.

Lastly, we need to consider Nishida's reaction to what had become his claim to fame. Within a few years of its publication, he explicitly rejected the thrust of his analysis in *Inquiry*, thereby taking his philosophy in a new direction. To understand why, we need to explore his tenor of mind, his philosophical motivations, and the way his own experience had an impact on his theory of experience. What had led him to the analysis he articulated in *Inquiry* and why did he later feel that the book had failed in its mission?

† See pages 418–25.

For convenience, I will refer to these as the three profiles of Nishida: the academic philosopher, the Japanese intellectual, and the independent thinker. If we can appreciate all three, we can better follow the various phases of his philosophical maturation. My goal is not to give a detailed overview of Nishida's philosophical systems, but only to present him in a way that allows us to appreciate the constellation of problems he addressed and his general approach in doing so. Through such an introduction, I hope to engage his thinking in a way that allows us to see him as both a prototypical modern Japanese philosopher and as an inspiration to many Japanese followers after him.

Profile 1: Nishida the Academic Philosopher

At the time of Nishida's hire at Kyoto Imperial University, the academic study of philosophy in Japan was highly derivative of western thought. Among his colleagues, therefore, there was only modest interest in the philosophical efforts of earlier thinkers from the modern period such as Inoue Enryō and Inoue Tetsujirō. Each had, as we have seen in Chapter 11, developed a scheme involving the term *soku* (as, qua, *sive*): Enryō's "principle *soku* matter-mind" and Tetsujirō's "phenomenon *soku* reality."[†] By Nishida's time, Ōnishi Hajime had already discounted both formulations for their lack of a logical foundation and so it is not surprising that neither the term *soku* nor either of the two Inoues were mentioned in Nishida's *Inquiry*.[37]

Yet, there is a sense in which the problem raised by those predecessors haunts the background of Nishida's first book, and arguably persists behind most of his later writings as well. This point becomes clearer if we ask not *what* the term *soku* means and instead ask *how* it functions in the philosophies of the two Meiji-period thinkers. What problem were those two philosophers addressing such that they resorted to using that term?

Inoue Enryō's major project was trying to locate different philosophical positions, East and West, into a single coherent schema. His garden at the Temple of Philosophy was in some ways a three-dimensional attempt to express materially what he was trying to work out conceptually. He came to his *soku* formulation as a way of referring to a single basis out of which philosophical thinking emerged, namely, a basis that was neither simply concrete (matter-mind) nor abstract (principle), but somehow both.

In other words, rather than trying to determine how to connect externally the realm of intellectual abstractions with the concrete realm of the senses, Inoue Enryō tried to discover a common, single ground from which both emerged. Not knowing how to articulate that ground, he simply resorted to using the

† See pages 419; 422–5.

Buddhist term *soku* to say that the abstract and concrete were not identical but not really separate either. Inoue Enryō never worked out his model in a philosophically satisfying way, but the question was worth posing. And, as we will see, Nishida took that question seriously.

In the case of Inoue Tetsujirō, his formula of "phenomenon *soku* reality" was offered as a catch phrase for his perspectivalism. For him, the world could not be engaged holistically and directly, but only as it appeared to a particular person taking a specific standpoint or perspective, that is, as its *phenomenal* appearance. Yet, to take a point of view, there must be something that is the object of the perspective, namely, *reality*. So Inoue Tetsujirō formulated his theory as "phenomenon *soku* reality." The remaining question, though, is who or what takes the standpoint that yields the perspective. Inoue was not able to answer that question.

Nishida did not refer to Inoue Tetsujirō any more than he had Inoue Enryō. Still, the idea that a judgment always arises from some place and the problem of who or what inhabits that place would be a nagging issue in most of Nishida's philosophical development.

In Nishida's own terms the problem was the nature of experience and the role of the self within it. A key issue was whether the relation between self and world was external or internal. If I accept the former option, do I and reality exist as separate entities? Is reality an *external* reality (that is, external to *me*)? If so, how do my self and the world come together so that I can engage the world: knowing it, participating in it, being affected by it and affecting it? This problematic we can call the *realist* alternative.

Or, accepting the second option, am I and reality not separate from each other at all, but rather two internally related points in a single unfolding event or system? If so, how can I understand my engagement in that single system without placing myself outside of it to analyze it? How can the system analyze itself? For reasons that will be explained later in this chapter, I will call this a "field" theory. Note that it foregrounds an internal relation between self and reality over an external, bifurcated relation. Moreover, it privileges engagement over detachment. One comes to understand the Way by working in it and through it, not by observing it at a distance.

Ultimately, Nishida came down on the side of the second alternative and he dedicated his philosophical career to trying to answer the questions that spin off from that basic philosophical orientation or commitment. At times, he even tried to show how he could relegate the first alternative to a subordinate position within his more inclusive system. To inspire his own thinking, he studied a wide variety of theories from the western philosophical tradition, usually taking them not to be alternative answers, but rather fingers pointing him in some direction.

To engage Nishida, therefore, we must try to think along with him, seeing how his answers to one set of questions always led to another set of questions and sometimes the answers to those questions led him to return and rethink his answers to the original questions. At times it might seem Nishida is hopscotching his way through the lexicon of western thought and western philosophy's hall of fame, but that would be the wrong impression. He is looking for trail markers and that sometimes means doubling back or trying another path.

Coincidentally, on the eastern edge of Kyoto, there is a pleasant path Nishida used to walk as he ruminated over his philosophical puzzles. It is known today as the *tetsugaku no michi*, "the Way of philosophy" (usually translated into English as "the philosopher's walk"). There is no mistaking the course of the trail as it winds its way along a brook with the traditional homes and shops on one side and the foothills of Kyoto's eastern mountains on the other. Although the site is most famous for its spectacular cherry blossoms, the lush summer foliage strikes me as a more appropriate representation of Nishida's philosophical path. It is a path that cuts right into the leafy overhangs, a bold march into the tangle of philosophy's perennial questions. (See photo on page 449.)

If only the course of Nishida's own thought over the decades had been as clearly marked and straightforward, things would have been much easier for him, not to mention for his readers. Even though the route of his philosophical journey may have been tortuous, the destinations were almost always clear. Before joining him on the path of his philosophizing, however, let us pause to learn more about this particular man with whom we will take our journey. More precisely, let us meet Nishida as not just an isolated individual thinker but as one who lived in Japan at a critical point in its cultural and civilization development. In other words, let us examine Nishida's profile as a *Japanese* intellectual.

Profile 2: Nishida the Japanese Intellectual

In his maiden work which won him such acclaim, *Inquiry into the Good*, Nishida developed his theory of pure experience which I will explain more fully later in this chapter. For now, however, our main interest is how that theory meshed with typical concerns in Japanese culture in the latter Meiji or early Taishō eras, namely, the first three decades of the twentieth century.

The style of "Inquiry into the Good": A new philosophical genre for Meiji Japan. In my initial discussion of Japan's road to modernity, I mentioned the literary innovation from that period known as the I-novel.[†] That genre grew out of naturalism, the theory that literature should try to be plainly descriptive

---

† See pages 436–7.

The Way of Philosophy

without resorting to figurative language, narrative conceits, or romanticist overlays of feeling. Rather than focusing on characters as playing out roles within a grand narrative or plot sequence, the Japanese I-novel described its protagonists from within the flow of their own experience.

Consider, then, how enthusiasts of the I-novel might have responded to the opening lines of Nishida's *Inquiry into the Good:*

To experience means to know facts just as they are, to know in accordance with facts by completely relinquishing one's own fabrications. What we usually refer to as experience is adulterated with some sort of thought, so by *pure* I am referring to the state of experience just as it is without the least addition of deliberative discrimination. The moment of seeing a color or hearing a sound, for example, is prior not only to the thought that the color or sound is the activity of an external object or that one is sensing it, but also to the judgment of what the color or sound might be. In this regard, pure experience is identical with direct experience. When one directly experiences one's own state of consciousness, there is not yet a subject or an object, and knowing and its object are completely unified. This is the most refined type of experience.

647–8

To some Japanese readers of the time, Nishida likely seemed to be approaching philosophy in a way parallel to how the I-novel was approaching literature, namely, describing experience "from inside." Whereas such writing was not unknown in the West (think of William James, or Rousseau, or even Augustine, for example), to his late Meiji-period audience Nishida's departure from the detached scholarly style of the Japanese academic philosophers of the time must have been stunning.

What had passed for academic philosophy in those early decades of the modern period was commonly scholarship *about* philosophy—descriptive, taxonomic, and interpretive. There was very little *doing* philosophy—constructive and provocative. Nishida presented to the Japanese academic world a new paradigm of how to be an academic philosopher. For example, in *Inquiry* Nishida mentioned more than fifty western philosophers and several theories or schools of thought. Yet, unlike a scholar of philosophy, he had a sustained discussion of none. Like the I-novel Nishida's *Inquiry* takes us into his own philosophical experience and gives little more than nods of recognition to those figures in passing as he reports the course of his own philosophical thinking.

Stylistically, *Inquiry* is probably Nishida's most engaging book; only some essays from his final years compare favorably. As a philosophical theory per se, however, *Inquiry* left much to be desired, as Nishida himself later admitted. Yet, it was immensely popular and went through several printings and new editions. Its presentation of a new style of Japanese academic philosophizing accounts for much of that popularity. Its content, though, was even more important. So let us examine it more closely.

Meeting the challenge to traditional Japanese patterns of relation. I have already mentioned a famous slogan of the Meiji era: "Japanese spirit, western ingenuity" (*wakon yōsai*). The catchphrase suggested that western ideas and techniques could enter Japan without corrupting its traditional value system. The motto implied western ideas and Japanese values could coexist by allocating each to its own domain.

In premodern times a popular metaphor for addressing the relationship among different philosophical contributions to Japanese culture was that of a tree. In that metaphor used by Yoshida Kanetomo and attributed to Shōtoku, the roots represented Shintō, the branches Confucianism, and the fruit Buddhism. As a Shintō thinker, Kanetomo thought the origins of the tree, the roots, to be most important, whereas the Buddhist Shōtoku thought the culmination, the fruit, to be most important. Yet, they agreed in thinking of Japanese intellectual culture as a single, growing organism developing from within.[†]

The Meiji slogan, by contrast, implied western science could be grafted onto Japanese culture from outside in a way that would not destroy the tree but would enable it to bear an additional fruit, namely, western technological prowess. The grafting would be an assimilation of western thought, allowing both the traditional and the newly imported ideas to maintain their integrity. In short, it was a model of assimilation by allocation.

By the time Nishida was writing *Inquiry*, Japan had unmistakably progressed significantly in the fields of industry, military readiness, and education. No longer vulnerable to colonization, Japan was on the way to being an imperialist colonizer in its own right. Although the social and political events were still volatile, there was at least the prospect that Japan was fast becoming a modern nation-state rivaling those of the West. Clearly, the graft of western ideas was

† See page 262.

bearing the fruit of modern science and technology, but was the rest of the tree really unaffected? Or, was the graft of western thought infecting Japanese traditional culture with a parasitic fungus that would invade the fibers of the tree, eventually rotting it down to its roots?

When *Inquiry* first appeared in print, it had already become clear to many Japanese intellectuals and cultural critics that traditional Japanese spirit and imported western ingenuity could not easily coexist after all. In fact, western science and technology, and the scientism accompanying it, brought in their wake cultural assumptions incompatible with how knowledge, self, and reality had been predominantly construed in Japan before the modern era.

For example, the western emphasis on a discrete self detached from reality was a direct threat to the model of engaged knowing. Science's atomistic approach analyzed the whole as consisting of isolated units linked only by external relations, seeming to have no place for the overlapping web of internal relations or the holographic model of ontology in which the part mirrors the pattern of the whole. Empiricism's separation of fact from value as well as intellect from affect threatened the heart of traditional Japanese ethical thinking.

If left unchecked, it seemed the influx of western technology and its new kind of thinking would undermine the philosophical footings upon which traditional Japanese cultural values had been constructed. Given Japan's modernizing investments in politics, imperialist expansion, education, and social reform, there would be no going back on the adoption of western ingenuity and scientific methods. If the westernization and modernization could not be stopped, however, could they at least be reined in somehow?

One strategy for doing so might be to accept the principles of "western ingenuity" but to relegate them into a system that would allow them only a status lower than at least some central Japanese values. Such core values might include, for example, the inseparability of self and world, or the internal relation between thinking and feeling, or the positing of a single field like *kokoro* as constituting the *in medias res* out of which experience, knowledge, and expression arise together.

Although Nishida did not directly address those issues, his personal path as a Japanese philosopher necessarily set out from the realities of his time and place. Nishida was insightful enough to recognize that western thinking could never be a simple branch grafted onto a Japanese tree; such a tree could never flourish. Yet, maybe a hybrid would, one that would incorporate both western philosophy and an appreciation of the kinds of experiences central to Japanese culture. A hybrid cannot be developed from outside like a graft, however. It involves modifying the genetic code of each species to transform them from the inside. As Nishida himself said it in his famous lines:

But is there not something fundamental in the cultures of the East that have nurtured our ancestors for thousands of years, something beneath the surface that can see the form of the formless and hear the voice of the voiceless? I would like to attempt a philosophical grounding to the desire that drives our minds continually to seek this out.[38]

The man who wrote those lines was the one I am calling Nishida the thinker, the Japanese philosopher who brought those cultural and academic issues into the stream of his own life and thought.

Profile 3: Nishida the Thinker

In 1943, nearing the end of his life, Nishida wrote the following:

Philosophy is a way for the self to become auto-aware and to live. Different philosophies place the emphasis differently, but it seems to me that they all come down to the same thing: the auto-awareness of a relationship between the individual self and the absolute One. Western cultures raised in Christianity see that relationship as an opposition that imposes duties on the self; life is rooted in *ought*.

Eastern cultures think of self-awareness as leaving behind one's customary, illusory self for a true self and returning to the One. Seen from western culture, this may seem like an abdication to nature, a loss of the self, the disappearance of morality. But this is where infinite activity and morality truly begin. Buddhism's *no-I* does not mean that the self disappears or merely resigns itself. Buddhist compassion means to see something by becoming it, to act by becoming one with what is acted upon. In contrast, duty—and even love—set up an opposition between self and other....[39]

When Nishida wrote those words, he was reflecting on the course of his own Way of philosophy, his own "philosopher's walk." Like Inoue Enryō, he had known from his early years that to make a hybrid of western philosophy and the types of experience nurtured in the East, he would have to establish a common intellectual basis for both. Yet, he did not want his philosophy to be vulnerable to Ōnishi Hajime's criticism of Inoue Enryō that without a *ground*, East-West philosophy was no more than mixing of "oil and water."† But where could Nishida the thinker find that ground? Perhaps in Zen Buddhist praxis?

As already mentioned, after completing his program of study at Tokyo Imperial University, Nishida found employment as a higher school teacher and at the same time started to practice Zen meditation more earnestly. Most of the time, he found his Zen praxis more frustrating than enlightening, having particular trouble with the kōan training because of his self-avowed "temptation

† See page 432.

to think."[40] He did make progress, however, and in 1903 he had a Zen insight (*kenshō*, "seeing your nature") as he cleared the *mu* kōan, the one he was first given back in 1897.[41*]

I mention Nishida's Zen experience not to imply Nishida was in some way "enlightened" by his praxis, granting him unique insight as a philosopher. Nishida did not even continue his Zen praxis throughout his life, never regarding his own thinking as somehow arising out of Zen. Nishida was no D. T. Suzuki, not to mention Dōgen. Yet, he did admit Zen was "in the background of his thought" even as he insisted it is "impossible" to "unite Zen and philosophy."[42] So, we cannot say Nishida found his answer in Zen, at least not directly.

As I see it, western philosophy gave Nishida a treasury of ideas; his Zen practice a reservoir of experiences. The goal was to develop that western philosophy so it could embrace the possibility of such experiences as part of his system. It may be impossible, as he said, to unite Zen and philosophy, but at least philosophy could be expanded so it would not be blind to the aesthetic, spiritual, and moral dimensions of the sort Zen and other Asian practices cultivated. That would be the impetus behind not only his first book, *Inquiry,* but also much of his later writings.

Around the time of his Zen insight, Nishida began his reading first of William James and then of Henri Bergson. That study likely influenced Nishida more than did his Zen praxis. In an interview in 1941, the day after Bergson died, Nishida said: "It was only after I familiarized myself with Bergson's thought that I was able to formulate my idea of pure experience."[43] The term "pure experience" itself he took from James. From both Bergson and James, therefore, (and admittedly maybe a little from his hours spent in quiet awareness of his own mental processes) Nishida concluded that he had found a way to resolve the conflict created by the bifurcation between subject and object. He thought he had discovered the unity of self as the basis of the unity of reality.

Nishida believed the solution lay not in the nature of the object of the experience, but in the structure of experience itself; not the subject of the experience, but in the experiential flow or field out of which the subject and object, the noetic and the noematic, were retrospectively abstracted out for analysis. This was his way of articulating the common ground beneath the projects of the German idealists, Bergson, James, and perhaps also Zen's stress on nothingness (*mu*). Faith in the reality of some such underlying field or ground, as we have seen, was a key assumption for most forms of engaged knowing in premodern Japan.

To frame this differently, consider again the previously quoted passage from the opening of *Inquiry*:

> In this regard, pure experience is identical with direct experience. When one directly experiences one's own state of consciousness, there is not yet a subject or an object, and knowing and its object are completely unified. This is the most refined type of experience.

Is this a description of the state of consciousness in Zen meditation? Is it a reference to Fichte's self-identity? Does it arise from the Yōmeigaku project of knowing the unity of mind and reality through introspection into principle? Is it Bergson's statement about the immediate givenness of consciousness? Is it Kūkai's *nyūga ganyū* ([the buddha-as-cosmos] enters me; I enter [the buddha-as-cosmos])? Is it James's vision of pure experience?

Even if Nishida knew enough of premodern Japanese philosophy to understand all the parts of those questions fully, I suspect his answer would be that it is none of those. Yet, he would insist pure experience is at the *ground* of all of them. So, let's now turn, finally, to the argument of *Inquiry* to see why he might have thought that. It may not be Nishida's most profound work, but if we follow his argument, we can gain insight into the trajectory of the line of thinking that defined his philosophical career.

"INQUIRY INTO THE GOOD" (1911): THE SYSTEM OF PURE EXPERIENCE

In *Inquiry* Nishida set forth his philosophical vision in terms of an analysis of "pure experience," a term he borrowed (and modified) from William James. In simplest terms, Nishida understood pure experience to be the foundation for every kind of event we ordinarily call an experience, whether it be knowledge of a fact, a unified intellectual intuition such as Goethe's composing a complete poem while in a dream, an act of will as simple as subtly shifting the eyes to see an object from multiple viewpoints, or a state of consciousness as complex and sublime as the religious desire for God.

As the ground of all experience, pure experience is unitary (no division between subject and object, experiencer and experienced) and unifying (the experience evolves of its own accord in the direction of maintaining unity and moving toward the goal of establishing ever-greater, more encompassing unities). The greatest unity would be the whole of what can be experienced, which is to say, reality.

If we think of the knower and known as in an internal relation of overlapping circles, in the ideal case the overlap becomes complete, which is to say, the two circles become one. Pure experience is direct experience, that is, there is no mediation through concepts or distinction-making reflections. Yet, pure experience is also the basis out of which thinking and reflection arise. That is, if thinking is not merely tacked on externally to the base-level pure experience, it can still arise of itself as part of pure experience's internal drive toward unity.[44*]

For example, if I am engrossed in playing the piano, I may be so intent in the act itself that there is no sense whatsoever of an "I" (the subject) who is playing the notes nor of the sheet music as a thing (the object) in front of me that I am reading. The experience obviously has the purity of a unified activity such that there is no awareness of the distinction between pianist and sheet music. Beyond that, there is a purity in a unifying impulse to attain a holistic perfection in which the music becomes self-expressive rather than merely played by anyone. It is as if the music itself is trying to play through me; that is, the "goal" of the pure experience is to create a greater unity such that there is just the music's self-performance (in the sense of auto-performance).

Now suppose this event of playing the piano is unfolding by the dimming illumination of twilight coming through my window until finally the room has so darkened I can no longer see the sheet music. I reach to turn on the piano lamp, an act itself so direct it is like scratching an itch on my leg without my ever consciously thinking "my leg itches." I turn the lamp switch knob and there is no change. I pause for a moment and my full attention abruptly shifts to the lack of light and my considering what just happened, or actually what did not happen. I turn the bulb a bit in its socket and the light comes on. Without missing a beat (well, actually missing several beats, but not very many), I am back to playing the piece, gradually losing myself again in reading the music and eventually letting the music play itself, with me as its instrument.

Such an experience is paradigmatic for Nishida. It is a common enough occurrence but nonetheless suggestive insofar as it can be recounted in two quite different ways. On one hand, the incident can be seen as a single event of a unified and unifying activity, a moment in life which I paradoxically found self-fulfilling even as I lost my sense of self.

On the other hand, the event can also can be readily analyzed into individual briefer experiences: my absorption in reading the sheet music, my feeling the music playing through me, the almost conditioned response of turning the lamp switch in reaction to the encroaching darkness, my reasoned maneuver of tightening the light bulb, and my trying to recapture the rhythm of the experience before the darkness had impinged on my absorption, and so on.

That latter way of looking at the event makes it seem more a series of interruptions than a single event: the darkness prohibits me from continuing in the flow of the experience; the failure of the light switch intrudes into the flow of my performance, forcing me to stop and think; the light's coming on and my having to start over again involves a conscious intent to recreate a process of which I was not self-consciously aware while it was happening.

So which interpretation better captures what happened? A sublime single event of experiential flow or a series of responses to interruptions in the purity of the experience? Nishida argues that both interpretations are correct. The critical point in the second take on the event is that the breaks in the pure experience arose internally from the experience itself and the responses were efforts to reestablish the broken unity. That is, my experience of the lamp's not responding when I turned the switch prompted me to think about the unlit lamp and to decide to try tightening the bulb. My intent was to end the disruption so as to reengage the flow of the pure experience.

Nishida wants to view such a phenomenon, therefore, as on one level a break in the pure experience requiring an intervention of thought, but on another level as pure experience's using part of itself (consciousness's capacity to think) to continue its internal flow. It is as if the pure experience were expressing itself as thought and that thought itself was a unifying activity.[45]

From that basic standpoint, *An Inquiry into the Good* analyzes a catalogue of experiences, showing that they all share such a dual-leveled characteristic. In so doing, he scrutinizes such functions as thought, will, and intellectual intuition as well as the awareness of facts, nature, spirit, God, and the Good to discover how, despite their surface appearances and apparent differences, they are all grounded in pure experience, that living flow which is both unified and unifying.

For example, consider what he says about the good:

> The good is the actualization of the person. Viewed internally, this actualization is the satisfaction of a solemn demand—that is, the unification of consciousness—and its ultimate form is achieved in the mutual forgetting of self and other and the merging of subject and object. Viewed externally as an emergent fact, this actualization advances from the small-scale development of individuality to a culmination in the large-scale unified development of all mankind.[46]

In other words, I become most fully a person via the impulse toward unification, a unification that ultimately entails breaking through the boundaries separating me from others. In that sense I and the other become one and I will treat others as myself. Such an explanation arises from an introspective, psychological viewpoint. Viewed from a social standpoint, we find that individuals merge increasingly with not just other individuals but also with humankind as a whole, establishing an impulse for world harmony. For Nishida, we discover here the notion of "the good" as arising from its ground in pure experience.

As for the "unifying" impetus in pure experience, Nishida connects it to (but does not identify it totally with) the idea of will.

I view any state in which the system of consciousness develops in actuality as the activity of the will. Even in thinking, the focusing of attention on a problem and the seeing of a solution is a form of the will. ... In comparison with ordinary knowing, the will is a more fundamental system of consciousness; it is the center of unity. The distinction between knowledge and volition does not lie in the content of consciousness—it is determined by their place in that system.[47]

For Nishida, because the will is the impetus behind the drive toward unity and unifying, it is even more basic than thought. Indeed will directs thought and makes it pure. In that respect we can sense his resonance with the voluntarist movement which made will the fundamental driving force not only of acting but also of thinking.

When juxtaposed with the other points I have discussed, of course, it follows that the will of Nishida's philosophy is not the ego-centered will that seeks the gratification of personal desire. Instead, it is the will of a person whose own impulse toward unity has dissolved the egocentric boundaries into the greater unity of personal actualization or service to humankind. As Nishida stated in his famous lines:

> As already discussed, pure experience can transcend the individual person. If so, though it may sound strange, by reason of its being able to know time, space, and the individual person, experience is beyond time, space, and the individual. It is not that there being the individual, there is experience; but instead that there being experience, there is the individual. The individual person's experience is no more than a special province within experience at large.[48]

In other words, I might ordinarily think of experience as something I as an individual produce or at least possess, but Nishida, like all the Buddhist thinkers we have examined in this book, claims that ordinary way of thinking is delusional. When we plummet the depths of experience, we find there is no individual there at all. Rather, the "individual" is a concept like other concepts such as "subject," "object," "mind," or "fact." The individual is no more than an idea isolated and subsequently extracted out of what was originally a unitary event. Admittedly, we can abstract the individual out of the unity of an experience, but that does not mean the individual exists as a discrete entity on its own. We can abstract the color red out of the apple, but that red does not exist apart from the shape or form. That we can think about color and shape separately certainly does not mean they exist separately.

Nishida assumes, more as an assertion than a justified belief, that even reality is grounded in pure experience, in fact, *is* pure experience. On this, he seems to be siding with the German idealists, Fichte and Hegel, in construing self-consciousness as identical with reality, that is, with the noumena or the things-in-themselves:

> As I stated before, reality is the activity of consciousness. According to the usual view, the activity of consciousness appears at particular times and then suddenly disappears... Does not this perspective lead us to the conclusion that such factors as our life experiences and, on the large scale, the development of the universe up to the present, are ultimately things that are in utter confusion without any sort of unifying base...? I contend that reality comes into being through interrelationship and that the universe is the sole activity of the sole reality.[49]

In other words, for there to be reality, for us even to have an *idea* that there is reality, we must conceive of a single, unified whole in which all things find their relation.[50] Relations, Nishida asserts, are formed in the mind, since the senses can only give us discrete chunks of unconnected data. And without relations, there is chaos, not reality. Hence, "reality is the activity of consciousness."

Beyond "Inquiry"

An early critique of Nishida's book came quickly and from an unexpected source, a graduate student in philosophy at Tokyo Imperial University, Takahashi Satomi (1886–1964). Takahashi had several criticisms,[51] but I will mention just one. He argued that Nishida's account is deeply flawed by an unresolved differentiation between what I will call for convenience "pure experience-in-itself" (pure experience as ground of all experience) and "manifest-pure-experience" (pure experience as those events by which disunity is recognized and resolved). Takahashi challenged Nishida for claiming pure experience is "without the least thought or deliberation" but also that thought can itself be a form of pure experience. Stated differently, how can Nishida be consistent in claiming all experience is pure experience and then also assert that pure experience is different from experience that is "adulterated" with thought?

In the final analysis, Nishida is far more Hegelian than he possibly would have liked to admit insofar as his conception of pure experience, like Hegel's spirit, seems to be progressing toward ever-greater unities. And it does so, as in Hegel, by somehow internally negating itself (depurifying itself?) as a means either to maintaining unity or to achieving a more inclusive unity (repurifying itself?). Alternatively, Nishida's position could be viewed in light of Fichte's self-identity, an identity that is established through change and, therefore, through perpetually negating what it has been in order to become something new. If pressed on the point, Nishida would likely have owned up to that latter influence.

As suggested by my distinction between "pure experience-in-itself" and "manifest pure experience," Nishida's account of pure experience resembles the Buddhist idea of the cosmic buddha as both reality-in-itself and as reality manifested for our heuristic use, an idea we have found in both Kūkai and Shinran, for example.[52*] Although Nishida might have been willing to admit a connection between his theories and those of the German idealists, he would not likely welcome an interpretation of his philosophy that would understand him to be advancing a well-known theory in Buddhist philosophy. Why?

Part of the reason was that creating a synthesis of western and Buddhist thinking—a philosophy both western and Asian—was not his intent. Rather, Nishida hoped to develop a (western-style) philosophy that would be capacious enough to be capable of analyzing experiences of the sort Buddhism cultivated. Nishida sought a philosophy able to embrace in its system the widest range of experiences, regardless of cultural origin. He was not motivated, for example, by the goal of synthesizing a new kind of philosophy from the ideas of all the world's philosophies. It is also worth bearing in mind how western was Nishida's academic training.

Starting as a teen, most of his philosophical education was carried out in English or German. The words for studying philosophy and the words for doing philosophy were overwhelmingly western words (or Japanese neologisms serving as tokens for those words) that were not attuned to the concepts and ideas of his own culture's tradition of philosophical reflection. As a result, Nishida would associate academic philosophy with western philosophy. That contrasts even with someone like Inoue Tetsujirō who had considered Asian thought to be part of the academic study of "philosophy."

But cultural patterns of thought do not have to be on the patent level of vocabulary. They can lurk deep in the syntax of the language, in the locutions of everyday affairs, or in the engrained patterns of behavior. If you grow up in Japan, you do not have to read Confucian texts to know about social roles and virtues. You do not need to read Kūkai to recognize the value of engaged knowing. Philosophical assumptions conceal themselves in how people live their culture.

Why am I being so hard on Nishida about his attempt to transcend or at least ignore his own culture when writing *Inquiry*? Because he might have more readily seen the problem and improved his theory had he known the work of a traditional Japanese philosopher like Kūkai. Almost totally absent in *Inquiry* is any clear sense of praxis, especially embodied praxis, as well as any place for metapraxis. As we saw, praxis was pivotal in Kūkai's establishing the difference between engaged and detached knowing (what he called the difference between the esoteric and the exoteric). As Kūkai had argued in his theory of the ten mindsets, one can *theorize* the interpenetration, the internal relatedness of all phenomena including self and world—as both Kegon and Tendai Buddhism had done—but the theory cannot be *grounded* without embodied praxis.[†]

Kūkai had realized that metaphysics (as Kant came to argue nearly a millennium later) cannot supply its own foundation; a metaphysical reason that justifies one's metaphysical system just leads to an infinite regress. According to Kant, by itself pure reason leaves us with metaphysical alternatives (antinomies) for which there is no rational basis in choosing one over the other. Kūkai's solution was that the ground of metaphysics can be known only by engaging in psychosomatic praxis. No conceptual construct alone can ground a metaphysical system. The German idealists of Kant's era had tried to conceive of an *active* self, but it was just that: a conception. The neo-Kantians pushed further in that direction to the extent of considering a social dimension as part of the self. Yet, their solutions were ultimately unsatisfying to Nishida and his purposes. As far back as *Inquiry*, Nishida was advocating a model of engaged knowing, but he kept trying to justify it in terms of western ideas rooted in a tradition of detached knowing. Hence, his philosophical frustration.

One of Nishida's philosophical inspirations, Henri Bergson, had recognized the importance of distinguishing two kinds of knowing[‡] and Nishida likely admired him in part precisely because he made such distinctions.[53] Yet apparently, Nishida had no idea that he was, in effect, trying to reinvent the wheel of which Kūkai had already fashioned a prototype. Admittedly, in twentieth-century Japan, it would certainly have to be a different kind of wheel in some ways—perhaps constructed with western not just Asian philosophical materials—but there was no need to start from scratch.

Fortunately, via a philosophical journey both tortuous and tortured, Nishida would eventually discover the missing wheel in his system: the realization that pure experience must be embodied through praxis or, as he put it, embedded in the historical world. But it would take him decades to reach that point. Had he known Kūkai's theories, he might have been able to find a shorter route to his destination.

Nishida's map of his own philosophical career. In any event, Nishida himself, provoked by his constructive exchanges with Takahashi, came to see the grave limitations of *Inquiry* and its theory of pure experience. To analyze Nishida's philosophical career as a thinker beyond his *Inquiry* phase, we can consider Nishida's own summary statement a quarter century later (1936) when he

† See pages 134–6.

‡ See page 42.

wrote a preface to a reprint of the book. Noting first that he believed *Inquiry* failed because it was limited to being a "kind of psychologism" (the theory that explains logical relations as psychological events rather than as necessary laws of reasoning), Nishida continued to discuss his subsequent publications as follows:

> In *Intuition and Reflection in Self-Consciousness* [1917], through the mediation of Fichte's *Tathandlung*, I developed the standpoint of pure experience into the standpoint of absolute will. Then, in the second half of *From That Which Acts to That Which Sees* [1927], through the mediation of Greek philosophy, I further developed it, this time into the idea of *place* [*basho*]. In this way I began to lay a logical base for my ideas.
>
> I next concretized the idea of place as a *dialectical universal* and gave that standpoint a direct expression in terms of *action-intuition* [performative intuition].[54] That which I called in the present book [i.e., *Inquiry into the Good*] the world of direct or pure experience I have now come to think of as the world of historical reality.[55]

Let us examine those self-described stages more closely.

The first period after *Inquiry* we can dispense with rather quickly. Frustrated with the philosophical problems of his first book, even while (a bit to his consternation) it was becoming ever more popular in the ensuing years, Nishida tried to find a stimulus for rethinking his system. Nishida, the academic philosopher, found himself surrounded by enthusiasts for the contemporaneous phase of German Kantian philosophy, the so-called neo-Kantianism of such thinkers as Wilhelm Windelband (1848–1915), Heinrich Rickert (1863–1936), Paul Natorp (1854–1924), and Hermann Cohen (1842–1918). (Nishida originally included Husserl as a member of that group as well, but came to realize phenomenology was better understood as a separate movement.)

Given the excitement over the neo-Kantians in Japan at the time, Nishida decided to study those thinkers in depth. Six years later, he concluded that his efforts were a fiasco. The best he could glean from them was an abstract idea of absolute will (which, on the surface at least, could be construed as suspiciously close to a new version of psychologism). Nishida's interest in the idea of absolute will, however, suggests he wanted to rethink his theory of pure experience such that it would be less a kind of knowing and more a self-expressive field of consciousness. (That idea of "field" was the germ of his *basho* theory that I will explain in the next section of this chapter.)

Nishida's movement from epistemology to ontological field also led him to a deepening appreciation for Fichte's theory of the fact-act (*Tathandlung*) as maintaining the inseparability between consciousness and self-consciousness and, by implication, the inseparability of consciousness and reality. In fact, Nishida changed the word he used for "self-consciousness"[56]: instead of *jiko ishiki* or *jiishiki* (which suggest consciousness's reflection on itself or on the self as its object), he now favored the more Buddhist *jikaku*, which implies "self awakening" or even better "auto-awakening."† In the end, though, Nishida felt he could not make his philosophical ideas any more logical and precise than his treatment of pure experience had been in *Inquiry*.[57] Burned out in his efforts, he wrote in the introduction to his 1917 *Intuition and Reflection in Self-Consciousness*:

> This work is a document of a hard-fought battle of thought. I must admit that after many tortuous turns I have finally been unable to arrive at any new ideas or solutions. Indeed I may not be able to escape the criticism that I have broken my lance, exhausted my quiver, and capitulated to the enemy camp of mysticism.[58]

And with the 1941 issue of the revised edition of *Intuition*, his new preface showed little change from his earlier evaluation:

> As I look back over this document of thirty years ago representing my hard-fought battle over several years, I cannot but have the feeling of exertion expressed by the famous phrase, "I have had fierce struggles, descending into the dragon's cave for you."[59]

It is easy to agree with Nishida's negative assessment of his time spent with the neo-Kantians. Perhaps the problem was not so much a lack of quality in their thought, but rather that the problems addressed in their philosophical agenda were incompatible with Nishida's needs. For their starting point, the neo-Kantians seemed to be still struggling with the legacy of modern western philosophy's bifurcation into self and world or into self-consciousness and object-oriented consciousness. Nishida's aim in his next phase of philosophy was, by contrast, to begin with a not-yet-bifurcated point of departure. Such a point of departure was, of course, also used in *Inquiry*'s theory of pure experience.

As we now turn to the crucial middle period of Nishida's thought, we must prepare ourselves to slog along with him through a terrain muddied with technical language, including some draconian phrases he likely picked up from his excursion into that aforementioned cave of neo-Kantianism. Fortunately, with a little care, we can keep our eye on the intended destination: finding the Holy Grail of prewar Japanese philosophy, namely, discovering the common ground between self and world, subject and object, and idealism and realism. That had to be a unity from which distinctions spring as well as the point to which thinking aims to return.

---

† For Shinran's use *ji* (自) as both "self" and "auto-," see page 204 and note 49 on page 629.

Following Nishida's own terminology, I will call this phase the development of his *logic* of experience. In my view, the theory of *basho* and the logic of the predicate from this middle period are the pinnacle of Nishida's speculative philosophical thinking.

THE LOGIC OF EXPERIENCE

According to the analysis of *Inquiry*, as we saw in the example of my playing the piano in the darkening room, pure experience shifts its profile depending on the standpoint we take. From one standpoint, it is unitary and undifferentiated; from another it is an impulse to deal with disunities and to work toward ever more inclusive unities. The problem in that description, Nishida came to believe, was that it was still explained from "my" standpoint as the agent interacting with the world and making decisions with regard to it. Essentially, Nishida's progress toward solving this issue was still stuck in the same quagmire beyond which Inoue Tetsujirō's perspectivalism could proceed no further.† That is, experience was still being construed as an event of my mind—the core idea of the psychologism Nishida wanted to avoid.

A better line of analysis, he thought, would be to think of experience as an auto-structuring field that gives form to both what we think of as self and what we think of as world. That is, for him, the I is not what constitutes experience, but rather, experience constitutes the I. Nor is it correct to think that reality supplies the data for *what* I experience. Instead, reality is the *way* experience takes form. He used a common Japanese word to indicate this self-aware and auto-formative field, namely, *basho*.

Basho is a Japanese word meaning "place" and in my account I will leave it untranslated. Others have translated it as variously as "place," "locus," or "*topos*," each having its advantages and limitations. By not translating the term, I hope its multiple nuances can be used as needed. I have already used *basho* in the sense of where or how an experience or a judgment in experience *takes place*. *Basho* also *topicalizes* an experience by establishing a standpoint or engulfing context for the way something is judged and it *localizes* every judgment in terms of its larger experiential context.

In the long run, rather than dwelling on how to translate "*basho*," it is vital we be clear about what Nishida meant by "logic" (*ronri*).[60] First of all, *ronri* does *not* mean "logic" in the sense of the academic subject usually taught in university philosophy departments. In Japanese the term for that would be *ronrigaku*, that is, *ronri* with the suffix for *–ology* (as "study of," or "science of"). Thus, symbolic logic, intuitionist logics, and so forth are considered part of the "science of

1260

---

† See pages 423–4.

logic," *ronrigaku. Ronri* in itself does not necessarily formulate explicit rules of inference, for example.

In understanding Nishida's sense of logic, it may help to think of an English expression: "I don't know why Harry is acting that way; there's no logic in it." In such a case, it may be true that Harry is not using syllogisms, but we more likely mean that we cannot find a *rationale*, a pattern of reasonableness in what he is doing that fits with the way things are. It helps to recognize that the *ri* in *ronri* is the term we have encountered often before in premodern Japanese where it has usually been translated either "principle" or "pattern," especially in the sense of the order of things that can be fathomed through reason.[†] The *ron* supplements that with a sense of "argument" or "rational discourse."

So, we could say *ronri* refers to the patterns in reasoning that (at least are intended to) reflect the patterns in things. The more technical *ronrigaku*, by contrast, would be the abstracted rules of inference or inductive reasoning. In the case of Kyoto School philosophers, the Japanese sense of "logic" is of the former sort and approximates Hegel's use of the term *Logik*.

The Logic of Basho

Nishida's "logic of *basho*," therefore, tries to find the patterns of how judgments take place within experience, determining, as the English idiom goes, "where they are coming from." Nishida is not talking about "judgments" in the sense of propositions or statements ("It is raining") but rather judgments in the sense of *experiences* (my making the judgment that it is raining). Once we properly understand Nishida's *logic of basho* in the way I have just described, it is clearer how aspects of German idealism, neo-Kantianism, and phenomenology seemed relevant to his project.[61*]

The basho of being(s). Accordingly, Nishida's basic question was this: in what *basho* of experience does any particular judgment *take place*? He considers three major options: the *basho* of the experienced empirical world (sometimes referred to as "the *basho* of being"), that of the idealist world ("the *basho* of relative nothingness"), and that of the ground of experience (the "*basho* of absolute nothing"). Although there is more sophistication to Nishida's analysis than I can go into here, the thrust of the theory is rather straightforward and I can try to explain it in terms of the leaves-outside-the-window example that I have used previously.[‡]

---

† See pages 301–2.
‡ See pages 423–4.

Let us start with my judging "there are leaves outside the window." From where does such a judgment arise? In what experiential space does that judgment become possible? Its place is the realm of empirical facts about physical objects. That is, the physical world takes place in the realm of empirical judgment of fact. Hence, says Nishida, the locus of empirical judgments is the "*basho* of being" (or "beings").

The basho of relative nothingness. Nishida's analysis then asks the following: Why is the locus of empirical judgments the right place to be for understanding physical reality? His answer: *because I see (or otherwise sense) physical objects.*

That hardly seems an earth-shattering claim, but notice what new wrinkles it has introduced into my analysis. For there to be a judgment that there are leaves out there, I must have a certain experience making that judgment possible (namely, my having sense experience of the leaves). Yet, that seeing is not part of the empirical judgment "There are leaves outside my window." In the world of empirical claims about reality, there is *no place* (no *basho*) for "I see" or "I hear" or "I taste," and so forth. Empirical claims are devoid of subjects having sense experiences and deal only with what is topicalized (*basho*-ized?) of those experiences as the domain of "beings." The trite claim about the importance of sensory consciousness for empirical judgments is now becoming more provocative. Let's see how.

Imagine a reality of physical things without any consciousness to observe them, no one to have *sense experience* of those things. There would be things, but no *facts* to be judged, indeed no *objects* (because there would be no subject to take a standpoint of objectifying them, of making them a focus). Therefore, for there to be a realm of physical facts (the *basho* of being), there has to be a domain of consciousness (the *basho* of consciousness) that makes those judgments of fact possible, even though the empirical realm excludes or ignores the role of that consciousness.

To summarize: from the standpoint of the *basho* of being, Nishida claims, the *basho* of consciousness does not exist. Or, to capture his technical terminology, *relative* to the *basho* of empiricism's judgments about beings, the *basho* of consciousness is nonexistent, a nonbeing, a *nothingness*. Yet, without the *basho* of consciousness, the empirical judgments could not take form and there would be no judgments of fact about physical objects. Hence, the *basho* of beings is enveloped by the *basho* of relative nothingness even though it does not recognize it.

In effect, Nishida has relegated empiricism to being under the umbrella of idealism. The facts of the material world are subordinated under the facts of consciousness. Idealism can explain materialism (which is a set of judgments) by saying that materialism is an idealism that has concealed the experiential environment that brought it into existence.[62] The empirical domain of judgments has *no place* for the experiencing subject who accesses the sense data that form the basis of all judgments about the material world. Empiricism is an idealism blind to its own sources.

It is important to see that Nishida is in no way attacking or refuting scientific empiricism. Relegation does not reject or refute, but rather finds a subordinate place for what was not originally part of its system. Indeed, Nishida is actually only affirming exactly what the scientific method has always maintained: empirical observation excludes or brackets out personal subjectivity. Nishida's clarification is that there is no observation without an initial personal subjective activity.

Stated differently, empiricism does not avoid or bypass subjectivity. Rather, *after the fact*, empiricism extracts the subject from the empirical observation, giving it "no place" alongside the judgments about physical things. It is not that subjectivity plays no role in science, but that once the sense data is collected (via the sentient "I"), the subjectivity is excised from the empirical study as if it had never existed.[63] Nishida's point is simply that science's forgetting or ignoring its origins in (idealism's) consciousness does not mean those origins do not exist.

To that extent Nishida has begun to extricate himself from the problem of the two Inoues. But he has done so, apparently, by becoming an idealist. So, he has not yet clutched the Holy Grail of modern Japanese philosophy: finding the common ground of *both* idealism and empiricism, of *both* the mental and the material. But Nishida is not finished; his idealism is only an intermediate step on the way to the *basho* of *absolute nothing*. Let us now turn to Nishida's next step and see whether he can not only progress but actually find his way out of the quagmire entirely.

The basho of absolute nothing. According to Nishida, our logical analysis cannot stop with the *basho* of relative nothingness and its inherent idealism. To simply subordinate the physical world to the experiential world leaves the door open to solipsism, that is, to the theory that the world is nothing other than the construct of my own individual mind. In other words, within the domain of relative nothingness, there is no rational reason to judge that the physical world is anything more than a mere dream or waking fantasy.

Nishida concludes, therefore, that there must be a still more fundamental *basho* that encompasses the other two, allowing the *basho* of relative nothingness and the *basho* of being their respective loci. He calls that most profound ground "the *basho* of absolute nothing." (I translate it here as "nothing" rather than "nothingness," because unlike "(relative) nothingness" which has an opposite—namely, "being"—nothing as "absolute nothing" is an absolute with no opposite against which it can be relativized.)

The *basho* of absolute nothing is not merely a field on which or in which something takes place, however. It is more analogous to a field in the sense of an electromagnetic field, a gravitational field, or a field in field-effect physics. The field itself is the event, not the place in which an event occurs. As we have seen time and again in Japanese philosophy, we have to change our mode of analysis from *what* to *how*: the *basho* of absolute nothing is a how, not a what.

Nishida sometimes calls that *how* the "performative intuition" or "action-directed intuition" (*kōiteki chokkan*).* The performative intuition defines the ground of all judging acts but yet, as a how, it can never be the object (a what) of any judgment. It is engaged when you recognize that you are located in and part of the world while simultaneously acting and performing in that world. The performative intuition is a field in which one aspect is data input (the intuition dimension) while the other aspect is your participation in the field (the performative aspect). And the two aspects are, by definition, inseparable.

As an analogy, I suggesst we consider how two gears function when they are engaged. Do the cogs (or teeth) on gear A *receive* the cogs of gear B into the gaps between its own cogs or do the cogs of gear A *penetrate* the gaps in gear B? That is, is gear A *being acted on* by gear B or is gear A *acting on* gear B? Obviously both. In fact, the receiving (like intuition's receiving sensations from the world) and the acting (like performing in the world) are *the same event* of engagement.

This brings us back to how the *basho* function in relation to each other. Why does Nishida believe we do not need yet a fourth *basho* to ground or envelope the third? Because the *basho* of absolute nothing is just that—*nothing*. It cannot become the object of any judgment because it is the engagement that is the source of all judging. In a terminology Nishida borrows from phenomenology, when we isolate absolute nothing's active, constitutive function, we find idealism's giving priority to the "noetic." The noetic is what Husserl calls the meaning-bestowing activity of the self or of the subject as constituting the object. If we stress its receptive dimension, on the other hand, we find empiricism's priority on the "noematic," that is, the objectified world of empirical facts.

In an interresponsive field characteristic of engagement, there is simultaneously both the vector extending from inside outward (what in Norinaga I called the "being in touch" aspect) and the vector extending from outside inward (what I called the "being touched" aspect). Alternatively, in Kūkai's terminology describing intimacy between self and reality (that is, between oneself and Dainichi), we found his phrase *nyūga ganyū*, "entering me; I entering."† Even when we think mechanistically of the engagement of gears, the cog from one wheel

† See page 120.

extends into the gap in the other wheel as the second wheel's gap accepts the cog, but that action itself is part of the larger activity wherein the second gear's cog extends itself into the first wheel's gap. When the two gears are engaged, it makes no sense to discuss which gear is engaging which.

Therefore, rather than settling for a philosophical system that is either idealistic or empirical, either mental or material, either subjective or objective, Nishida tried to define a logical system that would give the ground of all such dyads. It would reveal the basis of the philosophical positions generated by favoring one part of the dyad over the other. Such dyads arise from an artificial bifurcation, an abstraction drawn from what was originally a unitary event. In that respect, Nishida has finally formulated his response to the questions that Inoue Enryō and Inoue Tetsujirō had raised but could not yet answer. Nishida has found the Holy Grail.

The Logic of the Predicate[65]

In thinking through his logic for the performative intuition, Nishida realized that it had implications for logic in a different sense. He believed that western philosophy generally depends on the Aristotelian logic of substance-attribute, a dualism reflected in the grammatical form of the Indo-European sentence's subject-predicate structure. That is, the substance (expressed in the grammatical subject of the sentence) is primary and its meaning unfolds through attribution of its characteristics (expressed in the predicate of the sentence). Hence, our judgment that, for example, the horse is white and that it runs swiftly is that a substantial thing (horse) has the attributes of being white and running swiftly. We start with the what (the horse, the subject of the sentence) and add to it the how (is white; runs swiftly).

That Aristotelian form of logic, Nishida maintained, privileges the substance expressed in the grammatical subject over the attributes expressed in the grammatical predicate. Not surprisingly, this leads to a metaphysics of Being as primary, including the theological notion that God is the ground of that Being (as the theologian Paul Tillich put it). Nishida dubs that a "logic of the (sentential) subject" and notes that his system would be better described as a "logic of the predicate." By that he means the real ground is not Being, nor even its opposite—(relative) nothingness. Rather, the ground is absolute nothing—what cannot be characterized, what cannot be a subject of any sentence. That is, it is a pure predicate that is a field without subject, a pure activity without external agency.

Thus, with our bodymind, we engage that which is not verbalized (something like a not yet distinguished swiftly-running-white-horse) and that event unfolds judgmentally as swiftly-running→white→horse. That is, the "substance" as well as the subject of the sentence is an elaboration or addendum to the original judgment, rather than, as Aristotelian logic would assume, its starting point. Experience—the ground of all judgments—is, after all, not a thing but an event. Furthermore, how that event unfolds may be more important that what it is about. To focus on the *what* of experience is to isolate the object on which the experience focuses. But, as we have just seen in my description of the logic of *basho*, the experience itself in its fullness is better expressed as *how* I and world engage with each other. Since the predicate rather than the subject of the sentence better expresses the dynamism of that how, Nishida tried to develop a logic of the predicate rather than a logic of the subject.

Let us return to the running horse example, but interpret it in more detail now that we have a better idea of what Nishida was trying to achieve in his analysis. When we experience the swiftly running white horse with our body-minds, we have somatic sensations (hearing and feeling the stomping thunder, seeing the flash of color in a moving shape) and mental acts (seeing it as "swift" and categorizing it as "white" and "horse"). Then that event *expresses itself* naturally either from the noetic (subject) side of the *basho* of relative nothingness "*I see* a swiftly running white horse" or from the noematic (object) side of the *basho* of beings "The horse is white and swiftly running." Both the noetic and noematic expressions are derivative of something experientially more basic that precedes them, namely, the experiential field that takes expressive form as one or the other judgment (empirical or idealistic). By such an analysis, Nishida can characterize his logic of *basho* as a logic of the predicate rather than a logic of the subject. It gives priority to the event of the self-expressive absolute nothing, rather than to the stasis of Being as substance.

Lastly, in further developing his logic, Nishida drew on the terminology of the German Idealists, introducing into his system the Hegelian idea of "dialectic" and the "concrete universal." In discussing the relation between the concrete and the universal, Nishida again pitted himself against Aristotle. Aristotle believed the universal to be merely an abstraction of characteristics distilled out of concrete things, but like Hegel, Nishida maintained that the universal was not a thing at all, but an ongoing formative process by which concrete things emerge. The Hegelian addendum to his system introduced a temporal dimension, displaying again Nishida's commitment to the idea of process over stasis, event over thing, and becoming over being.

Nishida's analysis of concrete universals supported his attempt to bring an ontological dimension to his system. From the time of *Inquiry*, Nishida had the conviction that somehow experience was the common denominator of both mind and reality. His logic of *basho* worked quite well in addressing the mind half of the equation, but what about the reality half? Here he again looked for inspiration from the German idealists, not only Hegel's idea of concrete universals and Fichte's concept of self, but also Josiah Royce's American neo-

Hegelianism. In reading Royce, Nishida realized that to have a single system of mind-reality, the whole system had to be in some sense self-aware.

From the early 1920s, Nishida generally referred to the reflexive or "mirroring" (Royce's term) aspect of experience as self-awareness (*jikaku*), rather than self-consciousness (*jiishiki* or *jiko ishiki*).[66] Presumably, as I earlier noted, his objection to the two latter words was that they seemed to objectify the self of self-consciousness. Nishida wanted to find a term more suggestive of an agentless, objectless self-awareness. That led him to the word "self-awareness" (*jikaku*) in the sense of auto-awareness.[67*] Through that auto-awareness, Nishida believed, he could explain how the universals in his system could be "concrete universals" along the lines of those in Hegel's system. As we will soon see, however, that philosophical strategy raised even further issues in the eyes of Nishida's critics.

First, however, a comment about how well Nishida's logic fit assumptions we have seen in premodern Japanese philosophy.

Nishida's logic in its Japanese context. By identifying the ground as *zettai mu* or "absolute nothing," Nishida had, perhaps unwittingly, pointed toward some foundational orientations in premodern Japanese thought, especially the value placed on engaged knowing. Previously, I observed that his system had relegated western empiricism, accepting its truth only by demoting it to being a rarefaction of a kind of idealism. With his articulation of the *basho* of absolute nothing, by contrast, he introduced something akin to the basis of the traditional Japanese world view.

After all, what is the aesthetic of *kokoro* other than a performative intuition that can be engaged with bodymind but not defined intellectually? What is Dōgen's without thinking, as-ness, or even his *genjōkōan* (presencing of things as they are) other than the ground of thinking that cannot be objectified but which, once engaged, provides the basis for thinking itself to appropriately arise? What is Shingon praxis other than engaging the bodymind such that I have the inseparable intuition of the cosmos entering me and the activity of my entering the cosmos (*nyūga ganyū*).

Nishida's philosophy had seemingly met the agenda of Japanese modernity: he had found a place for western science by relegating it to being a part of a larger system valorizing the Japanese idea of "absolute nothing." His philosophy seemed to have secured the long desired goal of "Japanese spirit; western ingenuity."[†] Yet, as I have noted repeatedly, in articulating his system Nishida made no serious mention of its relation to the traditional Japanese ideas of *kokoro*, without thinking, or *nyūga ganyū*. Nor did he mention that his logic

† See page 416.

of the predicate resembled Motoori Norinaga's characterization of the Japanese language and its inherent syntactical capacity, centered in the sentence's verb, to blossom into a genuine engagement of reality. Nor did Nishida mention that his Roycean idea about the mirroring of self-consciousness was a way of expressing the holographic relation of whole as part and part as whole. Nor did he mention that his view of a self-aware or auto-aware reality parallels Kūkai's proprioceptive cosmos.†

Of course, on one hand, there is no need to criticize Nishida for his silence on his own tradition—it is his prerogative to decide where in the treasury of world thought he should go for his inspiration. On the other hand, his philosophical neglect of his own cultural *basho*, his ignoring his own embeddedness in a specific sociohistorical world, was potentially symptomatic of a problem within his philosophical system at large. Some of his contemporaries in the Kyoto School could see that.

Overlooking the cultural. In general terms the problem was that in introducing an embodied form of engaged knowing, Nishida had largely ignored the cultural dimension of human existence. Nishida may have addressed the how and what of experience and judgment, but he forgot the where. Consumed with his notion of the logic of *basho*, he neglected to find a place in his system for how culture functions as a major determinate of thinking.

At around this same time (late 1920s, early 1930s) in Japan as when Nishida was developing his logic of experience, some philosophers on the fringes of the Kyoto School were more directly addressing the relation between experience and culture. That circumstance resulted in tensions within the School itself, including one between its two major representatives. Here I can only briefly describe that dynamic, but since it eventually affected Nishida's own thinking, it merits some mention here.

As we will see in the next chapter, at Nishida's urging, Watsuji Tetsurō (1889–1960), Nishida's junior colleague in Kyoto, journeyed to Germany to study philosophy. Upon his return to Japan Watsuji openly criticized Heidegger's *Being and Time* for lacking an adequate account of how human existence is rooted in place and culture. Heidegger, Watsuji believed, had so emphasized the mental and temporal aspects of human existence that he had undervalued the relevance of the body and spatiality.

Along similar lines, Kuki Shūzō (1888–1941), Nishida's student at one point, criticized Heidegger for the same omission in his 1930 masterpiece on aesthetics, *The Structure of Iki.*[68] Kuki rejected the assumption that there are universal aesthetic values (such as the "sublime" in Kant's theory), arguing that we can

† See pages 377–8; 217–22; 120; 380–2; 32–4; 32–4; 126–9.

understand aesthetic terms only as they arise out of the life of a people in a specific time and place, what he called the "being of a people" (*minzoku sonzai*). Heidegger, Kuki claimed, had missed this dimension when he effectively reduced human existence to just *Dasein* (individual "being there") and *in-der-Welt Sein* ("being in the world"). Both criticisms of Heidegger could, with only minor adjustments be applied to Nishida's thinking at the time as well, but neither Watsuji nor Kuki did so.

Another Kyoto School figure and student of Nishida's, Miki Kiyoshi (1897–1945), abandoned Nishida's German idealism to study Marxism and its emphasis on the material and social dimensions of human existence. Those aspects had not been part of Nishida's own system and perhaps in its contemporaneous formulation could not be. In the end, Nishida's "worlds" were too much the realms of ideas and not enough the realm of material culture. Initially inspired by Miki, Tosaka Jun (1900–1945) turned even more sharply in the direction of historical materialism, criticizing Nishida's idealism in scathing terms.

No one was a more thorough critic of Nishida's transcultural system, however, than his departmental colleague, a longtime friend but eventual arch rival in the Kyoto School, Tanabe Hajime (1885–1962). His critiques of Nishida's philosophy were comprehensive and ongoing, far too complicated to explore here, but a few points merit our special attention since they affected Nishida's thinking in his final years.[69]

Criticisms by Tanabe Hajime

Tanabe's logic of the specific as critique of the logic of basho. In 1934–1935 Tanabe developed his "logic of the specific" as a critique of the universal-particular dynamic not only in Nishida, but also in most western philosophies as well. Tanabe's major contention was that any logical system such as the one Nishida proposed requires not only the dimensions of the universal and the individual, but also a third, intermediate layer between them, namely, that of the *specific* (or, to use the same Japanese word *shu* in its taxonomic sense, of the *species* level between the genus and individual). I can sketch in broad strokes the point of Tanabe's logic of the specific as follows.

On the generic (or universal) level, I am a human being. On the individual level, I am Tom Kasulis, an ontologically and genetically unique being. Most philosophies, western as well as Nishida's, recognize those two levels of identity. But on the level of the specific or of the species, I am an educated, white, early twenty-first century English-speaking American male. This specificity is not only fundamental to my identity, but is also in a crucial sense the starting point out of which the categories of my individuality and universality arise. To give a simple example, since my language as a native speaker of English (a cultural phenomenon at the level of the specific) is the medium for my words or categories, even when I speak of my individuality or my universal humanity, that conversation occurs at the level of neither. If I spoke from (not about) the individual level of my identity, I would be using a private language and unable to communicate at all. If I spoke from (not about) humanity, it would be in a non-cultural, nonnatural language incapable of nuance and subtlety. The twentieth-century linguistic experiment of devising a universal language, Esperanto, failed in practice partly because the language had no history, no literature, no evolution over time, no *culture*. Language must be grounded not in the universal, but the specific.

Tanabe also notes that the level of the specific is where the mediation of conflicting opposites occurs. Tanabe's point is commonsensical. After all, as an individual, there is no need for mediation—there is no one else for me to mediate with. And as a generic human being in a taxonomy which includes all other people, there is no alternative point of view to debate with. It is in the cultural, social, and ethnic realms that I mediate opposing ideas and identities, adjusting my behaviors accordingly. Moreover, that realm of the specific gives me a language in which to speak and think, an intellectual heritage upon which to draw, a sense of history beyond individual autobiography, and yet more particularized than the story of the human race at large. Families, communities, and nations all arise out of the realm of the specific. Thus, Tanabe's logic of the specific takes that for its point of departure.

Tanabe's full system of logic is too intricate to analyze here, but for understanding Nishida and the early development of the Kyoto School, the following is crucial. Tanabe highlighted the problem of integrating the historical, cultural, and ethnic into Nishida's system. The Kyoto School, he believed, had uncritically followed Hegel: the national, cultural, and ethnic were the endpoints rather than the points of departure for the progress of Spirit. Tanabe claimed that both Hegel and Nishida had started their respective logics from the standpoint of the universal (Being in Hegel, absolute nothing in Nishida) instead of the more concrete level of the specific. That left them with the irresolvable riddle of how to generate the specific from out of the universal. Furthermore, starting with Hegel but continuing with Nishida, the theory of concrete universals seemed to go directly from the universal to the individual, again by-passing the level of the specific entirely.

To Tanabe's way of thinking, nothing (*mu*) cannot be a thing or even, as Nishida would want it, a place. Rather it is the *function* of mediating or self-negating.[†] To isolate and objectify absolute nothing ignores the fact that there is

---

† For more on Tanabe's view of self-negation, see pages 527–30.

no world at all without culture. If absolute nothing is the point of origin for all judgments, how could cultural specificity even come about? Although he did not put it quite in these terms, one could say Tanabe was claiming that Nishida, despite his intentions, was slipping into making absolute nothing into a *what* instead of a *how*.

Tanabe's critique of Nishida's theory of self-awareness. Tanabe was equally critical of another central aspect of Nishida's philosophical system: his notion of self-awareness or auto-awareness (*jikaku*). To Tanabe, Nishida's auto-aware system of concrete universals emerging from an unarticulated ground of absolute nothing was tragically flawed. He accused it of being essentially a neo-Platonic metaphysics in which the oneness of being, reflecting on itself, emanates into becoming all the beings of the world.

Tanabe's critical sword on this point cut in two directions. First, it seemed to Tanabe that Nishida had transformed *mu* into Being, a something rather than a nothing.[70] Second, as the unkindest cut of all, Tanabe claimed that Nishida's philosophical system ended up being grounded in precisely the kind of mystical experience that Nishida had purportedly developed his logic of *basho* to avoid. In a sense, Tanabe was reiterating Ōnishi's critique of the *soku* formulations of Inoue Enryō and Inoue Tetsujirō: Nishida's system lacked a philosophical *foundation*. From Tanabe's standpoint, Nishida did not find the true Holy Grail after all.

Such criticisms started an extended, sometimes heated, debate between those two giants of the Kyoto School, the details of which need not concern us here. The ultimate effect was that such critiques moved Nishida into further refinements in his philosophical development.

MULTIPLE WORLDS

As Nishida began to expand his *basho* logic, he started to use the terminology of three "worlds" that were reminiscent of his triple-*basho* formulation, namely, the world of nature, the world of consciousness, and the world of the noumenal. In speaking of these as concrete articulations of universals, they are the realms, respectively, of the universal of judgments, of the universal of self-awareness, and of the universal of the noumenal. In the series as listed, each subsequent world embraces or encloses the one from before. Furthermore, the *basho* of absolute nothing is the infinite all-embracing *basho* that enfolds within itself all the other *basho*. Late in his life Nishida sometimes associated this *basho* of absolute nothing to the "world of religion."

In his reformulation, Nishida discusses the level of the noumenal to address some of the weaknesses in his earlier system. One new articulation of the function of the performative intuition is that, as an expression of the free self, it is a realm of opposing alternatives and possibilities. This seems to be where Nishida wants to locate the realm of conflict and mediation that Tanabe places on the level of species or of the specific. In this deepest, noumenal level of the self, we are aware of the self as ultimately unknowable. It cannot be fixed but is always in dialectical opposition among the alternatives posed by the will.

Earlier, in his middle period, Nishida had mentioned that, the more deeply the self penetrates the self, the more it becomes, in Nishida's terms, an "anguished soul."[71] Seeking self-determination to give itself stability, the noumenal self finds only that it is engulfed by a limitless *basho* of absolute nothing. That limitless indeterminability encountered at the same time as the anguished self is the source of the religious impulse. But Nishida came to realize that the religious self cannot be detached from the concrete, historical world of culture. That insight led to still further refinements in his system.

To address the criticism of his system's being an idealist castle in an empty sky, Nishida finally came to ground his system in the actual world, calling the three levels the "natural world" of things, the "life world" of conscious self-awareness, and the "historical world" of the self of contingency and indeterminancy. In the final few years of his life he concentrated his philosophical attention most on that last realm as it engaged him increasingly in questions about culture and history. He also was able to add further levels of sophistication to some of the issues of art and aesthetics that had interested him in his early phases of thinking. In those last years of his life for the first time he began to speak explicitly of Asian ideas, Japanese culture, and the basis of spirituality. Through the tortuous journey of a lifetime, Nishida had finally discovered the *basho* called home.

CONCLUSION

Nishida's impact on modern Japanese philosophy can hardly be overestimated. He transformed the study of philosophy in the modern Japanese academy from being just the scholarly study of ideas from abroad, into being a way of creative thinking. He changed western philosophy in Japan from a *what* that one studied in a detached manner to a *how* of intellectual engagement. To that extent, every philosopher in Japan today who thinks creatively and constructively is part of that legacy.

Second, throughout this chapter I have mentioned my persistent frustration over Nishida's not using the immense philosophical resources available to him from the premodern Japanese tradition. Yet, I still find it remarkable that he was able to take one core idea from that tradition and make it both philosophically respectable and a useful partner to a plethora of ideas taken from the West. I am speaking of his idea of absolute nothing.

As a concept, nothingness is not at all new to the West. As long as *Being* has been a prime category in western philosophy, there has been the occasional cameo appearance of its opposite, *Nothingness*. Even when the existentialist Jean-Paul Sartre brought it center stage for a marquee performance, it came once again with its sibling rival. The title of Sartre's book is, after all, *Being and Nothingness*. That nothingness is what Nishida calls "relative nothingness" and interestingly, Nishida placed relative nothingness in his *basho* of self-consciousness decades before Sartre had identified his nothingness with consciousness.

But absolute nothing—that is a nothing else entirely. It is akin to, but as Nishida demonstrates not identical with, infinity, the indeterminate, absolute freedom, and the unrestricted. If we try to pin it down, it escapes our grasp and flees into another place, where it becomes relative nothingness. But in the deft philosophical hands of Nishida, we can recognize that if we think deeply enough, fathoming the depths of self-consciousness with boldness even in the face of anguish and contingency, we know it is there, not as a what, but as a how. Perhaps Nishida's greatest accomplishment as a thinker is that he brought absolute nothing to our philosophical way of thinking. It became a hallmark of his followers in the Kyoto School.

The mention of the Kyoto School brings us to the final characteristic of Nishida's philosophy I want to underscore, namely, its lack of specificity. I mean that in two senses. First, Nishida's philosophy would have benefited from the inclusion of more, many more, specific examples. His language is too often so abstract and full of jargon (some borrowed, some of his own making) that his theory of intelligibility borders on being unintelligible. As readers, we may spend too much time trying to figure out what Nishida means and not enough on what difference it would make if he were right or wrong. More examples would decrease the time consumed by the former and help us come to a conclusion about the latter.

A second lack of specificity is of the sort criticized by Tanabe. Despite his attempted rebuttals to the contrary, Nishida never did in my opinion successfully bring into his philosophy the richness of culture and the social, the intricate way in which consciousness and intellectual heritage interact and mutually affect each other. In his later discussions of the historical world, Nishida introduced those dimensions, but he mainly talked *about* culture in his writings. He neither described nor specified with examples how the *engagement* with culture was foundational to all experience and judgments. Since Nishida's works are often devoid of concrete examples from everyday life, he never completely lifted the fog of lofty ideas that obscured his earthly concerns. That said, his final writings direct us clearly into the historical and concrete and we can only wonder what he might have done had he lived a little longer.[72]

Nishida's lack of specificity in both senses was, however, a major contributing factor to the development of the Kyoto School. His disciples worked diligently to bring to Nishida's primordial vision the connections to the particular, to the concreteness of the everyday, to the specifics of Japanese culture. To take one example, Nishitani Keiji took Nishida's anguished self, contextualized it into the religious language of Zen Buddhism as Hakuin's Great Doubt,[†] and brought to life Nishida's cryptic allusions to the religious world as that which lies both within and beyond the internal contradictions of life in this historical world.

You may well wonder, though, what modern Japanese philosophy would have looked like if it had started from a very different point of departure, namely, one of our being in the midst of culture, place, and time. It would be a modern philosophy that could recognize its own roots in the premodern Japanese philosophical tradition, drawing and expanding on its fundamental questions of knowledge and value. We have seen in this book the types of experiences that most inspired Japan's premodern thinkers. To Nishida's credit, he had after many struggles found the right "place," indeed a place of honor, for those experiences within his western-style philosophical system. What if instead, however, a twentieth-century Japanese philosopher had cross-pollinated the premodern styles of Japanese philosophizing with the western styles to create a strikingly new, hybridized form of philosophical thinking? You might wonder what such a modern Japanese philosophy would be like.

Actually, you need not speculate. The next philosopher we will engage, Watsuji Tetsurō, did exactly that. We meet him as a young man in a conversation with his father, a conversation that so embarrassed him that it altered his career path as a philosopher.

† See page 338.

13. Watsuji Tetsurō 和辻哲郎 (1889–1960)

Philosophy in the Midst

> Therefore, if human being is not simply the individual person, it is also not simply society. Within human being, these two are unified dialectically.
>
> Watsuji Tetsurō

As a young professor, Watsuji Tetsurō was visiting his family at the rural homestead outside Himeji. One evening he was having an intimate discussion with his father, a physician trained in traditional Chinese medicine and a devotee of the Confucian classics. Entranced by the literary arts even as a boy, Watsuji Tetsurō had fancied a career in fiction, displaying his literary and linguistic talent in middle school when he published translations of Byron and Shaw as well as his own creative works for the school literary magazine.

To no one's surprise, he gained admission to the prestigious First Higher School in Tokyo and subsequently to the premier academic institution in all Japan, Tokyo Imperial University. Watsuji's literary hero was the novelist, Natsume Sōseki (1867–1916), and he would eavesdrop on Sōseki's lectures from outside the window of the university lecture hall. He was thrilled when a year after graduation he was invited to join the discussion group that regularly met at Sōseki's home.

Yet, Watsuji had come to realize his true calling to be philosophy, a field in which he quickly made his mark. For his university degree, he had written a thesis on Nietzsche, but at the last minute the philosophy department rejected the topic, mainly because its chair, the aforementioned Inoue Tetsujirō, thought Nietzsche more literary than philosophical and not worthy of attention in his program. Under severe pressure of time, Watsuji wrote an entirely new thesis, "On Schopenhauer's Pessimism and Salvation Theory," thereby managing to graduate on time in July 1912.

He then defiantly published his *Studies on Nietzsche* the next year and in 1915 brought out his *Søren Kierkegaard,* establishing himself as Japan's foremost interpreter of European existentialism. Not yet even thirty years old, he had done much to make a father proud, having come a long way from his rural roots to being a young star in Japan's constellation of modern intellectuals.

The discussion between father and son took an unexpected turn, however. The father might have wondered who this urbane dandy in front of him could be. Where was the boy from the countryside nurtured in Confucian virtues, the son of a man who had dedicated his life to the alleviation of human suffering? The father looked deeply into his son's eyes and asked what he was doing to address the intellectual crisis of Japan. The country seemed to be abandoning traditional values to adopt western ways in a breakneck race to modernization. What would happen to those traditions that for so many centuries had sustained the country and its way of life? Would Japan as we have known it cease to exist? Watsuji's work was certainly fashionable, but to what end? Had he done anything to help his homeland recover from its cultural trauma?

The son looked back at his father at a loss for an answer, sheepishly bowing in silent respect. That encounter was part of Watsuji's change of heart, his "turn" as he called it. He pivoted to investigating more closely Japan's cultural and intellectual roots. Along the way, he was also becoming less a critic and expositor of others' philosophies and more a creative philosopher in his own right. To engage that philosopher, we need to examine more closely the contours of his subsequent intellectual development.[73]

Pilgrimages to Ancient Japan and Europe

To grapple with Japan's cultural identity crisis, Watsuji needed to better understand the factors at play. What western ideas and values posed the greatest threat to the traditional Japanese world view? And what exactly was that world view? In studying the classic western philosophers from Plato to the German idealists to the existentialists, Watsuji was already conversant with individualism, personal freedom, empiricism, and western political theory. For him the more difficult challenge was determining the traditions at the roots of his own culture. Taking a cue from such earlier thinkers as Kitabatake Chikafusa, Ogyū Sorai, and Motoori Norinaga, he tried to understand by returning to origins.[74] In 1917 Watsuji journeyed to Nara where he hoped to discover artifacts of Japan's cultural heritage at its point of inception in the eighth century. In 1919 he published his reflections as *A Pilgrimage to [Nara's] Ancient Temples,* a best seller.

Although Native Studies philosophers had also focused on eighth-century Nara as decisive in Japanese cultural development, Watsuji understood the importance of the period differently. For him, the quintessence of Nara culture was not in its *Man'yōshū* verses or its *Kojiki* myths, but was instead embodied in the Buddhist architecture and sculptures of the Tenpyō era (729–749). Confident that Japan's cultural foundation lay in the imported and transformed material culture of wood, ceramic, and bronze rather than indigenous words or narratives, Watsuji focused on the Buddhist Nara of Emperor Shōmu, the builder of the Great Temple to the East described and pictured in Chapter 2.[†]

In a salvo against the nativist quest for an ancient Japan untainted by foreign influence, Watsuji wrote:

> The world of the *Man'yōshū* and that of the Buddhist arts [of the same epoch] are completely different, and this difference is not merely because the one art is that of lyric poetry whereas the other is that of the plastic arts. It is rather a difference of interests, requirements, and aspirations—in short, in very basic things having to do with the mind and heart. This sort of contemporaneity of two "worlds" within one time-frame, however, should not come as anything of a surprise to people like ourselves—people who right now in front of our own eyes can observe two different and separate "worlds"....

Repudiating the nativist quest to discover a uniquely Japanese creative spirit in the Japanese ancients, Watsuji argued that in his study of ancient Nara, he found quite the opposite. In the Tenpyō art Watsuji found an openness to embrace and assimilate different people, ideas, and products from multiple sources, both abroad and home. He continued his point as follows:

> It seems to me that there is no need to insist always on the distinctive "creativity" of the Japanese. If, then, the culture of the Tenpyō era was the product of labor carried on cooperatively with foreigners, those foreigners became our ancestors and, therefore, when it comes to the question of what constitutes the culture of our ancestors this is no different from any other.[75]

Watsuji's pilgrimage to Nara also set him thinking about the anti-Buddhist iconoclasm of the Meiji period when nativist vandals had destroyed Buddhist images in cemeteries, roadside shrines, and even private homes.[‡] Even before publishing *Pilgrimage*, therefore, Watsuji wrote his response to iconoclasm in *Restoring the Idols*, a work likely inspired by Watsuji's reading of Nietzsche's *Twilight of the Idols*.

In *Twilight* Nietzsche had argued that creative religious symbols inevitably become stultified and must be destroyed, only to be unearthed and restored later. In that restoration, however, they become symbolic objects for aesthetic

† See pages 96–8.
‡ See page 417.

appreciation rather than foci of worship. According to Nietzsche, that was the history of the Greco-Roman statues of the gods. First, they were acts of spiritual creation, then overturned as objects of idolatry by Christians, and then finally revived in the Renaissance as exemplars of beauty.

Watsuji presumably imagined a similar transition in Nara's Japanese Buddhist images. Originally created as expressions of devotion, they subsequently became false idols defaced by the Meiji nativist iconoclastic movement, but now in Watsuji's Taishō era, they could be restored as artifacts of cultural value, enabling insights into the heart of traditional Japanese culture.[76] In taking that tack, Watsuji undermined the Native Studies (and subsequent State Shintō) disparagement of Buddhism as a "foreign" element polluting the "purity" of native Japanese spirituality.

Watsuji believed the defining impulse of Japanese traditional culture could be found in its continuous layering (*jūsōsei*) of ideas and values from multiple sources, a process we found in this book as far back as the Shōtoku *Constitution* in the early seventh century. Thus, for Watsuji, Japanese culture was not a primordial essence hidden by foreign "filth" as Motoori Norinaga had maintained, but instead an intrinsically syncretistic culture deriving its distinctiveness from the strata that have gone into its historical development.[77]

The trip to Nara inspired Watsuji's passion for rediscovering the basis of his culture, leading to such general works as *Japan's Ancient Culture* (1920), *Studies in Japanese Intellectual History* (1926), *Studies in Japanese Intellectual History—Continued* (1935), *A History of Japanese Ethical Thought* (1952), and *Studies in the History of Japanese Art* (1955) as well critical analyses of specific traditions such as his *The Practical Philosophy of Original Buddhism* (1927) and, for the sake of comparison, *The Significance of Original Christianity for Cultural History* (1926). His studies also treated the founders of philosophical-spiritual traditions, most notably his *Dōgen the Monk* (a collection of essays from 1920–1923)[78] and *Confucius* (1938).

Given our previous engagement with Dōgen, Watsuji's book about him is particularly noteworthy because it changed the way Japanese intellectuals viewed not only Dōgen but also premodern Buddhist thinkers in general. In a way, Watsuji could be said to have demolished Dōgen as a religious idol and then restored him as an object of secular, philosophical esteem. In Watsuji's own words:

> Concerning Dōgen's truth itself, which I am not confident of having understood, I am not claiming that my explanation is the only explanation. However, at least I may say I opened up a new way of interpretation. Because of this, Dōgen will become not Dōgen of one sect but Dōgen of the human race, not Dōgen the founder of a sect but our Dōgen.[79]

Thanks to Watsuji, for the first time in eight centuries, Dōgen was treated in a book-length study as a philosopher with importance beyond being just the founder of Japanese Sōtō Zen Buddhism. Inoue Tetsujirō had treated the Edo-period Confucians as philosophers in his trilogy,[†] and Inoue Enryō[‡] had considered some premodern Buddhist thinkers in a philosophical light, but Watsuji opened a line of interpretation that would have a lasting effect on a series of modern Japanese philosophers after him.

New Vistas

It might seem from what I have said that Watsuji was defining himself increasingly as a historian and critic of Japanese culture, but that impression would be mistaken because Watsuji's engagement with western philosophy was by no means over. Indeed his career as a constructive philosopher and creative independent thinker was just about to begin. In 1925 Nishida arranged an appointment for Watsuji at Kyoto University in the field of ethics and he subsequently urged his younger colleague to do research abroad. As a result, in 1927 and 1928 Watsuji spent eighteen months studying and traveling in Europe, mainly to Germany for its philosophy and to Italy for its contributions to the history of western art. The latter excursions led to a book on Italian cathedrals that he entitled, reminiscent of the earlier work on Nara, *Italy—A Pilgrimage to Its Ancient Temples* (1927).[80]

Of most relevance to Watsuji's later philosophical development, however, was his coming upon the thought of the German philosopher, Martin Heidegger. Watsuji was in Berlin in 1927, the year Heidegger's *Being and Time* appeared in print. Because of his earlier work in existentialism, Watsuji had already followed an intellectual trajectory that radiated from Kant's theory of the person, through the hermeneutics of Nietzsche and Wilhelm Dilthey, and into the phenomenology of Edmund Husserl. Watsuji had pursued that program of study long before he had turned to exploring Japan's cultural, aesthetic and spiritual roots. But now, when reading *Being and Time*, he felt something fit into place; seemingly separate strands of his career were about to be intertwined. Maybe he could even find a way to address the Japanese cultural crisis that so disturbed his father.

The Problem of philosophical anthropology. The issue piquing Watsuji's interest in reading Heidegger was not so much a single question as a theme: what it means to be a person. The philosophical exploration of that subject is known

---

† See page 422.

‡ See pages 418–20.

in German as *Anthropologie* and is commonly translated into English as "philosophical anthropology" to distinguish it from the empirical social science of the same name. (The Japanese language differentiates the two by calling the former *ningengaku* and the latter *jinruigaku*.) To appreciate Watsuji's perspective, it helps to be a little familiar with the succession of thinkers I just mentioned insofar as they had a bearing on his point of departure for developing his own philosophical anthropology: Kant, Dilthey, Nietzsche, and Husserl.

Immanuel Kant (1724–1804) had tried to disabuse philosophy of its fantasy that it could use pure reason to design grand metaphysical systems, urging it to concentrate instead on the categories we must use in making experience intelligible. As a chief architect of the modern western tradition of philosophical anthropology, Kant explored the dynamics whereby the "person" (the German word *Person* came to prominence in western philosophy partly through the efforts of Kant) served as the core agency in empirical knowledge, logical reasoning, ethical judgments, and aesthetic values.

Wilhelm Dilthey (1833–1911), along with other luminaries like Max Weber (1864–1920) and Emile Durkheim (1858–1917), developed the discipline of sociology to theorize the role of culture and society on the formation of that person, an influence that Kant had largely ignored in his emphasis on the individual. For such social thinkers, we understand ourselves and each other through our shared, collective experiences rather than through innate a priori categories. We become persons by living together either in community (*Gemeinschaft*) or society (*Gesellschaft*).

Nietzsche's (1844–1900) philosophical anthropology, by contrast, articulated an irresolvable conflict between the individual and the social group. Namely, the social tries to "herd" us into conformity for the sake of social stability while the authentic individual strives to transcend the herd through a free act of will. That free act enables a person to become "more than an ordinary human being," what he called the Overman (*Übermensch*).

Taking the viewpoints of those three philosophers together, it seems we can understand ourselves as either autonomous individuals or as a collectively educated, nurtured social group. Since both understandings seem appropriate, they might seem complementary. Yet, as Nietzsche suggests, the individual and the collective are not just competing definitions of how we are persons; they also point to opposing forces, each pulling at us from a different direction. The will pulls us toward asserting our individual freedom while the society pulls us toward following the approved behaviors and values of the collective. The relation between the individual and the collective serves as a fundamental problematic in Watsuji's attempt at a philosophical anthropology.

From Husserl, the fourth philosopher in the group, Watsuji did not glean a theory of what it means to be human as much as a method for how to approach the issue through a careful examination of the dynamics of human consciousness. Husserl's phenomenology is a sophisticated analytic technique for analyzing how we engage the world—how we extend our awareness outward with vectors of intentionality while experiencing reality as constructs of meaning. For Husserl, we live not in epistemic isolation wherein the world is "out there" and we impose "meaning" onto it, but rather we live in a web of meaning-bestowing acts (the noetic) and the products of those acts, the world of meaningful things (the noematic).[†]

More precisely, Husserl believed that we could not help but believe there is a world external to us causing our perceptions (a belief he called "the natural standpoint"). Yet, as phenomenologists, we must "suspend" that belief and not let it enter into our analyses of the invariant characteristics ("essences") within the structure of conscious events. As we saw in Chapter 12, many related issues concerning the subjective and objective aspects of experience were further explored in Japan by Nishida, Watsuji's senior colleague and his new mentor at Kyoto University.

Martin Heidegger took Husserl's phenomenology not only a step further, but in a new direction. A simple way to describe the difference between Husserl's and Heidegger's methods is to begin by thinking of Husserl as a cartographer of consciousness. That is, his goal was to map with objectivity and detachment[81] the vast variety of meanings emergent in conscious awareness. In phenomenology, one does that mapping without any assumptions about what objects outside my experience might have triggered those "meaning-bestowing acts" that comprise consciousness. That is, the phenomenologist is interested in how in experience we create meaning, not in what caused the experiences. Hence, it excludes any metaphysical considerations.

For example, in his *Idea of the Holy*, Rudolf Otto (whose application of phenomenological method Husserl endorsed) tried to reveal the nature of religion by analyzing the characteristics of the experience of the "holy" while bracketing out of his analysis the assumption of a transcendent entity (God, Brahman, etc.) that might arouse such an experience in a person. Or, on a more trivial level, through phenomenology I could analyze the commonality in my wife's and my experience of "having a favorite snack," even though for her that snack might be chocolate and for me popcorn. As for what they are in themselves, chocolate and popcorn have little in common, but in how they appear respectively in my wife's consciousness and my consciousness as "favorite snack," they are much alike. Clearly, the phenomenological method resonates well with the emphasis on *how* over *what* in premodern Japanese philosophy.

† See page 467.

As Husserl's student, Heidegger endorsed the basics of his phenomenological method, but as a quasi-existentialist,[82] he was not interested in Husserl's "scientific" project of mapping with objective detachment every kind of conscious activity. Husserl's method assumes every conscious event—like every mountain, river, or rock formation for a geographical cartographer—is equal in importance. Heidegger, by contrast, was interested in drawing a *treasure map* in which details would be stressed or ignored in terms of their value in locating the desired object, the spot marked "X" in his phenomenological charts. What was that X for Heidegger? Being.

For Heidegger "Being" (*Sein*) is not a thing; "beings" (*Seiendes*) are things. Yet, beings are not simply beings. As things, beings *exist*. When we say that, the "exist" is pointing to something that is not simply another being. It is an opening to Being itself, but not as another thing. Heidegger is critical of those who make Being into a thing, a metaphysical category that exists somehow in itself as a quality transcending ordinary existence. To connect with the vocabulary I have been developing in explaining Japanese philosophy, we can loosely say Being (as semantically primarily a verb that becomes a noun only when nominalized) is more a *how* that a *what* ("beings," on the other hand, are semantically always nouns). The recognition of this fundamental difference between Being and beings is part of how we human beings engage the world.

Certainly, most of the time, we do not think about that difference explicitly, but we always could. That possibility is how it is to be a human being in the world. That "being there" (*Dasein*) is distinctive to human being. Only a human can distinguish the existence in beings from just the beings. Only a human being could say, as President Bill Clinton did in his deposition, "it depends on what the meaning of the word 'is' is." Though Being in itself may be inexpressible (expressing it or describing it would make it a thing, a being), we can nevertheless keep circling back to it in our experience, unpeeling layers of meaning by fathoming more deeply our human being.

That certainly looks like a project in philosophical anthropology, the inquiry into the meaning of human being. Heidegger rejected that characterization, however, because of what that term had come to mean among some of his German contemporaries who were seeking an essence that defines our humanity. Philosophical anthropologists like Max Scheler had, Heidegger believed, reduced human being to just another thing, however special a thing. The ontological difference between Being and beings was therefore lost.

Still, despite Heidegger's objections, philosophical anthropology need not be essentialist in that way. Given the ways I have used the term in this book when considering the Japanese tradition, for example, Heidegger's profound analysis of *Dasein* as human being can easily fit a broadly construed sense of philosophical anthropology. Certainly, Watsuji was inclined to construe Heidegger in those terms.

Given his background, therefore, while in Berlin in 1927 Watsuji turned to reading Heidegger's new book, *Being and Time,* with high expectations. Heidegger was not only Husserl's most eminent student, but also, it was said, had had a falling out with his teacher over the future direction of phenomenology. *Being and Time* was rumored to be a trailblazing work that used phenomenology in a new way to address the qualities of human existence, to unravel the subtleties of living in the world. As he began his read, Watsuji was engrossed, but upon reflection he felt something amiss. Somehow this new Heideggerian philosophical anthropology did not jibe with the experience of this Japanese man studying philosophy in Germany, this cultural historian who had undertaken in recent years a series of studies of the ancient culture of Japan and, recently, of Italy.

According to Watsuji, for all its nuanced analysis of human existence, its interpretation of our "being there" (*Dasein*) and "existing in the world" (*In-der-Welt-sein*), Heidegger's book had an enfeebled understanding of both "there" and "world." Watsuji believed that Heidegger, preoccupied with his phenomenological study of consciousness and temporality, had undervalued the particularity of body and space. Moreover, Heidegger's "world" of human being was notably lacking a full accounting for the influence of culture. In Heidegger's *Being and Time*, the individual (*Dasein*) as opening to Being itself was the starting point and collective existence (*Mitsein*) a development within that individual existence. At least, that was how Watsuji reacted to Heidegger's project.

Given Watsuji's sensitivities and intellectual commitments, that simply would not do. Indeed, despite its fixation on anxiety (*Angst*) in ordinary human existence, Heidegger's *Being and Time* did not address the specific anxiety of cultural dissonance of the kind that had troubled Watsuji's father.[83] Nor did it deal with the dissonance between cultures. How could it? The book barely recognized culture as a primary dimension of human existence.

Watsuji began to formulate a counter to Heidegger's philosophical anthropology before he even started his journey home by sea in 1928, but the resulting book did not appear in print until 1935. Entitled *Fūdo* (translated as "Climates and Culture"), when the manuscript was completed in 1928, it was possibly the earliest book-length response to Heidegger's *Being and Time* written in any language.

FŪDO: THE MILIEU OF HUMAN EXISTENCE

Phenomenology as an Approach to Philosophical Anthropology

Watsuji's procedure for explaining *fūdo* was based in the phenomenological approach of Husserl, especially as re-envisioned through Heidegger's existentialist orientation. Both Heidegger and Watsuji were interested in human being, but they came to the issue from different directions. It is as if Heidegger began with human being as an access to Being and Watsuji with human being as being part of humanity.

The method of Watsuji's book "Fūdo." Though he would diverge sharply from Heidegger in his philosophical anthropology, Watsuji endorsed the basics of his existential-phenomenological method. The key variance was, as I already mentioned, that in speaking of human existence as "existing in the world," Watsuji digressed from Heidegger's version of what the world is and how that existence is lived. Watsuji found Heidegger's account of the world too cerebral and spatially homogenized, and most of all, too detached from any full-bodied notion of culture.

In response, Watsuji thought of a Japanese word that seemed a better description of the "in-the-world" of our existence, namely, *fūdo*. The Japanese term *fūdo* means "climate" but not in a simple meteorological sense.[84] Starting in the Nara period, that critical historical moment to which Watsuji had already looked for Japan's cultural foundations, the Japanese governmental offices had begun to compile regional documents called *fudoki* (records of *fūdo*), gazetteers that surveyed not only such items as topographical features, natural resources, and agricultural products, but also information about local folktales, dialects, and customs. Thus, they were regional geographies in our present-day sense of being more than maps and statistics; they were also overviews of the local *cultural* environment. So we could say *fūdo* does mean "climate" but only in its broadest sense of the milieu—physical and cultural—in which humans live.[85]

So *fūdo* is more than natural forces; it includes as well the human response within those forces, the human and natural forming a single field of mutual engagement.[86] For instance, the meteorological climate of much of Japan is rather temperate, but also humid and rainy. Those conditions accord with an architectural style having not only overhanging roofs to keep out the rain, but also walls of sliding paper panels to let in the light and air. That led to the possibility of opening the home's walls to a garden, bringing the outside world in. That, in turn, influenced the cultural attitude toward nature.

Those factors mutually affect each other, collectively constituting the *fūdo*. For Watsuji it was crucial that such a *fūdo* is part of the individual's existence from the very beginning. To make this point clearer, he analyzed the example of a cold human existence.

856–9 *A Phenomenology of cold.* Since phenomenology was known to only a few specialists in Japan at the time, Watsuji had to introduce the method to the readers of *Fūdo* so they could see the value in the project he would be undertaking. Recognizing that the phenomenological method is easier to show than explain, Watsuji did an extended analysis of what we call *cold*. He started with the disengaged understanding of the cold, the basis of the naturalistic or scientific view. If we take the cold to be an external physical object that exists outside us as a stimulus to our sense organs,

> ... it follows that the "cold" and "we" exist as separate and independent entities in such a manner that only when the cold presses upon us from the outside does the intentionality arise by which "we feel the cold." In that case, it is natural that we think of this as the influence of the cold on us.

857

Yet however appropriate that naturalistic approach may be to the sciences, it is only an abstraction from how we actually *experience* our environment, our *fūdo*.[87*] Watsuji continues:

> ... How can we know the independent existence of the cold before we feel cold? It is impossible. It is by feeling cold that we discover the cold. ... As far as individual consciousness is concerned, the subject possesses the intentional structure within itself and as a subject already "directs itself toward something." The "feeling" in "feeling the cold" is not a separate piece that results in a relation directed at the cold, but is in itself already a relation by virtue of its feeling something, and it is in this relation that we discover cold....

857

Therefore, for us to recognize the cold as cold, we must consciously attend to it. Experiencing the "cold out there" cannot be divorced from *my feeling* the cold. The cold and I are in internal, not external, relation. Does this mean that the cold is simply a mental construct? Not at all. What is cold is not my *idea* of the cold (an idea cannot chill me to the bone), but rather, the cold itself as something I experience as outside me. (Note that in the phenomenological method, we ignore the issue of whether the cold is *in reality* something outside my experience and focus instead on its being *experienced as* outside me. For phenomenology when I say something is objective, I am not referring to some essence in the thing itself but instead to an invariant characteristic of how something is experienced.)

Watsuji summarized the point this way:

> When we feel the cold, it is not the sensation of the cold that we feel, but directly the coldness of the outside air, "the cold" itself. In other words, the cold felt in intentional experience is not something subjective but something objective.... Therefore, from the start there is no problem in understanding how a feeling of cold supposedly comes into relation with the coldness of the outside air.
>
> Seen this way, the usual distinction between subject and object, or more particularly the distinction between "us" and "the cold" as independent of one another involves a certain misunderstanding. When we feel the cold, we ourselves are already dwelling in the coldness of the outside air. That we come into relation with the cold means that we ourselves already "stand out into" the cold. Our very way of being is characterized by what Heidegger calls "ex-sistere" (literally, "to cause to stand forth"), a feature of intentionality.

857–8

Furthermore, Watsuji insists that the engagement with the cold occurs in a shared human space such that the cold is what *we,* not just *I,* feel.

> ... But as we have been able to use the expression "we feel the cold" without any difficulty, it is "we" who experience the cold, not "I" alone. We feel the same cold in common.... Thus, it is not I alone but we—or more strictly, I when I am "we" and we when we are each an "I"—who are outside in the cold.
>
> What fundamentally defines our "ex-sistence" is this we, not an "I" by itself. Accordingly, to "ex-sist" means already to be out among other "I"s before it means to be out in some thing such as the cold. This is not the relation called intentionality, but rather an interrelation called *aidagara,* betweenness. It is primarily we in this mutual relationship of betweenness who discover ourselves in the cold.

858–9

Of course, Watsuji's phenomenological analysis applies not just to the phenomenon of cold, but to any phenomenon in the *fūdo.*

> I have attempted to clarify the phenomenon of cold, but we do not experience this phenomenon of the weather in isolation from others of its kind. It is experienced in connection with warmth or heat, as well as with wind, rain, snow, or sunshine, and so forth. In other words, the cold is simply one of the whole series of similar phenomena that we call weather.... [We] discover ourselves—our selves as interrelated—in climate.

859

Summing up what Watsuji has said up to this point, we find his method emerges from his conceiving experience to be a holistic field, embracing as a single event what we typically divide into subject and object.[88] *Cold,* Watsuji insists, is not external to me, impinging on me through the mediation of my senses. Such an account would be a detached understanding that treats *cold* and *I* as an external relation that has to be bridged in some way for the two to be linked. Rather, using his phenomenological method, Watsuji sees a single, internally related event in which cold and I are inseparably part of each other.

To hark back to language I used in explaining Kūkai, when I say "I am cold" I am not referring to the cold, but *conferring* with it. To feel the cold, to know the cold as cold, is to *engage* the cold, not detach ourselves from it. Yet, Watsuji points out, part of that event is that I can take a standpoint within it such that the cold is externally "there" to be felt, but—and this is the crucial point for him—whenever I externalize the locus of the cold, *at the same time* I must externalize myself as what is acted upon instead of as what is experiencing. If the cold is "out there" then I am "out there" with it in an internal relation to it. The cold and I exist together.

Yet, oddly enough, for me to see myself as "out there," I must also be "over here" looking at myself "out there." (Here some of Nishida's discussions of self-awareness seem parallel.[†]) That is, for me to experience the cold as external, I must externalize myself with it, thus implying the existence of a double *I*, the external *I* that is internally related with the cold "out there" and the *I* that is looking at the *I-cold* dynamic as existing outside itself. As I will explain later in this chapter, that polarity, an individuated self vs. a self within a shared field, will be crucial to Watsuji's later, more fully developed theory of what it means to be human and to be ethical.

There is a further step in Watsuji's analysis of cold that also has profound implications for his subsequent philosophy. As the character of my own experience allows this standing outside myself, I find myself not only within the cold but also within a social world in which I encounter other people who share the cold. I see them on the street, nod, and say "cold, isn't it?" while fully expecting some expression of agreement in return. Using our special terminology again, we could say my conference with the cold also includes my conference with others sharing that cold.

The very fact I use the English word "cold," even when thinking about it to myself, reflects that shared world with others. I express and even understand my experience in the medium of a shared language (in this case English) and that shared language is as much a part of the "climate" as is the arctic air in the atmosphere. Thus, *fūdo* is the shared field within which I, cold, and we exist together. That existence constitutes what Watsuji calls "betweenness" (*aidagara*) or being *in the midst*. The image is reminiscent of Norinaga's view of the *kokoro*

† See pages 461–2.

involved in the creation of a poem—the *kokoro* of the event, the words, the poet, and the audience resonate together to achieve expression.†

Most striking in Watsuji's analysis is how, on one hand, it is fully in accord with the phenomenological method developed by Husserl and his followers in twentieth-century Europe and yet, on the other hand, it is continuous with many hallmarks of philosophizing in premodern Japan: the emphasis of internal relations as primary, the focus on how instead of what, the embodied character of knowing, and the primacy of the interpersonal over the individualistic. Indeed, through a deft shift in terminology, Watsuji has transferred the method of engaged knowing from its traditional Japanese philosophical context to a contemporaneous western one.[89]

We find then a clear contrast between Watsuji's *fūdo* and Nishida's pure experience. Nishida, it seems, was interested in developing a western-style philosophy that could account for and analyze various *experiences,* some of which undoubtedly had been central in traditional Japanese culture with its range of aesthetic and religious sensitivities. Watsuji, by contrast, seemed more interested in translating *Japanese philosophizing itself* into a western medium. If that contrast is correct, then despite commonalities on specific points—overcoming the subject-object distinction, grounding abstraction in concrete experience, and the rejection of the primacy of the individual subject, for example—their projects inherently differed in intent.

In the rest of his book Watsuji reflected on the varying *fūdo* he encountered in his travels. Incidentally, in those accounts, like many of his other ruminations on the distinctiveness of this or that cultural form, Watsuji could be quite cavalier. At those times it is better to follow *how* he is approaching his description of something than focusing too much on the sometimes problematic details. His main concern was how in each instance, there was a fit among the components.

Watsuji specified three general types of climate: monsoon, desert, and meadow, reserving most of his analysis for the first type since it includes India, China, Japan, and the South Seas. This juxtaposition of similarities *and differences* among the monsoon type raised the question of Japanese uniqueness, the old bugaboo that had tormented the Native Studies thinkers. Watsuji ultimately concluded that Japanese uniqueness lies in the particular *fūdo* it exemplifies, not in some mystical underlying essence. That is, Japan is unique only through its particular combination of all factors: physical, cultural, linguistic, historical, and intellectual.

In *Restoring the Idols* Watsuji spoke of Japanese culture as consisting of various intellectual strata layered atop each other. In *Fūdo,* he used a more

† See pages 377–8.

horizontal image, namely, the field of the Japanese being in the midst of their environment, topography, meteorology, language, and cultural patterns. That Japan has a *fūdo* uniquely its own is not anything special about Japan, however. *Every* culture has its own *fūdo* and the world would be better, he believed, if each could play its own role in the global community.

In short: Japan, like every other culture, is unique, but it is not in any way uniquely unique. We need to celebrate cultural difference because, he says, the real demon is a homogenizing globalization that tries to erase those distinct particularities.

> But we must remain conscious of the significance of, and love, our destiny, our destiny to have been born into such a climate. In that this is our destiny we do not thereby become a chosen people without a match in the world; but we can, by maintaining and fostering this destiny, make contributions to the human culture of which no other people is capable. By such contributions we would first give real significance to the fact that every part of the world has its own distinctive character.[90]

In other words, Japan's role in the shared global community is to be itself even as it engages and is affected by other cultures, exactly as he saw the foreign and local elements intermingle in both the Buddhist sculptures of Nara and in the intellectual corridors of his own university. When viewed objectively without any nativist agenda, Japan discovers itself to be a multi-layered, interresponsive field consisting of many elements originally both foreign and domestic.

A remaining question is what specifically Japanese philosophy might be able to offer to the betterment of world culture. Watsuji's answer, and perhaps the basis for a solution to the cultural trauma that so disturbed his father, would be a Japanese contribution to philosophical anthropology, a contribution born of the Japanese *fūdo* but which might have value to people everywhere. To appreciate Watsuji's response, we will engage his theory of "being in the midst" or "betweenness" (*aidagara*) as the common core of both what it means to be human and what it means to be ethical, a theory that served as the cornerstone of his later thinking.

WATSUJI'S ETHICS AS PHILOSOPHICAL ANTHROPOLOGY

Unlike Heidegger, who generally avoided ethical issues, Watsuji believed that any adequate analysis of human existence necessarily involves ethical considerations.[91] As we have seen, Watsuji's analysis in *Fūdo* led to his emphasis on the field of betweenness (*aidagara*) as the basis of our existence, a field that includes our internal relatedness to others. Watsuji developed this argument further in such works as *Ethics as the Study of Human Being* (*Ningen no gaku to shite no rinrigaku*, 1934) and his *magnum opus*, the three-volume *Ethics* (*Rinrigaku*, 1937–1949).[92]

The central point of Watsuji's philosophical anthropology (*ningengaku*—literally the "study" [*gaku*] of "human being" [*ningen*]) can be summarized in the following quote from *Ethics as the Study of Human Being:*

> …Viewed in such a way, we can use the word *ningen* in the double meaning of world (*seken*) and individual person or persons (*hito*).† I would have to say that this best puts into words the essence of human being.
>
> Previously, I gave the historical background borne by the word *ningen*. This is how we try to show the concept of human being through words. *Ningen* means "in-the-world" (*yo no naka*) itself. Yet, it also means as well the individual person who is in the world (*yo no naka ni okeru "hito"*). Therefore, if human being is not simply the individual person, it is also not simply society. Within human being, these two are unified dialectically.[93]

As he had done in his earlier book with the words "being there" and "*fūdo*," Watsuji's point of departure in his ethical theory was to investigate keys terms like "human," "world," and "existence." Again he explored the root meanings of the appropriate Japanese words in contradistinction to Heidegger's etymological discussions of the German. In the Japanese words Watsuji uncovered references to a shared interpersonal space, what he called "being in the midst of person and person" or the "betweenness of person and person" (*hito to hito no aidagara*). That sensitivity to being-in-the-midst again drove Watsuji's philosophy in a direction radically different from Heidegger's.

In Heidegger, human existence was revealed as a being-there, an existence in-the-world but open to Being itself. As Watsuji read him, Heidegger's primary focus was on the individual human being whereas his own was on the interhuman. Watsuji reversed the vector of the analysis, starting with the interaction of betweenness and separating out from it the individual and world. For him, the *aidagara*, the internally related betweenness or in *medias res*, is the primary phenomenological term. Human existence does not discover a world or constitute a world. From its very beginning we find ourselves "in the midst" of a field of engagement.

Watsuji sees his perspective validated in the Japanese word for human being, *ningen*. The first sinograph *nin* (pronounced *hito* when occurring by itself)

---

† Watsuji commonly advances his analysis by spinning off and reconstituting the sinographs found in central compound words. In this case *hito* is an alternate pronunciation for the *nin* (人) of *ningen* (人間), while the *ken* 間 of *seken* (世間) is the same as the *gen* of *ningen* and the *aida* of *aidagara* (間柄). Thus, the vocabulary of *aidagara* has its own semantic *aidagara*.

means individual human being (or individual human beings) and the second character, *gen* (pronounced when occurring by itself either *aida* or *ma* in the sense of either "between" or "space") means a shared space. Thus, for Watsuji, the concept *ningen* suggests neither that society is simply a collective of individuals (as argued by the western political theory of social contract and by the individualism theory of existentialism, for example) nor that the individual is just a social construction (as presented, for instance, by Confucianism and Marxist theories of economic determinism). Rather, Watsuji insists, human being is foundationally a concrete event or field out of which we abstract both a commonly shared existence (the world both social and natural) and an existence as an individual. That abstraction then allows us to see those two in a dialectical interplay.

Let us think again of a magnetic field as an analogy. A magnetic field—a concrete single event—can be analyzed as the interaction between a positive and negative pole. That does not imply, however, that the positive and negative poles existed independently and came together to "make magnetism." The magnetic field is the concrete event, whereas the poles and the dynamic between them are subsequently abstracted out of that primary event for the purpose of explanation. The bipolar analysis is neither wrong nor useless, but it is critical to remember it is derivative of the original event, not preliminary to it. To theorize from the ground up, our point of departure should be the true ground: the magnetic field itself or, in the case of philosophical anthropology, the being-in-the-midst of *aidagara*. That is the thrust of Watsuji's analysis and it is not only creative, but also distinctive in the history of philosophy, either western or Asian.[94]

The Dialectical Nature of Watsuji's Ethics

As I explained in Chapter 12, the concept of absolute nothing played a key role in Nishida's later philosophy and the concept of nothing or nothingness continues today to be a keynote for the Kyoto School. In general, nothing or nothingness served two functions within their philosophies, one sometimes eclipsing the other. On one hand, as in Nishida's logic of *basho*, it can be the ineffable ground out of which differentiation emerges. On the other hand, as in Tanabe's logic of the specific, it can be the medium of negation (*hitei*), especially within a dialectical tension between opposing terms. In their personal systems, some individual Kyoto School philosophers preferred to discuss nothingness using the term *mu* ("nothingness") while others preferred *kū* ("emptiness"). Watsuji opted to use the latter.

In his philosophical anthropology, Watsuji uses "emptiness" as a descriptor of "betweenness" and, in doing so, stressed both senses of nothingness, that is, both as the ineffable ground and as the function of negation. As emptiness, betweenness in itself is not yet distinguished from anything else, but it becomes the basis for the bipolar distinction between the individual and social (like the magnetic field's being distinguished into positive and negative poles). Once the poles of the individual (*nin*) and social (*gen*) are established, the movement between the two is via dialectical negation, the other sense of nothingness. Simply stated, within betweenness, the person's change in orientation from the social to the individual is accomplished by negating the social; and the movement from the individual to the social is accomplished by negating the individual. That dialectical tension between opposites is the self-negating betweenness, the living in-the-midst that defines human being as *ningen.*

Let us therefore look more closely at that dialectical function since it is the central dynamic in Watsuji's ethical theory. To do so for the purpose of this chapter, some simplification is inevitable, but the overall structure is our main concern. Like any dialectical model, it is often initially more intuitive to follow its progressions by thinking of it as referring to a process through time. Therefore, I will first frame Watsuji's dialectic in terms of the course of life from birth to ethical maturity. The explanation is mine, but throughout his three-volume *Ethics*, Watsuji refers to most aspects of these life stages at some point or another so it is an explanation not at all alien to his thinking.

Life stages on the way to moral maturity. As human beings we come into existence as an inchoate, not yet defined but nonetheless real, betweenness. In *Climates and Cultures*, as we have seen, Watsuji used the term "being in the midst" or "betweenness" (*aidagara*) to express the field within which we live, a field that includes the comprehensive climatic milieu, both physical and cultural, as well as our being part of a collective "we." That notion continues into Watsuji's *Ethics*, but in that book he expands the notion of betweenness by associating it with "emptiness," thereby lending it a dialectical function.

At the outset of human life in pregnancy, we find a "person-to-person betweenness" (*hito to hito no aidagara*) in the relationship between the fetus and mother. The pregnant woman and her fetus are in the midst of a complex system in which a baby takes form while the woman's body undergoes striking changes in physiology. During the pregnancy the mother and fetus are so intertwined as to be indivisible. Only at birth does a separation between the two begin and the baby (let us assume for the sake of explanation a boy) now exists separately from the mother. Yet, the newborn remains totally dependent on the mother for his continued survival.

Still, that dependency is not completely unidirectional. As Watsuji notes, the mother is always watching for the child and the child for the mother.[95] So, the two humans, baby and mother, become a single social space—the *gen* of *ningen*.[96]

As our newborn grows into an infant, he gains some independence as an individual, showing the beginnings of a "personality" (*jinkaku*, which was also the word usually used to translate Kant's German word *Person*).[97]* Rather than an affirmation of a pre-formed inner essence as if it were the blossoming of a bud, the personality, according to Watsuji, takes shape through a process of negation. We can observe that negating of the social as the baby no longer always wants to be held, sometimes offering resistance to being picked up, for example. As he learns to speak, he asserts his freedom linguistically (most dramatically in the emphatic "no!" of the two-year old).

That radical individualism itself gets negated as the child learns manners and, to gain the approbation of his elders, willingly surrenders some individual autonomy to the social (the community of parents, siblings, playmates, teachers, etc.). The child learns to share and "play nice" with other children. School attendance emphasizes and reinforces this socialization, negating some options of radical egocentric individualism. For reasons I will explain below, Watsuji thinks this is the first appearance of the child as moral agent. Essentially, the child voluntarily negates some of his individualistic *nin* in favor of reengaging the social *gen*.

If the social pressure to conform (the *gen* side of *ningen*) becomes too strong, that can again lead to a negation that affirms the radically free individual over the social (perhaps the "rebel without a cause" of a teenager) but then the adolescent eventually gets pulled back toward the *gen* as he freely chooses to negate some individual freedom to join the workplace, start a family, and so on.

That ongoing dialectical tension, Watsuji claims, defines our lives as human betweenness, our living in-the-midst. Our humanity is not a what, but a how, whose character is to be continually *emptying* what it has been so it can be what it should be, an emptying (*kū*) defined in terms of the oscillation between *nin* and *gen*. If Watsuji were inclined to use the argot of the Kyoto School (and their German idealist exemplars like Fichte or Hegel), he might have lapsed into speaking here of "absolute contradictory self-identities." Perhaps his literary sensitivities restrained his indulging in such locutions.

Let us turn now more specifically to the ethical implications of being in the midst of that dialectic. In the first stage of moral development (the inculcation of moral values in the school child in my temporal characterization), we are pulled toward the social and communal, the *gen* side of the polarity. In that stage we learn the social norms of our society and conform to them either willingly or by submitting to externally imposed discipline. Watsuji believes that traditional Confucianism analyzes this stage of development very well, but according to him, runs the danger of never getting beyond it.

When pushed to the extreme, Confucianism can lead to a view wherein the social roles exhaust the meaning of who one is: the individual becomes no more than a unique collection of role-dictated behaviors. In that context what makes me different from you, for example, is that my filial piety is directed toward my parent and yours toward your parent, but the basic morality of filial piety (combined with the other "constant" Confucian virtues) defines ethics uniformly and universally. For Watsuji, that reduces *ningen* to merely *gen,* endangering the existence of individuality and personal expression (as well as, as I will discuss later in this chapter, nullifying a standpoint from which the individual can criticize the social status quo). One of Watsuji's critiques of Marxist socioeconomic determinism arose from a similar concern: it is susceptible to devaluing individual agency in the name of socioeconomic class consciousness. The same criticism would hold for any sociological reductionist whose social analysis of human existence obliterates the reality of autonomous individuals.

That danger of reductionism shows the need for a second stage of moral development, a negation of that social self as a move toward the individuality of the self, the *nin* of *ningen.* In that movement we find the emergence and expression of personal human freedom, a necessary aspect for any fully developed human being and a *sine qua non* for ethical conduct. Freedom (as in Nietzsche?) can only emerge as the negation of the inherited social order.

Watsuji believed the West, especially the United States, exemplifies this moment of the dialectic very well, but like the Confucians, runs the danger of becoming fixated in an extreme version of its position, creating an imbalance. In negating the *gen,* one can reduce the person to just *nin,* nothing more than an individual as in Søren Kierkegaard's self-chosen epitaph "That individual." By the attempt to preserve personal freedom and individual rights, however, the social dimension loses its priority as an essential feature of human existence. Again, the *aidagara* is brought into an imbalance and abandons its self-negating, self-"emptying" character.

Watsuji believes, as a result, that the fully moral human being only becomes possible when there is the "negation of the negation." That happens when the person moves on to the next moment in the dialectic, negating one's radical individualism as a *freely chosen* decision to rejoin the social. By doing so, one chooses to surrender some options of total freedom in order to find at least partial personal fulfillment in the social order. At this point, the person is once again in the *gen* side, but that *gen* is not compelled or imposed by an authority external to the individual, but instead, it is a *gen* that has been freely chosen by the *nin* from within the midst of its own individuality.

According to Watsuji, there is no true morality in either the *gen* or the *nin* alone. Ethics arises only when the original socially imposed, communally shared value system is negated in favor of the individual and then that individual *autonomously chooses* to be part of the social. There must be that double negation for the *ningen* to find its fullest human expression. In that respect, our humanity is both a given and an achievement. It is a given insofar as we are all born in the midst of that betweenness defining what we are, but it is also an achievement insofar as to maintain our humanity with full authenticity we must recognize and enact the double negation. To be a human being is to engage what we are (*ningen*), and to engage what we are is to be continually emptying ourselves into what we aspire to realize (*ningen*).[98] The end result is that ethics is the study of what it means to be really and fully human.

Ethics as Changing Interrelations

When I gave the thumbnail sketch of his philosophical anthropology as it could be applied to the moral development of an individual from birth to moral maturity, the implication was that the mutual negations between *nin* and *gen* would be ongoing. That is, after an initial double negation (for instance, in the transition from an infant as totally dependent on the mother—pure *gen*, as it were—to the two-year old who as *nin* says "no" in the face of adult authority, to the school child as *gen* who becomes socially well adjusted), there would be further double negations (from good student to rebellious teenager to responsible family head, and so forth).

We might try to explain those double negations as biologically predestined stages of physical maturity: accompanying changes in conceptual and linguistic capacity for the youngster or hormonal shifts for the adolescent, for instance. Yet, as we have seen in his critique of naturalistic environmental determinism, Watsuji rejects the premise that material factors alone can ever generate ethical norms. That was one of his criticisms of Marxism as well. So, what supplies the impetus for the negations at the heart of his theory of ethics? In answering that question, Watsuji delved more deeply into how negation works in our becoming fully human, living out that tension in the midst of *nin* and *gen*.

Watsuji's logic of negation. Watsuji understands negation in terms of its core emptiness:

> Indeed, there are three moments that are dynamically unified as the movement of negation: fundamental emptiness, then individual existence, and social existence as its negative development. These three are interactive with one another in practical reality and cannot be separated.[99]

He further stated the "basic principle of ethics" to be "the movement in which absolute negativity returns back through itself through negation."[100] What does that mean? Let us begin by returning to the way I characterized the development of the individual from womb to moral maturity.

In first explaining a complex dialectical system, I noted it often helps to think of the logical relations as a temporal sequence: "first this; next this; then that." Such an explanation can only take us so far, however, because logical relations are not inherently temporal. For example consider this if-then statement that clearly implies temporality: "If we finish the meeting early, then we will be home in time for the game." Finishing the meeting must occur before being home for the game. But contrast that with the following if-then statement "If it is raining, then there is moisture in the air." Such an if-then statement is strictly logical—the raining does not occur before the moisture's being in the air.

The raining is a *logical* but not temporal priority that could be expressed symbolically as follows. If (if p then q) is true, then whenever p is the case, q is the case; but if p is not the case, we cannot know if q is the case. Plugging in the variables and expressing the logical relation in language more akin to ordinary English we have: "assuming it is true that whenever it is raining there is moisture in the air, then if it is raining there is moisture in the air; but if it is not raining, there may or may not be moisture in the air." (For example, it might not be raining but only very humid or foggy.) Note that the sequence is logical with no reference to temporal succession.

In the quotation above in which Watsuji discusses the three moments of the dialectic, he was addressing its *logical* character, a character that is not necessarily temporal.[†] Temporally related facts (finishing the meeting vs. being home for the game) are separable, whereas strictly logical relations are not (the rain and the atmospheric moisture). The point for Watsuji is that *nin* and *gen* are logically interdependent terms and, as such, one cannot exist or have meaning without the other.[101]

For that reason, when my simplified account spoke of *nin* as negating *gen* or vice versa, the negating function could not logically *annihilate* the opposite pole. In Watsuji's theory, to be an individual is to be an-individual-as-opposed-to-the-social; to be the social is to be the-social-as-opposed-to-being-an-individual. If either pole were to completely eradicate the other, neither pole could exist. There cannot be a positive pole in a magnetic field without a correlated negative pole and vice versa. If the individual were to completely disappear into the social or the social into the individual, therefore, both poles would disappear into the foundational emptiness, the betweenness as what is not yet differentiated. That is a rather subtle and technical distinction. Why does Watsuji need to stress it?

---

† The word "moment" in the quotation above does not refer to a temporal instant. In dialectical logic, a moment is a pivoting point between a term and its opposing twin term.

For Watsuji, even as the social is negated for the sake of expressing the freedom of the individual, the individual—to maintain its identity as individual—must maintain a role for the social. To be an individual is to set oneself apart from the social. Without the social, the single human being is a loner, not an individual. Any movement toward individuality must stop short of completely abandoning the social. For example, even the aforementioned rebellious teenagers who claim to reject the values of U.S. society do so as *American* teenagers, drawing on the language of political or social rights, including its history from the dissidents of the American Revolution, through Henry David Thoreau's civil disobedience, up to Rosa Parks and her refusal to sit at the back of the bus. That is why a demand for personal expression often assumes the form of a counter-cultural *social* movement: the hippies, the early women liberationists, Green Peace activism, or today's Goths, for instance. To oppose and affirm the *nin* side over the *gen* side requires the *gen* to remain to some extent, even if only as the target of criticism.

If I oppose the social status quo, therefore, I have two options. First, I can dismiss the status quo while recognizing it (I can "drop out" but only insofar as I maintain the reality of what I am dropping out *of*). The other alternative is that I can be an agent of change who confronts the social as a critic, prophet, innovator, revolutionary, or whatever. In Watsuji's ethical system, the first option is amoral insofar as it tries to elude the dialectic of *ningen* by avoiding moral activity or conduct (*kōi*). By so doing, he insisted, I would be inauthentic to what I am as a human being. So, it is the second option—that of confrontational opposition—that interests him. To understand his position on this point, I must explain more fully his view of how conduct or moral action defines us as human beings.[102]*

For Watsuji, moral action is a distinctively human form of behavior because it involves more than animal activity or simple animated movements. Arising from the betweenness of *ningen*, moral action always contains a dual negation, simultaneously pulling us toward both the social and individual poles defining our human existence. That view of our ethical predicament differs somewhat from the way ethical dilemmas are often posed in western theory.

In the West we commonly think of an ethical problem as arising when I must choose between two or more actions in the future. I use my reason to imagine and analyze the alternatives, whereas my will enables me to pursue one option or another once I have reached my decision. For Watsuji, however, the ethical predicament is less about future action than about present self-definition: how am I to be? That question is inseparably both about me as free individual (the *nin* pole) and about me as a social being living in a particular collective and physical place (the *gen* pole). Thus, moral action is not simply a movement carried out by an individual; it must always occur vis-à-vis a social awareness as well. Whenever a human being acts ethically, the agency involves both an individual and social dynamic.

For that reason newborn infants, insofar as they have not yet fully differentiated the social and individual, are capable of human movements but not moral conduct.

> What can be said of the *movements of an infant? Moral conduct* can never be ascribed to an *infant*.... An infant does not stand in opposition to the mother or its baby-sitter as an individual. Even when it is fretful, an infant does not assume an attitude of acting contrary to the various connections with its protectors. What is recognized in the infant is its possibility of becoming an individual but not its actuality. For this reason, even though the movements as well as the attitudes of the mother... bear the meaning of moral conduct, the infant's movements corresponding to them are not to be regarded as moral conduct.

By that analysis, then, the mother is expected to act morally in her caring for the infant, even though the infant, not yet capable of such conduct, can only respond with reactive movements. The infant can react socially to the mother's actions, but cannot yet interpret those actions as constituting a social space against which it stands in its own individuality. Because the double negation of *ningen* has not yet crystallized, moral conduct is not yet possible. (Of course, the *possibility* of that conduct is discernible in the human infant and the process of child-rearing is aimed at actualizing that possibility.)

Besides that of the infant, Watsuji discusses another case in which the moral conduct paradigmatic of *ningen* is not realized, namely, that of a strictly defined, stultified social status quo in which people behave robotically without reflection or resistance. Watsuji acknowledges, of course, that the past influences present relationships, but that should never mean the past *determines* the present. If past social relations ever completely determine social relations in the present, then there is no room for the double negation that defines *ningen* and therefore no ethical conduct is even possible.

> If it is supposed that the past is an interactivity of subjects and that each of these activities is determined by the established relationships between these subjects, it is obvious that the moral conduct is burdened with the mutual relationships of the past. But this is not yet to establish moral conduct. The interactivities of subjects, no matter whether they move in the direction of revolting against each other or in coming into unity cannot be activities unless they involve in advance relationships that do not yet exist.[104]

In short: for ethical relations to occur, the relevant parties must recognize the impact of past interrelations, but only as part of an effort to establish new relations. There is no ethics in simply maintaining a status quo because, says

Watsuji, e*thical conduct entails changing the status quo of present interrelations.* An ethical agent is always, in that respect, an agent of change.

867–9

Such an ongoing reconstitution of interrelations, Watsuji maintains, can effectively occur only in a context of "trust" and "truth."[105]* Although those terms certainly have important roles in western ethics, when they appear in a modern Japanese context, the Confucian and Shintō overtones become critical. "Trust" is one of the primary Confucian virtues driving harmonious interpersonal relations while "truth" (as genuineness) is fundamental to all Shintō relations involving human beings.[106] Watsuji linked trust and truth by arguing that trust lies in one's relying on the other to be genuine and forthright. In effect, to be genuine is to be trustworthy.

324–8

In our historical overview, we have already seen Shintō and Confucianism fused in Yamazaki Ansai's seventeenth-century Suika Shintō.[†] The difference between Ansai's and Watsuji's projects is instructive, however. Ansai theorized that both Confucianism and Shintō derived from a common element of *reverence,* a human sensitivity to the transcendence of either the Confucian Heaven or the Shintō *kami.* Furthermore, he believed that the link between the transcendent and this world was related to the function of "principle" (*ri;* C. *li*). Thus, Ansai suggested reverence had a metaphysical anchor.

Watsuji's theory, on the contrary, has no role for a transcendent object of reverence outside this world. His philosophical anthropology recognizes nothing outside the human that one can revere. Even more strongly, Watsuji's discussion of truth, with its emphasis on the authenticity of *ningen,* precludes any consideration of something like *ri* that connects this world to a metaphysical reality. Consequently, although some of his terms—emptiness, trust, genuineness, and so forth—have associations with spiritual traditions, Watsuji's ethics is strictly humanistic (or secular) as opposed to religious. Still, even if ethics is not directed toward a transcendent value, it must, to be an ethics at all, be normative in some sense. There must be value *somewhere.* Where?

Watsuji had one obvious option: value must be found in the dynamic of *ningen* itself, a dynamic permeated with trust and reliance, both in oneself (the *nin* side human being) and in the collective (the *gen* side of human being). It is not in God (or *kami*) we trust, but in the interrelationality of *ningen.* We do not seek truth outside us (or in some abstract principle). Rather we discover it within us as *ningen,* our fundamental humanity living in the midst of those to whom we must be true. This brings us to the role of value in Watsuji's system.

† See pages 325–6.

Watsuji on Good and Evil

Let us begin by returning to Watsuji's description that ethical action or moral conduct creates new interrelationships. He pointedly said (in a passage previously quoted on page 501 above) that the innovation itself is the decisive aspect, "no matter whether [agents] move in the direction of revolting against each other or in coming into unity." In other words, although moral action is defined by its effort to change the status quo, that change can be either to make the interrelational bonds stronger or to subvert them.

I take this to mean that for your conduct to as moral or immoral, you must either be asserting your individual freedom against society's status quo or actively advocating society's norms against your present individual benefit. In other words, to act morally, you must either be actively changing yourself for the sake of society or actively changing society for the sake of your individual freedom. If you are not doing one or the other, there is no moral conduct involved, only amoral movement or change. That dynamism defining a person's being fully human and therefore fully moral as *ningen* brings us back to the issue of trust.

Watsuji explicitly rejects a common western notion that ethical human relations arise from trust. Instead he claims that trust is a *product* of being authentic to the inherent "laws" of relationality implied by the concept of *ningen*. Accordingly, he maintains that trust does not lead to relationships but, to the contrary, trust emerges from the dialectic of *ningen* and the relationships it generates. Simply stated, trust arises from the performance of yourself as *ningen*. This has implications for temporality.

For *ningen*, indeed even for either of the *nin* or the *gen* poles of *ningen*, to develop is to have a future. The future of *ningen* entails the trustworthy commitment of your individual dimension to consider the harmony of the collective and of your collective dimension to consider the freedom of the individual. That is, once we recognize human existence as *ningen*, we enter into a promissory relation of being both trustworthy and trusting. To deny that would be to ignore the universal character of human existence as *ningen*, in effect, to be a faulty example of a human being.

Watsuji's emphasis on changing the status quo (of either your individuality or of society) complements his earlier discussion about the double negation. Specifically, in the second negation—when *nin* moves back in the direction of *gen*—the individual may bring a new perspective that might inspire social reflection and a change in the status quo of the *gen*. Notice, however, that Watsuji is at this point defining moral conduct (*kōi*) itself, not necessarily *good* moral conduct. That is, he is distinguishing the moral from the amoral, not the moral from the immoral. "Moral conduct" in his restricted sense can be either good or evil.

Watsuji's ethics is at this point on the brink of going in a direction that will be a shock to readers who are deeply vested in the discourse of mainstream western ethics. To some such readers, Watsuji's position will seem patently wrong, even dangerous; to others, it might be considered descriptively true, but bizarre in its mode of expression. As I will now try to show, if we take some common western assumptions about ethics as our starting point, such reactions are understandable. But those very assumptions can also prevent us from truly engaging what Watsuji was trying to assert and, in a fundamental sense, our initial criticism would have no more validity than any other critique based in cross-cultural misrecognition.

In the final analysis, I too will claim there is a logical flaw in Watsuji's theory of ethics, but his error is far more subtle than the types of "problems" that would strike a typical western ethicist who came across Watsuji's conclusions. My project will, therefore, begin by presenting Watsuji's position as an advocate, presenting his case as best as I can without criticism. Only after that will I explain where I think his theory errs. That is, I urge us to engage Watsuji's thought so that we understand it as best as we can before we turn to criticizing it. To help us in that act of engaged knowing, let us consider Socrates as a case study for Watsuji's theory.

Culturally defined good and evil. A loyal citizen and military hero who fought in defense of Athens, Socrates subsequently developed a critical method and personal point of view that put him at odds with the social status quo in his city-state. Through his public philosophical interrogations, he was being true to himself ("know thyself" was his motto). Yet, his public questioning revealed that the generals (like Laches) did not know what courage is, the preachers (like Euthyphro) what piety is, or the sophists (like Gorgias) what rhetoric is. In other words, Socrates did not drop out of the social space of his society (as some Cynics later did, for example). Instead, he went public with critical questioning, bringing "philosophy" to the public forums of Athenian society.

That decision cost Socrates his personal freedom: first incarceration, then trial, and finally execution. Importantly, when given the chance, Socrates *freely chose* to ignore his personal welfare and not take the opportunity to escape from prison and his impending execution. In other words: in asserting his individual convictions, Socrates used the *nin* pole of his human identity to try to negate the uncritical and unreflective status quo of his society, the *gen* pole of his human identity. Subsequently, having failed to change the public value system of Athenian society, he freely submitted his individual freedom and his very life to the moral and political authorities to whom he owed his trust (the *gen* pole of his being a loyal Athenian).

Given the dialectical double negation between *nin* and *gen*, there can be no doubt that Socrates' actions qualified, by Watsuji's definition, as moral rather than amoral. Socrates was certainly acting to change the status quo while recognizing his dual obligations to both the *nin* and *gen* poles of his humanity. Moral conduct, unlike amoral behavior, can be categorized as either good or evil. The question: which was it in the case of Socrates?

First, let's review the basic facts. Socrates' extraordinary moral conduct (not mere amoral behavior) set into play a series of social and philosophical ramifications that eventually created a rift in the Greek's world view of the time, ushering in a new age of critical reflection (some call the change "axial"[107]). Socrates, therefore, changed Athenian thinking by opposing the harmony and stability of his society's status quo. At the time of his philosophical interrogations, his actions were so disruptive that in the minds of most Athenians, it justified his execution. After Socrates' death and upon further reflection, however, the Athenians came to see the insights behind his conduct, so much so as to crown him posthumously as a pioneer in the golden age of Greek philosophy.

Watsuji's system would have us assess the good or evil nature of Socrates' actions in the following way. When Socrates conducted his "Socratic method" in the streets of Athens, his actions *undermined the unity and harmony of the social community*, the city state of Athens. The society as a whole generally deemed his actions to be disruptive, immoral, and impious. The authorities warned him of such repeatedly, but Socrates persisted until put on trial and executed for his crimes against society.

From Watsuji's perspective, there would be nothing problematic here. Society defines the conventions that structure the collective aspect of our living together: the rules of language, the forms of proper behavior and etiquette, the models of education, the responsibilities for public service, and yes, the meaning of normative terms like *good* and *evil*. Only society can judge when conduct is within acceptable norms and when it requires sanctions. By that reasoning, the case of Socrates is clear. His conduct was criminally immoral and his punishment just. The Athenians executed a criminal for his evil conduct.

Watsuji's theory would not have us stop there, however. Socrates' behavior did eventually transform Greek society, leading it toward a new collective identity based on critical reflection and the open exchange of opposing ideas. At that point, the Athenians (indeed western culture at large) came to designate Socrates as *good*. Again, applying the same criteria as before, Watsuji would say that after society changed, Socrates' conduct had posthumously *become* good. Because Watsuji's system denies a transcendent source of principle or divine commands, normative evaluation belongs in the collective (*gen*) pole of our humanity. When society adjudicates an action to be good, it is by definition good; when it adjudicates it to be evil, it is evil.

Such an interpretation runs counter to how ethics is typically viewed in western accounts. Those western evaluations see Socrates as a *good* man who saw *evil* in his society and, at great cost to himself, created a positive change against what had been evil about that society. Watsuji, however, found such explanations circular or wrongheaded. They are circular because they beg the question: by what criterion is Socrates deemed to be inherently a good man even as he undermined the stability of his society? The only answer would seem to be because the society was in some sense bad and so it was good for Socrates to point that out and act to change it.

But that response just shifts the onus of the question. Who or what determines what is good or bad about a society? It cannot be simply *any* individual: we don't want to put Jesus in the same category as Hitler simply because they both addressed what *they* saw as evils in their respective societies. A response might be that only *good* people are morally justified in determining what evils exist in society and should be changed. But that just returns us to our original question: who or what determines which among us are good? If some set of criteria decides it, who picks the criteria?

Suppose it is God or some other transcendent source of value that sets the criteria for distinguishing good from evil. If so, who relates and interprets the divine mandate? The answer would seem to be some special set of prophets or a religious institution. But who decides which prophets or institutions are legitimate and authoritative? *We* do.[108] It seems that no matter how we look at it, good and evil are decided by the *gen* side of *ningen*, not by either the individual or by transcendent deities or universal principles of reason.

Watsuji believed western theories were in denial about how things actually work. The Aristotelians moved moral agency from the *polis* (of the *Politics*) to the individual (of the *Nicomachean Ethics*); Kant ensconced the good in the universal rational laws of the categorical imperative; religious ethicists looked to a nonhuman, transcendent deity for divine mandates. All were invalid attempts to avoid the fact that we as a collective *gen* determine what is good or evil.

The issue of ethical cultural relativism. Watsuji would likely qualify as a cultural ethical relativist in the eyes of many western ethicists. Cultural ethical relativism is the theory that maintains (1) culture defines what is good or evil and (2) there are no ethical universals across cultural differences. Hence, for such relativism, what is good in one culture or at one time may not be good in another culture or another time. Certainly Watsuji's theory fits the good and evil part of the definition. The question is whether if fits the second part.

To be fair, however, we must avoid any cultural misrecognition that derives from naïvely assuming central ethical terms can be applied straightforwardly across languages and cultures. Take, for example, the term *amoral*. When we investigate the definition and role of that term in Watsuji's ethical theory, we find that Watsuji does not so neatly fit the second part of the definition of cultural ethical relativist—the denial of any ethically relevant universals that hold across cultures and times.

In the western tradition the term *amoral* generally refers to some action or attitude that is neither good nor evil; what is *amoral* is outside the realm of morality altogether. As we have seen already, though, Watsuji gives the term a different emphasis. For him to be *amoral* refers to rejecting, ignoring, or (as in the case of a baby) being unable to distinguish the universal nature of *ningen*, and therefore also its attendant qualities of trustworthiness, reliance, and genuineness. Thus, for Watsuji the term "amoral person" is an oxymoron in a way that "good person" or "evil person" are not. To be a person is to live in the midst of *aidagara* and to authenticate it as such by preserving the two poles of the individual (*nin*) and the collective (*gen*).

In contrast to the western definition, then, an *amoral* individual for Watsuji is *incapable*, whether by disposition or by choice, of being either good or evil. While being always subject to the definition of a society and its particular *fūdo*, good and evil arise from a basis of authentic humanity, one which precedes cultural variation. Even if two people from different cultures would disagree whether a particular action is good or evil, they would both assume that human beings live in the midst of both an individualized and collective identity and that ethics is related to negotiating the tensions that entails.

Following that line of thought, Watsuji's theory would seem to imply sociopathic serial killers, for example, should be universally condemned, but not on the grounds of being evil or immoral. Rather sociopaths do not identify themselves as living in the midst of *ningen* and are therefore unable to recognize the trust and reliance on which the dialectic relation of *nin-gen* operates. For Watsuji the actions of such a murderer would not in themselves technically be "evil" but actually something (in his mind, at least) much worse. Such an agent would be "inhuman."[109]*

Such is the gist of Watsuji's ethical theory. There is, however, one point of slippage in his account, but I think it can be fixed with an analogy from a western philosophical position. The problem is that, when he is careful, Watsuji says the determination of good and evil is based in the *ningen,* but he also often speaks as if the judgment about good and evil lies in the *gen* side of *ningen* alone. In other words, when I said (on Watsuji's behalf) that *we* decide what is good or evil, is that the *we* of the in-the-midst *ningen,* that source of differentiation and dialectical tension between the individual and collective, or is it the *we* of the *gen* side of *ningen* (the "society")? I will try to explain Watsuji's final position, and also an give us insight into why the verbal slippage occurs, via an analogy with the western legal theory of civil disobedience.

Civil disobedience as a possible parallel. Who determines what is *legal*? "We" do. But sometimes an individual (or group of individuals)—part of the we as constituted by written or unwritten social contract—deems some law to be unjust. Then, in acts of civil disobedience, those individuals may break the law, committing an *illegal* act, fully expecting to be punished for it (by incarceration, for example). That is *freely accepted* in hopes of making the general society recognize the injustice in its present laws. If performing civil disobedience works as hoped, the *illegal* act will become the impetus for the society to change the law so that what was *illegal* will become at some future point *legal*.

For example, consider when Rosa Parks refused the white bus driver's command to give up her seat and go to the back of the bus. As a "Negro" in 1955 Montgomery, Alabama, she committed what was undeniably an illegal act in that time and place. Yet, if a bus driver in that same city today tried to force a person to sit in back of the bus on the basis of race, the *bus driver's* action would be illegal. In fact, Rosa Parks' illegal action was a factor in changing the society's view of justice such that what was illegal is now legal and vice versa. It would be strange to say Rosa Parks' conduct was legal at the time because we *now* consider it legal. Indeed, unless we recognize the illegality of Rosa Parks' action, we will miss the entire dynamic of how "we" make and change laws, of how the illegal can later become legal through the courage of individuals.

Indeed, if Rosa Parks, and other heroic people like her, had not knowingly and self-consciously violated the law, the Jim Crow laws might never have been repealed. Parks had identified an inconsistency in the U.S. legal system that supposedly maintained, on one hand, the principle that all people are created equal and, on the other hand, the legal enforcement of racial segregation. Typically, an individual who performs civil disobedience respects the rule of law as part of the community in which that person lives. Yet, *at the same time* that individual takes actions against some law that should be changed *for the community's own sake*, not just for that of the individual taking the action.

Of course, the violator of the law will likely be prosecuted and penalized (the publicity triggered by that prosecution may be part of the action's purpose). Given that ensuing punishment, it would seem the act of civil disobedience must be more than a desire for one's own personal well-being. Rosa Parks did not refuse to move simply because she was tired. That would have been no more than an affirmation of her individuality. No, her action was also an assertion of her being in the midst of the individual-society dialectic such that she was refusing the order on behalf of society as well as herself. Indeed, in such cases the individual as *nin* stands opposed to one aspect of the community as *gen*, even while affirming one's membership in that *gen*. If we substitute "good" and "evil" for "legal" and "illegal," the analogy with Watsuji's argument becomes clear.

Watsuji would find it strange to say Socrates' actions were "good" when he tried to rip apart the fabric of authority, the store of accepted knowledge, and bases of value in his contemporaneous Athenian society. Watsuji would also say that today it would be equally strange to say Socrates' social critiques, philosophical reflections, and argumentative dialogues were "evil." *Good* and *evil* are, we might say, defined by the intellectual and social *fūdo* of the time and place. and are, therefore, fluid.

Good and *evil* are, after all, words or concepts. Watsuji can find no special quality in their use or meaning that would set them apart from other words or concepts. If Watsuji's theory does something universal, it is in our recognition that we live in the ineluctable dialectic of *nin* and *gen*. To Watsuji's thinking, to live otherwise would be a denial of our humanity. Action emitting from the *nin* pole without regard for the *gen* would be simply criminal. Action emitting from the *gen* without regard to *nin* would be robotic. While he would not say that those who deny that dialectic are immoral, he would say they are amoral. And those who are amoral, by his definition, negate their own humanity.

Using the analogy of civil disobedience, we can better understand the shift in the meaning of the "we" as what determines good and evil in Watsuji's ethics. On one hand, we can consider where "good" and "evil" come from: the source of the distinction itself. As in civil disobedience's view of the law, good is always in the process of being defined in the mutual negating functions of the individual pole of our existence vs. the social pole. So, in that sense, "we" is the being in the midst of "I" and "the society," and that may require doing or saying what is "not good" as presently defined.

On the other hand, we can consider who finally articulates (in the present betweenness) the consensus of the society about what is good or evil. In that case, the court of last resort is the society as *gen*. As in the legal analogy, once the Supreme Court rules that the "law of the land" is such-and-such, no individual can argue that is *not* the law; one can only argue for a change in the law (or its present interpretation as established by precedent). Analogously, in Watsuji's ethics, once the society deems that something is good, the individual has no basis for saying otherwise. Rather, one can only hope (and act) to change the society.

I hope my efforts at contextualization and analogy have helped us engage Watsuji's theory enough that we have overcome any residual cultural biases that would lead us to dismiss it out-of-hand as simply patently false or descriptively bizarre. That said, it remains provocative and, to those encultured in western ethical philosophy, likely still disconcerting. Some of us may not be completely comfortable with the idea that good, like law, is an evolving conception based in an ever-changing social consensus about what is right, a consensus that can be affected by the disruptive ("evil") actions of individuals. Yet, we can now see it is at least an *arguable* position worthy of our understanding and evaluation. Let us turn now to how Watsuji expanded his ideas to a theory of the state, a theory that involves his understanding of "totality." After that, I can turn to what I see as the weak point in his theory.

FROM ETHICS TO THE STATE

To understand Watsuji's theory of the state, we need to be clear what he means by totality as contrasted with unity. If we think of unity as oneness, when unity is established, the parts constituting it dissolve into the whole like drops of water disappearing into an ocean. By contrast, a totality is a whole that preserves its parts without dissolving them into one: a magnet is a totality of individual molecules of iron aligned so that all their positive poles face in one direction and negative poles in the other. The individual molecules do not dissolve into the totality, but rather keep their "individuality." Similarly, in a mosaic the totality of the picture does not dissolve the individuality of the tiles, but those tiles are meaningless—they depict nothing—unless they are part of the totality.

In Watsuji's terminology, *individuality* refers to an individual within a totality. Thus, an individual person is not an isolated being (a pure *nin*, as it were), but only acquires individuality as he or she becomes part of the dialectical betweenness of *ningen*. In his evaluation of Hegel's philosophical anthropology, Watsuji criticized Hegel for making the political goal of his dialectical system an absolute that logically swallowed up or sublated the ethnic people (German. *Volk*; J. *minzoku*). We could say Hegel had generated an abstract, absolute ideal of the state without any concrete, actual people in it.[110]

Watsuji's idea of the state, by contrast, was a totality that included the "people" without dissolving them into an abstract unity. For Watsuji, there is no totality of the state (*kokka*) without the people (*minzoku*). The *minzoku* as defined in relation to the totality of the *kokka* has its own "individuality," what we commonly call a people's "ethnicity."

Watsuji ranked social totalities[111]* in terms of size and inclusiveness. For example, a family is a totality consisting of a small group with its own dialectical tensions between individuals and kin. A clan functions similarly but its group is greater in size and inclusiveness, a religion more so, and beyond that, the ethnic group or people (*minzoku*). Significantly, Watsuji stopped his hierarchy of totalities short of the totality of humanity at large. For him, to universalize humanity obliterates cultural differences and ends up being an empty abstraction, what he might disparage as Hegelianism.

A cultureless human being was to Watsuji an oxymoron. Since the greatest totality of *ningen* is the ethnic people, Watsuji made the people virtually equivalent to the state, the greatest political totality. As I will argue later, there are some serious philosophical problems with his theory of totality, but first, it is illuminating to see how Watsuji's standpoint gave him a stage for a critique against western imperialism.

Citing examples of empires ranging from ancient Rome to his contemporaneous United States, Watsuji argued that the western ideology of imperialism proceeds from a faulty philosophical anthropology and, therefore, is incapable of treating people morally. Specifically, that ideology assumes that there is a universal human nature underlying cultural difference and that such a universal quality should inform state organization. All people are understood to be alike in having the same needs and wants (whence comes a theory of universal human rights, itself often arising from thought experiments of the "state of nature" genre) and, as Hobbes argued, all people have the same dangerous inclinations such as greed and ambition (whence comes the authority of the state to impose sanctions).

Based on those assumptions, western imperialism sees the role of the state as bringing about material well-being, safety, and (following Francis Bacon) the dominance of nature through technology. The nations who are best at fulfilling that role are entitled, perhaps even obligated, to employ their system to regulate other countries through imperial expansion. Since all people are in essence the same, one system fits all. So why not have everyone under the same, most effective, system?

If one accepts that justification for western-style imperialism, colonization ultimately benefits the colonized by bringing them "civilization." Such civilizations are then typically ranked in terms of a universal set of criteria, evaluations that commonly privilege material excellence (size of monuments, efficiency of social organization, military strength, etc.) over cultural refinement.Such a way of thinking nullifies the role of culture in society. A mirror image of Hegel's idealist absolute, such a materialist absolute as a criterion for evaluating civilizations has no room for the diversity of cultures or the various ethnic peoples who live in dialectical interplay with them. Such, argued Watsuji, is the rationale behind western imperialist expansion from ancient times up to the present. He was sure Japan could pose an alternative.

Watsuji believed Japan could facilitate, at least in East Asia, a federation of nation states, each with its own cultural and political self-determination but united against western military expansion.[113*] The advantage of envisioning the state as a totality along the lines he outlined, Watsuji argued, is that such a state is internally all-inclusive of its people (all the Japanese people are included in Japan, for example), but it is self-contained and need not oppose the formation of other nation states, that is, other political totalities generated by other "peoples."[114] As we saw even in his early theory of *fūdo*, Watsuji's vision of globalism was that each country should be free to develop out of its own *fūdo*, including its own government structure, but to do so in a way that allows other peoples in other countries to do the same for themselves.

For Watsuji, the Pacific War (the Pacific theater of World War II) was a conflict over competing ideologies of empire, each arising out of its own philosophical anthropology. The first (western imperial) anthropology assumes that human beings, in all the most important and fundamental senses, are universally the same. So, global politics should develop in a manner guaranteeing that sameness (through universal human rights, for example), while using uniformity of needs and desires to build a worldwide network of technological and economic development, thereby improving the material well-being of everyone.

The other (theoretically, Japanese imperial) anthropology assumes that human beings, in all the most important and fundamental senses, attain their human individuality and dignity by being "of a people," by flourishing within an interresponsive field of local physical and cultural conditions. So, global politics should develop in a manner guaranteeing the preservation of those varying local conditions and the polities that have arisen within them. Global politics should take its mission to be truly inter-national, not trans-national, protecting local differences in human environments rather than trying to transcend them. It may be universally true that all *homo sapiens* share the need for a minimal daily intake of calories and nutrition, for example, but that does not mean everyone in the world should eat the same food.

As we will find in Chapter 14, a cohort of mid-twentieth-century Japanese philosophers viewed the War as one of competing ideologies of empire. For them, that conflict constituted a "moment of world history," that is, a pivotal point of global significance. For the first time Japan was playing a role on the *world* stage, in the vanguard against a form of western imperialism that had imperiled the sovereignty of Asian cultures for centuries. For the first time in modern history, they argued, there was an Asian nation that had mastered military technologies and could now stand up to the western imperialist powers.

Of course, if any of those Japanese intellectuals actually believed that the Greater East Asian Co-prosperity Sphere functioned in the way they idealized, that the Japanese expansion into the rest of East Asia and the Pacific was carried out in any way differently from any other imperialism, they were grossly deluded. Their theoretical support for a vision, however naïve, of what Japan could do for East Asia was quickly interpreted by the government as support for its military agenda. Watsuji generally seemed to accept that interpretation, tweaking his philosophy by including nationalistic catchwords. He also focused his criticism less generally at the West and ever more pointedly at the United States, the first western imperial power to enforce its will on Japan in the nineteenth century and its main adversary in the ongoing Pacific War. Watsuji's complicity in supporting government policies was even more visible in his valorization of the emperor system.

The Japanese Imperial System

The Japanese emperor system, Watsuji argued, is the most effective form of government for maintaining the highest level of totality, the state. To help us understand that claim, I first want to stress what Watsuji did *not* say. Unlike the official State Shintō ideology of the time, Watsuji did not accept the myths of divine origin as literally true; nor did he think of the emperor as an incarnate god sitting on the throne. Watsuji emphasized the *reverence* for the emperor more than the emperor himself. Again, though, it is important to recognize what Watsuji's emphasis on reverence is *not*. It is not a reverence directed toward an object beyond the human world as we find in the Confucian-Shintō syntheses of Yamazaki Ansai and Yoshikawa Koretari in the seventeenth century, for example.[†]

For Watsuji, the emperor was an open-ended symbol (actually a kind of emptiness) in this world, a creation of the people to focus and unify themselves into a state. In that respect, Watsuji believed the function of the emperor system to be primarily ethical, rather than religious or even simply political. The absoluteness of the emperor system, therefore, is in the *function* of the emperor, not the physical person of the emperor. Stated another way, for Watsuji, the emperor system is about *how* reverence creates a totality, not *what* is revered.

Revering the emperor is the absolutely totalizing function that makes possible a unified *Japanese* state. That is why, he thought, the Japanese system is not exclusivist like the "jealous God" of the Abrahamic traditions who will not tolerate other gods. The Abrahamic religions had made a divine person (rather than reverence for that divinity) into their absolute. As an absolute being, that God had to be perfect, infallible, completely just, and omnipotent. Given that metaphysical framework, there indeed could be no room for other gods.

Shintō, by contrast, has multiple deities who are not perfect, infallible, or absolute. Yet the Japanese people's *veneration* of them can be absolute. The emperor, therefore, symbolizes that venerating attitude and conduct (the emperor is not, as a person, the *object* of that veneration). In terms I have used

† See pages 325–7.

previously, the emperor symbolizes *how* the Japanese feel united in a totality not *what* makes them feel that way.[115]

Throughout Japanese history, Watsuji claimed, reverence for the emperor has remained a constant even alongside the flourishing of imported traditions like Confucianism and Buddhism. As he did when he spoke of the Japanese military expansion into the rest of East Asia and the Pacific, however, Watsuji often seasoned his philosophical analysis with the slogans of the imperial state. In doing so, he admittedly often gave those rallying cries his own spin, making them less fanatical, more reasoned than emotional. Again, it is important to remember that Watsuji was a secular humanist not prone to religious fervor of any hue. Still, he did little to disassociate his philosophy from the official state ideology and he continued to defend the imperial system vociferously even after the war had ended.

In designing his philosophical system of greater totalities, Watsuji committed a logical error, however. It goes back to the two senses of betweenness mentioned earlier: the betweenness of emptiness that logically precedes and makes possible the differentiation and logical tension between *nin* and *gen* (also called the *originary totality*) vs. the betweenness inherent in the collective pole, the *gen* of the *ningen*. That is, *ningen* is one kind of betweenness, namely, one that exists in the tension *between* the individual and the collective. The other kind of betweenness is that of collective itself (*gen*); as a collective, it is a totality between or among *people*. In my discussion of good and evil, I noted that Watsuji sometimes collapsed those two meanings of betweenness, but with the analogy of law in the western civil disobedience theory, I was able to offer a way of understanding Watsuji's point so that the conflation was not fatal to his system. That is not so easy to do in defense of his theory of the state, however, as I will now explain.

The danger in conflating the two senses of betweenness became critical when Watsuji introduced the assumption that a more inclusive totality supersedes a less inclusive totality because it involves a greater "unity of actions."[116]* That is, the greater the totality, the greater the number of people acting in unison with a common sense of purpose. What are these ever greater totalities? Presumably, Watsuji meant something like the following.

As a Japanese individual, I would yield some of my autonomy to my nuclear family, of my nuclear family to my extended family, of my extended family to my neighborhood, of my neighborhood to my city, and so on up to the level of the Japanese people at large. Or politically, each group (the political party, the military, the clergy, the intellectuals, etc.) yields some of its autonomy and distinctiveness for the sake of the greater totality, building up to the nation as a whole. As a consequence, Watsuji's system ends up equating the nation and the people; one's identity as a member of the Japanese people is fundamentally the same as one's identity as a member of the Japanese nation since both "nation" and "the people" refer to the same thing—the totality of Japanese.

This brings us to the critical issue. If human being is necessarily always *ningen*, what happens to the *nin* on this highest level of totality? As the totality grows larger, not only does the *gen* become larger, but so does the *nin*—expanding as I just suggested as an example from individual, to family, to region, to nation.† In effect, at the highest level of totality, the *nin* becomes all people (*the* people?) and *gen* the state. What then could the *nin* negate itself into or what could the *gen* negate itself into? If the people negates itself into the state or the state into the people, the totality is negating itself into an alternative description of what it already is. Like a computer glitch, the dynamism of Watsuji's dialectic freezes into a stasis.

It seems that the only conceivable relational change—and remember that Watsuji maintains that without change, there is no ethics—is the implosion of the complete totality from within. I can only imagine that to be all-out revolution and chaos in which the totality turns against itself. Watsuji's insistence on ever greater totalities, therefore, led him to a totalitarianism in its darkest sense, an authoritarian one in which there is no possibility of constructive alteration. An authoritarian totalitarianism that does not allow internal tensions to evolve can change only through self-destruction. Watsuji's ethical system led him to a vision of the state that was not ethical—indeed not even fully *human*—by his own definition.

I want to stress that this predicament does not result as much from Watsuji's ethical theory as from its (mis-)application. That is, if his theory of totality had not been pushed to the extreme of identifying the people with the state, but instead had maintained some tension between them, the *nin/gen* dynamic could still work and real ethical possibilities for change would remain.

For example, along the lines of a constitutional monarchy, the state (*gen*) could maintain the possibility of freely negating itself in the direction of the people (*nin*) through periodic democratic elections. That would allow for the possibility of the double negation to continue. That is, if the people could use the electoral process to prevent the state from overextending itself, that would be the first negation in the direction of *nin*. Once the election is decided, however, the people would then negate some of their political differences to support the state even when many individuals did not vote for the candidates who won the election. That would be the second negation, the movement from *nin* back to *gen*.

Such a model of the state would not *necessarily* be contrary to Watsuji's vision of philosophical anthropology, the symbolic function of the emperor, and the

---

† This progression may not be as obvious in Japanese as it is in English because the Japanese word *nin*—like most other nouns—can be either singular (a person) or plural (people) in meaning.

dialectic of the double-negation. In my earlier discussion of the atemporal logic of *ningen*,[†] I noted that Watsuji insisted that there could be no dialectical movement in which the *nin* pole *completely* negated the *gen* pole or vice versa. There is no magnetic field without both poles. What Watsuji did not see was that if his idealized view of a perfect totality identified the *nin* and the *gen,* that would also mean there are no longer two poles and the dialectical tension needed for ethics to occur would be lost.

Of course, Watsuji undoubtedly would not have been satisfied with a democratic endpoint for his system of ethics such as the one I suggest. Yet, I believe such an outcome would be logically consistent with his system, at least up to his final move when he made the totality into a unified absolute. Ironically, Watsuji's philosophical anthropology had failed in almost exactly the same way as he had earlier criticized Hegel's for failing, namely, by having the system move toward an absolute unity (or, in Watsuji's case, an absolute totality), the dialectic had nullified the individual.

CONCLUDING EVALUATION

I have previously mentioned the late nineteenth-century Japanese attraction to Mill's utilitarianism and Comte's positivism. At least two reasons for that appeal are likely. First, utilitarianism could resolve ethical dilemmas without recourse to a Confucian canon or Buddhist precepts, which many of Japan's new intellectual elite had come to see as antiquated artifacts of a bygone era. Instead, utilitarianism's methods lay in the comparative analysis of the benefits issuing from the available courses of action, choosing the one with the most utility. Second, in determining that utility, the method was empirical or positivistic, thereby reinforcing Comte's conviction that civilization had moved not only beyond the magical or superstitious stage but also beyond the metaphysical stage of finding value and truth in transcendent principles.

Many intellectuals in the newly constituted Empire of the Rising Sun were ready to welcome the dawning of such a scientistic age. The utilitarianism-positivism combination offered a this-worldly, secular, and humanistic ethics that seemed, to many, to present a viable future for the new Japan. It lost out rather quickly, however, to the ascendancy of State Shintō, interlaced as it was with a militaristic ethos of the Way of the Warrior. It is easy to attribute that ethnocentric shift to the continuing effect of Native Studies, but that is not the whole story, maybe even not the main part of the story.

The victory of the State Shintō ideology over utilitarianism and positivism can be traced as much to European as Japanese ethnocentrism. In the late Meiji

† See pages 499–500.

period many influential Japanese policy-makers and public intellectuals hoped to mold Japan into a modern (imperialist) nation-state along European paradigms: the United Kingdom of 1707, the Italian Kingdom of 1861, and the German Empire of 1871. Those modern nation states had used common language, contiguous territory, historical links, (supposed) blood ties, and claims to shared cultural heritage for nurturing loyalty to a central monarchical authority. To maintain the nation-state, that loyalty had to be vigorous enough to kindle a militaristic nationalism in which "the people" would be willing to make extraordinary sacrifices to "defend the homeland." Thus, the nation-state model typically melded national identity with folk identity. The newly conceived Japanese State Shintō with its *kokutai* ideology could, it was believed, succeed along parallel lines, allowing for appropriate local variations.

That context clarifies both the genius and the tragic application of Watsuji's ethical system. On the positive side, Watsuji had no use for the naïve belief in religious transcendence embedded in State Shintō mythology, nor the blind allegiance to canonical texts, whether the Chinese classics Sorai extolled or the Imperial Rescript on Education Inoue Tetsujirō helped promulgate. Neither would Watsuji countenance a formalistic kowtowing to the Confucian constant virtues or Buddhist precepts. Instead, like utilitarianism, Watsuji's ethical system was completely rooted in this concrete world of social and individual realities.

Unlike the detached, positivistic calculation and weighing of consequences that utilitarianism stressed, however, Watsuji emphasized an engagement with the betweenness of *ningen* that is both what we are and what we should be, a view of human existence that was always emerging from and modifying the *fūdo* in which it takes root. His inspiration was neither positivism nor utilitarianism (both of which purported to be transcultural and universal), but instead the existential and phenomenological project of understanding our human condition as it is lived in its particular physical, social, and cultural milieu. His was indeed an ethics of philosophical anthropology.

As the preceding two paragraphs suggest, there is much we can learn from, and perhaps philosophically salvage, from Watsuji's ethical theory. His system was not foolproof, however, and Watsuji himself was eventually fooled by it. A way to state the problem simply is that Watsuji let the logic of the double negation be overwhelmed by the *gen* of *ningen* in which the highest level of his dialectic transformed *nin* into "the people" (*minzoku*) and *gen* into "the state" (*kokka*), melding them into a totality of "allness" (he used the German *Allheit*).

From a strictly philosophical analysis of Watsuji's system, that result should not have been possible. He had gone to lengths to reveal the fundamental necessity of self-negating structures within both the *nin* and *gen* poles. Anything else would be less than "human." The over-dominance of the *nin* would result in anarchy and social dissolution to such an extent that the individuals had no society against which to define their separateness and uniqueness. The over-dominance of the *gen* would result in a static society unable to adapt to changing circumstances and thereby containing the recipe for its own self-destruction. A fully human society should have to be able to *learn* and *change*.

Without changing interrelationships, he said, there is no possibility for either authentic human beings or ethical conduct. Watsuji did see how the inability to change was poisoning Japanese wartime politics, but he attributed it to the dominant ideology of State Shintō and did not see it lurking between the lines of some of his own theorizing.* How could a philosopher of Watsuji's caliber not recognize that he was violating the implications of his own theory of ethics?

Several explanations suggest themselves. First, of course, is the reality of human frailty. We do not always act in accord with what our own clarity of reason demands and certainly the circumstances of the time propelled his analysis, perhaps leading him to not thoroughly think through all the implications of his ideas. Japan was at war. In fact, it had been involved in one war or another for much of Watsuji's adult life. Yet, the Pacific War (World War II) was the first to endanger Japan's sovereignty since Kublai Khan's failed invasions of the thirteenth century. In Chapter 14, I will address more fully some of those external influences on Japanese political philosophy in the late 1930s and 1940s, but in concluding this chapter, I want us to focus more narrowly on Watsuji's philosophy. Namely, was there something in Watsuji's philosophical system itself that could lead him in such a disastrous direction?

Some frame Watsuji's problem as his system's lack of transcendence: there is no standpoint outside the dialectic of *ningen* from which one might take a critical perspective on *ningen* itself. Watsuji's philosophy was indeed born of and remained within the *in medias res* of human existence. So, the obvious solution, one might think, is to posit something outside the human—some absolute moral imperative, a divine mandate, a transcendent set of rational principles, or a judging God perhaps—to give a standpoint from which one can criticize the system. Unfortunately, however attractive such an option might seem to many of us, such a way of "fixing" Watsuji's system is both simplistic and naïve.

The demand for an external, transcendent standpoint is simplistic for the following reason. Assuming (as I have argued in this chapter) Watsuji's project is to develop an account of ethics based in philosophical anthropology without recourse to any transcendent principle or standpoint, we cannot then say his system fails because it lacks transcendence. That would be like rejecting an argument for atheism on the grounds it lacks a proper place for God. Watsuji's main thesis is that *ethics does not require a transcendent reality*. So, in criticizing it, we have to show exactly how his argument fails on its own terms instead of asserting without proof that it was doomed to fail because its conclusion is false. In other words, we need a detailed analysis of the dialectical nature and inherent emptiness within *ningen*.

As for the naïveté, we should acknowledge the standpoint we take when we see the lack of transcendence in Watsuji's system, seeing it as the fatal flaw that makes criticism impossible. The assumption in that claim is that we cannot critique something unless we can stand outside it, viewing it from a transcendent vantage point. Here there are two problems. First of all, that assumption is false. A case in point: I can "criticize" the way you do something by simply demonstrating a better way to do it. When you see the improvement in results, you will be convinced I am right. No appeal to a transcendent standpoint is needed because the criticism comes from within the system. Parents and teachers correct children that way all the time. And even something as sophisticated and abstract as a geometric theorem can be disproved by showing it leads to a contradiction without having to stand outside geometry to prove a geometric theorem false. Many systems have within them the process to auto-correct.

The second problem in the naïve demand for transcendence is that it is more likely a preference for how to do criticism than the logical demand it is often purported to be. That is, in thinking transcendence is a necessary condition for criticism we are actually reflecting our own cultural *fūdo*, including how modern philosophy developed in the West. It is a cultural bias favoring detachment over engagement as a way of knowing. After all, to claim criticism requires a standpoint outside the system it criticizes is to say we must be disengaged from the system so we can "objectively" evaluate it from "outside." Thus, to criticize Watsuji for trying to build an ethical system without appeal to transcendence is not much more than saying our *fūdo* is better than his *fūdo*, a blustering act of vainglory and not much more.

All this is not to say I agree with Watsuji's overall philosophy of ethics. I do find his phenomenology of human existence to be astute and a powerful corrective to philosophical anthropologies that overly privilege the individual. Furthermore, his analysis highlights the importance of cultural differences and exposes the fantasy of socially constructed identities that assume universal human and social qualities. Watsuji presents us with a view of human existence, agency, and value that is somehow both commonsensical and profound in its implications.

Yet, in its push toward an absolute endpoint, a perfect integrated unity or totality, Watsuji's theory—like so many other rational systems—overextended itself with disastrous consequences. Should that lead us to rethink the nature and limits of reason itself? Can a premodern Japanese philosopher like Shinran, for example, shed any light on this issue? As we will see in the next and final chapter, Japan's defeat in the Pacific War triggered a sequence of cultural and philosophical reflections along those lines that continue up to the present.

14. Aftershocks and Afterthoughts

Postwar to the New Century

> [Japan] will be ... evolving a style more in
> consonance with Japanese traditions
> and really characteristic of the people....
> Frank Lloyd WRIGHT

There is a paradox in writing any history of philosophy. On one hand, the further we go into the past, the less rich is the repository of available details and more alien the context to today's readers. As a result, the historian of philosophy must excavate and sort through the philosophical remnants from the past, piecing together the thoughts of long ago, while devising creative ways to help the audience imagine what it was like to be a thinker in a time and place so distant from ours. On the other hand, in tracing the course of philosophy through the centuries, time assists the historian by eroding what does not endure, creating a record in various textures and hues of the historical strata which have shaped philosophy even as it has carved its way through them.

When dealing with more recent Japanese ideas and events as I will do in this chapter, the situation is reversed. On one hand, as a history of philosophy approaches the present, the resources for research swell and the social contexts of thought look more familiar. On the other, selection becomes more difficult and generalizations more precarious. Time's erosive effect on the present is too slow and too close for us to be sure of its eventual patterns. Are the ideas of today's most touted philosophers of the sort that will prevail to shape the future of philosophy? Or in the time to come will their theories be viewed as idiosyncratic, vapid fads like asking how many angels can dance on the head of a pin? Or even worse, as an epiphenomenon of a "Dark Ages" in which apparently there were few thoughts at all of lasting value.

It is probably a human trait to think always that our own times are groundbreaking, world-changing, and of great import, but as the Dark Ages example reminds us, it might not be so. Perhaps postwar Japanese philosophy, or perhaps postwar philosophy in the world at large, is like an automobile running on idle—consuming energy and generating heat, but going nowhere. Only time can tell for sure; certainly I can't.

In light of this situation, as I deal in this chapter with Japanese philosophy over the past seven decades, my comments will necessarily be more tentative and idiosyncratic. My interest becomes more thematic, rather than driven mainly by the hope of giving a rightful place to the most widely recognized important thinkers. But which themes are most worthy of attention in a book such as this? As I analyze my hunches about what to include, two criteria seem to have had the most weight.

First, all points being otherwise equal, I favor discussion of a theme that connects in some way with the tradition of Japanese philosophy previous to the postwar period. A Japanese philosopher's new twist on the understanding of self, for example, finds a more comfortable home in this book than would, by contrast, a new study in symbolic logic by the same philosopher (which likely would be readily accessible in international journals of logic written in western languages anyway). That criterion not only gives this chapter continuity with what precedes it in this book, but also reflects my own sense of how Japanese philosophy should proceed if it is going to be a vibrant tradition in the future. Simply stated: Japanese philosophers should more generally recognize that although philosophy is a global enterprise, its individual instances commonly reflect a regional flavor.

Consider an analogy from the West. However problematic the nomenclature may have become, full as it is with stark exceptions, it still makes some sense to distinguish an "Anglo-American" from a "Continental" tradition in philosophy. Why can there not be alongside those, again allowing for obvious exceptions, a "Japanese" tradition? Moreover, for the sake of convenience, many students of western philosophy speak unapologetically of, say, "British empiricism" or "German idealism." In a parallel fashion, I would argue, at some point we might identify some "Japanese $x$ism" that is an outgrowth of Japanese philosophy, both traditional and modern. Yet it would not necessarily be limited to Japan any more than German idealism, for example, is limited to Germany. The tendencies I outline in this chapter may be raw material for trends in Japanese philosophizing that could impact philosophy beyond Japan's shores. I will have more to say about this issue in the Conclusion of this book.

Therefore, a second criterion influencing what I include in this chapter is my estimation of whether the theme is presently or potentially of interest to current philosophical concerns outside, as well as inside, Japan. Incidentally, "current philosophical concerns" are not limited to what philosophers in academic philosophy departments write about. There might be an issue concerning the nature or function of language, for instance, that clearly has philosophical ramifications but is more commonly discussed in departments of linguistics, or in foreign language departments involved with translation issues, or in departments of literary criticism. If the faculty of western academic philosophy departments do not want to engage those issues, they may be doing so at the risk of becoming less relevant to their own society's intellectual milieu than they were a century ago, but their decision one way or another should have no bearing on deciding whether a particular question is "philosophical." What counts as "art," to take a comparable issue, is not limited to what academicians in university departments count as art. Art galleries, the news media, museums, and even consumers get to participate in the discussion as well. So should it be with philosophy.

With those prefatory remarks and admonitions behind us, I turn now to the main subject of this chapter, namely, developments in Japanese philosophy from the late war years up to the near present.

WARTIME IDEOLOGY AND ITS PHILOSOPHICAL EFFECTS

Most philosophy in Japan since 1945 has been affected either directly or indirectly by events during the wartime years of the 1930s and early 1940s. The two areas most obviously influenced by intellectual discussions from that era are political theories related to the meaning of national and ethnic identity as well as the broader analysis of what is usually called "modernity." In Chapter 13, I already broached the former in relation to Watsuji Tetsurō and in the chapter preceding that, I deferred discussing Nishida Kitarō's participation in political discussions because, unlike Watsuji, his ideas resonated with a whole school of philosophy (the Kyoto School) and are better understood in that context, which I will address in this chapter. That said, let us start with Nishida's philosophy of the state.

Nishida's Theory of Kokutai

By the 1930s, the Japanese intellectual world had unofficially crowned Nishida as Japan's most eminent philosopher. The government was anxious to enlist his illustrious name on their roll of intellectuals who, like Inoue Tetsujirō, had become outspoken supporters of the imperialist state and its military expansion into East Asia and the Pacific. Unlike Inoue, who was utterly obsequious in currying government favor, Nishida seemed to want to remain above the fray. That left the militarists unsure of exactly where he stood. As I explained in Chapter 12, by the 1930s Nishida was only beginning to leave the more rarefied issues of epistemology (including its relation to ethics and aesthetics) to engage human existence as embedded in concrete historical and social conditions.

Yet, even when he did turn to historical and social conditions, he often couched his theories in abstract and paradoxical terms (such as the "continuities of discontinuities" or the "absolute contradictory self-identity"). The government bureaucrats and censors likely could not make heads-or-tails of such locutions. Furthermore, if the government's ideological watchdogs thought they might judge the tree by its fruits, the political diversity among the Kyoto School philosophers would make ideological generalizations difficult.

For example, the aforementioned Tanabe Hajime (1885–1962), after Nishida the most senior and respected member of the Kyoto School, avidly supported the war effort with public speeches that spun off his logic of the specific and its stress on cultural identity. Judging from the venues of his speeches, he seemed to do so mainly to buttress the spirits of college students going off to war. Additionally, as I will show later in this chapter, among the next generation of Kyoto School philosophers, its most prominent member, Nishitani Keiji (1900–1990), drew on Nazi ideology to discuss the linkage among ethnicity, nationality, and morality.

On the other end of the spectrum, however, Tosaka Jun (1900–1945) broke ties with the Kyoto School to pursue Marxist materialism. Because of statements interpreted as critical of the imperial system and its agenda, he was incarcerated for "thought crimes" in 1938 under the Peace Preservation Law of 1925.[118] He died in prison in 1945. Miki Kiyoshi (1897–1945), another second-generation Kyoto School philosopher, favored the humanistic aspect of Marxism and openly supported a form of democratic socialism. Twice jailed for his leftist leanings, he, too, died in prison one month after the end of the war. Thus, there was simply not enough uniformity in the political ideology surrounding the Kyoto School to attribute definitively a political orientation to its founder.[119*]

By 1944, Nishida finally surrendered to the pressure to make an explicit statement about politics, the Japanese state, and Japan's role in future world history. In his famous essay "Theorizing the *Kokutai*,"† Nishida sated the government watchdogs by feeding them their restricted diet of imperialist terminology: "*kokutai*," "world historical mission," "Greater East Asian Co-Prosperity Sphere," and so forth. The right-wing ideologues drooled at the prospect of having brought over to their side Japan's premier philosopher at the precise point when the war was going poorly and nationalist morale needed boosting.

1025–7

A careful reading of Nishida's text, however, demonstrates how he put his own spin on the terms, situating them in a discourse that actually undermined many main tenets of the official state ideology. For example, he explicitly denied

---

† For the definition and explanation of *kokutai* and its role in Japanese political thought, see page 407.

that Japan was founded by *kami*, that *kokutai* is a unique form of government only able to exist in imperial Japan, and that the nation is built on a foundation of racial identity. For Nishida, race, nation, and *kokutai* were not metaphysical or theological categories, but rather constructs of identity that arise when a people reflect on themselves as having a shared mission in history. He sometimes said that the people make themselves into their own "world," that is, they forge themselves into a collective agency with a normative agenda.

Consequently, Nishida thought the idea of *kokutai* emerged from an interpenetration of religious and political ideologies, but it was unlike the divine right theory of the medieval West. According to Nishida, the divine right of kingship claimed a transcendent sacred source acting in the immanent world—God in heaven bestows authority on the king to rule over this world. Even the ancient Japanese myths recorded a similar pattern, that is, the *kami* ultimately put in place a human descendant to rule over Japan as emperor.

By contrast, in the *kokutai* theory as Nishida understood it, when the people desire an identity and purpose transcending their individual identities, they bestow spiritual-political authority on a human being as a focal point of the state—the emperor. Although the emperor himself is not absolute, the people collectively decide to extend absolute loyalty to him. Nothing supernatural is involved. The only transcendence in *kokutai* is the people's own desire to transcend their individual existence to be part of a unified people. According to Nishida's analysis, the people develop their myths of creation to give themselves a narrative of common origins and common history; so, too, they develop the special status of the emperor into a concrete, living symbol of their aspirations. That, he claims, is the real theory behind the governmental form called *kokutai*.

Consistent with that point of view, Nishida believed that other nations could, within their own historical contexts, find the resources to develop similar political structures for themselves, that is, develop their own form of *kokutai*: "The individuality of a nation is what constitutes a *kokutai*." To establish social and political unity, a people may draw on its own cultural and historical traditions to find its own manner of conjoining the spiritual and the political, thereby forming a nation. If that nation uses for its symbolic focal point a concrete person in this world without any metaphysical claims about transcendent spiritual authority, their nation is, by Nishida's definition, a *kokutai*.

1026

Thus, according to Nishida, the details of the *kokutai* in different nations will vary from one instance to the next. As there are different versions of democratic governments—republics, constitutional monarchies, federalisms, and so forth—each *kokutai* would have its own character.[120]* Japan's "mission in world history," in a sense its moral responsibility to the global future, would be to introduce the nations of the world to this new alternative form of polity, taking its place alongside other alternatives such as liberal democracy, divine-right monarchy, and communism. Importantly, Nishida noted, this would be the first time an Asian form of polity would be raised to the level of those previously developed in the West (and imperialistically imposed on the rest of the world as the only options). Such was to be Japan's role in the "new world order," as least as he imagined it.

In general, Nishida's political theory strikes me as somewhat similar to Watsuji's and potentially subject to the same criticism, the loss of the individual as a possible critical standpoint from which to negate the totality of the state. In fact, on one point of difference between the two, Nishida's position may be slightly more susceptible to that criticism than Watsuji's. I will begin by reviewing Watsuji's theory so my comparison with Nishida will be clear.

In Chapter 13 I argued that the logic of Watsuji's position was less problematic than the way he eventually applied it.[†] The reason was that Watsuji maintained in his logic of *ningen* an emptiness separating the *nin* pole from the *gen* pole, establishing a base out of which each side could negate the extremity of the other. Watsuji was concrete enough in his analysis that we can envision how this allowed the possibility of an individual's activism (from the *nin* pole) against the totalizing function of the state (the *gen* pole, as it were). Thus, I was able to develop the example of Socrates as standing in his individual freedom (as *nin*) against the status quo of the state that had overextended its *gen* character to thwart reflection and freedom of inquiry. At the time of his actions, Socrates was undermining the stability of society and hence was deemed evil. However, as time passed, that judgment was reversed when society later determined his actions as having had the well-being and improvement of the state at heart.

In Watsuji's case I found less problem with the logic of this argument than with the way he himself abandoned his own analysis in the latter part of his three-volume work, *Ethics*. That is, the problem was not that his ethical-political system itself did not preserve a place from which an individual could critically stand against the state, but rather, that Watsuji eventually abandoned the implications of that very system by transcending the dialectical tension between the individual and the collective in favor of an identity between the totality of the people and the state. His ideal state was a totality of people with no *ningen*.

In Nishida's case, however, the problem may be more intrinsic to the logic of his system itself. In his essay on *kokutai*, Nishida said that "the individual and the whole form an immediate *unity*. The more the two correlatives *become one*, the greater the creativity." For him, such creativity arises from the self-genera- tion of a single national identity, but that raises a logical problem. A unity does not allow a point from within itself to criticize that unity. (If it did it would not

1025

† See pages 513–16.

be a unity.) Nishida's system does not embrace, at least not explicitly, an internal polar tension like Watsuji's *nin* vs. *gen*. Admittedly, Nishida does (elsewhere) discuss a dynamic between the one and the many, held together as a unity by being a "contradictory self-identity." Yet, without more concreteness in his example-free account, I am unsure what that means for his political theory. For example, is the individual *kamikaze* pilot who dies on behalf of the *kokutai* "a contradictory self-identity"? If so, that is hardly the kind of political opposition that Watsuji's system allows as an option.

I do not believe Nishida condoned the military aggression and jingoism of his government in 1944, but either because of his explanations' typical lack of specificity or his own understandable cloaking of his views in the face of government oppression, I cannot see in his case (contra that of Watsuji) how his system could incorporate the possibility of political dissent against a totalitarian "unity." Ironically, of the two philosophers, Watsuji was likely more sympathetic to some of the government's ideology, but at least his philosophical system allowed me the room to use Watsuji's logic to argue against him. Nishida's system by contrast leaves me at a loss and all I can do is suspend judgment about what his logic implies on some political points. There is, however, much to be said in favor of his nontranscendent theory of *kokutai* and how his interpretation of it ran against the official ideology of the state at the time.

Whatever the case, even if we find weaknesses in Nishida's political philosophy, he was no pitchman for the official state ideology. Nothing in his position justified military expansion for the purpose of dominating the rest of East Asia and the Pacific. Nor did he regard the emperor's rule to be authorized by heaven (as is the case in Chinese Confucianism as well as western divine right theory). Rather, the emperor's status as *kami* derives from a completely human decision on the part of the people to transcend their separate identities for the sake of a common unifying symbol. Although radically different from Abraham Lincoln's vision of the republic, Nishida's vision of *kokutai* was still a government of the people, by the people, and for the people. If the emperor is *"kami,"* it is because the people freely decided to treat him as such, not because creator deities made him so.

One might even say that in Nishida's view, reverence for the emperor establishes political unity within *kokutai* similar to how pledging allegiance to the flag establishes unity within a liberal democracy like that of the United States or the valorization of the proletariat establishes unity within communism. For Nishida those alternative forms of political organization all legitimately serve solidarity. On the other hand, like the United States with its human rights "endowed by the Creator" and its idea of being "one nation under God," *kokutai* merges a spiritual component with its political, but does so without any appeal to divine transcendence outside this world. Like the Soviet state with its dialectical materialism, *kokutai* justifies itself within the human world, but does so without communism's denial of any role for the spiritual in politics.

I have tried to give a charitable reading of Nishida's analysis of *kokutai*. That is, I have interpreted him to be choosing his words with exquisite care in hopes of redefining the fundamental terms of the state ideology even while using those terms. Given the political climate and the threat of repercussions, the careful, somewhat cloaked, wording is understandable. Yet, the problem mentioned above—the lack of a concrete standpoint from which one can formulate a criticism of *kokutai*—still remains. Indeed, my reading of Nishida underscores his philosophy's inability to avoid that problem.

Despite Nishida's efforts to expose its misconceptions, the official state ideology prevailed. Indeed it seems the ideologues either ignored his criticisms or, given Nishida's subtlety, did not even recognize them. In the final analysis, there are no grounds for arguing Nishida promoted the state ideology. Scholars who claim otherwise, when we read them more carefully than they themselves have read Nishida's essay, seem to depend on a tendentious reading of his text supported by quotes taken out of context or even, when converted into English, mistranslated.

Tanabe's "Repentance" over Japan's Political Ideology

I have already mentioned that Tanabe Hajime was among the Kyoto   670–91
School figures who publicly supported the war effort. Many other philosophers who had backed the state ideology, including Watsuji, never recanted their views, but Tanabe's public repentance was a striking exception, beginning his change of heart and mind even before the war ended. Shinran's Shin Buddhist philosophy, it turns out, played a key role in his philosophical conversion.

In the preceding paragraph, I chose the words *repentance, change of heart and mind*, and *conversion* advisedly: they are all possible translations of Tanabe's key term *zange*, which he himself identified with the Greek term *metanoia*. In fact he tended to use the Greek and Japanese terms interchangeably in his book, *Zangedō toshite no tetsugaku* (*Philosophy as the Way of "Zange"*; published in English translation as *Philosophy as Metanoetics*). Tanabe started writing the book in 1943 and it appeared in print in 1945.

Tanabe's choice of the term *zange* resonates with a Shin Buddhist attitude that came late to his thinking. Like many other philosophers of the time including Nishida and Watsuji, Tanabe initially thought of Zen, not Shin, Buddhism as the most valuable intellectual resource for modern Japanese philosophy, writing an insightful book on Dōgen in 1939, *My View of the Philosophy of "Shōbōgenzō"* (*Repository of the Eye for the Truth*). In the latter years of the Pacific War, as Tanabe became ever more disillusioned with Japan's militarist policies, he wanted to speak out openly, but he also felt pulled by what he perceived to be his responsibility to support his country in time of war. Frozen in indecision about whether to make his criticism public, he languished in despair. But then...

> At that moment something astonishing happened. In the thick of my distress, I let go and surrendered myself humbly to my own inability. I was suddenly brought to new insight! My penitent confession—*metanoesis [zange]*—unexpectedly threw me back on my own interiority and away from things external.... The only thing for me to do in the situation was to resign myself honestly to my weakness, to examine my own inner self with humility, and to explore the depths of my powerlessness and lack of freedom...

689

Lest any of his readers not recognize the connection to Shinran's thought, Tanabe was explicit:

> To be sure, this is not a philosophy to be undertaken with self-power. One's own powers have already been abandoned in despair. It is rather a philosophy to be practiced through other-power, which has turned me in a completely new direction through metanoesis and has induced me to make a fresh start from the realization of my utter helplessness.... This other-power brings about a conversion in me that heads me in a new direction along a path hitherto unknown to me....
>
> My experience of conversion—that is, of transformation and resurrection—in metanoesis corresponds to the experience that led Shinran (1173–1263) to establish the doctrine of the Pure Land [Shin] sect. Quite by accident I was led along the same path... although in my case it occurred in the philosophical realm.

690

Reflecting his Kyoto School pedigree, Tanabe then tried to understand the "logic" of this *zange,* labeling it *absolute criticism.*

> Absolute criticism means that reason, faced with the absolute crisis of its dilemma, surrenders itself of its own accord. In the course of this critical task, the personal subject that is undertaking the critique of pure reason cannot remain a mere bystander at a safe remove from the criticism. The subjects of the critique cannot avoid getting tangled in their own web and exposing themselves to self-criticism. They cannot avoid being undone by the absolute dilemma of their own thought.

691

Reason's engagement in absolute criticism has even further implications, however. Tanabe points out that reason's self-criticism becomes, paradoxically, a form of affirmation in its own right.

> Yet in the very midst of this absolute disruption and contradiction, the power of contradiction is itself negated: the absolute contradiction contradicts itself. At this point an absolute conversion takes place and philosophy is restored,

through the power of the transcendent, as a "philosophy that is not a philosophy."

691

In Chapter 12, I recounted how Tanabe, like Takahashi Satomi before him, had criticized Nishida for seeming at times to make "absolute nothing" into an (empty) thing that is a source of other (not empty) things, rather than, as Tanabe viewed it, an ongoing mode of negating. Through his experience of *zange,* arising from within his philosophical thinking, Tanabe realized that his own thought, when pushed, would also necessarily *negate itself.* If we look carefully at the passage just quoted, his self-description suggests the initial moment of crisis irrupts when the self fails in its attempt to stand back in detachment as the agent which negates: if I negate everything, I must eventually negate myself, but then there is no agent to carry out the negation. I suppose that is consistent with Tanabe's own characterization of his being frozen in inactivity over what to do about the war.

But if I am negated, nothing—as the function of negating—no longer has anything to negate so "the power of contradiction is itself negated" and "philosophy is restored… as a philosophy that is not a philosophy." Tanabe's logic parallels Shinran's teaching that Amida-for-us exists to take us out of our ego-centered existence, so that self-power can surrender to the other-power of Amida's Vow.[†] But if there is no longer a "self," there cannot be an "other." So, Shinran claimed, the Amida-for-us disappears into the naturalness (*jinen*) of auto-power. In this regard, Tanabe's *zange* is much like Shinran's *shinjin* and Tanabe's "philosophy that is no philosophy" resembles Shinran's "practice that is no practice."

As is often the case with Tanabe's logical discussions, the level of abstraction can often obscure the practical import. As I see it, there are two key implications following from his theory. First, however strenuously they may try, philosophers cannot stand apart from reality, running through a dialectical process of affirming this by negating that. Such a view detaches the thinker from the objects of thought. If instead the philosophical criticism becomes absolute along the lines Tanabe envisions, nothing—not even the thinker who engages in the criticism—can stand outside the negating process. Thus, any philosophy based in self-power cannot stand. "One's own powers have already been abandoned in despair." Philosophy cannot reach absolute truth by thinking things through, that futile process Shinran called *hakarai.*[‡]

Second, the despair Tanabe mentions is itself the sign of fully engaging the flux of experience without ego, without detachment, and without objectification. Philosophical ideas can be no more than temporary *ad hoc* self-expres-

† See pages 203–4.
‡ See pages 185–7.

sions of reality that come and go of their own accord in response to surrounding conditions. Tanabe may have come to this position by his own disenchantment with political theorizing. Through that experience, however, he realized he had encountered a general failing of any philosophizing that presumes a detached form of knowing carried out by a discrete, disengaged self.

True to the Kyoto School method, when Tanabe discovered an error in thinking—be it psychological, moral, epistemological, or in this case political—he turned his focus to uncovering from what standpoint such a mistake could arise.[121] The Kyoto School is typically less interested in where ideas lead and more in where they come from.[122] The hope is to find the slip in logic that established a place for such misguided thoughts and actions in the first place. In this instance, Tanabe relearned the lesson Shinran had so painfully realized some eight centuries earlier. Namely, the error and its consequent anguish arises not from a mistake made by thinking, but rather, by our mistaking the nature of thinking itself. Thinking should not be the ego's standing apart from reality and figuring it out. Rather, properly employed, thinking happens of itself as we fully engage the natural flow of life.

Given his new understanding of thinking, Tanabe saw the implications for a new way of doing philosophy. Philosophy should not be the quest for the absolute, an ego-driven desire to figure out everything. Such an absolute would be a *what*, an endpoint or starting point, static in its detached perfection. Rather, Tanabe sees the "philosophy that is not a philosophy" as a process of negation that never stops, a *how* rather than a what. As the title of his book states, philosophy is the *Way* of *zange*, the auto-correcting "absolute criticism." For Tanabe, philosophy must not only continually criticize various philosophical positions, but it should also in an important sense turn against itself as an enterprise.

Philosophy should always be skeptical of reason itself. No philosophical system, however sophisticated and dialectical, can be trusted as an absolute or even fully adequate characterization of the way things are. To even try to create such a system is a folly of the ego's hubris. Philosophy is not a static *stand*point as much as a *walking* the path, a proprioceptive act of auto-aware engagement that is always adjusting, counterbalancing, and moving on. Philosophy's process of auto-negating is as natural, ongoing, and self-correcting as the shift from right foot to left foot to right foot in walking the Pure Land Way. Tanabe's critique of philosophy, even the Kyoto School philosophy of absolute nothing, is that philosophy should be more "natural" and *ad hoc* in Shinran's sense of *jinen*.

To review: in Chapter 13, we found Watsuji's political philosophy was intrinsic to his system of ethics and he might have developed some theory of the state even if Japan were not at war with a nationalistic ideology permeating the air. According to my interpretation in that chapter, however, were it not for the wartime context, Watsuji's political theory might have turned out somewhat differently because as it stands, it is inconsistent with the logic of his own ethical system.

In this chapter so far we have considered the two leading figures of the Kyoto School, Nishida and Tanabe. Because of its original emphasis on individual experience, epistemology, and logic, the Kyoto School did not initially involve itself much with political thought, but the spirit of the times eventually drew it into the thicket of ideological discussions, whether as critics or advocates. As I argued earlier in this chapter, Nishida did not directly endorse the military expansionist policies of the government and in his own highbrow way tried to subvert it. Tanabe, by contrast, endorsed the state ideology only later to repent.

That brings us to their most famous student, Nishitani Keiji, who endorsed the ideology and after the war was severely sanctioned for having done so. One way to read Nishitani is to see him as an ideological warmonger who, after having been punished, erased his former identity to become a philosopher of religion, eventually becoming the toast of East-West philosophy and an inspiration behind Buddhist-Christian dialogue.

713–32

Another way to read Nishitani, though, is to see him as having always been a philosopher of religion whose existential concern was the erosion of the spiritual dimension of humanity in the face of mechanization, atomistic individualism, and scientism—what the Japanese called the "problem of modernity." In that light, Nishitani's wartime writings can be understood as trying to frame the Pacific War as more than a conflict between the imperialist forces of the United States and Britain against Japan. More essentially, he thought, it was a conflict of ideas between the carriers of modernity and a Japan that wanted to accept modernity only as a waypoint to move beyond. This latter interpretation, I believe, better fits the full corpus of Nishitani's writings.

In reading Nishitani, what you see depends on where you sit when you read him. I suggest we start by sitting in the lobby of the Imperial Hotel, designed by Frank Lloyd Wright. From that vantage point, we can glean insights into what modernity meant to Nishitani's Japanese contemporaries and why so many of them considered it to be a "problem." Once we see the broader vista, we can more fruitfully turn to Nishitani's particular response to that modernity.

JAPAN'S PROBLEM WITH MODERNITY

Commissioned in 1916 and completed in 1923, Frank Lloyd Wright's Imperial Hotel sprawled just to the south of the grounds of the Imperial Palace, across the street from Hibiya Park. The Imperial court wanted the hotel to be a first-class hospitality center for visiting foreign dignitaries, a showplace for the world to witness Japan's new cosmopolitan and modern face. In replacing the old Imperial Hotel, a wooden structure in a European neo-Renaissance style,

Lobby of the Imperial Hotel Designed by Frank Lloyd Wright

the Japanese elite wanted an edifice more forward-looking rather than simply one aping the European past. It had to be grand, a symbolic expression that Japan was no longer just catching up with the West, but taking its place at the vanguard of global change.

Wright's design was (not surprisingly for him) eclectic in style, mixing elements of Mayan pyramids, art deco, and prairie design. Just as importantly, however, it drew on Japanese architectural elements as well, using long narrow corridors to link wings of the building in classical Japanese temple style. Wright had been first impressed with Japanese traditional architecture when he saw the Japan Pavilion at the Columbian World's Fair in Chicago in 1893. Even earlier, he had already begun assembling an extensive personal collection of Japanese woodblock prints. When Wright made his first trip abroad in 1905, therefore, it was not to Europe, but a two-month jaunt through Japan. From Wright's standpoint, Japan had much to offer architecturally and he hoped it would not be overwhelmed by modern western fads.

During his visit in 1913, before there was even a plan to build a new Imperial Hotel, the *Japan Advisor* reported in its interview with the American architect:

"The time of awakening must come sooner or later," continued Mr. Wright. "And then the country [of Japan] will be face to face with the costly necessity of getting rid of all these modern architectural monstrosities and evolving a style more in consonance with Japanese traditions and really characteristic of the people...."[123]

By the time Japan had begun erecting its new Imperial Hotel, it had shown itself a world power, victorious over China, victorious over imperial Russia, and the Asian power on the winning side in World War I, giving it the chance to take over the German railway holdings in China. To simply copy German forms as it had in its old Imperial Hotel's architectural style seemed no longer fitting to the New Japan. With the annexation of the northern island of Hokkaidō and the colonization of Korea and Taiwan, many of its leaders believed that Japan had finally taken its rightful place in the world. The Empire of the Sun was radiating its light throughout East Asia and the Pacific. Japan was ready to show its new face to the world and the Imperial Hotel would be a centerpiece in its public relations campaign.

The Emperor Shōmu, who had hosted Japan's first cosmopolitan debut at his Great Temple to the East in eighth-century Nara,[†] would have been proud of his descendant, the Emperor Taishō. As we sit in the lobby of the Imperial Hotel today, it is easy to imagine the excited anticipation for its Grand Opening. The hotel had started accommodating guests in June 1923 but the official opening was to be the first week in September.

The Kantō earthquake and its aftermath. Two minutes before noon on September 1st, in Sagami Bay off the shore of Yokohama and Tokyo, the earth lurched and the Great Kantō Earthquake was underway. The first shock, in which the ground rose vertically more than 2.5 meters with a force of 7.9 to 8.2 on the Richter scale (equivalent to 300 Hiroshima-size nuclear explosions), lasted for more than four minutes with hundreds of tremors continuing until another major shock 24 hours later. In Kamakura, the Great Buddha (see photo on page 247) lifted and moved about 2/3 of a meter. A 12-meter high tsunami swept in, leveling Yokohama and part of Tokyo.

Most Japanese households were cooking lunchtime meals over charcoal braziers in their wooden homes as the gas lines broke open, setting both Tokyo and Yokohama ablaze. Many rushed to the Sumida River for safety only to encounter a "dragon twist," a cyclone of fire and wind higher than a 30-story building. Before it was over, more than 140,000 people were dead, 3.3 million were homeless, and three-fourths of Yokohama and two-thirds of Tokyo lay in ashes and rubble. But the Imperial Hotel survived and George A. Lang took photographs from atop the building. Instead of its scheduled grand opening as a hotel, the Imperial became an emergency shelter, hospital, and food kitchen for survivors.

† See pages 96–8.

Photo from the Roof of Imperial Hotel after Great Kantō Earthquake (1923)
NGS photo: George A. Lang Collection No. 6

The devastation of the Kantō Earthquake affected the intellectual and political climate as well, creating a sharp political lurch to the right embracing nationalism and the valorization of the "ancient Japanese spirit." Facing a shortage of food and water, the people of Tokyo and Yokohama turned on each other as looting and assaults ravaged the cities.[124] When rumors spread that Korean residents were poisoning the water supply in retaliation for Japan's occupation of their homeland, throngs of thugs took to the streets in a rage, beating and stabbing every Korean they met: man, woman, or child. The estimate is that over 6,000 Koreans were murdered. To stop the mayhem, the government declared martial law.

In the face of such devastating events, the Japanese people searched for interpretation and explanation. How could such a disaster occur, right when it seemed Japan was entering an era of global eminence? How could this event be turned into a new beginning? Like the Silver Pavilion after Kyoto's Ōnin War,[†] the Imperial Hotel stood in the middle of the rubble, a *sabi*-like monument to darkened visions and dashed hopes of what now suddenly seemed like a dream from long ago. Politicians, religious leaders, journalists, and university professors all weighed in, eager to give the events context and meaning.

A surprisingly influential contingent of conservative and right-wing interpreters saw the earthquake as the vengeance of the *kami* who were chastising

† See pages 250–2.

the Japanese for their materialism and modern western ways, turning their backs on the time-honored Japanese values of morality, village lifestyle, and spiritual sensitivities. If it seems strange that such interpretations could have explanatory force, it is helpful to remember that the promulgation of the Imperial Rescript on Education and the official ideology of State Shintō were already in their third decade by this point. Responding to the claim that the disasters were the acts of angry *kami*, believers were given validation; skeptics, given pause. Why, some wondered, had the red-light district been so especially devastated? Was it a targeted message from a divine source or the result of the district's having been sloppily constructed on unstable, cheap land?

The only solution, the conservatives and right-wingers argued, was to rebuild the cities as models of moral education and everyday virtue, returning to the old ways while taking restricted advantage of modern technology. Neighborhood associations could bring back the village mentality which would cooperate with the state in monitoring and nurturing the moral behavior of the community. The echoes of Sakuma Shōzan's nineteenth-century slogan of "Japanese spirit; western ingenuity" (*wakon yōsai*) was like a phoenix's cry rising from the ashes. At least, so it was with some people.

Meanwhile some progressives and liberals argued that whatever the natural cause of the disaster, there was indeed an opportunity to rebuild, not to replicate what had been, but to embody the vision of the new Japan, where urban districts would no longer be demarcated by difference in social and economic class, where personal creativity could thrive in a harmonious society of free expression, and Japan could be a model for the blending of East and West. Standing upright above the rubble, the Imperial Hotel could symbolize the point of origin for this bold new venture. Unfortunately for those progressive visionaries, the city of Yokohama had been nearly obliterated. It had formerly been home to many western settlers and a number of Japan's more forward-looking thinkers and writers. Their intellectual network was in a state of ruin as much as the city itself. Meanwhile, the Diet (parliament) was in disarray and the military was eager to expand its base abroad, building on gains made with the victories over China, Russia, and (in WWI) Germany.

In the end, the militarists and conservatives won out by promising stability, security, and military command over the region. By 1925, just two years after the quake, the new Peace Preservation Law was in place, prosecuting "thought crimes" that threatened "national unity." In truth, it was a thinly disguised way to legalize the persecution of dissenters: anarchists, socialists, Marxists, and even some moderate liberals and progressives. Within a year the Ministry of Justice established an office dedicated to investigating and prosecuting thought crimes and the Tokyo District Court created a special division expressly for that purpose. As the aforementioned case of Tosaka Jun attests,[†] university professors were not immune. Tensions among faculty members increased as rewards and penalties became increasingly coordinated with national and international political policy. This returns us to the most notable second-generation philosopher of the Kyoto School, namely, Nishitani Keiji.

Nishitani Keiji (1900–1990) on Japan's Global Role

Nishitani Keiji came of age as a professor and scholar in the 1920s and 1930s under the tutelage of Nishida and Tanabe. The only intellectual climate he had experienced in his formative years was the one I just described. By the 1940s, with Nishida and Tanabe both retired, Nishitani had become the central figure of the Kyoto School and a philosophical voice to which some government factions turned for lending intellectual weight to their policy-making. That was the case with the so-called Chūōkōron Discussions (henceforth abbreviated CD). CD was a published record of a discussion group consisting of four second-generation Kyoto School professors including Nishitani.[125] They had three meetings: November 1941 (shortly before Pearl Harbor), March 1942 (when the Pacific War was going well for Japan), and November 1942 (a few months after the crushing defeat at Midway suggested the war would be not easy, nor victory assured). CD appeared in the journal, Chūōkōron, shortly after the series of meetings ended.

1078–84

The dialogue was originally suggested by the leadership of the Japanese navy who disagreed with the expansionist aspirations of the jingoistic army. The purpose was to rethink Japan's international position, the discussion centering on interpreting Japan's new role as a major player in global affairs. For the first time in modern history, a major global power was Asian rather than European or American. What were the implications of that situation for both the present and the future?

A major focus was on how Japan could have risen to such prominence even though no other Asian nation had yet been able to resist western exploitation. The obvious answer was that unlike China, India, southeast Asia, Korea, and the Philippines, Japan had been able to embrace and assimilate western science and technology rapidly and effectively. But why was Japan so distinctive in this accomplishment?

In the conversations recorded in CD, some credited the Japanese development of literacy and education in the Edo period. Others attributed the success—and Nishitani took the lead in this analysis—to the "moral energy" of the modern Japanese people. As a people, the Japanese had a vision of national destiny, see-

† See page 523.

ing themselves as not victims or passive players on the stage of global imperialism, but as agents of change in a "new world order." Since western technology would help them realize that vision, they jumped at the opportunity to make it their own. The other nations of the region, Nishitani believed, lacked that moral energy and national vision to take advantage of the same opportunity. Hence, he argued, Japan was in a unique position to lead the rest of the Asian countries in their own moral transformations.

The present problem, the interlocutors suggested, was getting the rest of the world to come to grips with that new global and regional reality. The West had to learn that in the new configuration of world politics Japan was an equal to the European and American imperialist powers and that the West had to cease meddling in East Asian affairs, leaving the countries to their own self-determination. Meanwhile, the rest of East Asia had to recognize that Japan was now their protector against western exploitation. Under the umbrella of Japanese protection, the other Asian countries could learn to find their own national moral energies and thereby define their own way into the community of modern nations.

As for catching up with technology, the group noted that the Chinese should recognize they could now learn from Japan and there was no need to depend on the West for their education. This, the panelists claimed, is the true idea behind the "Greater East Asian Co-Prosperity Sphere" (daitōa kyōeiken). Nishitani claimed that the English rendering of the sinograph ei 榮 as "prosperity" proved that the West did not grasp the real issue, using an English word that suggests no more than material well-being. Kōyama agreed, noting that the sinograph includes nuances of "moral honor" in the sense of "self-esteem, a moral pride, or even glory." Nishitani elaborated on that line of thought, adding:

> … to dilute the richness of the sinograph to "prosperity" is to reduce it to what one finds in the American value system. There is an especially strong danger that the economic aspect is given great weight. Economic power is playing an extremely important role in the present war, and the economic development of the Co-Prosperity Sphere is also a matter of great weight. Yet we must think beyond American values. For this is an ethical dimension…. 1077

Leaving aside the extent to which this caucus of four philosophers was deluded about contemporaneous events and the real intentions of the Japanese Empire, they had sketched a plausible theory. It was certainly true that the contours of world politics had changed and that it was critical to re-envision Japan's role in that reconfiguration. Moreover, it was fair to say that western imperialism had no real interest in the cultural self-determination of Asian countries. That is, the official ideology of western imperialism, to the extent it was articulated, was a mission of "civilizing" Asia, that is, making it fit the western cultural, social, political, and economic template. Japan held out the hope of being the shining counter-example to western cultural hegemony. It had proven that an Asian nation could technologically and socially modernize without becoming culturally western. As such, Japan could inspire other Asian nations to do the same. At least that was the way the panelists described the situation in their comments.

Although we might forgive Nishitani and his colleagues for being naïve when it came to realpolitik, a darker side of Nishitani emerged when he got down to brass tacks about what to do in practice. In this regard his professional philosophical education was likely a factor. In 1937, after being educated under Nishida and Tanabe and subsequently holding a lectureship at Kyoto University, Nishitani went to Europe for further training.

Nishitani's original aspiration was to study with Henri Bergson, but unfortunately, the French philosopher's health was already failing and so he decided to work with Martin Heidegger in Freiburg. I cannot help but wonder how Nishitani's political ideas might have differed if he had gone to France to study under a French Jew who, among other notable ideas, had introduced the distinction between "open" and "closed" societies. Instead, Nishitani found himself in Nazi Germany from 1937 to 1939.

From his student days in Kyoto, Nishitani had been a staunch Germanophile, having written his university thesis on Schelling. Now his time in Germany allowed him to steep himself in German mysticism, Kant, the German scholarship on the Greek and Hellenistic classics as well as, of course, Heidegger. In CD it is clear that he had accepted uncritically some racist theories prevalent in Germany at the time as well. The Nazi influence is obvious in some of his comments, including the theory that a nation's "moral energy" was linked with race, opening Nishitani to the possibility of there being a "master people" (*Herr-*1076 *envolk*).

When conceding that Japan's population was likely too small to fulfill its greater East Asian mission, Nishitani ruminated aloud about which races were superior to others and which might be fruitfully intermixed with "Japanese blood." Such people might best serve the Greater East Asian Co-Prosperity Sphere by being "half-Japanized." In his armchair reflections (he called his ideas "the fantasy of a complete amateur"—I shudder to imagine whom he would have considered a "professional" in such matters), he thought how productive it would be if the Koreans and the Takasago (native Taiwanese) could come to think of themselves as being of "one people" with the Yamato (Japanese).

Nishitani's enthusiasm for building an expanded population base of the master race seemed to trump his insistence in the earlier discussions that Japan's mission was to help each people achieve its own moral energy through self-determination. Nishitani did not seem to consider the possibility that some

Asian nationalities might, as part of their self-determination, not want to be of "one people" with the Japanese or that some might not want to be educated so as to become "half-Japanese." In fairness, it is important to bear in mind, however, that although Nishitani might have had scales on his eyes, he was not completely blind to the need for a "world ethic" in which nations were held responsible for being just and fair. That point is a little clearer in the "Symposium on Overcoming Modernity"[126] (henceforth, OM) to which we now turn.

1078-84

Also held in 1942, the symposium was a roundtable for a different group of intellectuals representing a broader range of academic disciplines. This one was the initiative of the editorial board of an academic journal rather than any government-related group. Of the fifteen members, Nishitani was one of the two philosophers, Shimomura Torataro (1902–1995), another member of the Kyoto School, being the other. They met to discuss the issue of "modernity" and its impact on both European and Japanese culture.

733-7

The term "overcoming" (chōkoku) in the title has the connotations of "getting through" or "getting over." In other words, the assumption was that modernity was a given and the challenge was not to ignore it, demolish it, or avoid it—that would have been both foolhardy and futile—but to live through it and to somehow get beyond it to achieve something newer and better. Unlike CD in which the participants showed agreement on most issues, in the case of OM, there was a wider spectrum of points of view. In his presentation for the symposium Nishitani returned to the link he imagined to exist between national moral energy and a world ethic.

> Moral energy is a concentration and strengthening of the nation as a community of people.... But if it is only that, it has no connection to a world ethic, and in certain circumstances can be linked to injustices such as making other peoples and nations objects of colonization, or serving the personal grudges of a nation. In our country today, the moral energy driving national ethics must at the same time directly energize a world ethic. Its character is a mutual entailment of nation-in-world and world-in-nation.

1082

Although that quote hardly undoes the ethnocentrism expressed in CD, the last sentence does clarify that Nishitani did not think his valorizing of the national moral energy was the final word on Japan's role in the new world order. On one hand, Nishitani believed such a Japanese moral energy may be necessary for his country's being able to fend off western imperialism on behalf not only of itself but also (in his interpretation) of all East Asia. That is what he meant by Japan-in-world. On the other hand, Nishitani seemed to recognize that such a moral energy could become a dangerous expression of dominance, leading to various evils. Japan must not become so caught up in its national moral energy that it does not recognize more universal responsibilities such as justice and the tempering of revenge. That is the ethical world-in-Japan dimension in Nishitani's statement.

For appreciating Nishitani's lasting contributions to philosophy, we should look away from his problematic political statements in the early 1940s and more closely at his analysis of the broader intellectual character of our times and its relevance to religion. Nishitani is best known in the West for his book *What Is "Religion?"* or, as it is entitled in the English translation, *Religion and Nothingness*. The thematic roots of the book can be seen even in his discussion of the problem of modernity in OM.

I already explained that the focus of the symposium was to explore the impact of modernity on both the West and on Japan as well as strategies for working through it. Each discussant had his own take on the problem, but two points recurred in their deliberations. First, we find the reappearance of the bugaboo of modern Japan: the fear of the loss of "Japaneseness" to westernization or modernization. Second, and this concern was understood to be as much a western problem as a Japanese one, was the anxiety over dehumanization, especially the mechanization and quantification brought about by technology and science.

For his part, Nishitani framed the issue as the challenge of identifying a spirituality that can serve as a basis both for humanism (with its emphasis on culture, history, and ethics) and for the unencumbered pursuit of science (with its emphasis on detached objectivity and abstract reason). He sought something that can resonate with what lies beneath both the idealistic emphasis on mind and the materialist emphasis on physical things. His analysis is lifted right out of Nishida's logic of *basho* as I described it in Chapter 13, which in itself traces back to the challenges first outlined by Inoue Enryō and Inoue Tetsujirō.[127] †

Like Nishida, Nishitani's solution to the dichotomy lies in a spirituality based in nothingness (*mu*) or emptiness (*kū*), the latter being Nishitani's preferred word.

> When we take away the body as a physical unit and the self-consciousness we usually call mind, it would seem that nothing remains. So it seems. But at the point where nothing remains, in fact, something does remain. Or rather, it is only here that appears the one and only thing that can in no way be objectified and is therefore incapable of creeping into the scientific field: namely, the standpoint of true subjectivity that is within us as subjects. We may call this the standpoint of subjective nothingness....

In continuing to explain, Nishitani did not refrain from making explicit references to Buddhist philosophical ideas:

† See pages 464–8; 418–25.

What is usually called "self" is thought of as some kind of substantial "being," like a thing. But true subjectivity lies on the other side of things and mind; it shows up in their negation as a "dropping off of bodymind," as a negation of the conscious self, as a "no-self" or "no-mind" that eradicates the petty ego.... When one transcends the self and awakens to the true self, there is no cutting oneself off from the body and its natural world, or from the mind and its cultural world.... This is not the working of a conscious self, but of a subject-in-nothingness....

1081

In speaking of the "subjectivity" of the self as nothingness, Nishitani reprises the Kyoto School perspective that thinking can present us with either a world of things or a world of ideas. On one hand, modernity's empiricism arises from placing knowledge in a *basho* where the self or mind is detached and considered irrelevant. The modern mind is no more than the disinterested recorder of the "facts" of science and the "human" element is no more than another "thing" to be studied empirically by the social sciences.

On the other hand, modernity's idealism arises from placing knowledge in a *basho* where the facts have no being in themselves, but rather, are known as the personal, cultural, and social constructions of the mind. Things are no more than what our minds create out of sensations, ideas, values, and intentions.

In both *basho* we find a disconnect between mind and matter, a detachment that leaves us with an incompatible either/or choice: either be personal or be factual; either be subjective or be objective; either be responsive to one's historical, cultural, social milieu or be attentive only to the measurable and quantifiable. In either alternative, the self is substantialized as an independent thing, a thing that either creates reality or simply witnesses it.

Missing in modernity's options is an understanding of active engagement. In Nishitani's terminology this is the "subjective nothingness." It is crucial to recognize the special sense in which he means "subjectivity" (and this usage is common to many Kyoto School thinkers).[128*] Theirs is not the subjectivity as opposed to objectivity that characterizes the idealistic *basho* as opposed to the empirical *basho*. In Nishitani's system, when he says nothingness is "subjective," he means it is an *acting*. Nishitani is again echoing Nishida, this time the latter's theory of "performative intuition."[†]

For both Nishida and Nishitani, there is no independently existing self that is the agent, no "I" who acts, but rather, to go back to the view we have found in almost all the Japanese Buddhist philosophers we have studied in this book, it acts *of itself*. It is a self-acting only in the sense of auto-acting. That explains Nishitani's references in the paragraph above to the general Buddhist view of

† See pages 467–8.

no-self, no-mind, and to Dōgen's "dropping off of bodymind. Unlike Nishida, Nishitani explicitly sprinkles his analysis throughout with references to premodern Japanese philosophy. Such an antiphony of western and Asian associations continued to be a hallmark of Nishitani's philosophy throughout his career.

The end of the war opened the hunting season on former political collaborators, both real and imagined. Nishitani was relieved not only of his professorial post at Kyoto University, but also of the impulse to write about political issues. The issue of modernity stayed with him, however. He saw it as a global challenge to western and Asian philosophies alike. The humanism-scientism dilemma he had discussed was no simple, transient sociohistorical issue, but (to use Nishida's word) an enduring "logical" one.

In 1949, while still not allowed to teach, Nishitani wrote *The Self-Overcoming of Nihilism,* a book arguing that the paradoxes and unresolved tensions of modernity would inevitably fold into themselves and collapse into nihilism. The collapse was obviously already patently visible in Japan. The war had demolished both the promises of Meiji modernity that had fueled the heady rush to technological advancement as well as the sublime exaltation over the indefatigable ideal of the ancient Yamato spirit. Both the physicality of science and the ideality of spirit had failed Japan—indeed Japan's demise arose from the inevitable mutual destruction of the two. All that was left was a void or "nihility," the object of a debilitating nihilism.

714–21

Nishitani believed the western victors in the war—especially the United States—would reap enough material progress from the turn of events that the underlying contradictions would be temporarily hidden from their sight. But eventually, in the very fruits of "success" would be discovered the hollow core of nihility as well. We might say that in 1949 Nishitani was already heralding the impending era of postmodernity in its darkest form, a retreat into the technology of distraction and self-indulgent relativism. What was the solution?

In his subsequent writings Nishitani developed further the analysis he had already outlined in OM. In Japan's case, there was a precious spiritual resource that had always recognized emptiness at the core of human existence, an emptiness that was not the vacuity that leads to nihilism, but instead an emptiness that was the opening up and clearing of a field for engagement with reality as-it-is. It was not intellectual but yet mindful; not materialistic but yet embodied. Furthermore, as I will explain later in this chapter when I discuss the postwar phenomenon of interreligious dialogue, Nishitani had found a few parallels to his idea of emptiness in western thought as well, such as in Saint Paul's kenotic (self-emptying) God and Meister Eckhart's apophatic (negatively approached) theology.

The Impact of the Occupation on Philosophy

Before we leave the lobby of the Imperial Hotel, I suggest we turn back the clock again, this time not to September 1923, but to March 1945. The city of Tokyo is again in flames. With the air defenses of the city already eviscerated by previous bombings, General Curtis LeMay realized that Tokyo, totally rebuilt after the earthquake but still consisting mainly of small wooden structures, was vulnerable to low-altitude fire bombings. He gathered his pilots on March 9th and told them the next day "You're going to deliver the biggest firecracker the Japanese have ever seen."

Analyzing details of the fires that had spread across the city from the earthquake two decades earlier, the military war strategy was to bombard Tokyo on March 10 in Operation Meeting House, using phosphorus bombs and the latest incendiary technology from Harvard's science labs: napalm. The reenactment of the earthquake fire was successful, down to the detail of creating another dragon twist. Even General LeMay admitted some time later that had the U.S. lost the war, he would have been deemed a war criminal. Below is an aerial photograph of Tokyo the next day.

About 40 percent of Tokyo homes were destroyed, and some 100,000 people died (more than in the atomic bombing of either Hiroshima or Nagasaki). Tokyo once again lay in rubble. But again the Imperial Hotel somehow endured. That was to the liking of General Douglas MacArthur, commander of SCAP

Aerial View of Tōkyō after the Operation Meeting House Firebombing[130]

(Supreme Command of the Allied Powers). He used it as officer barracks for his Occupation troops.

Incidentally, the lobby of Frank Lloyd Wright's Imperial Hotel in which I suggested we sit is today not in Tokyo, but in Nagoya's Meiji Mura (Meiji Village), a collection of representative buildings from all over Japan built in the Meiji or, in some cases like the hotel lobby, the Taishō eras. Frank Lloyd Wright's hotel was demolished in 1968, the encroaching high-rises of real estate development accomplishing what neither earthquake nor fire bombing had been able to do. The reflecting pool, entrance, and lobby were dismantled, however, and moved to Meiji Mura. Only one room from the original Frank Lloyd Wright building was preserved in today's Tokyo Imperial Hotel—the bar.

SCAP's agenda for the Occupation was to neutralize the militaristic and fascist elements in the society so that Japan could rebuild itself into an exemplary modern, democratic, and capitalist nation. For example, it disbanded the government system called Shrine Shintō, the institution that used Shintō shrines as centers for disseminating the State Shintō ideology; it prosecuted, incarcerated, and in some cases executed the military, political, and industrial leaders deemed to have been complicit in war crimes. The media was tightly monitored so that no plays could be performed or movies shown that the SCAP censors considered to valorize samurai, nationalistic, or anti-western sentiments. On the radio, the emperor formally declared that he was not *kami* and the Imperial Rescript on Education was banned, making room for a new school curriculum. The Constitution itself was rewritten under the watchful eye of the Occupation hierarchy.

Within universities, as I have already mentioned, professors like Nishitani who were identified as intellectual supporters of the militarist ideology during the war years were removed from their posts. Watsuji and Tanabe were spared the ignominy, perhaps in part because they had already retired. And, of course, Nishida had died shortly before the end of the war so his case did not even come up. (But that did not inhibit subsequent scholars from indicting him in their scholarly writings.)

Because SCAP's agenda was so extensive and, quite frankly, because philosophers seldom played an effective role in determining and carrying out government policy during the war, the initial screening of whom to submit to the Occupation's scrutiny was often left to the universities themselves. That is, professors and administrators to a large extent determined the fate of their colleagues. Persecuted for so long, the left-leaning academics suddenly had a say in the trajectory of their profession: who would teach, what kinds of scholarship would be encouraged, and how future academics would be trained. The academic fields like history, philosophy, religious studies, anthropology, linguistics, sociology, political science, and economics could now be pursued freely, even along Marxist lines if the scholars so wished, without fear of reprisals.

An important side-effect of this shift in academic philosophy is worthy of mention even though it is not directly within the purview of this chapter. It is a topic, however, that I will address more fully in the book's Conclusion because it has a bearing on the future of Japanese philosophy. I am referring to the fact that most philosophy programs in Japan's major secular universities today are almost exclusively limited to studying the western philosophical tradition. The interest in western thought is, of course, nothing new: serious scholarship on western philosophy in Japan dates back to the Meiji period (think of Nishida's thesis on Hume or Watsuji's books on Nietzsche and Kierkegaard, for example). Yet, the postwar fear of any resurgence of nativism led to a tendency to think of "philosophy" as *only* western philosophy. Of course, there are innumerable individual exceptions to this general bias toward the West among postwar Japanese philosophers and they are my focus in the rest of this chapter.[131]

Rethinking the religious

With the defanging of the State Shintō ideology and the dismantling of the state-supported Shrine Shintō system that promulgated it, the Occupation opened the way for Japanese intellectuals to again think freely about religion as they had in the Meiji and Taishō eras. Philosophical innovation occurred in two major areas. First, within the religious traditions themselves we find the Buddhist and Shintō equivalents of western philosophical theology (the study of philosophical first principles within a particular religious tradition) and religious philosophy (philosophy that is spiritually didactic or edifying for the followers of a designated religious tradition). Second, some philosophers have undertaken a more generalized analysis of the spiritual or religious as part of a new philosophical vision of their own, often a new philosophical anthropology. For convenience, I will label those two areas respectively philosophy *in* religion (encompassing both philosophical theology and religious philosophy) and philosophy *of* religion.[132] Postwar Japanese philosophy has contributed significantly to both and here I will do little more than highlight some innovations and refer interested readers to where they can find more details.

Philosophy in Religion

Since philosophy in religion arises from the standpoint of a commitment to a particular religion, for that writer, it is always philosophy in *my* religion. That is, its task is to understand the basic doctrines and values of one's own religious heritage in light of present-day issues, typically by drawing on contemporary philosophical ideas. The philosopher in religion asks: what does my tradition mean in today's terms and how can I make it relevant to our problems today? The answer involves both a firm grounding in the textual and historical aspects of one's own religious heritage (the scholarly side of the equation) as well as analysis of doctrine in light of major issues of the day (the philosophical side of the equation). Such philosophizing in religious contexts has been an important part of both postwar Shintō and postwar Buddhism.

Philosophy in postwar Shintō. As examples of postwar Shintō philosophy, I will mention two thinkers who represent radically different approaches: Orikuchi Shinobu (1887–1953) and Ueda Kenji (1927–2003). The four-decade gap in their years of birth helps explain their difference in agenda.

536–42

ORIKUCHI SHINOBU'S SHINTŌ PHILOSOPHY

Faced with the dire consequences of Japan's defeat and recognizing the role of Shintō and Native Studies in the militarist ideology behind that defeat, Orikuchi tried to discover where the Native Studies' dream of Restoration Shintō had gone wrong. His hope was to fix the problem to prevent a recurrence of such a disaster. During the war, Orikuchi had, like many other Shintō theorists, argued that Shintō was "not a religion," but rather a morality arising from the ancient sensitivities of the Japanese people. As such, the spiritual foundation of the state was moral, not religious. That conceit allowed the government to support the constitutional guarantee of the freedom of religion while also requiring all citizens to participate in State Shintō as part of their civic duty.

Following Japan's defeat, Orikuchi concluded that the American victory was due in part to its "Crusades" mentality. For the Americans, to Orikuchi's way of thinking, the war was ultimately religious, whereas for the Japanese it was merely moral. Since the passion of religious fervor would always win over the resolve of moral commitment, Orikuchi argued, Japan did not have a chance.

Orikuchi identified the error as following from the government's separating religiously devotional Sect Shintō from the Shrine Shintō constructed to support the official state ideology. The religious fervor of faith was thereby limited to private participation in Sect Shintō and excluded from the public life of Shrine Shintō. What postwar Japan needed, Orikuchi argued, was a renewed faith in Takamimusubi and Kamimusubi, the *kami* of creation who ensoul and continue to instill life in both people and things. His intention was to anchor postwar Shintō in the affirmation of life rather than the submission to imperial authority or loyalty to Japan, which were represented in his mind by State (or Shrine) Shintō's focus on Amaterasu (the imperial Sun Goddess) and Ame-nominakanushi (the First Deity). In short: Orikuchi hoped to restore Shintō's

541

vitality by excising its political connections.

Overall, his conservative approach offered no more than a corrective, a step back and to the side, of the path blazed by the Native Studies tradition of the nineteenth century. By contrast, Ueda Kenji's project in the 1980s and 1990s was to reformulate Shintō philosophy in a way analogous to how some theologians had reconstructed Christian theology to better fit the assumptions and concerns of today's world.

UEDA KENJI'S SHINTŌ PHILOSOPHY 543–9

Taking Paul Tillich, the Lutheran theologian, as his model, Ueda went to Harvard to study Christian theology under him. Ueda recognized that Native Studies had tried to give ancient proto-Shintō and folk Shintō a systematic philosophical articulation. Given the disastrous consequences of that venture in the form of State Shintō ideology, the danger was that Shintō would retreat to being once again a ritualistic tradition with little philosophical reflection and analysis. In response, Ueda tried to establish a more existential basis for Shintō praxis along the lines Tillich had done for his Christian faith.

Ueda articulated a new philosophical anthropology, grounding it in the internal relation between sacred beings (*kami*) and human beings. For him, the *kami* and the human share a communal field in which human beings and nature constitute an indivisible whole. As he put it: "Shinto does not consider human beings as anything that can be physically or psychologically isolated." Thus, there is no equivalent to the sin-guilt-repentance dynamic of the Abrahamic religions because such a spiritual process ultimately assumes a gap between the personal and the sacred, a dynamic of alienation and atonement. 545

Of course, as the *kami* may act in ways either beneficial or harmful to us, so can Shintō's life-power assume positive or negative features in us, either enhancing affirmation of life or working self-destructively against itself. Thus the life-power must be monitored and restrained. Through participating in Shintō rituals and festivals, one reaffirms and purifies that life-power. Based on this metaphysical and metapractical analysis, in his later life Ueda developed Shintō responses to today's environmental and biomedical issues. 546–9

Philosophy in postwar Buddhism. When the Occupation exorcised the demons of State Shintō from the universities, Buddhist philosophers, freed from the fear of being accused of thought crimes, began again to take center stage in religious philosophy. Two overlapping philosophical activities within Buddhist thought emerged, what I will call "philosophical scholarship" and "scholarly philosophy." Two professors from Tokyo University's program in Buddhist and Indic studies were especially adept at philosophical scholarship: Nakamura Hajime (1912–1999) and Tamaki Kōshirō (1915–1999). Philosophical scholarship here means the study of multiple Buddhist and western traditions with an effort to identify similarities and dissimilarities among them, perhaps evaluating their respective strengths and weaknesses from a philosophical standpoint.

117–24
125–32

THE PHILOSOPHICAL SCHOLARSHIP OF NAKAMURA HAJIME
AND TAMAKI KŌSHIRŌ

Encyclopedic in their grasp of every nuance of the Buddhist tradition in all its geographical and historical manifestations, Nakamura and Tamaki were renowned for their monumental works of pure Buddhist scholarship, covering the entire range of the Asian Buddhist tradition (and, especially in Nakamura's case, some Hindu philosophy also). Both also possessed a complementary knowledge of western philosophical history (and in Tamaki's case, Jungian analytic psychology as well). Linguistically gifted, (they both read philosophical works in the original languages, whether Asian or western), they were both also skilled in comparative philosophical analysis. Nakamura's focus tended to be on patterns of thinking, logic, law, and argument, whereas Tamaki's was more psychological and metapractical, focusing on self-transformation and its states of consciousness in relation to praxis.

The rubric of scholarly philosophy, as contrasted with philosophical scholarship, can be construed to include such postwar thinkers as Soga Ryōjin (1875–1971), Yasuda Rijin (1900–1982), Suzuki Daisetsu (1870–1966), Hisamatsu Shin'ichi (1889–1980), and Abe Masao (1915–2006), to name but a few. Unlike Nakamura and Tamaki, who were pan-Buddhist in both their scholarship and point of view, this group tended to identify in their writings with a particular Buddhist sub-tradition, bringing to it philosophical analysis supported by scholarly research. I will treat them in two groups: Shin and Zen Buddhist.

THE SCHOLARLY SHIN PHILOSOPHY OF SOGA RYŌJIN AND YASUDA RIJIN

Soga and Yasuda exemplify well the scholarly philosophy that is the Shin Buddhist equivalent to philosophical theology. Although they may have drawn parallels or contrasts with other traditions, including Christianity, their perspectives were self-avowedly anchored in Shin Buddhism. Yet, within that heritage, they often offered radically new takes on traditional doctrines.

273–9

Of the two, Soga was the pioneer and especially noted (and at times considered heretical) for his demythologizing of Shin Buddhism, framing the Amida narrative in historical and mythic rather than cosmic terms. In doing so, he was partly inspired by the "historical Jesus" movement in Christian thought.

280–5

Informed by western psychology and philosophy, Soga and his student Yasuda together brought a distinctively twentieth-century understanding of the self to analyzing the dynamics of Shin Buddhist faith. Their prewar works and postwar elaborations gave Shin Buddhism a philosophical-theological foundation that enabled it to participate in one of the more dynamic enterprises arising from postwar Japanese religious philosophy, namely, interreligious dialogue, especially Buddhist-Christian dialogue. Before turning to that phenomenon, though, I will comment on those who did for Zen Buddhism what Soga and Yasuda did for Shin.

THE SCHOLARLY ZEN PHILOSOPHY OF D. T. SUZUKI, HISAMATSU SHIN'ICHI, AND ABE MASAO

When speaking of Zen philosophy, it is helpful to keep in mind the distinction between those philosophers whose philosophy was inspired by Zen and those who used philosophy to help articulate their own Zen tradition, sometimes apologetically. The former include many philosophers of the Kyoto School, including some I have already discussed in some detail such as Nishida and Nishitani. Neither of those philosophers, however much influenced by Zen praxis and doctrines, considered himself to be doing "Zen philosophy." Watsuji is an even clearer example of the generalization to the extent he did not consider himself religious at all, but rather, was intrigued by certain Buddhist ideas, being interested in religion mainly as a cultural, social, and historical phenomenon.

In my previous analyses, we found such philosophers as Nishida, Nishitani, and Watsuji to be more engaged in advancing the philosophy of religion in general rather than philosophy in (their own) religion. The philosophers I will now briefly discuss—Suzuki, Hisamatsu, and Abe—better represent the latter. For them, however philosophical their discussions might be on some point, there is seldom any doubt that they speak from a Zen Buddhist perspective, either to develop it further philosophically or to advocate its teachings in the face of alternative spiritual or philosophical positions.

Suzuki Daisetsu (1870–1966), better known to the West as "D. T. Suzuki," had more impact on western culture than any other Japanese of the twentieth century. Fluent in English and having achieved an enlightenment experience authorized by a major Zen master, Suzuki was the perfect purveyor of Japanese wisdom to westerners, especially Americans, who sought an alternative value system to the scientism, dehumanization, and materialism of the late 1950s and 1960s. His books, many of which were written originally in English, were bestsellers in the United States and he served stints as a visiting professor at U.S. universities, most notably Columbia, which allowed him access to the country's intellectual and cultural media in New York. 214–20

To the Beat poets and writers, Suzuki was a font of creativity and inspiration. To Christian theologians looking to infuse a renewed spiritual life into their tradition, Suzuki was a provocative raconteur and conversation partner. To those seeking a personal spiritual rebirth, he was a guru. To academics interested in the Japanese arts, Suzuki was a valuable informant. In Suzuki's lifetime and due largely to his impact, the study of Buddhism within the American academy went from being an arcane subject studied in the nooks of only the most comprehensive research universities to having a curricular presence of some form in most colleges and universities today.

Suzuki was not an academic philosopher per se, and efforts by well-intentioned western commentators to think of him as one have only led to his being roundly discounted by professional philosophers in the West. It is better to think of Suzuki as an expositor and advocate of a variety of mysticism, one that he associated with the Rinzai Zen heritage (a historical claim that today many Zen scholars of both Japan and the West consider questionable).[133]

As an expositor and exemplar of the mystical life, Suzuki and his writings had, and I think still could have, a provocative influence on theology, psychoanalysis, and artistic creativity. In his own time, few people even in Japan thought of Suzuki as a philosopher, but he did have well-known close associations with some influential Japanese philosophers, especially those of the Kyoto School. Suzuki and Nishida grew up as schoolboys together in Kanazawa and remained lifelong friends. Furthermore, two philosophers influenced by Suzuki, namely, Hisamatsu and Abe, studied at Kyoto University and had ties to the Kyoto School. Because of those personal interactions with philosophers in Japan, Suzuki did occasionally raise philosophical issues in his works and his reflections sometimes had an impact on philosophers in both the Zen and Shin Buddhist traditions.

Suzuki's writings on Shin Buddhism are not as well known in the West as are his works on Zen. Yet, he did a fine English translation of most of Shinran's magnum opus, *Kyōgyōshinshō* (*The Teaching, the Practice, the Entrusting, the Enlightenment*) and wrote several provocative essays on Shin Buddhism. For this book, however, I mention him more to set the context for his two philosophical successors in the Zen tradition, Hisamatsu Shin'ichi and Abe Masao.

221–6 Hisamatsu Shin'ichi (1889–1980) studied philosophy under Nishida at Kyoto University and can thus be considered in the orbit of Kyoto School philosophy, but his deepest inspiration (encouraged by Nishida himself) was his Rinzai Zen praxis. Hisamatsu was not only an accomplished Zen meditator but also a Zen teacher. He never developed a systematic approach to philosophy; nor did he engage directly the epistemological and logical questions we associate with the Kyoto School. Yet, he did use the philosophical acumen honed at the university to address issues of spirituality in daily life and, most famously, the underlying Zen experience of emptiness as the basis for creativity in the Japanese arts. In those areas, Suzuki's influence is unmistakable. Teaching first at Kyoto University and then later at the Rinzai Zen university, Hanazono, Hisamatsu's philosophical interactions included a dialogue with the aforementioned Lutheran theologian Paul Tillich.[134] While at Kyoto, Hisamatsu also inspired a young philosophy student, Abe Masao, to shift his focus from Shin to Zen Buddhism.

After studying philosophy under Tanabe and Nishitani, and studying Zen
with Hisamatsu, Abe Masao (1915–2006) spent a short span in the mid–1950s
at Union Theological Seminary in New York, where he attended lectures by
Reinhold Niebuhr, Paul Tillich, and (fortuitously) D. T. Suzuki. Those different
elements from Japan and the U.S. melded into Abe's distinctive philosophical
perspective, a perspective he brought to his teaching in various institutions in
the U.S. for fourteen years after his retirement from Nara Educational University in 1980.

750–7

Abe's works in English, including a co-translation of several key fascicles
from Dōgen's *Shōbōgenzō* (*Repository of the Eye for the Truth*), played a major
role in introducing Japanese philosophy to the West. Most importantly, his
extensive knowledge of the western tradition, both philosophical and theological, as well as the ability to converse in English, made him a central figure in
Buddhist-Christian dialogue. Throughout his career of interacting with the
West, Abe was not merely an interpreter of Japanese philosophical ideas for a
western audience, but also a creative philosopher in his own right, articulating
his distinctive position always from within and in defense of Zen, but in light of
ideas from an array of philosophies, both Japanese and western.

BUDDHIST-CHRISTIAN DIALOGUE

Buddhist-Christian dialogue, in which Abe was an avid participant, functioned on two levels. Most commonly, especially in its early phase, it stressed
the interaction among participants who came to the dialogue as practitioners
of one or the other of the two traditions. That is, the Buddhists spoke as committed Buddhists and the Christians as committed Christians. A spin-off of
the interaction included sharing the praxis side of the two religions, Christian
monks in the life of Buddhist monasteries and Buddhist monastics in Christian
monasteries, for example.

Of more direct philosophical import was the theological discussion of specific topics such as the obvious difference between Christianity as a tradition
wherein the sacred is associated with absolute being and Japanese Buddhism as
a tradition wherein it is associated with absolute nothing. Buddhist participants
in one of the earliest discussion groups included Abe Masao and the American, Francis Cook, representing Zen, while Shin Buddhists included Takeda
Ryūsei from Ryūkoku University in Kyoto (also trained in process theology at
Claremont) and the Japanese-American Taitetsu Unno (Shin Buddhist priest
and Buddhism scholar trained at Tokyo University and teaching at Smith College). For the most part, the Christians were drawn from Harvard (Gordon
Kaufman), Chicago (Langdon Gilkey, David Tracy, Joseph M. Kitagawa), and
Claremont (John Hick and John Cobb, the convener of the group). The discus-

sions were most effective in identifying common themes and bringing about a clearer understanding of the relation between doctrine and praxis.

The second level of Buddhist-Christian dialogue functioned on a more exclusively philosophical or theological plane in which the personal religious convictions of the participants were less important than the mutual exchange and evaluation of ideas. That is, the focus was on understanding religion itself through the comparison of two rather different traditions. A central figure in this type of Buddhist-Christian dialogue in Japan has been Yagi Seiichi (1932–). A Christian theologian and biblical scholar in the vein of Rudolf Bultmann, Yagi has been developing a theory of the common point between Christianity and Buddhism as lying in the eradication of ego-centered existence.

1053–8

902–6

Some of his work has been inspired by Takizawa Katsumi (1909–1984), a Christian thinker who had studied under Karl Barth, but who developed a constructive criticism of the Kyoto School's philosophy of absolute nothing. Identifying Nishida's absolute nothing with God, Takizawa maintained that Nishida's analysis of the interpenetration of opposites failed to recognize the profound qualitative gap between the absolute and the relative such that the relative can depend on the absolute but not vice versa.

On the institutional rather than personal level, the Nanzan Institute for Religion and Culture in Nagoya, Japan, has been a major impetus behind Buddhist-Christian interactions by not only sponsoring a wide range of dialogues and publications within Japan, but of even broader significance, supporting the translation of many key philosophical works from Japanese into western languages, including the writings of the Kyoto School. By making such translations available in European languages, western philosophers and theologians no longer have to be in direct personal contact with Japanese religious thinkers to engage in the dialogue of ideas.

Translations like those from the Nanzan Institute have stimulated a different form of dialogue. Instead of being limited to what one or two interlocutors might say about some theme in Japanese Buddhist thought, the interested westerner can now read a variety of Japanese philosophers on an issue, determining for oneself what is most relevant. Furthermore, the translations present what the Japanese philosophers had originally written in Japanese for a Japanese audience. The difference in perspective gained is analogous to what a westerner can learn about Japan by watching Japanese feature films with subtitles as contrasted with what can be learned via English-language documentaries explicitly designed to explain Japan to foreigners. Many of those translated philosophical works best fit the category of philosophy *of* religion, the topic to which we now turn.

Philosophy of Religion

Alongside epistemology, the most prominent emphasis of Kyoto School philosophers has been the philosophy of religion. The philosophy of religion has had a long tradition in the West, especially in the modern era as medieval Christian and Jewish theology became no longer the only way of philosophically reflecting on the nature of the sacred. Despite its name, however, the western philosophy of religion has amounted to, at least to a great extent, philosophy *in* religion. That is, it has not completely freed itself from the categories of Judeo-Christian theology.

For example, a list of the common themes in almost any western textbook on the philosophy of religion reveals an Abrahamic bias: proofs for the existence of God, theodicy, free will vis-à-vis God's omniscience, and so forth. Such concerns obviously derive from religions in which monotheism is the norm and have little direct relevance to a nontheistic religion like, say, Buddhism. Therefore, when a Japanese, living in a Buddhist country, takes up the philosophy of religion, the meaning of "religion" necessarily expands beyond the Abrahamic cluster to become more inclusive and global.

Suppose a western-based philosopher of religion raises what is perhaps the most basic question in the field: what is religion?[135] Such a philosopher is likely to answer that question in terms of categories like "faith," or a "Supreme Being," or a "theory of salvation," or "transcendence." From a Japanese standpoint, that would seem like trying to explain what art is by only referring to cubist painting. How central is faith or a Supreme Being in Confucianism? A theory of salvation in Shintō? Transcendence in Zen? Therefore, as Japanese philosophers engage in analyzing the nature of religion, the result will naturally seem expansive and category-breaking from the standpoint of the philosophy of religion as it has commonly been practiced in the modern West. That shock on western categories has been one of the most striking effects of interreligious dialogue within philosophy at large.

Kyoto School philosophy of religion: Takeuchi, Ueda, Hase, and Ōhashi. The Kyoto School has been a leader in the Japanese philosophy of religion as I have just explained it. Not only Nishida and Nishitani, but also such figures as Takeuchi Yoshinori (1913–2002), Ueda Shizuteru (1926–), Hase Shōtō (1937–) and Ōhashi Ryōsuke (1944–). Both individually and collectively they have developed creative and insightful perspectives on the nature of religion in its broadest sense. When I survey their writings, two points stand out.

First, the point of departure for the analysis is usually a philosophical anthropology. Thus, in inquiring into the nature of religion, the inquiry is framed experientially (in the vein of William James) or phenomenologically (like Rudolf Otto). As a result, there is seldom a primary interest in religion as a social phenomenon, asking why society needs religion (as in David Hume), or how religion evolves over time (as in Hegel), or how religion justifies its core web of beliefs (as in the analytic philosophy of religion).

Instead the Kyoto School philosophers ask how individuals, especially people today, may draw on religion for addressing their deepest personal concerns. That question locates the commonality across religions not in a universal, albeit variously named, transcendent absolute (as in John Hick's or Huston Smith's perennialist philosophy of religion), nor in social function (as in Durkheim), nor in an innate human psychological mechanism (as in Freud). Instead, the impulse toward religion that interests the Kyoto School thinkers is more philosophical in the existential sense.

That is, for the Kyoto School philosophers, religion arises from reflection in our everyday lives and the consciousness that there is either something missing or something amiss. To this end, Hase Shōtō has analyzed the relation between grief and religiosity or between desire and faith, whereas Ōhashi Ryōsuke has focused on compassion as the core of religion as it is lived. Takeuchi Yoshinori, a disciple of Tanabe, explored the link between Buddhism and a special way of reflecting on our experience that he named a "Buddhist existentialism." Following the language of his mentor, he claimed that "Buddhist philosophy is a metanoetics," that is, "a conversion within reflective thought that signals a return to the authentic self" as no-I.

Takeuchi also applied much of his general philosophy of religion specifically to his own tradition of Shin Buddhism. To that extent, I could have easily included him in the previous category of being a philosopher *in* religion.[136] Yet, he did not draw on Pure Land teachings for the basis of his philosophy as much as he looked for an existential basis of religion that manifests itself in Shin Buddhism, but could just as easily manifest itself in Christianity. That seemed to be the overall thrust of his discussions with the German existential theologian, Rudolf Bultmann, for example.[137]

For Nishitani, as discussed earlier in this chapter, the common ground of religions lay in the encounter with the nihility or the void that religion transforms into an engagement with emptiness as the ground of human existence. Nishitani saw that transition not only in Buddhism but also in such Christian mystics as Meister Eckhart. The mention of Eckhart leads to a second common characteristic in the Kyoto School philosophy of religion, namely, an interest in western mysticism.

The philosophy of religion and mysticism. Ueda Shizuteru, Nishitani's student, wrote his doctoral dissertation on Eckhart while studying at Marburg University. An abiding interest in his philosophical career has been how prelinguistic experience, whether specifically mystical or more generally of the sort

785–91
792–8
744–9

765–84,
1017–18

represented by Nishida's pure experience, is transformed into other levels of the expressive world, whether in poetic language or conceptualized systems of thought. (Consequently, some of Ueda's more striking theories relate to his theory of language, a topic I will address later in this chapter.)

The Kyoto School's attention to mysticism traces back, I suspect, to a theme in Nishida's philosophy from its early theory of pure experience up through his analysis of the *basho* of absolute nothing. Nishida planted the seed of the theory that all thought arises out of reflections on a primordial, not-yet-conceptualized, experiential flow. The corollary is that such a core experience precedes articulation into different philosophical systems that vary not only generically (as in idealism vs. empiricism), but also culturally (as in Christianity vs. Buddhism). Thus, all religions arise as reflections on a similar core experience. Insofar as that experience is preconceptual, it is, technically speaking, without meaning.

If that is so, then meaning arises only when that core experience becomes reflective in the sense Takeuchi described when explaining the function of philosophy in Buddhism. This suggests that all religion arises initially from an encounter with that which defies interpretation, leaving the person with an anguished feeling of being rudderless in a stormy sea. Then, the content of that experience is transformed from the void of nihility into the pregnant ground of meaning that can only be called a meaningless "nothing" that is paradoxically the source of all meaning.[138*]

To Nishitani and his successors, if one is looking for a western parallel, one can be found in the mystics of apophatic theology like Meister Eckhart wherein we find a "negative theology" that cannot characterize God except to say what God is not. As we have seen so often in Japanese philosophy, the Kyoto School philosophers are less interested in *what* the mystic may experience as in *how* the mystic's experience unfolds and is subsequently expressed.

The interest in comparative mysticism within Japanese philosophy has not been limited to the Kyoto School, however. D. T. Suzuki wrote a book on the topic[139] and Izutsu Toshihiko (1914–1993), probably more than anyone else, brought a sophisticated philosophical analysis to an extraordinary range of religious traditions from all parts of Asia. Reputed to be fluent in some two dozen languages, he translated the *Qur'an* into Japanese, wrote a comparative study of Daoist and Sufi mysticism,[140] undertook studies in classic Japanese aesthetics (some coauthored with his equally able wife, Izutsu Toyoko (1925–),[141] and wrote in English one of the first books on Zen from a philosophical point of view.[142]

913–21

1220–7

In summation: the interaction between Buddhism and philosophical theories is extensive and varied. Some present-day critics, however, question the value of the whole enterprise. We turn our attention now to one such group.

Critical Buddhism

882–9

Ichikawa Hakugen (1902–1986) and other members of the intellectual movement called "Critical Buddhism" have rejected some ideas central to Zen and the Kyoto School.[143] Ichikawa believed that Zen's emphasis on emptiness and peace of mind led to a disengaged acceptance of the status quo even in the face of the atrocities occurring during the war years. The Critical Buddhists have at times gone so far as to condemn that brand of Buddhism as not Buddhism at all, saying that no such idea of nothingness had been preached by the founder of Buddhism twenty-five centuries ago. For Shakyamuni, they said (correctly), "emptiness" simply referred to the nonsubstantiality of all things, to the idea that reality is no more than a confluence of interdependent processes.

Critical Buddhists basically accused the Zen-influenced Kyoto School of treating absolute nothing as a *what* instead of a *how*, transforming what the Buddha had said about how things function into a claim about an underlying ground of experience. In its own defense the Kyoto School could say its point is not that absolute nothing is the underlying stratum of experience, but instead a primary *way* of experiencing, namely, one that does not impose categories.

102–3

Leaving aside the argument over who said what and how they said it, the more interesting point is why Critical Buddhists such as Hakamaya Noriaki (1943–) and Matsumoto Shirō (1950–) so stridently objected to such "non-Buddhist" ideas like emptiness and buddha-nature. Their worry, like Ichikawa's, was that such ideas contribute to two seriously flawed ideas that undermine the possibility of ethics and a socially engaged Buddhism. The first error is to assert that everyone (indeed everything) is, in some sense, already enlightened. For Hakamaya and Matsumoto, that dodges the real delusions and suffering in the world, insulating them from being seriously addressed and alleviated.

The second error pointed out by the Critical Buddhists is that the assertion of some ground that is either beyond or before distinctions, including the distinction between good and evil, eliminates the foundation for moral imperatives. Once Zen purports itself to be "beyond good and evil," the impetus to moral action dissolves.

Regardless of whether one agrees with the details of the Critical Buddhist arguments, many of which I find overly simplistic, it is a fact that from the publication of Nishida's *Inquiry into the Good* up to the present, the Kyoto School has not produced an adequate philosophy of ethics. (Watsuji is a separate case insofar as his system does not arise from the individual's preconceptual experience in the way assumed by the Kyoto School philosophers of religion I am discussing here.) That is, it is generally fair to say that among the Kyoto School philosophers, an intrinsic connection between religion and ethics has not been fully explored, not to mention explained.

The discussion of the individual's experience as the basis of the religious impulse brings us to another related theme in postwar Japanese philosophy, namely, the continuing philosophical discussion about the nature of the self.

PHILOSOPHIES OF THE SELF

In this book, we have recurrently encountered the question of the meaning of *I, ego,* or *self* in Japanese philosophy. The relevant Japanese notions with their accompanying philosophical anthropologies do not mesh well with the western, especially modern western, philosophical presumptions about who, what, and how "I am." Throughout this volume, I have argued that the dominant (but not universally accepted) Japanese epistemological model is that of engaged knowing rather than that of detached knowing. If I am right, we must account for the crucial difference between a self that is primarily viewed as a locus within an interresponsive field of reality as contrasted with a self that is primarily viewed as an objective observer of an external reality. Unless we confront that cultural gap between traditional Japanese thinking and western thinking, we cannot comprehend what a modern Japanese philosopher means by the "subject" of "subjectivity" or the "agent" of "agency." Modern Japanese philosophers are equally, if not more, aware of such differences so that the analysis of self in a comparative context has been a major theme in modern Japan, becoming if anything more pronounced in the postwar period.

The Embodied Self

A good example of a postwar Japanese philosopher who recognized the implications of the gap between the modern western and the Japanese understanding of self is Yuasa Yasuo (1925–2005). Initially a student in the two fields of ethics and economics at Tokyo University, Yuasa gravitated toward Watsuji Tetsurō, becoming one of his last and most important disciples. Although expert and talented in a variety of fields, both Japanese and western, Yuasa finally decided on philosophy for his career. A crisis in his thinking occurred in 1970 when he wrote his perspicacious survey, *Modern Japanese Philosophy and Existential Thought.* Although the book was successful by all accounts, Yuasa brooded over why it had been so difficult to write. He sensed there was some element in the modern Japanese philosophers he had analyzed that fit uncomfortably with most modern western notions of "philosophy."

943–51

Calling on his extensive knowledge of the history of both Asian and western thought as well as the analytic psychology of C. G. Jung (Yuasa was at one point president of Japan's Jung Society), he finally put his finger on the issue: modern Japanese philosophy is an *embodied* enterprise in a way that modern western philosophy typically is not. Furthermore, the understandings of the body in the two cultural traditions arise from different assumptions. Despite his familiarity with so many fields, Yuasa realized how much he *didn't* know in areas pertinent to exploring those cultural differences. So he spent, for example, an entire year studying nothing but neurophysiology. To that he added the study of traditional Asian medicine, both Indian and especially Chinese.

Early in his investigations, Yuasa realized that the difference between the western and eastern understandings of the body boils down to a simple distinction: in thinking about the mind and body, the modern western problem has been to identify what connects the two (note the language of external relation and *what*), but in the Asian (not just Japanese) case, the problem has usually been how mind and body are in a changing rather than fixed relation (note the language of internal relation and *how*). That is, the goal in traditional Asian philosophical thinking was not to connect the mind and body—they are already assumed to be intrinsically connected—but instead to make the overlap ever greater, with the ideal being the *unity* of bodymind.

Yuasa's point may be clearer if I give a simple example from everyday life. Right now I am writing this sentence while typing on a laptop computer. The western mind-body question is often something like: what connects the words in my mind to the movements of my body such that I can type the words I think? Now let us turn to what Yuasa believes is the more typical Japanese question. To do so, I first need to give a richer description of the typing event.

I think of what I want to write, my fingers hopscotch across the keyboard without my looking at them, and the words I am thinking wondrously appear on the screen—all spelled correctly with punctuation properly placed. Yet, I never thought about spelling, nor the layout of the keyboard, nor the punctuation. It is as if the mind thinks and trusts the body to "know" what to do to get the words onto the computer display.

Now consider this: if I remember back to the time in middle school when I first tried to touch type, the difference between then and now is as clear as day and night. Then, I had to think not words but letters (Shift-t, h, e, n, [space key] Shift-I [space key]h,a,d [space key]...); and I had to visualize the location of the letters on the keyboard, "telling" my fingers where to tap. It was as if the mind didn't trust the body and had to command what it should do.

Most traditional and modern Japanese philosophers, according to Yuasa, consider the following to be the interesting question about bodymind: how did the transition between those two modes of bodymind—my experience of learning to type vs. my experience of being an accomplished touch typist—occur? (Notice that again the question has shifted from a *what* to a *how*.) Yuasa calls the modality of bodymind in my middle school experience, "the bright consciousness" of the Cartesian *cogito* (the "I think" of Descartes' famous "I think; therefore I am"). If we seek, as Descartes did, "clear and distinct ideas," that is where we will find them. When I typed in middle school, each letter, each finger, each key on the keyboard was clear and distinct. If given a blank template of a keyboard, I could write in the location of the letters from memory.

Through "cultivation" (*shugyō*, the Japanese word for disciplined, embodied praxis or training), the clear and distinct mode becomes gradually so embedded in my second-nature embodied behavior that my typing starts to occur without self-conscious awareness. Indeed, as I type now, I am aware of my thoughts, but the agency in the transfer to the computer display through my embodied activity is hidden in what Yuasa calls the "dark consciousness." It seems to happen "of itself" (*jinen*). Indeed, if I am now filling in a blank keyboard template, I find it easier to move my fingers as if typing and then the right letter comes to mind. It is as if my *fingers* know where the keys are.

Yuasa developed those ideas in his career-changing book of 1977, *The Body: Toward an Eastern Mind-body Theory*.[144] According to Yuasa, when it comes to analyzing the process by which repeated, disciplined action becomes second-nature so as to achieve a unity of bodymind, western philosophers are, for the most part, in the dark about what to say. There are exceptions, though, and Yuasa explored some in the modern western tradition, such as the philosophers Maurice Merleau-Ponty and Henri Bergson as well as neurophysiological studies of conditioned responses and the Jungian theory of the subconscious.

Yuasa's book brought those western voices in conversation with an array of philosophies we have explored in this book including those of Kūkai, Dōgen, Nishida, Watsuji, and the classical aesthetics of *waka*. He also juxtaposed theories from traditional Asian medicine with modern western theories of psychosomatic medicine. In his later books, Yuasa drew further connections with athletic training and the martial arts as well as research into generative force (*ki*) as the underlying common element of East Asian metaphysics, traditional medicine, and cultivation practices.[145]

The mention of traditional Asian medicine raises another area of Japanese postwar reflection related to the body: bioethics. As we have seen, the traditional Japanese view is one of an engaged body rather than an objectified, physical object that can be studied from the outside in a detached scientific way. How does that affect the thinking about such contemporary issues like brain death or organ transplantation? In an essay written for *Japanese Philosophy: A Sourcebook*, Hayashi Yoshihiro highlighted three points that express long-standing cultural values relevant to today's Japanese debates about medical policy.

1231–45

First, in accord with what I have called in this book the holographic relation of the whole in every part, there is evidence that some Japanese think the whole of a person's identity is somehow in every part of the body. Thus, Yonemoto Shōhei in his book *Bioethics* quoted a woman whose brain-dead daughter was a liver donor: "I do not think of my child as dead but as fit and living inside of

1236

someone else's body."

1239–40

Second, philosophers like Kimura Bin (1931–), journalists like Nakajima Michi, and the historian of science Komatsu Yoshihiko have argued for the importance of the communal aspect of death. For them, death is not simply the shutdown of an isolated physical mechanism but an event of social meaning. For example, before an organ transplant is performed, the family has to recognize that death has occurred. Yet, in brain death, the body is still warm and flexible while respiration (though aided by machines) continues. The normal cycle of recognition and mourning is thereby disrupted, creating a cognitive and affective dissonance between the definition of death and the experiencing of someone as dead.

1236–7;
1241–2

Third, philosophers like Umehara Takeshi (1925–) as well as Yuasa himself have noted that the western justification for brain death as defining the point at which transplants are morally acceptable is based in a Cartesian model of the body as a soulless machine with interchangeable parts. Yet, as we have just seen, the traditional Japanese bodymind model of personal identity does not readily lend itself to such a mechanistic understanding. For example, if every organ is holographically mirroring the pattern of the person's whole bodymind complex, are body parts unproblematically interchangeable with those from another person?

For such culturally embedded reasons, although organ transplants based on the brain-death definition for the end of life have been legal in Japan since 1997, the number of actual transplants performed is much lower than in western countries with similar laws and available technology. When it comes to matters of greatest import, and certainly the issues of life and death qualify, cultural sentiments inevitably play a crucial role.

Yuasa's discussion of the role of embodied repetition resonates with an interest in postwar Japanese philosophers working in the aesthetics of *kata*, the patterns of movement that are practiced in preparation for, and in the realization

930–5

of, artistic performance. Minamoto Ryōen (1920–), a philosopher and intellectual historian trained in the Kyoto School tradition, wrote a comprehensive philosophical study about *kata*.[146] In it, he explores how the Japanese tradition of "no-mind" exemplifies the epitome of the transition from the ordinary mindfulness (which is also embodied but not fully integrated) to a complete integration of form into the bodymind. Ultimately, *kata* then becomes more than the individual movements of performance that are practiced repetitively (as in playing arpeggios on a piano, say); it becomes instead the entire flow of a bodymind event from preparation to the resonances continuing after the performance ends. The fullest expression of *kata* is then no longer just form but attains the status of being style.

In summation: thanks to the groundwork of such innovative thinkers as Yuasa, the embodied aspect of knowing has become a prevalent theme among many postwar Japanese philosophers. In recent years, incidentally, some western theorists have begun to show a similar interest in somatics, performance, and engaged knowing. Because, as we have seen throughout this book, the model of embodied, engaged knowing has been very much at the forefront of Japanese philosophy from its inception, that tradition might have a treasure trove of insights to stimulate the thinking of western philosophers interested in these issues. Such a dialogue between Japanese and western theorists could ultimately also enrich the West's understanding of agency, including the meaning of subjectivity, our next topic.

The Nature and Function of "Subjectivity"

As we have seen in surveying the history of Japanese philosophy, when a Japanese philosopher encounters a mistaken view, especially a particularly popular and enduring one, the first response is commonly not to simply reject it, but instead to understand its origins; not to rebut *what* is false, but to determine *how* the false idea came about. In terms of theories of the self, a pernicious error, according to many Japanese philosophers, is to consider the self as a discrete entity, separate from the world and from others, a detached observer of reality. Instead most Japanese think of the self as an interdependent being in a shared responsive state with other people and the world, an engaged participant in reality.

Perhaps it is revealing that in *Childhood and Society*, a western classic in the psychology of human maturation, Erik Erikson famously laid out eight stages of psychosocial development, labeling the highest stage "ego integrity." Although Erikson's theory is rich in nuance including, for example, the renunciation of the narcissistic self, my concern is not the theory but the terminology. From the perspective of many Japanese philosophers, both premodern and modern, the term *ego integrity* sounds more like a pathology than an aspiration. The choice of words conjures an image of exactly the kind of self most traditional Japanese philosophers have considered false.

The question: how could such a false notion originate? Putting this in Buddhist terminology, if no-I or *anātman* (J. *muga*) describes how things really are, how does the idea of "I" or *ātman* (J. *jiga*) arise? Some postwar Japanese philosophers have taken up that question as a central concern in their writings.

A good example of such a thinker is the already mentioned Kimura Bin (1931–), a practicing psychiatrist who has written extensively in the area of abnormal psychology, especially schizophrenia. Kimura is also, however, a serious student of both western and Asian philosophy, including that of the Kyoto

958–72

School. His professional practice and personal interest converge in his theorizing about the nature of self. My previous comment about the nomenclature in Erikson's extolling "ego integrity" is directly relevant here. From Kimura's perspective, to try to live as if one were primarily a discrete, individuated self is more likely to lead to a pathological rather than healthy self-image.

Rejecting the ideal of the isolated individual untouchable in his or her own integrity, Kimura stresses instead an image of healthy human existence as an identity that interpenetrates with others (a "being with"; G. *Mitsein*), a person who is deeply engaged in both the social and natural world. As a philosopher, Kimura wonders how such a false idea as that of the atomistic self or ego should be so persistent, not just in the West but seemingly in every culture. Wherein lies the psychological basis for such a distortion of what we are? He thinks a key lies in our tendency to reify events. Life is a flow of events (*koto*), but when we think about them or even put them into words, that event becomes a fixed object or thing (*mono*). We have to *stabilize* the flow of events so they can be remembered, described, or analyzed.

I have been reminded of Kimura's idea when trying to photograph a family event like a birthday party. The party is, as William James would put it, a "buzzing, blooming confusion"—a lived event. As I move in to snap my pictures, I make a thing of that event, a frozen birthday-party memory to be preserved in a photo album perhaps. In so doing, however, I am losing my engagement with the event of the party as it occurs. By definition, the photographer is an onlooker, not a participant. I am engaged in recording the party, not being part of the party. At times, if I am not careful, the party can end and I can feel I was never really "there." Fortunately, at least the photos of the party will always be there for me to engage at a later moment. Unlike the party, the pictures are not fleeting but they are also not alive.

Kimura's point is that the type of activity I just described is not idiosyncratic or rare, but is fundamental to our way of thinking. The record, that stabilizing and reifying activity, becomes my image of myself when I lose engagement with the flow of life. He summarizes his point in this way:

> Our consciousness does not seem to like this sort of instability. The reason may be that what we call "self" or "myself" or "I" is in fact not a thing but rather the event of "being myself" or "being I," something unstable without any clear form or whereabouts. The self, by nature unstable, tries to find a spot in the world in which to stabilize itself. But the world of events, far from supporting it, does nothing but increasingly expose its instability. That is why the self, as soon as it encounters an event, immediately takes distance from it and looks at it to change it into a thing.

Kimura's insight is reminiscent of Nishida's "anguished soul" that arises when one becomes self-aware of the openness and instability of the noumenal self.[†]

I mentioned Kimura's insistence that the self is not an individuated, isolated "I" but rather a "being-with." A postwar philosopher who has vigorously argued for the importance of recognizing the "collective subject" as part of a theory of self was the philosopher Hiromatsu Wataru (1933–1994), whose work on *mono* and *koto*, in fact, inspired Kimura Bin. I prefaced this discussion of the self with the general observation that Japanese philosophers, when encountering a wrong view, tend to look for the source of the error. Hiromatsu shifts the focus in that question to asking how it is even possible to judge another's understanding as a mistake. How does my experience of someone else's view as erroneous unfold?

973–8

Hiromatsu gives the example of an infant boy who mistakes a cow for a dog, calling it "doggie." For me to recognize that act as a mistake, Hiromatsu explains, I have to take a position outside my individual self in at least two ways. First, I have to be able to imagine what the child is trying to do, specifically, name the thing—or shall we say "event"—in front of him. To do so I must become a subject who is myself doing the naming. Thus, I establish a self-duality: the "I" who takes the position of the boy and the "I" who knows the animal is a cow, not a dog. But that is not all. I must also take the standpoint of "standard English speaker" to know that the correct word is "cow." That nomenclature is not of my own making as an individual, but rather derives from my acting as a "universal speaker of English," a posture for which my individuality is irrelevant.

Thus, I as the subject who judges that the child has committed an error, is at least a threefold I: the I as standard English-speaker, the I who imagines naming the animal, and the I who is the individual witnessing the utterance. Who judges the "mistake?" The threefold I as a collective subject, says Hiromatsu. Therefore, in even simple everyday acts, I am multiple, not singular.

In both Kimura and Hiromatsu, we have seen how their theories of self relate to language in some respect. In postwar Japan the philosophy of language has often honed in specifically on the nature of the Japanese language in comparison with other languages. This has typically been part of a larger theme, the nature of being "Japanese," the last topic I will address in this chapter.

BEING JAPANESE IN JAPANESE

1010–18

Japanese theories of language go back at least as far as Kūkai, but since the Native Studies movement and Edo-period Confucianism, Japanese philosophers have become especially preoccupied with language, often

---

† See page 475.

specifically with the Japanese language as compared and contrasted with other languages. In Native Studies that fascination intermingled with an attempt to define Japanese uniqueness and in the mid-Meiji period through the war years, it became part of a political ideology dedicated to defining Japan's singular mission in the modern world. The Meiji period and wartime ideology of Japanese uniqueness was characterized as "Japanism" (nihonshugi) by such advocates as Inoue Tetsujirō. Of course, after the war ended, such ideology was squelched.

By the end of the 1970s, however, a movement called "theorizing Japaneseness" (nihonjinron) reignited the smoldering embers from the earlier Japanist ideology. Not as blatantly political in its expressed intent, it nonetheless has sometimes attracted nationalistic and ethnocentric critics and scholars. Not everyone who participated in the discussions were right-wing, it should be noted, and some scholars and public intellectuals within the nihonjinron sphere held that there was not anything about being Japanese that was any more distinctive than any other national or ethnic identity.

As Watsuji had stressed even as far back as Fūdo: Japan may be unique, but not uniquely unique.[†] From that perspective, there is nothing dangerous nor necessarily ideological in studying the particularities of Japanese culture any more than there is something problematic about ethnic studies, linguistic studies, literary studies, gender studies, religious studies, or philosophical studies that concentrate on any other particular culture or subculture. Indeed, those who admonish Japanese scholars not to study what is characteristic of their own culture seem to be inadvertently making the bizarre claim that to study what is unique in one's own culture is uniquely dangerous for a Japanese. If someone really believes that, it seems that they themselves are making a claim for Japanese uniqueness.

Attempting to establish a neutral academic venue for the collaborative exchange among multiple disciplines and points of view concerning scholarship on Japan, in the 1980s some universities began to establish programs and departments in "Japanese Studies" (nihongaku—often translated in Japan as "Japanology"), loosely inspired by the idea of "American Studies" as taught in the United States as well as some European equivalents. In such Japanese Studies programs, one may still find lurking in the academic hallways and closets some scholars of the more ethnocentric or jingoistic ilk, but for the most part those reactionaries represent only one voice—clearly a minority voice—among researchers in that newly defined field.

The first department of Japanese Studies to be established in a national university, incidentally, was at Ōsaka University and its first director was the afore-

---

† See page 492.

mentioned Yuasa Yasuo, the student of Watsuji. It is in the spirit of *nihongaku*, not *nihonjinron*, and certainly not *nihonshugi* that I will discuss what some philosophers have said about the Japanese language in the postwar years.

I begin with Mori Arimasa (1911–1976). As we have seen, philosophers of language such as Hiromatsu and Kimura mostly focus on the nature of language in general. Although many of their points are more self-evident if one thinks of Japanese semantics and syntax, their aim was to analyze the complex structure of linguistic expression in *any* language. A couple of decades earlier, Mori Arimasa reflected on language in a somewhat different frame of reference. Tutored in French since a young boy, when Mori studied philosophy at Tokyo Imperial University, he wrote his thesis on Pascal. When it became possible to do so after the war, he gave up his teaching post at Tokyo University and moved to France in 1952 where he continued to teach until his death.

1047–52

As immersed in French language and culture as he was, Mori never lost his awareness of his Japanese roots. He taught about Japanese culture and language while in France and lectured in Japan during extended visits to his homeland in his later years, exploring in both venues the nature between "experience and thought," especially as manifest in language. Although not a linguistic determinist—after all he himself spoke and thought bilingually—he did recognize languages as having their own "mechanisms" normally hidden to speakers as they use the language, but able to be made visible upon reflection, especially by those who know more than one language and can compare them.

For example, he thought it significant (as had Norinaga[†]) that Japanese inflects verbal endings indicating tense, formality, and the social relation between speaker and audience, but neither number nor person. The implication is that even when a statement is made from a neutral standpoint ("It is Tuesday"), the Japanese verbal ending reveals something about the social relation in which the statement is uttered. If so, despite its apparent grammatical form, the statement is really not impersonal (not "third person" in orientation). Mori calls this the "slipping in of reality," the reality being that language is always by someone with someone else (a you-to-you or second-person orientation).

Mori's analysis is similar to Hiromatsu's in some respects, but Mori assumes it reveals something notable about the relation between the Japanese language and Japanese culture, whereas Hiromatsu assumes his points are about language in general. As I explained in Chapter 9, Motoori Norinaga discovered in the Japanese language various functions that Kūkai had claimed to be true of all languages, such as the assumption that language confers with, rather than refers to, reality. Is that a parallel for what is happening here—one philosopher

† See pages 380–2.

ethnicizes a linguistic function that another philosopher would consider universal? Not necessarily.

For Mori, the important point is that the "mechanism" of the interpersonal relation is on the surface in the Japanese language, whereas in French (or English), for example, it is hidden and has to be unearthed with an analysis such as the one Hiromatsu undertakes. That difference between patent and latent mechanisms, Mori thinks, affects speaking and thinking on some level. That is, in Japanese impersonal statements (such as purely logical, propositional statements) are difficult to make without seeming unnatural, abstract, or contrived. So an idea of language as conference rather than reference is more likely to seem intuitively right to a native Japanese speaker.

That does not mean, of course, that the Japanese people are determined by their language to think one way and English-speakers, for instance, another. As Hiromatsu's analysis and (I hope) my explanation of Kūkai's theory of language in Chapter 3 of this volume have shown, the conference theory of language can be persuasively argued in relation to English as well.

The previously mentioned† Kyoto School philosopher, Ueda Shizuteru, sheds some further light on how different languages bring philosophical insights to the surface in different ways. Like Mori, Ueda has also spent his philosophical career spanning two languages, in his case, German and Japanese. Earlier, I mentioned that Ueda has a special interest in mysticism and his larger concern was how the prelinguistic finds its way into the world of expression. That same interest also resonates with his experience of learning to write philosophically in German instead of his native tongue. As he explains, it was "more a matter of training myself in how to look at things than it was a matter of training myself in German." He discovered that what he eventually wrote was "different from, but not inferior to, how I would say it in Japanese." His bilingual training in philosophy has, in fact, become part of his way of doing philosophy.

1018

> In later years, I would have many occasions to write in German, but when doing so, I first let the matter at hand be situated in a position between Japanese and German (as a kind of *Vor-sache* ["pre-thing"]...). Then it could be expressed clearly in German or in Japanese, depending on which language I was writing in. This is not to say that what became clear in German always coincided with what became clear in Japanese. They could at times be different, but not completely different. Though each in its own way achieved a clarity, there remained a surplus in the intervening space of the *Vor-sache*. It was there that the clarities of German and the clarities of Japanese reverberate
>
> 1018
>
> against one another and intermingle.

† See pages 554–5.

That is, although what is said in German can be translated into Japanese and vice versa, how the meanings become clear in each case emerges through a different linguistic process.

Ueda also raises the issue of the expressive function of language more generally, making use of the Kyoto School notion of "absolute nothing" to speak of "the hollow." As his discussion of the "pre-thing" in the just previously quoted passage suggests, language normally makes things appear in our experience, escorting them from a pre-thing (or not-yet-meaningful) state into becoming a thing (with meaning). As the thing-with-meaning appears, it is more than a mere word and the need for the word recedes into the background, back into the meaningless hollow. After all, once the word brings us into engagement with the thing, we no longer need the word. The totality of things is what we call our "world."

766–84

For Ueda, therefore, our world emerges through the expressive function of language, but as it becomes world, language itself disappears. Of course, if for some reason, we need to point to a thing in that world, we can once again use the words to do so. In the actualized world, words can be linked to things easily because things come into the actual world through words. Yet, there are also other words that arise from the world but point beyond it.

For example, a fictional or metaphorical expression does not correspond to any actual thing but is "only" words. Ueda calls them "hollow words" since they break through the actual world of things-with-associated-words to a realm of just-words beyond actual things. As such they remind us of the meaningless hollow within which the actual world of things comes into being, but which itself is never expressible as a thing.

That is rather dense, but an example may help. Suppose I am a newcomer to Japan and a local friend is taking me for a hike through the woods. After walking for some time, he stops and looks at a rope tied around a tree with pieces of folded paper hanging from it. He points to the rope and says "*shimenawa.*" I realize that the rope marks a tree of some special spiritual significance. Unbeknownst to me, in the earlier part of the walk, we had twice before passed a tree encircled with a *shimenawa*, but I had not noticed them. They had not been part of my "world" as I was walking through this territory new to me. From that point on, however, I notice every other *shimenawa* we come across. Interestingly, I can't even recall the word *shimenawa* but the word is not so important now that the *shimenawa* themselves are part of my world. After all, the *shimenawa* itself is more than the word *shimenawa*.

Some hours later we return to town and I recount our hike to our wives who had not accompanied us. I start to explain about the *shimenawa* but cannot recall the word. As I struggle to think of it, my Japanese friend's wife kindly helps me out, "*Shimenawa.*" "Yes," I say, "*shimenawa.*" Ueda's point is that the word used the first time during the hike has a different function from the same word later uttered by my friend's wife. The first *"shimenawa"* brought a new thing into my world; the second just reminded me of a link between a thing in my world and the word everyone sharing that world uses to refer to it.

Now consider this example. A Harvard undergraduate, T. S. Eliot, is writing a poem at his desk and in describing the evening sky, he pens the words "a patient etherized upon a table." That phrase brings no new thing into our world when we read it for the first time. Nor is it linked to any actual thing in the way *shimenawa* is. The words are "hollow" in Ueda's terminology. Their function, however, is to call attention to themselves as words that break through the referential use of language into the hollow void from which all words and things emerge. Such is the language of poetry and religion. Ueda would say the poetic power of Eliot's phrase derives from its *not* being the way people in the actual world ordinarily speak of the evening.

In regard to how poetry can clear away the ordinary world and open up the locus of the hollow, consider the following statements by Yosano Akiko, the famed poet whom I mentioned previously in regard to the women's movement of the early twentieth century.[†] First, she notes how poetic language differs from ordinary language.

> …In the same way that painters fret over the purity of their colors, the thickness of the pigment on the face of the canvas, and the quality of the finished work, poets invest the same care in their work. A poem can never rest content with merely communicating a certain meaning the way a prose composition can.

1146

Yosano then continues to talk about what the poetic language can do in its erasing the ordinary world, using terms like "transparent" and "washing clean":

> Scholarship, which relies chiefly on reason, also enhances human life, but arts make our feelings transparent and as such wash our life clean in a more direct way. If one has only to read another's artistic expression to be emancipated from the narrow and oppressive world of the "useful," how much more so when one actually experiences the joys and trials of creativity!…

1147

For Yosano, it is one matter for Japanese philosophy to analyze creative forms of language, but quite another to use creative language as its own self-expression. In the above passage, Yosano seems to draw a hard distinction between the discursive qualities of academic "scholarship," which presumably would include most academic philosophy, as contrasted with artistic or poetic expression. Ueda, by contrast, seemed to think the mystical and the creative exist at

---

† See pages 433–4.

the threshold of ordinary experience and should, it would seem, be accessible to philosophers as well as to poets.

Those are points about language in general, but does the Japanese language pose any particular challenges to the philosopher? Some think so. The aforementioned Buddhist philosophical scholar, Nakamura Hajime,[†] for instance, thought there might be a problem with the Japanese language itself as a vehicle for logical and philosophical thinking. Of course, language is not a mental prison. If we want to escape the strictures of our native language, we can coin new words, devise new locutions, even over time change the syntax and grammar. (Think of the disappearance of *thee, thou, thy,* and *thine* in the modernization of English, for example.) So, Nakamura believed adjustments could be made if Japan "as a nation [would] develop the skills and linguistic tools for precise thinking." He saw no evidence of that change in 1964, however, when he wrote:

> Yet, even now, no one in Japan expresses philosophy in purely original Japanese words. We are, therefore, forced to conclude that Japanese has not been as fit for philosophical thinking as Sanskrit or Greek was or as German seems to be. 1016

Along similar lines, in the give-and-take part of the OM discussions, the literary critic Kobayashi Hideo accused the philosopher participants of writing in a Japanese that was stilted, unnatural, and difficult to understand. He wryly added, "We have the sense that Japanese philosophers really care very little for the fact that fate has given them a native language to write in." Nishitani defended himself by claiming, "[I]n order to be understood" philosophers often must be "forging a new language." Then he sniped, "Really, there is no time to bother writing in a way that general Japanese readers can understand." Who, then, was he hoping would understand? "To be frank, we feel as if we are writing for western intellectuals...." Since Nishitani's mentor was Nishida, that 1017 attitude might also account for some of Nishida's penchant for turgid locutions.

Perhaps no philosopher reflected more insightfully about the problems of writing philosophy in Japanese than Sakabe Megumi (1936–2009). Sakabe's 979–92 perspective was global in both the geographical and interdisciplinary sense. Renowned for his scholarship in western philosophy, especially Kant and contemporary critical theory, he was also a major interpreter of the Japanese philosophical tradition, especially the late-Edo through modern periods. His 1976 book on modern Japanese philosophy, *A Hermeneutics of the Mask,* had a major impact on how many subsequent philosophers viewed the period. His

† See page 548.

writings on Watsuji and Kuki Shūzō were also pioneering in their own way. At the same time, his interest in language, perhaps originating in his studies of European critical theory, expanded into various logical and linguistic issues. As a result, Sakabe's theory of language is rich and complex, but perhaps I can give us a taste of his approach by placing him in the context of the ideas we have been exploring in this part of the chapter.

First, Sakabe shares many assumptions with the philosophers I have been discussing even though he may not always specifically mention them. In fact, in many ways he is able to accept all their assumptions, even the ones that seem incompatible with each other, because he relegates them into a more comprehensive view of his own. For example, with Hiromatsu and Mori, Sakabe recognizes the collective subject and interpersonal space of linguistic discourse as a starting part. Sakabe calls that the "horizontal" parameter of the subjectivity within expression, associating it with Watsuji.

On the other hand, with Ueda and Yosano, Sakabe shares an appreciation of the creative function of language, in which the self transcends itself by a creative act that uses poetic language to break free of concepts and tap into the absolute, the ineffable emptiness at the source of the self. Sakabe speaks of that self-transcending movement as the "vertical" parameter of subjectivity within expression, associating it with Nishida's theory of self-transcendence in his "logic of the predicate." Returning to Kimura, we could say the predicate-based unfolding of language is a way of capturing the "event" character of experience before we reify it into things. This brings us to Sakabe's more technical linguistic analysis.

The postwar Japanese linguist who comes closest to Nishida's stress on the primacy of the predicate was, as Sakabe pointed out, Tokieda Motoki (1900–1967). Tokieda is well-known for two interrelated projects. First, as a scholar, he analyzed the much neglected traditional Japanese theories of grammar existing in the Edo period before the influx of western linguistic theory, indeed some theories going as far back as the poetics of the *waka* by Fujiwara Teika in the medieval period. There we find the emphasis on the predicate, the inflectional forms of the verbal, and the *te-ni-wo-ha* linking particles.

Tokieda's other contribution was as a constructive thinker who developed the "language process theory." That theory also emerges from the assumptions of the premodern Japanese grammarians and presents a process-based alternative to Saussure (at least as Tokieda understood him). Sakabe's critique of Tokieda's linguistic theory of the Japanese language is intriguing and will point us toward his interesting perspective on philosophizing in the Japanese language, but before addressing that I should cover a few other points preliminary to Sakabe's main analysis.

Sakabe was exasperated with using modern philosophical Japanese for actually thinking through and expressing the main tenets of Japanese philosophy. Sakabe believed, first of all, the vocabulary of modern Japanese philosophy is characterized by various kinds of "slippage." Most importantly, as western philosophy entered Japan in the latter half of the nineteenth century, neologisms had to be devised to translate the western terms. Both Nakamura Hajime and Sakabe believed the method for generating the new vocabulary was fraught with difficulties: basically, new compound words were created by juxtaposing traditional sinographs from China. The alternative—building the vocabulary for modern Japanese philosophy by creating neologisms out of native Japanese words—was never seriously pursued.

As Nakamura pointed out, in late medieval Germany when philosophy and theology were beginning to be expressed in the vernacular rather than in Latin, the new vocabulary was constructed out of ordinary German words. In fact, the aforementioned Meister Eckhart, the apophatic mystic on whom Ueda wrote his doctoral thesis and who was frequently cited by Nishitani and D. T. Suzuki, was a chief architect for building up the German philosophical vocabulary as we have it today. The question Nakamura and Sakabe asked was why something similar did not happen for the Japanese language when developing a modern vocabulary for its philosophizing. Nakamura surmised that although the native Japanese language "had a rich vocabulary of words denoting aesthetic or emotional states of mind," it nonetheless "lacked a vocabulary denoting intellectual and inferential thought processes," so it created neologisms that were spin-offs of Chinese Buddhist and Confucian terms.

1015

Sakabe's reading of the situation was different. First of all, he was more critical than Nakamura of the mismatch between western thinking and the Chinese sinographs brought to Japan through Buddhism and Confucianism. Sakabe's question was that since the Chinese sinographs were not such a good match anyway, why not try to use native Japanese instead? The real problem, he believed, was the entrance of western philosophy into Japan at the precise time that Native Studies (and the State Shintō associated with it) were fetishizing the native Japanese words (the *yamato kotoba*). Obsessed with purifying the ancient Japanese words and expunging the influence of Chinese on the "genuine" ancient Japanese language, it would only be a further defilement to use pure Japanese words to express ideas from yet another foreign source. Fetishism in the understanding of the Japanese language was also central to Sakabe's critique against Tokieda.

Sakabe was disappointed that Tokieda did not see a crucial implication of the historical part of his analysis, namely, that in premodern Japan, the grammars were not intended to be anything like a modern, scientific linguistic theory as Tokieda wished his language process scheme to be. Rather, the traditional grammars were part of a project in poetics, in effect, a metapractical reflection on the writing of poetry. To put it in terms I have used throughout this book, the traditional grammars were not primarily about *what* the rules and structures of the Japanese language are, but about *how* to use Japanese in poetic expression. The goal of the traditional works was not to have a detached understanding of the Japanese language, but instead to engage the Japanese grammar so as to realize the language's creative powers. Stated differently, we could say Sakabe wished the form of Tokieda's analysis (which after all was written in Japanese) to match the content of what he was analyzing.

Note, for example, Yosano's explanation of the evocative power of poetry in the paragraph quoted earlier in this chapter.[†] Sakabe's fear is that modern scientism has so colored our way of thinking that even when we read a work on the poetics of the Japanese language we transform the gist of that work into a scientific treatise. The fetishizing of the Japanese language continues in the form of scientific linguistics: we make the language into a thing external to us and analyze it as if we were bystanders instead of people engaged in using the language even as we are analyzing it.

Sakabe's hope, he told me in a conversation, was to try to figure out how to make the language of Japanese philosophy more "feminine" (*taoyameburi*) than "masculine" (*masuraoburi*). I warned him that those terms derive from Motoori Norinaga and have ethnocentric, maybe even nationalistic, nuances. He made it clear, however, that he was not seeking to bring out some Japanese uniqueness, but rather he wanted to return Japanese philosophy to the roots of its everyday language instead of having it entangled in contrived abstractions. In effect, I would say he wanted to find a language for philosophy that was more engaging than detached.

Sakabe thought Watsuji and Kuki Shūzō had begun to do that, but much more remained to be done. In 1987, about the time of our conversation, he wrote the following, beginning with his concern that the study of language has become a detached scientistic enterprise:

> The danger of straying into a cul-de-sac and idolizing words and the subject of linguistic practice had always been there, and the fully ripened cultural practice since the Edo period had great difficulty finding its place in a culture influenced by the spirit of (classic) modern science, which by its nature is unfamiliar with such things as free transposition of the power of imagination....

991

Noting the negative impact of that approach on the language of philosophers, Sakabe continues:

† See page 568.

Nor can philosophical thinking be divorced from this kind of critical circumstance. For example, Nishida's thought, which is extremely difficult to comprehend, and his style, which is deadly serious to the point of being suffocating, are emblematic of the vast distance that needs to be traversed in order to return to the foundation of the tradition of productive compositional or imaginative power in Japan.

992

Looking to the possibility of a new way of writing philosophy in Japan, Sakabe muses:

> On what kind of basis of linguistic or poetic compositional practice, on what kind of practice that in general has to do with community, would it then be possible in contemporary Japan to develop a truly free and productive subjectivity or mutual subjectivity?

992

Sakabe had hoped to not only write about this new language for philosophy, but also to write a book in that language. Sad to say, he died before his plan came to full fruition. I hope some Japanese philosopher will someday realize that dream for him. That last remark leads to the topic of asking what Japanese philosophy might be in the future. In so doing, we turn to my Conclusion.

15. Conclusion

In my honors philosophy seminar, I asked a blunt question of the venerable professor seated at the other end of the table. I was a college sophomore and my question predictably brazen. It was around the time for me to specify a major field of study, a decision that would likely both enrich and limit what I would be able to do the rest of my life as a career. Like many sophomores, I was at the time an existentialist by temperament, awash in radical freedom and constantly crashing against the facticity of reality. I was just twenty and Brand Blanshard, the retired philosophy professor who was our guest for that session of the seminar, was seventy-five. We had just finished reading his *Reason and Analysis*. Around the Yale philosophy department Blanshard was affectionately known as "the world's last living rationalist." He believed that all events everywhere are part of an interconnected whole and, furthermore, that reason is at least capable of penetrating every nook and cranny of that order. Clearly *not* an existentialist.

As the seminar drew to a close with time for one last question, I looked Blanshard in the eye, putting to him my sophomoric query, "Professor Blanshard, as you reflect on your philosophical career, what difference has it made?" He returned my look, replying without hesitation, "For whatever reason, I was born a rationalist. And should there ever be another one born, that person can read my writings and know what follows from that position." Recognizing the honesty and authenticity of his answer, I enrolled as a philosophy major later that week.

Now that former sophomore has himself just recently retired. The specter of my younger self glares, throws down the gauntlet, and asks of my philosophical career, "What difference has it made?" My shift of primary focus from the western to the Japanese tradition had at first seemed exotic, a turn toward a world of kōans instead of propositions, of mandalas instead of syllogisms, of *kokoro* instead of *cogito*. If I had thought I was escaping philosophy as I knew it, however, my Zen master in Kyoto quickly disabused me of that idea. In our first interview Kobori-*roshi* asked "What is Zen?" I could give no answer that would satisfy me, let alone him. Breaking into laughter, he said pointedly, "You're a philosopher. You know what Zen is—*know thyself*." The master had placed me between the two poles of Japanese and western philosophy, knowing that if I went too far toward one, the other would pull me back. For the time being, however, I was lost in the midst.

Max Mueller opined some 150 years ago that if all you know is your own religion, you know no religion. I have come to the conclusion you cannot fully understand philosophy either unless you also engage a philosophical tradition other than your own. How else can you uncover hidden cultural bias, imagine both the limits and possibilities of alternative terminologies, and evaluate major historical shifts in the history of philosophy as philosophers encountered ideas from other cultures? By walking down the path of Japanese philosophy, I began to see western philosophy from a new vantage point.

PHILOSOPHY AS WAY

When Socrates claimed philosophy boils down to knowing yourself, I take him to mean a philosopher—at least a good philosopher—does not think about philosophical issues, but instead thinks about ordinary issues in a philosophical way. Philosophy demands we plummet our inner depths, including how those depths bubble up through the specifics of our particular times and places. Evaluating Japanese philosophy, both classical and modern, has convinced me that at its best philosophy does indeed constitute a Way. It does not reduce to being a detached understanding of either reality or of other philosophers' ideas of reality.

I do not doubt most professional philosophers care deeply about their specialty. God have pity on us if we don't—what desiccated lives we would live. But the issue I am posing is not how we feel about philosophy, but rather how we feel about wisdom. After all, is not philosophy supposedly the love of wisdom? As an internal relation, does not love involve risk? Does the wisdom gleaned from philosophy transform who we are as persons? Or have we grown more aloof, safely examining philosophical puzzles from afar? Do we just analyze the problems the discipline generates, critiquing what others have said, and perhaps adding an idea or two of our own to the compost heap of once living ideas in hopes they might one day become fertile again?

When western philosophy came to Meiji Japan, the Japanese certainly took it to be a detached science, coining a new word for western-style philosophers: *tetsugakusha* or "scholars of wisdom." They did not choose to use *tetsujin* or "wise ones," a title for those who had mastered a Way, a *michi* or *dō*. A *tetsujin* might follow the Way of the Confucian sagely scholar, the Way of the *kami*, the Way of the Buddha, or even one of the Ways of artistry. A Way involves engaged knowing. The bodymind undertakes a disciplined training, modeling the forms of the masters or master texts, until it exemplifies the Way itself. Nishida likely knew that when he left his desk to take his daily stroll down the *Tetsugaku no michi*, "the Way of philosophy" (pictured on page 449).

At this point, I feel the pull back toward the western pole of the betweenness. After my excursion, however, I see some things I did not notice before in my home tradition. The Japanese idea of philosophy, that of the acquired wisdom discovered by means of the bodymind and expressed through it, strikes me as being closer to the original vision of philosophy in the ancient Greeks like Plato and Aristotle than it is to the modern emphasis on an impersonal, incorporeal knowing.[1] I'll begin with Plato, focusing not on *what* he said, but *how* he said it.

Plato wrote animated philosophical conversations. In his dialogues, most strikingly in those from his early and middle periods, Plato did not present his philosophy as a disembodied dialectic between opposing positions (as Hegel often did, for example). In Plato, ideas don't contend with each other; real flesh-and-blood people *with ideas* do. Plato wrote dramatically, crafting not only the words of the dialogue but also including what we might think of as stage directions, that is, descriptions of physical action.

Take Plato's *Republic* 336b, for example. Growing impatient listening to others around the table discussing the meaning of justice, Thrasymachus literally jumps into the conversation:

> ...[H]unched up like a wild beast, he flung himself at us as if to tear us to pieces. Then both Polemarchus and I [Socrates] got all in a flutter from fright. And he shouted out into our midst and said, "What is this nonsense that has possessed you for so long, Socrates?"[2]

So what does Thrasymachus argue? That might makes right, that justice is determined by the strong. Thrasymachus's beliefs match his personality, behavior, and method of persuasion. For Plato, philosophy is not simply *what* one believes; it is also *how* one lives it. Granted, in his final analysis, Plato regarded the body as the prison of the soul, assuming pure ideas are known only through intellectual contemplation. Yet even in making those claims, he expressed them through incarnate characters who flamboyantly flung themselves at others or who fluttered from fright in response. For Plato, however ethereal the final destination, the philosopher's journey departs from the concrete, not from the disembodied ideal.

Turning to Aristotle, because he always walked to and fro (*peripatētikos*) as he thought and lectured, even up through the Middle Ages his followers were commonly called the Peripatetic School. In today's parlance, it seems they not only talked the talk; they also walked the walk. What kind of philosophical school would be named after a bodymind activity? Aristotle insisted that both the philosophers and their ideas be materially embodied. Ethics for him was not the contemplation of metaphysical values or the Platonic Form of the Good. It was instead a matter of molding the right habits and dispositions (training in and through the bodymind). Part of Aristotle's philosophical agenda was to make virtue incarnate in his students, something that would not occur in disengaged, disembodied, cerebral knowers.

Such a description of philosophy as Way does not, however, characterize well the mainstream enterprise of philosophy in today's academy. Much more often than not, especially in the major research universities, departments of philosophy present their field as a *Wissenschaft* (an "-ology" or "science"), permitting it a place alongside the other disciplines in the university. Abdicating its role as the so-called queen of the sciences, philosophy has become just another *Wissenschaft* like the others, focusing mainly on itself, hoping to make progress in its own narrowly defined field. Rather than seeking the wisdom that transforms, philosophy has become more likely the search for knowledge about knowledge, an enterprise most generally known as *epistemology*. Yet, on what kind of knowledge does epistemology focus and how does epistemology study it?

We notice immediately that epistemology is yet another *-ology*, a scientific or detached study. The Greek term *epistēmē*, of which epistemology is the science, apparently derives from *epi-* (outside, beside, near) + *histanai* (to stand, to place). That etymology suggests epistemology specializes in the understanding of detached observers who posit reality outside themselves. In epistemology bystanders study the knowledge of bystanders by bystanders. It is a double detachment insofar as *what* it studies involves detachment and *how* it is studied is with detachment. Constructed of external relations, such a *Wissenschaft* paradigm maintains the integrity of the world and the integrity of the self, but at the loss of engagement. Without engagement, there is no self-transformation and, therefore, no love of wisdom, no *philosophy* in its archetypal sense.

Philosophy in the Academy—the United States

Today's philosophy departments in the United States (and probably in much of the West at large) seem to have lost the expansive mission that inspired the birth of the enterprise in Greece two and half millennia ago. First of all, the standard philosophy curriculum today often restricts itself geographically: courses in Asian philosophy are rare, at most amounting to only one or two offerings, and those typically at the undergraduate level. In effect, academic philosophy has made itself into a *regional studies* discipline focusing on western Europe and the United States.[3*]

In its regionalism, academic philosophy has even invented its own local dialects, a different one for "analytic" and "phenomenological" native speakers. Those dialects not only construct barriers within philosophy, but also make much of what philosophers say all the more unintelligible to nonphilosophers. Oddly, as scholarship and international awareness have become increasingly global, philosophy in the U.S. university has tended to be increasingly provincial.

Lastly, unreflective about its own historical roots, academic philosophy has often capitulated to the academy's newly arisen understanding of education itself. The increasingly hegemonic model within higher education today assumes that knowledge is the external relation between the knower and the known. As such, neither the knower nor the known is expected to be intrinsically transformed by the act of knowing. Furthermore, as an external relation, knowledge can be abstracted from the relation without loss.[†] It becomes no more than a packet of information delivered to students like an item acquired through the internet, boxed up, and dropped on their doorsteps.

Viewed in such a way, education loses the interpersonal dimension (what Dōgen called the "intertwining" of teacher and student "as they practice together"). It loses its capacity to question the questions (as in Hakuin's Great Doubt). It loses sight of its mission to *personally transform* students through the act of engaged learning (so one can "exchange civilities with the ancients" as Sorai put it).[‡] It even loses the interpersonal dynamic of the seminar that allowed me to ask my sophomoric question of Brand Blanshard.

In becoming just another academic *Wissenschaft,* philosophy has lost its Way. Philosophers no longer walk the path with their predecessors like Plato, Aristotle, and Kant, philosophical travelers who not only saw one Way, but who also recognized forks in the road, that is, pathways to different kinds of knowing. The *Wissenschaft* engineers have paved the one and only approved path through the forest of ignorance and philosophers have capitulated by staying on the prescribed pathways with nary a whimper.

I have likely exaggerated in painting such a bleak and pessimistic picture of western academic philosophy today. Perhaps with Japan's cultural emphasis on engaged knowing, western philosophy departments might learn to expand their self-imposed limits. Can Japanese academic philosophers bring something valuable to their western colleagues? Not likely, at least at present.

Philosophy in the Academy—Postwar Japan

In many respects, philosophy programs in Japan are even narrower in focus than those of the West. They often teach *no* classes in Asian philosophy alongside western philosophy. As I mentioned in Chapter 14, professional academic philosophers in postwar Japan do their technical work as if they were

† See the diagram of knowledge as external relatedness on page 28.
‡ See pages 236–7, 338, 348–9, and 574.

western philosophers working in outposts of European or American departments of philosophy. Philosophy departments in the West may be provincial, unable to see beyond the walls they themselves have built, but the situation in Japan is worse. Shackled by intellectual and cultural domination from abroad, philosophers in Japan's philosophy programs have too often been coopted into denying their own philosophical heritage. That is, they have been intellectually and culturally *colonized*. How did this situation occur? I can identify three factors.

First, immediately after the war, with the despair of utter defeat and hardship, Japan's government encouraged its people to jettison their old ways of thinking. Traditional Japanese ideas and values were simplistically equated with Native Studies, the samurai ethic, and its attendant tendencies toward jingoism, exceptionalism, and State Shintō—exactly what the new Japan was trying to expunge. Based on an ill-informed and naïve overgeneralization, the prejudice was often that any intellectual interested in premodern or even prewar Japanese philosophy was suspect of being a reactionary ethnocentrist. Given the sanctions against such philosophers as Nishitani Keiji, some professors likely thought it best to avoid controversy, thereby intensifying the Japanese suspicion of any philosophical ideas deemed "Japanese."

Second, to address that situation, the Japanese were encouraged to become more European and American in much the same way as they had been encouraged to do so in the Meiji period. Yet, the context today is different. In the latter decades of the nineteenth century and the early decades of the twentieth, the strategy was to learn how western philosophy might help Japan's modernization. What could be assimilated from the West (by allocation, hybridization, or relegation) that could make Japan stronger? Today, by contrast, it seems the philosophers who study abroad are not primarily hoping to bring back ideas of practical value to Japan, but rather aspire to become western philosophers. The goal is not to enhance Japanese philosophy, but rather to establish philosophical programs modeled on those in the West. It is more a strategy of *replacement* than assimilation. That approach may make sense in fields like physics or engineering, but there is no clear rationale for it when it comes to a humanistic, culturally embedded field like philosophy. Yet, philosophy has been treated in much the same way as the sciences.

Lastly, in Japan the study of Chinese and Indian philosophy, which Inoue Tetsujirō had originally taught as *tetsugaku* alongside western *tetsugaku,* typically spun off into their own programs. So professors in those areas generally became more associated with area specialists than with fellow philosophers. As for traditional Japanese philosophy, the universities commonly divvied it up piecemeal into such departments or programs as Aesthetics, the History of Japanese Ideas (mainly only ideas since 1600), Indo-Buddhist studies, and Ethics (or History of Ethics). Such an academic configuration makes Japanese ideas the focus of historical or cultural study, but preserves little room for constructive philosophizing in a Japanese vein. In Japan's academic world, Japanese philosophy is often just another object to be studied with detachment by various departments outside philosophy.

This leads me to a sad conclusion: someone who has carefully read this book will likely have a better understanding of Japanese philosophy than most professional philosophers in Japan's academic programs in philosophy or in professional associations for philosophy. As I have already said, the narrow focus typical of many philosophy departments in the West is an intellectual provincialism, the inability to recognize the value of any thought beyond the familiar horizons of home. By contrast, the western focus in Japanese philosophy departments is colonial. As with other forms of colonization, the colonized are often blind to their own regionality and past, having replaced them with the viewpoint of the dominant foreign regime.

There is hope, however. In Chapter 14 I focused on some individuals and trends that have run against the western colonization of philosophy in Japan. In postwar Japan a number of important philosophers have blazed their own Ways, creatively drawing on both western and Japanese philosophical ideas. The result has been hybrids that represent a new species of thought, ones with a parentage in both traditions, but no longer simply identified as one or the other. Some like Sakabe Megumi† paralleled the earlier course taken by Watsuji Tetsurō, establishing themselves first as major thinkers in the western tradition before turning increasingly toward their own Japanese roots, pointing out profound comparisons and differences, and often generating dramatic new insights of their own.

And of course, the Kyoto School continues. As a tradition intimately tied specifically to the philosophical systems of Nishida himself, however, it may be in its final stage of development. Today I generally find more *scholarship* about Nishida's systems than creative, innovative developments arising from within them. Yet, I recall from my first meeting with Nishitani in 1981 how he defined the Kyoto School, informing me that it is not the answers one gives to philosophical questions that define you as a member, but rather the kinds of questions you ask. In that respect, the Kyoto School could flourish for generations to come but only if, in my opinion, it is willing to expand its scope beyond the system of its founder. Nishida's philosophical questions and concerns can continue to inspire, but mining his writings for even more insights has become a project with diminishing returns. A promising sign for the future perhaps is that quite recently Kyoto's philosophy department has made formal efforts

† See pages 569–73.

to include more study of the premodern Japanese tradition, establishing the Forum for the History of Japanese Philosophy and a related journal, *Nihon no tetsugaku* (Japanese Philosophy).

Furthermore, beyond the new historical orientation emerging in Kyoto, in recent years new associations and institutions have begun to nudge Japanese philosophy in a new direction. Most striking is the University of Tokyo Center for Philosophy (UTCP), founded by Kobayashi Yasuo and assisted from the start by Takada Yasunari and Nakajima Takahiro. UTCP represents a new kind of philosophical institution in Japan, serving at once as a curricular center, a think tank, and a networking hub for international cooperation. Reflecting the expansive vistas of its founders, UTCP is both interdisciplinary and intercultural in design, bringing the Japanese ideal of Way to a new kind of thinking, collaborating, and philosophizing.

A continuing nexus for Japanese philosophy is the aforementioned[†] Nanzan Institute for Religion and Culture in Nagoya. It is an interdisciplinary and cross-cultural organization with international staff and visitors. Founded in 1975 and located in Nanzan University, one of Japan's few Roman Catholic universities, its purpose was inspired by the vision of its first acting director, Jan Van Bragt (1928–2007). From its origin, NIRC has been pioneering in its approach to Japanese thought in all its forms, making it a resource for collaborative philosophical and religious thinking. It is especially admired for bringing East and West into dialogue through its extensive list of journals, book series, colloquies, and symposia.

The Nanzan case is a good example of how Japanese philosophy is extending its reach well beyond Japan. For example, its *Frontiers of Japanese Philosophy* series of anthologies includes contributions from scholars in a wide variety of countries, both western and Asian. *Japanese Philosophy: A Sourcebook* (cited as JPS in this text) is a Nanzan publication through the University of Hawai'i Press and incorporates translations by a hundred scholars from around the world.

Another instance of the increasing impact of Japanese philosophy on the global stage is that of a new international publication, *The Journal of Japanese Philosophy*. The idea began as the initiative of two Chinese scholars in Hong Kong, Lam Wing-keung and Cheung Ching-yuen. Officially inaugurated in 2013, scholars from Japan, China, and the United States serve as its editorial board, led by the current editor-in-chief, Uehara Mayuko of Kyoto University. The journal itself is published in the United States.

Even as this book was about to go to press, yet another serial publication has sprung up outside Japan: *The European Journal of Japanese Philosophy*. EJJP is

† See page 552.

a publication of the European Network of Japanese Philosophy, itself a newly organized scholarly society. Under the editorship of Jan Gerrit Strala and Morisato Takeshi, the journal is distinctive in its policy of accepting articles in any of seven European languages as well as Japanese. For the foreseeable future, Japanese philosophy, especially in a hybrid form that traces its genealogy to both Japan and the West, will likely become an increasingly worldwide enterprise. In fact, research in Japanese philosophy need no longer be limited to Japan any more than Kierkegaard studies are limited to Denmark.

In light of that globalization, I will in this final section of my Conclusion mention a few ideas found in the Japanese tradition that strike me as provocative gateways for further reflection by philosophers of any country. These themes and even the approaches taken may not be unique to Japan, but given the evidence compiled in this book, it is fair to say Japanese philosophers have given them sustained attention and development. Anyone interested in such topics would do well to read what various Japanese philosophers have said.

THE FIELD OF JAPANESE PHILOSOPHY: SOME SEMINAL THEMES

Philosophical traditions build on elements that are discovered, engineered, combined, and adapted to meet the needs of their particular systems. For its elements, western philosophy has depended most on primary concepts like *things, facts, stuff, sensations, subject, object, being, substance, essence, attribute, quality, cause, effect, agent,* and so forth. As that list of elemental concepts became standardized, it has served as a glossary for future thinking and further philosophical initiatives. Philosophers may discover or even craft new elements, but they do so against that preexisting background, like filling gaps within the periodic table.

If you as a reader came to this book with an expectation that those are the key elements of philosophy in general, not of just western philosophy, you might have been startled to find how different the elemental concepts are in Japanese philosophy: *of itself* or *auto-* (jinen), *generative force* (ki), *pattern* (ri), *event-words* (koto), *the midst* (aidagara), the *interpenetration of thing with thing* (jijimuge), *conditioned co-production* (innen), *absolute nothing* (zettai mu), "howzit" (inmo), *as-ness* (nyoze), *interresponsive field* (kokoro), *the performative intuition* (kōiteki chokkan), *true working of nonworking* or *true meaning of nonmeaning (mugi no gi), no-I* (muga), *no-mind* (mushin), *pure experience* (junsui keiken), and so forth. Such terms arise from the conviction that reality is a field of interrelated processes, not a network of externally related things. So, it is not just that the western and Japanese traditions have different pictures of reality, but they also use different conceptual media to create those pictures.

As I have repeatedly noted throughout this book, the western list can be seen as more readily generating *what* questions and the Japanese list *how* questions. If I want to grow a plant, the western categories might serve me well in analyzing what kind of plant it is and what it needs to grow. On the other hand, the Japanese categories may be more helpful in asking *how* I can help a particular bonsai grow, *how* to interact with it and nurture it so that it finds its own ideal shape. This may seem like a difference that makes no difference or at least not much difference. I disagree. Consider the following anecdote.

Many years ago I was chatting with an electronics engineer who headed a research division at General Electric. At one point, I teased him with the following question: "Now, Jim, we both know all the major patents for videocassette recorders (which at the time were all the rage) are held by Japanese companies, either Sony or Panasonic. What were you guys at GE doing when all that R&D was going on in Japan?" Jim smiled sheepishly and explained the complexity of the VCR from an engineering standpoint: the mylar magnetic tape must travel from one reel to the other while passing across three spinning magnetic heads that do the recording and playback.

A consortium of engineers from several U.S. electronics companies had consulted, done the math and physics, and decided that a home VCR was scientifically impractical—the slightest vibration would cause the tape to get entangled in the spinning magnetic heads. VCRs would continue being limited to immovable desk-sized machines in television studios. The videodisk would be the home alternative, although there was at the time no way to make a disk-based machine that could record as well as play back.

Meanwhile, as Jim later learned, the engineers at Sony were working on the same problem. Rather than taking a math and physics approach, they assigned a small team to work with a prototype of a home VCR, experimenting with it until they could come up with a design that worked. After months, one engineer took a paperclip, bent it into a question mark-like shape and inserted it in the tape path within the cassette at a specific point. The tape stopped tangling, even when given a rather strong jolt. Jim said he will never forget what the Japanese engineer said, "We just kept watching the tape get entangled until we figured out a way to help it go where it wanted to go."

In that case, the cluster of Japanese elemental ideas apparently worked better than the western cluster. It amounted to being a difference between a detached knowing or controlling of reality as something external mediated by mathematical formulas vs. an engaged knowing that worked with reality more as potters do with their clay. The difference did make a difference pragmatically. It had what the American pragmatist, William James, called "cash value."

To sum up: the Japanese philosopher typically views reality as a complex, organic system of interdependent processes, a system that includes us as the knowers. Thus, we cannot begin our analysis with a separation of knower from known; to know reality is to work with it, not as a discrete agent, but as part of a common field, a *kokoro*. The tape in that Sony laboratory revealed its *mono no kokoro* (*kokoro* of things) and the engineer in the same field brought his *makoto no kokoro* (genuine human *kokoro*). The two resonated together to present the creative solution. The engineer had to intermesh with the tape, the common element of the conjunction between the tape and the engineer being the knowledge of the solution.

As Henri Bergson would have it, the engineer had to *enter into* the tape in order to know it.[†] In Japanese philosophy, the world is often more like light for the photographer than light for the physicist, more like words for the poet than words for the philologist, more like breath for the meditator than breath for the pulmonologist. Against that background image of the *field* of Japanese philosophy, let's consider some typical philosophical problems.

Bodymind vs. the Mind-Body Problem

As Yuasa Yasuo explained,[‡] modern western philosophy tends to consider the mind and body to be separate and that the challenge is to discover either what connects them or to prove one is illusory so that actually there is only body or only mind. By contrast, the Japanese philosopher (Yuasa thinks this is likely true in most other Asian traditions as well) starts with the experiential sense that the bodymind is a single complex. The mind part or the body part might be abstracted out of the whole and considered independently, but that does not mean they *exist* independently. So the question of what externally relates the mind and body does not arise.

Instead the primary philosophical issue becomes how the overlap of the internal relation in the bodymind functions. How does the bodymind transition into a unified whole so that it becomes difficult to think, even abstractly, of the body and mind as discrete? How, for example, does the novice pianist who has to think about the location of the keys become the accomplished player for whom the fingers seem to know where each key is? And then, how does that accomplished player become the virtuoso for whom the playing becomes a distinctive and innovative creative expression of the bodymind, working in conjunction with the musical score and the musical instrument?

Starting with Kūkai's Shingon Buddhism and continuing through and beyond Nishida's performative intuition theory, we have found a recurrent emphasis in Japanese philosophy on praxis and the theory of praxis (metapraxis). Through

† See page 42.
‡ See pages 557–9.

his metapractical theory, Kūkai bypassed the assumptions that led to Kant's problem of irresolvable metaphysical antinomies. Specifically, Kūkai's system implies that insofar as metaphysics is a product of detached knowing (what he calls the *exoteric*), metaphysics cannot establish its own ground. That would be like trying to fathom the working of bodymind by using only the mind, which itself only exists independently as an abstraction. Kūkai claimed that once we engage the bodymind in praxis (the *esoteric*), however, our engaged knowing will verify the foundation of its metaphysics. Only bodymind engaged in praxis can fully comprehend the nature of bodymind.[†]

The Agency of No-I vs. Autonomous Agency

If I am part of a single system of interdependent processes constituting reality, then there can be no substantial, discrete, independent "I." Sometimes this is called the relational self, but when we do so, we need to specify in the Japanese case this self is *internally* rather than externally related. Internal relations are initially more a matter of discovery than making. Although intensely personal, that moment of discovery gives them their objectivity. As engagement, relations take form out of the halves of intimacy of which Dōgen spoke. Once the preexisting connections are revealed, the relationship continues to be nurtured. The ideal, perhaps never realized, occurs when the overlap is so complete there is unity—the two circles of the internal relation intersect so much they become one. This adjustment in thinking of the self as *internally* relational has ramifications for aesthetics, ethics, and religious faith.

Aesthetics. We have in this book encountered a variety of aesthetic theories including the aesthetic of the Heian court, the poetics of *waka*, the Muromachi aesthetic of withdrawal, the aesthetic of the floating world, and Watsuji's appreciation of the material culture of ancient Nara temples. Yet, perhaps no one articulated the field within which all those theories took root better than Norinaga in his discussion of *kokoro*.[‡] The creativity in the work of art originates not in the artist but in the artist's engagement with a field that includes the medium, the auto-expressive character of reality, and the audience. All that together—artist, medium, reality, and audience—comprises *kokoro* in its fullest sense. The creativity within art originates not in the individual's self-expression but in *kokoro*'s auto-expression.

I spoke with a Zen master who specializes in making rock gardens. Admiring one of his masterpieces, I came right to the point, "How did you know where to

---

† See pages 133–4.
‡ See pages 377–83.

put the rocks?" He rejoined, "I put them where they wanted to be." Notice the similarity with the Sony engineers inventing the home VCR. Engagement is the common denominator between artistic creativity and knowing. In an important respect, creative expression is cognitive and cognition is creative. Their common source is what Nishida called the *performative intuition*.

Ethics. As many Japanese theories of creativity and knowing recognize the agency of no-I, so do Japanese theories of ethics. Ethics is also a form of engagement. If we try, we can rather easily pose most western ethical issues into *what* questions. What should I do? What principles apply? What action would yield the most favorable consequences? What is good? Again, with only a little effort, we can put Japanese ethical positions into *how* questions. How can I give up the ego so that my spontaneous actions will manifest Amida's compassion (Shinran)? How can I internalize the tradition of "Thou shalt not do evil" so that it becomes "you are such a person that you shall not do evil" (Dōgen)? How do I know the virtues of the ancient sage kings so that I can model myself after them in my present circumstances (Sorai)? How do I negotiate being in the midst between the collective and the individual self (Watsuji)?

With their emphasis on engagement and no-I, Japanese philosophers usually understand ethics more in terms of egoless responsiveness within situations rather than the individual's responsibility to follow rules, principles, or divine mandates. As we have seen, even the Chinese Confucian mandate of heaven (C. *tianming*; J. *tenmei*) never found a comfortable home in Japanese Confucianism. Because of this, of all the fields of Japanese philosophy, ethics is undoubtedly the hardest for many westerners to understand. Because it is literally true that Japanese ethical systems are typically without responsibility and without principles, it is tempting to see them as irresponsible and unprincipled. (That is, as immoral rather than amoral in the western sense.) I sympathize with that view very often myself, especially when considering a *bushidō* ethic claiming it is more important *how* you wield your sword rather than *on whom* you use it. Yet, my study of philosophers like Shinran has also shocked me into reexamining assumptions in my own western philosophical tradition and its approach to ethics.

In the ethical discussions we engaged in Chapter 5, Shinran focused on the problem of rationality in ethics. To think we can absolutely know what is right and to believe we have the ability to figure that out is, Shinran believed, as likely to lead to rationalizing evil as it is to doing good. Thinking (*hakarai*—trying to figure things out) is part of our ego-identity and, according to Shinran, ego is the fundamental obstacle to compassionate action.

In contrast to Buddhist responsiveness, responsibility derives from the idea of an individuated ego. Such an ego has frequently used reason to interpret principles in rationalizing reprehensible acts. Heinrich Himmler justified the actions of his SS agents on "principled" grounds, those principles deriving from the ideology of the Nazi state and its purported need to "defend" itself and its core national or ethnic values. In the final analysis, I suspect for every moral offense committed by a samurai in the name of spontaneous responsiveness there is another committed by someone's rationalization in the defense of some "principle."

In light of that analysis, on what grounds can we prefer one ethical theory over the other? Perhaps it comes down to Watsuji's claim that ethics is the manifestation of a philosophical anthropology. We derive our ethical theories from how we view what it means to be human. Presumably, that also implies how well that philosophical anthropology works in supporting our preferred theories of knowledge, aesthetics, and politics. Ethics cannot be a discrete field of philosophical inquiry. For Watsuji, it is inseparable from the field of *fūdo* from which we derive meaning as human beings in all aspects of our lives. Ethics is not what we do; it is how we live.

Religious faith. The Japanese foundational notion of the agency of no-I has ramifications in the religious realm, especially in relation to faith. Broadly speaking, the critical term for faith is *shin* 信, the root meaning of which is faith in the sense of *trust* (as when I say "I have faith in my dentist"). When Japanese philosophers hone in on specific texts for their inspiration (such as Norinaga and Sorai, for example), they have faith/trust in the authenticity and authority of their key texts (*Kojiki* or the Chinese classics, respectively). By contrast, because of their emphasis on the interpersonal transmission of engaged knowing, philosophers like Kūkai and Dōgen put their faith in their masters (and masters' masters—that is, the tradition of their transmission). Even a modern ethical theorist like Watsuji emphasizes having trust in others as the *sine qua non* for the dynamic of any ethical system. In the Pure Land tradition, Shinran had faith/trust in Hōnen and Hōnen in the texts of the Chinese Pure Land patriarchs. More provocative for the philosophy of religion, though, is Shinran's analysis of the "entrusting faith" (*shinjin* 信心; *shin* + mindful heart) directed toward the power of Amida's Vow.

First, it is crucial to underscore that entrusting faith is directed not to Amida Buddha (as we might expect in a theistic religion) but rather to the Vow. Only in Amida's heuristic form (the Amida-for-us) is Amida a person. In itself (as Amida-for-itself) Amida is formless, infinite light. Resorting to the "field" notion I have been developing in this Conclusion, entrusting faith allows me to relinquish my sense of my independent self (the *ji* as *jiriki* 自力) until I directly engage the field of as-ness or the self-so (the *ji* as *jinen* 自然). In other words as long as there is a subject having the entrusting faith, that faith directs itself to depend on the power of the object (the Vow of the personal Amida). But as the dependence on that objectified other-power becomes complete, the subject (the "I" who has the entrusting faith) dissolves. Yet, if there is no subject, the object must simultaneously disappear as well. The result is just the spontaneous naturalness of the agentless field, the "working of nonworking" (*mugi no gi*).

Shinran's account is certainly a powerful description for understanding "faith" in a nontheistic religion. Yet, even some theistic religions on the mystical end of the spectrum may speak of a God that disappears when engaged fully. As I noted, Kyoto School thinkers like Ueda Shizuteru and Nishitani Keiji pursued comparisons with Meister Eckhart on precisely those grounds. There is much here that lends itself to further interreligious reflection.

Political Theory

Within political theory there seems more variety in Japanese thought than in most other philosophical areas. We find in a Japanese Confucian thinker like Sorai a traditional characterization of the ideal state ruled by an educated elite, an approach I compared to both Machiavelli (following Maruyama Masao) and Plato. Meanwhile, Norinaga's theory of a state founded on aesthetic sensitivity is particularly striking and quite different from any of the mainstream western political theories.

In the modern era, we have engaged the political theories of both Nishida Kitarō and Watsuji Tetsurō. Both defended the imperial polity of Japan, but in different ways. Neither accepted the religious ideas of the State Shintō ideology nor claims about the uniqueness of the Japanese people. (As Watsuji argued, since every ethno-national group is unique, the Japanese are in no way uniquely unique.) Nishida's approach analyzed the people's self-conscious use of the symbol of the emperor as a way to support national unity. Watsuji's politics departed from his insight that ethics is the expression of a philosophical anthropology.

Language

One of the least Japanese statements Aristotle ever made is in his definition of *truth*:

> To say of what is that it is not, or of what is not that it is, is false; while to say of what is that it is, and of what is not that it is not, is true. (*Metaphysics*, 1011)

That statement is an archetypal expression of the theory that language refers (or fails to refer) to a preexisting reality. It is an assumption that has been challenged throughout the history of Japanese philosophy in a wide variety of ways.

Kūkai, for example, would reject the statement on the grounds that it assumes language is reference rather than conference. For him, language and reality are part of a single cosmic act, the resonance that both constitutes and expresses existence. Furthermore, Aristotle's statement does not account for the *sound* of the words spoken. In Kūkai's philosophy the resonating sound of the "truth words" (*mantras*) establishes the internal relation among sound, word, and reality.

From Dōgen's standpoint, Aristotle's statement does not account for language's fluidity of meaning that shifts and adjusts within ever-changing occasions. In present-day Japan Kimura Bin espouses a similar concern in his sophisticated analysis of how language transforms event (*koto*) into thing (*mono*).

Japanese exoteric Buddhists in general would find Aristotle's statement simplistic because it characterizes acts of speech without regard to audience. Yet, the same words mean different things to different people. For many Buddhist thinkers, it is a starting point for their hermeneutic that words about reality are typically heuristic expressions adjusted to the specific listeners or readers. In the twentieth century, Hiromatsu Wataru expanded on the complexity of audience in ordinary speech, showing how we can simultaneously take first, second, and third person perspectives in a single speech act such as when we correct a child's verbal misidentification of something.

Also from the modern traditions of Japanese philosophy, figures such as Yosano Akiko and Ueda Shizuteru would likely note how Aristotle's statement ignores the poetic and creative force of words. As we have seen, the spirit of words (*kotodama*) is an ancient theme in Japanese poetics and in the later theory of *waka* poetry. As a modern philosopher concerned with the same aspect of language, Ueda Shizuteru would say Aristotle overlooks language's ability to take the not-yet-meaningful "pre-thing" and to transform it into "thing." Only then can the word recede again into the "hollow," leaving the thing behind as the world of meaning in which we live. For Ueda there is "nothing" before the word. Furthermore, only in saying the word does the "what-is" arise.

Along the same lines, philosophers who stress sentences as emerging from the predicate rather than the subject such as Tokieda Motoki, Nishida Kitarō, and Sakabe Megumi would reject the stasis implied in Aristotle's statement. At the least I think they would say Aristotle needs to recognize that in this world of flux, what-is is a moving target for his words to point to. Only a predicate-oriented theory of language as itself an unfolding event might be able to explain how language can capture the instability of what-is.

I did not extract Aristotle's innocent, brief statement from its context just so I could bombard it with a salvo of critiques from a variety of Japanese perspectives. Rather, I wanted to demonstrate that Aristotle's formulation, which might seem so obvious as to be trivial or even tautological to a western reader of philosophy, would puzzle many Japanese thinkers. In general, Japanese philosophers would not think Aristotle is wrong as much as wrongheaded. Why, they might wonder, would anyone ever say such an odd thing, even if it were correct? For mainstream Japanese philosophers, language unfolds rather than restricts meaning. It creates a world rather than designates something that already is. Hence, poetry reveals language's true face; all other uses of language are just for the convenience of daily life. Given the sustained development of such Japanese theories, a philosopher of language from any culture can likely find riches of insight there.

THE SPECTER RETURNS

As this book comes to its close, the specter of my sophomore self has been waiting in the shadows, ready to put his question to me again about my career in comparative—western and Japanese—philosophy: "What difference has it made?" When I first engaged Japanese philosophy, I thought I was looking for something new outside the western tradition in which I had been trained. I did find that but in a most odd way. The more deeply I engaged Japanese philosophy, the less it was about Japan and the more about philosophy. Through Japanese philosophy, I have been reinvigorated as a philosopher, feeling I can reengage philosophy as I believe it was originally intended—as a Way. I went to Japan and found parallels to, for example, Plato's embodied dialectic, Aristotle's practical wisdom, Thomas Aquinas's "word" (*Verbum*), and David Hume's insubstantial self. Somehow I came to understand those western ideas anew.

One of my mentors, Tamaki Kōshirō, once told me that after our philosophical journeys, we sometimes must return to our "spiritual home village" (*seishin no furusato*). But not to worry, he said, it won't be the same place we left. A career studying Japanese philosophy in a comparative context—what difference has it made? Nothing. It is not a *what* that is different, but *how* the same has come to differ. I've somehow circled back to where I started, but yet, having traversed Japanese philosophy, nothing is any longer as it was when I set out. Maybe the record of my engaging Japanese philosophy can encourage others to find their own way back to their own *seishin no furusato*.

I conclude with a *waka* by Nishida Kitarō. It is etched on a rock along the Way of Philosophy he walked everyday:

人は人	*Hito wa hito*	People are people,
吾は吾なり	*Ware wa ware nari*	And I am just who I am.
とにかくに	*Tonikakuni*	Anyway, that said,
吾行く道を	*Ware yuku michi o*	In my case, I'm the walking
吾は行くなり	*Ware wa yuku nari.*	Of the Way that I travel.

Supplementary Notes

1. Engagement

1. Trans. in WILSON 2008, 3.

2. Trans. based on ZEAMI 2008, 62.

3. As I recall, the claim had been that in no possible world would a simple indexical like *this* or *that* be used such that one would be preferable or have more axiological value than the other. By nature, they must be completely neutral in value. Yet, in Chinese 是 (*shi*) means not only "this" rather than "that," but also "right" rather than "wrong," "positive" rather than "negative," or "fitting" rather than "unfitting."

4. The sharpest instrument in the philosopher's tool kit is formal logic, but in its technical notation, it is unfamiliar to most people and therefore of limited utility in a book such as this. But analogies may sometimes help in getting across the same point. An analogy may show the logical (or illogical) nature of a line of reasoning without the heavy-handed use of symbols.

A simple example: suppose someone claims "If we all have buddha-nature, then we are all enlightened; But we don't all have buddha-nature; So, we are not all enlightened." That is an invalid argument of the form: $p \supset q$; $\sim p$; therefore, $\sim q$. A reader who is not familiar or comfortable with symbolic logic might be more puzzled than convinced by that statement of the error. Suppose instead I said: "That argument is invalid. It would be analogous to saying 'If it is raining, the sidewalk is wet; but it is not raining, so the sidewalk is not wet.'" The invalidity of the argument is now probably clearer to most people. Obviously, the sidewalk could be wet from causes other than rain (like runoff from a lawn sprinkler system). Therefore, using an analogy without resorting to logical symbols can be a roundabout way of showing whether claims are logically valid.

5. That is a main argument developed in *Intimacy or Integrity*, KASULIS 2002.

6. Because of the emphasis on the "Way," an ill-informed philosopher might think such enterprises involve no more than technical know-how, what the Greeks called *technē*. But it is one thing to know how to use a potter's wheel and quite another to be able to make a pot that is a work of art. The latter involves not just technical know-how, but also practical wisdom (*phronēsis*) and probably even some intuitive insight (*nous*) into, say, beauty. Such qualities usually develop under the tutelage of a master who practices with the student.

That is not much different, incidentally, from how we learn to be philosophers. Making a valid argument or doing a straightforward logical analysis of a sentence is mainly a matter of know-how learned in a classroom, but a real philosopher adds insight to that skill and an eye for what is significant, qualities partly innate and partly acquired through praxis.

7. Being oblivious to the holographic relation of whole and part has led some present-day western scholars to culturally misrecognize the fundamental character of the emperor system in Japan, for example. With the advent of discourse analysis as a method, there is a tendency among some intellectual historians to interpret the relation between the emperor and the state to be one of synecdoche or metonymy. That is, the claim that the emperor is the state is taken to be a trope, a figure of speech, a metaphor. By that analysis, the emperor is *figuratively* spoken of as the state (as when one says in the western monarchical tradition that the "crown" has made a proclamation). Then, the analysis goes, the Japanese figure of speech about the emperor was used to develop an imperial ideology, usually one that the scholar enthusiastically (and perhaps rightly) criticizes.

The problem, though, is that premise of the argument—based in the analysis of tropes—is a misinterpretation, thereby making the rest of the argument irrelevant. To say the "emperor is the state" in the Japanese *kokutai* ideology is not a figure of speech, but an ontological claim based in a holographic analysis. If one wants to refute the imperialist ideology, one has to start with that ontological claim as such.

For example, when I say every cell in my body contains the blueprint (DNA) for my whole body, I am not engaging in metaphor. I am stating literally, not figuratively, an ontological relation. Similarly, most proponents of the emperor system do not understand themselves to be speaking figuratively when saying the emperor is the essence of state formation (*kokutai*). They believe (either rightly or wrongly) that they are asserting an ontological fact like the one I made about cellular DNA. The burden on the critic is to demonstrate, not assume, that the emperor-state relation is not holographic in the way that the cell-body relation functions in the DNA example.

8. The *reductio ad absurdum* form of argument differs in its refuting a *hypothetical* opposing position for the sake of argument, whereas an argument by refutation opposes an *actual* position.

9. BERGSON 1955, 21.

THE ANCIENT AND CLASSICAL PERIODS

2. Blueprints for Japan

1. In recent decades a number of scholars have questioned whether Umayado was actually the same person as Prince Shōtoku, the prince regent and heir apparent. Indeed, the very personage of Shōtoku may be the construction born of a political ideology from later in the seventh century. In this book, my main concern is the image of Shōtoku and the texts attributed to him, both of which were firmly fixed by the early eighth century, less than a century after the purported date of the *Constitution*. I will, therefore, follow the traditional narrative since that is what influenced so much of later Japanese thinking about Shōtoku and his contributions to Japanese culture and thought. For a summary of

the issues involved in the latest scholarship about the reality behind the Shōtoku legend, see YOSHIDA Kazuhiko 2006 and for a more thorough analysis of the iconic import of Shōtoku, see COMO 2008.

2. The name "Yayoi" refers to the location in Tokyo where archeologists first discovered the pottery distinctive to that period. Later digs show that Yayoi culture also existed in other parts of Japan, including the Yamato plain—today's Nara, Kyoto, and Osaka area—the cradle of the early Japanese state. Yayoi pottery is plainer in design than Jōmon: simple, elegant, and delicate rather than ornate. It was made on a wheel, hard-fired, and left unglazed in a natural reddish color. In fact, Yayoi pottery may remind non-experts of some simple styles found in Japanese tea ceremony over a millennium later.

Although the influence of Zen Buddhism on tea ceremony has been undeniable, too much has been made of Zen's development or introduction of an aesthetic of simplicity. Rather, it could be said that Zen's aesthetic was so attractive to the Japanese because it rejected the emphasis on elegance (*miyabi*) developed in the Heian period and returned to earlier sensitivities. See KASULIS 1998.

Dwelling places in the Yayoi period changed from the Jōmon pits and caves to thatched huts of pole-and-beam construction. Japanese architecture was beginning to look a bit more like the "traditional" Japan we associate today with its rustic hermitages and teahouses. The quantum leap in the sophistication of material culture and the widespread occurrence of that change suggests strong influence from abroad, probably from the Korean peninsula.

3. A fascinating, albeit cryptic, portrait of a late Yayoi period settlement is found in the Chinese accounts of continental explorers in the *Wei Zhi* (*Wei Chronicles*), the observations jibing with some archeological evidence. The text describes an area called "Yamatai" in the late second century CE. Although close in pronunciation to "Yamato," the location of Yamatai is an ongoing debate among archeologists as they assemble new evidence to support their theories. For a new translation of the *Wei Chronicles*, see KIDDER 2007, 12–18.

4. What we know of Himiko derives almost entirely from Chinese accounts. The Chinese recorded not only the previously mentioned visit to Yamatai, but also the visit of Himiko's emissaries to the Chinese court in 239. So there is little doubt about her existence. It seems to have been the Chinese understanding that her rule spread over diverse "lands" (*kuni,* often translated as "states" but such a term of political organization is anachronistic for the Japanese situation at that time).

Of course, the highly hierarchical Chinese bureaucrats of the Wei dynasty would have been quick to interpret Himiko as the monarch of the whole archipelago and to see her as bearing tribute to the Chinese empire from the land of Wa. Conversely, it would not harm Himiko's own status to present herself as the ruler of all Wa. An informative and extensively researched study of Himiko is KIDDER 2007. Based on archeological, historical, and mythological evidence, Kidder argues that her domain of Yamatai was in the general Yamato region rather than the other viable possibility, namely, the southern island of Kyushu.

5. The gendered difference in political role may suggest a rising male hierarchy in what had formerly been a strongly matriarchal society. Given the meager evidence, however,

that is still speculative. Certainly, the Chinese accounts (which, of course, could have been influenced by their own patriarchal assumptions) did not see the situation that way. According to them, Himiko came to rule not by matriarchal succession, but by virtue of a compromise among male warlords who chose her as an alternative to continued conflict.

However we might choose to read the issue of matriarchy, if we follow Takamure Itsue's (1894–1964) pioneering research, it is clear that ancient Japanese families were predominantly matrilineal, the husband's joining the wife's household (where she held hereditary rights). Takamure's ground-breaking 1938 work *Bokeisei no kenkyū* (*Study of the matrilineal system*) and her four-volume *magnum opus*, *Josei no rekishi* (*History of [Japanese] women*, 1954–1958) have shown that matrilocal marriages continued among the aristocracy until the eleventh century and even later among lower classes (see TAKAMURE 1938 and 1954). The medieval rise of the warrior classes was probably a major factor in undermining the system, later reinforced by the Confucian-influenced patriarchal assumptions of the Edo period (1600–1868).

In evaluating the gender roles within Himiko's sovereignty, it might also be relevant to consider them in light of the Japanese *himehiko* system of leadership found in many ancient kinship groups wherein a male-female pair (typically brother and sister) ruled in consort with a distinction in roles.

6. For example, the single term *matsurigoto* can refer to the "administration" of either religious rites or political institutions. As in the case of Himiko, throughout most of Japanese history, cunning politicos have used that dual administrative function to their advantage. By emphasizing the sacerdotal and *kami*-like functions of the emperor, they often claimed that the eminent sovereign should not be concerned with mundane political matters. Regents, shoguns, military "advisors," even parliaments, but not the emperors, have typically wielded actual political power in Japan through most of its history.

7. PIGGOTT 1997, ch. 5, shows that this process of making Amaterasu the national *kami* and of recognizing the sovereigns as having *kami* status themselves was not formally institutionalized until the reigns of Emperor Tenmu (r. 673–686) and Empress Jitō (r. 690–697). How much Shōtoku accepted this theory earlier in the century is a matter of conjecture.

Presumably, the most relevant documentation for the official view of his time would have been *Tennōki* (Chronicle of sovereigns) and *Kokki* (Chronicle of the country). Unfortunately, neither is extant. The *Nihonshoki* (Chronicle of Japan), compiled in 720, claims those two chronicles were compiled in 620 under the direction of Shōtoku and Soga no Umako, but destroyed by arson in 645.

8. Suiko's own political trajectory suggests the dynamics of the day and the ways of imperial intermarriage. Before becoming the ruling empress, Suiko had been the daughter of a previous emperor (Kinmei), the spouse of his successor (Bidatsu), and half-sister to a third (Sushun). Between Bidatsu and Sushun, incidentally, the emperor had been Yōmei, Shōtoku's father. Therefore, in a fifty-year period Suiko had been successively the daughter of an emperor, the wife of an emperor, a half-sister to an emperor, a sister-in-law to an emperor, and a ruling empress.

9. Unlike Chinese, Japanese is often considered a Ural-Altaic language linguistically connected to languages from Korea, Siberia, Finland, and Hungary. Although the exact

origins of the Japanese people themselves are uncertain, the linguistic similarity (along with other parallels such as architectural construction) supports an argument for at least some connection with those ethnic and racial groups. Because the Japanese archipelago once joined the mainland near Korea, such migration is even more probable. Some scholars also see indications of some very early South Pacific influences, another possible—though on a smaller scale—source of migration. There is no such persuasive evidence for any prehistoric mass immigration into Japan by the Chinese (Han) peoples.

Differences between the Japanese and Chinese languages include the following: Chinese is monosyllabic in its words or in the elements constituting compound words whereas native Japanese words are mostly polysyllabic; Chinese is tonal within the pronunciation of each syllable whereas Japanese is not (the only pitch variations are within strings of syllables in polysyllabic words or phrases); the Chinese word order is like English in that the verb precedes its object (subject-verb-object) whereas in Japanese it appears at the end of the sentence; Chinese verbs do not inflect, that is, they do not change their endings as in Japanese to indicate tense, voice, affect, etc. See also "About the Japanese Language," pages 685–95.

10. Important exceptions began to appear only in the thirteenth century, but even up to the mid-nineteenth century, some philosophical texts and many government documents continued to use Chinese (or *kanbun,* a Japanized style of writing derived from reading Chinese as if it were Japanese). Therefore, the ability to read and write in classical Chinese was a sign of sophistication among educated Japanese up through the early twentieth century. For a critical evaluation of the impact of this native vs. Chinese language use in Japan, see POLLACK 1986.

11. The very term "Confucianism" may be anachronistic here. It has even been argued that the idea of Confucianism as a discrete tradition might be a western projection onto Chinese culture, perhaps starting with Jesuit missionaries. See, for example, JENSEN 1997. The point here might be better stated that Chinese culture at this time was permeated with ideas found in several classic texts, many being part of the tradition of Confucius' *Analects* and its subsequent commentaries.

For our philosophical purposes I will, as the Japanese themselves came to do, identify "Confucianism" as a somewhat discrete philosophical tradition influential on both ancient and subsequent Japanese thought. It is probably fair to say, however, that Shōtoku's contemporaries were mainly trying simply to be *Chinese*-like, rather than exclusively Confucian, Buddhist, Daoist, Legalist, or Mohist.

12. The Chinese tradition attributes to Confucius not just the sayings collected in the *Analects* (*Lunyu*), the *Book of Filial Piety* (*Xiaojing*), and the *Book of Rites* (*Liji*). It also claims he edited many other classics such as the *Book of Changes,* (*Yijing*), *Book of History* (*Shujing*), *Book of Odes* (*Shijing*), *The Spring and Autumn Annals* (*Chunqiu*) as well as the sections of the *Liji* often treated as independent treatises, especially the *Doctrine of the Mean* (*Zhongyong*) and the *Great Learning* (*Daxue*). The ancient Japanese generally followed the Chinese in assuming a close connection between those Chinese classics and Confucius.

13. By the limited "religious" function of Confucianism, I mean the muted ritualization emphasizing reverence to the person of Confucius himself as at least a patriarch of the country's culture and at most an object of prayer and entreaty. Certainly, aspects of such

ritual were practiced in Japan in varied contexts (probably most strongly in the Nara and Edo periods). For the overwhelming stretch of Japanese history and for the vast majority of Japanese people, however, Confucianism has served more as a cornerstone for morality, pedagogy, and political or bureaucratic hierarchical structure rather than for religious practices. That is, Japanese religious rituals are overwhelmingly Buddhist, Shintō, and folk religious (the latter sometimes incorporating imported Daoist or Chinese folk religious elements).

14. In fact, we know of one explicit way in which even Shōtoku did not simply kowtow to China as a superior culture. In a letter from the Japanese court to the Chinese court, he addressed it as from the "emperor of where the sun rises" to the "emperor of where the sun sets." The Chinese court did not apparently appreciate that locution.

In general, though, Shōtoku held the Chinese Sui court in high regard and, as a result, Japanese emissaries as well as scholars and students were regularly sent abroad. In the seventh century Japanese official contacts with the Continent focused on China and Chinese intellectual currents, especially for the links between Buddhism and the state (see BLUM 2008). Because the Sui court favored Buddhism, Shōtoku's own efforts on behalf of Japanese Buddhism probably gained him prestige in the eyes of Japanese sinophiles.

15. A present-day western interpretation of this special form of relational ethics is sometimes called "role ethics." See AMES 2011.

16. A sixth virtue or excellence was sometimes included: excellence (*toku*) itself, i.e., the integration of all five other excellences. Shōtoku's awareness of the centrality of those five virtues to the Confucian ideal of society is reflected in his "twelve grades of cap ranks" (*kan'i jūnikai*) promulgated (like the *Constitution*) in 604. Shōtoku installed that system to establish a hierarchy of court ranks based on the service to the sovereign, using headgear to distinguish the ranks. The names of the cap ranks derived from the names of the six virtues (with two subdivisions of each). They purportedly rewarded performance, not merely hereditary entitlement as recognized by the earlier court rank systems. That innovation shows Shōtoku's conscious use of Confucianism to strengthen the centrality of the sovereign and subordinate the importance of clans.

17. Whenever we translate key terms from a culture whose value system and world view radically differ from those of English-speaking cultures, single word renderings are often problematic. For the English translation of the five excellences, I have tried to use English terms conveying some philosophical nuances of the original. These are followed by alternative translations corresponding to those most commonly found in older, standard works in English on Confucianism.

For my translations I am indebted to the terminology and interpretations developed by Roger T. Ames and Henry Rosemont, Jr. in their translation of *Analects* (CONFUCIUS 1999). For their rationale in rendering the terms as they do, see their "Introduction" to the translation. Of course, in this book we are most interested in not the original Chinese understanding nor even the western interpretations, but in the various *Japanese* interpretations. These will unfold as we progress in the book and it will be a primary focus in my discussion of Edo-period philosophy in Chapter 8 and of Ogyū Sorai in Chapter 9.

18. A difference between Japan and China in their imperial academies was that in

China admission was strictly based on performance in an examination, but in Japan, one had to be of aristocratic blood as well. That said, since in China typically only the elite could read, only they would likely pass the exam. So the practical difference in the admission standards was slight. Yet, in theory and sometimes in actuality, the Chinese ideal was a meritocracy open to anyone with the talent. That does not seem to have been how the system worked in ancient Japan.

19. I use the term "proto-Shintō" for the *kami*-worship traditions at this early point in Japanese history because it did not yet resemble well enough the institutionalized religion we now call "Shintō" to merit the use of that unqualified term. Yet, there is enough continuity in world view and value systems between this ancient tradition and contemporary Shintō that to always call it "*kami*-worship" without reference to what later became Shintō seems equally odd: it would be like calling pre-Constantinian Christians "Jesus of Nazareth followers" instead of "early Christians" since what we now think of as Christianity is more like its post-Constantinian aspects.

By the early eighth century, the proto-Shintō tradition had court-supported written narratives about the role of the *kami* in creation and in the formation of the State, a government bureau in charge of *kami*-related rituals, and a number of highly visible shrine edifices. It was decidedly not a completely discrete tradition but could easily have become one. In many ways proto-Shintō was further along in the formation of becoming an identifiable religion than Christianity was in the first three centuries of its existence (when it lacked a fixed canon, a universally accepted creed, an institutional structure recognized by the state, and an orthopraxis).

As we will see in our later chapters, this proto-Shintō tradition tends to blur into Buddhism by the end of the eighth century, but then it is partly systematized (in a highly syncretistic form) by medieval thinkers like Yoshida Kanetomo, whom I will discuss in Chapter 7. What we now think of as Shintō is more the result of Native Studies thinkers of the eighteenth and nineteenth centuries, especially Motoori Norinaga and Hirata Atsutane.

For a brief introductory treatment of the development of Shintō as a religious tradition, including its synergies with other strains of Japanese spirituality, see KASULIS 2004, Chapters 3–5. Recommended sources for a more detailed and scholarly treatment include PICKEN 2004; BREEN and TEEUWEN 2000 and 2010; and INOUE 2003.

20. Although the Japanese and Chinese languages are neither historically related nor grammatically similar, the ancient Japanese, having no orthography of their own, drew on Chinese for the writing system they eventually did devise. Thus, Chinese sinographs (*kanji* 漢字) were used by the Japanese to render both their own Japanese words (or the noninflected parts of those words) as well as words borrowed from China (or new compounds based on Chinese elements). As a result, the same character or group of characters in a word may have multiple pronunciations: either the reading drawn from the indigenous Japanese language (the so-called *kun* 訓 reading) or the reading drawn from one of the Chinese dialects (often generically called the *on* 音 reading). Thus the same compound 神道 might be pronounced as *kami no michi* in its *kun* reading, but "Shintō" in its *on* reading. When the distinction between words of "native Japanese" versus "foreign" origin became important in the ethnocentric movements of the eighteenth through

twentieth centuries, for example, the alternative readings of words assumed ideological significance. See also "About the Japanese Language," pages 685–95.

21. Scholars do not agree about the referent of the word *Shintō* in the oldest texts. Could it have been referring to popular religious practices from China, perhaps even to Daoism? Or maybe it referred simply to *kami*-worship without any institutional identity, orthodoxy, or orthopraxis? In an influential article, Kuroda Toshio (KURODA 1981) argued effectively that it is difficult to identify any kind of Shintō as an *independent* tradition before modern times. His argument exposes the wild conjectures found in the attempt of Native Studies scholars, State Shintō ideologues, and conservative politicians to claim Shintō is a pure, independent stream of Japanese religiosity going back "to the beginning." In Chapter 7 I will discuss Kitabatake Chikafusa as one of the earliest, if not the earliest, Shintō thinker to argue for the importance of going back to beginnings.

Unfortunately, in the conclusion to his essay, Kuroda overstated what his own evidence showed, asserting that before the modern institution, there was no such thing as Shintō at all. He claims that latter-day scholars constructed the idea by haphazardly picking up isolated bits of unconnected data and then called the grab bag *Shintō*. Kuroda was right to reject the essentialist definition of Shintō as having any application in the premodern period. Yet, he overlooked the possibility of a Wittgensteinian "family resemblance" type of definition, that is, a long list of ideas, values, and practices that all forms of Shintō share to a great extent, *but never in its entirety*. (See WITTGENSTEIN 1968, 33.)

Thus, as Kuroda admits, the term *Shintō* and closely related words were used throughout Japanese history even though those terms did not always refer to exactly the same thing. Yet, a family resemblance does not refer to a single characteristic either: some family members share the same shaped nose, others the same color eyes or hair, others the same physiognomy, and so forth. There is no one essential characteristic they have in common, yet collectively they look more like each other than they do to members of totally unrelated families. So, the different Shintos may share no one essence in common but have enough family resemblances to distinguish them from Buddhisms, Daoisms, and Confucianisms, for example. This position would be enough to refute the Shintō essentialism that is Kuroda's target, but would not go beyond the evidence he presented.

22. Daoism (formerly romanized in the Wade-Giles system as "Taoism") never achieved the independent prominence in Japan enjoyed by Buddhism and Confucianism. Absorbed into Japan as part of Chinese culture, Daoist ideas and ideals were assimilated for the most part into folk practices dealing with healing, augury, *yin-yang* practices, and so forth. There have indeed at times been Daoist sects in Japan and even government offices associated with its administration, but for the most part, they have not been influential as independent religious groups. See BOCK 1985 for a discussion of what Daoist rituals were practiced in ancient Japan.

As a philosophical tradition, much of the Daoist philosophy of Laozi and Zhuangzi was already absorbed into Buddhism in China and affected Japan mainly via that route. Furthermore, to some extent throughout history, Japanese philosophers (even non-Buddhists such as the Restoration Shintō philosopher Hirata Atsutane) have occasionally cited passages from Laozi and Zhuangzi to support their points, but more as a classical allusion than as any kind of distinctively Japanese Daoist philosophical or religious movement.

23. For a recent study of *tama* in English see IWASAWA 2011. For a discussion of *tama* in conjunction with two other key terms, *mono* and *mi,* see KASULIS 2004, 14–16.

24. According to the narrative in *Nihonshoki,* the *kami* Futsunushi and Takemikazuchi descended to the earth to quell the noisome flora and fauna. As the text says:

> But in that Land there were numerous Deities which shone with a luster like that of fireflies, and evil Deities which buzzed like flies. There were also trees and herbs all of which could speak.… The two Gods at length put to death the malignant Deities and the tribes of herbs, trees, and rocks. (Trans. in ASTON 1972, 64 and 69.)

For an insightful anthropological analysis of how the values expressed in the ancient myths continue to orient everyday Japanese life, see PELZEL 1986.

25. For a fuller discussion of *kokoro* as a key idea and value in Japanese culture, see VISHWANATHAN 1998 and KASULIS 2008.

26. The original Japanese for the poem is adapted from TAKAGI, GOMI, and ŌNO 1962, 1: 57–9.

27. The original Japanese text explicitly expresses the interfusion of wind and breath. Following TAKAGI, GOMI, and ŌNO 1959, 2: 57–9, I interpret its language in the following way. "With the wind from my sighs of grief" translates *"wa ga nageku / okiso no kaze ni"* literally, "in the wind (*kaze*) of the exhaling breath (*okiso,* i.e., *oki* "breath" + *uso* "blow forth") which I sigh" (*wa ga nageku:* the verb *nageku* probably deriving from *naga + iki,* that is, "a long breath"). Such a correlation between wind and breath occurs in many ancient cultures around the world. See FINDLY 2005. For a comment on the philosophical implications of the biblical use of terms for breath as correlated with spirit—*ruaḥ* (Hebrew) and *pneuma* (Greek) as well as *spiritus* in Latin commentary—see KASULIS 1992.

28. In appreciating how Japanese poetry may express the intimacy between the natural and human, we can consider the later classical literary device known as "pivot words" (*kakekotoba*), a regulated form of poetic word play. Because Japanese has a relatively small number of syllables (far fewer than half the number in English, for example), homophones abound. *Kiku,* for example, can be a form of the verb "to hear" or the word for "chrysanthemum."

> Through using double meanings, therefore, a poem (or a part of a poem) may be open to two completely different readings if one parses the phrases differently. Significantly, as in *kiku,* one reading may be about a person's experience, whereas the other describes a natural event or thing. The point of the pivot word is to shift the reader's attention back and forth between the two images, thereby creating an interfusion between them.

A striking example is this famous tenth-century poem by Sōsei Hōshi (Monk Sōsei) (*Kokinwakashū* no. 770):

> *Otoninomi*
> *Kikunoshiratsuyu*
> *Yoruwaokite*
> *Hiruwaomohini*
> *Ahezukenubeshi*

The three pivot words are *kiku* (from "to hear" and "chrysanthemum"), *okite* (from "to stay up" and from "to put") and *omohi* ("longing" and "facing the sun"). In understanding the poem, the Japanese reader pivoted between the two meanings in each case, melding them into a single statement. Thus, the pivot word is parsed as both the last word of the preceding phrase and (with a different meaning) as the first word in the succeeding phrase.

A rough rendering of what the Japanese would interpret is the following. The italicized words are the *kakekotoba* pairs and the English words in brackets have no corresponding Japanese word in the poem but are inserted for the translation to make sense. Moreover, English word order does not allow me to reflect the Japanese word order where the pivoting mechanism precisely hinges between its preceding and succeeding phrases.

> [I,] only *hearing* (*kiku*) of you [from others],
> *Stay up* (*okite*) all night,
> The glistening dew *clinging* (*okite*) to the *chrysanthemum* (*kiku*).
> [I,] unable to stand the daytime *longing* (*omohi*),
> [The dew, unable] to *face the sun* (*omohi*),
> [I and the dewdrop] must surely perish.

The poem's *kakekotoba* technique not only juxtaposes but also interfuses the human and the natural in a way that the English cannot easily render. That is, the same words are being read to refer simultaneously to the natural and the human, putting the two into an internal relation. The technique gives the poem a semantic density through which much of the poet-dew relation is intimated rather than expressly stated. The elliptical and suggestive rhetoric of intimation expresses an engaged knowing based in the internal relation among the poet, the words, and the audience. As Hasegawa Kai (see page 15) said of haiku, *waka* as well could be said to require a participative audience. Meaning arises in the overlap of reader and text.

In verses like the one above, the intimated affect internally, rather than externally, relates the human and the natural. In this case, the pivot word *omohi* interlinks the longing and facing the sun, while *okite* and *kiku* link the dew clinging to the chrysanthemum and the staying awake while thinking of what was heard of the woman. See original and notes in NKBT 8: 200.

29. I could use the word "magic" for "thaumaturgy" or "wonder-working," but that word often has connotations best avoided in this context. Part of the problem is that there is a long western, originally Near Eastern, tradition that associates magic with a struggle between the demonic as opposed to celestial or benign spiritual sources. Thus, even the early Christian literature tried to distinguish miracles performed through the grace of God from other wondrous acts achieved through the aid of demons or Satan. Note, for example, the claim by Jesus' critics that he healed through his lordship of demons rather than through the power of God (Mark 3: 22–3) or the story of the altercation between Simon Magus and St. Peter in Rome (Acts 8: 9–13). That dueling wizards scene is also reminiscent of the Hebrew account of the confrontation between Moses and the Pharaoh's magicians (Exodus 8: 7–13).

In Abrahamic cases, it seems the metaphysical source of the magical power determines its goodness or evil as well as its strength (good is stronger than evil). In the East Asian context, by contrast, the thaumaturgical power is usually understood to be by nature neutral (analogous to, say, physical muscular strength). Therefore, its use for good or evil derives not from the metaphysical source but from the person using that power (like a strong person using physical strength to either harm or help others).

The philosophical significance of this point is that the religious traditions of the Near East, so influential in western thought for the past three millennia (and even earlier if we think of Near Eastern and Egyptian influences on Greco-Roman mystery religions), assumed a bipolarity between good and evil. This often correlated with white (good) magic and black (evil) magic. Such a bipolar analysis is more typical of an integrity rather than intimacy cultural orientation.

In ancient Japan, by contrast, the *kami* could be either benign or harmful to humans, but they were intrinsically neither good nor evil. Their positive or negative quality of action emerged from the function in a particular context rather than from essential nature. The accounts of the *kami* at the time of creation as recorded in *Kojiki* suggest the harm done by the gods was commonly caused by mischief or whim rather than malevolence. In that respect, they more resemble the behavior of the Homeric gods and goddesses rather than the struggles between good and evil in, say, Zoroastrianism, Manicheanism, Judaism, Christianity, or Islam.

30. This refers to the ideal of the "[Dharma] wheel-turning king" (S. *cakravartin*; J. *tenrinjōō*) who rules the world with wisdom, benevolence, and compassion, rather than force.

31. *Nihonshoki* states:

> The following edict was made [by Shōtoku]: "We hear that Our Imperial ancestors, in their government of the world, bending lowly under the sky and treading delicately on the ground, paid deep reverence to the gods of heaven and earth. They everywhere dedicated temples to the mountains and rivers, and held mysterious communion with the powers of nature. Hence, the male and female elements became harmoniously developed, and civilizing influences blended together. And now in Our reign, shall we be remiss in the worship of the gods of heaven and earth? Therefore let our ministers with their whole hearts do reverence to them." (Trans. based on Aston 1972, 135.)

In this passage, the language suggests syncretistic elements in proto-Shintō, possibly intermixing some Daoist ideas with folk religious *kami*-worship.

32. Again, scholars are uncertain when and by whom the commentaries were written. See the brief comment in Como 2008, 164. Yet, they were attributed to Shōtoku, as was the *Constitution*, by the beginning of the eighth century, the importance of which is the commentaries and *Constitution* have often been interpreted in light of each other since ancient times. Because we are interested in the impact of the documents on subsequent Japanese philosophical thinking, I will follow that intertextual interpretation. See Hajime 2002, ch. 1, for a modern Buddhist scholar's reading along those same lines.

Historicist scholars can argue interminably about whether Shōtoku himself actually wrote the Buddhist commentaries and the *Constitution* himself. The answer may turn out to be trivial in either of two respects. First, as the regent, Shōtoku likely delegated many projects to trusted advisors. That does not in itself make him less responsible for the final product. For example, most famous quotations attributed to President John F. Kennedy were actually written by his speech writers such as Ted Sorensen. That Kennedy commissioned them and approved the final version justifies our attributing authorship to the president. Second, even if, say, the Buddhist commentaries were written long after Shōtoku died or were basically variants of Chinese or Korean commentaries, we still have to factor into a discussion of the evolution of Japanese philosophy that the great Japanese thinkers throughout history considered them to have been authored by Shōtoku.

Admittedly, the association of these works with Shōtoku's name might have originally been no more than a ploy to lend the documents greater authority. Just as likely, however, those who linked the *Constitution* and the commentaries perceived underlying commonalities in their ideas. Even alleged deviations in rhetoric or style could derive from different scribes being assigned the task of producing the documents. As I suggest in the ensuing discussion, I find the texts complementary in important ways, enough in my judgment that even Shōtoku's near contemporaries could successfully argue the two as having a common author. Until the twentieth century, no philosopher in Japan to my knowledge questioned the attribution of these texts to Shōtoku.

33. The original Sanskrit names for the three forms of texts—*kyō, ron,* and *ritsu*—are respectively *sūtra, śastra,* and *vinaya.*

34. For a helpful overview of the Korean background in the transmission of Buddhism to Japan in Shōtoku's times, see BLUM 2008.

35. This may be the first occurrence of a *reductio ad absurdum* argument in a Japanese text. As explained in Chapter 1, that form of argument is not as common in Japanese as western (or Indian) philosophical writings. Even its appearance here seems not to have had much immediate impact on Japanese rhetoric and logic, possibly because Shōtoku's commentaries, although commonly copied and mentioned, were not thoroughly analyzed until centuries later for their content. For an introduction and translation of Shōtoku's commentary on the *Śrīmālā Sutra,* see DENNIS 2011.

Of course, in the Nara period, with the introduction of originally Indian texts dealing with epistemology and logic, there are many more occurrences of *reductio* arguments, but my tentative impression is that they usually derive from the originally Indian text rather than from a Japanese commentator's own independent thinking.

36. Shōtoku's argument:

> When is one qualified for enlightenment: in a previous life, in a future life, or in the present life? If a previous life be recommended [as the answer], then it must be remembered that that life has already passed away. Hence, no causal basis that would qualify one for enlightenment exists now. If a future life be urged upon us [to explain when enlightenment can be attained], we must note that that life has not yet arrived. Thus, in this case too, there exists no causal basis of qualification for enlightenment. And even in the case of the present life, we must bear in mind that this life is momentary and transient. It is not abiding. Therefore, even here, there is no causal basis that would qualify one [permanently for enlightenment]. (Trans. based on NAKAMURA Hajime 2002, 18.)

37. Trans. in NAKAMURA Hajime 2002, 29.

38. Trans. in NAKAMURA Hajime 2002, 26.

39. Trans. in NAKAMURA Hajime 2002, 26. In that comment, Shōtoku reverses the meaning of the passage in the *Lotus Sutra* praising the contemplative life of detachment.

40. As Shōtoku expressed it:

> In the world one adorns one's own physical embodiment with seven jewels, but she adorns the cosmic embodiment with her various deeds. So, we call her "Queen Shōman" ("Queen Glorious Garland"). (Trans. based on NAKAMURA Hajime 2002, 25.)

41. Trans. based on NAKAMURA Hajime 2002, 25.

42. "The mind is the ground of all virtues. As the mind right now is pure, how can virtues originating in it not be pure also?" (Trans. based on NAKAMURA Hajime 2002, 25.)

43. Some readers might assume a Daoist element in such passages because of its reference to working in harmony with the cycle of the seasons. I don't think such a statement is enough to suggest a direct connection to Daoism, however. Confucianism as well emphasizes that harmony in the human realm of statecraft will coincide with harmony in the natural realm. The connection between those realms might be considered generically Chinese rather than specifically one tradition or another.

44. For example, the boysenberry seems to be a hybrid of a blackberry, loganberry, and raspberry. (And the loganberry itself is a hybrid of a blackberry and raspberry, but you cannot produce a boysenberry from just a blackberry and raspberry.) Some botanists believe the dewberry also played a critical role in the hybridization. As this example shows, a true hybrid, the parentage is often obscured and cannot be easily determined. It follows that a true hybrid cannot be "de-hybridized." A hybrid is a new species unto itself.

45. The Soga engineered the succession from Suiko to Emperor Jomei, and upon his death in 641 put his widow, Empress Kōgyoku, on the throne. Two members of the Soga family, Emishi and his son Iruka, worked the system and acquired ever increasing control of land, labor, and funds. Finally, in 645 Prince Naka no Ōe enlisted the help of Nakatomi no Kamatari to assassinate Iruka and force Emishi's suicide. The Nakatomi had joined the Mononobe in 522 against the Soga but, unlike the Mononobe, managed to survive after the Soga victory.

Naka no Ōe then installed his cousin, Emperor Kōtoku, on the throne with Kōtoku's sister, Empress Saimei, as his successor. So, the 37th sovereign, Empress Saimei, was the same person as the 35th sovereign, known as Empress Kōgyoku. Furthermore, she was Naka no Ōe's mother. When she died, Naka no Ōe assumed the throne himself and became the Emperor Tenji.

46. *Hentai kanbun* is a broadly applied term for certain literary forms of Japanese that draw extensively on Chinese as well as Japanese elements. Because it superficially looks like Chinese (until one tries to read it as Chinese) and because the term "variant Chinese" names the style, some writers mistakenly think it is a special form of Chinese, rather than of Japanese. Linguists generally agree, however, that if the text is read properly, it is read as Japanese with the addition of Chinese elements that had crept into the elite language because Chinese was previously the only written language in Japan.

As will be clear in Chapter 10's discussion of Motoori Norinaga, whether *Kojiki*'s language is essentially Chinese or Japanese became a matter of immense cultural importance. In the late eighteenth and ensuing centuries *Kojiki* came to be the chief canonical text of Shintō, esteemed as the first text to be written in the national language. It is certainly true that the insistence on the text's "Japaneseness" shaped its role in the ideology of the modern Japanese nation-state, but that does not mean the premise of the text's being a form of Japanese is wrong.

In their haste to expose the roots of modern Japanese nationalism, some intellectual historians have suggested that Norinaga, in effect, distorted an essentially Chinese text to make it into the primal text of the native Japanese spirit (*yamato damashii*). Whatever one might think about Norinaga's motives, it does not alter the fact that *Kojiki* was indeed written to be read aloud as Japanese, not Chinese. The historical linguist, Bjarke Frellesvig, explains:

> In an extreme type of logographic writing of Japanese, known as *hentai kanbun* "deviant Chinese text," stretches of text longer than single words are represented by strings of *kanji* in an order different from the word order in Japanese, making the texts appear more like Chinese than Japanese, but they are in fact complex representations of Japanese. (FRELLESVIG 2010, 13–14)

Christopher Seeley, another historical linguist of Japanese, puts it this way:

> It is clear from the above that [the editor] Yasumaro was at great pains to employ a form of writing in the *Kojiki* which would be easy, comparatively speaking, to read and understand as Japanese. Yasumaro considered writing in the Japanese style, in phonogram notation, but rejected this possibility for the main prose text on account of its prolixity. The format which he finally chose was a hybrid style written in an orthography which, while predominantly logographic, made use of phonogram notation extensively when compared with earlier texts. (SEELEY 2000, 44)

Perhaps no one else states the issue as pithily as the scholar of Japanese classics, Richard Bowring, when he writes that *Kojiki* is written "in a difficult hybrid style that retains a great deal of native Japanese beneath the cloak of a script borrowed from China...." (BOWRING 2005, 47)

47. For example, in 620 Shōtoku and Suiko had apparently commissioned two texts called *Tennōki* (Record of emperors) and *Kokki* (Record of the country). They in turn probably drew on even earlier texts called *Teiki* (Record of sovereigns) and *Kyūji* (Compendium of ancient times). Traditional accounts assert that all copies of *Tennōki* and *Kokki* were destroyed during the 645 coup, however.

48. The matter-of-fact locution in *Nihonshoki* demonstrates the voice of scholarly detachment:

> Izanagi no Mikoto and Izanami no Mikoto consulted together, saying: "...Why should we not produce someone who shall be lord of [what is under heaven]?" They then together produced the Sun-goddess, who was called Oho-hiru-me no muchi. Called in one writing Ama-terasu-oho-hiru-me no Mikoto. (Trans. in ASTON 1972, 18.)

Compare the miraculous account in *Kojiki*:

> Hereupon, Izanagi-nö-opo-kamï said: "I have been to a most unpleasant land, a horrible, unclean land. Therefore, I shall purify myself."
> Arriving at the plain of Apaki-para by the river-mouth of Tatibana in Pimuka

in Tukusi, he purified and exorcised himself. When he flung down his stick, there came into existence a deity named Tuki-tatu-puna-to-nö-kami. Next, when he flung down his sash, there came into existence a deity named Miti-nö-naga-ti-pa-nö-kamï…. Then when he washed his left eye, there came into existence a deity named Ama-terasu-opo-mi-kamï. (Trans. based on PHILIPPI 1968, 60–70.)

49. Actually, in some respects, *Man'yōshū*'s writing system, *man'yōgana*, was even more complex than the *Kojiki*'s system of *hentai kanbun*. This was not always due to some linguistic difficulty, but rather to a deliberate attempt to make a secret language reserved for those of the intimate circle.

To take one of the more quirky examples: the word *nikuku* (a suffix meaning "to be difficult") could be written in *man'yōgana* phonetically as 二八十一 (see *Man'yōshū* 11.2542). This is not "phonetic" in the straightforward sense since the individual characters might be read as, say, *ni, hachi, jū, ichi*, a rendering hardly like *nikuku*. However, the person in the know would recognize this as a clever pun, first parsing the character sequence into two numbers: two (二) and eighty-one (八十一), but then realizing that eighty-one is nine times nine. This gives us 2, 9, 9 pronounced phonetically as "*ni ku ku*." (See FRELLESVIG 2010, 18, for a brief discussion of this "rebus writing" in *Man'yōshū*.)

I cite this example not only because it is amusing, but also because it suggests at this crucial point in history, when the Japanese are first starting to make a point of distinguishing between Japanese and Chinese cultural elements, the writing system for the outside world is Chinese, but for "us," it is Japanese. In fact, in this case the language is not regular Japanese but a Japanese written for an intimate group, an "us"—a subgroup of the larger "us"—who is "in the know." Again, the outside face of Japan is "Chinese" and open, while the inner face is Japanese and intimate. By this time both are genuinely part of Japanese culture, but which side is presented depends on the context.

50. Saichō, Kūkai's contemporary and the founder of the Japanese Tendai Sect, also systematized Buddhist teachings by drawing on the analysis of the Tiantai Chinese philosopher, Zhiyi (538–597). Zhiyi in turn was inspired by the claim in the *Lotus Sutra* that all Buddhist paths are ultimately one. Kūkai's typology was, however, more philosophically sophisticated than Saichō's, whose classifications would be greatly enhanced by subsequent generations of Tendai thinkers. Furthermore, compared to Saichō's, Kūkai's scheme was more comprehensive, including even non-Buddhist views in his rankings of the "ten mindsets."

51. Exemplary of the government's wish to keep Buddhism from ordinary people was its treatment of the monk Gyōki (or Gyōgi, 668?–749). A Hossō charismatic Buddhist itinerant, Gyōki mixed with commoners, helping them with civil engineering projects, building monastic temples for monks and nuns, and performing miracles of healing. His sermons drew audiences in the hundreds and the government issued edicts against his practices for several years starting in 718.

Eventually, the aristocrats came to accept Gyōki, however, especially after he helped raise popular support for building the Great Temple to the East discussed later in this chapter. The emperor granted him the posthumous title of *bosatsu* (bodhisattva), the first to receive that imperial honor. See MATSUNAGA and MATSUNAGA 1974, 1: 118–19, and SJT–1, 115–17.

52. To speak more historically and less pejoratively of the schools of Indian Buddhism

that supposedly fit under the umbrella of the term *Hinayana* (S. *hīnayāna*), it would be best to find a different term. Some scholars favor "Conservative (or Orthodox) Buddhists." Others like "Nikāya Buddhists" (because they stress the version of the canon of early sutras preserved in Pali known as the *Nikāyas*). Still others prefer "Abhidharma Buddhists" (a term favored by some philosophers since their concern is with the earliest philosophical texts of the Hinayanists, which are called *Abhidharma* [P. *Abhidhamma*], texts that set the terminology and philosophical agenda later developed in Mahāyāna as well). "Early Buddhists" is also used, but it can sometimes be considered different from Hinayana, referring to Buddhists before the Mahayana and Hinayana traditions developed. "Mainstream Buddhists" has come into vogue recently. Although that term suits the Southasian context, it is not appropriate for Japan because Hinayana Buddhism was never mainstream there.

More important than the term is the way the idea of Hinayana functions in Japanese philosophical discourse. The name *Hinayana* became a way for Mahayanists (which include almost all Japanese) to designate what they are not. Thus, it functionally referred to what they considered to be Buddhist teachings lacking in profundity or practices lacking in optimal efficacy. This led to a host of straw man arguments in which Mahayanists criticized ideas, values, or practices as "Hinayanist" even though in some cases few, if any, of the members of the schools thought to be "Hinayanist" actually fit that description. The term *Hinayana*, therefore, is clearly pejorative and has not been commonly used as a self-designation by any significant and enduring group of Buddhists found in Japan.

So, we could say that for the purposes of tracing philosophical discussions in Japan related to Buddhism, the idea of Hinayana Buddhism was more or less a social construction of the Mahayanists, playing a crucial role in the development of their religious and philosophical imaginary. It allowed the grouping of a set of ideas and values that were admittedly Buddhist in origin, but not, except in rare cases, to be fully endorsed.

In the end, having to make a choice among no ideal candidates, I have decided to use *Hinayana* in this book. After all, it is the term (J. *shōjō* 小乗) used most often by Japanese philosophers in referring to the cluster of ideas and practices considered of lesser value than those they endorse as *Mahayana* (*daijō* 大乗).

53. To reiterate: the valence of the term "Hinayana" here is "non-Mahayana." Thus, it is not meant to refer to all the historical Hinayana schools that existed in India, some of which attached more metaphysical rather than this-worldly status to the Buddha.

54. To take one example, in advocating engagement in this world and its problems, Shōtoku's commentary on the *Yuima Sutra* used Hinayana asceticism as a contrast:

> Hinayana ascetics, hating the distractive world, escape into mountains and forests to practice careful disciplining of mind and body.... If they still think that various objects exist, and cannot give up that assumption, how can they rid their minds of such distractions, even if they stay in mountains and forests? (Trans. in NAKAMURA Hajime 2002, 24.)

55. Since the Hinayanists in this account heed the teachings, they are sometimes called "hearers of the [Buddha's] voice" (*shōmon*; S. *śrāvaka*). The term has the connotation of being part of a detached audience, however heedful, of the Buddha's message rather

than engaged participants in the world, relieving the suffering of others (the Mahayanist bodhisattva ideal).

The notion of nirvana underwent considerable adjustment as Buddhism moved from one cultural context to another. Speaking in broad generalities, one relevant shift in emphasis is that in Indian and Southeast Asia where the notion of rebirth was more strongly entrenched, the idea of nirvana often emphasized enlightenment as the release from the cycle of birth and death. In East Asia, however, there was no native belief in rebirth and so they placed more stress on the "awakening" aspect of enlightenment in this world. For a brief sketch of some of those and other changes in the idea of Buddhist enlightenment over time and cultures, see KASULIS 2005.

56. The more common English convention is to speak of the Buddha's three "bodies" instead of "embodiments." I have chosen "embodiment" over "body" because the English word has three apropos meanings. First, an embodiment is an incarnation, personification, or concrete symbol for something transcendent or abstract. This works well for the celestial and historical embodiments, especially when they are considered to be manifestations of a deeper essence, the reality or cosmic embodiment. In that case, *embodiment* is more suitable a term than *body* since it is more descriptive, implying subsistence as well as existence.

Another common English meaning for the word *embodiment* is to name the *process* of becoming incarnate, personified, or symbolized. In that sense "embodiment" refers not to a thing but an event. All the embodiments are the result of the Buddha's embodying itself in different ways. The cosmic or reality embodiment (S. *dharmakāya*; J. *hosshin*) has multiple meanings and different interpretations. It can be the intangible, transcendent principle or "emptiness" that lies behind reality and manifests itself as the various buddhas or even as the entire cosmos. Alternatively, it can be immanently all the buddhas and things of the cosmos itself. Thus, it either is that which embodies or is the embodiment itself. The term *embodiment* seems more suitable for that reason.

Lastly, the term *embodiment* can refer to an aspect of praxis. As this book will show, in Japanese religious philosophy, enlightenment and wisdom must typically be embodied, enacted, and engaged. Sometimes that process of embodiment, especially in esoteric Buddhism, mirrors the Buddha's (process of) embodiment.

57. In this book, I refer to the three embodiments as *historical, celestial,* and *cosmic.* Other commonly used names in English are, respectively, "transformational," "reward" (or "bliss"), and "dharma" (or "reality"). In Sanskrit, the terms are *nirmāṇakāya, saṃbhogakāya,* and *dharmakāya.*

58. Some western commentators involved in Buddhist-Christian dialogue have seen a parallel with Christian theories that discuss the so-called impersonal Godhead as the basis of the three persons of the Trinity, the essential unity that the Father, Son, and Holy Spirit share.

59. Consider this passage from the Shōtoku commentary on the *Yuima Sutra:*

> The reality of all things is emptiness. Hence, they are said to be "nonbeing." So, being is not really being. But why then should nonbeing be nonbeing? Accordingly, nonbeing is said to be not nonbeing.... [The meaning of] "being" and "nonbeing" is not definite. Nevertheless, both are born of causal relationships. (Trans. based on NAKAMURA Hajime 2002, 1.)

60. Nāgārjuna is often considered to be the first Indian Mahayana philosopher to make this argument. For a brief general treatment of his analysis as it influenced East Asian Buddhist traditions like Zen, see KASULIS 1981, ch 2. For understanding the more precise technical arguments of Nāgārjuna in his own Indian philosophical milieu especially as developed in his *Mūlamadhyamakakārikā*, see NĀGĀRJUNA 1995 or 2013.

61. For further explanation of this East Asian Buddhist concept of nothingness, see my analysis in KASULIS 1981, 3–52. There I distinguish the Indian Buddhist Madhyamaka view of *emptiness* (S. *śūnyatā;* C. *kong;* J. *kū*) from the Chinese Daoist notion of *Nonbeing* (C. *wu;* J. *mu*). I then argue that the East Asian (especially, but not exclusively, Zen) Buddhist idea of *mu* (which in that context I translate as *nothingness*) eventually collapses the two ideas into one. For a good account of the Daoist notion of creativity, see CHANG 1963.

62. For a philosophical take on the Buddhist theory of *upāya,* see SCHROEDER 2001. For a more textual approach, see PYE 1978.

63. The word *shū* was written in two different ways, suggesting two senses of the term at the time. One character 衆 means a collection of people, in other words, a group such as a study group. That term was more common in the Nara period. The other character 宗 is closer to the meaning of "sect" or "denomination" or "school of thought" and was also used sometimes in the Nara period, but later becoming the standard term.

64. The discussion of the teachings of these schools is here necessarily adumbrated. Fuller details in English are available in MATSUNAGA and MATSUNAGA 1974, 1: 26–137 and TAKAKUSU 1956, 57–125.

65. This differed from the context of the original Vinaya rules written in India. The original Vinaya established an autonomous religious system separate from the secular government. In Japan, during the Nara period (and often later) the government saw Buddhism as serving the country by performing rituals to protect the state and to effect prosperity. As a result, the state maintained significant control over Buddhist affairs and the secular-sacred dichotomy often so strong in Indian Buddhism did not apply to Japan.

The dynamics of the relation between Buddhism and the state during the Nara period are far more complex than can be described in this brief overview. For a more thorough account in English of state-clergy relations up through the Nara period, see BOWRING 2005, ch 3.

66. There is some similarity here in the debate between the scholastic realists and nominalists in western medieval philosophy.

67. Bodhisena (704–760) was in Japan as the result of a pilgrimage to find Manjuśri, the bodhisattva of wisdom, who purportedly resided in earthly form at Mt Wutai in China. Told that the bodhisattva had left the mountain to move east, Bodhisena ended up in Japan. Landing in Osaka harbor in 735, he met Gyōki, whom he recognized as Manjuśri and called him *bosatsu* (bodhisattva). That apparently was the origin of that title's being bestowed posthumously by the emperor. See note 51 above. The story is recounted in TAKAKUSU 1956, 109.

68. It was by Nakamaro's counsel that Kōken abdicated the throne in 758 in favor of Prince Toneri's son and Nakamaro's son-in-law, Emperor Junnin. Prince Toneri, a chief compiler of *Nihonshoki* (working with others, such as Ō no Yasumaro), had been

instrumental in getting Empress Kōmyō her title as nonreigning empress. It seems, then, that Toneri, Nakamaro, and Kōmyō were united in their support of Junnin's rise to sovereignty. Kōmyō died in 760 and the arrangement started to unravel.

69. Toby 1985 argues convincingly that the purpose of the move to Heian was not simply to avoid the power of the Six Nara Schools, as earlier scholars had often assumed.

3. Kūkai (774–835)

70. Trans. from Shiba 1975, 3. An abridged English translation of this work is Shiba 2003 (the corresponding passage here appears on page 1). Shiba Ryōtarō was a noted author of historical and biographical books supported by his quite extensive reading in scholarly sources. Thus, his work falls between the clear demarcations of fiction, nonfiction, and personal editorializing. As such, Shiba certainly took liberties with technical details and often generalized ideas without their technical nuance. Yet, this semi-fictional, semi-nonfictional work captures aspects of the spirit of Kūkai and his thought especially well, in some ways better than any strictly nonfictional biographical study could.

71. Tsunoda Bun'ei has raised a doubt as to whether the Saeki kinship group to which Kūkai belonged was the same Saeki clan related to the Ōtomo. Yoshito S. Hakeda, however, gives textual reasons for rejecting Tsunoda's view. See Hakeda 1972, 13–14, n. 2. Shiba gives a rather spirited account of the intricate issues involved. See Shiba 2003, 1–6.

72. For a brief description of the curriculum and Kūkai's own mention of his focused dedication to study at the time, see Abe Ryūichi 1999, 69–74. For a discussion of the bureau of the *daigaku* in the early tenth century, its selection procedures, the constitution of its faculty, its curriculum, and its semi-annual ritual in veneration of Confucius, see Bock 1985.

73. In fact, a little later, the Ōtomo/Saeki family with which Kūkai was affiliated was allegedly involved in the assassination of Fujiwara no Tanetsugu in 795. Because of this, the emperor stripped the Ōtomo of many of their titles. These were subsequently reinstated about a decade later, but such turmoil was typical around the time of Kūkai's tenure in the capital.

74. Actually, the draft of this work (called *Rōko shiiki*) was probably written in 797. With the exception of the prologue, the text is nearly identical with the *Sangōshiiki* compiled much later but still dated 797. For a discussion of the dating of these manuscripts, see Hakeda 1972, 16–17.

75. He expresses this preference in these excerpts from one of his well-known Chinese poems written later in life:

Why i go into the mountains
You ask, "Teacher, why do you go into that deep cold—
That unsafe place among the deep, steep peaks
Where the climb is painful and the descent difficult,
That place where the mountain *kami* and tree spirits are at home?"
......
Oh, don't you know? don't you know?

Human life being what it is, how long can you go on?

Thinking, thinking of this, day and night, gnawing at your guts;

Like the sun setting in the western mountains, your life is half-gone.

Like a walking corpse, your years are half-spent.

There's no point in staying on and on [in the city].

I must go. I must. I cannot stay.

So, this teacher of the great emptiness (*kū*) does not stay; no, he does not.

This child of [Shingon Buddhism's] milky sea (*kai*)

Does not weary of seeing Mount Kōya's rocks and pines,

And is continually moved by its clear-flowing streams.

Do not take pride in the poison of fame and gain.

Do not be consumed in the fiery world of delusion.

Taking up the secluded religious life,

One quickly enters the realm of the Buddha's cosmic embodiment.

Trans. from kz 3: 406–7; kkz 6: 732. For an alternative translation of the whole poem, see Hakeda 1972, 51–2.

76. Trans. in Abe Ryūichi 1999, 106.

77. Japanese Shingon Buddhism, unlike Tibetan Buddhism, generally does not consider itself a *tantric* tradition, however. Tantrism is rooted in Indian Hindu and Buddhist secret practices. There are indeed important connections between Shingon and Indian tantrism, but it is probably not appropriate to call Kūkai a "tantric Buddhist philosopher." In fact, most scholars who are themselves Shingon Buddhists avoid that characterization. There are at least two main reasons for this.

First, as will be clear from the rest of this chapter, probably no distinction is more important to Kūkai than that between esoteric and exoteric. Yet, the distinction does not occur, at least so sharply, in India. Indeed, there is no Sanskrit equivalent to the term *exoteric* (J. *kengyō*).

Second, compared with most tantric masters from Tibet and India, Kūkai's collected writings contain relatively few specific, step-by-step instructions for esoteric rituals (the *tantra*). One might expect that, as the founder of Japanese Shingon, Kūkai would have taken pains to ensure a perfect transmission of the praxis. Overall, however, he seems to have been more concerned about the theory of praxis, the metapraxis. Perhaps Kūkai's own youthful experience in the mountains of Yoshino convinced him of the futility of esoteric praxis without a theory of metapraxis and an accompanying metaphysics.

78. Huiguo's disciples were an unusually diverse international group. See Abe Ryūichi 1999, 122.

79. Trans. in Abe Ryūichi 1999, 126.

80. For an account of the interaction between Kūkai and Tokuitsu, see Abe Ryūichi 1999, 204ff.

81. Abe Ryūichi 1999, 212.

82. The technical term for Kūkai's present status is *nyūjō* (entrance into meditation). Morita Ryūsen brought the techniques of modern scholarship to bear on the history and doctrinal significance of this phenomenon. See Morita 1973. On the development of the Kūkai mythos, see also Kitagawa 1966, 182–202.

83. Trans. from KKZ 2: 149; see also English translation in GIEBEL and TODARO 2004, 17. Besides the sampling of selections in JPS, there are presently two useful, more complete translations for most of the works discussed in this chapter: those by Hakeda Yoshito in HAKEDA 1972 and the translations by Giebel in GIEBEL and TODARO 2004. On one hand, the former is superior for its hundred-page introduction and for the religious or spiritual suggestiveness used in translation of many key terms. On the other hand, the latter is more philosophically precise and has the advantage of being complete in the essays it translates, including all the scriptural excerpts Kūkai includes in the original.

In this chapter, I usually follow the latter translation. However, in many cases, for the sake of consistency with English terminology used in this book or to capture one particular nuance rather than another in the original, I translate the passage myself from KKZ. When doing so, for the convenience of the English reader, I also cite the page number where the same passage occurs in Giebel's translation.

84. The four-sinograph slogan is a traditional East Asian way to express the heart of a key teaching. In the case of *hosshin seppō* 法身説法, the first and last characters are the same: *hō* or "dharma." Thus, the phrase utilizes the multiple meanings of that term. The buddha's dharma (reality)-embodiment [which is the same as all dharmas, that is, the cosmos] expounds (or teaches or preaches) the dharma (true teachings) [which in this case is also all the dharmas as the totality of phenomena constituting reality]. Hence, the phrase comes down to meaning something like "reality is the buddha's teaching the truth as all phenomena," or alternatively "the cosmic buddha preaches the truth as all phenomena."

85. See TAMAKI 1974, 12–17.

86. Trans. from KKZ 2: 150; See also GIEBEL and TODARO 2004, 17–18.

87. In this book I reserve the English word "secret" to translate the term *himitsu* 秘密, literally, "obscure" + "intimacy."

88. In modern Japanese the word *shō* or *koe* (声) usually means "voice," but the sinograph is sometimes used even today more broadly to indicate the sound of something such as rain (雨声), a gun (銃声), stringed instruments (絃声), or a bell (鐘声). In Buddhist terminology, the term is commonly used for anything audible, in other words, *sound*. In the present case, the voice of Dainichi constitutes the sounds and resonances of the universe. So, both "voice" and "sound" are viable translations. Here I follow GIEBEL and TODARO 2004 and HAKEDA 1972 in using "sound" rather than ABE Ryūichi 1999 and JPS which use "voice." Since he is interested in pursuing a semiotic and discourse analysis, Abe's choice of "voice" is certainly more apt in that case.

89. Kūkai's earlier works only mention five seed mantras, the sixth (*hūṃ*) being added only from around the time of his writing *Sokushin jōbutsugi* (*The Significance of "Attaining Buddhahood with This Very Body"*) in 817. This point will be discussed later in relation to Kūkai's adding "consciousness" (*shiki*) to the list of basic elements. See KANAOKA 1979, 230–1.

90. The points made here are limited to considerations directly relevant to our interest in Kūkai. For a general phenomenology of auditory experience, see IHDE 1976.

91. Of course, from the scientific standpoint, we know that the light reflected off an object must also come to us for it to be visible; yet, experientially, we feel like we are look-

ing at a tree, not that a tree is coming to us. Contrast that with the experience of hearing the bird singing in its branches.

92. For an analysis of different kinds of speech acts and how Kūkai would understand them, see KASULIS 1982. That article also contrasts Kūkai's view with the one Plato develops in *Cratylus*, suggesting that in Kūkai and Plato's understanding of philosophical language, the two cultural traditions began to diverge in significant ways.

93. The Chinese tradition has multiple lists of elements: the number usually varying from four to six. Originally, Kūkai favored the five element list (not including "consciousness") commonly cited in the *Dainichi Sutra*. Why then the switch to six?

Presumably, Kūkai realized that, as the activity of the enlightened Buddha Dainichi, the universe must be permeated with consciousness and that consciousness could not be easily reduced to any combination of the other five elements. Therefore, he subsequently opted for the more inclusive six-element list. Since his first writings after returning from China used the five-element system, it may well be that the shift to six elements was his own idea, rather than something learned from Huiguo. In any case, I consider that shift to be a critical point in the development of Kūkai's philosophical system.

94. In HAKEDA 1972, Hakeda translates *kaji* as "grace." That is a provocative rendering, especially if we think of grace as universal instead of predestined. Like universal grace, *kaji* is available to anyone who recognizes it and chooses to participate in it through ritual. Such a perspective illumines the sacramental character of Shingon practice: ritual is the form for participating directly in sacred power.

It is not surprising that the first Roman Catholic missionaries to Japan in the sixteenth century, relying on the advice of their Shingon fisherman interpreter, tried for a time to translate "God" as "Dainichi Buddha." Although the similarities between God and Dainichi Buddha are not trivial, the missionaries abandoned that translation after a couple of decades. The most telling difference is that Dainichi is not a creator as we will see when I explain the arguments of Fukansai Habian in Chapter 8, pages 294–8. There was no point at which Dainichi created reality; nor is Dainichi in any way willing reality to be as it is. The world merely follows from Dainichi's style of existence as an intimation of what is innermost to Dainichi's being. Dainichi is not an artist; the world is not Dainichi's handiwork. There is no planned design, only the pattern of enlightenment that flows spontaneously and necessarily from Dainichi's person.

Still, there remains the possibility of fruitful dialogue between Roman Catholic sacramentalism and Shingon esotericism. For an interesting collection of essays along this line, see KADOWAKI 1977. Also, see my essay comparing Kūkai's criteria for the ten mindsets and Karl Rahner's criteria for the "anonymous Christian" (KASULIS 1984).

95. For an astute philosophical study of attunement in relation to the philosophies of Kūkai and Dōgen, see NAGATOMO 1992.

96. This explanation could account for malevolent powers as well. The thaumaturgist can willfully work against the natural harmony, causing the neighboring phenomena to be more off-key, as it were, resulting in disease or even death. In the world view of Kūkai's age, due consideration would be given to negative as well as positive miraculous phenomena.

97. In expressing this idea, Kūkai wrote:

To play with the sharp sword of the mind of oneness is the exoteric teaching; to brandish the *vajra* of the three intimacies is the esoteric Buddhist teaching. If a man takes pleasure in the exoteric Buddhist teachings, he is bound to spend a period as long as three aeons before he attains enlightenment; but, if he commits himself to the esoteric Buddhist teaching, he may attain enlightenment quickly by means of sixteen spiritual rebirths [in this one lifetime]. The most sudden among the sudden approaches is the esoteric Buddhist teaching. (Trans. based on HAKEDA 1972, 150.)

The contrast between the exoteric use of the mind as sword and the esoteric use of empowerment as *vajra* (a ritual implement used in esoteric praxis) is particularly striking. It points to a difference between two modes of understanding, namely, conceptual analysis or detachment vs. ritually engaging the world with the three intimacies of body, mind, and speech.

98. In "On the Significance of *Sokushin jōbutsu*," Kūkai quotes from the *Dainichi Sutra*:

Without forsaking this body,
You attain the supernatural
And roam freely through the great void.
Furthermore, you achieve the secret of the body (*shin himitsu*).
......
If you want to enter perfection in this life,
Comply with the Buddha's empowerment and contemplate on it.
After receiving the mantra personally from your reverend teacher,
Meditate on it until you become united with it.
Then you will attain Perfection.
(Trans. based on KŪKAI 1975, 16–17.)

99. Kūkai was not always consistent in distinguishing the three terms. I suspect that was due, at least in part, to his frequent quoting of passages from texts that may not use them as he does. In any case, looking at his philosophical discussions as a whole, I believe the differentiation I explain here generally fits his system.

100. Trans. from KKZ 6: 759.

101. See the eighth definition under the entry for *shiki* (識) in NAKAMURA 1975, 1: 577–8, where its meaning is akin to a generalized spirituality. That meaning is close to the line of interpretation I will pursue here. As for thought and intention, they are not included in the bodily intimacy, but rather in the mental (*i* 意 or sometimes *shin* 心).

102. KKZ 1: 14.

103. *Jūjūshinron* is not available in English. *Hizō hōyaku*, in a much abridged form, is translated as *The Precious Key to the Secret Treasury* in HAKEDA 1972, 157–224 and is available in a full translation by Rolf W. Giebel in GIEBEL and TODARO 2004, 133–215.

104. Yuasa Yasuo explains the dynamic as follows:

What is distinctive to Kūkai's view, however, is that the ascending process in [spiritual] cultivation is simultaneously taken to be the descending process of the Buddha's compassion and salvation. In [*The Precious Key to the Obscure Treasury*], for example, Kūkai explicitly takes the advance to a higher religious experience as being the Buddha's power disclosed to the cultivator, and guiding him or her to that state. For example, [in reference to the move from the fourth to the fifth mindset] Kūkai says, "If you happen to encounter the Tathāgata's wonderment, your mind turns to the generosity of the bodhisattva.".... (YUASA 1987, 152)

105. There is a difference in emphasis between the two texts delineating Kūkai's theory of the mindsets. *The Theory of the Ten Mindsets*, true to the mandala formula, emphasizes that within any mindset, there is the kernel of Dainichi's activity that can pull you directly into the esoteric (tenth) mindset without traversing the other exoteric mindsets 1–9. To take the extreme example, the lust and desire driving the first mindset can evolve into affection. If pushed still further, that could lead to a love that establishes an internal relation with all things, the foundation for switching over from the detached knowing of exotericism to the engagement of esotericism in the tenth mindset. Esoteric enlightenment is always available to anyone right here and now.

Meanwhile, the argument in *Precious Key* tends to show more the internal logic of each mindset as capable of discovering a shortcoming in its view that leads one naturally into the next higher mindset, a type of self-negating process that would be common in some later Japanese philosophies, especially in the modern era. Of course, in that text as well, Kūkai insists that the esoteric is everywhere available right now, but that is not as major a focus as it is in the *Ten Mindsets* text.

106. Trans. from KKZ 1: 14.

107. The titles I give here of the ten mindsets are translated from those given in *Precious Key*, which are almost identical with those from *Ten Mindsets*. The descriptions, however, are my own summaries of Kūkai's characterizations of each mindset.

108. How would Kūkai the mature Shingon master have located the mindset of his younger self who wrote the *Three Aims*? The other-worldliness of Buddhism, so sharply delineated in the *Aims*, is not visible in the higher five levels of the Ten Mindsets. That leads me to surmise that the mature Kūkai would have evaluated the young Kūkai as living in a fifth-level mindset, that of a hermit buddha. Of course, biographically speaking, that is exactly what he was until he found his master in China.

109. WHITEHEAD 1979, 39.

110. The most prominent and astute Japanese intellectual historian of the postwar period, Maruyama Masao (1914–1996), recognized something similar, but his evaluation was radically different from what I present here. Maruyama labeled the submerged archaic as a *basso ostinato* (JPS, 922-9). It represented for him a stratum of Japanese culture that enabled it to resist the acceptance of transcendent principles and spiritual modernization. His musical description is formulated from the standpoint of the audience who identifies it as an "obstinate" and "stubbornly repetitive ground bass" that does not harmonize or enhance the melody, but rather, somehow invisibly shapes it in some way. By speaking instead of a riff, I shift the focus from the standpoint of the detached listener to that of the engaged performer, seeing the archaic riff as a source of creativity rather than resistance to constructive change.

As a postwar theorist, Maruyama was committed to trying to liberate Japan from the ideologies that had brought such horrific destruction in the preceding decades. He wanted a new Japan based in democratic principles and empirical reasoning. He was acutely aware of the social, political, and moral issues at stake, but he tended to overlook the epistemological tension between engaged vs. detached knowing that underlies all of them. Instead of engaging the riff and transforming it into his vision of a new Japan, he stood back from it and saw it only as an obstacle to his agenda. Maruyama's *basso ostinato* is a way of *referring to* the esoteric layer of ancient Japan, whereas the riff is a way of *conferring with* it.

4. Shining Prince, Shining Buddha

111. Trans. by LaFleur in SAIGYŌ 1978, 20.

112. In Chapter 2 of Lady Murasaki's *The Tale of Genji,* there is a famous discussion among Prince Genji and his cohorts about ranking the qualities of various ladies of the court.

113. This is not to say no men wrote Japanese texts in the native language. The most prominent exception is probably Ki no Tsurayuki (872?–945), a poet, editor, and political figure (see JPS, 1168–70). He not only wrote Japanese poems in Japanese (which was not so unusual), but he also wrote his introduction to the *Kokinshū* in Japanese (the first work on poetics written in Japanese rather than Chinese). He also wrote *Tosa Diary,* a fictionalized account of a journey presented in the Japanese voice of a woman courtier

114. All passages I quote from *Genji* are in Royall Tyler's translation, MURASAKI 2001, 461. For an alternative translation of just this passage about fiction, see that of Ivan Morris excerpted from his *World of the Shining Prince* in SJT-1, 201–2. For original, see MORRIS 1964.

115. My colleague at the Ohio State University, Naomi Fukumori, was the first to suggest to me the blog analogy.

116. As I will explain in Chapter 8, for example, in the Edo period the relation between author and subject matter in Bashō's aesthetic is closer to Murasaki's while Saikaku's is more like Sei's. See pages 283–4.

117. See page 607, n. 51 for the example of the populist monk, Gyōki.

118. Because of the transmission routes of Buddhism, with few exceptions, Tibet's Buddhist developments occurred in isolation from Japan's. Thus, if there are similarities between, say, esoteric Buddhism in Tibet and Japan, it is mainly because of common roots for the two traditions rather than direct interaction.

119. The Sanskrit and Japanese names for the three sutras:

> *The Larger Sutra of Immeasurable Life* (S. *Sukhāvatīvyūha sūtra*; J. *Daimuryōju kyō*)
>
> *The Amida Sutra* (S. same name as the preceding text, but a different, shorter work, sometimes also called in English *The Shorter Sutra*; J. *Amida kyō*)
>
> *Sutra of Contemplation on [the Buddha of] Immeasurable Life* (no extant Sanskrit version; J. *Kanmuryōju kyō*; often abbreviated to *Kangyō, Contemplation Sutra*).

120. The Japanese name "Amida" traces back to two closely linked buddhas in the Indian tradition: Amitābha and Amitāyus, the buddhas of "immeasurable light" and of

"immeasurable life." The name "Amida" is taken from the common element "immeasurable" in the two names.

121. The "five grave offenses" (*gogyaku*) are acts so heinous that, according to some Buddhists, their perpetrators can never subsequently achieve enlightenment. A common version specifies the offenses of patricide, matricide, killing an enlightened monk, wounding a buddha so he bleeds, and subverting the harmony of the Buddhist monastic community.

122. Three Chinese Pure Land commentators are best known in Japan by the Japanese pronunciations of their names: Tanluan (J. Donran, 476–542), Daochuo (J. Dōshaku, 562–645), and Shandao (J. Zendō, 613–681).

123. For a study of the development of the notion of *mappō* in Buddhist history, see NATTIER 1991. MARRA 1988 focuses on the development of the idea in Japan.

124. Under Emperor Wuzong's vicious persecution of Buddhism in China, Ennin found himself in the wrong place at the wrong time. As a foreign Buddhist monk living in China, Ennin was denied access to many holy sites (including Mt Tiantai, the intended main destination of his trip), was refused permission to go back to Japan, and was even sometimes briefly put under house arrest. For the life of Ennin, see REISCHAUER 1955, SWANSON 2005, and KASAHARA 2001, 80–4.

125. A variation was a one-week retreat every lunar month. This became the more common practice.

126. For a comprehensive work in English on this historically crucial figure in the institutional development of Heian-period Tendai, see GRONER 2002.

127. Paul Groner traces the history of how these examinations and debates developed on Mt Hiei. See GRONER 2002, 128–66.

128. The wide dissemination of this idea, at least in this formulation, seems to have been largely via a text called *The Awakening of Faith in Mahayana*, a highly influential sixth-century Chinese work. Although it purports to be a translation of a Sanskrit text from India written by Aśvaghoṣa, most scholars today agree that it is likely of Chinese authorship and not a translation at all.

129. This idea came to be expressed in terms of the doctrine of *sōmoku jōbutsu*, "the grasses and trees become buddhas." For a discussion of this theory and its eventual connection with *hongaku* theory, see STONE 1999, 29–31.

130. For an excellent discussion of many of these technical issues related to *hongaku*. See STONE 1999. Her analysis explains clearly and thoroughly the evolution of this idea, its proponents, and its critics.

131. This work, written in 978, was *Inmyō ronsho shisō iryaku chūshaku* (Comments on the Four Kinds of Logical Error Discussed in [Kuiji's] "Commentary on Buddhist Logic"). See GRONER 2002, 151–2. For Groner's discussion of "logic" texts in East Asian Buddhism see pages 153–6.

132. Kakuban's Shingon system, including its integration of Amidism, is most fully developed in his late work, *Gorin kuji myō himitsushaku*, translated as *The Illuminating Secret Commentary on the Five Cakras and the Nine Syllables* by Dale Todaro in *Shingon Texts* GIEBEL and TODARO 2004, 257–328. A more technical translation with extensive

commentary and notes is in chapter 5 of VAN DER VEERE 2000. The point under discussion here is expressed clearly in Kakuban's prologue to this work:

> The exoteric teachings consider Amida to be different from Śākyamuni. In the treasury of esoteric teachings, Dainichi is Amida. One should know that the pure lands in all directions emanate from the one Buddha [Dainichi]. All buddhas are wholly this Dainichi. Dainichi and Amida are different names for the same substance. Amida's Pure Land and [Dainichi's] Realm Adorned with Intimate Enlightenment are the same place with different names. (Trans. based on VAN DER VEERE 2000, 136.)

133. For example, the "short mantra" is "*Oṃ Amrita tese kara hūṃ.*" For a discussion comparing *nenbutsu* and Amida's Shingon mantras, see VAN DER VEERE 2000, 119.

134. The *locus classicus* for Kakaban's analysis of the meaning of Amida from a Shingon standpoint is his short work, *Esoteric Explanation of Amida* (*Amida hishaku*). For an abridged translation of the key sections, see JPS, 75–7. The full work is translated in SANFORD 2004, 120–38; alternative translation in VAN DER VEERE 2000, 111–15.

135. This line of thought was at the heart of what became a schism within Shingon. Critics of Kakuban's analysis claimed that by putting total focus on only one of Dainichi's manifestations, in this case Amida, you lose direct access to the teachings of Dainichi as *hosshin seppō*, "the cosmic Buddha preaches the dharma." In effect, they claimed Kakuban had confused the medium of the message with the message and its true origin. Defenders of Kakuban's teachings, on the other hand, rebutted that the medium *is* the message and that to separate the two violates the inseparable relation between Dainichi and Dainichi's manifestations. That dispute led Kakuban's followers to form the Shingi ("new teachings") branch of Shingon.

Certainly, the schism had nonphilosophical causes as well. Most notably, Kakuban had risen to such prominence in the Shingon institution and was so favored with imperial sponsorship that he simultaneously served as abbot of both Kyoto's Temple to the East and the Mt Kōya monastery, a departure from precedent. That resulted in internal dissent and attempts on his life that helped trigger the schism.

136. The Taira and Minamoto both traced their families back to aristocratic roots. In the early ninth century, due to the plethora of imperial consorts, the number of imperial progeny underwent a baby boom. In part to limit the possible claimants to the throne, and the inevitable political maneuvers and assassinations, the court trimmed branches of the imperial line. Having lost their imperial status, those court outcastes were given family names. Taira (also called Heike or Heishi) and Minamoto (also called Genji) were the two main ones. Members of their families received as recompense provincial appointments. As the centuries passed, their status transmuted into samurai.

137. KEENE 1960, 202–3.

138. Using the holographic relation of whole and part, Ryōnin's formulaic statement about interpenetration was the following:

> One person is all people; all people are one person; one practice is all practices; all practices are one practice. This is what explains the experience of Birth in the Pure Land by reliance upon Amida's power. All living beings are included in one thought. It is because of this mutual interconnection between all things, including the

buddhas themselves, that if one but calls upon Amida's sacred name once, it has the same virtue as if one did it a million times. (Trans. in WATTS and TOMATSU 2005, 80.)

Ryōnin was philosophically astute enough to discern the epistemological implication in this theory of interpenetration. "All things are really as they appear. There is no subjective and no objective. It is here that all virtue and all merit may be found" (WATTS and TOMATSU 2005, 80). In effect, this is an appeal to an intimate, internal-relations form of engaged knowing which rejects the independence of subject and object and maintains instead their inseparability and overlap. This is a case where a metapraxis to justify the *yūzū nenbutsu* (namely, the idea that one practice is all practices) leads to a metaphysical understanding of the nature of reality (an interfusion of all things including self and other). That understanding in turn not only informs the praxis but leads to a change in it (the move to communal chanting for the rebirth of everyone, not just oneself).

139. Trans. in NISHI HONGWANJI COMMISSION ON THE PROMOTION OF RELIGIOUS EDUCATION 1974, 47–8. This selection is from *Kurodani shōnin gotoroku* (*Record of the Saint of Kurodani* [i.e., Hōnen]). Other translations of Hōnen's works include the old, but still useful, COATES and ISHIZUKA 1925, as well as HŌNEN 1997, 1998, and 2011. Snippets of translation organized within an overview of Hōnen's teachings are available in WATTS and TOMATSU 2005. A good introduction to Hōnen's life and thought as well as some comparison with western religious ideas is MACHIDA 1999.

140. The term *shōdō* 聖道 literally means the "saintly" or "holy" (*shō*) "Path" or "Way" (*dō*). For the Buddha's Noble Eightfold Path, for example, the Sanskrit term for "noble" was rendered as this sinograph *shō*. Thus, the thrust of the Pure Land position is that the path outlined by the historical Buddha can no longer be effective in our present situation of decline. Applied to the Japanese case, this would mean the praxes followed by the dominant Buddhist sects such as Hossō, Shingon, Tendai, and Kegon were no longer effectual.

The distinction between the easy and difficult paths is Tanluan's, while that between the Gate to the Pure Land and the Gate to the Path to Self-perfection is Daochuo's. Yet, the two distinctions are easily correlated. As Hōnen said, "… the words differ but the meaning is actually the same." (Trans. in HŌNEN 1997, 13.)

141. Found in NST 10: 87–164 (Japanese rendering with notes); 257–82 (original Chinese). For an English translation, see HŌNEN 1998.

142. Throughout the classical and medieval periods, the principle of selection was central to the critical literary practice of compiling poetry collections as well. The aesthetic value of a poetry collection—whether it be *Kokinshū, Shinkokinshū,* Fujiwara no Teika's *Hyakunin isshu* (Hundred Poems by a Hundred Poets)—was both in its selection of quality poems and the juxtaposition of the poems to bring out nuances that might otherwise have been missed. Hōnen's *Passages* used selection and juxtaposition not as an aesthetic technique but instead a form of philosophical exposition and argumentation.

143. The reference here is that nuns were not expected or even allowed to be scholars, but knew only enough of the teachings to carry out the praxis authentically. In this passage Hōnen explains that as an advantage instead of a disadvantage over scholars. Although here working within the sexist assumptions of his time and tradition, it should

also be noted that Hōnen emphasized Amida's inclusion of women to be saved by the power of his Vow. See the discussion and citations in WATTS and TOMATSU 2005, 50–60.

Yet, Hōnen and his disciple Shinran still generally upheld the traditional belief that only a male could become a buddha. Hence, Amida would have to transform women into men before they could reach enlightenment. (Since one does not actually attain enlightenment until leaving the Pure Land and returning to this world, it is not clear whether women are transformed into men upon entrance into, or departure from, the Pure Land.) See also the discussion of the status of women in Hōnen, Shinran, Dōgen, and Nichiren in KASAHARA 2001, 292–8.

144. Both passages: Trans. in HŌNEN 1998, 13.

145. In India, by contrast, schools often coalesced around particular philosophical theories and were named accordingly.

146. Once a school assumes its own identity, an *ex post facto* interpretation of the tradition's history and lineage usually ensues. These are seldom literally true in a historical sense, but become instead an organizational device for the institution as well as a heuristic for talking about continuity in praxis and metapraxis. For an account of how scholars understand this to have worked in the Chinese Chan tradition, see MCRAE 2004.

147. For my overview of this development and its relation to the East Asian understanding of creativity, see KASULIS 1998.

148. He made his defense in two essays, *Shukke taikō* (Essentials of Monastic Life) and *Kōzen gokokuron* (Treatise on the Propagation of Zen to Protect the Nation).

149. While the Kamakura shogunate may have controlled the reins of political, economic, and military power, the Kyoto imperial court still served as the heart of culture and spiritual charisma. The military government was acutely aware of this imbalance and tried to build up their military center in Kamakura as a second center of culture.

150. An obvious exception to this would be Zen Master Musō Soseki (1275–1351), the founder of the major Rinzai Zen temple Tenryū-ji, whose life overlapped the Kamakura and Muromachi periods. In this book I will treat him as a Muromachi figure, especially because of his relation with Ashikaga Tadayoshi, the founder of the Muromachi shogunate.

151. This manifest (*shaku* or *jaku*) versus essential (*hon*) distinction is the same terminology used in the aforementioned *honji suijaku* theory that interpreted the Shintō *kami* as "trace manifestations" of the buddhas who were the "essential ground." (See pages 145–6.) As in that earlier case, the *shaku/hon* polarity is a rhetorical or logical frame for relegating one (the *shaku*) to being a merely surface manifestation of the true source (the *hon*).

152. The term for "attaining enlightenment in this very body" is the same as that of Kūkai's esotericism.

153. See his "Letter from Sado" for his discussion of *shōju* versus *shakubuku*. The discussion of the pen and sword analogy is found in the English translation: NICHIREN 2003, 1: 34.

154. Masaharu Anesaki, one of the first scholars to write about Nichiren in English, constructively used the ancient Hebrew prophets as a comparative paradigm for explaining Nichiren's fiery style of rhetoric. See ANESAKI 1916.

155. One of Nichiren's most famous works was his "Treatise on Opening Your Eyes" (*Kaimokushō*). For an English translation see NICHIREN 2003, 2: 29–117.

156. Although the school is commonly known today by the name "Nichiren School" or "Nichiren Sect" (*Nichirenshū*), it was in the first few centuries of its existence called the "Lotus School" (*Hokkeshū*). See STONE 1999, 447, n. 2. For simplicity, I will use the term "Nichiren School (or Sect)" throughout.

157. This comparison exemplifies the importance of metapraxis in constituting the meaning and value of a given practice. Even an ostensibly identical praxis can have a different significance depending on the metapraxis associated with it. For example, the liturgical distribution of bread and wine may look similar in a Roman Catholic, a Lutheran, and a Calvinist church—even to the extent of voicing the same words. Yet, the metapraxis, the theory that explains what is happening and how it is important, differs sharply in the three cases. In the end, that variation in metapraxis makes them distinct liturgical traditions, whatever their superficial similarities may be.

158. For comparison see, for example, Nichiren's discussion of the individual sinographs *myō* and *kyō* in his letter "The Daimoku of the Lotus Sutra," translated in NICHIREN 1996, 31–51. Note, however, that although he treats the full incantation as mantric in most respects, he does not, as Kakuban did with the Amida mantra, break it down into seed mantras of individual syllables. Instead, he uses the interpretive model of the whole-in-the-part, explaining for example that *kyō* ("sutra") in the *daimoku* contains *all* sutras (*kyō*). "Within this single sinograph *kyō* are contained all the sutras in the entire universe" (NICHIREN 1996, 37).

159. Jacqueline Stone explains the significance of Nichiren's use of the term *gyōja*:

> In contrast to the more conventional term *jikyōsha*, one who "holds" the sutra and recites it as his or her personal practice, *gyōja* for Nichiren meant one who lived the sutra through one's actions, experiencing in one's own person the great trials that it predicts. His later writings would call this "reading with the body" (*shikidoku*) (STONE 1999, 252).

Incidentally, Pure Land Buddhists, including Hōnen, also used the term *gyōja* in referring to those taking the Pure Land Gate.

THE MEDIEVAL PERIOD

5. SHINRAN 親鸞 (1173–1262)

1. See DOBBINS 2004, 26–7.

2. Scholars disagree about how close to Hōnen's innermost circle Shinran might have been. He did allow Shinran to copy his central work, *Senchakushū*, the aforementioned collection of the most important passages related to Pure Land teachings. And Hōnen did allow Shinran to have a personal portrait made of himself, a privilege reserved only for his special students. Furthermore, when Hōnen was exiled, Shinran was one of the small number of disciples also covered by the edict.

Yet, in historical records related to Hōnen and his closest followers, Shinran's name rarely occurs. By contrast, in Shinran's writings Hōnen's name is ubiquitous. There is no doubt that in their own time, Hōnen was the charismatic public figure and Shinran obscure. For example, Nichiren-targeted Hōnen, not Shinran, in his vitriolic attacks on Amidism.

3. This was the culmination of a series of events starting two years earlier when the establishment schools of Tendai on Mt Hiei and of Hossō at Kōfuku-ji in Nara brought formal charges against the heretical doctrines and behavior of the "exclusivistic" (i.e., single practice only) *nenbutsu* groups. Up to January 1207, Hōnen had been able to defend the movement by publicly apologizing for any individual's deviant behavior, by clarifying the teachings actually expounded, and by promising not to attack the doctrines of other schools. Hōnen was a respected and revered figure in the capital, with some members of the court loyal to him. This time, however, things went badly for him and his followers.

As for the question of the two ladies of the court, when the emperor was away, two of his consorts became involved with two of Hōnen's disciples. As to the precise kind of involvement, the historical facts are not clear. Was there some moral impropriety? Or did the courtesans convert to Hōnen's group and become nuns? Or both? In any case, whatever happened seems to have precipitated the imperial sanctions. For discussions of these events, see DOBBINS 1989, 14–18; TAKAHATAKE 1987, 75–83; and KEEL 1995, 40–3. Dobbins's discussion includes the near contemporaneous account of the events by Jien (1155–1225).

4. The Echigo region was a popular site for exile. Later, Nichiren was sent there as well. When the punishment called for even further isolation, as it did for Nichiren, they sent exiles offshore from Echigo to the island of Sado. See location on map, page 697.

5. Since one extant version of *Shinran muki* seems to be in Shinran's own handwriting, it is presumed authentic. There is some question, based on Shinran's wife's account, as to whether this revelatory event might have occurred at the same time as the previously discussed event in the Hexagonal Hall. For a translation of the verse in question, see DOBBINS 2004, 171, n. 65.

6. TAKAHATAKE 1987, 43.

7. Texts like the late 13th-century *Shasekishū* (*Collection of Sand and Pebbles*) show that monks during this period did sometime take wives, but only in secret and usually only in old age for the sake of companionship and nursing care. Shinran did so openly and lived as a family man, a scandalous act for clergy at the time.

8. CWS 1: 289.

9. In Japan there was by this time a well-established system designating a class of people as *eta* ("filth") or, more delicately, *burakumin* ("hamlet people"). Often those outcastes were employed in the slaughter of animals, the processing of animal skins, the disposition of corpses, and so forth. Hence, they were directly involved in activities either of harming sentient beings (a Buddhist prohibition) or of handling blood and the dead (taboos in Shintō). Since the outcaste status was determined by birth, it is moot whether the stigma preceded or followed from their livelihoods.

The discriminatory practices against the *burakumin* (limited rights, forced to live in ghettos, bans against intermarriage outside their class, etc.) remained the law until after 1945 and even today can be a source of discrimination. The point is that Shinran, in contrast with many of his contemporaries, directly reached out to these people and welcomed them into the Pure Land movement.

10. Trans. in SHINRAN 1984, 6; CWS 1: 659. The passage is from *Tannishō* (Lamenting the Deviations). Shinran's follower, Yuien, compiled this text of Shinran's sayings in response to what he perceived to be misunderstandings of his teacher's ideas. The text is traditionally considered a reliable source of Shinran's own words and I will treat them that way in this book. For the translation of *Tannishō*, I generally draw on Taitetsu Unno's translation in SHINRAN 1984, but also include for convenience the reference to the same passage in CWS as well, another reliable translation.

11. The Japanese term *bonnō* traces to the Sanskrit Buddhist term, *kleśa*. As explained in CWS 2: 172, *bonnō* is a comprehensive term descriptive of all the forces, conscious and unconscious, that propel unenlightened people to think, feel, act, and speak—whether in happiness or in distress—in such a way as to cause uneasiness, frustration, torment, pain, and sorrow. Thus, the effects of *bonnō* are comprehensive, affecting the cognitive, emotional, spiritual, and even physical well-being of both oneself and those with whom one is in contact.

12. For a convenient anthology of textual excerpts arranged by topic and spanning the entire Pure Land tradition, including Shinran's writings, see BLOOM 2014.

13. Hōnen asserts that if we recite the *nenbutsu* continuously, it will deepen our sense of dependence on the power of Amida's Vow. For example, he speaks of the value of keeping count of one's recitations with prayer beads, comparing it to keeping the beat in musical performance:

> A string of prayer beads must be held in one's hand at all times. In song and dance, there must be a beat to guide you in rhythm and timing. In the repetition of the *nenbutsu*, the prayer beads are considered to be the score that guides your tongue and hands. (Trans. in HŌNEN 2011, 369.)

> The number of recitations is not essential. Copious *nenbutsu* encourages incessant practice. If one does not keep track of numbers, one may become lax; therefore, counting the prayer beads encourages the recitation of a large number of *nenbutsu*. (Trans. in HŌNEN 2011, 301–2.)

To account for the texts that say even one recitation is enough to ensure rebirth in the Pure Land, Hōnen maintains that teaching refers only to those who have not been devoutly reciting the *nenbutsu* throughout life, but do so once on their deathbed. Even they, says Hōnen, will be reborn in the Pure Land:

> The issue of birth in the Pure Land through *nenbutsu* at the time of death refers to the case of a nonbeliever who did not desire birth in the Pure Land or recite *nenbutsu* in daily life. Though he is ignorant, the nonbeliever will still achieve this birth if he meets in his final moments a virtuous teacher who encourages him to recite *nenbutsu* and he utters *nenbutsu* for the first time. (Trans. in HŌNEN 2011, 220.)

The preferred option, however, is to continuously chant the *nenbutsu* throughout your daily life (many thousands of times a day). Then, even if circumstances are such that one cannot recite the *nenbutsu* at the point of death, the cumulative merit of a lifetime of recitations will guarantee Amida's coming at the point of death to take one to the Pure Land.

"Through the merit of *nenbutsu* frequently recited in daily life, Amida Buddha is certain to come to take us to his Pure Land at our time of death." (Trans. in HŌNEN 2011, 220.)

14. I cannot in this book go into detail whether the view I am calling Hōnen's position was actually what he meant. For the most part, the non-Shin Buddhist disciples of the Pure Land tradition thought it was, but Shinran (and many of his followers) thought it represented those disciples' interpretation and not necessarily Hōnen's intent. In the end, my view is that it does represent what Hōnen taught, at least most of the time.

That said, we have to take with a grain of salt Shinran's claim that he was merely repeating what Hōnen taught. He would have two motives for saying that, regardless of whether it was completely true. First, Shinran would want to express his sincere admiration and gratitude toward the saintly mentor who had indeed saved Shinran's spiritual life. Second, there was a typical Kamakura-period rhetorical conceit that "I am not teaching anything new." The nature and significance of that discursive ploy will be clearer when I discuss in Chapter 8 how it contrasts with the Edo-period philosophical discourse that stressed innovation (see pages 285–6).

15. In his *Hymns of the Dharma Ages*, Shinran writes:

> The saying of the Name [i.e., the *nenbutsu*] arising from true and real entrusting faith
>
> Is Amida's direction of virtue to beings;
> Therefore, it is called "not directing merit,"
> And saying the *nenbutsu* through own-power is to be rejected.
> (Trans. based on CWS 1: 408.)

16. Trans. in HŌNEN 2011, 372.

17. Hōnen's disciple, Ryūkan (1148–1227), reinforced this interpretation by maintaining that although the *nenbutsu* could be practiced in a way based in self-effort (as it was in the *nenbutsu* discipline on Mt Hiei, for example), it has no efficacy when so performed. Only when practiced out of an entrusting in Amida's power does the *nenbutsu* assure rebirth in the Pure Land. See the discussion in CWS 2: 35.

18. In his Translator's Introduction to HŌNEN 1997 (pages 4–5), Morris J. Augustine explains the difference between Shinran's and Hōnen's theories of the *nenbutsu* as follows:

> Shinran declares that the practitioner in our Age of Degeneration cannot even wish to recite the Nembutsu, much less perform more difficult works, without the enabling omnipresent power of Amida's Original Vow to save all sentient beings. Hōnen, however, insists throughout [in the *Senchaku hongan nenbutsu shū*] that men and women can and must recite the Nembutsu as the one and only "practice" left within their power. Whereas he does see this recitation as based on Amida's Other Power, he nevertheless uses the same terminology (e.g., "practice") and the same manner of thinking as that used by others within his mother Tendai sect. In other words, people retain some small power of their own to do good, and thus an absolutely total break with traditional Buddhism was avoided.

19. As a spontaneous vocalization arising from an inter-responsive field between the individual's turning to other-power and the power of Amida's vow, this understanding of the vocalized *nenbutsu* parallels in its formal structure the spontaneous dynamic of

aware discussed in Heian aesthetics. (See pages 140–2.) Moreover, in the terminology I used to explain Kūkai's view of language (see pages 118–19), we might also say that when a Shin Buddhist spontaneously exclaims the *nenbutsu* ("I take refuge in Amida Buddha"), the *nenbutsu* does not *refer to* Amida as much as *confer with* Amida.

20. In his *Passages on the Selection of the Nenbutsu of the Original Vow*, in fact, Hōnen cites Kūkai in support of his claim for the spiritual power of reciting the *nenbutsu*. Hōnen compares the *nenbutsu* to what Kūkai (following the *Sutra of the Six Paramitas*) called the "*Dhāraṇī* [mystic phrase] Gate" to enlightenment, the medicinal "ghee" of the various Buddhist paths and the only one able to help the most sinful of human beings:

> The Nenbutsu is the same [as the medicinal ghee]. In the teaching of Rebirth, the Nenbutsu Samādhi is like a *dhāraṇī* or like ghee. Without the medicinal ghee of the Nenbutsu Samādhi, it would be extremely difficult to cure the sickness of deep and grievous crimes such as the five deadly sins.
>
> ... [If] the Nenbutsu Samādhi destroys even grievous sins, how much more will it destroy minor sins! (Trans. in HŌNEN 2011, 101.)

On this one point, then, we can see a trajectory from Kūkai's mantrayāna Buddhism to Kakuban's esoteric Amidism (stressing a mantra practice directed toward Amida) to Hōnen's *nenbutsu* (as generating merit and having spiritually transformative power). That trajectory seems more transitional than one of disruptive change.

By contrast, Shinran clearly departs from that trajectory in denying the function of *nenbutsu* as a merit-producing practice necessary to being assured rebirth in the Pure Land. It is the result, not the cause, of that assurance. That said, Shinran did write fifteen short hymns lauding the practical benefits of reciting the *nenbutsu,* but his suggestion of the *nenbutsu*'s having such effects is certainly more the exception than the rule. See CWS 1: 352–5.

21. A common practice in Shin Buddhism today is repeating the *nenbutsu* in what seems to be a mantra-like repetitive pattern (often counting the incantations on a rosary). That makes the practice outwardly seem like Hōnen's continuous reciting of the *nenbutsu*. However, Shinran's interpretation is that repeating the *nenbutsu* in such a ritual way does not "do anything," but is rather an expression of gratitude for the presence of the power of Amida's vow. Hence, it is not connected to any idea of producing "merit." It technically has no direct connection with whether the person doing the incantation will or will not be assured rebirth in the Pure Land.

22. Trans. based on CWS 1: 107.

23. Shinran writes:

> The idea of Amida's coming at the moment of death is for those who seek to gain birth in the Pure Land by doing religious practices, for they are practicers of own-power. The moment of death is of central concern for such people, for they have not yet attained true entrusting faith. We may also speak of Amida's coming at the moment of death in the case of those who, though they have committed the ten transgressions and the five grave offenses throughout their lives, encounter a teacher in the hour of death and are led away at the very end to utter the *nenbutsu*.
>
> The practicer of true entrusting faith, however, abides in the stage of the truly settled, for he or she has already been grasped, never to be abandoned. There is no need to wait in anticipation for the moment of death, no need to rely on Amida's

coming. At the time entrusting faith becomes settled, birth [in the Pure Land] too becomes settled; there is no need for the deathbed rites that prepare one for Amida's coming. (Trans. based on CWS 1: 523.)

24. Trans. in HŌNEN 2011, 220.

25. "One thought-moment" is *ichinen* as in the Tendai doctrine of *ichinen sanzen* "all realms of existence in one thought moment" (see page 163). The Pure Land term refers to either one-saying of the *nenbutsu* or, in other cases, one moment of holding Amida in mind.

26. Trans. based on CWS 1: 110–11.

27. Trans. in CWS 1: 114, but I substitute throughout my discussion "lateral" for its "crosswise" and "forward" for its "lengthwise."

28. Trans. in HŌNEN 2011, 261.

29. Trans. based on CWS 1: 550.

30. Trans. in SHINRAN 1984, 6; see also CWS 1: 659.

31. Trans. in SHINRAN 1984, 14; see also CWS 1: 665.

32. Trans. in CWS 1: 125.

33. Trans. based on SHINRAN 1984, 35; see also CWS 1: 679.

34. See, for example, the following passage from Shinran's *The Teaching, the Practice, the Entrusting, the Enlightenment* (*Kyōgyōshinshō*):

The karmic-consciousness of true and real entrusting faith is the inner cause. The Name and light—our father and mother—are the outer cause. When the inner and outer causes are united, one realizes the true body in the fulfilled land. (Trans. from CWS 1: 54.)

As suggested by this passage wherein Amida is referred to as both mother and father, in Japan the gender of buddhas can be ambiguous. Biographically, Amida was formerly the bodhisattva Hōzō, a man. Hence, Amida is generally considered male and is referred to as "he" among English-speaking Shin Buddhists. Portrayals of Amida in painting and sculpture are generally male. See the two statues of Amida in the photographs found in Chapter 7, page 247. Amida as a buddha, however, technically transcends gender so Amida can be thought of as either mother or father.

The situation is complicated further by the general disuse of personal pronouns in Japanese so Japanese grammar seldom, if ever, forces one to make a gender distinction. (See pages 692–5 for a discussion of sentence subjects in Japanese.) Broadly speaking, when Amida does have a gender, Amida is thought of as male, however. For this book, I will stay with the use of the male pronoun since the neuter form would depersonalize Amida in the mind of most western readers—a far more misleading interpretation than the problem of slightly over-masculinizing Amida's gender.

35. Hōnen, following Shandao, also spoke of the "intimacy" between Amida and the person vocalizing the *nenbutsu*:

Master Shandao interpreted the intimacy relationship, one of the three kinds of karmic relationships between Amida Buddha and a *nenbutsu* devotee, as follows:

When sentient beings worship Amida Buddha, he sees them. When they recite the name of Amida Buddha, he listens to them. When they are mindful of

Amida Buddha, he is also mindful of them. Therefore, the three categories of acts [the physical, verbal, and mental] exercised by both Amida Buddha and the *nenbutsu* devotee unite into one. Since this relationship between Amida Buddha and a *nenbutsu* devotee is like that between parents and their children, it is called the "intimate karmic relationship."

... Thus, we must strive to be seen and to be within the awareness of Amida Buddha in order to benefit from his benevolence. To accomplish this [intimate karmic] relationship a practitioner must recite *nenbutsu* continually in order to bring harmony between Amida Buddha and the three categories of acts of a *nenbutsu* practitioner. The three categories are physical, verbal, and mental acts. (Trans. in HŌNEN 2011, 393–4.)

The three categories of act here are what Kūkai discussed as the "three intimacies" (*sanmitsu*), which were for him the shared event of Dainichi's self-expression and the harmonized ritual performance of the Shingon Buddhist. (See pages 113–16.) Thus, in both Shingon and Hōnen's Pure Land Buddhism, the intimacy between the self and Buddha is characterized as a convergence of the activity between the Buddha (whether Dainichi or Amida) and the Buddhist practitioner.

36. *Lamenting the Deviations* (*Tannishō*), chapter 6, reads:

As for myself, Shinran, I do not have a single disciple. If I could make others say the *nenbutsu* through my own devices, they would be my disciples. But how arrogant to claim as disciples those who live the *nenbutsu* through the sole working of Amida's compassion. (Trans. in SHINRAN 1984, 11; see also CWS 1: 664.)

37. Trans. based on CWS 1: 107.

38. Trans. based on SHINRAN 1984, 8; CWS 1: 663.

39. Trans. based on SHINRAN 1984, 24; CWS 1: 671.

40. Trans. based on CWS 1: 553–4.

41. See the discussion in *Lamenting the Deviations* (*Tannishō*), chapter 13 on how the karmic effects of the past limit our ability to do good or evil.

42. See, for example, this passage from chapter 13 of *Lamenting the Deviations*:

The gist of this statement is that when we think good thoughts, we think we are good; and when we think evil thoughts, we think we are evil, not realizing fully that it is not these thoughts but the inconceivable power of the Vow that makes our salvation possible. (Trans. based on SHINRAN 1984, 24.)

43. Trans. based on SHINRAN 1984, 8.

44. Trans. in CWS 1: 665.

45. As we saw in Chapter 4 (see pages 156–8) Kakuban, because of his distinctive focus on Amida, differed from Kūkai somewhat. By equating Amida with Dainichi's wisdom (and ultimately, through the holographic relation with Dainichi as a whole), Amida was for Kakuban the reality embodiment, but that is true only insofar as Amida is really Dainichi. Separate from Dainichi, Amida would not have that status.

46. Trans. based on CWS 1: 534.

47. The *Lotus Sutra*, as I mentioned in Chapter 2 (see page 82), depicted a cosmic Shakyamuni of which the historical Shakyamuni was a special manifestation. Addition-

ally, in his esoteric system, Kūkai sometimes prefers a theory of the fourfold embodiment of the cosmic buddha as a substitute for the exoteric historical-celestial-cosmic embodiment theory.

48. The terminology in this passage is so technical that an English translation can be almost unintelligible without extensive explanation. In the rendering here, I have tried to make the point easier to follow via various simplifications. First, the passage characterizes Amida in terms of two cosmic embodiments: *hōben hosshin* 方便法身 and *hosshō hosshin* 法性法身. The former, in formal terms, is the "heuristically expressive cosmic body" and the latter, the "dharma-nature cosmic body." Since the former is Amida in the embodiment adapted to our needs, I call it simply "Amida-for-us." The latter is Amida in its own nature without expedience and so I call it "Amida-in-itself." In addition, I simply deleted or collapsed other nomenclature that adds technical precision not necessary to the basic point. For a more technical and complete translation of this passage see CWS 1: 461–2. Except for the changes noted, I follow that translation closely.

49. Shinran's terminology allows a connection that is not obvious in English translation, specifically, the polysemous nature of the sinograph 自. It can be the *ji* of *jiriki* (self- or own-) power as contrasted with the *ta* (other) of *tariki* (other-power), a sinograph for *mizukara* (to do something for oneself) as well as for *onozukara* (to happen of itself as in the English prefix *auto-*). Given those meanings we can say that through entrusting faith, we surrender our *own power* (*jiriki*) to the vow of Amida-for-us (which is other than us, hence *tariki*). To us it seems that through *tariki* we surrender to Amida's own-power (*jiriki*), but since Amida is enlightened, that *ji* is not a self-power but an agentless activity. Hence, once *shinjin* is fully realized, there is no self- vs. other-power. Rather, the fully realized *shinjin* is *onozukara* (of-itself), occurring as *jinen* ("naturally"). *Jinen* is written in sinographs as 自然,—literally, an "of itself sort of thing").

50. Trans. in CWS 1: 453.

51. Trans. based on CWS 1: 165.

52. Trans. from SSZ 2: 630. See also CWS 1: 461.

53. Abridged and adapted from CWS 1: 62.

6. DŌGEN 道元 (1200–1253)

54. Trans. based on DŌGEN 2001. For the original see DZZ 6: 15.

55. The term 故 is usually translated "reason" or "source" or "basis," but I have chosen the less common "provenance" because it has a nuance of being a source in which something is engendered, that is, where it comes from and belongs. That organic, generative, or creative aspect is, as I interpret him, crucial to Dōgen's meaning.

56. Trans. based on DŌGEN 2001; DZZ 6: 14, 16.

57. A general difference between the Hindu and Buddhist understandings of ignorance arises from the distinction between "illusion" and "delusion." For many classical Hindu philosophies, reality (*brahman*) has an illusory appearance (*māyā*). Therefore, knowledge entails our understanding deceptive appearances for what they are and not letting them mislead us.

Consider the following example. If we are driving along a hot blacktop road on a sunny day, puddles of water seem to be on the pavement ahead of us. Once we understand this illusion to be the result of heat waves bending light above the hot road, puddles will continue to appear, but we will know them to be not really puddles. Analogously, the goal for many Hindu philosophies is to know the difference between reality and its illusory appearance.

For most forms of Buddhism, by contrast, the problem of ignorance has more to do with delusion than illusion. Since reality generally presents itself as it is without false appearance, ignorance must arise from our projecting delusions onto reality. Our own delusional projections, not the false appearance of reality, fools us. That is, we delude ourselves. Therefore, if we eliminate our false projections, what remains is just reality as it is.

Suppose I have the delusion I am Napoleon and I even see myself as Napoleon when I look in the mirror. When I am cured of my delusion, however, the appearance of Napoleon in the mirror will disappear. What remains in the mirror is the image of someone taller and less historically significant. Yet, that image reflects to me who I really am. That contrasts with the puddles-in-the-road example because in that case, the puddles will continue to appear, though I know them to be a false appearance.

58. The term *shinjin datsuraku* merits some analysis. *Shinjin* means "body and mind," "body-and-mind," or "bodymind." The first rendering is appropriate to many ordinary contexts (Chinese does not need to specify the conjunctive "and" as a separate word). In most of his writings, however, Dōgen clearly considers the body and mind to be distinguishable but inseparable. That is, because their relation is internal, not external, they overlap with no third thing connecting them. Hence, we sometimes find translators resort to the rendering: "body-and-mind." Yet, Dōgen also refers to a "oneness" or "unity" of the two. When doing so, he suggests an even stronger connection, namely, that there is a single process or event; "body" and "mind" are no more than qualities or factors abstracted from that single event. That line of thought leads to the "bodymind" translation used, for example, in SHANER 1985.

Let us now consider the *datsuraku* part of the term. In common parlance, *datsuraku* can refer to one's "dropping off" a piece of clothing such as a robe or cloak as well as a snake's or insect's "molting" its skin. This leads some to construe the full term as some variant of "dropping off (or sloughing off) body-and-mind." Such a translation can in some passages lead to a misunderstanding in either of two ways. First, it seems to convert the Chinese grammatical subject (*shinjin*—bodymind) into an English direct object, thereby leaving the impression that *shinjin datsuraku* is something that someone does to or with the bodymind rather than something that bodymind does of itself. Second, and more crucially, according to Dōgen a person is not an agent who *does* something in *zazen*. Indeed, when the ego stops acting as an agent, bodymind drops away. In that regard, I think Dōgen's term *shinjin datsuraku* borrows more from the use of *datsuraku* to describe a natural function such as an animal's molting an old skin or autumn leaves' dropping off the tree as part of their spontaneous development. Furthermore, since this is not for Dōgen a once-and-for-all event but occurs repeatedly in *zazen*, it is a natural process of life and growth. Thus, in KASULIS 1981 I used "molting."

Regardless of which translation we use, we need to be clear about two points. First, *shinjin datsuraku* is a spontaneous event describing what bodymind does rather than what someone does *to* bodymind. Second, *shinjin datsuraku* is a recurring event spontaneously enacted whenever one does *zazen*. In this book I will use "bodymind dropping away" or "bodymind drops away" to translate *shinjin datsuraku*.

In fairness, I should point out that Dōgen also sometimes reverses the phrase into *datsuraku shinjin*, (five times in *Repository* as compared with eleven occurrences of *shinjindatsuraku*). In those cases, it might be understandable to translate it "sloughing off bodymind." The number of occurrences are taken from the concordance KATŌ 1952.

59. Dōgen wrote these instructions for *zazen* in Chinese in his little essay *Fukanzazengi* and in the Japanese *Repository* essays *Zazengi* and *Zazenshin*. Subtle and suggestive variations appear in these texts over Dōgen's lifetime, showing shifts in emphasis revealing much about Dōgen's changing interactions with his Zen contemporaries. Dōgen wanted to distinguish his school's understanding of *zazen* from that of his Zen competitors in both Japan and China. As the competition changed, Dōgen adjusted his emphases (and criticisms) accordingly. For an authoritative discussion of these shifts, including translations of the relevant writings, see BIELEFELDT 1988. Since these historical details take us outside our present philosophical concerns, though, I will not go into them here.

60. A kōan refers here to a jarring incident or saying, serving as a focal point in Zen praxis and usually taken from the Zen Buddhist canon of student-master exchanges. (See also the discussion of *kōan* in the term *genjōkōan* later in this chapter.) Many kōans seem contradictory or paradoxical, defying ordinary logical analysis.

Zen masters have used the kōan in various ways. Sometimes it is the focus of concentration during *zazen* (often connected with so-called *kanna zazen,* of which Dōgen did not generally approve). Sometimes (often in conjunction with the first use) it serves as a test in the master-disciple relation. In such instances, the master demands the student respond to the kōan by displaying an insight outside mere logical or intellectual understanding. In yet other contexts, the kōan serves as a provocative theme for a Zen master's lecture, sermon, or essay (the most common use in Dōgen's *Repository*). Lastly, Zen students may study the kōan as part of a textual heritage comprising a *de facto* Zen Buddhist literary canon. This latter use is reminiscent of textual study in some Chinese literati (Confucian and neo-Confucian) traditions and I will discuss this briefly in Chapter 7 when treating the "Five Mountain" tradition of Rinzai Zen. (See pages 270–3.)

If there is a common element in these uses, it is that the kōan forces an engagement with the uniqueness of the present stimulated by a resonance with paradigms from the Zen tradition. The best discussion of kōan use in the Japanese Rinzai tradition is HORI 2003. For the most comprehensive scholarship in English on Dōgen's relation to the kōan tradition, see HEINE 1994.

For this case, Dōgen discusses the original *kōan* on which this is based in the opening section of his *Repository* essay, *Zazenshin* ("The Lancet [or Acupuncture Needle] for [Treating Mistaken Ideas about] Zazen"):

> Once, when the Great Master Hongdao of Yaoshan was sitting [in meditation], a monk asked him,
> "What are you thinking of, [sitting there] so fixedly?
> The master answered, "I'm thinking of not thinking.

The monk asked, "How do you think of not thinking?

The Master answered, "Nonthinking [or "Without thinking]."

(Trans. in BIELEFELDT 1988, 188–9.)

61. This line of justification is a main theme in Dōgen's first substantive essay written upon returning from China, his *Bendōwa* ("Discussion on Pursuing the Way in Praxis") later included in the longer *Repository* collection. English translations include those by Waddell and Abe (DŌGEN 2002A, 7–30) and Tanahashi (DŌGEN 2010, 3–22).

62. Some western readers may be tempted to consider this claim about without-thinking in a present-day philosophical context. In doing so, however, we need to be both precise and cautious in making comparisons. For example, a deconstructionist follower of Jacques Derrida may interpret Dōgen's position as denying the reality of presence entirely. But what kind of presence is Dōgen or Derrida then purportedly denying?

The nub of the issue is whether we should construe "presence" as *meaningful* presence, that is, a presence that contains within itself its own meanings. If that is the sense of presence intended by Derrida, Dōgen's without-thinking theory is consistent with Derrida since without-thinking's presence is devoid of meaning. In that sense both could be said to deny there is presence before language. Derrida's "absence" then would be the absence of meaning in the content that arises within without-thinking. Heidegger, in arguing for a "letting go" (*Gelassenheit*) of intentionality, speaks of the "thinging of things." This creative turn of phrase points to a presence that is not (at least not yet) meaningful.

Another way to understand Derrida would be to take him to mean that a non-conceptual experience is impossible. If we interpret Derrida in that way, Dōgen presents a contrast rather than comparison. See note 75 below.

63. Dōgen's "Buddha-nature" essay is one of his most trenchant. A careful translation with extensive notes aimed at mining some of its deeper philosophical implications is by Waddell and Abe (DŌGEN 2002A, 59–98). See also the complex analysis of this fascicle in ABE Masao 1992, 35–76. In claiming impermanence in itself is buddha-nature, Dōgen is citing and analyzing a quotation from Huineng, the sixth ancestor of the Zen tradition.

64. Trans. from NST 12: 222; DZZ 1: 203.

65. Trans. from NST 12: 222; DZZ 1: 203–4. In my translation, I try to reflect Dōgen's vocabulary and orthographical distinctions for the first person by following this convention: われ="I" as the everyday sense of the changing self that is also first-person agency; 我 = "the I," "ego," "substantial self," often used as an equivalent to the Sanskrit *ātman* which Buddhism considers unreal; 吾 = "I" in roughly the same sense as われ but primarily used when quoting or discussing Chinese rather than Japanese texts.

As the first philosopher to write sophisticated philosophical texts in Japanese rather than Chinese, Dōgen was likely careful in not only his choice of words but their orthography. For example, although today the hiragana *ware* (われ) and the sinograph for *ware* (我) can often be interchangeable, as the first thinker to write philosophically about the self in Japanese, Dōgen may be distinguishing the two. For more explanation about translating premodern philosophical Japanese, especially in Dōgen, see KASULIS 2010.

66. Dōgen uses *genjōkōan* as either a noun or a verb (usually by adding the verbal ending *su* to the compound). The English gerundive form, *presencing*, preserves both

possibilities and so I generally favor that translation. The simple nominal "presence" might be mistaken to mean a characteristic of things, namely, that they are present rather than absent. That misses the vitalism Dōgen reads into the term.

67. This interpretation of the meaning of *"kōan"* is attributed to Dōgen in a conversation with one of his disciples. The point is discussed in one of the earliest commentaries on Dōgen's *Repository* as explained by Waddell and Abe in DŌGEN 2002A, 39–40.

68. Compare this view of experience with William James' analysis of the flow of experience, its focalized aspect, and the present yet peripheralized "fringe." The primary source of his discussion is vol. I, chapter 9 of *Principles of Psychology*, the chapter entitled the "Stream of Thought" (JAMES 1890, 224–90). Apparently Nishida first grew interested in James when D. T. Suzuki recommended he read *Varieties of Religious Experience* (JAMES 1958). The comparison between Zen and James will be particularly relevant in Chapter 12 when we engage the 20th-century philosopher, Nishida Kitarō. Nishida built his first systematic philosophical theory around the notion of "pure experience," inspired in part by his reading of James' *Principles of Psychology* and also his 1904 essay, "A World of Pure Experience" (JAMES 1971, 23–48).

69. When Dōgen uses the actual term *kōan* in his *Repository* writings, he almost always uses it in conjunction with *genjō,* either as a single compound term or as two terms closely linked in syntax. When discussing the traditional kōans in his comments within *Repository,* he seldom uses any generic name for them, but instead just relates them as "Master so-and-so said, ..."

70. The English phrase "the issue at hand" is Thomas Cleary's translation for the term *genjōkōan.* See DŌGEN 1986, 29.

71. Trans. from NST 12: 35; DZZ 1: 2.

72. The phrase "pattern in the way of things" renders the term *dōri,* a fairly common word in Dōgen (and indeed in many East Asian texts), but difficult to translate. See the comment on the term in the glossary found in DŌGEN 2006, 283. My rendering is, I believe, quite close to the sense Ōhashi and Elberfeld intend in translating *dōri* as *Sachverhalt* ("state of affairs"). In general, their glossary (indeed their whole book) is especially insightful for readers wanting to understand the philosophical implications of Dōgen's idiosyncratic terminology and conceptual field.

73. Trans. from NST 12: 36; DZZ 1: 3.

74. Ōhashi Ryōsuke and Rolf Elberfeld in DŌGEN 2006 find a "middle voice" dimension in Dōgen's Japanese. The middle voice, as found in ancient Greek or Russian, for example, is neither active voice nor passive voice. Instead it is a form arising from the expression of the activity itself without distinguishing who or what is acting upon what or whom. So, rather than the active "I bought a book" or the passive "the book was bought by me," languages with a middle voice have a third option not available in English, one in which the event is expressed without clear active or passive specification. Most linguists find no such *grammatical form* for the middle voice in the medieval Japanese language such as what we find in Greek or Russian. Yet, few would disagree that the usage of the language in many of Dōgen's sentences resembles the middle voice *in intent.*

75. Many present-day philosophers and scholars doubt not only whether there can be any "authentication" outside concepts, but also whether there can be any nonconceptual

experience at all. A striking counter-example to those who deny the possibility of non-conceptual experience is the neurological infliction known as *blindsight*. Patients with that condition have suffered traumatic injury to the part of the brain that conceptually processes visual perception. As a result, they can receive visual sensations and even act on them, but are unable to use concepts to structure the data. Unable to conceptualize visual input, the patients describe themselves as *blind*.

Yet, patients with blindsight are often able to negotiate their way across a crowded room without bumping into anyone or anything. When they do this, they insist they had used no conceptual process at all; they cannot even name or identify in words the objects "seen" in the room. In fact, they insist they "saw nothing," that they are "blind" and merely "guessed" correctly where obstacles lay in their path. Their account matches what we know about the brain function—or lack of it. In such cases, their injured brains are able to respond to sensory input without resorting to any conceptualization either at the time or later. One theory is that the patients use visual processing located in the so-called *reptilian* sector of the brain, a part that is not normally used (or only minimally used) by humans without blindsight.

The importance of the blindsight phenomenon is that it places the burden of proof on those who deny the possibility of nonconceptual experience. Arguments appealing to logic or speculations about the impossibility of something lose their force in the face of empirical evidence to the contrary. For a pioneering study on blindsight, see WEISKRANTZ 1986. For an excellent overview of, and bibliography for philosophical inquiries into nonconceptual experience, see BERMÚDEZ and CAHEN 2012.

Some cultural theorists refuse (on *a priori* grounds, it seems) to accept the very *possibility* of the without-thinking type of experience or mode of consciousness, leading them to the Foucaultian line of analysis that such claims are no more than rhetorical ploys for establishing power and authority. For example, FAURE 1991 reduces the Zen Buddhist emphasis on "immediacy" to being a mere rhetorical strategy not based in any actual experiential validation or verification.

Of course, if we can empirically verify the existence of nonconceptual experiences, as the studies above suggest, Faure's argument becomes moot. Appeals to Derrida's rejection of "presence" outside language would be trumped by this empirical evidence as well. (See note 62 above.) After all, the blindsighted are somehow aware of objects in the crowded room (insofar as they avoid bumping into them), but act without language or concepts. In short: a nonconceptual awareness of "something present" is verified in the neurological study of blindsight.

Some modern comparative discussions about presence and absence in this vein focus on Buddhist phrases like "the emptiness of emptiness." The Buddhist position, however, is neither to affirm absence nor to affirm presence, but instead to *neutralize* the distinction. That is presumably why Husserl calls such a modality the *neutrality modification* in *Ideas* vol. 1, § 109 (HUSSERL 1981, 257–9).

76. Trans. from NST 12: 20; DZZ 2: 546.

77. The original term for "profoundly realize" is a verb based on the noun *daigo* ("great realization" or "great *satori*"). In his *Repository* essay by that name, Dōgen comments on a *kōan* about "what happens when someone who is enlightened becomes deluded again." In his own analysis, Dōgen makes such comments as the following:

"Great realization is not nondelusion."

"You should understand there is a great realization that consists of becoming intimate with *becoming deluded again*."

(Trans. from NST 12: 120, 121; DZZ 1:95. See also: Trans. in DŌGEN 2010, 299.)

78. Trans. from NST 12: 35; DZZ 1: 2–3.

79. With the strong esotericism permeating Japanese Buddhism at the time (see especially pages 149–51), the notion of "esoteric words" of transmission from teacher to student was obviously not only a Zen phenomenon.

80. Trans. from NST 13: 57, 58; DZZ 1: 491, 492–3.

81. Trans. from NST 12: 37; DZZ 1: 4–5.

82. To this extent we might be tempted to say that Dōgen is a realist who maintains the reality of the "external world." Yet, that term ill fits Dōgen's world view. Because Dōgen maintains the relation between self and world is inherent or internal rather than external, the world cannot possibly exist as a reality totally external to the self.

In the argot of empiricists who use the term "external world," the point is to reject idealism. That is, in affirming the reality of the external world, such empiricists insist there is a reality or presence existing before or outside the construction of it by human ideas and interpretation. To that extent, Dōgen might be loosely characterized as accepting "the reality of the external world."

As the ensuing analysis in this chapter shows, however, Dōgen's view of how meaning is generated in relation to that external reality is more sophisticated than what passes for that relation in the less rich forms of empiricism such as logical positivism. For Dōgen, we cannot think of meaning as a simple "correspondence" between ideas and external reality. In the first pioneering book in English on Dōgen's philosophical position, Heejin Kim used the phrase "mystical realist" to try to capture the ambiguity expressed here (KIM 1975). The qualifier "mystical," however, is not satisfactory for my purposes because the ineffability essential to mysticism takes us away from, rather than into, the issue of expressiveness.

83. Dōgen does at least once in *Repository* refer specifically to the idea of *issuishiken*, or at least does so elliptically (writing only *shiken*—"four views"). See part 1 of his essay *Gyōji* (Conduct and Observance), NST 12: 170; DZZ 1: 150.

84. The Yogācāra position is often characterized as *vijñapti mātratā* in Sanskrit (J. *yuishiki*), "mental constructions only." That is, there is no reality without mental constructions. Dōgen would probably prefer to say there is no *meaning* without mental constructions. The presencing of things as they are is real, albeit not a mental construction. Admittedly, it is in itself meaningless, but without it, no meaning could arise.

85. The term *jisetsu* is the Japanese pronunciation of a common Chinese term for "when," but Dōgen seems to give it extra significance, playing on the meanings of the individual sinographs (*ji* 時 = time; *setsu* 節 = node, as in a bamboo stalk; hence a "crux in time" or "occasion"). In Dōgen the term specifies the spatiotemporal locus which occasions a phenomenon to have a specified meaning. See the first two lines of the essay *Genjōkōan*, for example. For a detailed analysis of the opening three lines of that essay and how to translate it, see Kasulis 2010.

In the essay from *Repository* where he does focus directly on temporality, Dōgen concentrates his analysis on the term that serves as the essay's title *uji* 有時 "being-time" or, as Rein Raud ingeniously renders it, "the existential moment" (JPS, 148–51). Dōgen glosses this temporal term *uji* in a provocative but idiosyncratic manner. He takes that Chinese term for "sometimes" or "there are times when," and breaks it down into its component parts "being" (or "existence"—*u*) and "time" or "a unit of time" (*ji*). Hence, "sometimes" becomes "being-time" or "the existential moment."

Dōgen's main points in the essay are the following. First, to think either of being or of time in isolation from the other is the height of abstraction and can lead to philosophical nonsense. One might talk separately about the temporal or the existential aspect of something, but that does not mean that either exists without the other—any more than color exists separately from shape. There is only the temporality of all experience and all presencing.

In other words, time and being are inseparable. Being without time would be an unchanging permanence or eternity. Yet, we have no direct experience of any such timelessness. Time without being would be something according to which temporality flows or is measured. This leads to misleading metaphors such as "time flies" or *tempus fugit*. Dōgen muses that if time flies, then how fast is its fleetingness? By what time can we measure the velocity of time's flight? (JPS, 150)

Dōgen's second point is that when *uji* is properly discussed (that is, when it is tied to having a specific meaning in a specific context), it presents either of two profiles: time as "the now of right now" (*nikon no ima*) or time as "flowing," "ranging," or "shifting" (*kyōryaku*). The *right now* sense of temporality is the experience of a "moment" that has within it a fullness or ripeness of time. If we think of it as a moment, though, we should not consider it an abstracted or infinitesimal moment (like the *dt* in a calculus formula for physics, or the infinitesimal moment—*kśana*—in some Hinayana Buddhist systems of thought). Instead, it more resembles the Greek *kairos* in that it is a sense of temporal appropriateness that makes this present time special (and often complete in itself), a moment outside the flow of diachronic or linear time that goes from past to present to future.

The other profile of time is one in which the past-present-future flow or shift into each other. Memory, for example, is about the past but occurs in the present; hopes are about the future, but arise in the present. So, the past flows into the present and the future into the present. The present (as the intentionality of focus of memory or expectation) flows into past and future as well. Therefore, if the right now is the epitome of discreteness and specificity, the flowing, ranging, or shifting of time is the epitome of interconnectedness.

Dōgen seems to find those two profiles of time to be the most authentic in characterizing temporality, each having its appropriate place or context but each also maintaining the inseparability of time and being. They contrast, for example, with notions of time empty of being, whether the time be momentary or passing. The former is the theoretically instantaneous moment (which even the ancient Greeks realized can lead to insolvable contradictions like Zeno's paradoxes); the latter is the complete desiccation of temporality so it becomes no more than the "clock time" that exists independent of events (and which obscures the lived reality of "having a long day" or the quickness of a "New York minute").

In this book I do not deal with Dōgen's theory of *uji* in any detail but it has already been thoroughly discussed among scholars and philosophers in western languages. See, for example, HEINE 1985 and STAMBAUGH 1990. For an insightful comparison between Dōgen and Nishida on some of these issues, see Raud 2004.

86. Trans. from NST 12: 37–8; DZZ 1: 5.

87. The word *toku* 徳 means "virtue" primarily in the sense of a thing's being what it is with its inherent capacity, as when we say in English, "by *virtue* of its chemical structure, wood is easily combustible." Therefore, a thing's *toku* is what allows it be what it can be. For humans, this includes the moral sense of virtue, that is, the sense of fully realizing one's humanness. Compare the English word "virtue" (from the Latin *virtus*) which itself derives from the Latin word for "man" (*vir*).

88. Trans. from NST 13: 59; DZZ 1: 493.

89. Trans. from NST 13: 59; 1: 493.

90. In saying "his or her" to refer to the Zen master I am not being merely inclusive for stylistic reasons. In his *Repository* essay *Raihai tokuzui* (Getting the Marrow by Doing Obeisance), Dōgen explicitly criticizes males who think they cannot learn from a female master. For an English translation in the Soto Zen Text Project, see DŌGEN 2002B.

91. Trans. from NST 12: 425; DZZ 1: 416–17.

92. This phrase *skin-flesh-bones-marrow* is referring to a narrative about Bodhidharma, the first Chinese ancestor in the Zen lineage, and his four disciples. Bodhidharma asks his students to express their insight. In reply to the first student's response, Bodhidharma says "You have attained me in my skin." To the second, "You have attained me in my flesh." To the third, "You have attained me in my bone." To the fourth, Huike, "You have attained me in my marrow." Since Huike is generally recognized as Bodhidharma's successor, the usual interpretation is that each successive answer was more profound.

In the *Repository* essay *Kattō*, Dōgen offers a different interpretation. He argues that since Bodhidharma says each "attained me," they each attained *all* of Bodhidharma—one cannot attain part of enlightenment. The difference among Bodhidharma's disciples is not, therefore, one of depth of insight, but rather of shifting contexts or occasions, or even differing personalities within equally enlightened individuals. (JPS, 162)

93. Trans. from NST 12: 428; DZZ 1: 420.

94. In light of note 85 above, we can see a similarity between the two ways of talking about a sequential numerical pattern and the two profiles of *uji*, namely "the now of right now" and the "ranging," "shifting" or "flowing."

95. The term I translate "buddhas-in-action" is *gyōbutsu*, which can mean "practicing buddhas." Yet, in Dōgen's theory all buddhas are necessarily practicing, since praxis and enlightenment are inseparable. Practicing buddha is being a buddha. In my translation of the term, I am stressing that buddhahood is an activity in which we participate with the buddhas, that is, we are buddhas in our engaged action.

96. Trans. from NST 12: 87; DZZ 1: 59.

97. Trans. from NST 12: 87; DZZ 1: 59.

98. Trans. from NST 12: 87; DZZ 1: 59.

99. Note the phrase once again stresses *how* rather than *what* as defining the self.

100. Trans. from NST 12: 89; DZZ 1: 62.

101. Note the similarity to Shinran's image of the personal Amida who disappears into egolessness when we surrender our ego in perfect entrusting faith. See Chapter 5, pages 203–4.

102. Trans. from NST 12: 89–90; DZZ 1: 62.

103. Trans. from NST 12: 36; DZZ 1: 3. For a fuller explanation of this passage, see KASULIS 1981, 87–93.

104. Trans. from NST 12: 356; DZZ 1: 343.

105. Trans. from NST 12: 356; DZZ 1: 343.

106. Trans. from NST 12: 357; DZZ 1: 344.

107. Dōgen here writes "do no evil" in Japanese (*shoaku tsukurukoto nakare*) rather than leaving it in its sinicized pronunciation *shoakumakusa*. In this way he can be explicit about how ordinary people hear it or interpret it. Of course, for Dōgen, however you understand what something means, that can never be *all* it means. Hence, the ensuing discussion.

108. Trans. from NST 12: 357; DZZ 1: 344.

109. On an interreligious note, it is provocative to contrast Dōgen's view of evil as "something added" (through delusional projections from an ego) with the traditional Christian view that evil is "something missing"—the absence of or alienation from the goodness of God. Although the two traditions agree the problem is within the corrupted human self, it is intriguing that the evil function of the ego is viewed in almost opposite terms. For Zen, that ego function creates what is not real (delusions); for Christianity, it rejects what is real (God).

110. Dōgen uses as his pivotal term for his analysis of the second line the basic meaning of "do" (*bugyō*) in "do good" (*shuzenbugyō*). The *bugyō* refers to "devoted action" or "performance," or alternatively as William Bodiford aptly puts it, "devout practice" (JPS, 156–60). Therefore, once again, Dōgen shifts the focus from the what (in this case "good") to the how (of practice, of being a buddha-in-action). The third line, "keeping your own intentions pure" needs little further elaboration as it basically reaffirms the point of Dōgen's reading of the first two lines. That is, it expresses the "how" of nonproduction and devoted action.

111. Trans. from NST 12: 362; DZZ 1: 352.

112. For a somewhat fuller analysis of the ethical theory that emerges from Dōgen's treatment of *shoakumakusa*, see KASULIS 1981, 93–9.

7. Refuge from the Storm

113. From *Tsurezuregusa* (*Essays in Idleness*). (Trans. in YOSHIDA Kenko 1967, 7.)

114. Both poems are found in SJT-1, 390–1 but retranslated here. For a fuller literary interpretation (on which my comments are based) see LAFLEUR 1983, 97–8; Haga Kōshirō in SJT-1, 391; and IZUTSU Toyoko in JPS, 1224–7.

115. Trans. in YOSHIDA Kenko 1967, 115–18.

116. For Paul L. Swanson's translation and commentary on the seminal work for the *shikan* meditation tradition, see T'ien-t'ai Chih-i, 2007.

117. The notion of "having heart" (*ushin* 有心) resembles the Zen "no-mind" (*mushin* 無心) when used as an aesthetic term, as in Zeami's previously quoted statements about Nō and no-mind (see pages 255–6). The oddity is that the sinographs for *u* and *mu* are generally oppositional. For an explanation of how these two seemingly opposing terms, *ushin* and *mushin,* came to have similar meanings, see KASULIS 2008.

118. Thanks to the work of a number of scholars in the past three or four decades, the connection between Buddhism and the medieval arts, especially the literary arts, is now well documented. Important studies include: MARRA 1981; LAFLEUR 1983; RAMIREZ-CHRISTENSEN 2008; LAFLEUR 2003; and SANFORD, LAFLEUR, and NAGATOMI 1992.

119. For a thorough discussion about the pronunciation *Shintō* as well as a general overview of the development of Shintō over the centuries, see TEEUWEN 2003.

120. For a translation of this work see KITABATAKE 1980.

121. Chikafusa's authorship of this text is sometimes questioned. More important, however, is its close connection to Watarai Shintō discussed below. In fact, Varley points out that it is "based almost entirely on *Ruiju Jingi Hongen* (Collection of *Kami* Origins) by Watarai Ieyuki (1256–?), a major thinker in the school. See KITABATAKE 1980, 13. The philosophical point of interest is that Chikafusa, the *Gengenshū*, and the Watarai School developed their positions by arguing from *origins,* a hallmark of Shintō thinking from this point forward.

122. See TEEUWEN, 1993. Also, for a book-length study of Watarai Shintō, see TEEUWEN 1996.

123. Buddhism has not typically emphasized cosmogonic theories, considering time to have had no beginning. Consequently, Buddhism generally lacks creation narratives and creator buddhas.

124. Buddhism may have shown comparatively little interest in explaining the *origins* of the universe or of the world, but it certainly has been attentive to the *sources* of ideas, world views, delusions, knowledge, wisdom, and so forth. Discussions of such psychological or experiential sources figured prominently in the analyses by Kūkai, Dōgen, and even Shinran. The end result is that what the Watarai Shintō philosophers meant by "origins" is not at all comparable to what Japanese Buddhist philosophers meant by "sources."

125. Trans. based on YOSHIDA Kanetomo 1992, 153.

126. Although the metaphor is the same, the emphasis is quite different. Shōtoku, applauds the fruit (Buddhism) as the religious and philosophical culmination, but Kanetomo praises the root (Shintō) as the religious or philosophical origin.

127. Trans. based on YOSHIDA Kanetomo 1992, 138–9; 144; for original see NST 19: 211–2, 221.

128. For the details about Kanetomo's account of the relocation of the Sun *Kami* and the Food *Kami*, see GRAPARD 1992, 43–4.

129. For a selection of essays on various aspects of secrecy in Japanese religion, see SCHEID and TEEUWEN 2006.

130. Sometimes the Kamakura thinkers are characterized as "reformers," but that may not be the best description of their intent and their impact. For a balanced and probative analysis of how best to characterize the "new religions" of the Kamakura period in terms of "reform," see FOARD 1980.

131. This amalgam of Buddhist traditions defining the religious establishment at the time of the Kamakura reformers is sometimes called, following the influential historical analysis by Kuroda Toshio (1926–1993), *kenmitsu* (exo-esoteric) Buddhism. See KURODA 1981. Basically, Kuroda's theory is that ritual throughout the period maintained its esoteric qualities, especially those related to purported thaumaturgical powers. Yet, atop that esoteric praxis was an overlay of exoteric theories, each distinctive to the respective Buddhist denomination. As Kuroda has shown, that religious form continued to dominate throughout the medieval period, despite the gradual rise of the "new Buddhisms" developed by such figures as Hōnen, Shinran, Dōgen, and Nichiren.

One of Kuroda's points is that the *kenmitsu* cluster of beliefs and practices crossed sectarian lines and mixed esoteric and exoteric elements. He also argues that aspects of this cluster were later picked up by the nativists and interpreted as being "original Shintō," something preceding Buddhist influences from the mainland. (This is the type of enterprise we found in Yoshida Kanetomo's Yuiitsu Shintō, for example.)

Kuroda maintains that *kenmitsu* Buddhism is the real ancient Japanese religion and that what we now call Shintō is in fact an outgrowth of it. That line of analysis eliminates the need for the classification "proto-Shintō" as used in this book. (See notes 19 and 21, pages 599–600.) Kuroda's careful historical research and his interpretative structures are invaluable correctives on some historiographical distortions by both some Native Studies/Shintō advocates as well as some Buddhist scholars stressing the Kamakura "reformers" as overthrowing the whole Buddhist establishment of their time.

For tracing *philosophical* developments in Japanese history, however, Kuroda's interpretation is not as helpful. First, it minimizes the preexisting animistic tradition in Japan with which Kūkai's esotericism resonated so well. I have called this aspect of Kūkai's project "philosophizing in the archaic." See KASULIS 1990, EISENSTADT 1996, and BELLAH 2003. Second, as a philosophical term, *kenmitsu* is problematic. As we have seen, it is a technical term used by Shingon and Tendai with specific philosophical meanings, not all of which are appropriate to Kuroda's broader usage. So, it might be confusing for this book to use the term in both its technical Shingon sense and Kuroda's more general historiographical sense.

Moreover, by interpreting the esoteric to function primarily on the level of praxis (minimizing its metapractical doctrinal dimension), Kuroda overlooks the crucially important philosophical distinction between *kengyō* (exoteric teachings) and *mikkyō* (esoteric teachings). Thus, the compound term *kenmitsu* may in the end be too vague to carry much hermeneutic weight. Are there not in the medieval period purely exoteric as well as purely esoteric theories and purely exoteric as well as purely esoteric practices? If so, the term *kenmitsu* must imply some synthesis between the two philosophical dimensions. But precisely what kind of synthesis? Does one tradition relegate the other? Are they each allocated their own role? Or is it a true hybrid? Or are there multiple species of *kenmitsu*?

For addressing such questions, Kuroda's term is too imprecise. All this is not to refute Kuroda. His theoretical formulation may be particularly useful in characterizing praxis and doctrine on the level of everyday religious life, for example. But such a focus does not in this case shed much light on the philosophical concerns of this book. That is why I do not make more use of Kuroda's theory in this work. For a helpful critique of Kuroda's theory as it applies to Japanese medieval Buddhism, See MATSUO 2007, 52–7.

132. For a collection of essays on Rennyo see BLUM and YASUTOMI 2006.

133. The "Ikkō Sect" here does not refer to an earlier independent group of Shin Buddhists founded by the thirteenth-century Pure Land leader, Ikkō Shunjō (1239–1287). That Ikkō Sect was an aggressively antinomian circle that Rennyo explicitly refuted. Yet, through a sequence of associations, Shin Buddhism in general commonly came to be called the Ikkō Sect until modern times. See DOBBINS 1989, 110–11. Perhaps some of the confusion derives from the common use of the term *ikkō* (single-mindedly) in many Pure Land texts, including Shinran's.

134. The phrase's origin seems to be either the Ikkō sect (see preceding note) or the Chinzei branch of Honen's Pure Land sect. See the discussion in DOBBINS 1989, 146–8.

135. Rennyo wrote:

> There is no doubt that one who with firm faith prays for rebirth, knowing salvation to be the one great issue, will indeed attain the blessed state in the next life. But in addition the *nenbutsu* naturally functions as a kind of prayer that ensures world blessings without our asking for them. (Trans. based on KASAHARA 2001, 206.)

Material blessings in this world were part of the benefits promised in the Hokke sect, going all the way back to Nichiren's teachings. With only a couple of minor exceptions, Shinran generally frowned on the idea that material benefits may accrue from Shin Buddhist praxis.

136. Seeing trouble brewing already in the previous year (1473), Rennyo issued eleven rules to guide his followers. To disregard any of them would be grounds for expulsion from the local Shin Buddhist group. The sixth rule was: "As *nenbutsu* adherents, do not denigrate the provincial governor (*shugo*) or constables (*jitō*)."

137. By 1386, the list stabilized as follows: Nanzen-ji (Kyoto) was at the pinnacle, above being counted in the system itself. The Kyoto Five Mountain Temples (in descending order) were: Tenryū-ji (founded by Musō Soseki and dedicated to the deceased spirit of Emperor Go-Daigo), Shōkoku-ji (the Ashikaga family temple), Kennin-ji (Eisai's first temple), Tōfuku-ji (historically linked to the Fujiwara), and Manju-ji. For temple rankings in Kamakura the list was: Kenchō-ji, Engaku-ji, Jufuku-ji, Jōchi-ji, and Jōmyō-ji. For a synopsis of the system, see BOWRING 2005, 400–4. A comprehensive study in English is COLLCUTT 1981.

138. Not every major Rinzai Zen temple in Kyoto was part of the Five Mountain system, however. For example, partly by choice Daitoku-ji (Temple of Great Virtue) and Myōshin-ji (Temple of the Marvelous Mindful Heart) remained outside the system, claiming an emphasis on the purity of their Zen praxis. In reality, however, they were generally as involved in literary and artistic studies as the Five Mountain temples. For an account of the founding spirit of Daitoku-ji, see the excellent biography of Daitō in

KRAFT 1992; and for an excerpt from one of the great medieval Rinzai iconoclasts also of Daitoku-ji, see the selection from Ikkyū Sōjun (1394–1481) in JPS, 172–7. For a biography of Ikkyū, see SANFORD 1981.

139. See *Zhuangzi (Chuang-tzu)*, chapter 2.

140. For a brief discussion of this Zen capping phrase, see HORI 2003, 14–15. In general, Hori's book is the most thorough and insightful book in English dealing with kōan practice in Rinzai Zen, its historical development, its practical purpose in Zen training, and its metapractical justification. The theme of the book most directly relevant to my discussion of Musō is pithily expressed by Hori as follows:

> Although it is true that one can only grasp a kōan by becoming it, that one cannot grasp a kōan merely through intellectual understanding, nevertheless there is an intellectual language, both technical and symbolic, for talking about the many aspects of Zen awakening. Intellectual understanding of the kōan and the experience of the nonduality of subject and object are not opposed to each other, the one excluding the other. Without realization of the point of the kōan, there can be no intellectual understanding of the kōan. With realization comes understanding. (HORI 2003, 15)

Therefore, the same words that entangle us in self-delusion are transformed in meaning and purpose once we "get it." Then those words become expressively revealing and part of the communications among the adept. This approach to paradox is not, among religions, unique to Zen. See KASULIS 1997.

141. Is this approach different from Dōgen's "cutting through *kattō* with *kattō*" as described above on pages 236–7? It is as if Dōgen claims that the knot can be cut through with the rope, that language can cut through our being entangled in language, whereas Musō (and most other Rinzai masters) use a weapon to cut through language (the kōan, hitting, shouting, etc.). Sōtō and Rinzai Zen clearly differ in both traditional rhetoric and the emphasis on specific techniques of praxis.

Yet, it seems to me, the two traditions have the same goal: returning us to *where* we were, but not *as* we were, before the praxis. Some of this interpretation was developed in KASULIS 1981 in my comparison between Dōgen and Hakuin (an eighteenth-century Rinzai master who seems to be, on these points at least, fully in accord with Musō). For exploring Musō's philosophy, including his theory of language, see MUSŌ 2010.

142. Musō writes of how people may relate to a garden differently. Some are interested for the sake of owning a splendid garden with rare rocks. That is just a "love for worldly things." Others have no interest in such secular things, but have the refined taste so that they get "nourishment for their souls" through poetry or gardens. "But if such people are lacking in the spirit of the Way, even such refined qualities became the basis for future rebirths in the samsaric [delusional] world." Others use gardens as a technique in practicing the Way—to ward off sleepiness or boredom while practicing, but they also "cannot be called true Way-followers." Finally, there are those who

> regard mountains, rivers, grass, trees, tiles, and stones to be their own original nature. Their love for gardens may resemble worldly affection, but they employ that affection in their aspiration for the Way, using as part of their practice the changing scenery of the grasses and trees throughout the four seasons. One who

can do this is truly an exemplar of how a follower of the Way should consider a garden. (Trans. in Musō 2010, 133.)

For Musō's similar attitude toward words in Zen praxis, see Musō 2010, 104.

THE EDO PERIOD
8. The Open Marketplace of Ideas

1. On the peasant uprisings during the Edo period, see Bix 1986 and Vlastos 1986.

2. A rich resource for exploring many dimensions of the Tokugawa legal system is the monumental 21-volume work under the general editorship of the famous American jurist, John Henry Wigmore (1863–1943). See Wigmore 1967. Wigmore, incidentally, was brought to Japan by the government to teach in Keiō University Law School from 1889 to 1892. During that time he began compiling his collection of Tokugawa legal rulings on all major areas of law including contracts, property, legal precedents, torts, penal law, and so forth. The vast selection of court rulings shows both the shogunate's respect for record keeping and for the value of establishing legal precedents.

3. Consider the following example: under Tokugawa law merchant-class ladies were prohibited from dressing in the elegant brocade of the elite and they were restricted in the colors they could wear. But where there is a market, there is a way. The textile industry developed stylish kimono out of silk dyed in rich indigo, browns, and grays and patterned in a painterly style using rice paste or wax. The stylish result was as stunning as any embroidered seven-layered kimono from the old Heian court. In the end, the shogunate proved itself more adept at controlling armed forces than market forces.

4. A particularly innovative and insightful analysis of the Tokugawa intellectual scene in terms of the sociology of philosophical networks is found in Collins 1998, 347–69.

5. As the etymology of the name suggests, *terakoya* ("temple children's schools") evolved out of the medieval system in which monks gave children their basic education. *Terako* literally means "temple child," but by the Edo period meant generally any student.

6. This long-held claim may need to be hedged in light of recent research. Part of the problem is what defines *literacy* in Japanese with its multiple writing systems. For example, mastery of the *kana* syllabary is enough for a very basic level of literacy. Because the syllabary glyphs correspond to the syllables of the spoken language (unlike many alphabetical spelling systems where the same letter may correspond to a number of different sounds), if one can speak Japanese and knows the approximately fifty signs of the syllabary, one can read or write a message in the syllabary with little trouble.

However, Japanese is not typically written in just the syllabary but as combined with the sinographs, of which there are thousands. Moreover, in the Tokugawa period, official documents, most scholarship, and many traditional texts (such as Buddhist sutras) were written in Chinese-Japanese hybrid writing systems. So, at what level should we peg the *literacy* benchmark?

Recent research has shown that literacy varied less by class than by location. In some provincial domains, many of the samurai were not literate, even at the minimal level of mastering the syllabary, whereas in other domains, a fairly large percentage of even the peasants were at least minimally literate. See Rubinger 2007 for both a thorough description of literacy in rural areas as well as (in Chapter 5) an analysis of the revealing literacy tests administered at the beginning of the modern period as part of military conscription.

7. This is not to say that education in Buddhist temples did not continue on some level. Sōtō Zen continued to run grammar schools in many of its mostly rural temples and Rinzai Zen, in the Five Mountain tradition, continued a high level of learning, especially in the Chinese classical style. The big change, however, was that the Edo period ushered in a wide range of options for secular education that did not exist in any vigorous form previously.

8. Note that today's highest Grand Master rank of *yokozuna* did not exist in the Edo period. The program depicted here is from a printed copy, the original of which is in the archives at the Komaba branch of the Tokyo University Library. (See Noguchi 1993, 11.)

9. In many ways, a more useful system of classification would be not in terms of "schools" at all, but instead associations of thinkers with interpersonal connections. That is the approach of the historical sociologist, Randall Collins, who is especially perceptive in discussing the new educational institutions of the period and their market dynamics (Collins 1998, 347–69).

Collins's analysis has the weakness of ignoring the function of the incursion of Christianity and western learning, an important dimension in the Edo turn toward empiricism. Some ideas may be "in the air" and *au currant* enough that philosophers would respond to them without necessarily formulating them into an easily identifiable philosophical position, interpersonal network, or school. Thus a cluster of ideas may indirectly connect people across networks in ways that should not be overlooked.

10. The Japanese translation called *Kaitai shinsho* (New Book of Anatomical Dissection) was published in 1774.

11. The career of the Portuguese Jesuit, João Rodrigues (1561?–1633), exemplifies the missionaries' linguistic prowess. Rodrigues came to Japan as a cabin boy on a Portuguese trading vessel in 1577, became a Jesuit during his stay in Japan, and attained such skill in Japanese that he served as an interpreter for both Hideyoshi and Ieyasu. His *Arte da Lingoa de Iapam* published in Nagasaki in 1608 became a standard for the grammatical and cultural study of the Japanese language well into the nineteenth century.

Other Jesuits assembled the impressive Japanese-Portuguese dictionary of some 33,000 entries. Published in Portuguese in 1603 and 1604, it subsequently appeared in both Spanish and French editions as well. The dictionary was called *Vocabulario da Lingoa de Iapam com a declaração em Portugues* and was known in Japanese as *Nippo jisho* (*Japanese-Portuguese Dictionary*).

12. For the sake of communicating the primary values and historical events of Japanese culture, Fabian translated the popular medieval war epic, *The Tale of the Heike*, into colloquial sixteenth-century Japanese, writing the text in roman letters rather than Sino-Japanese script. Since the foreign missionaries needed a command of spoken Japanese for their proselytizing, the texts allowed Fabian's novices to become quick studies in the use of Japanese for practical purposes. As the translator of the text, he listed his

name as "Fucan Fabian." That is the origin of the western convention of calling him "Fabian." A classic study of Fabian in English is ELISON 1973.

13. There is an irony in this argument that may not have been lost on Fabian. When Francis Xavier and the first Jesuits came to Japan, their guide and interpreter was a Japanese fisherman they had met in Macao. They tried to explain to the fisherman the meaning of "God" so he could suggest a good translation. Being of Shingon background, the fisherman suggested "Dainichi," the cosmic buddha in Kūkai's tradition. After being in Japan awhile, the missionaries were horrified to find that their Christianity was being interpreted as some weird offshoot of Shingon Buddhism, so they quickly changed to using the untranslated "*Deus*" to refer to God.

14. As mentioned earlier, Fabian had studied in the Kyoto Rinzai Zen monastery Daitoku-ji, famed for its thinkers Daitō Kokushi and Ikkyū (JPS, 172–7). Although Daitoku-ji, like another major Rinzai monastery in Kyoto, Myōshin-ji, did not participate in the Five Mountain system, the doctrine of "original mind" was prevalent in all traditions of Rinzai Zen.

15. It is intriguing to speculate on how the Jesuit missionaries in Japan might have fared if they had been given more time and circumstances had differed. The Jesuit strategist and administrator for the East Asian missions was the Italian, Alessandro Valignano (1539–1606). Valignano insisted that his missionaries learn the language and culture of their potential converts and, whenever and however possible, to integrate those elements into Catholic teaching and praxis.

Of those who followed Valignano's strategy, one of the most successful was Matteo Ricci (1552–1610). Ricci spent some three decades in China, mastering the culture so expertly that many Chinese intellectuals accepted him as an equal and colleague. Ricci was most prominent for his knowledge of western science, his stress on education, and for his constructive participation in what we might today call interreligious dialogue.

Valignano made three administrative visits to Japan (1579–1582, 1590–1592, and 1598–1603), but his followers there never enjoyed Ricci's level of success and stature. Of course, a key consideration is that the political climate from the Warring Domains through the early Edo periods lacked the cultural stability necessary for true intellectual exchange. How might the Jesuits have fared in the cultural and philosophical renaissance of, say, late seventeenth-century Japan, assuming the shogunate would have permitted their activities?

16. For an overview of the Chinese Legalist school, see the anthology of essays in GOLDIN 2014.

17. As one might expect, within the *daigaku*, the imperial training academy for court officials, there was at least a modest interest in what was happening within the Chinese Confucianism of the time. As a result some of Zhu Xi's neo-Confucian writings entered Japan even in the Kamakura period, but they had little appreciable impact until centuries later. See NOSCO 1984A, 6–7.

18. Hayashi Razan, one of the pioneering Japanese neo-Confucians, expressed the traditional correlation of principle in mind with principle in reality as follows:

> Accordingly, within people's minds, the principles of the myriad things are endowed; the *ki* of heaven and earth is the *ki* of humanity; and the mind of

heaven and earth is the mind of humanity. Invariably the principles of the Way and the mind of humanity are a unity, without change. Illuminating this mind in thought, speech, and action so that it is never darkened is called "manifesting bright virtue."(JPS, 314)

19. The ideal of building a society in which painful hard work would be rewarded with subsequent enjoyment was captured by the classic phrase (derived from Chinese poetry) of "hardship first, enjoyment later" (*sen'yū kōraku*), suggesting that ideal rulers should deal with hardships until they can see their subjects able to enjoy themselves. Only then should they allow themselves such relaxation and pleasure.

The slogan was taken up as a motto by Tokugawa Yorifusa (1603–1661) when he built his grand garden in Edo, Kōrakuen (Garden of Enjoyment Later). Yorifusa was Ieyasu's eleventh son and became the founding daimyō of the Mito branch of the Tokugawa family, which centuries later would play a key role in the ideology behind imperial restoration.

(Koishikawa) Kōrakuen survives today as a scenic respite from Tokyo's hectic lifestyle. It is adjacent to Kōrakuen Park, an amusement park and site of the Tokyo Dome, home of the Yomiuri Giants baseball team. Thus, the phrase, *sen'yūkōraku* exemplifies both the impact of Chinese ethical norms in politics as well as the Edo-period consciousness that enjoyment is a primary goal in an ideal society.

The word *yū* in *senyū* is, incidentally, also pronounced "*uki*," as in the aforementioned characterization of the medieval world as *ukiyo* in the sense of "melancholy world" as contrasted with the Edo-period *ukiyo* meaning the "floating world." (See pages 282–3.) It might not be too clever an interpretation of the phrase *sen'yūkōraku* to note that first was the medieval world of hardship, then the Edo-period world of enjoyment. Whether or not that is a historically accurate way to view the two periods, I do suspect such a rationale was part of the "floating world" zeitgeist lived out by the townspeople.

20. This literary emphasis in the Five Mountain system also reinforced the *kōan* study's connection to the literary tradition of Rinzai Zen. Students could express their insight for their master's evaluation in the form of a spontaneous gesture or word, but also as a poem, a painting, or very commonly, a creative expression based in the collection of classic Zen sayings. This latter practice has some formal similarities with Japanese poetry competitions practiced since Heian times. Instead of the Fujiwara Teika's classic *waka* poetics of "expressing new meanings with old words," we might say here we have something like a Zen practice of "expressing new realizations in old words."

21. Donald Keene credits Seika's punctuating the Chinese classics and making them available to the wider public as a crucial part of that propagation. The ancient Chinese texts are unpunctuated, making them difficult to read because Chinese is uninflected and the same sinograph can function as either a noun or a verb, for example. Word order in the sentence is the determining factor, but if you do not know where the sentences begin and end, you find yourself in a vicious cycle of having to know what the text says before you can read it and only by reading it can you know what the text says.

Thus, traditionally, you can learn to read such texts only by studying under a master who will help you decipher the sentences by adding the appropriate punctuation. In the medieval period, this was often done in a covert, intimate relation between master and apprentice. By making the punctuation public, Seika let the secret out of the bag and made the texts available to a much wider reading public. Again, we have an example of the Edo period as opening up information and scholarship to the public marketplace of ideas. See KEENE 1984, 120–2.

22. The institution was originally located in the Yushima section of Edo, near today's Ueno Park, but moved to its present Ochanomizu location in the late seventeenth century.

23. The site is so named because it is where water was fetched for the shogun's tea. The hegemons and Tokugawa shoguns, even the ruthless Oda Nobunaga, had a fondness for tea and its ritual. There is a story that a man once scheduled for execution was able to save his own life by spontaneously offering Nobunaga a famous, highly treasured kettle for boiling water in the tea ceremony.

As for Hideyoshi, he was especially close to the aforementioned tea master Rikyū (see pages 252 and 298), taking lessons from him in the Way of tea. Ordinarily obsessed with his own status, Hideyoshi even submitted to the egalitarian ritual praxis of entering the small door to the teahouse by crawling on hand and knee. Yet, he never did fathom the more subtle aesthetics of tea.

To celebrate his master's art, for example, he once decided to invite Rikyū to serve a party of friends and associates. Rikyū was likely stunned when he learned that meant a party of ten thousand. Another time Hideyoshi showed his devotion to Rikyū, as well as his lack of insight into *wabi,* by giving Rikyū a tea house whose interior was gilt in gold. Perhaps not surprisingly, given what we have already seen of Hideyoshi's fickle nature toward the Christians, for reasons still debated by scholars, he terminated his relationship with Rikyū by ordering his ritual suicide.

24. Herman Ooms can be credited with refuting this common misperception about the centrality of *Shushigaku* thought in the intellectual foundations of the Tokugawa shogunate. A major reason for the error was that the Hayashi school did an excellent job of marketing itself as being more important than it was. Later scholars had naïvely accepted their accounts without sufficient suspicion.

Furthermore, as Ooms also points out, part of the issue was that the Tokugawa regime did not have *any* clear ideology of its own, not to mention a Hayashi-centered one. He attributes that misperception to scholars' assuming that any successful government as authoritarian and complex as the Tokugawa shogunate must have had some single ideology driving it. Ooms shows that it basically didn't. See OOMS 1985.

25. Moreover, the shogunate had built in the mountains of Nikkō an elaborate, ornate Shintō shrine for the resting place of Ieyasu's spirit after death. The Tokugawas had apparently planned to use Shintō to enhance their charismatic authority in much the same way as had the imperial court in earlier centuries.

26. As a sign of the times, it is significant that in Edo and modern Japan, loyalty was given as much or more prominence as the classical Confucian "five cardinal virtues." Loyalty was indeed a traditional Confucian virtue and recognized as such in China, but there it was typically subordinate rather than equal to the five cardinal virtues.

27. This view is exemplified, for example, in Jinsai's treatment of "principle" in his *The Meaning of Terms in the Analects and Mencius*:

The notion of the Way is a living word capable of describing the reproductive and transformative mysteries of living things. Principle, in contrast, is a dead word.... It can neither convey nor capture the mysteries that heaven and earth produce through productive and transformative life.... (JPS, 352)

28. For a good overview of Ekken and his thought see M. E. TUCKER 1989.

29. Even Hayashi Razan, when introducing Zhu Xi's thought to Japan, had his doubts about this apparent dualism between principle and generative force, saying the two are so interdependent that neither can exist prior to the other. See JPS, 305. The same can be said of the *Yōmeigaku* philosopher, Kumazawa Banzan (1619–1691). See JPS, 329–34.

30. For examples of such writings, see his selections in SJT-2, 254–68. *See* JPS, 330.

31. The title is less cryptic when given in full rather than the abbreviated form by which it is commonly known. The book's full title is "Notes on What Was Heard in the Shadow of Leaves" (*Hagakure kikigaki*), suggesting passing down the teachings in an intimate, perhaps secret, master-apprentice setting.

32. The temple, following many popular accounts, celebrates the anniversary of the assassination as December 14, but historians agree it occurred several weeks later on January 31st.

33. It is not surprising that in the *banzuke* depicting philosophers as sumō wrestlers (see pages 286–7), the designated referee for the match was often a member of the Hayashi family. Always politically astute, the Hayashi family leadership tried to stay above the fray in most major controversies.

34. For an extensive selection of readings on the Akō Incident, see SJT-2, chapter 31 from which this passage is taken (444–5).

35. Trans. in SJT-2, 448.

36. As Naokata put it:

The Asano family had revered Yamaga Sokō's teachings on military science. Ōishi had thus studied these teachings from the start. [The forty-seven men's] plot arose out of their virulent reaction to the prospect of being reduced to the status of masterless samurai. Their attack was a product of calculation and conspiracy; it did not arise from any real sense of loyalty (*chūgi*) to their lord or from any feelings of commiseration with their lord in his misfortune. Someone who presumes to be a samurai should instead analyze things in detail and make clear distinctions so that he can resolve the confusion clouding the common people. (SJT-2, 451)

37. SJT-2, 461.

38. For a detailed discussion of how the *giri/ninjō* dynamic functions in Chikamatsu's plays, with special attention to the neo-Confucian social context, see KEENE 1984. The classic philosophical study of *giri/ninjō* in Japanese is MINAMOTO 1969.

39. Keisai believed that the Way is universal but could still vary from one country to another. For him Confucianism's universality lay in its ability to accommodate ethnic and cultural differences. That is, no single country's version of the Way could be considered definitive for the whole tradition. Therefore, although he was a dyed-in-the-wool Confucian, Keisai insisted he was a *Japanese* Confucian. Nothing in his Confucianism was exclusively Chinese. As a country, Japan had its own points of superiority to China,

especially how, consistent with his point about the Akō Incident, Japan had uniquely developed the strong bond between lord and vassal.

40. For a brief, but precise, account of Koretari's position, see NOSCO 1984B, 172–4.

41. Trans. in NOSCO 1990, 48.

42. Nosco refers to the "metaphor of China," resembling in some ways what I am calling the "imaginary" of China.

43. An important exception was the presence of Chinese Zen Buddhist monks, such as the Rinzai master, Ingen (1592–1673). Ingen is considered the founder of so-called Ōbaku (C. Huangbo) Zen in Japan. See page 338.

44. An early source for this assessment of *waka* is found in Mujū Dōgyō (1226–1312) in section 5A.12 of his *Sand and Pebbles Collection* (*Shasekishū*):

> When we consider *waka* as a means to religious realization, we see it has the virtue of serenity and peace, of putting a stop to the distractions and undisciplined movements of the mind. With a few words, it encompasses its sentiment. This is the very nature of mystic verses or *dhāraṇī*.
>
> The gods of Japan are Manifest Traces (*suijaku*), the unexcelled Transformation Bodies (*ōjin*) of buddhas and bodhisattvas.... Japanese poems do not differ from the words of the Buddha.... If the Buddha had appeared in Japan, he would simply have used Japanese for mystic verses. (Trans. in MINER, ODAGIRI, and MORRELL 1985, 163–4.)

For a brief philosophical discussion of this passage in English and its relation to the theory of *waka-dharani*, see YUASA 1987, 101–4.

45. Keichū wrote, for example, the following:

> Japan is the land of the *kami*. Therefore in both our historical writing and our public matters, we have given priority to the *kami* and always place humans second. In early antiquity, our rulers governed this land exclusively by means of Shintō. Since it was not only a naïve and simple age but an unlettered age as well, there were only the oral traditions called "Shintō," and there were no teachings like those in Confucian classics and Buddhist writings. (Trans. in SJT-2, 482.)

The passage suggests that imperial rule was ultimately divinely inspired and not the result of human reasoning and ingenuity. The basis for the claim lay in the ancient culture's being illiterate. The connection between orality, Shintō, and ancient rulership would be a common theme among many Native Studies thinkers.

46. See CADDEAU 2006, 23–4.

47. An abridged version of the "Petition" in English translation can be found in SJT-2, 486–9.

48. This brief summary follows Mabuchi's own characterization as explicated in Nosco 1990, 123–4.

49. Trans. in NOSCO 1990, 130.

50. See, for example, the excerpts in SJT-2, 491–6. Also, see the discussion of Mabuchi's opinion of Laozi in NOSCO 1990, 142–3.

51. For an excellent synopsis of these "ten good precepts" and Jiun's analysis of them, see WATT 1984, 200–12.

52. For the most comprehensive treatment of Linji in English, see LINJI 2009.

53. For a brief description and analysis of Hakuin's techniques in light of their philosophical purpose, see KASULIS 1981, 104–24.

54. For a summary of how education was disseminated outside the formal academies, see SAWADA 1993, 9–27.

55. The term *shingaku* (心学) was Tōan's term whereas Baigan usually used *seigaku* (性学, "inherent nature learning") instead. Tōan's term was chosen for its familiarity to ordinary people but did not, at least directly, imply any connection with the neo-Confucian tradition of *shingaku* (C. *xinxue*).

56. Fortunately, there is a good book in English for focusing on each aspect. For the popular morality side of the movement (especially Baigan's contribution) and how it laid the groundwork for Japan's transition into a modern industrial society in the nineteenth century, see BELLAH 1957. For a treatment of the spiritual praxis and metapraxis, especially as related to Tōan, see SAWADA 1993.

57. Michael Pye's helpful introduction to Tominaga and the translation of his two major extant writings can be found in TOMINAGA 1990.

9. OGYŪ Sorai 荻生徂徠 (1666–1728)

58. Trans. based on LIDIN 1973, 22.

59. The common terminology today is different. The text in its original Chinese form is "*kanbun*" (Chinese text). When one reads it so it comes out more like Japanese, it is called "*kanbunkundoku*" (Japanese reading of *kanbun*). This reading typically uses little marginal marks to guide the reader in making the transformation called "*kunten*" (Japanese marks), what Sorai called "cat whiskers" messing up the clean lines of the original text. The markings require the reader's eyes to jump from the text to the adjoining *kunten* and to shift up and down as the syntax gets rearranged. As a result, it is also common today to reorder the text so it can be read directly as *kanbunkundoku* without the *kunten*. This is called *yomikudashibun* (read downward text). This format allows the reader to read the *kanbunkundoku* straight down the page as one would normally read Japanese, with no visual hopscotching along the *kunten*. This system is still often used today. In the main, Sorai failed in his attempt to get most Japanese to read Chinese as Chinese.

60. This difference between Chinese and Japanese syntax allowed the creative "going back over the reading" (*yomikaeshi*) technique for interpreting excerpts of Chinese Buddhist sutras and commentaries. As we have seen, this was common among Kamakura-period philosophers like Dōgen and Shinran. For example, when Dōgen read the phrase normally understood in Chinese to mean "all beings have buddha-nature" as "all of being is buddha-nature," he did not have to change a word of the Chinese text (the *kanbun*), but only changed the Japanized (*kundoku*) reading of it. This process created new meanings for the Chinese sacred writings so that the texts could now be taken to signify what the original writer could not have foreseen (or would necessarily have even endorsed).

Even so, the *yomikaeshi* method lent the appearance of being true to the literal Chinese text. This exegetical technique made philology a creative tool in support of new philosophical ideas. It served the purpose of renovating, rather than deconstructing or restoring tradition. For an analysis of how Dōgen used this technique in the "Do No Evil" fascicle of *Repository*, see pages 240–2.

61. Sorai snidely remarked that the unfamiliarity of the Heian-period Japanese language to his contemporaries added a luster of false profundity to texts from that era. Trivial remarks sound profound when spoken with somber tones in an antiquated tongue. To Sorai, texts like *The Tale of Genji* are just "obscene stories about rouge and powder and affairs in the bed chamber" (Trans. in YOSHIKAWA 1983, 112), but readers think there is a deeper level to them because of the archaic language. Sorai's comment is like someone today claiming that even television soap operas would seem to have a profound message if intoned in the Elizabethan English of Shakespeare or in the language of the King James Bible. See Pastreich 2001 for a good account of Sorai's pedagogy.

62. It is not clear exactly when Sorai began to learn modern Chinese oral pronunciation. On one hand, it seems unlikely he could find a person with native Chinese language skills in isolated Kazusa, but once relocated, he could easily seek out some Chinese monks from the Ōbaku Zen sect, for example. There is evidence he emphasized the importance of native Chinese pronunciation early in his Edo teaching career. Hence, he either learned Chinese pronunciations before returning to Edo or almost immediately upon his arrival there. For a discussion of the possibilities, see YOSHIKAWA 1983, 121–2. We also know that later one of Sorai's students, Okajima Kanzan (1674–1728), tutored him in modern Chinese. In 1716 Kazan wrote a treatise on colloquial Chinese.

63. Trans. based on YOSHIKAWA 1983, 147, 148.

64. In retrospect Sorai wrote of his early years of exile as a positive force in his life, for which he was grateful to Tsunayoshi:

> [Because of its prosperity], however, Edo is a cesspool of iniquity, indolence, and pleasure-seeking that prevail all over the rapidly growing city. Had I been immersed in that environment, I would have ended up as a plain Edoite like a frog inside a well. However, having been a son of an exile, I had an experience that no other scholars have had, and thanks to that, I learned to read all kinds of books with great facility.
>
> So here I am today with my humble name known nationwide. I always think that among the many favors I had received from [Tokugawa Tsunayoshi] including the honor of frequently having audience with him, the greatest was that he had sent me down to the countryside in south Kazusa. (Trans. based on YOSHIKAWA 1983, 99.)

65. Hakuseki's close ties to the shogunate perhaps factored into his holding the highest rank of *ōzeki* in the Scholar's Sumō Program rankings pictured on page 287.

66. Hakuseki acerbically criticized the methodological approach of Sorai and his followers:

> …[W]anting to copy "Chinese pronunciation," [they] learn to mumble with bad accents a few phrases of the sort of Chinese spoken by the crews of the ships that come to Nagasaki…. What is called "Chinese pronunciation" is the vernacular spoken by Chinese of this kind of low station…. To refer to the language spoken by the crew and sailors who come to Nagasaki as "flowery [Chinese] sounds" is

to regard our country as barbaric.… There could be nothing else so disloyal and lacking in propriety toward our country. (Trans. in OGYŪ 2006, 46.)

67. One of Hakuseki's more contentious recommendations was that Ienobu be addressed by foreign dignitaries as "his highness, king of Japan" (*Nihonkoku ō denka*) instead of the then common title for such purposes "great ruler of Japan" (*Nihonkoku taikun*, the origin of the English word "tycoon"). Ienobu's agreeing to follow this recommendation triggered a controversy known as the "[Shogun's] Title Incident" (*shugō jiken*).

Hakuseki's major scholarly projects included the task of formulating a historical justification for shogunal, rather than imperial, rule. His detailed historical analysis of governance in Japanese history traced the structure of political power from ancient times up to Tokugawa rule. His analysis supported the guiding principle that the shoguns should revere the emperors and the emperors should grant all political governance to the shoguns. For further analysis and a translation of Hakuseki's major history, see ARAI 1982; for a translation of Hakuseki's autobiography, also by Joyce Ackroyd, see ARAI 1979.

68. Itō Jinsai and Sorai both held the second highest rank of *sekiwake* in the Scholars' Sumō Rankings, Jinsai representing the Western Division (Kyoto and Osaka) and Sorai the Eastern (Edo). (See page 287.)

69. For J. L. McEwan's commentary and translation of extended excerpts from these two works arranged by topic, see OGYŪ 1962.

70. Trans. based on OGYŪ 2006, 137.

71. John A. Tucker has demonstrated convincingly the debt of Jinsai and Sorai (as well as the Japanese Shushigaku scholar Hayashi Razan) to the lexicographical mode of philosophical argument developed by the Chinese neo-Confucian Chen Beixi (1159–1253). See, for example, J. A. TUCKER 1993. For Tucker's general description of the importance of philosophical dictionaries as a way to present a philosophical position, see OGYŪ 2006, 6.

72. Richard H. Minear fruitfully analogizes Sorai's mix of philology and faith to that of Erasmus. See MINEAR 1976, 48–57.

73. In ancient China there was a belief, at least among some groups, in an "Emperor (or Lord) Above" (the literal meaning of *shangdi*). In subsequent periods the Confucians disagreed (1) whether there actually is such a being; (2) whether he is a personal deity who acts on his own; and (3) whether he is merely an executor who follows either principle (*ri*) or the command [mandate] of heaven (*tenmei*). The importance of Shangdi diminished over time and by the early centuries of the Common Era was seldom a focus of philosophical discussion.

Because Sorai emphasizes the Six Classics (in which Shangdi enjoyed some prominence), however, he could not ignore the issue completely. Generally, when putting the issue in his own terms, the key point was that he wanted to affirm that heaven had intention or mind.

As we have seen in my discussions of Buddhism in earlier chapters, however, for the Japanese intellectual tradition, the presence of "mind" or "consciousness" does not necessarily entail a sense of personhood that we would commonly associate with it in the modern West. For example, consider the use of "mind" as "mindset" in Kūkai's system as well as his proprioceptive sense of cosmic consciousness (see pages 126–9).

74. Yamashita points out that this critique against the Daoist valorization of naturalness could also be a critique of Zhu Xi (and by extension most followers of Shushigaku) as well. Zhu Xi wrote, for example, "the Way is the nature of heaven and principle" and "the Way is the path of nature." See OGYŪ 1994, 40, n. 9.

75. For Confucianism in general, and often for Sorai, the term *shōjin* (C. *xiaoren*) has a pejorative sense because it literally means "small people" and is glossed as "small-minded" or "people of little aptitude." In his *Distinguishing Names,* Sorai defines *shōjin* as follows:

> On the other hand, "small people" is a term referring to the people at large. The people consider making a living as their fundamental concern. Therefore, their sense of purpose is directed only at completing themselves, without concern for bringing peace and security to all people. Thus, they are called small people because their purpose is small. Although they may attain high rank and status, if their minds remain like this, they will still be called small people. (Trans. based on OGYŪ 2006, 334.)

From this perspective Sorai goes on to say that even latter-day Confucian masters who put their own interests above society's are *shōjin* as well.

76. OGYŪ 1994, 41.

77. Trans. based on OGYŪ 1994, 41.

78. Sorai did leave open the possibility that someone of a different class could become an accomplished one. See, for example, Sorai's definition of *kunshi* in chapter 33 of *Distinguishing Names*:

> "Prince" [*kunshi,* "an accomplished one"] thus suggests high rank and status. However, if a person's rank is low but their virtue is sufficient to make them superior to others, they too are deemed princes. Thus, the term also refers to virtue. (Trans. in OGYŪ 2006, 333.)

Although he may have held that position theoretically, in practice he stressed only the training of samurai.

79. See, for example, MARUYAMA 1974, *passim.*

80. A problem in using the political thought of Machiavelli to illuminate the position of Sorai is that scholars do not agree on how to interpret Machiavelli. Should we, for example, follow his recommendations for dictatorial rule in *The Prince,* or should we rely more on his work extolling the republican form of government in ancient Rome as in his *Discourses on First Ten Books of Livy?* Even when one focuses on the former, there is still debate about how to interpret the work. How much of it, for example, is meant to be ironic? Was Machiavelli being descriptive or prescriptive on various points? And so forth.

For the comparison with Sorai, I am assuming the more established image of Machiavelli, that is, the Machiavelli who talked about being ruthless while presenting the veneer of virtue, of using state propaganda to deceive the people about what was happening, of pandering to the populace's lower instincts, and of ruling through fear of retaliation.

81. Maruyama's interpretation of Sorai's differentiation between the public and private is, I think, a point well taken and strongly argued. See MARUYAMA 1974, especially

102–12. Maruyama identified that difference as a telling aspect of Sorai's "modernist" tendency.

I find less convincing, however, Maruyama's claim that this is more a bifurcation than a distinction, a division between two distinct realms rather than an interactive bipolarity. Too often Maruyama overlooks another contrast important to Sorai (and many other Confucian thinkers), namely, the difference between the "sage" and the "accomplished one."

Only sages can create the Way and there are no more sages, according to Sorai. He repeatedly says rulers can only adapt the Way of the sage kings; they cannot innovate. Whether they do that adaptation well or poorly depends upon their innate virtue and the development of that virtue through learning. As Maruyama himself points out, from his first days as advisor to Tsunayoshi, Sorai held rulers responsible for whether their policies brought harmony or disharmony. If the economy fails and people are driven to crime because of dire poverty, the primary failure is in the character of the ruler, not the people. In that respect, the public (political) and private (moral) are not as sharply separated as Maruyama sometimes suggests.

82. Trans. in MARUYAMA 1974, 111–12.

83. Trans. in MARUYAMA 1974, 111.

84. In the *Responsals*, Sorai says:

> From ancient times, there has been talk of the generative force of *yin* and *yang*, the actions of ancestral and heavenly spirits, and the various kinds of animals thought to possess animal power. Heaven and earth are active phenomena that are divinely mysterious and beyond our ken. We have contemplated these phenomena with our limited knowledge and generated the several theories presented earlier. Yet all of these are conjecture; none is a sure thing. This being the case, all one can say is that what is called the learning of the accomplished ones involves studying the way of pacifying and governing the country, and human affairs is difficult enough. (Trans. based on OGYŪ 1994, 51–2.)

85. OGYŪ 2006, 232.

86. Trans. based on OGYŪ 2006, 140.

87. For a discussion of the difference between mastery words and ordinary words, see YOSHIKAWA 1983, 158–63. The English translation here has difficulty communicating all the nuances in the passages Yoshikawa cites. His argument is, therefore, somewhat clearer in the original Japanese version of his text. See YOSHIKAWA 1975, 131–4.

88. Sorai finds the ancient language to be corrupted on two fronts. First, a written language becomes increasingly verbose as it develops over time. For example, the Chinese ancient literary style used fewer particles (linguistic units functioning somewhat like prepositions in English) than in later times such as the Song period when the Zhu Xi school flourished.

Second, the spoken language tends to cultivate superfluous verbiage. (Compare, for example, how the English colloquialism "at this point in time" now often replaces the simple "presently" or even "as of now.") Incidentally, Sorai also claimed that even spoken modern Chinese, however colloquial and loose, is still terse and refined as compared with even the best Japanese written language. Such examples of sinophilia were easy targets for Sorai's critics having a pro-Japanese ethnocentric agenda.

89. Trans. based on YOSHIKAWA 1983, 171.

90. There is some similarity here to when Kūkai rejects the exoteric discourse of heuristic expression (*hōben*) as losing esoteric discourse's ability to conform directly with reality (Dainichi) on its own terms. Both Kūkai and Sorai ground language in praxis and both want to avoid the tendency of language to respond only to previous language and no longer directly to reality. Such a spiral effect ultimately leads one away from plainly describing the way of things.

91. This disdaining of metaphysical speculation in favor of total engagement with the practical issues of governance and social harmony has led to a popular interpretation of Sorai as an early pragmatic thinker in Japan. He has been interpreted as helping to lay a theoretical foundation for the rapid modernization movement in the late nineteenth and early twentieth centuries. Of course, during that period Sorai's ideas also came under fire by those wishing to reject his Confucian and sinophilic orientation in favor of a State Shintō ideology. For a comprehensive overview of the status of Sorai in later Japanese thought, see John A. Tucker's discussion in OGYŪ 2006, 46-134.

Perhaps a simpler interpretation would be to stay within traditional Japanese Confucian categories. We could then see Sorai as a representative of the philosophical mode of thinking known as *jitsugaku*, "practical learning," a category too broad to be considered anything like a school of thought. It did fit very well, however, the practical mindset of much of Edo thinking explained in Chapter 8. *Jitsugaku* may in the end be more an axiom about the goal of philosophizing than a separate philosophy itself. In fact, many of the principle (*ri*)-oriented thinkers Sorai criticized would also fall under the *jitsugaku* umbrella when understood as developing a method analyzing the practical issues of politics, ethics, and even natural science. For a collection of essays treating *jitsugaku* thinkers from throughout East Asia ranging from Zhu Xi through to Fukuzawa Yukichi in late nineteenth-century Japan, see DEBARY and BLOOM 1979.

92. My interpretation here follows closely that of YOSHIKAWA 1983, 80, 155, 161.

93. YOSHIKAWA 1975, 80, expresses his understanding of *kaku* as 自己のものとしてやって来るように. The English translation renders that phrase as "assimilating oneself with" things (YOSHIKAWA 1983, 80) whereas my description avoids a straight translation in favor of a more nuanced explanation of Yoshikawa's interpretation.

In any case, the point is that Sorai rejects the idea that we should investigate things as something outside us, a type of disengaged, detached knowing. Instead, we should let ourselves be impressed by them so we can express ourselves through them. In this regard, his point is akin to Dōgen's saying: "To practice-authenticate all things by conveying yourself to them is delusion. Realization is for all things to come forward, practicing-authenticating you." NST 12: 35; DZZ 1: 2. I discussed that passage on pages 223-4.

94. Trans. based on OGYŪ 2006, 166.

95. Sorai was a student of both Chinese history and, to a lesser extent, Japanese history. Since the ancient ways have to be adjusted to modern circumstances, future rulers need to understand how present circumstances came to be. For that, the study of history

is vital. Sorai concludes *Distinguishing the Way* with the following conciliatory words toward some of his philosophical adversaries:

> Ancient and modern times are distant. (Parts of) the Six Classics are corrupt. Essentially, we cannot avoid making inferences (about the Six Classics) on the basis of their principles.… If we make our inferences more and more refined, how would we possibly make the mistakes of the Song Confucians and the various other scholars? Moreover, the way of scholarship esteems thought. When we think about these matters, even the words of the Daoists and Buddhists, along with all others, must be considered worthy of serving as our aids. How much more so is this true of the accounts of the Song Confucians and various other scholars? (Trans. in OGYŪ 2006, 167.)

96. For an interpretation of Sorai's account of this case, see MARUYAMA 1974, 70–1.

97. Trans. based on MARUYAMA 1974, 110–11.

98. See OGYŪ 1962, 132–44, for excerpts of Sorai's proposals on educating samurai.

99. Trans. based on YOSHIKAWA 1983, 90.

100. Trans. based on MARUYAMA 1974, 132.

101. Trans. in YAMASHITA 1994, 41–2.

102. Trans. in MARUYAMA 1974, 98.

10. MOTOORI Norinaga 本居宣長 (1730–1801)

103. Trans. based on YOSHIKAWA 1983, 268.

104. Norinaga did later write briefly about the meeting, but his wording signals to scholars that his account of what Mabuchi said cannot be accurate since it uses terms Mabuchi, to our knowledge, never used. Either Norinaga consciously embellished what Mabuchi said in order to make it seem he supported the *Kojiki* project more than he actually did or perhaps it simply reports what Norinaga heard Mabuchi to say, even though Mabuchi did not actually say that. For a good analysis of the main points at issue in Norinaga's account, see NOSCO 1990, 174–7.

105. Trans. based on NOSCO 1990, 130.

106. For a more detailed discussion of the complicated relation between Norinaga and Mabuchi, including some brief quotes from Mabuchi's letters, see MATSUMOTO 1970, 68–76.

107. See MATSUMOTO 1970, 13–16, for more details about his relation to the *kami* Mikumari.

108. Scholars have discovered Norinaga's handwritten notebooks on Sorai's philosophy. See the comment in MOTOORI 1997, 3, and Sey Nishimura's reference to Ōno Susumu's discussion of the matter.

109. Trans. in SJT-2, 507.

110. I mentioned in Chapter 4, pages 144–5, that today many Japanese think of the Heian period as the epitome of Japanese high culture and aesthetic elegance. To a great extent, that is a result of Norinaga's construction of Japan's cultural history. One could

well argue that Norinaga, more than any other premodern figure, influenced what became the mainstream interpretation of the history of Japanese literary culture.

111. The term found in *The Tale of Genji* is just *"aware"* rather than *"mono no aware."* By the mid-Tokugawa period, the term had lost many of the aesthetic nuances important to the Heian culture as Norinaga understood it and had come to be associated only with sadness and grief. Thus, it had become a term of affective subjectivity, having lost its sense of being a resonance between things and persons. In light of that situation, Norinaga added the *mono no* ("of things") to the term to capture the sense of the original Heian use and dissociate it from the idiom of his day. See entry *"mono no aware"* in *Kodansha Encyclopedia of Japan*.

112. Trans. in NOSCO 1990, 178.

113. Trans. in MOTOORI 1987, 483.

114. Trans. in NOSCO 1990, 180 *fn*. 33.

115. Trans. in YOSHIKAWA 1983, 272.

116. AYER 1952, 107–8.

117. WITTGENSTEIN 1961, 151.

118. In his book, *On the Way to Language* the philosopher Martin Heidegger relates a fictionalized dialogue with a Japanese (presumably, the young philosopher, Kuki Shūzō). (See pages 471–2.) Their conversation focuses on the philosophical nature of language (HEIDEGGER 1971, 1–56). The Japanese view of language presented in the essay, "A Dialogue on Language between a Japanese and an Inquirer," is basically like what we find here in Norinaga.

For a provocative comparative study of how language is used in Pure Land Buddhism with reference to Heideggerian ideas, see HIROTA 2006.

119. This is the translation found in AMES and ROSEMONT 1999, 78.

120. The original Chinese is 温故而知新、可以為師矣. Taken literally the characters mean approximately "cherish-old-and-know-new; can-befit-a teacher." Other English translations illustrate the point just as well. Edward Slingerland translates it as "Both keeping past teachings alive and understanding the present—someone able to do this is worthy of being a teacher" (CONFUCIUS 2003, 11), whereas Arthur Waley renders it, "He who by reanimating the Old can gain knowledge of the New is fit to be a teacher" (CONFUCIUS 1938, 11). Clearly, there is no serious disagreement over the meaning and each translation into English must in a similar way add words that do not correspond one-to-one with each original sinograph.

121. The website interprets it in modern colloquial Japanese as「昔の出来事や学説を研究して、現在にも通じる新しいものを発見すれば指導する立場になれるだろう」 (http://ja.wikibooks.org/wiki/中学校国語＿漢文/温故知新, accessed December 27, 2014).

122. It is noteworthy that Japanese uses an array of sentence-ending particles (*joshi*) like *ne, wa, nee, zo, kana, kashira, yo*, *ya*, and so forth to express the affective aspect often relegated to intonation in spoken English. In Japanese, however, these are linguistic units in the sentence that can be used in written as well as spoken Japanese. As a result, although limited to a mere seventeen syllables, Japanese *haiku* often reserve a few of those precious syllables for such sentence-ending particles because they are so effective in helping the reader enter the shared *kokoro* expressed by the poet, the words,

and the phenomena. For further discussion of aspects of the Japanese language relevant to philosophy, see "About the Japanese language" in the "Pointers" section of this book, pages 685-95.

123. Trans. based on YOSHIKAWA 1983, 268.

124. In speaking of words (*kotoba*), behavior (*waza*), and mind (*kokoro*), Norinaga's analysis follows the structure of the Buddhist analysis of personal action as involving word, deed, and thought. Norinaga's argument, like Kūkai's concerning the three intimacies, is that the three dimensions are so interlinked you can engage all three via any one of them.

125. MOTOORI 1987, 475–6.

126. Trans. in SJT-2, 509.

127. Trans. in YOSHIKAWA 1983, 268.

128. Because the Native Studies movement emphasized the naturalness of sentimentality over the regulative mentality of Confucianism, it was commonly accused of being a disguised form of Daoism. Mabuchi, in fact, drew directly on Daoist sources in his critiques of Confucianism. See NOSCO 1990, 142–3.

Norinaga vigorously denied the association, however, believing the Daoists renounced not only rationalism, but also culture itself. From Norinaga's standpoint, the Daoists had in effect developed a counter-ideology just as dangerous as the ideology they criticized, making their emphasis on the natural into an "-ism," a naturalism labeling all human production as artificial.

129. See HAROOTUNIAN 1988, 114–17, for a discussion of the idealized society envisioned by Norinaga.

130. Trans. in YOSHIKAWA 1983, 273.

131. "The basic function of the *uta* [Japanese ode or poem] is not to assist in government, nor is it intended to improve the person. It is the outward expression of thoughts in the mind and nothing else." Trans. in SJT-2, 505.

132. NOSCO 1990, 170.

133. Trans. in MARUYAMA 1974, 168.

Note that I am here discussing merely Norinaga's sense of *ideal* community. When addressing the shogunate structure in place during his time, he was explicitly supportive of it. The latter decades of the eighteenth century were politically unstable and hardly progressive. Tokugawa power was waning. Peasant uprisings, sometimes joined by townspeople, were increasingly frequent.

In 1790 the Tokugawa shogunate issued the Kansei Edict forbidding all philosophies except the strain of neo-Confucianism taught in the shogunate's official academy. Although the Edict had little practical effect, it was a sign of increasing political and social insecurity. In that volatile context, Norinaga's invocation of the "ancient Way" was straightforward and conservative—the people should follow the rule of the emperor unquestioningly:

> In ancient times, all the Japanese people, down to the lowest subjects, wholeheartedly followed the will of the emperor and devotedly respected his decrees. And under his gracious shelter, they also worshiped their respective ancestor-kami. Thus the people, doing properly what they ought to do, lived in this world quite

peacefully and happily. Can there be anything more than this to be especially taught and practiced as the Way? (Trans. in MATSUMOTO 1970, 103.)

From Norinaga's standpoint, the Japanese emperor was *kami* and as such beyond the human criteria of good and evil. If the emperor performed what seemed to us evil, that was irrelevant and we should continue to be loyal and obedient. In contrast with the Confucian theory developed by Mencius, for Norinaga a revolution against the emperor could never be justified under any circumstances.

How then did he evaluate the Tokugawa shōgun's claim to political entitlement? Again, Norinaga took a conservative position. Referring to Tokugawa Ieyasu by his posthumous title as a *kami*, "Azumateru kamumioya no mikoto," Norinaga praised him for his loyalty to the emperor and for serving the imperial family so well. In so doing, Norinaga granted the Tokugawa shogunate legitimacy, but only a legitimacy derivative of the imperial family's authority.

In 1787 Norinaga responded to a daimyō's request to write a treatise on the social and political aspects of the ancient Way. In that work, *Hihon tamakushige*, Norinaga mentioned the increasing number of uprisings and blamed not the common people, but their masters, for the problem. He argued that the peasants would, if properly ruled and their needs met, be subservient to their lords. Oddly, this was similar to Sorai's position decades earlier. (See page 367.) "Each uprising was the fault not of the people below but exclusively of those above." (Trans. in MATSUMOTO 1970, 152.) This did not justify the peasant uprisings, but neither did it blame the peasants for their unruliness. In effect, Norinaga criticized the revolts but in a way that would not justify any further oppression of the peasantry. For translations of some of Norinaga's key works see Norinaga 1987, 1988, 1991, and 1997.

134. Of course, as is commonly the case for such a complex and historically crucial text, especially when someone claims to be interpreting literally, it is still a matter of scholarly debate how much of Norinaga's reading was simple exegesis (extracting meaning from the text) and how much eisegesis (inserting one's own meaning into the text).

135. Norinaga's term returns to the ancient Japanese pronunciation: *inishie no michi* and is often written in the syllabary to avoid using sinographs. The Chinese term in its sinified Japanese pronunciation is *kodō* 古道, a Confucian word referring to the Way of the Chinese ancients (or of the sages in the case of Sorai).

136. YOSHIKAWA 1983, 279.

137. The following passage from *Uiyamabumi* is one of many that make the connection between the Age of *Kami* and classical poetry:

> The Way of the Gods contains no trace of Confucian or Buddhist logic that crudely judges good and evil, right and wrong. The Way is simply abundant, elegant, and expansive in nature, and the poetic style of Man'yoshu accords with it particularly well. (Trans. in NORINAGA 1987, 476.)

138. Norinaga stated this point as follows:

> Almost every man, no matter how intelligent he may be, is not much different from women and children if we search into the depth of his mindful heart. All beings are thus effeminate and frail. (Trans. in YOSHIKAWA 1983, 270.)

[That men have become alienated from their true natures] is attributable to the temperament of the samurai class in recent ages and also the arguments of the Chinese Confucians. (*ibid.*)

139. See Yoshikawa 1983, 270, for a discussion of this point with relevant quotes.

THE MODERN PERIOD

11. Black Ships, Black Rain

1. Tayama Katai, from his story "One Soldier," written in 1908, based on his experience in the Russo-Japanese War. Translated by G. W. Sargent in Keene 1956, 150.

2. Any stipulated date is just that—a stipulation. Depending on your interests, you could easily find signs of modernity back to the early Edo period: urbanization, development of a regulated market system, high literacy, secularization, and so forth. For that reason, the Edo period is now commonly called "Early Modern Japan."

For a history of philosophy, however, that nomenclature might be more confusing than helpful since "modern Japanese philosophy" (*gendai nihon tetsugaku*) has a fixed meaning in the discipline to refer to thought after the major influx of western philosophy in the post-1868 era. That is also the point when philosophy became its own discipline in Japanese universities. Hence, in speaking of philosophy, an "early modern thinker" would be someone from the Meiji period (1868–1912), not from the "Early Modern" period of Edo. To avoid that confusion (similar to the type that arises when a philosopher and a literature scholar talk about "modernism" in the West), in this book I do not use the nomenclature of "Early Modern" to designate the time before 1868.

3. Note the Confucian elements in both Ōshio's analysis of the problem and his justification for reacting violently:

> Forgetting the "humaneness that unites all beings as one body," the officials of the Osaka magistrate's office are conducting the government for their own selfish ends. They send tribute rice to Edo, but they send none to Kyoto, where the emperor himself resides. On top of this, in recent years the moneyed merchants of Osaka have accumulated vast profits from interest on loans to the daimyō and appropriated great quantities of rice, living a life of unheard-of luxury.... Knowing no want themselves, they have lost all fear of Heaven's punishment and make no attempt to save those who are begging and starving to death on the streets.... (Trans. in sjt-2, 560.)

In that passage we find a general Confucian value that those higher in the political hierarchy should care for the interests of those below. In this following passage we find a specific reference to the Yomeigaku emphasis on the innate knowledge of good.

> In studying the Way of the sages, we entrust everything to our innate knowledge of the good. Therefore we are like someone crazed (*kyōsha*) in our efforts to make public what we perceive to be right and wrong. Accordingly, we have no way of telling how much trouble from other people this will bring upon us. Nevertheless, to end up diminishing our sensitivity to right and wrong just because we are afraid of the trouble it will cause us is something that a man of character (*jōfu*) would

consider shameful. And what honor (*menboku*) would we have to be able to meet the sages in the afterlife? Therefore, I concern myself with nothing but following my resolve (*kokorozashi*). (Trans. in SJT-2, 565.)

4. Of course, Atsutane was not Norinaga's only early critic among the Native Studies thinkers. For example, Fujitani Mitsue (1768–1823) challenged Norinaga for his naïve literalism in reading *Kojiki*. (See JPS, 493–508.) Mitsue introduced a hermeneutical criterion somewhat like Rudolf Bultmann's "form criticism" for reading the Bible in the twentieth-century West. That is, Mitsue said that we must distinguish the different *forms* statements might take in a text like *Kojiki*: many might be straightforwardly historical, but others might be metaphorical, for example. The truth of *Kojiki* must be evaluated in light of such different genres. Mitsue was also critical of Norinaga's idea that morality would flow naturally without instruction as long as one had a genuine mindful heart.

5. A fascinating and well-researched example of Atsutane's methods and assumptions can be found in Wilbur Hansen's *When Tengu Talk*. *Tengu* are mountain goblins and Hansen's book concerns Atsutane's own account of his encounters with the *"Tengu* Boy," Torakichi, a fourteen-year old who claimed he had been raised by *tengu* for eight years. Torakichi became for Atsutane a key informant about "the other world" and the beliefs and practices of itinerant, mystical "mountain people" (*sanjin*). See HANSEN 2008.

6. I explore the philosophical differences in a bit more detail in KASULIS 2004, 119–30. An outstanding Japanese resource for comparing Norinaga and Atsutane is KOYASU 1977. HANSEN 2008 compares differences between the two Native Studies thinkers that are brief but sound and to the point. HAROOTUNIAN 1988 gives a stimulating discourse and ideological analysis of Native Studies in which Atsutane and Ikuta Yorozu figure prominently along with Norinaga. That book is somewhat controversial among scholars who find Harootunian's readings of some texts to be tendentious and misleading. I agree in part with that evaluation, but still believe the book's basic argument is sophisticated and merits serious consideration. For shedding light on the philosophical concerns of my account, however, Harootunian does not analyze enough the differences between Norinaga and Atsutane on issues of language, ethnocentrism, violence, and metaphysics.

7. HANSEN 2008 *passim* gives several references to points in Atsutane's theories that were likely culled from his access to Christian sources.

8. For a description of those conditions, see MCCLAIN 2002, 248–56.

9. Some 2000 schools were destroyed in the riots. See GORDON 2003, 68.

10. See GORDON 2003, 78–9; SJT-2, 671–2; GOTO-JONES 2009, 54–5; MCCLAIN 2002, 155–7. Of these quality histories of modern Japan, Goto-Jones is the most succinct, and also the most sensitive to influences on philosophical thinking. PIOVESANA and YAMAWAKI 1997 (revised) is the classic starting point for an overview of Japanese philosophy in the modern period.

11. This way of approaching western philosophy, we may note, would relegate it to a subordinate place in Japanese culture at large. Here we have a seldom considered twist on the claim there was no *philosophy* in Japan before the western tradition was imported in the latter nineteenth century. Namely, when we compare western philosophy to that of Buddhism, Confucianism, and Native Studies, the Asian philosophies are more inclusive, touching on all dimensions of being human: our practices as well as our theories,

our feelings as well as our intellect, our poetry as well as our prose, our character as well as our rules of good behavior. So, philosophy in the western sense seems to be too narrowly academic to be placed alongside the richer tradition of the Asian Ways.

If western philosophy had entered Japan before the western Enlightenment, that is, before it had become an academic discipline in European universities, the Japanese might have accepted it as more akin to their own thought in the premodern period. In some respects it is fair to say, premodern Japanese philosophy and premodern (ancient and medieval) western philosophy have more in common than either have with modern western philosophy. See my Conclusion to this book for a fuller argument.

12. For a thorough and well-balanced historical analysis of the Buddhist persecutions during the Meiji period as well as the various ways Buddhist institutions and individuals navigated those dangerous waters, see KETELAAR 1990.

13. For details see KETELAAR 1990, 46–65.

14. The rise of State Shintō ideology and the division into "sect" and "shrine" Shintō is too complex to discuss here. For an overview of the relation of Shintō to the state ideology and the philosophical ideas behind it, see KASULIS 2004, 119–40. For a fuller and more nuanced discussion, including the reactions among the general populace, see HARDACRE 1989.

15. The "scientific" and therefore "modern" aspects of Buddhism were often highly touted in the Meiji period, partly in defense of its place in the "new" Japan of the times. Even when D. T. Suzuki's Zen master, Shaku Sōen (1859–1919), gave his lecture at the World Parliament of Religions in Chicago in 1893, he emphasized the "scientific" character of the Buddha's theory of conditioned co-production (dependent origination).

16. Inoue Enryō on this point is likely indebted to the Huayan (J. Kegon) analysis of the four phenomenal worlds developed by Dushun in China. (See page 93.) Inoue's characterization of "principle *soku* matter-mind" is like Dushun's theory that on the deepest level, principle disappears altogether into the interpenetration of thing and thing (C. *shishiwuai*; J. *jijimuge*). Perhaps this explains why Inoue Enryō placed the Kegon Buddhist Shaku Gyōnen in his "Arbor of Three Teachings" to represent Japanese Buddhism. See note 18 below.

17. Kapila was an ancient Indian sage, traditionally associated with the founding of the Sāṃkhya school of orthodox (Hindu) philosophy.

18. Shaku Gyōnen (1240–1321) was a Kegon monk scholar of the Kamakura period who could be considered one of Japan's earliest "buddhologists" in that he wrote extensively and fairly about all the Buddhist groups of his time (the Six Nara Schools, Shingon, and Kegon). See GYŌNEN 1994.

19. Inoue maintained that religion and philosophy are not fully discrete but rather overlapping circles of internal relation. Thus, much of philosophy is not religion and much of religion is not philosophy. Nonetheless, they overlap and we can talk about, for example, either the "philosophical" or the "religious" part of Buddhism. See his diagram of that internal relation in JPS, 620.

20. Before Inoue Tetsujirō's efforts, dictionaries had been not much more than glossary lists of Japanese equivalents to western philosophical terms. Inoue's editions, by

contrast, included definitions—some quite extensive—that were often contributed by Japan's leading authorities on the topic.

21. Despite Inoue's original plan, philosophy departments in Japan often ended up having Indian and Chinese philosophy taught in separate programs from western philosophy. The study of Japanese philosophy, by contrast, came to be sprinkled across the departments of the History of Japanese Thought, Ethics, Buddhist Studies, and Aesthetics. The ramifications on the development of Japanese academic philosophy will be explored in my Conclusion.

22. An excellent and succinct explanation of Inoue Tetsujirō's theory is WARGO 2005, 17–25. Here I am giving only the most general description of the issue for the sake of explaining a general problematic that runs through the thinking of many modern Japanese philosophers.

23. Although, to my knowledge, no Japanese philosopher ever attempted to make a formal system of logic based on *soku,* it seems like it could be done. Indeed, the skeleton of such a system has been presented in JONES 2004.

24. This statement seems to be a hybrid between the *Kojiki* account of creation and Sorai's theory about the relation between the ancient Chinese virtues and the ancient sage kings. *Kojiki* says nothing about the *kami* as planting virtues and Sorai said nothing about the creation of Japan along the lines presented here.

25. A proof text for this was Ōshio's rationale for the Osaka uprising quoted in note 3 on page 660. Ōshio criticized the government's hoarding rice for itself while sending "none to Kyoto, where the emperor himself resides." Ōshio is implying the emperor's status was being demeaned by the shogunate, a righteous reason to rebel.

26. Around this time it is said Inoue's colleague in Tokyo Imperial University's philosophy department, Raphael von Koeber, a man known for his acerbic tongue, said of Inoue Tetsujirō: "He's not a bad man, just stupid." See KUMANO 2009, 29.

27. Inoue would later turn against utilitarianism in favor of the Confucian virtues highlighted in his three-volume study of Japanese Edo-period Confucianism. Still later, once the German idealist tradition had taken hold in Japan, neo-Kantianism would be the western tradition Inoue most used to buttress his analysis of Japanese values.

28. For a discussion of the philosophical aspects of Japanese identity as filtered through language, politics, and religion, see JPS, 1005–99.

29. Inoue had also criticized Christianity on the grounds of individual statements, most taken out of context, that seem to place God above everything else including loyalty to family or state. Ōnishi's response to those criticisms was twofold. First, he pointed to different biblical passages that emphasized the idea that God's kingdom is "not of this world" and hence, by definition, cannot be a competitor to any kingdom in this world. As he put it:

> To say that Christianity has not any especial tendencies toward the State is different from saying it is completely against the State. *Not* is quite different from *against.* (Trans. based on KŌSAKA 1958, 260.)

Ōnishi then argued that Christianity presents for Japan a new kind of thinking and that the real conflict is not between Japanese morality and religion, but between an antiquated conservative thinking represented by people like Inoue and a new universal thinking represented by Christianity (as well as Buddhism).

30. I do not think Inoue Enryō was trying to unify the two as much as claim that originally the two were not separate. That is, I suspect he was trying to formulate a position that emerges from the *in medias res* in which there is no such bifurcation. For my explanation of the *in medias res* form of analysis, see Chapter 1, pages 39–41. See also the philosophy of Watsuji Tetsurō, the focus of Chapter 13. More than most other Japanese philosophers, Watsuji not only uses the *in-the-midst* form of analysis, but also justifies it.

31. For a sampling of translated pieces from the journal *Seitō*, see BARDSLEY 2007.

12. NISHIDA Kitarō 西田幾多郎 (1870–1945)

32. An outstanding intellectual biography of Nishida is YUSA 2002. Pages 41–4 include a translation of Nishida's reminiscence about his days as a special student.

33. Yusa explains how sales of Nishida's book rose sharply after Kurata wrote of the work with such unbridled enthusiasm as the following:

> In the arid, stagnant Japanese philosophical world, shamelessly filled with the smell of worldliness, he whose work gives us pure joy, moral support, and even a slight sense of surprise is Mr. Nishida Kitarō. His work is like the finely scented pale blue bellflowers growing out of the dried-up, sterile earth in the mountain shadows. (Trans. in YUSA 2002, 130.)

34. For a helpful and probing overview of Nishida's thought throughout his career, including an up-to-date bibliography, see John C. Maraldo's entry in the on-line *Stanford Encyclopedia of Philosophy* (MARALDO 2012).

35. For a succinct and insightful synopsis of the Kyoto School, see DAVIS 2012.

36. Moreover, having only special student status, Nishida was not the close protégé of any prominent philosopher. Japan traditionally values the so-called *onshi-deshi* relation of master and disciple that is especially strong within academic and artistic contexts. Although Nishida himself did not have an *onshi* in his own university years, he became the beloved *onshi* of many advanced philosophy students at Kyoto University, undoubtedly one reason a school of philosophy grew up around him.

37. Nishida did take up later the issue of the meaning and function of *soku*, particularly when inspired by an essay written by his friend, D. T. Suzuki (Suzuki Daisetsu). See JPS, 214–18.

38. Trans. from NKZ 3: 255.

39. This passage is condensed from NKZ 9: 461–3 and 406. It was been abridged and translated by James Heisig, whose translation (with a few small adjustments for consistency with my text) has been followed here. See HEISIG 2015, 156–7.

40. YUSA 2002, 69.

41. The *mu* kōan, from the time of Hakuin at least, became a major part of Rinzai Zen praxis in Japan. The source of the kōan is the anecdote of the Chinese Zen master, Zhaozhou (778–897). When asked whether a dog has buddha-nature, he responded "*Mu!*" In the Kyoto school the term *mu* is usually interpreted as "nothingness" but its

general meaning also extends to "nonbeing" or even the negative "no." The term would become central to the mainline of Kyoto School philosophers, starting with Nishida and continuing through Tanabe Hajime, Nishitani Keiji, and Ueda Shizuteru. See JPS, 643. For a focused treatment on nothingness in the Kyoto School, see HEISIG 2001. For my brief discussion of the *mu* kōan in Hakuin's regimen of Zen praxis, see KASULIS 1981, 118–19.

42. These comments were in a letter to Nishitani Keiji in 1943. For a fuller context of the quote, see the paragraph translated in YUSA 2002, xx. The original letter can be found in NKZ 23: 73.

43. Trans. in YUSA 2002, 97.

44. Although the main argument is strikingly like Dōgen's analysis of thinking/not-thinking/without-thinking, there is no evidence that Nishida ever read Dōgen. That may be an influence from D. T. Suzuki, Nishida's friend since childhood and his guide for most things Zen. I have heard first-hand reports from two people referring to two different occasions when Suzuki was dismissive in a conversation about Dōgen, saying there was no need to study him "since he was not enlightened." Whatever the truth of that may be, Dōgen became very popular among Nishida's major students such as Nishitani Keiji.

45. Nishida says the following in his *Inquiry* chapter on "Thinking":

Probably everyone agrees that the primordial state of our consciousness and the immediate state of developing consciousness are at all times states of pure experience. The activity of reflective thinking arises secondarily out of this. ... Consciousness, as stated above, is fundamentally a single system; its nature is to develop and complete itself. In the course of its development various conflicts and contradictions crop up in the system, and out of this emerges reflective thinking. But when viewed from a different angle, that which is contradictory and conflicted is the beginning of still greater systematic development; it is the incomplete state of a greater unity.... [T]he groundwork of a great unity has been laid. (Trans. in NISHIDA 1990, 16.)

46. Trans. in NISHIDA 1990, 142; NKZ I: 131.

47. Trans. in NISHIDA 1990, 28.

48. Trans. from NKZ 1: 28; see also NISHIDA 1990, 19.

49. Trans. in NISHIDA 1990, 59.

50. As we saw even in Kūkai, an adequate view of reality must include even wrong views of reality. However erroneous, they still exist as real views.

51. Robert J. J. Wargo summarizes the key ones and gives the gist of Nishida's response in each case. See WARGO 2005, 53–6.

52. Let's do consider at least one comparison with Kūkai, however brief. As I suggested in Chapter 3, I think Kūkai was a major reason the engaged form of knowing took root so deeply in subsequent Japanese thought. Indeed, it was so entrenched that it has become almost second nature in the thinking process of most subsequent Japanese philosophers. As westerners may commonly use the concept of *potential* for example, that does not imply they all know it to be originally an Aristotelian idea. That may be like what happened to Nishida in this. I will offer here just one of many possible parallels: Kūkai's understanding of Dainichi and Nishida's of God.

I'll begin by reviewing a few key points from Kūkai's system. Reality (the-cosmos-as-buddha and buddha-as-cosmos) consists of three interlinked activities: thought, word, and deed. Since those functions or intimacies exhaust the meaning of Dainichi-in-himself, Dainichi is, in effect, the unity of the three interrelated intimacies (*sanmitsu soku ichimitsu* as Kūkai, put it). When we humans think of our own thoughts, words, and deeds, we call it *experience* and when we think of Dainichi's thoughts, words, and deeds, we call it *reality*. In that sense we can say that reality, as Dainichi, is one unified experience and that as individuals we are a subset of that experience. As Nishida claimed, because there is experience, we are individuals, not vice versa.

For Kūkai, reality as Dainichi's experience is intrinsically in harmony with itself (what Nishida's calls "unity"?), but very often *our* experience is not; we are in disharmony, what Buddhism calls delusion, the source of our anguish. Accordingly, our goal is to reharmonize our subset of reality with reality itself, to re-attune ourselves as part of the universe.

A comparison between Kūkai's Shingon system and Nishida's theory of pure experience may seem far-fetched. For reasons I will explain in a moment, no one more than Nishida would find it so. Yet, before we abandon it as pure fancy, consider these following quotes from *Inquiry* wherein Nishida characterizes God in relation to the unifying factor in pure experience. As the following four excerpts show, Nishida's philosophical description of God approaches Kūkai's characterization of Dainichi Buddha.

> …God is the foundation of the universe… [not] a transcendent creator outside the universe, for God is the base of this reality. …The universe is not a creation of God but a manifestation [or "expression" as Kūkai would say?] of God.…

> Construed in terms of the auto-awareness in God's personality, each of the unities in the phenomena of the universe is none other than God's auto-awareness.…

> Granting that facts of pure experience are the sole reality and that God is their unity, we can know God's characteristics and relation to the world from the characteristics of the unity of our pure experience or the unity of consciousness, and from the relation of that unity to its content. [cf. our experience of unity within us reflects the unity of cosmos-as-buddha—an experiential holographic entry point?].…

> Considering the relation between the world and God in the above way, how should we explain individuality? … Although there is probably no independent individuality separate from God, our individuality should not be regarded as a mere phantasm; rather, it is part of God's development, one of God's activities of differentiation.… The relation between God and our individual consciousness is the relation between the entirety of consciousness and one part of it. In all mental phenomena, each part stands in the unity of the whole, and at the same time each must be an independent consciousness.[cf. the holographic relation between Dainichi and individual?] (Trans. in Nishida 1990, 158, 162, 167, 170.)

The parallelism with Kūkai casts Nishida's theory in a new light. First, the similarity between Nishida and Kūkai is all the more striking since Nishida's *Inquiry* made no mention of earlier Japanese thinkers or even of general Buddhist principles. Nishida framed his philosophical problem and proposed solution strictly in western terms. Did he have the Asian ideas in mind, but just, for whatever reason, decided not to mention them? Not necessarily.

To my knowledge, Nishida was unfamiliar with Kūkai's thought. Admittedly, because of the historical connection of esotericism through Tendai Buddhism and then into Zen, some esoteric Buddhist ideas likely drifted into the vocabulary of his Zen praxis, others perhaps in communications with his friend, D. T. Suzuki. Because at the outset of the modern period there was no academic call to study the history of Japanese philosophy, however, there was no academic reason for Nishida to look for such connections and make them explicit, certainly not in the way he was expected to treat western philosophical ideas.

53. Nishida seems not to have quoted Bergson on the two kinds of knowing, but he knew Bergson's *Introduction to Metaphysics* and the book's first page contains the quotation I gave on page 42.

54. James Heisig was the first to translate *kōiteki chokkan* as "performative intuition" (HEISIG 2015, 177). I previously had used "acting intuition," others "active intuition," but I think "performative intuition" better captures Nishida's intent. See also note 64 below.

55. Trans. based on NISHIDA 1987A, xxxii–xxxiii.

56. Actually, Nishida does use the term *jikaku* in *Inquiry* toward the end of the book, particularly in his discussion of *God*. He uses it as a general term for describing self-consciousness, however, only in his subsequent works.

57. Nishida's later concern for "historical reality" probably also had its roots in his reading of the neo-Kantians, but he did not focus on that issue at the time of this initial reading of them.

58. Trans. in NISHIDA 1987A, xxiii.

59. *Ibid.*

60. Consider what Nishida says about logic in 1945, the last year of his life:

Aristotelian logic appears to be the formulation of the linguistic self-expression of a world expressing itself symbolically—logic par excellence. Kant's own transcendental logic is no longer Aristotle's. And Hegel's dialectical logic stands opposed to what Aristotle took the discipline of logic to be. Contradiction is not permitted in Aristotelian logic, while in a dialectical logic, it is the proper formulation of self-development. Are not the logics of Kant and Hegel logic? We have to try giving some thought to what logic is. It is a formulation of our thinking. To make clear what logic is, we have to begin from the essence of our thinking. (JPS, 669.)

61. Nishida's position is not something completely new in the history of Japanese thought either. To find premodern parallels, we need only think of Kūkai's mapping of the ten mindsets (see pages 129–34) or Dōgen's characterization of what the ocean means as experienced from different standpoints (see pages 228–30). In both cases the philosopher focuses on the mindset (in Kūkai's case) or the context (in Dōgen's case) that leads to a particular judgment.

62. To draw a parallel again, in his ten mindset theory, the inability of a particular mindset to give the foundation for itself was, for Kūkai, what can propel a person from one mindset into the next, more inclusive, mindset. (See pages 133–4.)

63. One scientific method that "removes" the input of subjectivity is to have others

redo or replicate the observation. In effect, it replaces a subjective "I" with a subjective "we." When the "we" is large and diverse enough, we call it "objective." The "I" of the *basho* of relative nothingness then cloaks itself in that "we" of the scientific community that takes its place within the *basho* of being.

Up to this point Nishida's analysis is quite compatible with Husserl's phenomenology. However, in the next step, the transition to the *basho* of absolute nothing, they part ways. Nishida feels that he must diverge from the typical phenomenological model because, in the end, Husserl's theory remains an idealism in opposition to a realism. Nishida seeks the originary ground out of which that opposition emerges.

64. Again, translation is important. *Kōiteki chokkan* was once commonly translated "active intuition" but that rendering is ambiguous because it might seem to be in contrast with "passive intuition." In Japanese the root of the adjectival form *kōiteki* is *kōi* which means "action" in the sense of conduct or deed, not active as contrasted with passive (which is a different adjective, *katsudōteki*). Hence, we have the improved translation as *performative intuition* or, as suggested by John Maraldo in some of his writings, "the action-directed intuition." See note 54 above.

65. The most thorough treatment of Nishida's logic of the predicate in English is Wargo 2005.

66. For an excellent description and analysis of Nishida's notion of the mirroring aspect of self-awareness, see MARALDO 2006. For a detailed and remarkably clear account of Nishida's overall notion of self-awareness as a cornerstone in his thinking, see ODAGIRI 2008.

67. Note again that Nishida is unknowingly following the line of analysis that Kūkai took when he realized that reality must in some sense be conscious. That led to Kūkai's characterization of what I called the "proprioceptive cosmos." (See pages 126–9.) Alternatively, one could say Nishida's move from self-consciousness to auto-awareness parallels Shinran's from one's own power (*jiriki*) to auto-power as *jinen*, "happening naturally of its own accord." (See page 204.)

I wonder if on some subliminal level, Nishida may have sensed this compatibility with the Japanese Buddhist philosophers when he chose to use *kaku* for "awareness," a term meaning awakening or enlightenment in the East Asian Buddhist lexicon. (It is, for example, the *kaku* in the distinction between *shi-kaku* and *hon-gaku* [initialized vs. inherent enlightenment]. See my explanation on pages 151–2.)

In drawing on Royce's conception of consciousness as a self-mirroring, recursive system, Nishida again approaches the ideas of some premodern Japanese thinkers, especially Kūkai, but occasionally Nishida seems to slip into speaking of the self as *doing* something (perhaps a remnant of his former preoccupation with the German idealist focus on the will?). Technically, of course, that is not what his system implies. In Shinran's terms, on Nishida's deepest level (his third *basho*, or what he starts calling the "noumenal world"), the *ji* (自) must always mean "self" in the sense of "auto-" (*onozukara*) and not "self" in the sense of the "self" as oneself (*mizukara*) or as autonomous agent (*jiko*).

68. For an English translation, see KUKI 1997.

69. For an excellent treatment of Tanabe's philosophy, including his debates with Nishida, see HEISIG 2001.

70. In his own logic of the specific, Tanabe in effect puts the negating, dialectical function of *mu* on the level of relative nothingness, thus obviating the need for Nishida's *basho* of absolute nothing. As Tanabe puts it:

> Since the absolute, as nothingness, must act as an absolute mediating force, it presupposes relative being as its medium. In contrast with the doctrine of the creation of the world maintained by the theist, or the theory of emanation propounded by the pantheist, historical thinking must begin from present historical reality in order to reconstruct reality in practice…. For historical thinking, the absolute and the relative, nothingness and being, are interrelated each with the other as indispensable elements of absolute mediation. (Trans. in TANABE 1986, 23.)

71. NKZ 4: 141. For a good discussion of this concept as it appears in Nishida's middle period, see ODAGIRI 2008.

72. For translations of some of those latter writings, see NISHIDA 1986 and 1987B.

13. WATSUJI Tetsurō 和辻哲郎 (1889–1960)

73. Watsuji's own account of this episode can be found in WATSUJI 2012, 10.

74. This "return to origins" was rampant in western thought at the time. For example, some linguists searched for the *Ursprache* out of which all languages evolved and Martin Heidegger delved into the pre-Socratics for the source and meaning of philosophy.

75. Trans. in LAFLEUR 1990, 250–1.

76. One point that LaFleur does not make but is worth mentioning here is that Watsuji's "restoring the idols" was in no way an act of personal religious commitment. Like Nietzsche, Watsuji understood himself as restoring cultural and artistic artifacts, not objects of devotion. He even thought the state should take possession of the Buddhist images and preserve them in a museum, much to the consternation of the temple communities that had revered them for over a millennium. See the discussion of this event by one of Watsuji's main disciples, Yuasa Yasuo, in Watsuji 1996, 312.

77. See the discussion in LAFLEUR 1990, 254–5.

78. Trans. in WATSUJI 2011. For the original see WTZ 4: 156–246.

79. Trans. in WATSUJI 2011, 28.

80. 『イタリア古寺巡礼』, WTZ 8: 257–407.

81. Husserl referred to phenomenology as "a pure science" (*eine reine Wissenschaft*).

82. Heidegger came to disassociate himself from the European movement of existentialism as it had come to be defined. For the introductory purpose of this account and for our interest in how Watsuji interpreted Heidegger, however, the link with the earlier "existentialists" that Watsuji had studied—mainly Nietzsche and Kierkegaard—is helpful. Hence, I will continue to treat Heidegger as connected to that movement.

83. His father's death in 1927 was a main reason for Watsuji's early return to Japan.

84. *Fūdo* 風土 is a compound word composed of the sinographs for "wind" and "earth." That in itself suggests more than merely atmospheric weather. For designating meteorological climates, Japanese uses different words, especially *kikō* 気候 ("generative force" + "weather/season").

85. This is probably why Geoffrey Bownas's revised English translation of the book changed the title (simply *Fūdo* in the original Japanese) from *Climate* to *Climate and Culture: A Philosophical Study.* No single English word seems to capture the fullness of the single Japanese term and so an elaboration of the title for English readers is necessary to prevent confusion.

86. On not being a simple physical determinist regarding climate, Watsuji wrote:

> The point of this book is to clarify the nature of *fūdo* as the structural point of origin for human existence. So, our issue here is not about how the physical environment determines human life. (Trans from WTZ 8: 1)

In fact, the sinograph for *fū* in *fūdo* can mean not only "wind," but also "manner" or "fashion" as in the medieval term for "stylistic refinement" (*fūryū* 風流) discussed in Chapter 7. (See page 250.)

87. Husserl applies the term "the natural standpoint" to an account of reality that begins with the assumption that there is an external world that impinges on me and causes my experiences. Phenomenology excludes, suspends belief in, or "brackets" out of its analysis such a standpoint. Phenomenology does not deny the natural standpoint, but simply ignores it for the sake of the phenomenological exploration of the experience. Husserl compares this to having to draw a particular right triangle for reference in a geometric proof, but nothing about that *particular* triangle is allowed into the proof itself. That is, the proof must apply to all right triangles, not just the one drawn.

88. In Watsuji's philosophical project of revealing what precedes the distinction between subject and object, it is hard not to think of his commonality with Nishida. Watsuji's method seems to draw most directly on western phenomenology, but at the least, it is reinforced by Nishida's general treatment of pre-bifurcated experience as far back as his maiden work, *Inquiry into the Good,* written in 1911. (See pages 454–8.)

89. For example, Maurice Merleau-Ponty's stress on embodied knowing parallels the traditional Japanese view. Yet, there was no direct influence of Japanese philosophy on his theories. I will discuss the theme of embodiment in the next chapter when I briefly consider the philosophical contributions of Yuasa Yasuo.

90. Trans. in WATSUJI 1988, 207.

91. For an astute statement of Watsuji's relevance to philosophical ethics from a comparative standpoint, see CARTER 1996. In addition, Erin McCarthy has insightfully compared Luce Irigaray and Watsuji in terms of their views of self, body, and ethics (McCARTHY 2011). For a fuller discussion, see also McCARTHY 2010.)

92. About two-thirds of the first (arguably most important) of the three volumes is available in English translation: WATSUJI 1996. The original of the full work is located in WTZ, vols. 10 and 11.

93. Trans. from WTZ 9: 20.

94. Although Watsuji made references to western anthropologies throughout his works, including his three-volume *Ethics,* his critique of a variety of western theories of philosophical anthropology and their application to ethics is most sustained and discrete in his short monograph, *Ethics as the Study of Ningen* (人間の学として倫理学) found in WTZ 9: 1–192.

95. Watsuji wrote:

> A mother and her baby can never be conceived of as merely two independent individuals. A baby wishes for its mother's body and the mother offers her breast to the baby. If they are separated from each other, they look for each other with all the more intensity. (WATSUJI 1996, 61)

96. Watsuji compares the mother-child relation as like the field defining an atom:

> If it is thinkable that a nucleus, with its electrons circling around it, constitutes one atom and not just separate individuals, then it is equally permissible to think that a mother's body and her child's are also combined as one. To isolate them as separate individuals, some sort of destruction must occur. (WATSUJI 1996, 62)

97. In the Meiji period, with the introduction of western thought, the Japanese struggled to coin terms appropriate to an array of western words referring to aspects of personhood. Relevant to the present instance, in translating Kant's writings, *jinkaku* was a common translation for "person" (German. *Person*) and *jinkakusei* for "personhood" (German. *Persönlichkeit*). Watsuji's close associate, Abe Jirō (1883–1959), was a leader in the Japanese personalist movement called *jinkakushugi* 人格主義 "*jinkaku*-ism."

More psychologically oriented literature in the early twentieth century, however, often rendered "personality" as *jinkaku,* the dominant meaning of the Japanese term today. In the face of such fluid shifts in terminology, when giving the equivalents between Japanese and western philosophical terms, we need to be sensitive to the time period and the context of a word's use. Simple one-to-one correlations can sometimes mislead.

98. The passage from Dōgen's *Genjōkōan* essay quoted on page 239 is similar in spirit:

> To model yourself after the Way of the buddhas is to model yourself after yourself.
> To model yourself after yourself is to forget yourself.

99. Trans. in WATSUJI 1996, 117.

100. Trans. in WATSUJI 1996, 119.

101. Watsuji demonstrated the failure of western philosophical attempts to either construct the social (*gen*) out of the plurality of individuals (multiple *nin*) or, conversely, construct the individual (*nin*) out of functions derived totally from the social (*gen*). His main targets in that discussion were Gabriel Tarde, Georg Simmel, Leopold von Wiese, and Émile Durkheim. See WATSUJI 1996, 101–18.

102. Watsuji discusses this issue most pointedly in a subsection of *Ethics* called "human conduct" 人間の行為 *ningen no kōi* (literally, "human [*ningen*] conduct"). It is found in Volume I, Main Discussion, part Two, chapter 6 (WTZ 10: 246–78) or chapter 12 in the English translation, WATSUJI 1996, 235–63. That English translation renders *kōi* throughout as "act" but since *kōi* is more specifically *ethical* action (the French *action morale*), I usually translate it in my discussion in this chapter as "(moral) conduct" when it is being discussed theoretically and "(moral) deed" when it is used to describe a specific action.

Because I stress Watsuji's connection to phenomenology, I also hope to avoid confusing *kōi* with the term *act* (German. *Akt* or *Handlung*) as used in phenomenology and psychology or in Fichte/Nishida's compound *fact-act* (German. *Tathandlung*). *Sayō* 作用 is the more common Japanese term for "act" in that sense and it does not necessarily imply any moral dimension. Moreover, when *kōi* is being contrasted with *dōsa* 動作, I translate the latter as "movement" or "move" rather than as "motion" as it appears in the English translation. Thus, I pose the *kōi* vs. *dōsa* distinction in English as "deed" vs. "movement" rather than "act" vs. "motion."

103. Trans. in WATSUJI 1996, 239. I added the italics from Watsuji's original Japanese text that were dropped in the English translation.

104. Trans. in WATSUJI 1996, 241.

105. "Trust" (*shinrai* 信頼) and "truth" (*shinjitsu* 真実) are the focus of Volume I, Main Discussion, Part II, chapter 6 found in WTZ 10: 278–98 (chapter 13 in the English translation, WATSUJI 1996, 265–82).

These two Japanese terms are more or less synonymous with the common Confucian and Shintō terms, but use different (though related) sinographs. For "trust" or "good faith" the classical Chinese term is just the first sinograph of *shinrai*, the *rai* adding the nuance of "reliance." The ordinary word for "genuineness" or "truth" in Shintō is *makoto*, which can be (but is not commonly) written with the second sinograph of *shinjitsu*. In that case, the *shin* sinograph intensifies the sense of "true." Watsuji often engages in word play and may here be making associations with another word pronounced *shinjitsu*, namely 信実, which has the sense of honesty or sincerity and is a compound consisting of the first sinographs of the two words under discussion. In any case, Watsuji himself directly connects the word *shinjitsu* here with *makoto*. See the following note.

106. Watsuji explicitly discusses truth (*shinjitsu*) in terms of *makoto*, the idea of genuineness to which the Shintō and Native Studies scholars had given so much weight. (See, for example, pages 327 and 331 above.) See WATSUJI 1996, 274.

107. The notion of the "axial" has in recent years become an increasingly valuable parameter for historical sociological studies of Japan. Most prominently, S. N. Eisenstadt in his *Japanese Civilization* has argued that Japan might be called a "non-axial" society. Following the same line of that analysis, Robert N. Bellah wrote an incisive introduction to his collection of essays, *Imagining Japan*, that first reviews the "axial" vs. "nonaxial" distinction and then applies it perceptively to various points in Japanese intellectual history with special emphasis on recent history. See EISENSTADT 1996 and BELLAH 2003, 1–62.

108. The same can be said for Plato's impersonal but transcendent Form of the Good. In the *Republic*, Plato charges the Guardians with interpreting the Good. Again, who gives them the authority to do so? *We do.*

109. Such an inhuman being would be outside the "realm of human beings" (insofar as that realm contrasts with the realm of beasts, ghosts, and demons, for example). That "realm of human beings" in Buddhist terminology is an original meaning of *ningen*.

110. Kierkegaard criticized Hegel along similar grounds when he used the image of Hegel's system as a grand castle on the hilltop while people lived in hovels at the foot of the mountain.

111. Watsuji used two different words to express totality, namely, *sōtaisei* (correlated with the German *Allheit* in the quotation in note 116 below) and *zentaisei*. Of the two, he used *zentaisei* (which has the nuance of "wholeness") more frequently and when he did, he often embedded it in the phrase "*originary* wholeness" (*honrai no zentaisei*). He

also frequently spoke of *zentaisei* as a wholeness to which ethics ideally returns us. The *originary* wholeness within *ningen* would likely be the wholeness of emptiness (*kū*).

Yet, emptiness itself is not exactly a totality; it has no parts. Indeed the point is that it is completely empty. As the source of all negation, however, emptiness (in its negating function) initiates the dynamism that fuels the dialectical movements of individual-social, *nin* and *gen*. For that reason, I think Watsuji means that the dialectic between *nin* and *gen* brings about our return to the original betweenness that is not *nin*, not *gen*, nor *ningen*, but rather the holistic emptiness out of which those distinctions arise. If that interpretation is correct, the influence of Nishida's view of absolute nothing (*zettai mu*) is unmistakable.

112. In his comparison, the imperial monuments of Rome are vacuous displays of material power as compared to the more refined art found in the culture of Athens. Watsuji places the United States in the same category as Rome, investing its pride as a civilization in its monuments (including skyscrapers) and technological achievements.

113. Oddly enough, Watsuji's version of the theory behind the Greater East Asian Co-prosperity Sphere resembles the rationale behind an organization the West later developed vis-à-vis the Soviet bloc, namely, the North Atlantic Treaty Organization (NATO). Of course, the western political institution has a completely different geneal-ogy, tracing back to previous confederations of nations, the federation of American colonies (which became the United States), and even to notions of tribal confederations developed by Native American groups like the Algonquins (who gave English the word *caucus*, for example). Obviously, similar ideas do not necessarily share common origins.

114. As I explained in *Intimacy or Integrity,* some intimacy systems establish a line of integrity around themselves to prevent the incursion of other intimacy systems. See KASULIS 2002, 148.

115. One might argue that he was doing his own phenomenology of the experience of "the holy" in the vein of Rudolf Otto, but applying it specifically to the Japanese experi-ence of the emperor system.

116. One way Watsuji expresses this link between the totalities and the unity of moral deeds is as follows:

> This sort of conduct means the *unity of moral deeds.* The unity of moral deeds is the *unity of the will* and, hence, the unity of personhood. This unity is precisely the final purpose at which ethics aims. However, this unity has nothing to do with that unity (*Einheit*) which is regarded as the "one" and which makes its appearance in Kant's scheme of categories. Rather, it should be called individuality (*Einzel-heit*). Individuality belongs to multiplicity (*Mehrheit*) and multiplicity acquires its unity in totality (*Allheit*). Therefore, unity makes its most evident appearance in totality. The unity of moral deeds lies not in individual behavior but as the totality in the nexus and connection of behavior. "It is not one hand (*eine Hand*) that enables moral conduct (*Handlung*). Rather, many hands (*Hände*) must be connected with each other for this purpose." (Hermann Cohen's *Ethik des reines Willens,* page 184.) In this connection the unity of moral conduct as well as that of the will is established for the first time.... (Trans. based on WATSUJI 1996, 253. Original found in WTZ 10: 266–7.)

117. Watsuji's criticism of the inability of Japan's wartime ideology to learn and adapt in the face of empirical evidence can even be found, surprisingly, in a speech to graduates of the naval academy in December 1943. The essay based on the lecture アメリカの国民性 (The National Character of the American People) is in WTZ 17: 451–81. The speech has typically been interpreted as Watsuji's total capitulation to the ethnocentric and militaristic nationalism of the government. In it are some of his most blatant and inflammatory criticisms of U.S. culture, offered as an argument for why Japan's cultural superiority would necessarily prevail against such an inferior people and nation.

Leaving aside the point that some of his sharpest criticisms of the actions of the United States are historically valid (*e.g.*, that it expanded its territories with an ideological policy of racial aggression including the enslavement of Africans and the genocide of the Native American peoples), he also made positive comments about the U.S. culture's commitment to empirical feedback.

If you do not read Watsuji's words carefully, encapsulated as they are in an otherwise scathing critique of Americanism, you might take him to be merely echoing the Japanese militarist ideology that the Japanese spirit would necessarily dominate over American materialism. A more discerning reading, however, reveals that Watsuji actually says that American scientific thinking, indebted to Baconian experimentalism, is actually a *strength* of the culture. Because of that commitment to empirical verification, the United States could change its military and political policies in the face of empirically discernible negative results from past tactics. The Japanese navy leadership had bemoaned the fact that such adjustments in the face of previous failures were not the standard protocol for Japan. Under the influence of the army, it believed, Japan was so poorly executing the war that disaster was looming on the horizon (which, of course, it was).

During the war, straightforward criticism of Japanese military actions or official state ideology resulted in prompt imprisonment or worse. Therefore, we should read Watsuji's comments in that context, being on the lookout for distinguishing between what he may seem to be saying on the surface with, at least sometimes, what he actually means, although stated in a covert form. Unfortunately, from the postwar period up to the present, many scholars in both Japan and the West, sometimes influenced by their own ideological assumptions, have shown themselves to be blind to Watsuji's rhetorical strategy and submit the speech as incontrovertible evidence of Watsuji's collusion with the government. At the least, the situation is more complicated than that.

My interpretation of Watsuji's speech is indebted to the incisive and, to me, convincing reading developed by William R. LaFleur. See LAFLEUR 2001.

14. Aftershocks and Afterthoughts

118. The law imposed imprisonment up to ten years to any who "formed an association with the objective of altering the *kokutai* or the system of private property." By the end of the decade, the law was revised to allow the death penalty for the crime. The 1925 law was the second by that name, the 1887 version serving as the legal basis for Nakae Chōmin's banishment from Tokyo for two years. See pages 427–8.

119. For an excellent collection of essays on the politics of the Kyoto School during the war years, see HEISIG and MARALDO 1995. The anthology includes a balance of representative positions about how complicit the various philosophers were in promoting the government ideology. Those who read all the essays, by both Japanese and western experts, will get a fair picture of the situation in its complexities and ambiguities.

The scholarly literature, in both Japanese and western languages, on the involvement of major Japanese thinkers in support of wartime ideology is extensive. Unfortunately, not all of it is reliable. The problematic analyses are flawed in various ways. One common error is to clump all the Kyoto School thinkers as being of one political stripe—which they weren't. For instance, Mutai Risaku (1890–1974) developed a logic that blended Nishida's and Tanabe's logics for the purpose of developing a "cosmopolitan" and more pacifist humanism. See JPS, 692–701 and KOPF 2009.

A second problem is that some scholars seem to have an ax to grind and write tendentious arguments, taking quotes from the Kyoto School philosophers out of context or sometimes, when writing in English, (willfully?) mistranslating key terms or passages. A third problem involves analyses colored by either implicit or explicit moralism, often confusing a moral imperative with a wish for the supererogatory. That is, the critics often collapse what the Japanese thinkers were ethically obligated to do and what they could have heroically done, perhaps at enormous cost to themselves, their families, and their students. It is, of course, legitimate to require of people that they behave ethically, but not to demand they act in a supererogatory or heroic manner. *Heroism*, by definition, applies to actions that go beyond the call of duty or obligation.

I noted two thinkers associated with Nishida or the Kyoto School, namely, Tosaka Jun and Miki Kiyoshi, were convicted for criticizing the government and subsequently died in prison. It is hypocritical for present-day western scholars, safely ensconced in a tenured professorship within a country guaranteeing freedom of expression, especially scholars who have personally never been imprisoned or physically punished for their political beliefs, to pontificate how others should have risked career, freedom, familial well-being, and their own lives to do something beyond what morality minimally requires.

The political circumstances of Japan in the late 1930s and early 1940s must be realistically assessed before making simple-minded accusations about the morality of individuals from the Kyoto School during that period. (See Parkes 1997.) Before passing judgment, it is incumbent on the critics not only to analyze all the possible options open to the philosophers in question, but also to evaluate the probable consequences. Second, the critics should offer a frank statement of their own ideological perspectives and assumptions. And most importantly, they should analyze the relevant texts in their proper political context to determine whether the apparent surface message may differ from what a more nuanced philosophical reading would reveal.

In Chapter 13 I attempted such a reading by following William LaFleur's interpretation of Watsuji's essay "National Character of the American People" (see page 674, note 117) and in this chapter, I have given a similar reading of Nishida's "Theorizing the *Kokutai*." To use terminology from the official state ideology but giving the key terms a different interpretation seems to have been a rhetorical strategy among some philosophers in negotiating the fine line between being critical of the state and avoiding criminal prosecution. Ueda Shizuteru has called this a "tug-of-war over the meaning of words" (HEISIG and MARALDO 1995, 90). By the latter war years, for example, one could not criticize the concept of *kokutai* without being silenced and imprisoned. One could, however, try to reframe the concept and neutralize its venomous implications. That, in my reading, is the subversive layer of Nishida's essay "Theorizing the *Kokutai*."

120. Although Nishida is not fully clear on this point, it would seem his theory distinguishes between a *kokutai* and a constitutional monarchy on the following grounds. In the latter, the loyalty of the people divides its focus between the parliament and the monarchy (and in many cases is primarily directed toward the parliament). In the *kokutai* model, by contrast, the loyalty directly focuses on the emperor. It would seem that any loyalty to parliamentary legislation is only through the authorization of the emperor. I would imagine that within Nishida's definition, the emperor could even dissolve the parliament and still maintain a *kokutai* form of government (which, of course, cannot occur in a constitutional monarchy).

What happens in the *kokutai* system, however, if the people oppose the imperial edicts? Presumably, since Nishida's delineation of the *kokutai* system requires unquestioned loyalty to the emperor, the only option would be to dissolve the *kokutai* system itself. Without the people's free decision to extend absolute loyalty to the monarchy, there could be no *kokutai*.

121. In fact, we can trace that philosophical proclivity—to pursue the origin of an error rather than simply to refute its conclusion—in Japanese philosophy back to Kūkai's relegation technique in the *Ten Mindsets*. (See pages 129–34.)

122. In KASULIS 1989, I argued that the Kyoto School's dialectical thinking typically proceeds back to "whence" in contrast with Hegel's dialectic which proceeds forward to "whither." I then explained how that difference affected Nishitani's view of history in his *Religion and Nothingness*.

123. PBS website http://www.pbs.org/flw/buildings/imperial/imperial_response.html. June 20, 2013.

124. Joshua Hammer has made a thorough analysis of the sociopolitical and ideological impact of the earthquake: HAMMER 2006. See also SCHENCKING 2008.

125. Besides Nishitani, the other participants were Kōsaka Masaaki (1900–1969) Director of the Institute for the Humanities (JPS, 708–12), Suzuki Shigetaka (1907–1988) lecturer in western history, and Kōyama Iwao (1905–1993) who taught in the philosophy department with Nishitani (JPS, 738–43).

126. An English translation of the whole symposium is available in CALICHMAN 2008.

127. Of western scholarship on Nishida, WARGO 2005 best highlights this connection between the two Inoues and Nishida.

128. Although it is not always so, in many cases Japanese philosophers use different words for the two senses of "subject," namely, *shukan* 主観 (the epistemological subject as in "the subject-object distinction") and *shutai* 主体 (the subject as the incarnate being who acts). The sinograph *kan* in the former suggests looking, while the sinograph *tai* in the latter suggests embodiment. Neither, of course, should be confused with "subject" in the sense of the grammatical subject of a sentence which is *shugo* 主語.

129. This book has been translated into English (NISHITANI 1990) with an excellent introduction by Graham Parkes.

130. Public domain: U.S. army photo, Tokyo_1945-3-10-1.jpg; accessed through Wikipedia Commons.

131. In recent years, some programmatic alternatives to the Eurocentric mainstream of philosophy in Japan have arisen. I will mention a couple in the Conclusion to this book.

132. In Japanese, the single term *shūkyōtetsugaku*, literally "religion-philosophy," can be used to cover both. This is helpful since in some cases an individual's philosophy seems to qualify as both philosophy in religion and philosophy of religion.

133. For an overview of Suzuki's reception among western, especially U.S., readers over the decades, see KASULIS 2007.

134. Originally carried out in 1957, the dialogues were translated and published in TILLICH and HISAMATSU 1971.

135. As noted above on page 540, Nishitani's most famous work was *What is Religion?* Its English translation, *Religion and Nothingness,* was one of the early successes of the Nanzan Institute for Religion and Culture in its mission of nurturing further Buddhist-Christian dialogue.

136. The previously treated Hase Shōtō might even fit the alternative characterization and belong in this category instead of philosophy of religion.

137. TAKEUCHI 1991, 130–3.

138. Some interpreters, primarily in the West, have seen this as akin to the postmodern deconstructionist claim that (arguing against Husserl) there is no "presence." Nothing is given; everything is constructed. The problem with that comparison is that there is a difference between the denial of presence and the affirmation of a meaningless presence. In Nishitani's terminology, the former is the void or nihility of nihilism; the latter is the emptiness at the core of religious experience. The latter, in engaging its *basho* or context, will autonomously generate meaning of itself (*jinen*) in variegated ways (as it autonomously takes form in its interactive field of responsiveness). The formation of meaning does not need an external agency any more than the water within its field of space and gravitational pull needs another agency to form itself into pools. It happens "naturally."

139. See SUZUKI 1957.

140. IZUTSU Toshihiko 1984. Some of Izutsu's thinking about mysticism is closely linked to his theories about the origin and primary purpose of language in relation to magic. See IZUTSU Toshihiko 1956.

141. The most notable publication in this regard is IZUTSU Toshikiho and IZUTSU Toyoko 1981.

142. IZUTSU Toshihiko 1982.

143. For a fine treatment of the many sides of the Critical Buddhism movement, see the collection of essays in HUBBARD and SWANSON 1997.

144. YUASA 1987.

145. See, for example, YUASA 1993.

146. MINAMOTO 1992.

15. Conclusion

1. See HADOT 1995 and HADOT 2002.

2. PLATO 1991, 13.

3. In earlier times, even recent earlier times, the provincialism of western philosophers was not so marked. Thomas Aquinas read in translation the Arab philosophers and theologians, Leibniz the Chinese neo-Confucians, Hegel and Schopenhauer the Indian *Upanishads* and the *Bhagavad Gīta*, as did also many American transcendentalists. It seems the scientism of the mid-twentieth century and the rise of American political-economic dominance after WWII contributed to the American tendency to think there is little of philosophical value in Asia.

Reference Material

Pointers for Studying Japan

My comments here are designed mainly to help readers new to Japanese studies, although a few points, especially those in the second and third sections dealing with names and language, may interest more experienced readers as well. I start with some crude guidelines for pronouncing Japanese words and terms. The goal is not to start you on the path to Japanese conversational fluency, but something more modest. In reading this book you will encounter a large inventory of names and terms. If you pronounce them correctly right from the start, you will then easily recognize those items if you hear them mentioned orally. Furthermore, you would more likely be understood when using them in conversation.

The next section of "Pointers" addresses the thorny issue of Japanese names. I have included it for two reasons. First, many westerners are confused by Japanese names. Why, for example, do we call the author of *The Tale of Genji* "Murasaki Shikibu" when neither Murasaki nor Shikibu was her actual name? It is not even her *nom de plume*, that is, if she had heard the appellation "Murasaki Shikibu," she would likely not have known it was meant to refer to her. In considering Japanese naming practices, furthermore, we will glean some further insights into personal identity in Japan, a topic worthy of explanation in its own right in a philosophy book such as this.

In the third and final section I address a few basic issues about the nature of the Japanese language itself. I do so not because I think language somehow determines Japanese thought, but because I would like to offer novice readers enough information about the language so they can better understand the context of Japanese philosophers' discussions about language generally and the Japanese language specifically. Again, though, my analysis in that section will occasionally take us into deep waters relevant to the philosophy of language in general, so philosophers of that specialty, regardless of their interest in Japan, might be provoked to think about language in new ways.

Pronouncing Japanese in the Hepburn Romanization

Since Japanese does not use roman letters but instead sinographs representing words and *kana* representing sounds, the Hepburn romanization system was devised to enable an English speaker to approximate the correct pronunciation of Japanese names and words. Fortunately, the system is straightforward and only a few clarifications are necessary. The paragraphs preceded by (*) are probably the most essential; if you violate those rules, your pronunciation of a term or name might be unintelligible to a native speaker.

Syllables

A Japanese syllable contains one and only one vowel sound. So a syllable in the Hepburn romanization may be a single letter (a vowel) or a grouping of a vowel preceded by one or two consonants. All syllables end with a vowel sound, never a consonant, and every syllable has equal stress. Hence, flower arranging in Japanese, *ikebana*, is pronounced more like "eek-kay-bah-nah" than "eek-kay-BAH-nah." (In some cases, the vowel sound is silent but still given a beat and so Hepburn drops the vowel and uses a double consonant as, for example, *ittai.* The sound of the *tt* approximates the common quick pronunciation of *tt* in an English word like *outtake,* when the first *t* is swallowed but still takes a beat in length.)

Vowels

Vowel sounds. There are five vowel sounds, all familiar to English speakers. Pronounce "*o, e, i, a*" as in the notes of the musical scale "do, re, mi, fa." Pronounce "*u*" as in the English "put." So, "*sake*" (Japanese rice wine) is pronounced "sah-kay" not "sah-kee."

Nasalized vowels. A vowel may also be nasalized and elongated to two syllables in length. This is indicated by adding *n'* to the end of the syllable. If the *n'* occurs at the end of a word, the apostrophe is dropped. For example, *hon* sounds roughly like the English word *honk* without the final *k* sound. This is not to be confused with the regular consonant sound *n* which occurs always before a vowel or the consonant y followed by a vowel.

Long vowels. The vowels *o* and *u* (and less frequently *a, e, i*) also occur as long vowels two syllables in length. The long vowel is designated with a macron such as *ō* and *ū*. The vowel sound is unchanged but simply extended to twice its usual length. For example, *ō* is like saying in English "hello over there" when the two "*o*" sounds merge into a single "*o*" double in length.

Diphthongs. There are no diphthongs in Japanese (combinations of vowels like *ou* pronounced together in one syllable as in the English *ought* or *pout*). Instead, each occurrence of a vowel is a new syllable. So, *geisha* is pronounced "gay-ee-sha" not "gay-sha" or "gee-sha."

Consonants

Most consonants are pronounced about as in English (although generally a little more forward in the mouth). Only a few need special comment.

*g is always hard like the first, not the second, *g* in the English word *garage*. (For the sound of the second *g*, Hepburn uses *j*.)

*y is always a consonant followed by a vowel sound as in the English *yo-yo*. It is never a vowel as in the English *baby*. Hence, the Japanese pronunciation of the city Tōkyō is "toh [vowel held for two syllables]-kyoh [held for two syllables]," not the "toh-kee-yoh of the Anglicized pronunciation.

f is somewhere between an English *f* and *h* (as if one says the English *f* sound without biting the lower lip).

n is like the English consonant and not to be confused with the *n'* nasalizer following a vowel. It never occurs at the end of a syllable because all syllables end in vowel sounds.

r is a difficult sound for English speakers (as is the English *r* for Japanese speakers). An approximation is when a British person might say "very good" so that it almost sounds like "veddy good." Sounding a little like a soft *d*, it is made in the mouth quite differently—the tongue rolls forward over the palate instead of snapping against the front teeth.

Understanding Japanese Names

Your name commonly serves two purposes. First, it is a designator for a particular person, setting you apart from most or even all others. In addition, your full name commonly suggests at least some other people connected with you: your relations. Thus, in names of English speakers, the last name (surname) designates a familial relation and the first name the individual in that relation. A middle name may further narrow the familial subset to better specify the individual.

Names in Japan can ordinarily play a similar function except the order is reversed, that is, the surname comes first and the given name second. In many cases, however, those two names are just the beginning of the story. Samurai names, for example, were particularly complicated. In translating Arai Hakuseki's autobiography, Joyce Ackroyd found it necessary to explain at the outset the multiple names used to designate the same individual in her study:

> The Japanese samurai had (1) a sept or clan name (as Minamoto); (2) a surname (as Arai); (3) a childhood name (as Hi-no-Ko); (4) a personal or familiar name (as Kageyu); (5) and a given or legal name (as Kinmi). They often

adopted a literary pseudonym (Hakuseki). On retirement, some became lay priests and adopted a Buddhist name (as Jōshin).[1]

In addition, even today many Japanese upon death are bestowed a Buddhist ordination name (called *kaimyō*) to take with them in the afterlife.[2] To add to the confusion, adults may be adopted into another family, thereby bringing about a change in surname. That practice is common among families lacking a son or in artistic traditions where the master may use the adoption process as a way of naming a successor.

The traditional practice for aristocratic women's names involves further complexities. Take the case of the Heian-period author of *The Tale of Genji*. Murasaki Shikibu (as we now know her) was not likely the name by which she was known in her own lifetime. Her name was probably Tō no Shikibu, the *Tō* (wisteria) indicating her connection to a lower branch of the Fujiwara (wisteria) family. Shikibu is not a name, but a title, and her title only by association at that. *Shikibu* is from *shikibushō*, the court's Ministry of Rites, an office in which both her father and brother served. Her personal given name is not known to us.

For women of the court, the given name was shared only with those in a most intimate relation such as one's immediate family and one's betrothed. As for the Murasaki (which means "purple") part of her name, that sobriquet seems to have been added only in the century following her death. Various theories account for its choice, including that it reflects the color of wisteria (pointing to the family connection again) or the name of a main character in her novel that may be a literary surrogate for the real Murasaki, the author.

Using multiple names for the same person does not present a major problem for readers of this book, however, since I follow the common convention of using the philosopher's pen name or ordination name for premodern figures. (Incidentally, I am primarily discussing names in relation to the elite; commoners and townspeople did not typically even have surnames until legally required in the 1870s).

Even these limited comments about naming customs suggest two significant points about Japanese identity. First, the naming practices suggest personal identity is highly fluid. Many historical figures were addressed by several different names in their lifetimes (and, as in the case of Murasaki, even after their lifetime). The main purpose was, it seems, to place individuals within their appropriate social contexts. In the case of a self-chosen name, the new name may indicate how the person wishes to mark a transition to a new context or role. A famous example is the woodblock artist Hokusai (1760–1849), who used some thirty different names over his career, often to mark shifts in his artistic style. The fluidity of Japanese personal names readily supports such a re-inventing of the self.

The second point about naming is that what people are called may involve levels of respect and intimacy. I noted that Murasaki's personal name was known only to her intimates. That suggests affection may be most linked to the personal name, while role identity and the public respect toward superiors may be linked more to context-dependent names. For example, even today in Japan, one commonly refers to one's superior by role (such as *buchōsan*—Mr./Ms Department Head) rather than by name. Moreover, a younger sibling still often refers to an older sibling not by name but by status (*nēchan*, familiar form for "older sister," for instance).The elder sibling in the family, by contrast, commonly refers to a younger sibling by the given name (such as "Masao" or with the endearing form, "Masao-kun").

In Ackroyd's brief account of samurai names, using Hakuseki as her case study, we see that as the samurai male moved across different social groups and associations, and as he joined the literary or artistic community, the name he went by might change. That certainly underscores the importance of social place in personal identity: where and how I am contributes to who I am. By comparison, in English if I use a middle name along with my given name and surnames, that helps distinguish me as an individual from others with similar names. The middle name is *added* to my other two names for further specification (not unlike the taxonomic nomenclature for an animal species). In Ackroyd's discussion of samurai names, however, we find that the new names generally *replace* rather than supplement the old. (In the West, this occurs most often in the case of pen names or pseudonyms.)

In Japan, the social context of interrelations define the person's activities and roles, often trumping that person's individuality. For Murasaki, for example, we do not even know the part of her name that is independent of family, the family's social position, or the name given by her fond readers. Nor should we. Her "real name" (*jitsumyō*) is only for those in her innermost circle.

I am not claiming that the complex naming practices are still as rigorous in Japan as they were a couple of centuries of ago. The samurai as a class are long gone and democratization has undercut many of the old classist practices. Yet, although the specific naming regimens may have eroded, I believe the ideals behind those practices persist: the fluid self, the sense of defining one's role contextually (a major purpose of business cards to this day), and the sensitivity to formal social hierarchy.

ABOUT THE JAPANESE LANGUAGE

The Two Strata in the Japanese Language

Both English and Japanese can be considered to have two main layers in their historical formation. English has one stratum from before the Norman invasion (which for convenience only I will here call Anglo-Saxon English) and one stratum from after (the Latinate or Romance language part of English, which also had previously incorporated many ancient Greek words). In English those two eventually merged but we still find a few scattered remnants of their duality. In the terminology of common law, for example, some compound terms drew on both constituents of the language, perhaps as an aid in bridging the language gap: *aid* (Latin) and *abet* (A-S), *breaking* (A-S) and *entering* (Latin), *murderous* (A-S) *homicide* (L), and so forth.

Today, however, the two strata of English have combined rather seamlessly into a single language. One distinction that does remain is that simple, concrete words (e.g., *think*) are more often than not Anglo-Saxon in origin while more abstract or specific terms (*e.g., cogitate, ruminate*) tend to be Latinate.

Turning our attention to Japanese, the two layers of the premodern language[3] are the preliterate, indigenous Japanese language (often called, somewhat problematically, the Yamato language) and the imported Chinese language with its sophisticated writing system. Each layer contributed its own vocabulary. For example, as we would expect, before the Chinese influence the preliterate Yamato language already had a word for *dog* (*inu*) but not *book*. So, the Japanese used the Chinese sinograph for *dog* (犬) and pronounced it *inu*. But in writing the word for *book* (which, having adopted writing, they now needed), they borrowed the Chinese word and its written form 本, pronouncing it in what they considered a semblance to its Chinese pronunciation (*hon*). Yet, in Chinese the word for *book* is the same in both pronunciation and written form as the word for *source* or *origin*, for which the Yamato language did have its own word, *moto*. The result was that the same Chinese sinograph 本 could be pronounced as either *hon* (meaning either *source/origin/basis* or *book*) or as *moto* (meaning *source/origin/basis*). Complicating matters further, the Japanese continued to add more Chinese words through the centuries (using again Japanized pronunciation), borrowing especially compounded sinographs for complex, highly specific, or abstract ideas.[4*]

As a result, the distinction between the more specific or concrete vs. the more general or abstract was sometimes correlated with the difference between Yamato vs. Chinese words. In *very* broad terms this resembles the distinction between the Anglo-Saxon vs. Latinate in English. Yet, because of the historical and cultural context, the Japanese are a bit more aware of the difference between words of Chinese origin and indigenous words, even to the extent of sometimes using different dictionaries for accessing the technical details about a single word depending on the stratum of the language from which it derives.

The dual-layered aspect of Japanese was foregrounded as an issue at least thrice in the history of Japanese philosophy. In ancient and medieval Japan, the standards of poetics required poems in Japanese (*waka*) to use only Yamato words, reserving China-derived words for poems in Chinese (*kanshi*). In the Edo period scholars and philosophers often stressed philology and the history of language. Both the classicist Confucians and the Native Studies theorists frequently discussed the differences between the Chinese and Japanese languages and this carried over at times into the differences between the two substrata within Japanese. For example, the nativists maintained the Yamato words of the Japanese language reflected a richness of spiritual nuance that the words borrowed from China could not. The sinophiles, on the other hand, lauded the superior concision of Chinese over Japanese.

The differences between the Yamato and Chinese-derived words also became crucial a third time when western thought flooded into Japan in the latter half of the nineteenth century. The Japanese needed to develop quickly a large lexicon of neologisms to express the newly imported ideas expressed in European languages. The protocol was to create new technical terms by designing compound words consisting of sinographs rather than constructing new words out of Yamato terms. Some later Japanese philosophers such as Sakabe Megumi[†] believed that decision tended to distance philosophy in Japan from the openness and concreteness of the everyday in favor of the precision and abstract quality of the Chinese derived layer of the Japanese language. For less technical words, a common practice has been to import foreign words wholesale, writing them in the *katakana* syllabary, which functions in this case much like italics in English as a marker of foreign words.

Japanese Syntax and Kana

Although the Japanese both used Chinese sinographs for creating their own writing system, that does not mean Japanese is at all similar to Chinese. For example, Chinese verbs do not inflect, that is, they do not add endings to verb stems to indicate such differences as tense. On the other hand, Japanese verbs do inflect. Originally, since only sinographs were available for writing Japanese, they were added after verbs (which were also written in sinographs) to supply the inflection. In that function, the sinographs were meant not to be read as words but as sounds only (like the letters in the English alphabet, for example).

Thus, eighth-century texts used individual sinographs within the same sentence as either strictly semantic or strictly phonetic units. That was extraordinarily difficult to decipher and by the early ninth century, a new writing system for phonetically representing syllables (*kana* in either the *hiragana* and *katakana* form) was developed. It was then possible to write Japanese entirely

[†] See pages 569–73.

in *kana* (as women and occasionally men did in the classical period). Yet, using only *kana* produced very lengthy texts (a single sinograph might be four syllables long in its Japanese pronunciation and hence take four *kana* to write). In the end *kana* came to be used mainly as supplements to the sinographs, expressing mainly inflections of verbs, some words of Yamato origin, and the grammatical particles know as *joshi,* my next topic.

The Function of Particles (joshi)

The particles (*joshi*) are Japanese linguistic units serving two major purposes. First, they are one- to three-syllable grammatical units used after nouns to designate their syntactical function (much as endings are added to nouns to designate case in Latin, for example). Because some common *joshi* are *te, ni, wo,* and *ha,* the *joshi* were classically known as just that: *te-ni-wo-ha.* (The philosophers in this book often called them that.) Because the *joshi* originally derive from the syntax of the Yamato language and because Chinese has at best inexact equivalents in form and meaning, the *joshi* are written in the *kana syllabary* rather than with sinographs.

The *joshi* have a second use, however, one that is considered especially significant by some Japanese philosophers. Sociolinguistically and grammatically, they may express the affect and gender of the speaker, the mood of the situation, or the relative status of speaker and listener. In that function they often occur at the end of the sentence. Thus even a simple statement in Japanese may, because of the *joshi,* acquire extra nuances not contained in the statement's propositional communication about a state of affairs.

In spoken English much of the work *joshi* do in Japanese can be shouldered by intonation. Take the simple statement: "It is already Friday." Now consider the various feelings or moods in the situation you can communicate with those same four words by moving the stress to different places within the sentence, by altering pitch, or even saying the sentence at different speeds. Your voice could communicate *relief* or *excitement* (the weekend's almost here); *dismay* (the project is due at five o'clock); *surprise* (I thought it was only Thursday); *matter of factness* (the clock just struck midnight); *thinking aloud to yourself* (figuring out what to do next, given the time); *seeking confirmation or agreement* (planning with others what to do). And so forth. In each case, exactly the same four words may be spoken, but the intonation (along with body language) could suggest more than the mere empirical claim inherent in the sentence. In conversations the Japanese use intonation for the same purpose, but the *joshi* add a further dimension.

In comparing Japanese and English on this topic, I want to stress four points.

1. No matter how the four words are said in English, in a strictly logical sense, the proposition expressed remains constant. It is simply either true or false that it is Friday, regardless of how you say it or why you say it.

2. Allowing for variation in intonation and gesture, an English speaker and Japanese speaker can express much the same range of affects or mood in saying just a few words.

3. Most of the similarity between Japanese and English with regard to point (2) disappears when the English sentence is written instead of spoken, however. Written English is limited in how to definitively communicate affect and situational mood. Its only options are underlining the word or putting it in italics, writing the word totally in upper case, and using one of the three sentence-ending punctuation symbols (period, exclamation point, or question mark). In the example above, for instance, the utterances showing excitement, dismay, and surprise might all be written "It is already FRIDAY!" But even that typography does not definitively distinguish which of those three moods is being expressed. The Japanese situation is different. Since the effect can be achieved by the inclusion of the appropriate *joshi,* and since the *joshi* are used in written as well as spoken Japanese, a writer can express affect or mood as explicitly in writing as in speaking. Therefore, in communicating affect, the gap between oral and written expression is not nearly as great in Japanese as in English.

4. Japanese culture has long appreciated the power of *joshi* to be more than mere grammatical particles. A case in point: a *haiku* is limited to just seventeen syllables, yet often lines of the poem end with emotive *joshi.* Indeed many *haiku* use three or even four of its precious seventeen syllables to include *joshi* that literally refer to nothing, but express so much about the poet's state of mind, the situation's mood, and (ideally) the reader's responsiveness.

Those four points have ramifications for how the written language of philosophy can affect how we understand what is central to the nature of language. In English the gap between the written and oral can be so great that the written denatured statement may seem a natural expression. By *denatured statement* I mean one in which the sentence means nothing more, and the writer/speaker intends nothing more, than the proposition contained in it. Yet, no matter how fashionable that way of thinking about language might be in some philosophical circles, it is blatantly nonsense to think a natural language actually functions (or maybe even *can* function) that way.

To be provocative, I'll state my point baldly. Whereas it is true that in the course of history many denatured statements may have been written, none has ever been spoken. When it comes to spoken language, through some means—whether intonation, *joshi*, facial expressions, gestures, or whatever other sociolinguistic device the human cultural imagination has created—the contextualizing affect and mood is communicated along with the proposition, lending it a texture or hue, we might say. Denatured sentences are like an assembly line that carries propositions to plug into lines of syllogisms. The natural sentences of ordinary discourse cannot be reduced to that.[5]

Perhaps because of the ubiquity of the *joshi* in natural language and their power to communicate nuances beyond the merely referential, most Japanese philosophers have shown little interest in analyzing denatured statements and propositions. They seem too artificial and concocted. On the other hand, Japanese philosophers have frequently been fascinated with language's capacity to open us to new meanings and to engage in rich intimations of indirect communication. Still, at the danger of repeating myself, I want to be clear that I do not believe this is just a "Japanese" sensitivity, but something more generally human. I will hazard an example from pop culture that strikes me as particularly revealing.

As is often the case, popular culture may be ahead of the philosophers. In this digital age, people have noticed that the concision of a text message on a smart phone often produces denatured sentences. Wishing to express affect and mood more explicitly while using as few keystrokes as possible, software designers have gifted us a new kind of *joshi,* one that spans all natural languages. We call them *emoji* (☺).[6*] In just one keystroke, they reflect the affective mood the writer wants to communicate.

Such considerations bring us to the sociolinguistic dynamic between the speaker and the audience.

The Speaker-Audience Relation

It seems obvious enough that except in rare moments of reflective soliloquy, annoyance, or self-deprecation, language is spoken (or written) by someone to someone else. Indeed, the words are not just *to* but also *for* someone. That commonplace characteristic of language is more explicitly built into the semantics and syntax of Japanese than in many other languages. For example, every Japanese verb is inflected not just for tense, but also for levels of formality, respect, and intimacy. If the situation is informal, I may say *iku* ([someone] goes); if more formal, I would likely use the longer form of the same verb, *ikimasu.* When showing deference to who is going, I can use a different verb, which also has informal and formal forms: *irassharu* or *irasshaimasu.* If the person going is either myself or someone from my ingroup, I might show diffidence or humility in the presence of an audience of respected outsiders by using yet another verb with two forms, formal and neutral: *mairimasu* or *mairu*.

There are also clusters of nouns that show varying degrees of deference or humility. If I am conversing with you about our wives, I would likely not use the generic, detached word for wife (*tsuma*), but words that have built into their use a recognition of our mutual relation. That is, I would use the humbling word *kanai* to refer to my wife or the wife of someone in my intimate group and would refer to your wife with the respectful word *okusan*. So functionally speaking, *kanai* means "my wife" and *okusan* "your wife."[7]

Reinforcing what I have already said earlier in this discussion of the Japanese language, the recognition of the social context and audience is intrinsic to the semantics and syntactics of most sentences. As Mori Arimasa observed, that characteristic lends a second-person feel to Japanese sentences: "you" as the audience is always affecting how I speak or write.[†] That again supports a Japanese philosopher's tendency to be less interested in the denatured, proposition-asserting aspect of language than in how language responds within an interpersonal, always shifting, social field. To understand what any statement means, we would do well to consider not just the words, but also the context and audience of those words. Without an audience, words have not yet attained their full function as meaning.

To once again be clear, I am *not* claiming that Japanese philosophers are interested in certain aspects of languages more than others because their language *determines* them to think along those lines. With some exceptions, Japanese philosophers delve into the nature of *language*, not just the Japanese language. All people, regardless of culture, ethnicity, gender, class, or nationality, share in multitudinous ways of using words. Meaning depends on who is speaking, to whom one is speaking, and the conditions that occasion the linguistic expression. For example, those conditions would inform the English speaker whether to say, "thank you so much," "thank you," or "thanks" or even to just nod and smile. Language is used to soothe the distressed, to buck up the timid, to spiral off into or out of a maelstrom of depressing thoughts. We use language to make us laugh or cry, to hurt or to feel good, to uplift or to dampen, to demand or to plead, to reveal or to conceal.

Yes, of course, we certainly also use language to refer to states of affairs, to point out aspects of reality. Yet, the denatured sentence is only one arrow in language's quiver—the logical part. Logic is part of language, but language is never just logic, no matter how much we might try to denature it.

† See pages 565–6.

My claim then is that a denatured sentence may stand out more sharply as unnatural when written in Japanese rather than, say, English. Consequently, an English speaker might more readily slip into the false view that denatured sentences are natural sentences or that linguistic expressions are propositional statements with some extra emotive frills that can be jettisoned with little or no philosophical loss. Still, granting all the differences between Japanese and English, it is true in *both* languages that a denatured sentence is not an adequate paradigm of what language, any language, is or how it functions. That general insight into language is not determined by the particular language one speaks.

The Primacy of the Verb or Predicate

English (like many other languages, living and dead, in which western philosophy has traditionally been written) requires as a rule both a subject and a predicate in every sentence. Hence, the minimum sentence in English requires at least two words, paradigmatically a noun for the subject and a verb for the predicate.† The bridge, the external relation between the subject noun and predicate verb, forms the nucleus of the English sentence, the remaining words in the sentence ultimately modifying that nucleus. (For those familiar with the grammatical exercise of diagramming English sentences, the diagram begins with the polarity of subject and predicate as its template, having all the other words in the sentence serve as branches sprouting from them.)

Suppose you live where the cultural orientation privileges external relations and also favors a metaphysics in which self-existing things (substances) are understood to have discrete, essential properties (attributes). Furthermore, suppose you are enculturated to assume events can be analyzed into the agency performing the activity and the activity itself. If your native language happens to be English or some other Indo-European language with the embedded subject-

---

† To prevent confusion, I should add that I am not referring to elliptical statements which superficially seem to lack either a subject or predicate. For example, consider this brief exchange. "Is that Tanya or Michelle standing over there?" "Tanya." The second, declarative statement is actually asserting a full sentence that, for convenience, has omitted some words already said and now assumed. The full sentence is "(The person standing over there is) Tanya." It is *elliptical* (as in an ellipsis …) because, given the context, the words omitted from the full sentence, were they uttered, would indicate nothing additional. Indeed, they have already been part of the initial question in the conversation and the information is known to both participants in the dialogue.

Furthermore, in some languages, the verb inflects for person (I, you, she, he, it, we, they). In that case, the verb has two parts, the verb stem (with its tense) and person. The person part of the inflection contains the apparently missing subject of the sentence. Hence, the Latin *cogito* means "I think." If I add the understood pronoun and say *ego cogito*, I have brought no new propositional meaning to the sentence. That shows the original sentence is elliptical.

predicate structure I just described, you would likely speak of the substances and agencies in terms of nouns that form the subjects of sentences. Conversely, you would speak of the attributes of substances and the actions of the agencies in terms of verbs forming the predicate of those sentences. (Remember that the copula *is* acts as a verbal link with an adjective or noun in a predicate such as *is red* or *is a fruit*.)

Given that happy convergence between the philosophical ideas and the language in which they are expressed, as a philosopher you would likely feel secure in your view of the world and your ability to articulate it. But suppose you have second thoughts. You start entertaining the possibility that reality is more like an interdependent cluster of self-generative processes than static things or agencies and that relations are more likely internal than external. For articulating that perspective, the structure of your native tongue does not make it easy for you. Certainly, no language can *prevent* you from thinking and expressing your ideas. Your thoughts are never fully determined by your language; like a poet, you can generate creative ways of speaking within that language that allow you to say what your language has not yet been fully shaped to say well.

To develop your philosophy to any extent, however, you would have to leave the linguistic comfort zone that has been traditionally used to support a world view you no longer hold. You will have to find how to make processes the subject of sentences without attributing discrete, independent agency. You will need to develop strategies for using language to highlight events rather than substances. This, of course, can be done. Process philosophers have already done it, often pushing the comfortable limits of their language: Hegel and Heidegger did it in German, Bergson in French, and Whitehead in English, for example.

Now consider the cultural mirror image of this situation. In Japanese the verb that would be the predicate in a subject-predicate language, even if it is only a single word, can be a sentence in itself. For instance, the verb *iku* ("goes") can stand alone as a complete sentence. As Japanese verbs do not inflect by person, *iku* does not in itself specify whether what goes is I, we, you, he, she, it, or they. Any words added now to expand the sentence are essentially modifying that verb as the syntactic nucleus, bringing to it greater specificity. It is critical to understand that in Japanese *iku* is not simply elliptical, leaving out what has been said already; instead, the sentence opens to elaboration only as deemed necessary in the particular context, saying what has not been said up to now, but given the circumstances, *has* to be added for the sake of further elaboration.

Unlike in English, the Japanese subject cannot be conceived as independent of the predicate, but rather is an outgrowth of it.[8*] In effect, the subject of the Japanese sentence is just a modifier of the verbal predicate on a par with other modifiers such as the temporal, locative, or instrumental. The subject lacks the privileged status it enjoys in the bridge-like English sentence linking subject and predicate. In Japanese the subject plays an almost adverbial role; it becomes part of the how of the happening instead of the what that makes something happen.

A rather bizarre little anecdote might bring the point home. One late evening in Tokyo I was riding the subway, fortunately not crowded at the time, and two young Japanese women sat in the seats next to me, engrossed in conversation. My sleepy eyes were almost closed as they continued their chitchat, speaking in hushed yet animated tones, sometimes giggling. I suspect they assumed that either I was asleep or did not understand Japanese, or both. At least I rather hope so. From the snippets I picked up, it seems they were talking about the intimate details of a mutual acquaintance's recent sexual adventures.

The detailed exchange continued for a couple of minutes. My dreamy state of mind drifted with the conversation and, frankly, at some points I was trying to picture what they were talking about, but could not do so clearly. The problem was that I did not definitively know if they were talking about a man or a woman. *They* knew which it was, of course, and probably in the first sentence or two of their conversation before boarding the subway, they even mentioned the person's name. So they were being elliptical, not repeating what had already been said and understood.

The point I want to underscore, though, is that their Japanese language did not require a subject for their sentences and they did not bother giving one, at least in the part of the exchange I overheard. I doubt that any comparable conversation in English that went on for so long, however elliptical the speakers' sentences might have been, would not have slipped in a personal pronoun or personal name somewhere to refer to the agent of the activities, to give a subject to the predicates. The demands of English syntax—no predicates allowed without subjects—could not have been resisted for such a stretch of verbal exchange.

As it stood, though, when I came to my subway stop I left without knowing whether the women were talking about a *he* or a *she* or—omigosh!—a *they*. For a short span of time, I had found myself an accidental eavesdropper on events minutely detailed. The predicates were bursting with vivid verbs, adverbs, adjectives, and nouns. Yet, what we might consider the star of the show—the unnamed subject of the sentences and the agent of the actions—was conspicuously absent. I knew a lot about *how* the unmentioned subject of the sentences behaved, but not *who* or *what* that subject was.

By contrast, in English we certainly could, if we were skilled enough writers, describe an action or event without specifying the subject or agent. But it would be difficult. As a native speaker of a subject-predicate language, when I hear or read a predicate I connect it back in the sentence to the subject. If I hear a subject, I anticipate a predicate. As a bridge, the sentence cannot be a bridge to nowhere. I must have two endpoints to span. That propensity has to be at least somewhat mitigated if we are to engage Japanese philosophy and not merely think about it in a detached manner.

In this book, I often remind us to try to stop looking for a *what* as the missing answer to a philosophical question and instead to be on the lookout for a *how*. The *how* departs from the verb not the noun, throwing us into the midst of the event so we can think through it, not about it. If we do that, we engage Japanese philosophy, not only in its content, but also through its mode of expression, even when its language is translated into English.

NOTES

1. ACKROYD 1979, x.

2. For an anthropological study of the use of *kaimyō* in Japan today see the dissertation by Erica SWARTS 2001.

3. A third strata was added to the Japanese language with the inundation of European words entering the country in the modern period. Those words are almost always written in *katakana* to distinguish them from the other two strata of the language. In effect, that is comparable to the English practice of writing foreign words in italics. Thousands of these words are in common use in Japan. Since they do not have a strong influence on philosophy in Japan (except in using technical European terminology with no Japanese equivalent), I will not discuss them further here.

4. As the Chinese dynasties rose and fell, the capital moved to different regions of China with different dialects. At the same time Japanese traders and spiritual seekers also expanded their range of travel within that country. So new words imported from China came with new pronunciations of the sinographs based on differences in the Chinese dialects. (In general, the dialects use the same sinographs but pronounce them according to their local conventions.) Because the "Chinese" pronunciation of words newly introduced to Japan would reflect those variations, the consequence was that even more pronunciations came to accompany the identical sinographs already in Japan.

The history of the varying Japanese pronunciations of sinographs is certainly a treasure trove for philological and lexical studies, but the question is whether it has any philosophical significance. Sometimes it seems so. To take one example, the sinograph 明 has three common pronunciations, namely, *akira*, *myō*, and *mei*. The first is a Yamato or *kun* pronunciation; the latter two are Chinese with different pronunciations reflecting the word's itinerary and time of entry into Japan.

Regardless of pronunciation, the basic denotation of the sinograph 明 is rather constant, however: it refers broadly to "bright clarity." Yet, the same sinograph has different connotations when it used by Shintō, Buddhist, and Confucian philosophers. That itself is not necessarily remarkable. Yet, because Shintō, Buddhist, and Confucian ideas have different timelines for their main appearance in Japan, the Shintō thinker is more likely (with admittedly *many* exceptions) to pronounce the sinograph *akira* (or *akari*), the Buddhist *myō*, and the Confucian *mei*. That is, the written sinograph secures the basic denotation, but the voiced reading gives the term a connotative place within the Shintō, Buddhist, or Confucian worlds of meaning. If we know the sinograph, we know to what it refers, but if we know the pronunciation as well, we sometimes have a clue as to other terms with which it is likely to intersect. In Frege's terminology, the written sinograph in such cases is more linked to the *Bedeutung* and the pronunciation more to the *Sinn*.

Another example would be the term "ancient Way," a concept important to both Japanese Confucian and Native Studies philosophers. It is originally a Chinese-derived term written 古道, pronounced by the Confucians as *kodō*. When the term is picked up and used by Shintō thinkers like Motoori Norinaga, however, it is given a Shintō reading *inishie no michi*, as if it were a Yamato word preceding the influx of Chinese Confucianism (which, to my knowledge, it isn't). To camoflage the Chinese connection further, *inishie no michi* is most often written in *kana* instead of the sinograph.

That this distinction between written and voiced form occurs only occasionally and only with some terms makes the phenomenon less than astounding, but that the differentiation ever occurs at all is still noteworthy. At the least, it shows another way sound in Japan plays a special role in conferring meaning.

5. Some people such as those with severe autism may have difficulty processing a spoken sentence as anything but denatured. Lacking a sensitivity to the social cues embedded in intonation, gestures, facial expressions, and so forth, such individuals may not be able to readily go beyond the literal meaning to see how that meaning is nuanced by context or feeling.

6. *Emoji* is a word of Japanese origin. It means picture (*e*) + character or letter (*moji*). They were invented in the 1990s by the Japanese mobile phone company DoCoMo when consumers wanted a way to communicate emotions with pictures while using only a single keystroke, an important consideration in messages restricted to a fixed number of characters.

7. Literally, *kanai* means the "one within the household" as contrasted with the husband who is the "master" (*shujin*) of the household in interactions with outsiders. *Okusan*, on other hand, means the "honorable mistress of the interior (of the household)" while the husband is honorifically called *goshujin*, the "honorable master" representing the house to those outside one's intimate group.

8. Nishida's terminology misleads us a bit in speaking of the "logic of the predicate" as contrasted with an Aristotelian "logic of the [grammatical] subject." The Aristotelian designation is acceptable because Aristotle's logic assumes the subject-predicate bridge. If we follow Nishida's line of analysis, however, there really cannot be a "logic of the predicate" because there can be no predicate without a subject and he has the subject emerge out of the predicate. Yet, without a subject, it is peculiar to refer to a *predicate*. He gets around this problem in some ways by ultimately identifying the predicate with absolute nothing, thereby reminding us that the predicate opens up to the rest of the sentence.

Map of Japan

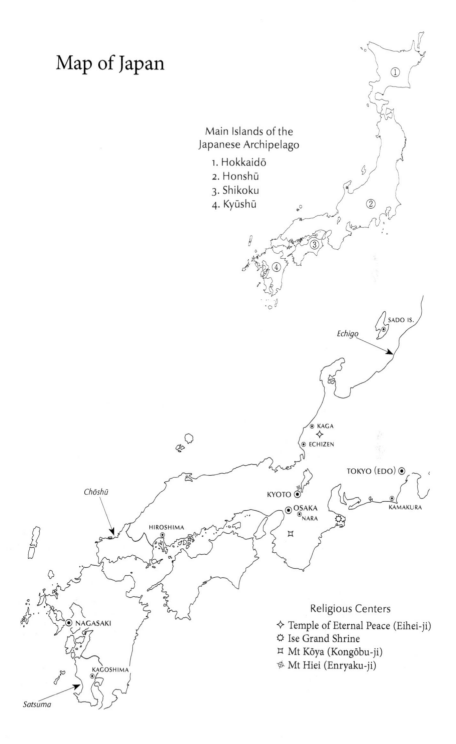

Main Islands of the
Japanese Archipelago

1. Hokkaidō
2. Honshū
3. Shikoku
4. Kyūshū

SADO IS.

Echigo

KAGA
ECHIZEN

TOKYO (EDO)

Chōshū

KYOTO

OSAKA
NARA

KAMAKURA

HIROSHIMA

Religious Centers

✧ Temple of Eternal Peace (Eihei-ji)
✿ Ise Grand Shrine
⌑ Mt Kōya (Kongōbu-ji)
⚘ Mt Hiei (Enryaku-ji)

NAGASAKI

KAGOSHIMA

Satsuma

697

Bibliography

Abbreviations

CD 　『世界史的立場と日本』[The world-historical standpoint and Japan] (Tokyo: Chūōkōronsha, 1943).

CWS 　*The Collected Works of Shinran*, trans. with introductions, glossaries, and reading aids by Dennis Hirota (Kyoto: Jodo Shinshu Hongwanji-ha, 1997), 2 vols.

DZZ 　『道元禅師全集』[Complete works of Zen Master Dōgen] (Tokyo: Shun-jūsha, 1989–1991), 7 vols.

ER 　Lindsay Jones, editor in chief, *The Encyclopedia of Religion* (Farmington Hills, MI: Macmillan Reference), 15 vols.

JPS 　*Japanese Philosophy: A Sourcebook,* James W. Heisig, Thomas P. Kasulis, John C. Maraldo, eds. (Honolulu: University of Hawai'i Press, 2011).

KKZ 　『弘法大師空海全集』[Complete works of Kōbō Daishi Kūkai] (Tokyo: Chikuma Shobō, 1983–1985), 10 vols.

KZ 　『定本弘法大師全集』[Complete works of Kōbō Daishi, standard ed.] (Waka-yama: Kōyasan Daigaku Mikkyō Bunka Kenkyūjo, 1991–1997), 10 vols.

NKBT 　『日本古典文学大系』[Library of Japanese classical literature] (Tokyo: Iwa-nami Shoten, 1957–1969), 102 vols.

NKZ 　『西田幾多郎全集』[Complete Works of Nishida Kitarō] (Tokyo: Iwanami shoten, 2003–0), 25 vols.

NST 　『日本思想大系』[Library of Japanese thought] (Tokyo: Iwanami Shoten, 1970–1982), 77 vols.

OM 　Kawakami Tetsutarō 河上徹太郎, et al., 『近代の超克』 [Overcoming modernity] (Tokyo: Fuzanbō, 1994).

SJT-1 　*Sources of Japanese Tradition,* Wm. Theodore de Bary et al., eds. (New York: Columbia University Press, 1964, 1st edition), vol. 1 of 2 vols.

SJT-2 　*Sources of Japanese Tradition,* Wm. Theodore de Bary et al., eds. (New York: Columbia University Press, 2001, 2nd edition), vol. 2 of 2 vols.

WTZ 　『和辻哲郎全集』[Complete works of Watsuji Tetsurō] (Tokyo: Iwanami Shoten, 1961–1991), 22 vols.

General reference works in western languages

1983 　*Kodansha Encyclopedia of Japan* (New York: Kodansha), 9 vols.

2006 *Encyclopedia of Philosophy.* Donald M. Borchert, editor in chief (Detroit, MI: Macmillan Reference), 10 vols.

1995– *Stanford Encyclopedia of Philosophy.* Online: https://plato.stanford.edu.

Other sources

BLOCKER, H. Gene, and Christopher L. STARLING

2001 *Japanese Philosophy* (Albany, NY: SUNY Press).

BOWRING, Richard, and Peter KORNICKI

1993 *The Cambridge Encyclopedia of Japan* (New York: Cambridge University Press).

BRÜLL, Lydia

1989 *Die Japanische Philosophie. Eine Einführung* (Darmstadt: Wissenschaftliche Buchgesellschaft, 2nd edition), 1993.

CRAIG, Edward

1998 *Routledge Encyclopedia of Philosophy* (London; Routledge), 10 vols.

GONZÁLEZ VALLES, Jesús

2000 *Historia de la filosofía japonesa* (Madrid: Tecnos).

HAMADA Junko 濱田恂子

1994 *Japanische Philosophie nach 1868* (Leiden: E. J. Brill).

HEISIG, James (ed.)

2004 *Japanese Philosophy Abroad* (Nagoya: Nanzan Institute for Religion and Culture).

PAUL, Gregor

1986 *Zur Geschichte der Philosophie in Japan und zu ihrer Darstellung* (Tokyo: Deutsche Gesellschaft für Natur- und Völkerkunde Ostasiens).

Works cited in the text

ABE Masao 阿部正雄

1992 *A Study of Dōgen: His Philosophy and Religion,* ed. by Steven Heine (Albany, NY: SUNY Press).

ABE Ryūichi 阿部龍一

1999 *The Weaving of Mantra: Kūkai and the Construction of Esoteric Buddhist Discourse* (New York: Columbia University Press).

ACKROYD, Joyce

1979 "On Samurai Names" from *Told Round a Brushwood Fire: The Autobiography of Arai Hakuseki.* (Tokyo: University of Tokyo Press).

AMES, Roger T.

2011 *Confucian Role Ethics: A Vocabulary* (Honolulu: University of Hawai'i Press).

ANESAKI Masaharu 姉崎正治

1916 *Nichiren: The Buddhist Prophet* (Gloucester, MA: P. Smith).

ARAI Hakuseki 新井白石

1979 *Told Round a Brushwood Fire: The Autobiography of Arai Hakuseki*, trans. by Joyce Ackroyd (Tokyo: University of Tokyo Press).

1982 *Lessons from History: The "Tokushi yoron,"* trans. and commentary by Joyce Ackroyd (St Lucia; New York: University of Queensland Press).

AYER, Alfred Jules.

1952 *Language, Truth and Logic* (New York: Dover Publications).

ASTON, W. G.

1972 *Nihongi: Chronicles of Japan from the Earliest Times to A.D. 697* (Rutland, VT: C. E. Tuttle).

BARDSLEY, Jan

2007 *The Bluestockings of Japan: New Woman Essays and Fiction from Seitō, 1911–1916* (Ann Arbor, MI: Center for Japanese Studies, The University of Michigan).

BELLAH, Robert N.

1957 *Tokugawa Religion: The Values of Pre-industrial Japan* (New York: Free Press).

2003 *Imagining Japan: The Japanese Tradition and Its Modern Interpretation* (Berkeley: University of California Press).

BERGSON, Henri

1955 *An Introduction to Metaphysics,* trans. by T. E. Hulme; with an introduction by Thomas A. Goudge (Indianapolis: Bobbs-Merrill).

BERMÚDEZ, José, and Arnon CAHEN

2012 "Nonconceptual Mental Content" in *Stanford Encyclopedia of Philosophy* (Spring 2012 edition), ed. by Edward N. Zalta (http://plato.stanford.edu/entries/content-nonconceptual/).

BIELEFELDT, Carl

1988 *Dōgen's Manuals of Zen Meditation* (Berkeley: University of California Press).

BIX, Herbert P.

1986 *Peasant Protest in Japan, 1590–1884* (New Haven, CT: Yale University Press).

BLOOM, Alfred, ed.

2004　*Living in Amida's Universal Vow* (Bloomington, IN: World Wisdom).

BLUM, Mark L.

2008　"When the Dharma Comes: Contextualizing the Public Transmission of Buddhism in Japan" in Dorothy C. Wong, ed., *Hōryūji Reconsidered:* 法隆寺の再検討 (Newcastle, UK: Cambridge Scholars Publishing), 193–235.

BLUM, Mark Laurence, and Shin'ya YASUTOMI, eds.

2006　*Rennyo and the Roots of Modern Japanese Buddhism* (Oxford: Oxford University Press).

BOCK, Felicia G.

1985　*Classical Learning and Taoist Practices in Early Japan: With a Translation of Books XVI and XX of the "Engi-shiki"* (Tempe, AZ: Center for Asian Studies, Arizona State University).

BOWRING, Richard J.

2005　*The Religious Traditions of Japan, 500–1600* (New York: Cambridge University Press).

BREEN, John, and Mark TEEUWEN

2000　*Shinto in History: Ways of the Kami* (Honolulu: University of Hawai'i Press).

2010　*A New History of Shinto* (Malden, MA: Wiley-Blackwell).

CADDEAU, Patrick W.

2006　*Appraising Genji: Literary Criticism and Cultural Anxiety in the Age of the Last Samurai* (Albany, NY: SUNY Press).

CALICHMAN, Richard

2008　*Overcoming Modernity: Cultural Identity in Wartime Japan*, ed. and trans. by Richard Calichman (New York: Columbia University Press).

CARTER, Robert E.

1996　"Interpretive Essay: Strands of Influence," in *Watsuji* 1996, 325–54.

CHANG, Chung-Yuan

1963　*Creativity and Taoism: A Study of Chinese Philosophy, Art and Poetry* (New York: Julian Press).

COATES, Harper H., and Ryūgaku ISHIZUKA (trans.)

1925　*Honen, the Buddhist Saint: His Life and Teaching* (Kyoto: Chion-in), 2 vols.

COLLCUTT, Martin

1981　*Five Mountains: The Rinzai Zen Monastic Institution in Medieval Japan* (Cambridge, MA: Harvard University Press).

COLLINS, Randall

1998   *The Sociology of Philosophies: A Global Theory of Intellectual Change* (Cambridge, MA: Belknap Press of Harvard University Press).

COMO, Michael

2008   *Shōtoku: Ethnicity, Ritual, and Violence in the Japanese Buddhist Tradition* (New York: Oxford University Press).

CONFUCIUS

1938   *The Analects of Confucius,* trans. and annotated by Arthur Waley (New York: Random House).

1999   *The Analects of Confucius: A Philosophical Translation,* trans. by Roger Ames and Henry Rosemont, Jr. (New York: Ballantine Books).

2003   *Analects: With Selections from Traditional Commentaries,* trans. by Edward Slingerland (Indianapolis, IN: Hackett Publishing).

DAVIS, Bret

2012   "The Kyoto School" in *Stanford Encyclopedia of Philosophy* (Winter 2014 edition), Edward N. Zalta, ed., (http://plato.stanford.edu/archives/win2014/entries/kyoto-school/).

DEBARY, William T., and Irene BLOOM, eds.

1979   *Principle and Practicality: Essays in Neo-Confucianism and Practical Learning* (New York: Columbia University Press).

DENNIS, Mark W. (trans.)

2011   *Prince Shōtoku's Commentary on the Śrīmālā Sutra, Taishō* 56.2185, trans. by Mark W. Dennis (Berkeley: Bukkyō Dendō Kyōkai America).

DOBBINS, James C.

1989   *Jōdo Shinshū: Shin Buddhism in Medieval Japan* (Bloomington, IN: Indiana University Press).

2004   *Letters of the Nun Eshinni: Images of Pure Land Buddhism in Medieval Japan.* (Honolulu: University of Hawai'i Press).

DŌGEN 道元

1986   *Shobogenzo: Zen Essays by Dogen,* trans. and annotated by Thomas F. Cleary (Honolulu: University of Hawai'i Press).

2001   "Instructions for the Cook," trans. by T. Griffith Foulk (Sotoshu Shumucho http://web.stanford.edu/group/scbs/sztp3/translations/eihei_shingi/translations/tenzo_kyokun/translation.html).

2002A   *The Heart of Dōgen's "Shōbōgenzō,"* trans. and annotated by Norman Waddell and Abe Masao (Albany, NY: SUNY Press).

2002B   "Getting the Marrow by Doing Obeisance," trans. by Stanley Weinstein (Sotoshu Shumucho: http://web.stanford.edu/group/scbs/sztp3/translations/shobogenzo/translations/raihai_tokuzui/rhtz.translation.html).

2006   *Shōbōgenzō: Ausgewählte Schriften. Anders Philosophieren aus dem Zen,* ed. and trans. with commentary by Ōhashi Ryōsuke and Rolf Elberfeld (Tokyo: Keio University Press).

2010   *Treasury of the True Dharma Eye: Zen master Dogen's "Shobogenzo,"* trans. by Tanahashi Kazuaki (Boston: Shambhala), 2 vols.

EISENSTADT, S. N.

1996   *Japanese Civilization: A Comparative View* (Chicago: University of Chicago Press).

ELISON, George

1973   *Deus Destroyed: The Image of Christianity in Early Modern Japan* (Cambridge, MA: Harvard University Press).

FAURE, Bernard

1991   *The Rhetoric of Immediacy: A Cultural Critique of Chan/Zen Buddhism* (Princeton, NJ: Princeton University Press).

FINDLY, Ellison Banks

2005   "Breath and Breathing," in ER 2: 1041–7.

FOARD, James H.

1980   "In Search of a Lost Reformation: A Reconsideration of Kamakura Buddhism, *Japanese Journal of Religious Studies* 7/4: 261–91.

FRELLESVIG, Bjarke

2010   *A History of the Japanese Language* (Cambridge: Cambridge University Press).

GIEBEL, Rolf W., and Dale A. TODARO

2004   *Shingon Texts* (Berkeley: Numata Center for Buddhist Translation and Research).

GOLDIN, Paul, ed.

2014   *Dao Companion to the Philosophy of Han Fei* (Dordrecht: Springer).

GORDON, Andrew

2003   *A Modern History of Japan: From Tokugawa Times to the Present* (New York: Oxford University Press).

GOTO-JONES, Christopher S.

2009   *Modern Japan: A Very Short Introduction* (Oxford: Oxford University Press).

GRAPARD, Allan G.

1992 "The Shinto of Yoshida Kanetomo," *Monumenta Nipponica* 47/1: 27–58.

GRONER, Paul

2002 *Ryōgen and Mount Hiei: Japanese Tendai in the Tenth Century* (Honolulu: University of Hawai'i Press).

GYŌNEN 凝然

1994 *Essentials of the Eight Traditions,* trans. by Leo M. Pruden (Berkeley, CA: Numata Center for Translation and Research).

HADOT, Pierre

1995 *Philosophy as a Way of Life: Spiritual Exercises from Socrates to Foucault,* ed. by Arnold I. Davidson, trans. by Michael Chase (Malden, MA: Blackwell).

2002 *What Is Ancient Philosophy?,* trans by Michael Chase (Cambridge, MA: Harvard University Press).

HAKEDA, Yoshito S.

1972 *Kūkai: Major Works,* trans. by Yoshito S. Hakeda (New York: Columbia University Press).

HAMMER, Joshua

2006 *Yokohama Burning: The Deadly 1923 Earthquake and Fire that Helped Forge the Path to World War II* (New York: Free Press).

HANSEN, Wilburn

2008 *When Tengu Talk: Hirata Atsutane's Ethnography of the Other World* (Honolulu: University of Hawai'i Press).

HARDACRE, Helen

1989 *Shinto and the State, 1868–1988* (Princeton, NJ: Princeton University Press).

HAROOTUNIAN, Harry D.

1988 *Things Seen and Unseen: Discourse and Ideology in Tokugawa Nativism* (Chicago: University of Chicago Press).

HEIDEGGER, Martin

1962 *Being and Time,* trans. by John Macquarrie & Edward Robinson (New York: Harper & Row).

1971 *On the Way to Language,* trans. by P. D. Hertz (New York: Harper & Row).

HEINE, Steven

1985 *Existential and Ontological Dimensions of Time in Heidegger and Dōgen* (Albany, NY: SUNY Press).

1994 *Dōgen and the Kōan Tradition: A Tale of Two Shōbōgenzō Texts* (Albany, NY: SUNY Press).

HEISIG, James W.

2001 *Philosophers of Nothingness: An Essay on the Kyoto School* (Honolulu: University of Hawai'i Press).

2015 "Nishida's Philosophical Equivalents of Enlightenment and No-Self" in *Much Ado about Nothingness: Essays on Nishida and Tanabe* (Nagoya: Nanzan Institute for Religion and Culture), 153–89.

HEISIG, James W., and John C. MARALDO, eds.

1995 *Rude Awakenings: Zen, the Kyoto School, and the Question of Nationalism* (Honolulu: University of Hawai'i Press).

HIROTA, Dennis

2006 *Asura's Harp: Engagement with Language as Buddhist Path* (Heidelberg: Universitätsverlag Winter).

HŌNEN 法然

1997 *Senchaku hongan nembutsu shū: A Collection of Passages on the Nembutsu Chosen in the Original Vow,* trans. by Morris J. Augustine and Kondō Tesshō, BDK English Tripitaka 104–II (Berkeley, CA: Bukkyō Dendō Kyōkai and Numata Center for Buddhist Translation and Research).

1998 *Hōnen's "Senchakushū": Passages on the Selection of the Nembutsu in the Original Vow,* trans. by the Senchakushū Translation Project (Honolulu: University of Hawai'i Press).

2011 *The Promise of Amida Buddha: Hōnen's Path to Bliss,* trans. by Jōji Atone and Yoko Hayashi (Boston, MA: Wisdom Publications).

HORI, Victor S.

2003 *Zen Sand: The Book of Capping Phrases for Kōan Practice* (Honolulu: University of Hawai'i Press).

HUBBARD, Jamie, and Paul L. SWANSON

1997 *Pruning the Bodhi Tree: The Storm over Critical Buddhism* (Honolulu: University of Hawai'i Press).

HUSSERL, Edmund

1982 *Ideas Pertaining to a Pure Phenomenology and to a Phenomenological Philosophy—First Book: General Introduction to a Pure Phenomenology,* trans. by F. Kersten (The Hague: Nijhof).

IHDE, Don

1976 *Listening and Voice: A Phenomenology of Sound* (Athens, OH: Ohio University Press).

INOUE Nobutaka 井上順孝, ed.

2003 *Shinto: A Short History,* trans. by Mark Teeuwen and John Breen (London: RoutledgeCurzon).

IWASAWA Tomoko 岩澤知子

2011   *Tama in Japanese Myth: A Hermeneutical Study of Ancient Japanese Divinity* (Lanham, MD: University Press of America).

IZUTSU Toshihiko 井筒俊彦

1982   *Language and Magic: Studies in the Magical Functions of Speech* (Tokyo: Keio Institute of Philological Studies).

1984   *Sufism and Taoism: A Comparative Study of Key Philosophical Concepts* (Berkeley: University of California Press).

1982   *Toward a Philosophy of Zen Buddhism* (Boulder, CO: Prajña Press).

IZUTSU Toshihiko, and IZUTSU Toyo(ko) 井筒豊(子)

1981   *The Theory of Beauty in the Classical Aesthetics of Japan* (Boston: Martinus Nijhoff Publishers).

JAMES, William

1890   *The Principles of Psychology* (New York: Henry Holt & Co.), 2 vols.

1958   *The Varieties of Religious Experience* (New York: The New American Library).

1971   *Essays in Radical Empiricism and A Pluralistic Universe,* ed. by Ralph Barton Perry (New York: E. P. Dutton).

JENSEN, Lionel M.

1997   *Manufacturing Confucianism: Chinese Traditions and Universal Civilization* (Durham, NC: Duke University Press).

JONES, Nicholaos J.

2004   "The Logic of *Soku* in the Kyoto School," *Philosophy East and West* 54/3: 302–21.

KADOWAKI Kakichi 門脇佳吉

1977   『密教とキリスト教：神秘思想の現代的意義』 [Esotericism and Christianity: The present-day significance of mystical ideas] (Osaka: Sōgensha).

KANAOKA Shūyū 金岡秀友

1979   『空海辞典』 [Kūkai dictionary] (Tokyo: Tokyodō Shuppan).

KASAHARA Kazuo 笠原一男, ed.

2001   *A History of Japanese Religion* (Tokyo: Kosei Publishing Company).

KASULIS, Thomas P.

1981   *Zen Action, Zen Person* (Honolulu: University of Hawaiʻi Press).

1982   "Reference and Symbol in Plato's *Cratylus* and Kūkai's *Shōjijissōgi*," *Philosophy East and West* 32/4: 393–405.

1984   "Kōbō Daishi and Karl Rahner: The Ground of Spirituality" in Goonki

Kinen Shuppan Hensan Iinkai 御遠忌記念出版編纂委員会, ed.,『弘法大師と現代』[Kōbō Daishi today] (Tokyo: Chikuma Shobō), 57–74.

1989 "Whence and Whither: Philosophical Reflections on Nishitani's View of History," in Taitetsu Unno, ed., *The Religious Philosophy of Nishitani Keiji: Encounter with Emptiness* (Berkeley: Asian Humanities Press), 259–78.

1990 "Kūkai (774–835): Philosophizing in the Archaic" in Frank Reynolds and David Tracy, eds., *Myth and Philosophy* (Albany, NY: SUNY Press), 131–50.

1992 "Philosophy as Metapraxis" in Frank Reynolds and David Tracy, eds., *Discourse and Practice* (Albany, NY: SUNY Press), 169–96.

1997 "Intimations of Religious Experience and Interreligious Truth" in Thomas P. Kasulis and Robert C. Neville, eds., *The Recovery of Philosophy in America: Essays in Honor of John Edwin Smith* (Albany, NY: SUNY Press), 39–57.

1998 "Zen and Artistry" in Roger T. Ames with Thomas P. Kasulis and Wimal Dissanayake, eds., *Self as Image in Asian Theory and Practice*, (Albany, NY: SUNY Press), 357–71.

2002 *Intimacy or Integrity: Philosophy and Cultural Difference* (Honolulu: University of Hawai'i Press).

2004 *Shinto: The Way Home* (Honolulu: University of Hawai'i Press).

2005 "Nirvāṇa" in ER 10: 6628–35.

2007 "Reading D. T. Suzuki Today" *The Eastern Buddhist* 38/1–2: 41–57.

2008 "Cultivating the Mindful Heart: What We May Learn from the Japanese Philosophy of *Kokoro*" in Roger T. Ames and Peter D. Hershock, eds., *Educations and Their Purposes: A Conversation among Cultures* (Honolulu: University of Hawai'i Press), 142–56.

2010 "The Ground of Translation: Issues in Translating Premodern Japanese Philosophy" in *Classical Japanese Philosophy*, ed. by James W. Heisig and Rein Raud (Nagoya: Nanzan Institute for Religion and Culture), 7–38.

KATŌ Shūkō 加藤宗厚編

1952 『正法眼蔵要語索引』[Concordance to *Shōbōgenzō*] (Tokyo: Risōsha), 2 vols.

KEEL, Hee-Sung

1995 *Understanding Shinran: A Dialogical Approach* (Fremont, CA: Asian Humanities Press).

KEENE, Donald

1984 "Characteristic Responses to Confucianism in Tokugawa Literature" in *Confucianism and Tokugawa Culture*, ed. by Peter Nosco (Princeton, NJ: Princeton University Press), 120–37.

1960 *Anthology of Japanese Literature, From the Earliest Era to the Mid-Nineteenth Century* (New York: Grove Press).

1956   *Modern Japanese Literature: An Anthology,* ed. by Donald Keene (New York: Grove Press).

KETELAAR, James Edward

1990   *Of Heretics and Martyrs in Meiji Japan: Buddhism and Its Persecution* (Princeton, NJ: Princeton University Press, 1990).

KIDDER, J. E.

2007   *Himiko and Japan's Elusive Chiefdom of Yamatai: Archaeology, History, and Mythology* (Honolulu: University of Hawai'i Press).

KIM Hee-jin

1975   *Dōgen Kigen: Mystical Realist* (Tucson, AZ: University of Arizona Press).

KITABATAKE Chikafusa 北畠親房

1980   *A Chronicle of Gods and Sovereigns: Jinno shotoki of Kitabatake Chikafusa,* trans. by H. Paul Varley (New York: Columbia University Press).

KITAGAWA, Joseph M.

1966   *Religion in Japanese History* (New York: Columbia University Press).

KOPF, Gereon

2009   "Nationalism, Globalism, and Cosmopolitanism: An Application of Kyoto School Philosophy," in *Confluences and Cross-Currents,* ed. by Raquel Bouso and James W. Heisig (Nagoya: Nanzan Institute for Religion and Culture), 170–89.

KŌSAKA Masaaki

1958   *Japanese Thought in the Meiji Era,* trans. by David Abosch (Tokyo: Pan-Pacific Press).

KOYASU Nobukuni 子安宣邦

1977   『宣長と篤胤の世界』 [The world of Motoori and Atsutane] (Tokyo: Chūō-kōronsha).

KRAFT, Kenneth

1992   *Eloquent Zen: Daitō and Early Japanese Zen* (Honolulu: University of Hawai'i Press).

KŪKAI 空海

1975   *Kukai's Principle of Attaining Buddhahood with the Present Body,* trans. with introduction and annotation by Hisao Inagaki (Kyoto: Ryukoku Translation Center, Ryukoku University). See also GIEBEL and TODARO 2004.

KUKI Shūzō, 九鬼周造

1997   *Reflections on Japanese Taste: The Structure of "Iki,"* ed. by John Clark and trans. by Sakuko Matsui and John Clark (Sydney: Power Publications).

KUMANO Sumihiko 熊野純彦

2009　『日本哲学小史──近代 100 年の 20 篇』[A short history of Japanese philosophy: Twenty topics from the past century] (Tokyo: Chūōkōron Shinsha).

KURODA Toshio 黒田俊雄

1981　"Shinto in the History of Japanese Religion," trans. by James C. Dobbins and Suzanne Gay, *Journal of Japanese Studies* 7/1: 1–21.

LAFLEUR, William R.

1983　*The Karma of Words: Buddhism and the Literary Arts in Medieval Japan* (Berkeley: University of California Press).

1990　"A Turning in Taishō: Asia and Europe in the Early Writings of Watsuji Tetsurō," in J. T. Rimer (ed.) *Culture and Identity: Japanese Intellectuals during the Interwar Years* (Princeton, NJ: Princeton University Press), 234–56.

2001　"Reasons for the Rubble: Watsuji Tetsurō's Position in Japan's Postwar Debate about Rationality," *Philosophy East and West* 51/1: 1–25.

2003　*Awesome Nightfall: The Life, Times, and Poetry of Saigyō* (Boston: Wisdom Publications).

LIDIN, Olof G.

1973　*The Life of Ogyū Sorai, a Tokugawa Confucian Philosopher* (Lund: Studentlitt).

LINJI 臨済

2009　*The Record of Linji*, trans. and commentary by Ruth Fuller Sasaki, ed. by Thomas Yūhō Kirchner (Honolulu: University of Hawai'i Press).

MACHIDA Sōhō 町田宗鳳

1999　*Renegade Monk: Hōnen and Japanese Pure Land Buddhism*, ed. by Ioannis Mentzas (Berkeley: University of California Press).

MARALDO, John C.

2006　"Self-Mirroring and Self-Awareness: Dedekind, Royce, and Nishida," in James W. Heisig, ed., *Frontiers of Japanese Philosophy* (Nagoya: Nanzan Institute for Religion and Culture), 143–63.

2012　"*Nishida Kitarō*" in *Stanford Encyclopedia of Philosophy* (Summer 2012 edition), ed. by Edward N. Zalta, (http://plato.stanford.edu/archives/sum2012/entries/nishida-kitaro/).

MARRA, Michele

1981　*The Aesthetics of Discontent: Politics and Reclusion in Medieval Japanese Literature* (Honolulu: University of Hawai'i Press).

1988   "The Development of Mappō Thought in Japan," *Japanese Journal of Religious Studies* 15/1: 25–54, 15/4: 287–305.

MARUYAMA Masao 丸山真男

1974   *Studies in the Intellectual History of Tokugawa Japan,* trans. by Mikiso Hane (Princeton, NJ: Princeton University Press).

MATSUMOTO Shigeru 松本 滋

1970   *Motoori Norinaga, 1730–1801* (Cambridge, MA: Harvard University Press).

MATSUNAGA, Daigan, and Alicia MATSUNAGA

1974   *Foundation of Japanese Buddhism* (Los Angeles: Buddhist Books International), 2 vols.

MATSUO Kenji 松尾剛次

2007   *A History of Japanese Buddhism* (Folkestone: Global Oriental).

McCARTHY, Erin

2010   *Ethics Embodied: Rethinking Selfhood through Continental, Japanese, and Feminist Philosophies* (Lanham, MD: Lexington Books).

2011   "Beyond the Binary: Watsuji Tetsurō and Luce Irigaray on Body, Self and Ethics," in Bret W. Davis, Brian Schroeder and Jason M. Wirth, eds., *Japanese and Continental Philosophy: Conversations with the Kyoto School* (Bloomington, IN: Indiana University Press), 212–28.

McCLAIN, James L.

2002   *Japan, A Modern History* (New York: W.W. Norton & Co.).

McRAE, John R.

2004   *Seeing through Zen: Encounter, Transformation, and Genealogy in Chinese Chan Buddhism* (Berkeley: University of California Press).

MINAMOTO Ryōen 源 了圓

1969   『義理と人情――日本的心情の一考察』 [*Giri* and *ninjō*: a consideration of Japanese sentiments] (Tokyo: Chūōkōronsha).

1992   『型と日本文化』 [*Kata* and Japanese culture] (Tokyo: Sōbunsha).

MINEAR, Richard H.

1976   "Ogyū Sorai's Instructions for Students: A Translation and Commentary" *Harvard Journal of Asiatic Studies* 36: 5–81.

MINER, Earl R., Hiroko ODAGIRI, and Robert E. MORRELL

1985   *The Princeton Companion to Classical Japanese Literature* (Princeton, NJ: Princeton University Press).

MORITA Ryūsen 森田龍僊

1973 『弘法大師の入定観』 [Observations on Kōbō Daishi's passing into nir-vana] (Kyoto: Yamashiroya Bunseidō).

MORRIS, Ivan I.

1964 *The World of the Shining Prince: Court Life in Ancient Japan* (New York: Knopf).

MOTOORI Norinaga 本居宣長

1987 "First Steps into the Mountains: Motoori Norinaga's *Uiyamabumi*," trans. by Nishimura Sey, *Monumenta Nipponica* 42/4: 449–55.

1988 "The Jeweled Comb-Box: Motoori Norinaga's *Tamakushige*," trans. by J. S. Brownlee, *Monumenta Nipponica* 43/1: 35–44.

1991 "The Way of the Gods: Motoori Norinaga's *Naobi no Mitama*," trans. by Nishimura Sey, *Monumenta Nipponica* 46/1: 21–41.

1993 『本居宣長全集』 [Complete works of Motoori Norinaga], ed. by Ōno Susumu 大野晋 (Tokyo: Chikuma Shobō, 1968–1993), 23 vols.

1997 *Kojiki-den: Book 1*, trans. by Ann Wehmeyer (Ithaca, NY: East Asia Program, Cornell University).

MURASAKI Shikibu 紫 式部

2001 *The Tale of Genji*, trans. by Royall Tyler (New York: Viking).

MUSŌ Soseki 夢窓疎石

2010 *Dialogues in a Dream*, trans. by Thomas Yūhō Kirchner (Kyoto: Tenryu-ji Institute for Philosophy and Religion).

NĀGĀRJUNA

1995 *The Fundamental Wisdom of the Middle Way: Nāgārjuna's "Mūlamadhya-makakārikā,"* trans. by Jay L. Garfield (Somerville, MA: Wisdom Publications).

2013 *Nāgārjuna's Middle Way: Mūlamadhyamakakārikā*, trans. by Mark Siderits and Katsura Shōryū 桂紹隆 (Somerville, MA: Wisdom Publications).

NAGATOMO Shigenori

1992 *Attunement through the Body* (Albany, NY: SUNY Press).

NAKAMURA Hajime 中村元

1975 (ed.) 『佛教語大辞典』 [Dictionary of Buddhist terms] (Tokyo: Tokyo Shoseki), 3 vols.

2002 *History of Japanese Thought 592–1868: Japanese Philosophy before Western Culture Entered Japan* (London: Kegan Paul), 2 vols.

NATTIER, Jan

1991 *Once upon a Future Time: Studies in a Buddhist Prophecy of Decline* (Berkeley, CA: Asian Humanities Press).

NICHIREN 日蓮

1996   *Letters of Nichiren*, trans. by Burton Watson et al., ed. Philip B. Yampolsky (New York: Columbia University Press).

2003   *The Writings of Nichiren Daishonin* (Tokyo: Soka Gakkai), 2 vols.

NISHI HONGWANJI COMMISSION ON THE PROMOTION OF RELIGIOUS EDUCATION

1974   *Shinran in the Contemporary World* (Kyoto: Nishi Hongwanji).

NISHIDA Kitarō 西田幾多郎

1986   "The Logic of Topos and the Religious Worldview." trans. by Michiko Yusa, *Monumenta Nipponica* 19:2 1–29; 20:1 81–119.

1987A   *Intuition and Reflection in Self-Consciousness,* trans. by Valdo H. Viglielmo, Yoshinori Takeuchi, and Joseph S. O'Leary (Albany, NY: SUNY Press).

1987B   *Last Writings: Nothingness and the Religious Worldview,* trans. by David A. Dilworth (Honolulu: University of Hawai'i Press).

1990   *An Inquiry into the Good,* trans. by Masao Abe and Christopher Ives (New Haven, CT: Yale University Press).

NISHITANI Keiji 西谷啓治

1990   *The Self-Overcoming of Nihilism,* trans. by Graham Parkes and Setsuko Aihara (Albany, NY: SUNY Press).

NOGUCHI Takehiko 野口武彦

1993   『荻生徂徠: 江戸のドンキホーテ』[Ogyū Sorai: The Don Quixote of Edo] (Tokyo: Chūōshinsho 1161, Chūōkōronsha).

NOSCO, Peter

1990   *Remembering Paradise: Nativism and Nostalgia in Eighteenth-Century Japan* (Cambridge, MA: Council on East Asian Studies, Harvard University).

1984A   (ed.) *Confucianism and Tokugawa Culture* (Princeton, NJ: Princeton University Press).

1984B   "Masuho Zankō, a Shinto Popularizer," in P. Nosco, ed., *Confucianism and Tokugawa Culture* (Princeton, NJ: Princeton University Press), 166–87.

ODAGIRI Takushi 小田桐拓志

2008   "From Self-Reflexivity to Contingency: Nishida Kitarō on Self-Knowledge," in James W. Heisig and Uehara Mayuko, eds., *Origins and Possibilities* (Nagoya: Nanzan Institute for Religion and Culture), 73–93.

OGYŪ Sorai 荻生徂徠

1962   *The Political Writings of Ogyū Sorai,* trans. by J. R. McEwan (Cambridge, MA: Cambridge University Press).

1994   *Master Sorai's Responsals: An Annotated Translation of "Sorai sensei tōmonsho*," English trans. by Samuel Hideo Yamashita (Honolulu: University of Hawai'i Press).

2006   *Ogyū Sorai's Philosophical Masterworks*, trans. by John A. Tucker (Honolulu: University of Hawai'i Press).

Ooms, Herman

1985   *Tokugawa Ideology: Early Constructs, 1570–1680* (Princeton, NJ: Princeton University Press).

Parkes, Graham

1997   "The Putative Fascism of the Kyoto School and the Political Correctness of the Modern Academy," *Philosophy East and West* 47/3: 305–36.

Pastreich, Emanuel

2001   "Grappling with Chinese Writing as a Material Language: Ogyū Sorai's *yakubunsentei.*" *Harvard Journal of Asiatic Studies* 61/1.

Payne, Richard K., and Kenneth K. Tanaka, eds.

2004   *Approaching the Land of Bliss: Religious Praxis in the Cult of Amitābha* (Honolulu: University of Hawai'i Press).

Pelzel, John C.

1986   "Human Nature in Japanese Myths," in Takie S. Lebra and William P. Lebra, eds., *Japanese Culture and Behavior: Selected Readings* (Honolulu: University of Hawai'i Press, revised ed.), 7–28.

Philippi, Donald L.

1968   *Kojiki* (Tokyo: University of Tokyo Press).

Picken, Stuart D. B.

2004   *Sourcebook in Shinto: Selected Documents* (Westport, CN: Praeger).

Piggott, Joan R.

1997   *The Emergence of Japanese Kingship* (Stanford, CA: Stanford University Press).

Piovesana, Gino K., and Naoshi Yamawaki 山脇直司

1997   *Recent Japanese Philosophical Thought, 1862–1996: A Survey, Including a New Survey by Naoshi Yamawaki,* "The Philosophical Thought of Japan from 1963 to 1996," (Richmond, Surrey: Japan Library, revised ed.).

Plato

1991   *The Republic of Plato*, trans. by Allan Bloom (New York: Basic Books, 2nd ed.).

Pollack, David

1986   *The Fracture of Meaning: Japan's Synthesis of China from the Eighth through the Eighteenth Centuries* (Princeton, NJ: Princeton University Press).

PYE. Michael

1978   *Skilful Means: A Concept in Mahayana Buddhism* (London: Duckworth).

RAMIREZ-CHRISTENSEN, Esperanza

2008   *Emptiness and Temporality: Buddhism and Medieval Japanese Poetics* (Stanford, CA: Stanford University Press).

RAUD, Rein

2004   "'Place' and 'Being-time': Spatiotemporal Concepts in the Thought of Nishida Kitarō and Dōgen Kigen," *Philosophy East and West* 54/1: 29–51.

REISCHAUER, Edwin O.

1955   *Ennin's Travels in T'ang China.* (New York: Ronald Press Company).

RUBINGER, Richard

2007   Popular Literacy in Early Modern Japan (Honolulu: University of Hawai'i Press).

SAIGYŌ 西行

1978   *Mirror for the Moon: A Selection of Poems,* trans. with an introduction by William R. LaFleur (New York: New Directions Books).

SANFORD, James H.

1981   *Zen-Man Ikkyū* (Chico, CA: Scholars Press).

2004   "Amida's Secret Life: Kakuban's *Amida hishaku*" in PAYNE and TANAKA 2004, 120–38

SANFORD, James H., William R. LAFLEUR, and NAGATOMI Masatoshi, eds.

1992   *Flowing Traces: Buddhism in the Literary and Visual Arts of Japan* (Princeton, NJ: Princeton University Press).

SAWADA, Janine A.

1993   *Confucian Values and Popular Zen: Sekimon Shingaku in Eighteenth-Century Japan* (Honolulu: University of Hawai'i Press).

SCHEID, Bernhard, and Mark TEEUWEN,eds)

2006   *The Culture of Secrecy in Japanese Religion* (London: Routledge).

SCHEINER, Irwin, ed.

1974   *Modern Japan: An Interpretive Anthology* (New York: Macmillan).

SCHENCKING, J. C.

2008   "The Great Kanto Earthquake and the Culture of Catastrophe and Reconstruction in 1920s Japan," *The Journal of Japanese Studies* 34/2: 295–331.

SCHROEDER, John W.

2001   *Skillful Means: The Heart of Buddhist Compassion* (Honolulu: University of Hawai'i Press).

SEELEY, Christopher

2000   *A History of Writing in Japan* (Honolulu: University of Hawai'i Press).

SHANER, David E.

1985   *The Bodymind Experience in Japanese Buddhism: A Phenomenological Perspective of Kūkai and Dōgen* (Albany, NY: SUNY Press).

SHIBA Ryōtarō 司馬遼太郎

1975   『空海の風景』 [Kūkai's landscape] (Tokyo: Chuōkōronsha).

2003   *Kukai the Universal: Scenes from His Life,* trans. by Takemoto Akiko 武本明子 (New York: ICG Muse).

SHINRAN 親鸞

1984   *Tannisho: A Shin Buddhist Classic,* trans. by Taitetsu Unno (Honolulu, Hawai'i: Buddhist Study Center Press).

STAMBAUGH, Joan

1990   *Impermanence Is Buddha-Nature: Dogen's Understanding of Temporality* (Honolulu: University of Hawai'i Press).

STONE, Jacqueline

1999   *Original Enlightenment and the Transformation of Medieval Japanese Buddhism* (Honolulu: University of Hawai'i Press).

SUZUKI (Teitarō) Daisetsu 鈴木 (貞太郎) 大拙

1957   *Mysticism: Christian and Buddhist* (New York: Harper).

SWANSON, Paul

2005   "Ennin," in ER 4: 281–2.

SWARTS, Erica Diehlmann

2001   *Kaimyō (Japanese Buddhist Posthumous Names) as Indicators of Social Status.* Dissertation, The Ohio State University.

TAKAGI Ichinosuke 高木市之助, GOMI Tomohide 五味智英, and ŌNO Susumu 大野晋

1962   『萬葉集』 [*Man'yōshū*] (Tokyo: Iwanami Shoten, 1957–1962), 4 vols.

TAKAHATAKE Takamichi 高畑崇導

1987   *Young Man Shinran: A Reappraisal of Shinran's Life* (Waterloo, ONT: Wilfrid Laurier University Press).

TAKAKUSU, Junjirō

1956   *The Essentials of Buddhist Philosophy,* ed. by Wing-tsit Chan and Charles A. Moore (Honolulu: University of Hawai'i Press, 3rd edition).

TAKAMURE Itsue 高群逸枝

1938   『母系制の研究』 [A study of the matrilineal system] (Tokyo: Kōseikaku).

1954　『女性の歴史』[A history of (Japanese) women] (Tokyo: Kōdansha), 4 vols.

TAKEUCHI Yoshinori 武内義範

1991　*The Heart of Buddhism,* ed. and trans. by James W. Heisig (New York: Crossroad Publishing Company).

TAMAKI Kōshirō 玉城康四郎

1974　『日本仏教思想論 上』[On Japanese Buddhist ideas, vol. 1] (Kyoto: Heiraku-ji Shoten).

TANABE Hajime 田辺 元

1986　*Philosophy as Metanoetics,* trans. by Takeuchi Yoshinori, Valdo Viglielmo, and J. W. Heisig (Berkeley: University of California Press).

TEEUWEN, Mark

1993　"Attaining Union with the Gods: The Secret Books of Watarai Shinto," *Monumenta Nipponica* 48/2: 225–45.

1996　*Watarai Shintō: An Intellectual History of the Outer Shrine in Ise* (Leiden: Research School CNWS, Leiden University).

TEEUWEN, Mark, et al.

2003　*Shinto: A Short History* (London: RoutledgeCurzon).

T'IEN-T'AI CHIH-I

2017　*Clear Serenity, Quiet Insight* [C. *Mo-ho chih-kuan*; J. *Makashikan*] trans. and commentary by Paul L. Swanson (Honolulu: University of Hawai'i Press).

TILLICH, Paul, and HISAMATSU Shin'ichi 久松真一

1971　*Dialogues, East and West: Conversations* (Kyoto: The Eastern Buddhist Society).

TOBY, Ronald P.

1985　"Why Leave Nara?: Kammu and the Transfer of the Capital," *Monumenta Nipponica* 40/3: 331–47.

TOMINAGA Nakamoto

1990　*Emerging from Meditation,* trans. by Michael Pye (Honolulu: University of Hawai'i Press).

TUCKER, John A.

1993　"Chen Beixi, Lu Xiangshan, and Early Tokugawa (1600–1867) Philosophical Lexicography," *Philosophy East and West* 43/4: 683–713.

TUCKER, Mary Evelyn

1989　*Moral and Spiritual Cultivation in Japanese Neo-Confucianism: The Life and Thought of Kaibara Ekken, 1630–1740* (Albany, NY: SUNY Press).

VAN DER VEERE, Henny

2000   *A Study into the Thought of Kōgyō Daishi Kakuban: With a Translation of His "Gorin kuji myō himitsushaku"* (Leiden: Hotei Publishing).

VISHWANATHAN, Meera

1998   *"Kokoro,"* in Edward Craig, ed., *Routledge Encyclopedia of Philosophy* (London: Routledge), 5: 291–3.

VLASTOS, Stephen

1986   *Peasant, Protests and Uprisings in Tokugawa Japan* (Berkeley: University of California Press).

WARGO, Robert

2005   *The Logic of Nothingness: A Study of Nishida Kitarō* (Honolulu: University of Hawai'i Press).

WATSUJI Tetsurō 和辻哲郎

1988   *Climate and Culture: A Philosophical Study,* trans. by Geoffrey Bownas (New York: Greenwood Press).

1996   *Watsuji Tetsuro's Rinrigaku: Ethics in Japan,* trans. by Yamamoto Seisaku and Robert E. Carter (Albany, NY: SUNY Press).

2011   *Purifying Zen: Watsuji Tetsurō's Shamon Dōgen,* trans. by Steve Bein (Honolulu: University of Hawai'i Press).

2012   *Pilgrimages to the Ancient Temples in Nara,* trans. by Hiroshi Nara (Portland, ME: MerwinAsia).

WATT, Paul B.

1984   "Jiun Soja (1718–1804): A Response to Confucianism within the Context of Buddhist Reform," in NOSCO 1984A, 188–214.

WATTS, Jonathan, and Yoshiharu TOMATSU, eds.

2005   *Traversing the Pure Land Path: A Lifetime of Encounters with Honen Shonin* (Tokyo: Jodo Shu Press).

WEISKRANTZ, Lawrence

1986   *Blindsight: A Case Study and Implications* (Oxford: Oxford University Press).

WHITEHEAD, Alfred North

1979   *Process and Reality: An Essay in Cosmology,* ed. by David Ray Griffin and Donald Sherburne (New York: Free Press).

WIGMORE, John Henry

1967   *Law and Justice in Tokugawa Japan: Materials for the History of Japanese Law and Justice under the Tokugawa Shogunate, 1603–1867* (Tokyo: University of Tokyo Press).

WILSON, Robert D.

2008 "An Interview with Hasegawa Kai," *Simply Haiku: A Quarterly Journal of Japanese Short Form Poetry* 6/3, Interview by Robert D. Wilson (http://simplyhaiku.com/SHv6n3/features/Kai.html).

WITTGENSTEIN, Ludwig

1961 *Tractatus Logico-Philosophicus,* trans. by D. F. Pears and B. F. McGuinness (London: Routledge and Kegon Paul).

1968 *Philosophical Investigations,* trans. by G.E.M. Anscombe (New York: Macmillan, 3rd edition).

YOSHIDA Kanetomo 吉田兼俱

1992 "*Yuiitsu shintō myōbō yōshū*," trans. by Allan G. Grapard, *Monumenta Nipponica* 47/2: 137–62.

YOSHIDA Kazuhiko 吉田一彦

2006 "The Thesis that Prince Shōtoku Did Not Exist," *Acta Asiatic* 91: 1–20.

YOSHIDA Kenko 吉田兼好

1967 *Essays in Idleness: The Tsurezuregusa of Kenko*, trans. by Donald Keene (New York: Columbia University Press).

YOSHIKAWA Kōjirō 吉川幸次郎

1975 仁斎·徂徠·宣長 [Jinsai, Sorai, Norinaga] (Tokyo: Iwanami Shoten)

1983 *Jinsai, Sorai, Norinaga: Three Classical Philologists of Mid-Tokugawa Japan,* trans. by Tōhō Gakkai (Tokyo: Tōhō Gakkai).

YUASA Yasuo 湯浅泰雄

1987 *The Body: Toward an Eastern Mind-Body Theory*, ed. by Thomas P. Kasulis, trans. by Shigenori Nagatomo and Thomas P. Kasulis (Albany, New York: SUNY Press).

1993 *The Body, Self-Cultivation, and Ki-Energy,* trans. by Shigenori Nagatomo and Monte S. Hull (Albany, NY: SUNY Press).

YUSA Michiko 遊佐道子

2002 *Zen and Philosophy: An Intellectual Biography of Nishida Kitarō* (Honolulu: University of Hawai'i Press).

ZEAMI Motokiyo 世阿弥元清

2008 "Transmitting the Flower through Effects and Attitudes," English trans. by Tom Hare, in *Zeami: Performance Notes* (New York: Columbia University Press), 24–73.

Index